GW00992337

To Neal

Best wishes

EU P

CO PARKER

9 FEB 2015

Commodity Derivatives

Documenting and Understanding
Commodity Derivative Products

Consulting Editors **Edmund Parker** and **Marcin Perzanowski**

Consulting editors
Edmund Parker and Marcin Perzanowski

Publisher
Sian O'Neill

Editors
Carolyn Boyle, Jo Moore, Elizabeth Rutherford-Johnson

Marketing manager
Alan Mowat

Production
John Meikle, Russell Anderson

Publishing directors
Guy Davis, Tony Harriss, Mark Lamb

Commodity Derivatives: Documenting and Understanding Commodity Derivative Products
is published by
Globe Law and Business
Globe Business Publishing Ltd
New Hibernia House
Winchester Walk
London SE1 9AG
United Kingdom
Tel +44 20 7234 0606
Fax +44 20 7234 0808
Web www.globelawandbusiness.com

Printed by Antony Rowe Ltd

ISBN 978-1-905783-37-3

Commodity Derivatives: Documenting and Understanding Commodity Derivative Products
© 2010 Globe Business Publishing Ltd

All rights reserved. No part of this publication may be reproduced in any material form (including photocopying, storing in any medium by electronic means or transmitting) without the written permission of the copyright owner, except in accordance with the provisions of the Copyright, Designs and Patents Act 1988 or under terms of a licence issued by the Copyright Licensing Agency Ltd, 6–10 Kirby Street, London EC1N 8TS, United Kingdom (www.cla.co.uk, email: licence@cla.co.uk). Applications for the copyright owner's written permission to reproduce any part of this publication should be addressed to the publisher.

DISCLAIMER
This publication is intended as a general guide only. The information and opinions which it contains are not intended to be a comprehensive study, nor to provide legal advice, and should not be treated as a substitute for legal advice concerning particular situations. Legal advice should always be sought before taking any action based on the information provided. The publishers bear no responsibility for any errors or omissions contained herein.

Table of contents

All authors are (or recently have been)
lawyers working at Mayer Brown

Preface

Edmund Parker

Commodities are used by everyone. The price of commodities such as coal, gas, power, agricultural products and metals affects the price of goods, and whether businesses are profitable or make losses.

High power prices may be good news for a power utility, but bad news for a manufacturer. A ship owner may be delighted at high freight prices, while a coal importer despairs of them. A mining corporation borrowing to finance a gold mine may lose its shirt if the price of bullion falls and it cannot repay the loan.

So there is a large global market of parties which are willing to forgo a potential upside to hedge themselves against a potential downside. They combine with well-organised, sector-specific markets using standardised documentation and standardised underlying assets to make commodity derivatives a rich, diverse and deeply interesting derivatives asset class.

This book focuses on the 2005 ISDA Commodity Definitions, but also looks at the other documentation platforms used in the commodities market, such as the platforms provided by the Futures and Options Association (FOA), the European Federation of Energy Traders, the Zeebrugge Hub and the Forward Freight Agreement Brokers Association.

This book is intended for legal practitioners, traders, treasurers, finance professionals, students and all end-users of derivatives – from mining corporations looking to hedge the price of precious metals to steel makers protecting themselves against a rise in the cost of emissions allowances under the EU Emissions Trading Scheme and ship owners guarding against a fall in freight rates.

All of the authors are (or recently have been) lawyers working at Mayer Brown, forming part of the firm's derivatives and structured products practice. I am privileged to work with so many bright and talented lawyers, and I would like to thank them all for their hard work and excellent contributions. I would also like to thank my co-editor Marcin Perzanowski for his immense dedication to this project, in terms of both editing and writing.

Edmund Parker is a partner at Mayer Brown International LLP; he heads the London office's derivatives practice and co-heads the global derivatives and structured products practice. Mr Parker advises on complex over-the-counter credit and equity derivatives, commodity derivatives, Islamic derivatives, and insurance and pensions-linked derivative structures. He also advises on repackagings, as well as distress situations affecting derivatives.

According to UK Legal 500 (2008), *"the [derivatives] practice has been transformed by the arrival of [Parker]", and he "brings a reputation for structured credit and equity derivatives". It has also been said that he "would easily fit into any top-tier derivatives practice" and "he has great expertise"* (Chambers UK (2009)).

Mr Parker has written extensively on derivatives and related matters, and is sole author of Credit Derivatives: Documenting and Understanding Credit Derivative Products *and sole editor of* Equity Derivatives: Documenting and Understanding Equity Derivative Products.

Overview and introduction to commodity derivatives

Edmund Parker

1. Introduction

1.1 Introducing commodity derivatives

The father of communist theory, Frederick Engels, wrote that "a commodity is a thing that has *use-value*; the latter exists in all forms of society, but in capitalist society, use-value is, in addition, the material depository of exchange-value".[1] This is a good definition. Things that have a use value as well as an exchange or tradable value include:

- bullion and metals, such as gold and aluminium;
- agricultural products, such as wheat, grain, livestock and cotton; and
- electricity and gas.

Twenty-first century commodities trading has broadened this definition to include freight pricing, permits for carbon dioxide emissions and other asset classes.

Many economists and political theorists have analysed commodities: Adam Smith in *The Wealth of Nations*, Karl Marx in *Das Kapital* and Lenin are all quoted in this book. Relatively little has been written to provide an understanding of commodity derivatives. Even less time has been spent analysing and discussing the documentation of commodity derivatives, even though commodity derivatives have existed for thousands of years and have been popular in Europe and the United States since the 19th century and before. This book fills the gap.

Throughout the book, we define a commodity derivative as:

- a financial instrument;
- referencing an underlying commodity asset or other variable;
- from which the financial instrument's price or value is derived; and
- entered into by the parties for a purpose.

We analyse those underlying commodity assets in detail, from freight rates to bullion to gas, electricity, weather indices and more.

We also analyse the commodity derivative contracts – the financial instruments – and their documentation in detail, examining 'over-the-counter' (OTC) financial instruments such as swaps, forwards and options. We analyse and explain negotiable instruments (eg, structured notes issued from a bank's medium-term note or warrant programme), and examine exchange-traded contracts (eg, options and forwards

---

1   *Synopsis of Capital* by Frederick Engels (1868).

traded on the London Metals Exchange).

In addition, we cover the more esoteric products now classed as commodity assets (eg, emissions trading and weather derivatives), as well as the standardised documentation platforms provided by trade bodies such as the International Swaps and Derivatives Association, Inc (ISDA), the Futures and Options Association (FOA) and the European Federation of Energy Traders (EFET).

Finally, in a period when we are seeing perhaps the biggest changes to the derivatives regulatory environment ever, we also cover in depth the regulatory and tax environment surrounding commodity derivatives.

1.2 The book's structure and rationale

We defined commodity derivative above as:

- a financial instrument;
- referencing an underlying commodity asset or other variable;
- from which the financial instrument's price or value is derived; and
- entered into by the parties for a purpose.

This definition (slightly longer, but more logical than the norm) is the thread running through this book.

The first part of the book provides an overview of commodity derivatives, as well as a discussion of the reasons for using commodity derivatives and the value which can be derived from commodity derivatives contracts.

The second part of the book focuses on the financial instruments themselves (ie, OTC derivatives, structured products and exchange-traded derivatives).

The third part of the book covers ISDA's documentation platform for OTC derivatives, looking in detail at the 2005 ISDA Commodity Definitions and its related documentation in detail. ISDA's documentation platform references a broad range of underlying commodity assets; we take the opportunity here to discuss in detail the most complex of them, with specific chapters on bullion, weather indices, gas, power, emissions allowances and freight rates. Each chapter corresponds to the related ISDA sub-annex for that underlying asset.

ISDA is not the only trade body to provide a documentation platform for commodity derivatives. Other bodies providing comprehensive platforms include the FOA and EFET. The fourth part of the book includes specific chapters covering the documentation platforms of these two organisations, together with a further chapter that examines the commodity derivatives documentation platforms provided by the International Emissions Trading Association (IETA), globalCOAL and the Forward Freight Agreement Brokers Association.

The purposes of use and the underlying commodity assets themselves necessitate that commodity derivatives are subject to regulatory and tax treatment which is not only complex but varies between Europe and the United States. The fifth part of the book looks at the regulatory regimes for commodity derivatives in Europe (in particular, the United Kingdom) and the United States, as well as the UK tax regime. Strong regulatory winds are blowing and momentous changes are coming into force in 2010, including a push towards central counterparties, data repositories and exchange clearing on both sides of the Atlantic. We capture and analyse the latest developments.

Please note that in this book, the terms which are defined in the 2005 ISDA Commodity Definitions are denoted by the use of quotations marks when used for the first time. Thereafter, those terms are spelled without using any capital letters or punctuation marks.

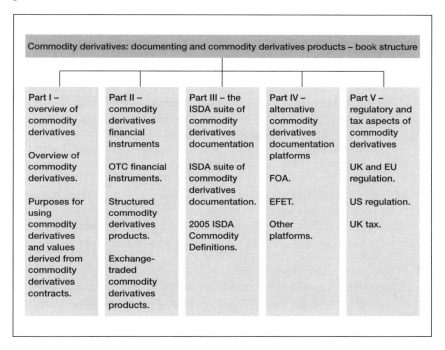

2. The size and history of the commodity derivatives market

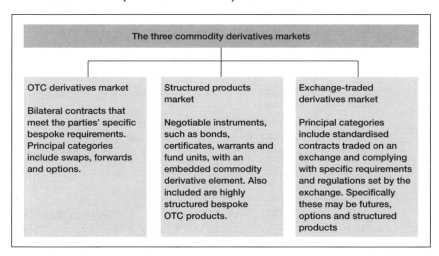

There are three categories of commodity derivatives financial instrument, each with different market sizes, characteristics and history:

- OTC derivatives;
- structured products; and
- exchange-traded derivatives.

2.1 OTC derivatives

OTC commodity derivatives (ie, bilateral privately negotiated contracts) are nothing new. Bilateral forward contracts have been around for centuries and long precede the credit and interest-rate derivatives markets. Forward contracts, where farmers agreed to sell their crops for an agreed price once harvested, were documented in ancient Egypt. Certainly brokers have entered into forward and option contracts referencing freight rates (the cost of carrying goods by sea) since the 17th century.

The popularity of these products has increased significantly, as with all derivatives asset classes. The Bank of International Settlements' semi-annual reports provide the most reliable data on the overall size of the OTC market. Its end-of-year report for the first half of 2009 disclosed more than $3.7 trillion of outstanding OTC commodity swaps, forwards and options. This is a decline on previous years and in numerical terms is likely to continue as standardised commodity derivatives instruments are forced towards exchange clearing through regulatory stimulus. More complex and bespoke transactions, though, will always be documented off-exchange.

2.2 Structured commodity products

The market for structured commodity products is growing. Each different negotiable financial instrument (eg, certificates or fund units) is called a 'wrapper'. Structured commodity products also include OTC derivatives contracts, which show a greater level of sophistication than so-called 'vanilla' products.

With many products privately traded and tailored to specific investor requirements, it is difficult to estimate the market's precise size.

Many major financial institutions have incorporated commodity derivative provisions into their medium-term note programmes. They can then issue debt where the return is linked to the performance of an underlying commodity asset, such as the gold price, a commodities index or the relative performance of a basket of commodities or indices. Major players in this area include Goldman Sachs, Morgan Stanley and Deutsche Bank, among others. Some, including Goldman Sachs, also have commodities warrant programmes.

These programmes began in the 1980s and the more popular issue hundreds of series of notes, certificates and warrants to investors every year. These institutions will also structure bespoke OTC swaps for certain clients, providing a complex investment strategy in certain commodity assets.

2.3 Exchange-traded commodity derivatives

The financial markets of the 16th to 18th centuries introduced organised derivatives contracts trading with commodities and equities at the forefront. There are now several major players in the exchange-traded commodity derivatives market. These include ICE Futures Europe, a regulated futures exchange for global energy markets which lists the leading global crude-oil benchmarks and handles half the global trade in crude oil and refined-product futures. Present too is the London Metal Exchange (LME), which traces its origins to 1571 and the opening of the Royal Exchange. The LME offers futures and options contracts for base and non-precious metals such as aluminium, copper, nickel, tin, zinc and lead, plus two regional aluminium alloy contracts. In 2007 it achieved volumes of $9.5 trillion.

The London International Financial Futures and Options Exchange (LIFFE) – now called NYSE LIFFE and part of NYSE Euronext following its takeover by Euronext and Euronext's merger with the New York Stock Exchange – trades a number of commodity futures and option contracts, including a range of agricultural commodity contracts.

Eurex is a global derivatives exchange which is jointly operated by Deutsche Börse AG and SIX Swiss Exchange. Popular contracts traded on the exchange reference emissions allowances, bullion and agricultural derivatives.

CME Group Inc (formed through the merger of the Chicago Mercantile Exchange (CME) and the Chicago Board of Trade (CBOT)) also owns NYMEX. The CME is a financial and commodity derivative exchange based in Chicago. It was founded in 1898 and trades a variety of commodity derivative products. CBOT, which was established in 1848, is the world's oldest futures and options exchange and also trades a wide variety of contracts. NYMEX is a futures and options exchange comprising two divisions: the NYMEX division and the COMEX division. The NYMEX division trades coal, crude oil, electricity and uranium futures and options contracts. The COMEX division trades futures and options contracts referencing gold, silver, aluminium and copper.

3. Understanding the four constituent parts of a commodity derivative

We define a commodity derivative as: a financial instrument referencing an underlying commodity asset or other variable, from which the financial instrument's price or value is derived, entered into by the parties for a purpose. By setting out the definition in this way, we show that a commodity derivative is made up of four constituent parts:

- a financial instrument;
- referencing an underlying commodity asset or other variable;
- from which the financial instrument's price or value is derived; and
- entered into by the parties for a purpose.

This allows us to analyse each constituent part in turn to form a fuller picture of the nature of commodity derivatives.

The financial instrument – the first constituent part – will fall into one of the three main categories of commodity derivative financial instrument:

- OTC derivatives;
- structured products; and
- exchange-traded products.

In the case of an OTC derivative, the financial instrument will be a swap, forward or option. In the case of a structured product it will be a note, certificate, warrant, fund unit or bespoke swap. In the case of an exchange-traded product, it will be a future, an option or one of the structured products.

The second constituent part – the underlying commodity asset or other commodity variable – will be a commodity such as bullion, other metals, agricultural products, freight prices, paper, gas, power, emissions allowances or a weather index. The commodity itself will be commoditised. For example, it might be a metric tonne of a certain grade of cocoa or a specific freight route in a vessel of a particular size for a specific weight of cargo.

The price or value of the underlying commodity asset from which the financial instrument derives its value – the third constituent part – may be the change in the price or an underlying commodity or future referencing it, or the level of an index over a period of time or between specific dates. Alternatively, it may be the relative price or level of different underlying assets over a period of time or specific dates; or the total return on single or multiple underlying assets (eg, indices or futures contracts) over a period of time. These prices or levels may be determined on specific or multiple dates and often in accordance with a formula.

The fourth constituent part – the purpose for which the parties enter into a commodity derivative transaction – can be many and varied. Reasons might include:

- commodity producers such as mining companies looking to hedge against sale proceeds being insufficent to cover production costs;
- manufacturers hedging against rises in raw material prices which would erode sale margins;
- speculators making leveraged investments in particular commodity asset classes, such as oil; or
- funds looking to diversify their investments away from traditional asset classes such as debt and equities.

We now look at each of the four constituent parts of commodity derivatives in further detail.

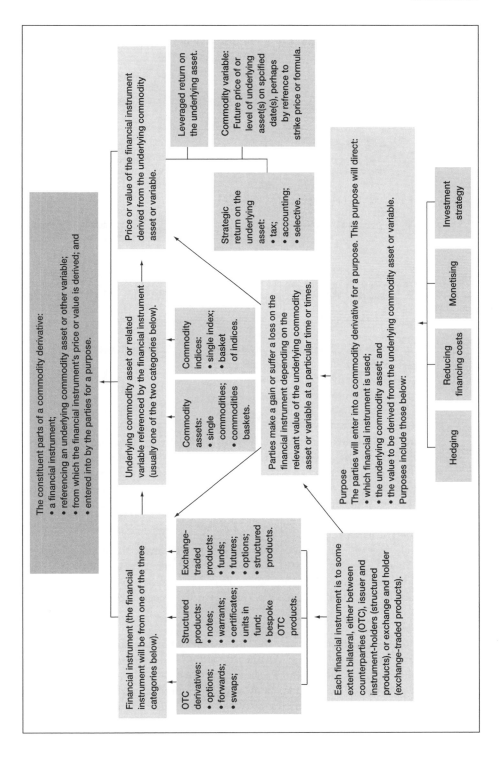

4.   The first constituent part of a commodity derivative: the financial instrument

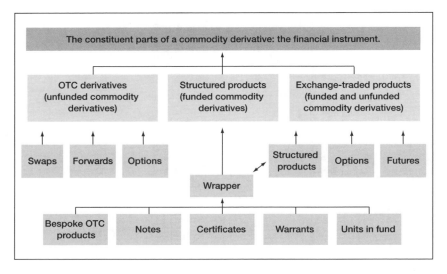

Any commodity derivative financial instrument will be a sub-type of at least one of the three commodity derivatives categories:

- OTC derivatives;
- structured products; and
- exchange-traded products.

An OTC derivative financial instrument will be a swap, a forward or an option. A structured product financial instrument will be a note, a certificate, a warrant, a unit in a fund or a bespoke OTC product. An exchange-traded product financial instrument will be a future or an option or, if it is listed on an exchange, one of the four types of structured product financial instrument.

4.1   OTC derivatives

There are three categories of commodity derivatives OTC financial instrument: options, forwards and swaps. Each type has various sub-types. Sub-types of option are European, American, Bermudan, Asian and barrier options. Among the sub-types of forward are contracts for difference, while sub-types of swap include index-linked and basket swaps.

(a)   Options

An option is a bilateral contract. The buyer of the option acquires a right to buy (or sell to the seller of the option) a defined amount of an underlying commodity asset at a price agreed at the contract's outset (the strike price). This price will be either a specific price or one determined by reference to a formula or set of rules set out in the confirmation. The underlying asset is usually a single commodity or basket of commodities, or an index or basket of indices.

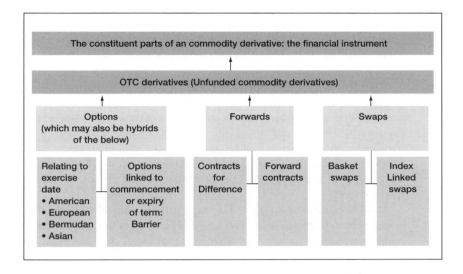

The option buyer pays an amount of money (a premium) to the option seller, as determined in the relevant transaction confirmation, to compensate it for providing the option.

Options are either call options or put options, and are also either cash settled or physically settled.

In a physically settled put option the buyer has a right to sell a specified quantity of a commodity or basket of commodities (eg, one metric tonne of coal) to its counterparty at an agreed price (the strike price) on a future date. In a physically settled call option, the option buyer has a right to buy the same at the strike price.

Whether the option buyer chooses to exercise its option will depend on whether the underlying commodity asset is trading above or below the strike price. Naturally, the call option is worth exercising only if the underlying asset is trading above the strike price on the exercise date. Likewise the put option is worth exercising only if the underlying asset is trading below the strike price on the exercise date.

In a cash-settled option, a put option buyer has the right to demand a payment from its counterparty if the settlement price (ie, the trading price of the underlying commodity or future, basket of commodities or futures or the level of a commodities index) is lower than the strike price (as provided in the confirmation) on the exercise date. Conversely, a call option buyer can demand a payment when the actual price (the settlement price) is higher than the strike price on the exercise date.

Options are also categorised by when they can be exercised. The three most common types are American, European, Bermudan and Asian.

An American option can be exercised on any trading day during the option's term; this means that it can be exercised at any time before its expiry. However, a European option can be exercised only on the day of its expiry (ie, its expiry date).

A Bermudan option is a half-way house between a European and American option. It can be exercised on specific days, as provided in the confirmation; these are called potential exercise dates.

Options can be categorised using the method by which the strike price or exercise price is determined (if this is not specifically set out in the transaction confirmation). For example, an Asian option looks at the average price of the underlying asset over a period of time or on specific dates.

Another category of option is a barrier option (which has sub-sets called 'knock-in' and 'knock-out' options). In a knock-in transaction, a payment or delivery is contingent upon the occurrence of a knock-in event on any knock-in determination day (usually a trading day or predefined period or range of dates). In a knock-out transaction, the transaction will terminate without the option being exercised if a knock-out event occurs on any knock-out determination day. Knock-in and knock-out events will usually be the level of a share or index going above or below a specified level.

Options can also be categorised by being part of a particular trading strategy. For example, in a straddle, a derivatives user can purchase both a call option and a put option referencing the same underlying asset and with the same strike price. The strategy protects the derivatives user against volatility above or below a specific level in the trading price of the underlying asset.

(b)   Forwards

A forward transaction is a bilateral sale-and-purchase contract. In a physically settled transaction, one of the parties agrees to sell and the other agrees to buy a defined amount of the underlying commodity at a defined point in the future for a specified price (if the transaction is physically settled). In both cases, sale prices can instead be determined by reference to a formula or an average price over a number of dates.

In a cash-settled transaction, the parties exchange the difference between the actual trading price of the underlying commodity asset at the future date and the price set out in the confirmation.

A forward can also relate to an index (in which case it will be cash settled), and the parties will instead exchange payments based on a settlement price related to the level of the index at the future date as compared with the level set out in the confirmation.

(c)   Swaps

A commodity swap is a bilateral contract that allows a party to acquire economic exposure to an underlying commodity asset without the need to buy that asset. There are several variations.

Under these types of transaction, the swap references a commodity underlying asset, which can be a single commodity or basket of commodities, or an index or basket of indices. One or several measurement dates are set out in the transaction confirmation.

There are many bespoke variations depending on the underlying commodity asset. These are described in the underlying asset chapters set out in Part IV of this book. The most complicated structures are set out in the chapters on weather index transactions, freight and emissions trading.

Generally speaking, though, each transaction has two parties: a fixed amount payer and a floating amount payer. On each payment date a fixed amount is paid. If the value of the underlying commodity asset has risen above a set level on a particular measurement date, the floating amount payer will pay the fixed amount payer an amount equal to the positive differential (multiplied by the transaction's notional amount and any mulitplier). If the value of the underlying commodity asset has fallen below the set level on the particular measurement date, the fixed amount payer will pay the corresponding value of that differential to the floating amount payer.

Different underlying commodity assets are treated differently from one another. Bullion swaps, EU emissions allowances, freight and other derivatives all have their own market norms. These are driven partly by market traditions and standards, and partly by the esoteric nature of the underlying asset itself.

(d)   *Documentation platform for options, forwards and swaps*

Much of the OTC commodity derivatives market has standardised norms and documentation. The principal documentation platform for OTC derivatives is provided by ISDA.[2] Documentation platforms for other underlying commodity asset classes have been provided by, among others:

* EFET for energy derivatives;
* the International Emissions Trading Association (IETA) for emissions allowances; and
* the Forward Freight Agreement Brokers Association (FFABA) for freight derivatives.

(i)   *ISDA*

ISDA, founded in 1985, is a latecomer to the commodity derivatives market. It accompanied the new players, the financial institutions and hedge funds – the traditional brokers were using commodity derivatives long before and already had their own market norms, traditions, documentation and trade bodies. The ISDA platform therefore was specifically designed to harmonise with existing market practices and trade organisations, while trying to add greater documentation sophistication developed in other derivatives areas, such as equity derivatives.

ISDA's suite of documentation for commodity derivatives consists of three inter-linking platforms: a primary platform, a secondary platform and a tertiary platform. The primary platform – a master agreement amended by a schedule and possibly a credit support document – is an umbrella agreement applicable to all derivatives areas covered by ISDA (eg, interest, foreign exchange, currency and credit). All transactions entered into under the master agreement form a single transaction, allowing amounts payable under the same currency to be netted in the same transaction and, if the parties elect, all transactions. On an early termination (eg, as a result of the bankruptcy of one of the parties), the amount due can be netted to a single amount.

The secondary platform consists of the 2005 ISDA Commodity Definitions. The 2005 definitions are designed to be used with OTC confirmations relating primarily to option transactions, forward transactions and commodity swaps governed by an

---

2   The ISDA documentation platform is discussed in depth in Part III of this book.

ISDA master sgreement already entered into by the parties.

The 2005 definitions provide a framework of agreed terminology, together with market standard fallbacks for when prices cannot be obtained or, for example, trading days for exchanges or the calculation of indices are disrupted.

The tertiary platform essentialy consists of best-practice statements and guidance prepared by ISDA, to provide support for market participants in case there are any market disruptions.

(ii)   *EFET*

EFET is a non-profit organisation whose membership is made up of more than 90 energy trading companies from 23 European countries. EFET's documentation platform operates in a similar manner to ISDA documentation.

It utilises a primary platform of general agreements. These operate similarly to the ISDA Master Agreement, except that they are product specific and relate to gas or electricity only. These general agreements are then amended, modified or supplemented through separate election sheets and/or appendices, just as one would amend the ISDA Master Agreement through the ISDA Schedule.

For gas, there is the EFET General Agreement Concerning the Delivery and Acceptance of Natural Gas. This governs all transactions for the purchase, sale, delivery and acceptance of natural gas. This general agreement also has an allowances appendix to facilitate emissions trading through the trading of EU emissions allowances. For electricity, there is the EFET General Agreement Concerning the Delivery and Acceptance of Electricity, which performs the same function.

EFET's secondary platform consists of a confirmation under which each individual transaction is documented. Each confirmation supplements and forms part of the relevant general agreement.

4.2   Structured products

For structured products, the financial instrument is called a wrapper. The wrapper may be a certificate, note or warrant or, for more bespoke OTC commodity derivatives, the standard ISDA documentation framework. The specific format that a wrapper takes will depend on investor preference, efficiency, liquidity, and tax and regulatory issues.

Although notes or certificates can be issued as standalone instruments by an issuer (usually a financial institution or one of its specially created subsidiaries), for reasons of documentation efficiency they are more commonly issued under a programme. The programme will establish a master documentation platform, under which future issues of instruments will be documented.

The programme will have a prospectus which will be listed on a stock exchange. In Europe, this is most commonly the Luxembourg Stock Exchange or the Irish Stock Exchange. The prospectus will set out the conditions of any instruments issued under the programme. These conditions will usually adapt many of the provisions from the 2005 ISDA Commodity Definitions to make them suitable for inclusion in a certificate, note or warrant. The prospectus will also contain risk factors and disclosure on the issuer and any other relevant parties.

The programme will also have an agency agreement which will set out the roles and responsibilities of the various other parties to the transaction – such as the calculation agent and paying agents.

Each time the issuer issues instruments to investors, it will complete a final terms document. This will make various elections contained in the conditions (set out in the prospectus) and will set out the pricing information and specific terms (eg, the identity of the underlying asset) for the particular issue.

The final terms together with the conditions will be attached to a global instrument (which will represent all of the securities for a particular issue), and will be deposited into a clearing system. In Europe, this will usually be either one or both of Euroclear and Clearstream. The instruments can then be traded.

Sometimes, but not always, the individual issue of securities will be listed on the same stock exchange as the programme. This helps to make the securities more liquid and also meets the investment requirements of many institutional investors. This means that commodity derivatives structured products can also be exchange-traded products.

Another form of commodity derivatives structured product relates to investments in commodity funds. This is where an investor purchases units, or alternatively shares or preference shares, in a fund located in a low-tax or no-tax jurisdiction such as the Cayman Islands or Jersey. Alternatively, the fund may be located in a European Economic Area (EEA) jurisdiction as an Undertaking for Collective Investments in Transferable Securities III scheme. The fund will invest in commodity underlying assets such as gold or copper; or it may track the performance or relative performance of various indices, or indeed follow various commodity investment or commodity derivative strategies, to generate an enhanced return for investors. The instruments issued by the fund will derive their value from the value of the fund. If the instruments issued to investors are listed on a stock exchange, the fund will be an exchange-traded fund. The listing allows increased liquidity for the fund's units.

An alternative structure can involve establishing a cell company, which then creates a separate segregated cell for each issue, whose assets are ring-fenced from the other cells. Other less common forms of wrapper include:

- structured deposits with financial institutions, the returns on which are usually linked to commodity indices;
- life insurance policies with returns usually linked to the performance of commodity indices; and
- trust certificates, which operate in a similar manner to protected cell companies (with a separate sub-trust be established for each issue and segregation between different sub-trusts).

4.3 Exchange-traded products

Exchange-traded commodity derivatives are commodity derivatives traded on an organised exchange. They provide, just as with trading in the underlying commodities, standardised contracts, tradable through a central clearing house (also known as a central counterparty). The principal exchange-traded commodity derivative products are futures, options and structured products.

Forwards and futures are similar, the main difference being the way in which they are traded. Forward contracts are OTC private bilateral contracts where each party takes a credit risk on the other. Futures contracts are standardised exchange-traded contracts with limited credit risk, as they will have the benefit of a central counterparty.

The futures markets developed promoting efficiency, market regulation and increasing investor confidence. The pricing, delivery provisions and other elements of each futures contract are standardised. Delivery of the underlying asset rarely occurs, with the initial contract being hedged.

While forwards have both credit risk and market risk (with the credit risk arising from exposure to the counterparty), futures aim to eliminate credit risk as far as possible, leaving only market risk. The central counterparty will transact only with brokers – these are institutions which are members of the exchange. Central counterparties are usually a part of an individual exchange or third-party entity, which acts as a buyer to every seller and a seller to every buyer. They minimise counterparty risk by taking margin payments in line with underlying exposure. The central counterparty therefore takes a limited credit risk on each broker and the brokers take a limited credit risk on their clients. No party takes any credit risk on an unknown party. Each broker will take an initial margin payment in the form of cash or securities from its client, which it holds in a margin account.

Central counterparties are also relevant where standardised derivatives contracts are not traded on exchange. There are strong regulatory initiatives on both sides of the Atlantic to push as many standardised products as possible towards central clearing and exchange clearing as possible.

5.   The second constituent part of a commodity derivative: the underlying commodity asset

In the case of commodity derivatives, the underlying asset being referenced by the financial instrument is almost always a single commodity or a basket of commodities, or a single commodity index or a basket of commodity indices.

In equity derivatives transactions, the underlying asset is fairly simple: shares or indices related to them. The complexity lies in the regulation, extreme volatility of the underlying asset and the sophisticated structures set up to manage these. In commodity derivatives, the most complex area is the variety of underlying assets and the adaptation of derivatives financial instruments to work with these – in particular, the different market norms which can exist in the mature markets that relate to them.

The most common assets underlying commodity derivatives transactions are agricultural products, energy, freight, metals, paper, emissions allowances and weather indices.

Commodity derivatives generally reference the price of an underlying commodity asset. To do that, the commodity must be standardised (ie, traded by reference to a specific price and quality (or grading)). The quantity and quality will be specific to the particular underlying asset.

5.1 Agricultural products

Mature markets for trading agricultural derivatives have existed since the 19th century, and many of the older commodity derivatives exchanges were set up to trade futures and options referencing agricultural products. Some of the most popular underlying agricultural commodities include canola, cocoa, coffee, corn, cotton, livestock, milk, oats, orange juice, rubber, soy beans, sugar, sunflower seeds, wheat and wool.

Within these categories are various sub-categories of traded commodities:
- within coffee, there is washed arabica coffee and robusta coffee;
- within corn, there is yellow maize and white maize; and
- within livestock, there is dressed carcase, feeder steers, live steers and lean value hog carcasses.

Each commodity is traded in a standardised quantity. For example, cocoa is traded in tonnes; corn is traded in bushels; cotton and sugar are traded per pound; and cattle are traded on a per-kilogram basis.

Standardisation is vital in commodity derivatives and so financial instruments referencing individual agricultural commodities will almost always reference one of the prices published by a commodities futures exchange. These are then republished by information providers such as Reuters. Definitions for the most popular commodity prices are set out as commodity reference prices in Sub-Annex A to the 2005 Definitions.

The commodity reference price for cotton, for example, is set out as:

"COTTON NO.2-NYBOT" means the price for a Pricing Date will be that day's Specified Price per pound of deliverable grade cotton No.2 on the NYBOT of the Futures Contract, stated in U.S. cents, as made public by the NYBOT and displayed on Reuters Screen "0#CT:" on that Pricing Date.

Several things are apparent from this definition:
- the standardised quantity (pounds);
- the grading (deliverable grade cotton No 2 is a set of quality standards);
- that the dollar pricing is the trading price of the related futures contract; and
- that the commodity reference price is that republished on the specified Reuters screen.

5.2 Energy

Some of the most popular underlying energy derivatives include benzene, coal, diesel fuel, electricity, fuel oil, gas oil, gasoline, heating oil, jet fuel/kerosene, methanol, naphtha, natural gas and oil. Within these categories are many sub-categories of traded commodities.

Electricity, for instance, is divided into several groups of tradable commodity reference prices based on geography, with trading markets in particular for Australia, Europe (with sub-groups for the Benelux countries, France, Germany, the Nordic countries, Spain, Switzerland and the United Kingdom) and the United States.

The commodity reference prices for each group reference the price per megawatt for physical delivery of electricity. Each country or area will have several different commodity reference prices. For example, Sub-Annex A to the 2005 definitions specifies four different traded prices for UK electricity commodity reference prices, relating to prices calculated by the London Energy Brokers' Association for the UK Power Indices:

- the Day Ahead Window Index;
- the Working Days Index;
- the Monday–Friday Peak Index; and
- the All Days Index.

There are many tradable electricity commodity reference prices and these represent just four. These prices are not necessarily published with derivatives in mind and are widely used in the spot markets.

Each of the other energy commodities also has several tradable commodity reference prices. Oil, for example, has:

- Brent crude oil;
- Dubai crude oil;
- baskets of crude oil imported into Japan, known as Japanese Crude Cocktail (Provisional); and
- West Texas intermediate light sweet crude oil.

5.3   Freight

Freight rates are the prices charged for carrying goods on a ship and are the underlying asset in freight derivatives; and freight derivatives involve a financial instrument which derives its value from the underlying asset of a freight rate. The complexity of the underlying assets and how these are traded makes freight derivatives a particularly complex area of commodity derivatives. The discussion below demonstrates both the difficulty and importance of understanding the intricacies of the underlying asset, both when dealing in the particular product and when documenting any particular transaction.

Freight rates are filled with nautical terminology. They are quoted on the basis of cost per metric tonne for transporting cargo on an agreed route, in a vessel of a particular size. These rates will differ according to the following, among other factors:

- whether the route is on a voyage basis or a time charter basis;
- the size of the particular vessel transporting the cargo; and
- the route taken.

Freight rates are volatile: prediction of future demand rests on sentiment about the future direction of world trade and the global economy, with unreliable and differing forecasts in this area correlating to volatility in the future direction of freight rates. Ships run on fuel, so movements in oil prices directly impact on freight rates. Particular freight rates are often directly referenced to the commodities being carried (eg, coal or iron ore). So movements in the pricing of the underlying commodity can also impact on freight rates.

Trading in freight derivatives is possible only if reliable market prices are available. These come from published indices, freight rates and trading prices. The principal provider of current freight market information is the Baltic Exchange (located in London and a centre of freight trading for hundreds of years). For tankers, Platts (an information provider) is important; and for wet route rates published by both the Baltic Exchange and Platt's, the prices published by Worldscale are used as a nominal base.

Worldscale is a joint venture between Worldscale Association (London) Limited and Worldscale Association (NYC) Inc. It operates as an online platform providing more than 320,000 flat rates for previously requested freight routes, on the basis of a standard-sized vessel carrying a standard cargo being charged at a daily hire rate. These rates are published annually and are supposed to represent the average market rates at the time of publication. Worldscale operates on a system of 'points of scale'. Parties then negotiate these dollar figures by adjusting them by Worldscale points. Each point away from 100 represents a percentage point of adjustment to the published rates. For example:

- 100 points means the published rate itself (or Worldscale Flat);
- 40 points means 40% of the published rate; and
- 180 points means 180% of the published rate.

These figures are expressed with the prefix 'WS', so in the preceding examples these would be expressed as WS100, WS40 and WS180.

5.4   Metals

Some of the most popular underlying metal commodities comprise aluminium, copper, gold, lead, palladium, platinum, silver, steel and tin.

Within these categories are various sub-categories of traded commodities, which are tradable commodity reference prices. For example, within aluminium there is high-grade primary aluminium traded on COMEX or the LME, and also aluminium alloy traded on those exchanges. For copper, there is grade-A copper and high-grade copper.

Bullion is one of the more complex categories of metals. Gold and silver are defined by reference to gold (or silver) bars or unallocated gold (or silver) complying with the rules of the London Bullion Market Association relating to fineness and good delivery.

Palladium and platinum are traded as palladium (or platinum) ingots or plate or unallocated palladium (or platinum) complying with the rules of the London Platinum and Palladium Market relating to good delivery and fineness.

The bullion market trades in ounces. However, 'ounce' has one meaning for gold and another for precious metals: for gold it means a fine troy ounce, while for silver, platinum or palladium it is just a troy ounce. This is a fine distinction, but one which reflects that there are many distinct trading environments for commodity assets and that commodity derivatives financial instruments must accommodate them.

5.5   Paper

The most popular type of underlying paper commodity assets include containerboard, newsprint, pulp and recovered paper. Each category has several types of widely traded price in the commodity derivatives market.

5.6   Emissions allowances

Emissions trading derivatives consist of financial instruments such as swaps, options and forwards which derive their value from the underlying asset of permits giving the right to emit a defined quantity of a greenhouse gas.

Commodity derivatives trading involving emissions allowances is highly complex, as far as the underlying commodity asset is concerned. Currently the biggest area is based around the EU Emissions Trading Scheme (ETS). This is the European Union's compulsory cap-and-trade project for trading carbon dioxide emission allowances. To date, it is the most ambitious and comprehensive emissions trading scheme ever created, although the United States is making strong efforts to develop its own scheme.

Each allowance represents the right to emit one tonne of carbon dioxide and each participating installation must surrender allowances equal to its actual carbon dioxide emissions. If its allocated allowances are not sufficient to cover its actual emissions, the affected installation must go into the market and purchase additional allowances to cover the shortfall. Failure to surrender sufficient allowances to cover emissions incurs a penalty per tonne of carbon dioxide emitted, as well as a requirement to make good the allowances in the following year. If the affected installation has an excess of allowances, perhaps through generating efficiencies, it can sell these into the market for a profit. The scheme aims to reduce carbon dioxide emissions by financially rewarding affected installations that reduce their emissions and penalising those that do not.

These permits have a tradable value, which varies based on their perceived scarcity. This makes them ideal underlying assets for commodity derivative transactions.

5.7   Weather indices and catastrophe swaps

Weather risk is hard to include as a commodity, but it is justified by the derivative market because of the impact that weather can have on the pricing of goods.

In the world of weather derivatives, the underlying commodity asset referenced is the variance in an index which measures the differences in temperature, precipitation, snow or wind as recorded at meteorological stations. The 2005 definitions reference 28 of these – for example those in Austria, Australia, Belgium, Canada, Switzerland, the Czech Republic, Germany, Denmark, Italy, Japan, South Korea, Mexico, New Zealand, Spain, Finland, Sweden, South Africa, the United Kingdom and the United States.

Two types of weather derivative are commonly traded. Under the first type, an aggregate weather variable for temperature, precipitation, snow or wind is measured over an agreed period of time at a meteorological station. The variables are compiled together by a calculation agent, with each increment of the variable above or below a threshold adjusting the number of weather index units in a notional index. If the number of weather index units is above or below a pre-agreed level at any measurement date, then one party will make a differential payment to the other, based on an amount per weather index unit.

Under the second type of weather derivative transaction, if a specified adverse weather event, such as a hurricane, occurs during the transaction's term, the party which is the seller will pay the other a fixed amount, based on the event's severity.

Weather indices, like emissions allowances and freight rates, are particularly complex assets.

5.8   Commodity indices generally

Investors in a commodity derivative often want the diversity of exposure to more than one commodity, perhaps to follow an investment strategy. This can be achieved by the financial instrument referencing movements in a commodity index or basket of commodity indices. Commodity indices are compiled by specialist index providers. These are usually financial institutions (eg, Goldman Sachs and Morgan Stanley).

The constituent items in a commodity index are not typically the trading price of the physical commodity, but instead the trading price of a commodity-linked futures contract. The constituent items are weighted as specified by the index's rules. The most commonly referenced commodity indices include the S&P GSCI (previously, the Goldman Sachs Commodity Index) and the Commodities Research Board Index.

6.   The third constituent part of a commodity derivative: the value to be derived from the underlying asset

Under a commodity derivatives contract, one party will pay the other an amount linked to the value of the underlying commodity asset. This amount may be based on many types of election, which are agreed by the parties at the outset.

Examples of common values referenced to or extracted from the underlying asset	
Type	Description
Single commodity	• The total return on a single commodity futures contract. • The difference in trading price of a single commodity or commodity future on or between specific dates or against a specific price or formula.
Basket of commodities	• The total return on the basket of commodities or commodity futures. • The difference in trading price of the basket of commodities or commodity futures on or between specific dates or against a specific price or formula. • The difference in trading price between the constituent parts of the basket on or between specific dates, against a specific price or formula, or against each other.

Examples of common values referenced to or extracted from the underlying asset	
Type	Description
Single index	• The total return on the single index (eg, the value of the return on the individual commodity futures comprising all or part of the index). • The difference in trading level of the single index on or between specific dates or against a specific level or formula.
Basket of indices	• The total return on the basket of indices (eg, the value of the return on the individual commodity futures comprising all or part of each index). • The difference in trading level of each of the indices on or between specific dates, against a specific level or formula, or against each other.

7. The fourth constituent part of a commodity derivative: purpose[3]

7.1 Who are the market participants?

To understand why parties enter into a commodity derivatives contract, we must first look at who those parties are (ie, the key market participants in the commodity derivatives market).

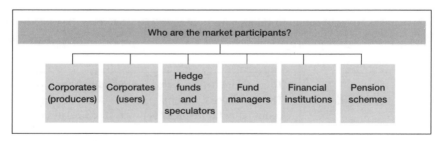

Almost all participants fall into one of the following categories:
- corporate entities (commodity producers);
- corporate entities (commodity users);
- hedge funds and speculators;
- fund managers;
- institutional clients; and
- pension schemes.

---

3 The purposes for using commodity derivatives are discussed more fully in the chapter entitled 'Reasons for entering into commodity derivatives transactions'.

(a) *Corporates (commodity producers)*

Corporates that produce commodities are major users of commodity derivatives products. A commodity producer has many fixed costs in producing a commodity, and falling commodity prices can adversely affect profitability.

Owners and operators of coal mines may wish to forgo the potential upside of future increases in the coal price, to protect themselves against a potential market decline. An oil producer may wish to do the same by entering into an oil forward contract to hedge against a fall in oil prices. An electricity producer may wish to enter into a weather derivative to hedge against a mild winter reducing the demand for electricity. A ship owner may wish to enter into a forward freight agreement to hedge against a decline in freight rates eroding the profitability of its fleet.

(b) *Corporates (commodity users)*

Corporates that use commodities are major users of commodity derivatives products. A commodity user has many fixed costs in producing its product, and falling commodity prices can adversely affect profitability.

A steel producer will see increased costs if the price of coal increases and may wish to enter into a coal forward, agreeing to purchase coal at a fixed price on a future date. An airline might prefer to enter into a cash-settled jet fuel swap to lock in current jet fuel prices over an extended period, rather than pass fuel price increases onto its customers in the form of a surcharge. A coal importer may wish to enter into a forward freight agreement with the ship owner so as to hedge against an increase in freight rates eroding the profitability of its business.

Corporate commodity users are the natural end counterparties of corporate commodity producers. Here lies the great strength of derivatives: the ability of parties to trade risks and protect themselves against the unforeseen.

(c) *Fund managers*

Fund managers are increasingly establishing funds that reference and trade different types of commodity. This represents an alternative asset for investors to invest in. This is something which has been particularly attractive during the 2007–9 credit crunch, with several commodities such as gold performing at record levels while equities and bonds have languished. Investment is generally in commodities futures. However, fund managers also make use of other derivative financial instruments for hedging and leverage purposes.

(d) *Hedge funds and speculators*

The line between hedge funds and asset managers has become blurred in recent years, with hedge funds sometimes moving towards traditional long strategies and asset managers looking to participate in leveraged and shorting strategies.

Traditionally, hedge funds have looked to make returns from any type of market:
- in an upward market through leverage (perhaps through the use of options);
- in a downward market through shorting strategies; and
- in times of market volatility through leveraged trading strategies.

Hedge funds and other investors that look to make profits from movements in the value of an underlying asset alone are not popular with regulators and politicians. For example, in 2008 US Senator Byron Dorgan introduced the End Oil Speculation Bill of 2008, which would have cracked down on speculative commodity derivatives trading. It never made it into law. However, new US legislation now allows regulators to impose position limits on commodity derivatives. It remains to be seen how this will affect hedge funds and speculative traders.

In their defence, these users argue that they bring liquidity to the market, which in the end benefits those participants that are hedging actual risk.

(e) **Financial institutions**

Commodity derivatives can form a large part of a financial institution's business and relate to a significant source of its profits.

A financial institution may use commodity derivatives as a market maker, acting as a buyer to sellers and a seller to buyers. Here the financial institution makes its profits from being able to sell exposures to an underlying asset at a better rate than it purchases them.

An example of this would be a financial institution that enters into a forward freight agreement with a ship owner, where it agrees to pay the negative differential below a fixed freight rate at a future date, while the ship owner agrees to pay the financial institution the positive differential above the fixed freight rate at the future date (should that be the case). Simultaneously, the financial institution will enter into a back-to-back transaction with another of its clients, a coal importer, which is exposed to increases in the same freight rate. Here the financial institution agrees to pay the positive differential above the fixed freight rate at the future date, while the coal importer agrees to pay the financial institution the negative differential above the fixed freight rate at the future date (should that be the case).

The financial institution can charge favourable pricing differences in both transactions because it is making a market and is itself isolated from any movement in the freight rate. Alternatively the end users – the ship owner and the coal importer – may be matched up by two financial institutions entering into a forward transaction with one another and then entering into corresponding transactions with the end users, creating a chain of transactions.

Financial institutions may also enter into commodity derivatives transactions on a proprietary basis, perhaps as part of an investment strategy.

(f) **Pension schemes**

Pension schemes invest the majority of their funds in equities. However, they are increasingly diversifying their assets to avoid overexposure to the equity markets. Investing in commodities as a separate asset class is likely to gain in popularity.

7.2   Reasons for using commodity derivatives

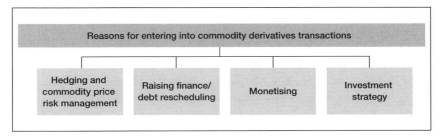

The principal reasons for entering into commodity derivatives contracts usually include one or several of the following:

- hedging, and commodity-price risk management;
- raising finance/debt rescheduling (or increasing debt capacity);
- monetising; and
- investment strategy.

Some of these overlap and, depending on the type of market participant, the importance of each motivation is likely to have different significance.

(a)   *Hedging, and commodity-price risk management*
There are various reasons why a market participant may choose to hedge a commodity price. These include:

- reducing volatility in earnings;
- ensuring minimum cash flows;
- hedging a fixed proportion of production, guaranteeing prices to customers; and
- keeping the price of goods within a predetermined price range.

Hedging is principally done in relation either to end-users' expenses or to earnings depending on a commodity price.

(b)   *Raising finance/debt rescheduling (or increasing debt capacity)*
This area overlaps with hedging. Banks are usually more willing to lend to companies exposed to movements in commodity prices, which have effectively hedged themselves against those risks – or the banks are at least willing to lend at more favourable rates.

Where a borrower or debt issuer is particularly exposed – perhaps because it is a raw materials producer, such as a mining company – commodity-linked risk management instruments embedded in bond and loan structures can allow borrowers and lenders to decouple their exposure to commodity prices from the ability to pay.

These instruments embed a commodity derivative into the overall transaction structure.

For example, if a gold mining corporation enters into a facility agreement at a fixed or floating rate of interest, it faces gold price risk exposure. If the price of gold falls below the cost of production, then it will not generate enough revenue to repay the principal and interest on the loan.

For banks and borrowers to protect themselves against this risk, as part of the overall transaction structure, the borrower could enter into a cash-settled gold swap with a notional amount equal to the principal amount of the facility agreement. Under this swap, the mining corporation would pay the positive cash differential between the actual gold price on each measurement date above a set level (multiplied by the notional amount) and the hedging bank would pay the equivalent negative differential if the actual gold price happened to be below the set level on the relevant measurement date.

The hedging bank would in turn enter into equivalent opposite transactions with other market participants, making a return on the differentials between these two prices. The gold swap would remove some of the exposure to the underlying gold commodity price for both the mining corporation and the banks.

Other commodity-linked structures can involve the return of principal or return being linked to an underlying commodity price or basket of prices; or, in lieu of interest, investors having the right to exercise a cash-settled call or put option.

Commodity bonds have also been used as part of debt-rescheduling programmes to reduce repayment obligations. Examples have included long-dated bonds issued by foreign-exchange-poor raw-material-rich countries, which link repayment of principal and payment of interest to the particular commodity export prices.

(c)   *Monetising*

Commodity prices can be very volatile. In recent years we have seen extreme movements in the price of oil, for example. This volatility can make hedging essential for certain market participants. If the hedging proves useful, though, individual hedging contracts can themselves gain great value. For instance, if an oil producer entered into a series of options giving it the right to sell thousands of barrels of oil at $100 a barrel in three-month intervals, this contract would have little or no value if oil were trading at $120 a barrel. However, as has happened in recent times, if oil were trading at $50 a barrel, then if sold the contract would have significant value, entitling the new counterparty to sell oil at $50 a barrel less than the current price.

Market participants will from time to time seek to monetise these values. Indeed, in the structure described above, the mining companies and the banks involved might choose to sell on the embedded derivatives contracts if the price of gold collapsed, and use the resulting profits to pay down the principal of the loan. This practice was common in early 2009 as financial institutions sought innovative ways to rebuild their balance sheets.

(d)   *Investment strategy*

Commodity derivatives may form part of a fund's, corporate's or financial institution's investment strategy. Commodity derivatives can allow a user to achieve leverage, allowing for greatly enhanced returns (and, potentially, losses too).

Commodity derivatives can also allow users to pursue certain strategies taking a view as to the relative performance of one commodity or commodity future over the performance of other commodities or commodity futures within a basket.

Commodity derivatives can help investors to follow sophisticated strategies which decouple the risk of an individual commodity producer from the price risk of the underlying commodity it produces. An example of this is where an investor enters into a commodity future which provides it with the upside return on a commodity (eg, coal) while selling short a particular gold producer's shares (ie, borrowing these shares, selling them into the market and hoping for a decline in price). This strategy would allow the investor to take a view that the commodity producers shares would decline in value relative to the value of the underlying commodity asset it produces, while hedging itself against an increase in the share price due to an unrelated increase in the price of the underlying commodity.

8.   Additional and inherent risks of commodity derivatives

We have discussed the constituent parts of a commodity derivative in detail. Surrounding these constituent parts, though, are various additional and inherent risks and other relevant factors, which any user of commodity derivatives ignores at its peril. To some extent, these may even negate or temper the effectiveness of any applicable purpose for using commodity derivatives and must therefore be considered seriously.

The five relevant areas here can be divided into:
- structural and strategic factors;
- regulatory and tax risks;
- operational and documentation risks;
- counterparty risks; and
- liquidity risks.

Inevitably, there is some overlap.

8.1   Structural and strategic factors

The third limb of the definition of a commodity derivative: "from which the financial instrument derives its value" – provides users with the opportunity to make gains as well as unexpected losses. And the ability of commodity derivatives to leverage losses as well as returns, mixed with the complexity of any strategy, means that there is an opportunity to get it badly wrong.

The complexity of strategies followed in commodity derivatives transactions can also make it more difficult for any user to accurately gauge the risks involved. This is particularly so where the institutional approvals given to enter into transactions may be sanctioned by personnel with a lesser degree of knowledge than those structuring these products.

For example, a commodity derivative which bases its return on the worst-performing of three commodity derivative indices, by reference to a complex formula, may be particularly risky if bought by a pension fund that does not habitually engage in these types of finance transaction but that is attracted to the potentially high return.

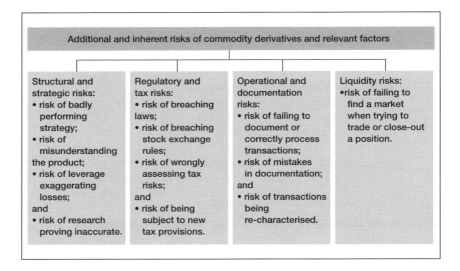

Many financial institutions which are leading market participants produce commodity derivatives research as one of their key client products. This research can cover ideas for new transactions and strategies, or may consist of analytical reports and briefings for new products. The risk that any research proves to be incorrect is significant in any commodity derivative.

8.2   Regulatory and tax risks

Part V of this book concentrates on the regulatory and tax aspects, respectively, of commodity derivatives. The size and complexity of these sections demonstrate the risks involved both in relation to a commodity derivative's underlying asset and in relation to the tax domicile of the parties themselves.

(a)   Regulatory risks

Since 2009 there has been an increasing regulatory focus on transparency, with regulators shining a light on the participants in the derivatives markets and the size of their exposures. Regulators on both sides of the Atlantic are also pushing for standardised trades to be traded through central counterparties and for certain transactions to be traded on an exchange. Transparency is being enforced through the use of data repositories.

The extent to which commodity derivatives transactions can be prohibited, preventing hedging of risk, or limited by forcing standardisation of trades (which prevents hedging of actual exposures by end users) will become an increased risk in commodity derivatives transactions. Further risks may arise where speculative trading is restricted and this results in reduced liquidity in the market, making it more costly and difficult for participants to close out transactions when they no longer have a need for them.

(b)   *Tax risks*

Where a commodity derivative allows a gain or loss to be deferred, failure to obtain proper tax advice can lead to a product user not obtaining the desired gains. Such arrangements can also run the risk of being re-characterised as tax avoidance techniques, leaving a product user perhaps subject to a large bill and/or proceedings against it.

8.3   **Operational and documentation risks**

(a)   *Operational risks*

What happens when a derivative product becomes a victim of its own success? The product grows so quickly that the IT, back-office and middle-office support cannot keep pace with the product's growth: trades can no longer be tracked and/or documented as quickly as parties enter into them. Inevitably, in these circumstances, operational risk increases. This is what has taken place in the credit derivatives market and equity derivatives market; it is also a concern in the commodity derivatives market.

Operational risk also arises where transactions are entered into without proper authorisation or due diligence being carried out, or where delays in the documenting of transactions mean that there is uncertainty as to the terms which were agreed. These can occur due to the sheer volume of transactions entered into by a market participant.

The first area is most apparent where two institutions enter into a relationship trading commodity derivatives (and perhaps other derivatives contracts as well) but the documentation process of agreeing and negotiating an ISDA master agreement (or other trade body standard documentation) and carrying out the requisite due diligence as to creditworthiness and legal risk does not proceed at the same pace.

The second area of confirmation backlogs has caused some concern. Without a confirmation in place, the process of ascertaining what was actually agreed between the parties can become open to dispute and extremely difficult to determine.

(b)   *Documentation risks*

The first major question is whether the commodity derivatives documentation will work. Does it do what is intended and is it legal, valid, binding and enforceable? The OTC commodity derivatives market is now well established and the standardisation efforts of ISDA have reduced these risks as much as possible (eg, ISDA has obtained legal opinions in more than 40 jurisdictions around the world on various enforceability issues). However, there is still a risk – particularly with regard to more bespoke products and/or where UK or New York law is not used as the governing law – that documentation will not perform as intended and will not be legal, valid, binding and enforceable. Similar concerns exist for the documentation produced by other trade bodies.

8.4   **Counterparty risks**

In OTC commodity derivatives transactions, both counterparties are exposed to one another's credit risk. An option buyer, for example, is exposed to the risk that the seller will not be in a position to pay any cash-settlement amount or physically deliver the commodity.

To a certain extent, counterparty risk is inherent in all derivatives transactions. The parties can deal with this risk using existing ISDA documentation architecture (ie, the credit support annex and/or other collateral and credit support-related documentation), or the margin provisions provided in other market-standard documentation. The push towards the use of central counterparties arising from the Euro-American regulatory initiatives of 2009 and 2010 is likely to reduce these risks to some extent.

A further risk is that a counterparty does not have the correct legal authority to enter into a commodity derivatives transaction. The early landmark cases relating to derivatives and capacity occurred in the 1980s and apply to derivatives in general. Proper diligence on any counterparty is essential and will depend to a large extent on the type and jurisdiction of the relevant reference entity. Otherwise, the risk remains that any commodity derivatives contract could be unenforceable and/or that any payments due may not be recoverable.

Commodity derivatives structured products are often issued under the arranging financial institution's Euro medium-term note (EMTN) programme. This exposes the noteholder to the credit risk of the issuing entity. Where a commodity derivatives structured product is issued by a special purpose vehicle (SPV), the financial institution arranging the transaction will usually also enter into an commodity swap with the SPV, pursuant to which the noteholder will be taking the credit risk on that swap counterparty.

8.5 Liquidity risks

Commodity derivatives and OTC structured products may not be as liquid as the underlying commodity futures they reference. This may mean that the price of a commodity derivative against the relevant underlying obligations may become distorted and prone to wider fluctuations in price that the market price of the underlying asset.

9. Restrictions on the development of the commodity derivatives market

The main restrictions that are preventing development of the commodity derivatives market can be summarised as follows:

- lack of knowledge;
- inadequacy of trading systems and trade infrastructure;
- lack of liquidity in the market in general;
- pricing issues;
- regulatory issues;
- documentation inadequacies, particularly in relation to new products; and
- complexity of accounting and tax treatment of commodity derivatives.

9.1 Lack of knowledge

The perceived complexity of certain commodity derivative products actively prevents many potential market participants from purchasing or using products.

Whereas these entities may be entirely comfortable with the mainstream commodity markets, the perceived dangers of leveraged losses may stop many entities from using commodity derivatives, even where products can hedge against losses of existing commodity exposures.

9.2 Inadequacy of trading systems and trade infrastructure
The costs of putting appropriate structures in place will deter many potential market participants from the market, as will the perceived risk if the infrastructure and systems do not prove sufficiently robust.

9.3 Lack of liquidity in the market
Concern regarding how easy it would be to close out or sell a particular commodity derivatives product can deter potential users of commodity derivative products. Whereas an exchange-traded option may be easy to trade, a structured commodity-linked note may not be.

9.4 Pricing issues
Return and losses on commodity derivatives products may be linked to bespoke and complex mathematical formulae. Difficulty in understanding these and the related risks involved will deter many users (in particular, retail users) from purchasing commodity derivatives products. Additionally, issues of opacity relating to how certain formulae are structured may also lead to concerns.

9.5 Regulatory issues
Changes in the global regulatory regime for derivatives in 2010 are momentous and have been rushed through at breakneck speed. It will take time for these changes to bed down and in the meantime uncertainty is likely to hinder the future development of the commodity derivatives market. In the longer term, though, it is hoped that the greater transparency will attract new entrants.

9.6 Documentation inadequacies, particularly in relation to new products
Derivatives documentation is structured for ease of use. This has the benefit of reducing the costs and related timeframes for documenting products. It also makes it easier for experts to understand quickly how a product works. However, the documentation is not constructed to be easily understood by the general user.

The effect of this can be to make the documentation extremely difficult to understand for non-derivatives specialists, even when they are finance lawyers. This can mean that necessary credit approvals for the usage of commodity derivative products can be difficult to obtain.

9.7 Complexity in the accounting and tax treatment of commodity derivatives
As with the regulatory concerns described above, the multi-jurisdictional nature of many commodity derivatives can magnify the difficulties in applying the correct accounting and tax treatment to commodity derivatives products.

Reasons for entering into commodity derivative transactions

Sabine Bertin
Aaron McGarry

1. Introduction

Any business, as part of any commodity sale/supply chain, will face risks associated with that commodity. A jewellery manufacturer is exposed to a rise in the price of gold; a mining corporation is exposed to a fall in the price of gold; a ship owner is exposed to a fall in the cost of transporting freight; and an exporter is exposed to rises in the cost of transporting goods.

Commodity risk is the risk that a business faces from an adverse change in a commodity price. Commodity prices are volatile for many reasons, including floods, droughts, war, technological improvements, the global economy, and supply and demand disruption of distribution or production.

Commodity prices can be even more volatile than interest rates or foreign currency rates. The smaller size of the many different commodity markets alone (eg, gold, silver, copper and cocoa) is partially responsible for the high volatility of commodity prices. Thus, a disruption in any one source of supply may greatly affect the price, since many commodities are dominated by only a few suppliers.

Various economic actors have or seek exposure to commodity risks:

- Commodity producers face price risks in respect of the output – sale proceeds may be insufficient to cover the production costs.
- Processors face price risks in respect of both the input and output – their processing margins depend on variation in the two prices. Moreover, a processor, even if fully integrated into a particular supply chain, will face offsetting price risks.
- Consumers/end users face price risks in respect of the input – the purchase price of the commodity they need may be higher than expected and may therefore increase their expenses.
- Exporters and importers face price risks associated with the holding of inventories.
- While the above economic actors wish to reduce their exposure to commodity risks, investors (eg, large financial institutions, hedge funds, pension funds and other investment funds) seek to exploit the opportunities created as a result of commodity price fluctuations.

Exposure of economic actors in the gold supply chain

A commodity derivative, as opposed to any other derivative, is a financial instrument whose value is determined, at least in part, by fluctuations in the value of some underlying assets or other variable linked to commodity prices.

Commodity derivatives were first created for farmers to offer them protection against crop values falling below the cost of growing the crop. That story goes back thousands of years. Protection came in the form of derivatives contracts covering commodities such as white pepper, wheat, rice, coffee, cotton and many others.

Progressively, the commodity derivatives market has been seen as a direct and pure way to invest in commodities rather than investing in the companies engaged in the production of, or trade in, those commodities. It is easier to forecast the price of commodities based on their demand and supply projections as compared with forecasting the price of the shares of a company – which depends on many factors other than just demand and supply of the products it manufactures, sells or trades.

In this chapter, we look at the purposes for which parties enter into commodity derivative financial instruments and contracts and describe the broad spectrum of uses, from hedging solely to mitigate price risks to engaging in proprietary trading.

2. Reasons for entering into commodity derivatives transactions

The undesirable exposure to commodity risks provides two major business concerns for many market participants. Firstly – and most obviously – there is the risk of incurring a financial loss following adverse price fluctuations (eg, the expected cash flows of a gold producer could be dramatically reduced in the event of a gold price crash). Secondly, the presence of the commodity risk itself creates an uncertainty that hampers the ability to make long-term plans, limits financial strength and can even restrict the capacity to raise debt. There are times when a market participant may want to monetise its commodities by putting a value on them immediately or to predict future valuation. Commodity derivatives are used in a variety of ways as

[handwritten margin notes]

investment strategies, and increasingly they are being opened up to new entrants and new markets – there is no better example of this than carbon trading.

2.1 Hedging, or commodity-price risk management

The objectives of a hedging transaction can be diverse, from reducing earnings volatility to protecting a specified minimum cash flow, hedging a fixed proportion of production, guaranteeing prices to customers or keeping within predetermined price ranges.

In simpler terms, a variation in commodity prices can affect a commercial project or business on two levels – expenses and earnings:

- *Expenses* – for example, if the project or business is dependent on the supply of a certain commodity (eg, a jewellery chain on the price of gold). It must be assured of a supply of raw materials and utilities at costs within an acceptable price range; a shift in price of raw materials could be detrimental to profitability.
- *Earnings* – for example, if a project's or business's income depends on a commodity (eg, the price at which a gold mine can sell its gold). Movements in commodity prices have fundamental implications for estimating future cash flows, and price shifts can thus affect project and business profitability and creditworthiness.

The remainder of this section sets out some simple examples from the perspectives of producer versus seller and consumer versus buyer

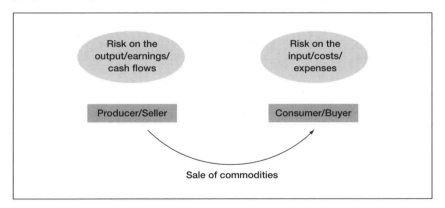

The diagram above shows the opposite risks of the producer/seller and the consumer/buyer. To avoid this uncertainty on the price of the input and output, a company will often seek to hedge these risks.

Various hedging strategies available in the derivatives markets can be employed to reduce commodity pricing risk (eg, options, swaps, forwards and futures). However, managing a hedging programme can be costly.

Below are some examples of commodity price hedging strategies and instruments.

(a)   Hedging 'input risk': the perspective of the buyer/consumer of commodities

Hypothetical example: the oil refinery and the fixed-for-floating swap
Bosphorus Refinery wants to establish a new marketing programme for its key industrial customers to strengthen these long-term relationships. The programme consists of locking in the price that those customers pay to Bosphorus Refinery for a specified quantity of oil products for the next two years.

As Bosphorus Refinery buys its crude oil at spot index prices, it will suffer a loss if this price exceeds the locked-in price it has 'guaranteed' to its customers.

To protect itself, Bosphorus Refinery enters into a two-year fixed-for-floating swap with Bank Caspian to hedge 10,000 barrels of crude oil per month at a fixed price of $80 per barrel.

Under the swap agreement, Bosphorus Refinery makes a monthly fixed payment to Bank Caspian equal to $80 per barrel. Bank Caspian in exchange makes a monthly floating payment to Bosphorus Refinery based on the arithmetic average of the daily settlement prices of the prompt NYMEX crude oil futures contract for each of the pricing periods for which the reference price is quoted.

Bosphorus Refinery continues to purchase crude oil from its usual suppliers at spot index prices. On each settlement date, Bosphorus Refinery and Bank Caspian exchange payments equal to the difference between the monthly average of the spot index price and the fixed $80 per barrel swap price.

The floating payment received from Bank Caspian should closely approximate to the spot index based payment that Bosphorus Refinery discounts to its suppliers for the physical purchase of crude oil.

Bosphorus Refinery receives a positive pay-off from the swap if crude oil prices rise. However, Bosphorus Refinery forgoes opportunity gains if oil prices fall.

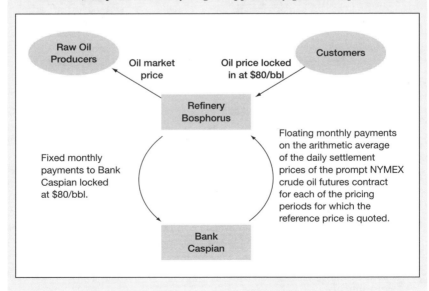

(b)   *Hedging 'output risk': the perspective of the seller/producer of commodities*
Similarly, a market participant may wish to hedge the price of commodities that it produces and sells.

Hypothetical example: the gold mining company and the floor agreement
In a gold mining project financing, the project value (and ultimately the probability of repayment of the project loans) is highly linked to the gold price. The project finance lenders will often require the gold mining company to hedge against falling gold prices to lock in the project value.

Gold mining company Pact'Aulus expects to commence production in 2011 at an originally planned production rate of 10,000 ounces of gold per month for two years. Pact'Aulus finds itself exposed to the risk of falling gold prices in two years; if this happens, it will significantly impact on the company's cash flows and ability to repay the project loans. Pact'Aulus has determined that a gold price under $800 per ounce is likely to be a threat to its ability to survive and pay the production costs and repay the project loans.

To achieve downward price protection, in 2009 Pact'Aulus enters into a two-year $800 per ounce floor agreement with Bank Phrygia for 10,000 ounces per month at a $1.25 per ounce premium starting on the production commencement date, scheduled to happen in January 2011.

During the term of the agreement:
- Pact'Aulus will continue to sell 10,000 ounces of gold per month to its regular customers at agreed-upon index prices;
- Bank Phrygia will receive a $1.25 per ounce premium for providing the price protection under $800 per ounce;
- at the end of each month, if the average of the mean is above $800 per ounce – the floor price – no payments will be due under the floor contract. Pact'Aulus will sell its gold at market price and benefit fully from the high prices; and
- if the average of the mean falls below $800 per ounce, Bank Phrygia will pay Pact'Aulus the difference between the market price and the floor price.

A floor agreement entered into between Pact'Aulus and Bank Phrygia will establish a minimum average sale price for future gold production. This will provide full protection from falling prices, while allowing Pact'Aulus to benefit fully from increases in gold prices.

The chart on the next page indicates in diagrammatic form how the two parties to the transaction interact.

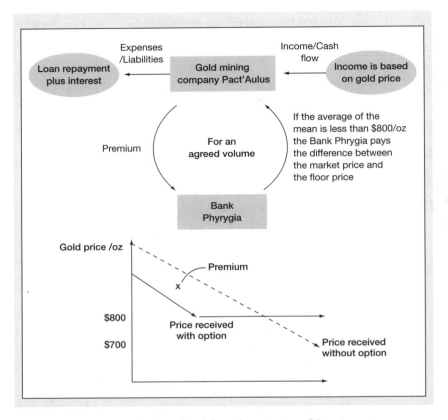

(c) *Managing simultaneously the price risk at the output and input*
The example below describes a complicated set of risks associated with the production of aluminium.

> **Hypothetical example: the gas-fired power plant and the aluminium-gas swap**
>
> Company New NRJ has obtained approval to build a new gas-fired power station in Essex. The gas-fired power station will produce 1 gigawatt of electricity. The output (electricity) is sold to an aluminium smelter on an aluminium-indexed price. The input (gas) is purchased at a floating oil-linked price.
>
> New NRJ faces two risks in this project:
> - that the project value will decrease if the price of aluminium falls; or
> - that the production costs will increase if the price of gas rises.
>
> A customised solution to this set of risks is to enter into a combination of forward contracts (an aluminium–gas swap).
>
> New NRJ will pay Green Bank the floating aluminium price. In exchange, it will receive from the swap counterparty a floating fuel price for the agreed

volume. As a result, New NRJ is fully hedged against the risk of a rise in the price of fuel and a fall in the value of aluminium.

(d) *Hedging strategies in response to specific hedging objectives*

In addition to the examples described above, a variety of risk hedging strategies and instruments exist to suit every market participant and specific hedging objective.

Set out below are five examples of commodity derivatives instruments catering for specific hedging objectives. We have used the same hypothetical example as in section 2.1(a): Bosphorus Refinery and Bank Caspian.

A participation swap would give Bosphorus Refinery a right to participate in favourable price moves below a specified participation price level at an agreed participation rate:

Objective	Solution	Explanation
To achieve a price protection from any increase in crude oil prices above $80/bbl to also participate in the downward price move	The refinery can enter into a **Participation Swap** with a Counterparty	The participation swap establishes a maximum average purchase price forward while offering the refinery the right to participate in favourable price moves below a specified participation level at an agreed-upon participation rate

Example	
Maximum average purchase price forward = $80/bbl Specified participation level = $80/bbl Participation rate = 25% Pricing period = month	

43

A cap agreement would give Bosphorus Refinery the opportunity to minimise exposure to unanticipated increases in oil prices without any loss in participation in favourable moves:

Objective	Solution	Explanation
To achieve a price protection from any increase in crude oil prices above $80/bbl and to be able to fully benefit from downward price moves	The refinery can enter into a **Cap Agreement** with a counterparty	The cap agreement establishes a pre-determined price at which the commodity can be purchased if the refinery decides to exercise the option
Example Maximum average purchase price = $80/bbl		

A spread swap would entitle Bosphorus Refinery to lock in the spread between commodity prices at two different dates:

Objective	Solution	Explanation
To lock in the differentials between the commodity prices at different times (eg, between the time the crude oil is purchased and the time it is refined)	The refinery can enter into a **Spread Swap** with a counterparty	In the spread swap, the refinery pays a pre-agreed fixed spread level in exchange for a floating spread level from a counterparty
Example Pre-agreed fixed spread level = £0.50/bbl Spread value = arithmetic average of (Closing Settlement Price Futures Contact (M) – Closing Settlement Price of Futures Contract (M+12) on each day of the calendar month)		

A collar agreement would ensure that the commodity price range stayed within a maximum and minimum limits:

Objective	Solution	Explanation
To achieve a fixed price range for crude oil purchases at no monetary costs	The refinery can enter into a **Collar Agreement** with a counterparty	The collar agreement establishes a minimum possible purchase price (floor price) and a maximum possible purchase price (ceiling price). For prices within the range, the refinery achieves the market price

Example	
Cap strike price = $90/bbl Floor strike price = $70/bbl	

Hybrid instruments combine the basic swap-based or option-based contracts to create highly customised financial products that market participants can use to meet specific hedging objectives.

Hybrids can take a variety of forms. The most common hybrid structures include extendable swaps, double-up or double-down swaps, participating collars, swap options, cross-commodity indexed swaps, range swaps, extendable collars and barrier or 'knock-out' options.

Hybrid instrument	Explanation
Extendable swap	Similar to the fixed-for-floating swap, except that Bank Caspian has the right to extend the swap maturity for a pre-specified amount of time at the end of the stated maturity.
Double-up swap	Similar to a basic swap, except that it offers Bosphorus Refinery the opportunity to improve significantly its effective purchase price. Under a double-up swap, Bosphorus Refinery's swap fixed price is set lower than for an otherwise identical conventional swap. In exchange, Bosphorus Refinery agrees to buy on any settlement date pre-specified additional quantities of the commodity at the swap fixed price, if Bank Caspian elects to sell these additional quantities.

continued overleaf

Hybrid instrument	Explanation
Participating collar	Allows for index flexibility within a specified price range and provides a predetermined percentage gain from any favourable price moves.
Swap option	Provides the right, but not the obligation, to buy or sell a swap at a predetermined fixed price, in exchange for a premium payment.
Cross-commodity indexed swap	Allows Bosphorus Refinery to shift synthetically revenues from one commodity to another to reduce price risk and volatility.
Range swap	Bosphorus Refinery buys a swap at a level below the current market, but the swap ceases to exist if the market settles above the predetermined level in any individual month.
Barrier or 'knock-out' option	Similar to a conventional option, except for the addition of a second expiration feature which makes it cheaper to purchase. In addition to the usual option terms, an 'out' price level is specified. If the commodity price is at or moves through the 'out' price level at any time during the life of the option, the option expires immediately. Otherwise, the barrier option offers the same protection as a conventional option.

2.2 Raising finance/debt rescheduling (or increasing debt capacity)

An industrial consumer of crude oil, such as a transport company, operates in an environment subject to adverse price movement in the international oil market. This risk exposure reduces the company's ability to make long-term plans, dampens its appeal to investors and makes gaining access to debt markets more difficult – uncertainty must be paid for! As a result, there is a real incentive and added value to such a company to manage efficiently exposure to fluctuating crude oil prices.

In this instance and in contrast with section 2.1, commodity derivatives are a means of increasing the predictability of an enterprise's future commodity-linked cash flow, rather than a means of stabilising commodity prices. We set out below some examples of commodity price hedging strategies and instruments.

(a) Corporate hedging programmes or long-term business planning

Hedging enables a company to secure its objectives, to measure performance and to reduce the cost of capital (eg, in terms of both capital raising and reserves to cover the risk of a commodity price variation).

In general, 'corporate commodity hedging' can be defined as a reduction in dependence between uncertain future corporate profits and random market prices.

The entry into selected derivatives contracts aims to manipulate certain features of the probability of distribution of the company's future cash flows or earnings. A selected derivative financial instrument can also ensure that a specified debt covenant is not breached.

This is different from speculative policies that increase the company's exposure to price fluctuations and that might result from advantages in information about future prices (see section 2.4).

For example, a project finance transaction comprises two phases: a construction phase and a production phase. Given the time gap between the date of utilisation of the loan for the construction phase by the project company and the commencement of production (source of revenues), the project lenders run the risk that the commodity prices will fall dramatically, thus impairing the project company's ability to repay the project loans.

A hedging strategy enables the project developer to reduce the volatility of the cash flows, thereby reassuring the project lenders that there will be a lower probability of default.

Although banks are normally more willing to lend to companies that have reduced their risks by hedging, a general hedging policy can still be regarded as insufficient by lenders, insofar as the hedging proceeds are not linked to the repayment of the loans and there is no 'guarantee' for the lenders that the borrower will indeed apply the hedging proceeds to repayment of the loans.

Commodity-linked risk management instruments such as commodity bonds and loans can provide a useful tool to decrease the credit risk from the lender's perspective and the default risk from the borrower's perspective. These instruments are usually used for finance raising or debt restructuring, and are not primarily intended to manage price risk in commodity trades. Price management elements are built in the bond or loan to provide greater security to lenders that the borrower will be able to meet its commitments even in the event of unfavourable price developments. Thus, commodity bonds and loans can act as a creative vehicle to obtain access to capital on easier terms.

(b) Raising finance through debt (loans or bonds)

(i) Providing security to lenders

Debt instruments with an embedded commodity derivative can provide greater security to prospective lenders that the commodity-exposed borrower will be able to meet its commitments.

If a commodity producer/seller borrows at a fixed rate, it faces commodity price risk exposure – that is, the price of its output may fall below the break-even cost of production. If it borrows at a floating rate then, in addition to commodity price risk exposure, it faces the risk of a rise in interest rates. Commodity-linked bonds and loans can provide a hedge against both rising interest rates and rises or falls (as the case may be) in the commodity price.

Commodity-linked bonds and loans tie the repayment of a loan or bond and the payment of interest/coupons to commodity prices. Take a conventional bond or loan. The bearer of the conventional bond (or the lender, in the case of a loan) receives fixed/floating coupon (or interest, in the case of a loan) payments during the life of the bond (loan), and face value (principal, in the case of a loan) at maturity. Commodity-linked bonds (or loans) will differ from conventional bonds (or loans) in terms of their pay-offs to the holder (or lender, in the case of a loan).

Therefore, the structural difference between the two bond/loans is that the nominal return of the conventional bond/loan held to maturity is known with certainty (although the real return is unknown due to inflation uncertainty), whereas both the nominal and real returns of the commodity-linked bond are unknown.

Commodity-linked bonds and loans in reality consist of a large number of non-standardised instruments, often with complicated specifications.

Principal/face value: The principal of a commodity-linked bond/loan may be paid in either the physical units of a reference commodity or its equivalent monetary value. For instance, the Giscard gold bond issued by the French government in 1973 carried a 7% nominal coupon rate, but the redemption value was indexed to the price of a 1 kilogram bar of gold.

Interest/coupons: Similarly, the coupon payments may be in units of the commodity to which the bond is indexed.

For instance, a copper-linked bond could have its principal and interest payments indexed to copper. The bond could be 4% copper-linked, with an aggregate principal of 1,000 ounces of copper. Interest payments could be payable annually. Bearers of these bonds could have the option to receive both interest and principal in either the monetary value of the specified amount of copper indexed to the bond, the physical quantity of copper referenced or even units of a copper exchange-traded fund.

Bonds/loans embedding of an option (call or put): There are two types of commodity-linked bond: forward based and option based. With the forward type, the coupon and/or principal payment to the bearer of the bond is based on the price of a stated amount of the reference commodity. With the option type, the coupon payments are similar to those of a conventional bond, but at maturity the bearer receives the face value plus an option to buy or sell a predetermined quantity of the commodity at a specified price. Alternatively, to minimise the default risk, the borrower may be given the option to pay the minimum of the face value and the value of the reference amount of the commodity at the maturity date. Here are two examples:

- *Gold warrants* – gold warrants are another type of gold-indexed security. A company issues 1,000 preferred voting shares. Holders of these shares are entitled to an annual dividend of $1 and one gold warrant per share. Each warrant, when exercised, guarantees the holder 0.01 ounces of gold from a mine at a price of $800 per ounce.
- *Option-based bond* – another company owns a large silver mine. It issues silver-indexed bonds to hedge against fluctuations in the price of silver. Each $100 bond is indexed to 10 ounces of silver, pays a coupon rate of 8.5% and

has a maturity of 10 years. At maturity of the bond, its bearer receives the maximum of the face value of $100 or the market value of 10 ounces of silver. The bonds can be redeemed after 10 years only if the average silver price for 30 consecutive days is higher than $20 per ounce.

Therefore, from a commodity producer/seller's perspective, if the commodity price rises, the commodity-linked debt becomes more expensive to repay, but that is offset by an increase in revenues; and if the price of the commodity falls, the debt will cost less to repay. Win–win.

A further example: an aluminium company, concerned about a drop in the price of its product, may issue commodity-linked bonds whose interest rates rise and fall with the price of aluminium. When the company's revenues decrease as a result of a drop in aluminium prices, its cost of borrowing also declines. Commodity bonds and loans act as a natural hedge for future revenues and production. Risk transfer: one of the best drivers of all derivatives products.

The primary motivation for a commodity producer to issue a commodity-linked bond is to raise investment capital while ensuring, through the use of a single instrument, that the investment's return is not affected by changes in the price of the commodity. Therefore, the ultimate objective in using this instrument is to acquire protection from adverse movements in interest rates and spot commodity prices. Commodity-linked bonds have also been used to repay debts. The aim is to create for the debtor a positive correlation between all its debt service obligations and commodity prices. This has been used particularly in debt rescheduling of emerging countries heavily dependent on a certain commodity price (see section 2.2(c)).

(ii)   *Reducing the cost of financing/funding*
Forward-type commodity bonds are often issued for risk hedging by the company or producer (or country) involved in producing the commodity to secure the means of repaying a financing; option-type bonds are instead used to reduce the cost of financing (eg, lower coupons).

With option-type bonds, the bondholder receives the nominal face value of a conventional bond and has the possibility of choosing whether to exercise an option to buy or sell a certain amount of the designated commodity at a predetermined price at maturity or at any predetermined date before that.

This option has a positive effect on the cost (interests/coupons) of financing.

Hypothetical example: the aluminium producer and the commodity-linked bond
Alumni Corporation is an aluminium producer and needs to borrow $100 million to develop a mining project.

If the project is financed by a simple bank loan and aluminium prices fall, Alumni's ability to repay the loan will be impaired. To avoid this risk, Alumni will enter into an aluminium-linked syndicated loan structure, in which liabilities and cash flows are directly linked.

Bank Intermediary and Alumni sign an agreement pursuant to which Bank Intermediary receives the aluminium-linked payments from Alumni, while paying Lender Ultimate the $100 million principal repayment plus interest.

From the perspective of Alumni, the financing consists of a commodity bond and a put embedded in the bond:

- On Day 1, Alumni makes a drawdown of $100 million financing from Lender Ultimate.
- During the 10-year term of the loan, Alumni repays portions of the loan every six months (December and June).
- Each instalment is calculated according to a formula which effectively implies that:
  - if the aluminium price falls below $1,800 a tonne (the reference price being the arithmetic average of the London Metal Exchange official cash settlement price for all business days during the previous six months), the reimbursement amount declines in tandem (for each dollar that the reference price is below $1,800, the loan reimbursement is $10,000 lower);
  - if the aluminium price is between $1,800 and $2,000 a tonne, the amount repayable increases. For each dollar that the reference price is above $1,800, the loan reimbursement is $10,000 higher. Alumni gives all the benefits of prices above $1,800; and
  - if the aluminium price is above $2,000, Alumni benefits from all further increases in aluminium prices.

The structure is implemented as follows:

- a swap arrangement between Bank Intermediary and Alumni, in which Bank Intermediary links Alumni's reimbursements to the income from its expected aluminium production while giving Lender Ultimate a debt service which is not linked to the aluminium prices;
- a series of options (put options with a strike price at $2,000) embedded in the deal, which ensure that if aluminium prices increase above $2,000, Alumni's loan repayments will no longer increase, allowing the company to benefit from large price increases. (The premium for these options is, in effect, part of the financing). Thus, Alumni has the choice of paying either the repayment amount or the market value of the designated commodity.

The structure has the following benefits:

- It guarantees a minimum price for Alumni production.
- It links repayment amount with ability to pay, making budgeting easier and reducing the credit risk exposure taken by Lender Ultimate, leading to more favourable pricing of the loan (lower interest rates).
- It locks in the borrower's repayment cost.
- It gives Alumni unlimited advantages if prices increase above $2,000 (which is the level the company believes that aluminium prices will reach in the medium term).

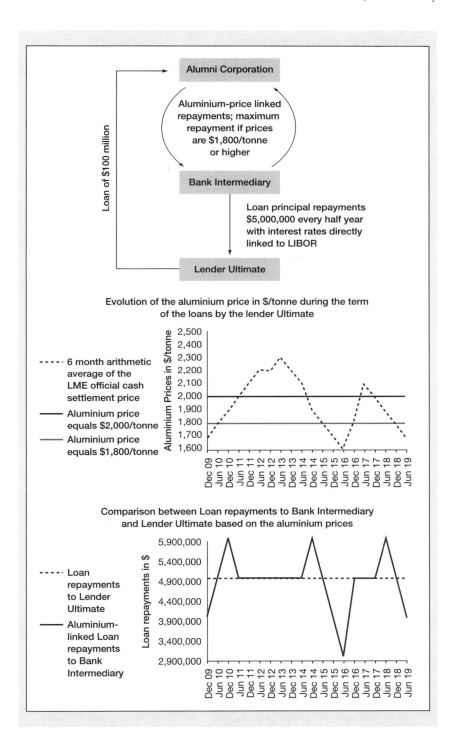

(c)   *Debt rescheduling/restructuring*

Commodity bonds can be used as part of debt rescheduling programmes to reduce a borrowing country's debt service obligations. For example, in 1990, as part of the Brady Plan, banks which agreed to receive lower principal repayments or interest payments on their existing loans to Mexico and Venezuela were given in return new 30-year bonds from the governments of these countries carrying the right to receive supplementary payments tied to oil export prices.

In other terms, banks agreed to a debt-for-bond exchange at a discount price in order to ameliorate the interest payments and principal repayments on new or modified debt contracts.

> **Examples: Brady bonds or the use of a commodity-linked bond as debt restructuring**
>
> Brady bonds are named after US Treasury Secretary Nicholas Brady, who – in association with the International Monetary Fund (IMF) and the World Bank – sponsored the effort to restructure outstanding sovereign debt and interest arrears into liquid debt instruments:
>
> - Creditor banks exchanged sovereign loans for Brady bonds incorporating principal and interest guarantees and cash payments. Brady bonds were issued by the Mexican government.
> - Principal and interest on the Brady bonds were collateralised by US Treasury zero coupon bonds and other high-grade instruments.

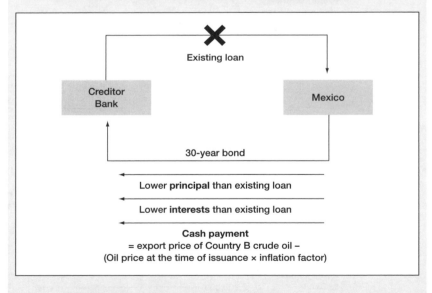

Brady bonds incorporated value recovery rights or warrants, which granted bondholders the right to recover a portion of debt should the debtor Mexican government's debt servicing capacity improve. In effect, these are known as 'oil warrants' because they are linked to oil export prices and thus to the oil export receipts. These oil warrants gave the holder a cash payment based on the difference between the export price of Mexican crude oil and a reference price. The reference price was calculated by the price of oil at the time of issuance multiplied by an inflation factor calculated by the IMF.

As a result of this debt restructuring, debtor governments had their principal, interest and interest arrears reduced.

(d) Raising finance through equity

Investors generally prefer to invest in the shares of companies that perform as planned. Leaving aside speculative shareholders seeking an exposure to commodities, most institutional shareholders focus on sustainable growth. For instance, in the case of a mining company, shareholders will analyse the ability of a company to fund and execute its exploration and development of quality mining assets, and subsequent profitable extraction and processing of its ore reserves. From a company's perspective, this justifies a hedging programme if and when projected risk capacity (cash-flow generation) might potentially curtail the company's ability to fund and execute its planned investor rate of return-positive projects while meeting other critical financial targets.

(e) Obtaining short-term export financing

A futures or forward contract is a legally binding agreement for delivery of a certain commodity in the future for an agreed price that satisfies the requirement of a sales contract. In most countries, a sales contract is necessary to obtain access to government pre-export finance. Forwards can offer considerable flexibility to a seller when it expects prices to decrease, because they permit the seller to have a sales contract without having to lock in prices. Particularly in executable orders, the price is determined as a function of the published price – generally, a price of one of the futures exchanges. An example is a sales contract for a certain volume of raw coffee signed in December 2009 for delivery in June 2010, with a price clause establishing that the price will be the raw coffee price of a July 2010 futures contract on a specific exchange at a specific but still to be determined date. Either the buyer or the seller may fix the price at which the contract will be executed at any time before the end of June. Executable orders offer considerable flexibility.

Similarly, an export sales contract is a document necessary in the application process to obtain pre-export financing from private lenders (execution of a spot export contract will be a condition precedent to the drawdown of a loan). However, there is no requirement for the price of the commodity to be determined at time of loan making. The price may be agreed not when the export contract is signed, but when the commodity is delivered. In this event, the export contract should specify how the price will be calculated. A futures or forward contract can be used for this purpose.

2.3   Monetising

(a)   Mining derivatives

One of the key characteristics of commodities is that historically they have been price volatile and subject to market fluctuations. Oil is an excellent example of an especially volatile commodity, with a recent history littered with price spikes and troughs as world events play into the world markets. However, it is not just oil which suffers extreme price variations: since the turn of the century, copper, aluminium, zinc, gas and, consequently, the price of the delivery of electricity have all seen rapid price rises and falls. The consequences of such price volatility can play havoc with income streams for mining companies that extract such commodities, making it difficult to put in place long-term strategies for exploration, production volumes and setting guaranteed prices for customers.

To mitigate this market volatility, mining companies in particular enter into hedging arrangements. A variety of different derivatives can be entered into, including specific 'over-the counter' contracts, exchange-traded derivatives, which are more standardised, and commercial hedging built into loans or other commercial contracts such as offtake agreements. All of these different types of derivative will help to protect the hedge taker against whatever aspect it wishes to cover – whether that be price, volume or time risk, to name a few. Since mining companies are actually producing the commodity in question, they have in fact covered any derivative position they take. This is not the case, however, for speculators that enter into commodity derivatives and are looking to make a profit out of anticipated price movements in commodities as discussed above.

In addition to hedging such risks, entering into such derivatives can also help to put a monetary value on the commodity in question before it has left the ground.

Hypothetical example: a gold mining company and monetisation
Lafonde Mining Inc decides to open a new gold mine with the price of gold standing at $100 an ounce.

Lafonde Mining enters into futures contracts with a number of counterparties as follows:

- Lafonde Mining agrees to deliver 10,000 kilograms of gold.
- The delivery date is August 1 2010.
- The price is also $100 an ounce.
- As this is a future, both parties must fulfil the obligations of the contract.

Lafonde Mining does this in order to protect itself against price volatility in the market.

It is possible, of course, that the price of gold may have gone up by the time Lafonde Mining comes to deliver on the gold futures on August 1 2010 and as a result it will lose out on such an upside.

However, if the price has gone down, it has insulated itself against the fall and can rely on the fact that, as long as it delivers the 10,000 kilograms of gold agreed on, it will still be paid $100 an ounce.

This provides a host of benefits to Lafonde Mining, including:

- price stability;
- guaranteed income streams; and
- predictability in a volatile market.

In addition to the above, however, it also puts a definite value on the commodity that the company is seeking to mine. Among other things, this should make it easier to obtain loans, as the company can point to an already locked-in value for the raw material itself; and it can facilitate a more stable valuation of the company, making it potentially easier to raise money in the capital markets should it wish to do so.

As such, a well-thought-out and coherent hedging strategy is a vital tool for mining companies in the commodities market as a way to overcome often turbulent markets by monetising the raw materials themselves, with a view to ensuring price and company stability.

(b) Weather derivatives

Weather derivatives are a sophisticated method of monetising through derivatives. An ice-cream seller could help to overcome poor London summers with above-average numbers of cold days, leading to reduced sales of ice creams, if only he had access to the weather derivatives market. His counterparty is a large financial institution that enters into many thousands of different weather derivatives of all types, and that at any one time will hold large positions and exposure to such derivatives. This financial institution market-makes by entering into weather derivatives, but without net exposure. It can avoid net exposure in a number of ways, such as entering into back-to-back derivatives with a third party, often with another financial institution; or through exchange-traded transactions where its exposure will be matched, again to a third party.

A third way of offsetting the risk while at the same time monetising the value of the basket of weather derivatives on their balance sheet is to issue a weather bond. Weather bonds work in the same way as catastrophe bonds, a product present in the market for years and used by insurers to avoid traditional catastrophe reinsurance – and indeed by reinsurers themselves to transfer risks they take on natural disasters, such as earthquakes and hurricanes.

The structure of a catastrophe bond, and in turn a weather bond, is that a special purpose vehicle (SPV) – generally located in a tax-efficient jurisdiction – issues bonds to investors. This SPV will hold the bond proceeds. These are invested in collateral in the form of highly rated securities held by a custodian. The bonds pay a coupon to investors over the life of the bond, providing them with a healthy return on their principal investment – if all goes well. However, in the case of a catastrophe bond, if an earthquake occurs in Japan, for example, which is exactly what the catastrophe insurance underlying the bond references, the investors will lose much, if not all, of their principal and the bond proceeds will be used to pay out on the earthquake insurance. In the same way, therefore, baskets of weather derivative risks can be transferred to bondholders. At the same time, though, the weather bond has the added benefit of valuing the derivatives and monetising them so that if the financial institution is out of the money at any point on the underlying weather derivative transactions (with pub chains and ice-cream sellers), the SPV will pay out to it under a swap agreement.

Few weather bonds have reached issuance stage, with the first being arranged in 1999 by Koch Energy Trading. However, there are plans to issue a weather derivative for excess rainfall from the Caribbean Catastrophe Insurance Facility, which is Caribbean owned and helps Caribbean governments to assist with weather-induced emergencies. At the time of writing, it is anticipated that such a derivative could well be repackaged into a weather bond and it will be interesting to see whether this comes to issuance. Certainly, with the seemingly increased occurrences of weather-induced disasters around the world, weather derivatives and bonds to monetise the risk look set to become more common in the future.

So weather derivatives can match those who need rain with those who need blue skies; those who need sun with those who need rain; and those who need to stand in the middle with insurers, investors and those who want money for nothing going wrong in world. And they can all offset their risk against each other – the magic of derivatives!

2.4   Investment strategy

(a)   Proprietary trading/trading volatility

Inflation – especially high inflation – undermines the value of currency, assets and stocks. Although a small amount of inflation every year can be a good thing, consistently high or unexpected spikes in inflation have a negative impact on the economy. They erode the purchasing power and therefore the value of a portfolio of assets that an investor might hold, and as such any investor should look to protect itself from inflation. Investing in commodity derivatives can be one way of doing this. The principal reason for this is that as demand for goods and services increases – the underlying cause of inflation – so the price of commodities rises as producers look to secure the necessary commodities to produce the goods and services required. A knock-on effect is that commodity derivatives also see price rises as they are heavily traded in the market – again, as producers look to secure supplies of necessary commodities and the increased demand drives prices higher.

Many commodity derivatives investors will be doing so on a speculative basis, investing in 'paper' commodity futures in particular as part of their broader portfolio of investments. These investors rarely look to receive physical delivery of the commodity in question and will look to sell on the contract at a higher price: 100,000 tonnes of cocoa delivered to the City of London could be a problem!

Although commodity prices are more volatile than other underlying assets, they can be still be an effective inflation hedge, because commodity price hikes drive up inflation. Placed in a portfolio of investments, commodity derivatives can protect the purchasing power of any capital invested in them as they rise in price alongside rises in inflation. As such, they can be an effective way of diversifying a portfolio of investments that might include more traditional stocks, bonds and gilts which will be negatively affected by rises in inflation rates.

(b) *Asset-based trading for optimisation/trading to optimise an asset position*

This term is usually associated with energy companies and their trading strategy of optimising the usage and capability of the assets they own. These assets may be gas storage facilities, power plants, wind energy farms or others. On the face of it, speculative trading while looking to optimise assets seem at odds. Speculation by its very nature is high risk and high in volume, and ignores the asset capabilities of an energy trading company – the usual driver in asset-based trading. Pre-Enron, speculative energy trading was big; but then the bubble burst. The market is still picking up the pieces. Current themes are still 'trading around the assets', as it is termed, to optimise storage space or power capabilities and attempting to capture an arbitrage in location, time and transportation factors, among others.

For example, Domini Gas and Griffiths Emissions both own gas storage facilities and both purchase forward gas contracts to be delivered in the summer time, but at the same time sell forward gas contacts to deliver that gas in the winter. As a result, both companies will hopefully benefit from the summer/winter arbitrage in gas prices based on usage at those times of year, while being able to use their storage facilities in the meantime.

This is a very simple example, but it shows how such commodity derivatives can become embedded in the assets themselves. This is contrary to a purely speculative trade, which may also be done by an energy trading company buying gas forwards; but the difference is it may have no storage facilities and hope simply to sell on the forward when prices move in its favour, providing a profit.

(c) **Short selling**

Short selling, and especially naked short selling, has become a very controversial form of speculation in recent years. It has been blamed by the ill-informed (including some regulators) for a variety of distortions in the market such as the food and oil price spikes in 2007–8 and even as a major factor in the collapse of Lehman Brothers. While such views are debatable – sometimes true on both sides – short selling can be an effective form of protecting against falling prices. As such, if an investor or trader feels that commodity prices may be about to fall – perhaps as a result of a slowing economy, and therefore falling demand for commodities to produce goods and services – he might consider short selling his positions in any commodity derivatives he holds; he doesn't just have to make money on the back of good news. Often in short selling – although not always – the investor or trader does not actually own the financial instrument and may actually borrow it from a broker for a fee with a view to selling it into the market at the current (higher) price and hoping to buy it back at a future date when it has fallen in price. The financial instrument can then be returned to the owner and the investor/trader comes out of the process having made a profit off the back of the falling prices.

(d) **Market access**

As a rule, derivatives may seem too complex and intricate to become involved in for all but the most sophisticated investor: our ice-cream seller might agree. However, new derivative products are emerging for a variety of different scenarios and asset classes, and can open up the possibility of using derivatives to whole new classes of business and investor that may never have considered using them.

Weather derivatives are a good recent example. These break down into many different climatic products, but the most common type by far is still based on temperature. They work by calculating how many heating degree days and how many cooling degree days there are on average above or below a set and agreed temperature. To focus the derivative even further, the contract is usually limited to a set place over a set period of time – usually one month, or possibly over a winter or summer season.

Many businesses rely on temperature. Let's take a very obvious example: our ice-cream seller. He would clearly be very keen to see long, hot summers every year (as would most of us), in order to sell as many ice creams as possible and maximise his revenue. However, especially in the United Kingdom, he cannot rely on that being the case and his revenues will fluctuate from summer to summer, depending on how many hot, sunny days there actually are. A temperature-based weather derivative could help out our ice-cream seller during bad summers where there are few hot days and prolonged periods of below-average temperatures. Such a derivative could look like this:

> **Contract period:** Five months, from May to September
> **Average temperature and average amount of cooling degree days over the set period:** 15 degrees centigrade with on average 50 days that are cooling degree days (ie, days that have temperatures below 15 degrees centigrade)
> **Place:** London

The ice-cream seller's derivative with his counterparty will therefore see him receiving a payment if the average number of cooling degree days over the period exceeds 50 days. He will make no payment at all if the number of such days either is on the average or below 50 days. However, the ice-cream seller will have to pay the counterparty a premium for entering into the derivative in the first place. Premiums can vary depending on the counterparty, but typically range from 10% to 30% of the absolute limit that could be expected to be paid out by the counterparty.

As a result, it is possible to see how weather derivatives of the temperature-based variety can be of use to businesses – whatever they be – that are so exposed to the vagaries of the weather. The ice-cream seller might not enter into the derivative; but the ice-cream manufacturer might!

2.5 New entrants – the carbon trading market as an example

Carbon trading is a global attempt to reduce world emissions of greenhouse gases, particularly carbon dioxide (CO_2). This has in turn led to derivatives on carbon trades being developed and has opened up the derivatives market to a whole new class of users.

Under the Kyoto Protocol, which came into force in 2005, most developed nations committed to cut their emissions by 5.2% by 2012. The Kyoto signatories also agreed to adopt a cap-and-trade system to effect this reduction. This operates whereby a central authority – usually the government or supra-national body such as the European Union – sets a cap on the amount of greenhouse emissions that a country can emit. It then issues emission credits for those pollutants. It is up to the individual polluters to stay within the credits they are provided. The trade aspect of the system comes in where, for example, a particular company may find it needs to emit more CO_2 than it has credits for. In such a situation it can buy emission credits from another company that has been emitting less CO_2 and has decided it will not need to avail itself of all the credits it has in its possession. The obvious upsides and downsides here are that those that pollute more end up having to pay for doing so by purchasing the extra credits, while those that pollute less are rewarded through selling their redundant credits.

The EU Emissions Trading Scheme (ETS) was set up in 2005. All EU members have subscribed to the ETS as their unified response to meeting their obligations under the Kyoto Protocol. Under the ETS, each member state submits a national allocation plan to the European Union for approval, after which the European Union will issue an EU allowance (EUA) permitting a polluter to emit one tonne of CO_2. The EU ETS is by far the largest such scheme operating in the world today, accounting for more than 70% of the volume and more than 78% of the value of this 2.9-billion-tonne trading market.

Considering the above, therefore, there clearly needs to be a liquid market in place to allow for the trade element of this cap-and-trade system to operate efficiently and effectively, so that sellers and buyers can more easily come together. Four exchanges exist across the European Union where EUAs and derivatives on them can be traded: the European Climate Exchange and the Climate Spot Exchange, both in London; the Climex in Amsterdam; and BlueNext in Paris.

When it is also considered that, under the ETS, failure to hold sufficient EUAs on a predetermined compliance date results in a €100 fine per excess tonne, the value of derivatives as a means for emitters to hedge the risk of failing to comply becomes more apparent. As such, the two most popular and beneficial derivatives to use for EUAs are futures and options.

(a)   EUA futures

A future in this scenario gives the holder of such a contract the right and obligation to buy EUAs at some predetermined date in the future for a predetermined price. A future differs from an option in that both parties must fulfil the contract: the buyer must buy and the seller must sell the EUAs at the agreed price on the agreed date. One EUA futures contract under both BlueNext and the European Climate Exchange contains 1,000 EUAs, so on fulfilment of the contract it allows a polluter to emit 1,000 tonnes of CO_2. The benefits of such a contract for a participant in the EU ETS are clear. It stabilises the price of an EUA for the emitter by locking in a price per 1,000, so that when it comes to exercising the future the emitter knows exactly what it needs to pay to buy them – or indeed what it will receive, should it be selling. This hedges against the constant fluctuations of the market, which might force an emitter to pay a significantly higher price per EUA at the time of compliance when it finds it does not hold the requisite amount of EUAs for all of its emissions. It also has the benefit of providing the buyer with comfort that it will indeed hold the required number of

EUAs needed, and will almost definitely provide a significantly cheaper way of staying within the rules of the EU ETS rather than just paying the fine. Of course, this process can be taken to its next logical step: there is also a secondary market in the trading of carbon futures on the same exchanges. By following the prices of EUAs and futures, emitters that actively manage their carbon trades can actually end up making money if they buy and sell futures and EUAs at the right time.

(b)   *EUA options*

An option on an EUA is similar to a future, but differs in one vital respect, in that the holder of an option has the right to exercise the contract on or prior to a set settlement or expiration date. In other words, both parties are not obligated to fulfil the contract on a set date for a set price; rather, only one party must fulfil its side of the bargain and only then if the holder of the option decides to exercise its right thereunder. Again, like a future, the underlying asset can be an EUA and very frequently is so, being fulfilled on the same exchanges named above that help the carbon cap-and-trade system to function.

The advantages are similar, if not identical, to those for futures, but this time the option holder has an element of flexibility, since it is not obligated to pay the agreed price for delivery of the EUAs should it find that it does not in fact need additional EUAs. Instead, it will pay a premium for entering into the contract and for the privilege of having the option in the first place. Like a future, in the long run this can mean a financial saving: by paying the relatively small price of the premium, the option holder ensures it will have a plentiful supply of EUAs should the need arise, thus avoiding the much heavier financial penalty of an EU fine.

Again, the next logical step can be made, whereby options can be taken on EUA futures themselves. The price paid for this type of option is the trading price of the specific future being sought at the time the option is exercised.

As can be seen, derivatives in the form of futures and options with underlying EUAs can be a very effective way of hedging against possible price volatility in the carbon trading market. They also ensure compliance with the EU ETS and the avoidance of potentially significant financial penalties. These advantages should open up the possibility of their use to one of the newest markets in the world today – and one that is surely set to grow.

3.   Conclusion

3.1   Trade-off between risk and return

A key element in any hedging strategy is to determine the desired level in the trade-off between risk and return. In addition, any potential user must decide whether the instruments are to be primarily used for price hedging, as part of a wider marketing strategy (eg, establishing long-term trading relationships) or for price hedging in combination with other financial deals, including raising investment funds.

3.2   Risk

Several firms using derivatives in an attempt to manage such risks have suffered huge losses of late – on paper at any rate. Among the hardest hit have been airlines, many of which paid to protect themselves from higher fuel prices last year when the oil price peaked at $147 a barrel. Because oil now costs much less, many have had to write down the value of those contracts, even if they are not due to be settled for years (*The Economist*, June 19 2009).

3.3 Cheap financing: current situation

By the second half of 2009, such hedging declined for the first time since 2001, according to ISDA. The bankers' reluctance to participate in such transactions stems from the nature of hedging contracts, which although not officially loans, nonetheless create liabilities between banks and their customers that grow or shrink as the underlying variable changes. The hedges that are available have become much more expensive. Banks are explicitly charging for the credit risk that they assume when writing a derivative contract.

Over-the-counter commodity derivatives

Marcin Perzanowski

1. Introduction

Do over-the-counter (OTC) derivatives really involve walking into a shop and asking the proprietor for a commodity-linked forward, swap or option? This is not too far from the truth! A financial institution, acting as a market maker, is the shop and it offers derivative products to meet the wants and needs of its customers – corporates, other financial institutions and hedge funds.

The institution is not unlike a New York delicatessen, which offers its customers sandwiches with a vast array of fillings: a wide choice of cheeses, meats and pickles, all laid out across a vast display cabinet. In the case of OTC derivatives, the choices include semi-annual or quarterly payment dates; index-linked underlying assets, single assets or baskets made up of gold, wheat or gigajoules of electricity; or perhaps a range of maturity dates, strike levels and premiums – anything which takes the customer's fancy or meets its requirements.

The delicatessen makes much of its profit from selling packaged ingredients to customers for more than the purchase price. So too the commodity derivatives market-making financial institution: if it can sell a cash-settled gold derivative put option for a better price than it purchases a cash-settled gold derivative call option, it will turn a profit.

OTC derivatives are highly customised, privately negotiated, bilateral contracts designed to meet particular needs of sophisticated parties. They take the form of forwards, swaps and options.

OTC derivatives referencing commodities are very similar to OTC derivatives referencing other derivative underlying asset classes such as equities, foreign exchange or interest rates. The main difference is that although equity and credit derivatives have complex derivative instruments, their underlying asset is relatively simple – for example, bonds or loans of a referenced entity in a credit derivative, and shares or indices in an equity derivative.

In commodity derivative transactions the underlying assets may be more complex while the derivative financial instrument is comparatively simple. Of course, there are straightforward underlying commodity assets, such as agricultural products and metals. There are also the highly regulated electricity, gas and emissions trading markets, which are referenced in OTC commodity derivatives, not to mention weather indices and freight rates underlying commodity derivative asset classes.

Documenting and understanding these types of commodity derivative requires an in-depth understanding of the underlying commodity market, and these markets are discussed in detail in dedicated chapters of this book. This chapter provides an overview of the main types of commodity OTC financial instrument and of the commodity derivatives market itself.

2.   OTC commodity derivatives transactions: is there a future?

Guilty fingers have been pointed at OTC derivatives by many politicians and regulators, and while some of the most hysterical accusations have died down, further regulation of the market is on the horizon, with central clearing, increased use of exchange trading and greater disclosure being common themes across the globe. But is this the end of OTC derivatives, or at least the non-cleared OTC transactions? Far from it.

The standardisation of derivatives is essentially a continuum starting with exchange-traded contracts, such as futures, where only the price is negotiated. Those transactions are always centrally cleared, as the cash flows and structures are generally rather straightforward. To the right of them, there are cleared OTC transactions. They are also relatively standardised, but the parties negotiate not only the price but also other items such as quantity and duration. They are entered between market participants on an arm's-length basis and are subsequently transferred to a central clearing-house.

Finally, there are customised OTC derivatives, which are not standard and are incapable of being centrally cleared. They often need to conform exactly to the underlying asset or liability. What is capable or not of being centrally cleared essentially depends on the capacities of a clearing-house and changes as central counterparties become more and more sophisticated. Bearing in mind, however, that there is an indefinite number of combinations for OTC trades, it is practically impossible for all of them to be centrally cleared.

Buying and selling commodity derivatives on exchanges or through a central clearing platform, as opposed to the non-cleared OTC market, has its advantages. Firstly, it makes the entire process more transparent. Exchange-traded derivatives are standardised documents with uniform sets of terms. Transparency is created through disclosing trading volumes and prices to the market. This is also the case with standardised transactions cleared through a central counterparty.

Secondly, trading on an exchange or with a central counterparty theoretically minimises credit risk, as each party 'gives up' the transaction by entering into a mirror transaction with the clearing-house – a central counterparty. Thus, the exchange's central counterparty acts as a buyer to every seller and as a seller to every buyer. The exposure of each participant is only to a central counterparty, and not to any other market player, and the central counterparty minimises credit exposures by taking a margin. As no exchange or central counterparty has ever become insolvent (at least to date), a bankruptcy of even the biggest financial institution should not affect any of these types of transaction.

This explains why governments and regulators want to push most derivatives trading onto such platforms. In fact, they have been quite successful so far. According to the Bank of International Settlements, as of the end of the first half of

2009 the total volume of OTC commodity derivatives had decreased. So, if exchange-traded commodity derivatives and central counterparties are such a godsend, why do we think that predictions of the demise of non-cleared OTC derivatives are exaggerated?

Firstly, on an exchange or centrally cleared platform, a market participant can enter into contracts only for a standardised amount of a commodity asset for a fixed duration. The counterparty cannot enter into a customised trade that would match its unique risk profile. This means that it cannot protect its financial position effectively – its ability to hedge is reduced. OTC commodity derivatives provide far more flexibility and allow the parties to structure each transaction as they see fit. Their existence is essential for hedging purposes.

Secondly, exchanges and central counterparties demand the posting of the daily margin, which is often not a requirement for OTC trades. Although daily margin calls minimise the counterparty's risk, they can be quite cumbersome in practice and act as a deterrent to hedging.

Thirdly, a number of contracts either do not exist on an exchange and central counterparty platform at all or have limited liquidity. Again, the OTC market, with its inherent flexibility, offers a solution. When an investment bank or a hedge fund speculates on the price of a given commodity, exchange-traded derivatives are probably exactly what it needs. However, if, for example, an airline needs to ensure fixed costs for fuel or a gold mine wants to ensure that it will obtain a minimum price for its gold, a very bespoke, customised OTC commodity derivative transaction may be the only solution.

The documentation of OTC derivatives referencing commodities has been standardised for some time now. The International Swaps and Derivatives Association Inc's (ISDA's) suite of commodity documents is the most popular platform for OTC trades on commodities, but other industry bodies, such as the Futures and Options Association, have produced their own standard forms. These are analysed elsewhere in this publication.

The standardised and easily commoditised derivatives contracts will be forced onto exchanges. Other contracts will also be pushed onto centrally cleared platforms. However, the regulators will not ban all non-cleared OTC contracts. As centrally cleared platforms will accept only standardised contracts, non-cleared OTC derivatives contracts will exist in the form of:

- more bespoke transactions;
- transactions which meet specific hedging needs; and
- new and innovative types of transaction. As these become traded in sufficient volumes, they will become commoditised and moved onto central and exchange-clearing platforms.

The volume of OTC transactions will decrease, but the format of centrally cleared derivatives will be similar to non-cleared OTC derivatives – and the most interesting and bespoke transactions will remain within the non-cleared OTC arena.

3. Market for OTC commodity derivatives transactions

The overall size of the OTC derivatives market is huge and the commodities represent only a small share of it. According to the Bank of International Settlements, as of June 2009 the amount outstanding of OTC derivatives stood at $605 trillion, which included only $3.7 trillion of commodity derivatives positions. This grossly underestimates the role of commodities in the modern economy for the last few decades, if not centuries.

The Bank of International Settlements began putting together the statistics for OTC trades in 1998 and the picture is revealing. In 1998 the total outstanding amount of commodity derivatives was less than $0.5 trillion, but gold accounted for almost half of that figure. By June 2008 the total volume had increased by 1,400% to reach more than $13 trillion, with gold and other precious metals representing just over $0.8 trillion. This was followed by a sharp drop in the second half of 2008 and, as of June 2009, the total notional outstanding equalled $3.7 trillion, with gold and precious metals accounting for only 8% ($0.3 trillion).

This sudden decline in the total notional for commodity trades occurred at the same time as the credit crunch took its toll on the global economy. This is no coincidence. Many derivative positions were liquidated involuntarily at that time as credit lines for the funds holding the instruments or the banks issuing them were suspended or reduced. This, coupled with a sharp decline in most commodity prices, caused the total notional amount for all OTC commodity trades to fall by two-thirds.

The historical data provided by the Bank of International Settlements also highlights another interesting fact. Whereas gold represented only 1% of the global value of world commodities between 1998 and 2000, at that time it accounted for between 42% and 45% of the total value of commodity derivative transactions. This is mostly because gold, unlike other commodities, is primarily seen as a financial asset, akin to currency or government bonds, rather than a typical commodity.

In addition, at the turn of the millennium the commodities markets were in turmoil, which affected other commodities more than gold. The bear market was quickly followed by a bull market, with prices peaking in mid-2008. The massive jump from $0.5 trillion in 1998 to $13 trillion in 2008 was also due to an increased incidence of energy transactions referencing, in particular, gas, electricity and coal.

The future direction of the OTC derivatives market is still uncertain. Although commodity prices have slowly started to rise together with the notional amount of derivative positions, regulators and national governments have put enormous pressure on trading to move into regulated exchanges and centrally cleared platforms, as explained above. In any case, gold, precious metals and energy derivatives continue to be traded primarily on the OTC market, at least for now. Considering the dramatic changes reflected in the Bank of International Settlement's figures for the past 11 years, the future will be equally exciting.

4. Main OTC products

There are no surprises here – the main OTC products in the area of commodities, as well as in any other derivative field, are forwards, options and swaps. All three instruments are similar in many respects and one can often achieve the same commercial effect by using any one of them or a combination. They are all bilateral contracts allowing a party to acquire economic exposure to an underlying commodity asset. Considering that each of them is an individually negotiated OTC transaction, the number of variations is limited only by the imagination and commercial needs of the market participants.

This section provides a brief summary of each product and presents the standard variations which are characteristic of commodity derivatives transactions.

4.1   Sales on 'spot' or forward basis

Sales on a 'spot' basis are not technically derivatives instruments: essentially, they are just sale-and-purchase transactions, where one party undertakes to buy a specified amount of commodity from another. Consumers enter into a number of 'spot' (or 'immediate') commodity transactions every week – for example, when they buy groceries or fill their cars with petrol.

The difference between a spot and a forward transaction is merely a matter of the timing of the delivery. Under a spot trade, the parties agree the current price for a specified amount of commodity to be delivered immediately. Under a forward, the parties agree a price for a specified amount of commodity to be delivered at a defined point in the future (in the case of a physically settled transaction).

Standard derivatives documentation platforms, such that produced by the ISDA, often provide the same template agreements for both spot and forward transactions. In each case the documents include a similar amount of information and specifications relating to the underlying commodity. The major difference between them is merely the point in time at which the amount of goods is to be delivered.

A forward agreement need not necessarily reference traditional commodities, such as agricultural products, paper or oil. Both spot and forward trades are also often entered into on electricity or greenhouse gases allowances. This is explained in detail elsewhere in the publication.

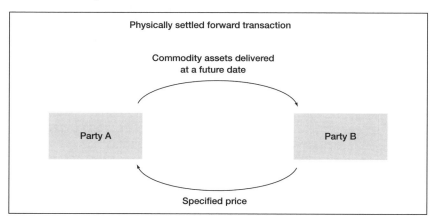

(a)   Variation: cash settlement

Contract parties can decide to settle their transaction physically by delivering an agreed amount of commodity asset at a specified time for a pre-agreed price (eg, 1,000 barrels of oil at $80 a barrel in one month's time). If oil is trading at $90 a barrel at the settlement date, the buyer will have done well; if it is trading at $70 a barrel, the seller will have done well. However, to take advantage of these price movements the parties must actually buy and physically deliver oil.

They could achieve a similar economic result if they agreed to exchange the corresponding price difference at that time (ie, the difference between the pre-agreed price and the market price at the time of settlement). Therefore, the purpose of cash settlement is to put the parties financially in the same position as if they actually transferred the commodity.

Cash-settled forwards work as follows. At the outset of each forward transaction, the parties decide the price of the commodity to which the trade relates. At the time that the delivery would otherwise occur, they check the market price of that commodity. If the current market price exceeds the amount agreed in the contract, the forward seller makes a payment to the forward buyer. If, however, the agreed price is lower than the current market price, the buyer pays a defined amount to the seller. This payment is equal to the difference between the actual trading price of the underlying commodity asset at the settlement date and the price set out in the agreement.

Hypothetical example: Ksarina Jewellery Corp and Sophiyah Mining
Ksarina Jewellery Corp is a chain of jewellery stores in Scotland. Ksarina is concerned that the price of silver may exceed $20 per ounce, which would adversely affect its profits. Therefore, early in 2010 it enters into a physically settled forward transaction, through a broker, with Sophiyah Mining, under which Ksarina undertakes to buy 100,000 ounces of silver for $20 per ounce from Sophiyah on October 18 2010. On October 18 the price of silver is $22 per ounce. Nonetheless, Ksarina pays only $20 per ounce for the amount it has agreed to buy. Therefore, Sophiyah needs to deliver 100,000 ounces of silver in exchange for the sum equal to $20 per ounce × 100,000 ounces = $2 million.

Alternatively, instead of entering into a physically settled transaction, Ksarina could conclude a cash-settled agreement, perhaps because it wishes to maintain its relationships with its existing suppliers. In that case, on the settlement date Sophiyah would not deliver any silver but it would make a payment equal to the difference between the market price as of October 18 and that agreed in the agreement ($22 − $20 = $2), multiplied by the specified number of ounces: ($22 per ounce − $20 per ounce) × 100,000 = $200,000.

Now Ksarina could just go to the market and buy the required amount of silver itself from suppliers.

(b)   *Variation: transactions on indices*
Forwards referencing commodity indices instead of assets are always cash settled. In general, there is little difference between a cash-settled forward referencing an actual commodity and a forward on an index. In both cases the ultimate payment will be determined by reference to the value which represents either the price of commodity or the level of an index at the relevant time.

A commodity index generally tracks not a single asset, but rather a basket of different commodities. To be precise, the constituents are not commodity assets but, rather, futures contracts on those assets. The indices are also weighted in accordance with a specified methodology.

There are a number of popular commodity indices, including the S&P GSCI (previously the Goldman Sachs Commodity Index), the Rogers International Commodity Index and the Commodities Research Board Index. Their constituent parts are often diverse. For example, as of January 22 2010 the S&P GSCI consisted of 24 commodities grouped in five main categories: energy, industrial metals, precious metals, agriculture and livestock. The weighting is proportional to the production and consumption of each commodity in the market at the relevant time.

An OTC forward transaction referencing an index gives an investor a chance to get exposure to the selected sector without the need to buy the actual commodities or to enter into a set of separate forward contracts for each asset. However, in the market it is more common to enter into OTC swaps on indices, rather than forwards; but considering that both products are cash settled, in practice the difference between them is rather small. In particular, a swap can be categorised as a series of forward contracts.

4.2 Option transactions

An option is similar to a forward contract. It is a bilateral transaction entered into between two market counterparties on agreed terms, under which they gain exposure to a specified commodity or commodities. Under a forward, each party is exposed to market fluctuations and may suffer their consequences; however, under an option the option seller is at much greater risk to unfavourable price movements than the buyer.

(a) Call and put options

The buyer of a call option acquires a right, but not an obligation, to buy from the seller of the option a defined amount of a commodity asset at the price agreed (the strike price). This price will be either a specific price or one determined by reference to a formula or set of rules set out in the agreement. The underlying asset is usually a single commodity or basket of commodities, or an index or basket of indices.

In a put option, the buyer has a right to sell (ie, to 'put') a specified quantity of a commodity asset (eg, 100,000 oil barrels) to its counterparty at the agreed strike

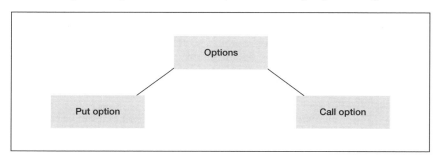

price on a future date. In a call option, the option buyer has a right to buy (ie, to 'call') the same at the strike price. If the strike price is less than the agreed price at the future date, the buyer will not exercise the option. However, it will have lost its premium and it is this amount to which the buyer will be at risk.

(b)   *Cash-settled and physically settled options*

The economics behind a physically-settled option are simple. If it is a call option and the strike price is lower than the actual price at the relevant time, the buyer exercises the option and physically takes the assets. If the strike price is higher, it lets the option expire.

The difference between a physically settled and a cash-settled option is that the underlying asset under a cash-settled trade is not the actual commodity. Instead, it is a futures contract for that commodity and the price is determined accordingly.

If the parties enter into a cash-settled transaction, its commercial effect is generally identical to that of a physically settled trade. On the date when the option can be exercised, the parties look at the price of the specified commodity and compare it with the strike price agreed in the contract. If the buyer decides that it wants to exercise the option, it will not acquire the physical asset; instead, the seller will pay it the difference between the strike price and the actual price at the relevant date.

In a put option, the buyer has a right to demand a payment from its counterparty if the actual price is lower than the strike price on the exercise date. Conversely, a call option buyer can demand a payment when the actual price is higher than the strike price on the exercise date.

(c)   *American, Asian, Bermudan and European options*

Options are categorised by reference to the time when they can be exercised and the value ascribed to them at that point. The four most common types are American, Asian, Bermudan and European.

A European option can be exercised only on the day that it expires. For example, if parties enter into a call option referencing gold on January 1 at a price of $850 per ounce with an expiry date of October 30, the option buyer will be able to exercise the option and buy the gold only on October 30. If the trade is cash settled, the buyer will exercise the option if the price of gold at that point in time exceeds $850 per ounce.

An American option can be exercised on any trading day during the option's term. This means that the option buyer in the foregoing example will be able to exercise it on any business day between January 1 and October 30.

A Bermudan option is a halfway house between a European and American option and can be exercised on specific days, as provided in the agreement. For example, the parties can decide that the option will be exercisable on May 1, July 1 and October 30. If the Bermudan or American option is cash settled, the parties take the price of gold on the date when the option is exercised in order to determine the value of the instrument.

The Asian option is similar to the European option as it can be exercised only on the day that it expires. However, its value is determined by reference to the average price of the commodity throughout the term of the trade. If on October 30 the price of gold stands at $855 per ounce, but the average price from January 1 to October 30 is only $844 per ounce, the option buyer will not normally exercise the option.

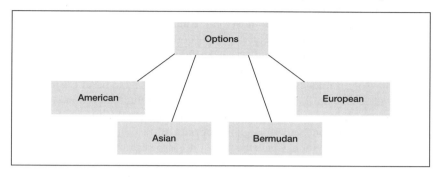

Types of option	Day when option is exercisable	Day or days relevant for calculating the prices
American	Each day during the term of the transaction	Day when the option is exercised
Asian	Last day of the transaction	Each day during the term of the trade
Bermudan	On such dates as are specified in the contract	Day when the option is exercised
European	Last day of the transaction	Day when the option is exercised

(d)   Premium

The option buyer pays an amount of money (a premium) to the option seller, as determined in the relevant transaction confirmation, to compensate it for providing the option. The option buyer need make no other payments under the terms of the transaction, unless it chooses to, and its risk is limited only to the value of the premium paid at the outset of the transaction. This means that the option buyer essentially purchases insurance against the increase or decline in the price of a chosen commodity. Although in legal terms this is definitely not a contract of insurance,[1] to some extent this is its commercial effect. A farmer can buy an insurance policy against his house burning down and can also buy an option to protect his financial position against the drop in the price of produce.

---

1   The analysis is complex, but as the seller need not have any exposure to the underlying asset, and indeed may not do so at the option's exercise date, there is no insurable interest and the contract is not one of insurance. In cases of doubt, an opinion from a law firm is advisable.

(e)   *Value of an option*

Each option has an intrinsic value. This will be determined by two main factors: the actual price of the underlying asset at any point in time and the length of time until the option's expiration. Both factors are important when determining the premium paid at the transaction's outset and the option's value throughout its term.

The first factor is calculated by analysing the relationship of the strike price to the current price of the underlying asset. If the strike price is equal to the current price of the underlying commodity, the option is said to be 'at the money'. Its value will be zero unless the market has a view on the future direction of the underlying commodity's price. Naturally, the relationship between the strike price and the market value will vary throughout the term of the transaction.

For a call option, where the strike price is lower at any time than the actual price of the referenced asset, the trade is 'in the money' for the option buyer. If, however, the strike price is higher than the market price at a given time, the option is 'out of the money' for the buyer. The converse would apply for a put option.

The second aspect is the length of time to the expiration of the contract. The general principle is that the longer the term, the longer the uncertainty. Therefore, the premium paid by the option buyer is usually directly proportional to the option's duration. The seller will assume larger risk and wish to be compensated accordingly.

(f)   *Exercise and set-off of options*

If the option is 'out of the money' on an exercise date, the buyer will not exercise it. Instead, it will let it expire and possibly buy or sell the relevant commodity on the market. Some standard documentation platforms do not even allow for exercise of an out-of-the-money option.

A more complicated scenario occurs when the option is in the money. The buyer has two possibilities: it can exercise the option or it can sell it. Exercise is straightforward: the buyer notifies the seller that it has decided to settle the transaction. Settlement then takes place either by effecting the physical delivery of the underlying commodity or by making the relevant payments. Standard documentation often provides for the automatic exercise of options, as long as they are in the money.

Alternatively, the buyer may decide to sell an in-the-money option to realise accrued profits. In practice, many buyers prefer to sell the option, rather than to exercise it, to avoid losing any remaining time value.

(g)   *Variation: baskets and indices*

There are a number of popular variations for options, options referencing baskets of commodities or commodity indices being the most standard. For basket trades, the option will reference more than one commodity asset. In most cases these products are cash settled and, if the option is in the money at the end of transaction, the buyer will receive a payment determined by reference to the value of all items in the basket.

Options on indices are another way of referencing more than one commodity asset, as most specialised commodity indices have a number of components. This is outlined in section 4.1 above on forwards. As with forwards, all options referencing indices must be cash settled and the payment, if any, is calculated by comparing the difference in the level of the relevant index at the outset and on the day the option is exercised.

Standard commodity documentation produced by ISDA also covers options on EU emissions allowances and options referencing indices on weather and other exotic assets. In terms of mechanics, all options operate as set out above. For example, an option referencing a weather derivative is nothing other than an option on an index with the relevant precipitation or temperature levels. Even for the most complex underlying assets, an option is nothing more and nothing less than a right to buy or sell a specified asset.

(h)   *Variation: exotic options*
Exotic options, by definition, are bespoke, many and varied, so this section considers some of the most popular ones. Exotic options are modifications of standard options. For example, an exotic option may make the commencement or expiration of an option conditional on the occurrence of a specified event or may change a transaction's valuation mechanics.

Perhaps the most popular exotic options are barrier options. These are also known as 'knock-in' and 'knock-out' options. In a knock-in transaction, a payment or delivery is contingent on the occurrence of a knock-in event on any knock-in determination day (usually a trading day or predefined period or range of dates). In a knock-out transaction, the transaction will terminate, without the option being exercised, if a knock-out event occurs on any knock-out determination day. Knock-in and knock-out events will usually be the level of a commodity price or index going above or below a specified level. When combined, they are called 'KIKO' (knock-in/knock-out) transactions.

Another popular exotic product is a rainbow option, which is easily confused with a simple basket trade. A rainbow option also references a number of commodity assets, but the difference is that the buyer can exercise the option only in relation to one asset. The contract will set out the conditions as to how identify this asset, which is usually the best- or worst-performing item.

Lookback and binary options change the valuation method of the instrument. A lookback option allows the buyer to look back at the price of the referenced asset during the term of the trade and to choose the optimum value.

Lookback options can be further subdivided into fixed and floating types. Under a fixed lookback option, the strike price is fixed at the outset of the transaction, but at the option's expiry the buyer can choose the point in time at which the instrument shall be deemed to have been exercised. In the case of a floating lookback option, the buyer chooses the strike price on the basis of the best price (either the highest or the lowest) during the life of the instrument.

Binary options are much simpler. If the option is in the money on the exercise date, the seller pays a specified sum to the buyer which has been agreed at the outset of the transaction. If the option is out of the money, it expires and the buyer receives nothing. For this reason, it is often referred to as an 'all or nothing' or a digital option.

(i) Standard hedging strategies using commodity options

Options can be used as effective hedging strategies against the risk of either rising or falling prices. A put option can constitute protection against the risk of the decline in prices, whereas a call option ensures that the option buyer will be able to buy the specified commodity at the agreed strike price, even if market prices rise in the meantime.

For example, if a farmer grows corn, he needs to be sure that he can sell it at a profit. He may be concerned that between the planting of the seeds and the harvest, the price will fall and he will be unable to recoup his original investment in seeds and agricultural equipment. To protect his position, he can enter into a put option – either cash or physically settled – with a strike price that represents the minimum amount that he needs to receive to make an overall gain.

Another farmer needs corn to feed his pigs and is worried that the price of corn will rise and his business may make a loss as a result. To protect himself, he can enter into a call option at a price that represents the maximum price that he is prepared to pay for the corn so that he still makes enough profit overall.

The two farmers can enter into these transactions through their brokers. In the cases of both put and call options, the farmers would not exercise their options if the actual market price is more favourable from their perspective. They will just let them expire.

(j) Advanced hedging strategies using commodity options

There are a number of examples of sophisticated option strategies, the aim of which is to hedge a party's position, to make a gain through arbitrage or to speculate. This section explains the following two hedging possibilities:

- protection against selling too soon; and
- a collar (or fence) strategy.

Let's continue with the example of the farmer trying to sell his corn. Assuming that he has found a buyer, he could sell the corn right away and make a profit. However, he thinks that the price of his produce will go up and he does not want to lose out as a result. Naturally, instead of selling he could just enter into a put option to sell his produce later in the year at the specified price. However, he does not want to go through the trouble of storing the corn. Therefore, he sells the corn at the outset at the market price, but at the same time buys a cash-settled call option referencing corn, which is out of the money at that time. If the price of corn exceeds the specified strike price during the term of the option, he can exercise it and make an additional profit. If not, the option simply becomes unexercised. This strategy is also often referred to as a 'synthetic' put.

The collar (or fence) strategy can be used to provide a higher downside protection at the expense of the upside price potential. To make sure that he can sell the corn at the desired price, the farmer could simultaneously:

- buy a put option with a strike price representing the minimum amount that he would like to receive from the corn; and
- sell a cash-settled call option with a higher strike price.

As long as the price of corn remains within the collar constituted by both strike prices, the options remain unexercised.

If the actual price drops, the farmer can exercise his put option and sell the corn at the lower strike price. However, if the price of corn suddenly rises, the buyer of the call option will exercise it and the farmer will need to make the relevant payment. Therefore, the farmer's potential profits are limited by the amount representing the strike price under the call option. However, if the call option is exercised, the price of corn is high enough for the farmer to sell the corn and to make enough profit to pass some portion of it to the call option buyer. At the same time, he will have received a premium for selling it, which in turn increases his overall gains.

> **Hypothetical example: Roderick Plantations Corp**
> Roderick Plantations Corp owns sugar cane plantations in Latin America and is concerned that the price of sugar may drop from the current high price of $350 per tonne. It would like to hedge against this risk so, through a broker, it enters, into two cash-settled European options with hedge fund Alexander Investments Corp.
> On January 1 Roderick buys a put option with a strike price of £300 per tonne. At the same time, it also sells a call option on the same amount of sugar with the strike price of £400. Both options expire on October 30. The premium amounts payable by Roderick and Alexander have cancelled each other out, so effectively Roderick has obtained the protection for free. Three scenarios are possible:
> - *The price of sugar is less than £300 per tonne* – The scenario feared by Roderick has occurred and the price of sugar on October 30 stands at £250 per tonne. Roderick sells its sugar on the market for that price and exercises the option. Now Alexander makes up Roderick's loss by paying £50 per every tonne of sugar to Roderick.
> - *The price of sugar is between £300 and £400 per tonne* – In this case both options will expire unexercised. At the same time, Roderick has obtained free protection against the decline in the value of sugar.
> - *The price of sugar is more than £400 per tonne* – The price of sugar has rocketed and stands at £420 per tonne as of October 30. This means that Alexander will exercise its option and demand a payment from Roderick. Therefore, Roderick sells its produce at £420 per tonne and makes a payment to Alexander equal to £20 per every tonne of sugar.

4.3   Commodity swap

In their purest forms, a forward is an obligation to buy or sell an asset and an option is a right to buy or sell an asset (or an obligation to do so, if the option seller). A swap is an instrument analogous to a series of forwards on the same terms. Generally, commodity swaps are cash settled.

A commodity swap references a commodity asset. This can be a single commodity or basket of commodities, or an index or basket of indices. There are many bespoke variations depending on the underlying asset. Those variations are described in the asset-specific chapters set out in Part III of the book. The most complicated and different structures are set out in the chapters on weather index transactions, freight and emissions trading.

Different underlying commodity assets are treated differently. Bullion swaps, EU emissions allowances, freight and other derivatives all have their own market norms. These are driven partly by market tradition and standards, and partly because of the esoteric nature of the underlying asset itself.

Below we describe the most popular types and variations of commodity swaps.

(a) ***Fixed-for-floating swaps***
'Fixed for floating' is the most common type of commodity swap. Under its terms, there are two parties: a fixed-rate payer and a floating-rate payer. They make payments of a fixed amount and a floating amount, respectively. This swap is used mainly as a hedging strategy under which the floating-rate payer assumes the risk of the fluctuation in prices of the underlying commodity. The fixed-rate payer always pays a specified fixed amount, whereas the amount of the floating payments depends on the actual price (ie, trading price) of the commodity on the relevant date.

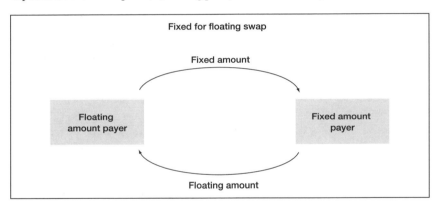

On the payment date both values will be netted against each other so that there is only one payment. If the value of the underlying commodity asset has risen above the fixed level on a particular measurement date, the floating-amount payer will pay the fixed-amount payer an amount reflecting the positive differential. If the value of the underlying commodity asset has fallen below the fixed level on the particular measurement date, the fixed-amount payer will pay the corresponding value of that differential to the floating-amount payer.

Hypothetical example: Dan Oil Inc
Dan Oil Inc is an oil producer which sells crude oil to its customers at the current market price. This means that any fluctuations in the price of oil have a significant impact on Dan's cash flows. To make the revenues more predictable, it enters into a one-year swap with Uta Holdings at a fixed price of $70 per barrel. The parties have agreed for the notional amount to be equal to 100,000 barrels and for the payments to be due each month, with Dan being the floating-rate payer and Uta the fixed-rate payer.

If after a month the market price of oil stands at $71 per barrel, Dan makes a payment to Uta equal to the difference between the market price and the fixed price, multiplied by the notional amount: ($71 – $70 per barrel) × 100,000 barrels = $100,000.

However, suppose by the following month the price of oil has dropped to $65 per barrel. This time, Uta will need to make a payment equal to the difference between the fixed price and the market price, multiplied by the notional amount: ($70 – $65 per barrel) × 100,000 barrels = $500,000.

This means that each month Dan effectively receives $70 per barrel for the crude oil it sells to its customers. If the price falls below $70, then even though the customers still pay the market price, Uta pays the difference. The downside is that Dan is unable to make extra profit when the price rises.

(b) Commodity-for-interest swaps

'Commodity for interest' swaps are similar to standard equity swaps but are less common in the market than fixed-for-floating swaps. Under a commodity-for-interest swap, the total return on a commodity is exchanged for a specified money market rate (which may also include a spread). This can be used by a market participant either to gain exposure to a particular commodity asset or to hedge against the price fluctuations in the asset.

For example, a hedge fund may want to acquire long exposure to a particular commodity index (eg, S&P GSCI). It enters into a swap with a bank and whenever the level of the index rises, the bank makes a payment to the fund. If, however, the index level falls, the hedge fund must pay the difference in the value to the fund. In order to compensate the bank for providing this exposure, the hedge fund also makes a regular payment by reference to the specified money-market rate (eg, the London interbank offered rate or the Euro interbank offered rate) to cover the bank's funding costs, together with a defined spread.

Alternatively, a commodity producer may want to protect itself against any fluctuations in the market. Accordingly, if the selected commodity price rises, it makes a payment to the bank. If the price falls, it receives a corresponding payment. In this way, the producer can not only lock in a price for its product but also hedge against rising rates on the company's debt.

(c) Variation: commodity caps, collars and floors

Under a standard commodity swap, a payment can be triggered by even the slightest movement in prices. The parties can use caps, floors and collars to limit the circumstances when any amounts are payable. This allows for a better management of risk and can decrease any premium payable on the entry into any hedging arrangements.

For example, if an airline enters into a standard fixed-for-floating commodity swap as a fixed amount payer, it will receive a payment if the oil prices rise in a particular time period. If at the beginning of a year the price of oil is $50 per barrel and it rises to $52, the airline will receive $2 per barrel.

The premium payable by the airline could be lower if the airline were prepared to accept some portion of the risk. One of the ways of doing so would be to agree a cap price of, for example, $70 per barrel. In that case, the counterparty would need to make a payment to the airline only if the price of oil rose above the level of $70 per barrel. The payment would be equal to the excess of the current price over the cap price.

Similarly, a gold manufacturer may be worried that the price of gold may go down. Assuming that the current price is $1,000 per ounce, the manufacturer can enter into a fixed-for-floating swap with a floor of $900. Its counterparty will then need to make a payment only if prices decline below $900. The payment will be equal to the excess of the floor price over the market price.

The parties can also agree to enter into a collar transaction. In that case one party pays a floating amount based on the cap price, whereas the other pays a floating amount based on the floor price. Thus, one party will make a payment to another if the price of the commodity rises above a certain level (the cap price), and the other party must make a payment to the first only if the price falls below a defined threshold (the floor price). If, however, the price of the commodity stays within the collar (ie, it does not rise above the cap price and does not fall below the floor price), no party needs to make any payment to the other.

(d)   *Variation: basis swaps*
Basis swaps (or floating-for-floating swaps) are similar to fixed for floating swaps, but there is no fixed payment; instead, the value of the payment of each party is different on each payment date. For example, one party might make payments calculated on the basis of a gold price, while the other does this for silver.

This form of swap may be essential in order to fine-tune price risk management, especially when a company is exposed to price differentials between two different commodity assets. Among fund managers, it is popular to enter into a basis swap referencing the return on both gold and on the S&P GSCI.

(e)   *Variation: indices, baskets and physical settlement*
As with forwards and options, instead of entering into a swap confirmation referencing a single commodity asset, the parties can reference a basket of different commodities or a commodity index (or a basket of indices). These are relatively standard instruments through which an investor can gain exposure to the wider commodities market, rather than just to one asset.

Swap transactions referencing baskets are usually cash settled, whereas those referencing indices must always be cash settled. If a party wishes to obtain the actual commodity, an option or a forward generally provides a better mechanism than a swap. However, for various tax, structuring or other reasons, the parties may want to structure a physically settled transaction as a swap.

(f)   *Variation: exotic swaps*
There are a great number of different types of more or less exotic swap that market players can use to meet specific hedging objectives. Generally, most exotic swaps can be divided into five broad categories:

- swaps with obligations that are conditional or deferred;
- swaps which allow the parties to participate in the fluctuations of the relevant prices;
- swaps which allow the parties to change the maturity of the instrument or the referenced quantity;
- swaps relating to price differential between different commodities; and
- hybrid instruments involving different asset classes.

(i)   *Swaps with obligations that are conditional or deferred*
The first grouping includes, for example, 'swaptions' and forward swaps. A swaption is an option on a swap transaction. This means that one party sells to the other an option which, when exercised, triggers the underlying commodity swap. A forward swap, in turn, is a swap which starts in the future.

Examples of more sophisticated instruments in this category include so-called range swaps, digital swaps and cliquet swaps. Under a range (or fairway) swap, one of the parties is obliged to make a payment to the other only if the chosen reference price is within the pre-agreed range. In a digital swap, a specified amount is payable only if the underlying return has reached a certain level. The prices under a cliquet swap change during the term of the instrument and depend on the previous return on the underlying commodity.

(ii)   *Swaps which allow the parties to participate in the fluctuations of the relevant prices*
As referred to above, a swap is the perfect instrument for hedging. For example, an oil producer which sells crude oil to its customers can enter into a swap to lock in a price for a barrel of oil at $80. Whenever the price is less then $80 per barrel, its swap counterparty must make a payment to it equal to the difference. If, however, the price rises above $80, the producer must make the corresponding payment.

The protection against the price falling below $80 costs the oil producer the additional profits when the oil price is above $80. Even if the price is at, for example, $110 per barrel, the producer receives only $80, as it must pay the rest to the swap counterparty.

However, if the producer wants to make the extra profit on upwards price movements, it can enter into a participation swap or a participation collar. These instruments can provide for a pre-agreed percentage gain from any favourable price movements. For example, the oil producer could retain 15% of the relevant portion of the notional amount if the price crosses the $80 threshold.

(iii)   *Swaps which allow the parties to change the maturity of the instrument or the referenced quantity*
Another popular type of swap is where some of the main terms of the instrument can be amended at a later stage. Examples include extendable swaps, extendable collars and double-up or double-down swaps. Essentially, these are plain swap transactions, which include an embedded option allowing one of the parties to change some of the fundamental details of a transaction.

Extendable swaps and extendable collars allow one of the parties to extend the maturity of the transaction. Financial institutions offering hedging protection like this sort of instrument, as they can decide to prolong the swap if it is in the money for them. In return, the pricing of the product is more favourable to the client.

A double-up or double-down swap performs a similar role. It allows one of the parties – usually the financial institution – to increase (in the case of double-up swaps) or decrease (for double-down swaps) the notional quantity of the referenced commodity. If the prices move in favour for the financial institution under a double-up swap, it can exercise the option and make an additional profit; in the case of a double-down swap, it can limit its losses. In return, however, the client gets a more favourable fixed price as compared with the scenario where its counterparty did not have the option.

The parties can also enter into a swing swap, which allows one of the parties to specify the notional amount of the trade at its maturity.

(iv)   *Swaps relating to price differential between different commodities*
Swaps referencing more than one commodity asset can be helpful when a party is exposed to the price differential between two commodities. In addition to the basis swap mentioned in subsection 4.3(d) above, there are also other, more sophisticated products, such as cross-commodity swaps, crack spread swaps or spark spread swaps.

Cross-commodity swaps are popular among manufacturers whose profits depend on two variables:
- the price of the commodity they produce and sell on the market; and
- the price of another commodity, such as natural gas or oil, that they need in order to operate.

If the price of the commodity that they sell falls at the same time as the price of the commodity that they use rises, they can soon become insolvent. This is why they often enter into cross-commodity swaps to hedge this exposure. An example would be an oil refinery which buys crude oil and produces refined products, or a power station which produces electricity but uses up coal, gas or oil.

Crack spread swaps and spark spread swaps also provide sophisticated ways for the parties to fix a difference between the average price of one commodity against the average price of another commodity.

(v)   *Hybrid instruments involving different asset classes*
The popularity of other hybrid instruments is growing constantly as market participants aim to hedge against a number of variables at the same time. Using the fixed-for-floating swaps referred to above, parties can protect themselves against fluctuations in the funding rates and commodity prices simultaneously. However, parties often try to combine other asset classes, with typical examples being a cancellable credit default swap triggered by the level of oil or an interest rate-amortising swap triggered by the level of crude oil.

4.4   Contracts for difference

The term 'contract for difference' (CFD) is rather imprecise and has different meanings depending on the context. The definition provided under the UK Financial Services and Markets Act 2000 and related regulations is very wide and would capture almost any cash-settled derivative instrument. Generally, however, a CFD allows an investor to take a view on the future price movement of the underlying asset.

Using a CFD, an investor can take either a long or a short position, which means that it can benefit from both the falling and rising pricing of the referenced asset. By definition, CFDs are always cash settled and were originally developed to speculate on the values of shares. CFDs referencing commodities are a relatively recent phenomenon but are gaining popularity among smaller investors.

A commodity CFD is really a cash-settled swap and is most similar to the commodity-for-interest swap discussed in subsection 4.3(b) above. A CFD provider allows an investor to obtain exposure to a particular commodity asset. CFDs have a relatively short term – usually one day – but they can be rolled over indefinitely. In addition, they are subject to margin payments which consist of the initial deposit and then daily variable margin calls, depending on the price of the underlying commodity asset.

Structured commodity derivatives

Sabine Bertin
Dharini Collins

---

1. Introduction

'Structured commodity products' is a loose term that means different things to different people. Broadly speaking, we would define a 'structured commodity product' as a financial instrument, taking the form of a tradable certificate, note, bond, loan or unit in a fund, which derives its value from an underlying commodity product, such as the level of a freight index or the price of oil or wheat. We call the financial instrument the 'wrapper'.

The way in which the financial instrument derives that price can be simple (eg, a return earned for each point that the underlying commodity index increases in price), or complex. And the level of complexity can be immense, with a return or loss being generated through the relative performance of different commodity prices, as determined by complex formulae.

The financial instrument used in a structured product will normally be funded – that is, the investor will pay an upfront amount which covers its potential exposure in the transaction.

This chapter discusses structured commodity products: their background and development, how they work, what they are, who uses them and why.

Unfunded instruments such as over-the-counter (OTC) derivatives contracts can also be highly structured in the technology they use for gaining exposure to the underlying commodity asset. For this reason, the more complex OTC tailored commodity derivatives contracts are sometimes (although not universally) also referred to as 'structured commodity products'. Although OTC derivatives are discussed in detail elsewhere in this book, we also cover the more complex structures here.

1.1 Growth of structured commodity products

Commodity investment has become increasingly popular over the past decade. This is partly due to the consumption of commodities at unprecedented levels and the resulting scarcity of the underlying commodity. The developing economies of China and India have both contributed to the elevated demand for commodities (particularly in raw materials to fuel their growth). The Iraq war has kept petroleum prices volatile, which in turn has impacted on the pricing of almost all other commodities (since the transportation of goods is inherently linked to the price of crude oil).[1]

---

1   www.wtrg.com/prices.htm.

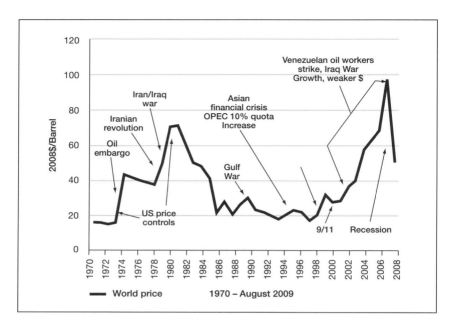

Another reason for the explosion of interest in commodities as an asset class arises from the perceived negative price correlation between commodity prices and equity or bond prices. That is, when standard asset classes are underperforming, investors look towards investments in commodities to diversify their portfolios. Unlike other asset classes, commodities are real assets which tend to continue to capture value despite inflationary pressures – for instance, investments in gold (and consequently, gold prices) soared in 2009 in tandem with the decline in the value of the US dollar and concerns over the health of the US economy.

Historically, the commodities market has centred around perishable goods or agricultural commodities and the need to find buyers (and sellers) for these goods ahead of their delivery date. Today, the commodities market caters for investments in metals, energy, carbon emissions, plastics, the weather and catastrophes, to name a few.

As the market for commodities has grown, new investors have been attracted to commodity investment. Those investors often wish to gain exposure to this market through structured commodity products.

There are various reasons as to why a party may wish to participate in the commodities market. For instance, a commodity producer may wish to hedge a particular trading risk (eg, a Costa Rican coffee farmer entering into commodity futures contracts in order to lock in prices for the sale of future deliverable stock); or a sovereign state holding large exposures to US dollar-denominated debt may be concerned that future inflation may continue to erode the US dollar's value, and in such a case, investments in precious metals – particularly in gold – may provide a hedge against such a risk.

Investments in equities are considered to be subject to country-specific economic pressures. Commodities, on the other hand, are exposed to more global economic

Five-year gold price history in US dollars per ounce[2]

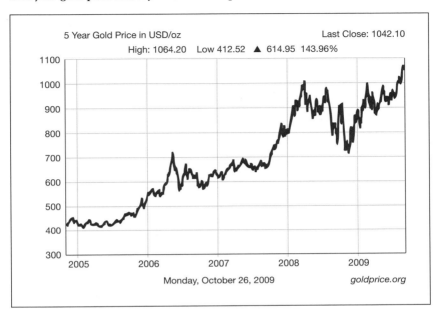

5 Year Gold Price in USD/oz · Last Close: 1042.10
High: 1064.20 Low 412.52 ▲ 614.95 143.96%

Monday, October 26, 2009 · goldprice.org

trends, which removes a layer of volatility/uncertainty as compared with the equity markets. In addition, the development of structured commodity products has opened a new area of investment, creating access to difficult-to-reach commodities and broadening the types of investor that can invest in commodities.

Structured commodity products offer investors the opportunity to participate in the commodities market and can provide creative structured solutions tailored to the specific requirements of that investor.

There is no specific form that a structured commodity product must take in order to be classed as such. The scope of structured commodity derivatives is wide ranging and dynamic. Structures can vary from jurisdiction to jurisdiction, depending on a number of factors, including local laws, investor appetite and the evolution of a particular product in that jurisdiction.

There are limitless ways in which structured commodity products can take shape; some of the most common structures are outlined further in this chapter. For instance, because commodities are a non-interest-bearing asset, investors will be relying on the capital appreciation of the commodity in order to secure a return. In order to provide an investor with an income stream linked to the commodity, a coupon-bearing security linked to the price of a particular commodity or a commodity index could be created.

Investment banks typically offer a wide range of such structured solutions to

---

2   www.goldprice.org/gold-price-history.html.

their investor base, as they have the tools available to offer a variety of structurally and legally different products to investors and in return make a profit from any embedded fees in the product itself, or from providing market-making facilities and trading the structured product on the secondary market.

1.2 Users of structured commodity products

The commodities market has a more diverse set of participants than most other asset classes and is said to be the largest 'non-financial' market in the world. Participants include traditional producers of commodities (eg, our Costa Rican farmer), end-users of commodities, corporate entities with commodities exposures, banks, brokers and investment funds.

New investors have been attracted to commodities as a result of the extensive range of new products on offer. These new investors include institutional investors, high-net-worth individuals and retail investors.

(a) Institutional investors

Pension funds have large volumes of assets under management, and in certain continental European jurisdictions and in the United States there appears to be significant appetite from pension funds to invest in this area. In other jurisdictions, the regulatory regimes may have an impact on whether pensions funds can participate in this market. For instance, the Hermes Commodity Investment Fund was designed for investment by pension funds and was set up with a £1 billion investment from its parent, the BT Pension Scheme.[3] Its objective is to deliver a return linked to the S&P Goldman Sachs Light Energy Index, giving pension fund investors exposure to the asset class which this index represents. Insurance companies are generally subject to heavier regulatory restrictions in relation to the range of investments they can make. Fixed-income-style collateralised commodity obligations have proved to attract investment from this type of institutional investor.

(b) High-net-worth individuals

Sophisticated investors with large amounts to invest sometimes find that investing directly in exchange-traded futures or options on commodities is beyond their reach due to large contract sizes or because of the procedural requirements of exchanges/clearing-houses. Even some investments into index funds may have minimum investment amounts. These investors have often sought to gain exposure to the market through a structured note. The note will be tailored to the investor's requirements with respect to denomination, leverage and payout. High-net-worth individuals typically invest in the market through capital-protected structures or indirectly through hedge funds.

(c) Retail investors

Investment in commodities by retail investors is relatively advanced in certain continental European jurisdictions. However, as with high-net-worth individuals,

---

3   www.hermes.co.uk/ic_hcif.aspx.

there are limits in terms of the range of products that this class of investor can take advantage of. The recently launched exchange-traded commodities (ETCs) or exchange-traded funds (ETFs) have been developed to cater somewhat to this segment of investors.

2. Methods of investment in commodities

An investor has as its disposal a wide range of options, from 'traditional' commodity investment products to highly customised structured commodity products. A structured commodity product is a financial instrument whose investment return derives from the performance of underlying commodity-linked assets. Typically, such commodity-linked assets happen to consist of the traditional investment alternatives described in section 2.1 below, and a structured commodity product 'wraps' such customary commodity investment alternatives into a new investment vehicle. Commodity indices are described further in section 2.2.

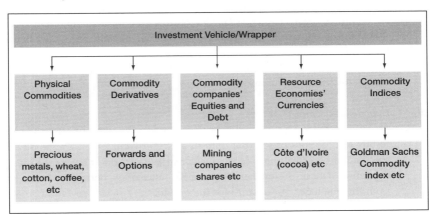

2.1 Traditional commodity investments

Traditional investments in commodities available to investors include the following, each described further below:

- investment in physical commodities;
- investment in commodity derivatives contracts;
- investment in commodity companies' equity and debt; and
- investment in resource economies' currencies.

(a) Investment in physical commodities

An investor may wish to buy the commodities directly (eg, it could decide to purchase an oil and gas well or acquire gold bars). Although this appears to be the purest way of investing in a commodity, this option presents some significant hurdles.

Some investors may be prohibited from owning physical commodities, or the minimum investment size (eg, gold bars) may prevent an investor from taking this route. Furthermore, some commodities cannot be physically owned (eg, weather risk or carbon emissions). The purchase and transfer of certain physical commodities may also have tax-adverse consequences for the investor. Finally, this option could involve significant costs of storage and insurance (eg, an investor acquiring precious metals would in reality store them in a bank, warehouse or depository and be issued a vault receipt as evidence of ownership of the precious metal).

(b) **Investment in commodity derivatives contracts**

A commodity derivatives contract is a contractual agreement that derives its value from an underlying commodity. There are two basic types of commodity derivatives contracts that an investor can invest in: forward-based contracts and option-based contracts.

(i) *Forward-based contracts*

A forward contract is an agreement to exchange a certain volume of a commodity at a specific date in the future on terms specified at inception of the contract. Forward contracts are typically negotiated directly between the buyer and the seller.

A futures contract is a special type of forward contract which has standardised terms and is traded on an exchange, rather than directly negotiated between the buyer and the seller.

A 'swap' can be thought of as a series of forward contracts, typically based on commodity prices or commodity index levels.

(ii) *Option-based contracts*

An option contract gives the holder of the option the right, but not the obligation, to buy (call option) or sell (put option) a certain volume of a commodity at a pre-specified price, called the exercise price or strike price, on or before the pre-specified expiration date of the option. The original seller of an option receives a premium from the purchaser in exchange for the option.

(iii) *General observations*

Investment in derivatives contracts is a popular way of investing in the commodities market. It is a pure play on the underlying raw commodity: the investor's future profit or loss is entirely dependent upon fluctuations in the underlying commodity price. The investor can also benefit from leveraging its exposure to the underlying commodity by investing in a derivatives contract. In addition, one advantage of future trading for an investor is that the futures market is highly liquid and the future contracts can be sold on again at any point before the final delivery date.

However, there are some inherent issues with investing in commodity derivatives contracts. Certain commodity derivatives contracts as futures are traded on separate, specialist exchange markets, such as the New York Mercantile Exchange, the InterContinental Exchange and the London Metals Exchange, rather than on regular stock exchanges, and these markets may not be accessible to most investors. For instance, some derivatives contracts have minimum investment amounts and on-exchange trading requires the posting of margin on a regular basis, and selling restrictions and other regulatory restrictions may prevent certain classes of investors from accessing the market in this way.

(c) ***Investment in commodity companies' equity and debt***

A typical investment medium for investors that wish to gain exposure into commodities is share trading. An investor can buy shares in certain companies that derive their income from the production of the coveted commodity, such as mining companies, oil exploration companies or agricultural producers.

The main advantage of share trading is that most such shares are traded on the major stock-exchange markets and therefore this is often a highly liquid investment.

However, there is a noteworthy disadvantage. There is a difference between the value of a share in a gold mining company at a certain time and the gold price at the same time. The value of the share is distorted by the presence of company-specific factors such as management decisions, capital structure, profitability and other commingling market conditions.

An investment in a corporate bond issued by a commodity producer company (eg, a gold miner) is another way of gaining exposure to a particular commodity.

(d) ***Investment in resource economies' currencies***

Some countries' gross domestic products (GDPs) are heavily dependent on the exportation of commodities (eg, the production of cocoa represented 15% of GDP and 35% of exports for Côte d'Ivoire in 2007[4]). As a result, the national currencies of these countries are affected by the price fluctuations of such commodies. Investing in the currency of such a country is an indirect investment into commodity prices.

2.2 Commodity indices

From exposures to the price fluctuation of a particular commodity, the commodities market has progressively seen the development of commodity indices. A commodity index is a statistical measure of the price changes in a portfolio of commodities or commodity-linked derivatives (eg, futures) representing a market or a portion of the overall market.

A commodity index is defined by its constituent commodities (index components), the respective weightings of such commodities (eg, equal weightings, predetermined weightings, fixed weightings, price-based weightings) and the type of commodity value to be tracked (eg, spot price, futures price). A commodity index can be regularly rebalanced.[5]

There is a wide range of commodity indices on the market, with each varying by its components and respective weightings. For example, the Reuters/Jefferies CRB Index is traded on the New York Board of Trade and comprises 19 different types of commodity, ranging from aluminium to wheat. The Goldman Sachs Commodity Index is a composite index of commodity sector returns which represents a broadly diversified, unleveraged, long-only position in commodity futures.

The primary route available for investing in commodities has become investment

---

4   http://siteresources.worldbank.org.
5   This, however, creates 'rebalancing costs' due to the inflow and outflow of the underlying commodity-linked securities for any structured product that attempts to mirror the index. Rebalancing costs depend on the number of index components likely to change, the frequency of such changes and the likely cost of the sale and purchase of index components.

in a commodity index. However, 'investing in an index' is something of a misnomer. To invest in an index, an investor does not buy units of the index – instead, it may:

- invest in a portfolio of securities to replicate an index – the investor thus creates a portfolio of commodities that best represent the index, with the kind of commodities and the weightings of the allocations being the same as in the actual index (this manner of investing uses the 'traditional' investment products described above);
- invest in units or shares of index-based funds, which are a type of investment fund which tracks the performance of a particular index; or
- invest in an index-linked ETF or an ETC, which are types of exchange-traded security that track the performance of an index.

These two last options are types of commodity structured products and are further discussed below.

3. Structured commodity products

A structured commodity product can provide a structured solution to some of the disadvantages of investing in commodities through the traditional ways described above, depending on the investor's investment strategies and/or inherent constraints.

In addition, there are some inherent advantages to using structured commodity products, including access to difficult-to-reach commodity markets (commodities that cannot be invested in through the traditional investment alternatives), flexibility based on creativity, and high customisation and optimisation of the investor's risk–return objectives. The variety of structured commodity products indeed provides an investor with the opportunity to reduce its risk and maintain the same potential at the same time (eg, by using capital-protected notes).

Typical types of structure are products with a full or conditional capital guarantee, participation, products with a maximal guarantee and leveraged products. Apart from these classical forms, new kinds of structured products with different structures are constantly being launched.

Some of the typical commodity structured products available to investors that wish to invest in commodities are described next.

3.1 Types of wrapper

The legal structure which a structured commodity can take may vary and will depend in part on the local laws, regulatory requirements and tax considerations in the jurisdiction of the issuer of the structured product and the jurisdiction of the investor. The evolution of a particular product in that jurisdiction may also affect the form in which that product is 'wrapped' and sold to an investor.

The forms of wrapper may include:

- OTC derivative contracts;
- loans;
- transferable securities, including in the form of notes, warrants or certificates;
- units in an investment vehicle such as an index (mutual) fund or a hedge fund;

- ETFs, ETCs or exchange-traded notes (ETNs);
- shares or other interests in various entities; or
- structured deposits or trust certificates.

The types of wrapper which structured products utilise are varied and the structured products can become quite complex as a result. However, use of these products permits bespoke solutions to be offered to meet the needs of a particular investor or investment class of investors.

A 'wrapped product' can permit the tailoring of cash flows and facilitate the transfer of other financial characteristics of the underlying commodity to the investor. A structured product may also give an investor access to a particular underlying or market segment which it may not otherwise be permitted to deal in directly.

3.2   'Structured product' as a combination of plain-vanilla derivatives contracts

There is no universal definition of a 'structured product'. The definition at the beginning of this chapter tries to encompass the idea of a financial instrument capturing a highly structured and customised response to a complex set of risks.

The example below describes a complicated set of risks associated with an oil refinery and introduces an 'extendable swap'. Extendable swaps are similar to fixed-for-floating swaps, except that the swap counterparty has the right to extend the contract maturity for a specified period of time for the same reference quantity.

Hypothetical example: Smart Refinery and Callaghan Bank

Smart Refinery uses about 10,000 barrel of crude oil per month. The price of its refined products has remained constant in the past year, while crude-oil prices have nearly doubled. Projected increased demand is likely to raise the prices of its refined products in the next two years. In the meantime, however, Smart wishes to hedge against potential rising prices over the next three years to protect margins.

The current price of a two-year fixed-for-floating swap for $20 per barrel is higher than what Smart is willing to pay. An alternative is to enter into a two-year extendable swap with a counterparty called Callaghan Bank in which Smart pays a fixed price of $19 per barrel on 10,000 barrels of crude oil per month. In exchange, Callaghan has the right to extend the swap for an additional year at $19 per barrel.

As a result, starting from January 2010 and until December 2011, Smart continues to buy crude oil from its regular suppliers at index prices.

At the end of each month, if the average crude-oil price is above the $19-per-barrel fixed price, Smart Refinery receives a payment equal to the difference between the swap price and the average price. If the monthly average crude oil price is below $19 per barrel, Smart is obliged to make a payment equal to the amount by which the average is below $19 per barrel. The extendable swap agreement ensures that Smart is, in effect, paying $19 per barrel for its crude oil.

Near the end of 2011, Callaghan Bank must notify Smart Refinery whether it intends to extend the swap through 2012.

The advantage of the extendable swap is that the swap fixed price is lower than that of a conventional swap.

3.3 Commodity-linked loans

A commodity-linked loan is a credit/loan instrument whose repayment schedule or principal/interest payment amounts are contingent on the value of an underlying commodity or portfolio of commodities. There are many ways to tie the repayment of a loan to commodity prices. For instance, a loan can be reimbursed with the value equivalents (using a reference price) of fixed amounts of a commodity. In addition, the repayment structure can embed an option (call or put) that provides a payoff if the commodity price rises above or drops below a predetermined strike price. In such an event, the payoff is applied directly to the loan or credit instrument.

Such a structured commodity product is used in the agricultural sector. Indeed, because of the high volatility of certain agricultural products, agribusiness firms (eg, farmers) face two types of risk: a commodity price risk and a debt repayment ability risk. Even though agribusiness firms might engage in crop insurance or commodity markets to stabilise their returns, there are no guarantees that any gains from hedging or any proceeds from insurance will be used first or be sufficient to meet the firm's credit needs. From the agricultural lender's point of view, commodity-linked loans have the double advantage of tying reductions in the agribusiness firm's business risk to the minimisation of its credit risk.

Hypothetical example: Collins Farm and Bertin

Collins Farm specialises in swine livestock in New Zealand. A recent swine flu outbreak has impaired the prospects of the swine demand in the food industry. As a result, Collins is facing wide commodity price fluctuation for pigs, which makes its return from investment vulnerable and impairs its debt repayment ability. In addition, Collins Farm has insufficient collateral to support a loan. The presence of such risks limits Collins' access to capital.

A practical solution to this issue is to obtain a commodity-linked credit/loan with a built-in price protection – that is, the repayment risk is effectively hedged by structuring the repayment of the loan with swine price fluctuation.

Agricultural lender Bertin agrees to make a loan to Collins Farm with the following terms of repayment (also show overleaf in diagrammatic form):

- The loan is a five-year loan of NZ$50,000 with an annual repayment amount of NZ$10,000.
- If, in any year, the swine commodity price falls below NZ$0.50 per pound, the principal repayment required in that year is reduced to NZ$5,000.
- If, in any year, the swine commodity price rises above NZ$0.60 per pound, the principal repayment required in that year is increased to NZ$15,000.

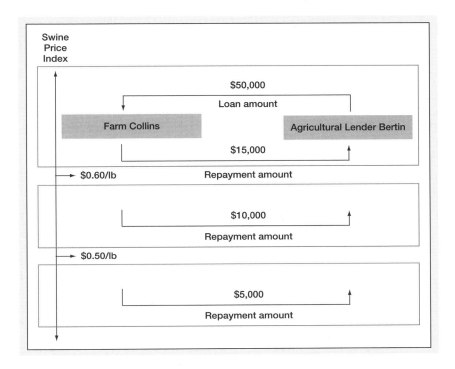

3.4 Debt and hybrid securities

The meaning of the term 'securities' has varied over time and the specific definitions of 'note', 'warrant' and 'certificate' are subject to change depending on the market in which such terms are used.

(a) Debt securities

A 'debt security' is a type of security whereby the issuer of the security owes an amount of money to the holder of that security. Notes and bonds are forms of debt security instrument. Bonds are typically long-term obligations (of five years or more maturity). Notes are medium-to-long-term obligations. Debt security instruments are usually for a fixed term, at the end of which the issuer will redeem the security in return for a pre-agreed payout on maturity to the note holder. Debt securities are normally structured so as to provide a coupon, or income stream, to the note holder; however, zero-coupon debt securities are also available and are often used in conjunction with other forms of investment as a structured solution for an investor.

(b) Hybrid securities

Warrants, convertibles and certificates are forms of hybrid securities, in that they contain elements of debt and equity securities:

- Warrants typically give the holder the contractual entitlement either to purchase or to sell the underlying on predetermined terms.
- Convertibles typically allow the holder to convert the security into the

underlying (or another form of security) at a predefined trigger event.

- Certificates can be structured in a number of different ways, but they are most often structured as discount certificates which track a particular underlying and return a payout to the holder in line with the value of the underlying. However, the initial investment by the holder is at a discount to what the holder would pay had it invested directly in the underlying.
- A debt security with an embedded derivative will sometimes also be referred to as a hybrid security.

Sub-section 3.4(e) below gives more details on certificates and warrants.

(c)   *Securities offerings*

Investment banks often underwrite the issuance of securities into the capital markets. An offer of securities can be by way of either public offer or private placement. A more stringent set of rules and regulations will apply in the case of publicly offered securities.

An offer of securities may be made through a standalone issuance or by way of a multiple issuance programme. Standalone issuances can be quite costly and result in delays in issuance of the product. In the mid-1980s the European capital markets developed the use of medium-term note (MTN) programmes to expedite and simplify the process of issuing structured securities to the market. The issuer under an MTN programme is typically an entity which is usually a financial institution or a special purpose vehicle with either a strong credit rating or a bankruptcy-remote structure. The MTN programme may be approved by one or more of the rating agencies for issuing rated structured products.

The documentation for structured commodity-linked product issuances through an MTN programme must comply with relevant securities laws. European securities offerings may need to comply with the EU Prospectus Directive (2003/71/EC) and US securities offerings would, among other things, need to comply with the US Securities Act of 1933. Customarily, documentation consists of the framework programme terms, which incorporate similar provisions to those in the 2005 ISDA Commodity Definitions. The terms of each individual issue of securities can then be contained in a relatively short-form document, in Europe, in the form of final terms or a supplementary prospectus.

Securities may be listed on a stock exchange or unlisted. If listed, the securities may theoretically be bought and sold on-exchange. In reality, there is limited secondary trading in many issues of these securities, with the attraction of listed securities stemming from greater disclosure and the requirements of many investors (including mutual funds) to invest only in securities listed on a regulated exchange.

Listed securities are subject to certain listing rules and regulations of the relevant exchange.

The key element of this type of structured product is that securities are negotiable – that is, they can be bought and sold on the secondary market without the consent (and usually knowledge) of the issuer – unlike OTC products, which require a specific novation of that derivative, agreed to by both parties, to transfer it from one party to another.

Securities can be issued in two forms: bearer securities and registered securities.

Bearer securities are issued in paper form and the promise to pay the bearer of such instrument is evidenced on the paper. The person in possession of the bearer note or certificate is the legal owner of that security, and transfer is effected by delivery of that certificate to another person. Under English law, bearer securities technically constitute 'choses in possession', even though they are in fact debt instruments that are somewhat intangible in nature.

That, at least, is the theory. Usually, however, a bearer security is settled via a clearing system. Where this is the case – and it will be so for almost all securities issues – the bearer certificate will be held by a common depository (acting on behalf of the clearing system), and the certificate will be held in global bearer form (ie, representative of the entire issue size of the securities) and not in definitive form. The common depository – or rather, the relevant clearing system – then holds the relevant security on behalf of the underlying note holders. Note holders can then trade their interests in the securities by the clearing system crediting and debiting the relevant accounts within the clearing system. Definitive securities are printed and delivered to the note holders only if the clearing system is shut for a period of 14 days or if there is a default under the relevant instrument.

With registered securities, in contrast, the certificate or note evidences the debt owed by the issuer to the holder of the security and legal ownership is not given by possession of the registered certificate. A register will be maintained (with the issuer), and details of the holders of the securities will be entered into that register evidencing legal ownership. Transfer of a registered security is effected by amendment of the register. Under English law, registered securities are considered to be 'choses in action'.

(d) Commodity-linked notes

(i) Zero-coupon bond plus a commodity option

One of the more basic forms of commodity-linked note is a zero-coupon bond with an embedded option (normally a call option). This product is designed so that some or all of any positive return in the case of a call option, or negative return in the case of a put option, on the note is tied to the performance of a specific commodity or commodity index.

This structure is typically capital protected – that is, the amount invested by the note holder on the issue date of the note will be guaranteed to be returned to the note holder on the maturity date of the note. This is achieved by the issuer investing a portion of the issue price of the note into a zero-coupon bond. This is possible because, for instance, if the issue price of the note is €1,000, the issuer may invest €900 into a zero-coupon bond which, taking into account the present value (discounted time value) of the bond, will result in a principal payment to the issuer of €1,000 on the maturity date. The issuer is then free to invest the remaining €100 in an option linked to a commodity or commodity index, which it can do by paying a premium equal to €100. It then gains the right to exercise that option. If, in the case of a call option, the market price of the commodity exceeds the strike price, the option will be exercised, passing on any up-side profit in the underlying commodity or commodity index to the note holder.

At maturity, investors receive par value on the zero-coupon bond and a variable return based on the commodity component. In circumstances where the option does not become exercisable, note holders simply receive their original investment (ie, the payout under the zero-coupon bond).

Hypothetical example: zero-coupon bond and call option premium

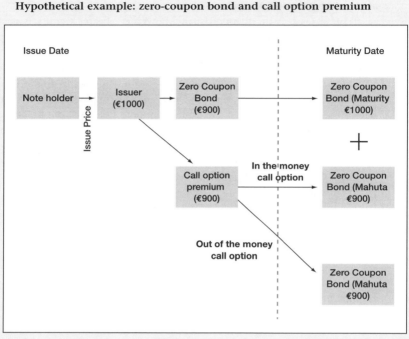

In the example above, the payment of the call option premium enables the issuer to acquire 100 futures contracts, with a strike price of, say, €10 per contract. The exercise date of the option is typically set to coincide with, or pre-date, the maturity date of the zero-coupon bond. If, at maturity, the call option is in the money by €3 per contract – that is, €300 in total – then the note holder will receive a final repayment amount of €1,300 (ie, the zero-coupon bond pay-out plus the option settlement amount).

However, if in the above example the call option is out of the money (ie, the underlying futures contract price is lower than the strike price), the option will not be exercised. The note holder will receive the final repayment amount of €1,000 (ie, just the zero-coupon bond payout plus the option settlement amount). In this case, the investor still receives the initial principal (issue price) invested; however, having received no interest on that initial principal, the investor has 'lost' the opportunity to make a return on that initial investment. For instance, had the initial issue price been invested in an interest-bearing deposit account or a government bond, the investor would have made a return on its investment. By forgoing this opportunity, the investor gains instead the ability to make a potentially higher return on its investment, provided that the option element of this structured product is in the money at maturity.

There are numerous variations on the zero-coupon bond plus embedded derivative structure. One of these is to structure the note so that there is a contingent coupon payable at various intervals during the term of the note. In this case, as above, an amount is invested in a zero-coupon bond to ensure principal protection at maturity. However, multiple options must be purchased, with expiration dates coinciding with interest payment dates. If the relevant option is in the money on the related coupon-payment date, the investor will receive a coupon amount on the note. Conversely, the note holder will not receive a coupon amount if the option is out of the money on the relevant coupon-payment date.

Another common variation of this product is the use of a 'barrier' option. In this case the option incorporates a knock-in and/or knock-out feature. This means that the option is activated only at a pre-specified knock-in level, or it is no longer exercisable if the knock-out level is triggered. The latter is a common feature and enables the issuer of the note to maintain some limits on the amount of up-side or down-side return that is payable to the investor.

Finally, a 'cliquet' note allows for gains and losses on the underlying derivative to be locked in and averaged out over the life of the note. For instance, a five-year note has bi-annual valuation dates. On each valuation date the value of the underlying commodity or commodity index is calculated (whether it be a gain or a loss). Then on the maturity date, all positive and negative amounts are aggregated to calculate the final coupon amount. This type of structure allows investors to protect against volatility of a particular underlying asset class.

(ii)   *Dynamic note structures, including CPPI products*
Note structures can take the form of actively managed strategies. For example, a note linked to a basket of shares in zinc mining companies may have an additional feature

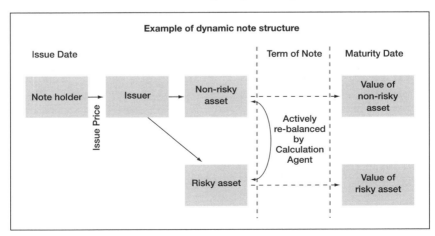

that the issuer (or calculation agent appointed by the issuer) of the note re-weights the constituents of the basket periodically, based on past performances of the underlying shares. This would be a form of actively managed note (see diagram on previous page).

Constant protection portfolio insurance (CPPI) structures are a form of actively managed note. Most CPPI structures offer capital protection. As shown in the preceding diagram, the issuer of the CPPI note invests a portion of the issue price of the note in a non-risky asset. This could be a zero-coupon bond or a money market instrument which will return an amount equal to par-value of the note on maturity. The remaining portion is invested in a riskier, performance-based commodity-linked asset.

During the term of the note, on specified dates, the issuer (or calculation agent) rebalances the proportions in which the note is invested *vis-à-vis* risky versus non-risky assets. For instance, if on the issue date 90% of the note is invested in, and therefore linked to, the non-risky asset, and on the first 'rebalancing date' the risky asset is performing well, the calculation agent may re-weight the constituents so that only 80% of the note is linked to the non-risky asset and 20% is linked to the risky asset. If on the following rebalancing date the risky asset is performing badly, the calculation agent may rebalance the constituents again so as to increase the proportion of the note invested in the non-risky asset. The rebalancing is carried out by the calculation agent using a set formula or mathematical algorithm (ie, a CPPI note is non-discretionary and is rules based).

At maturity, investors receive the sum of the values of the risky asset portion of the note and the non-risky asset portion of the note.

The term 'bond floor', which is used in connection with CPPI products, denotes the value below which the note should never fall in order to ensure the payment of all future due cash flows (including principal protection at maturity). The term 'cushion' denotes the reduction in value which the note can absorb before hitting the bond floor.

The size of the allocation to the risky asset will be determined by a multiplier (the size of which will be related to the volatility of the underlying 'risky asset' class). Therefore, in practice, the allocation to the risky asset will be equal to the cushion times the multiplier.

If the risky asset starts to perform badly, assets will be reallocated to the non-risky asset. However, if the value of the risky asset falls dramatically and the calculation agent has not had time to re-weight the constitutions, the issuer may incur a loss – this is referred to as 'gap risk'.

(iii)   *Fund-linked note structures*
The structures described previously in this sub-section (d) presuppose that the derivative element of the note will be invested in commodity-linked futures contracts, options contracts or another security linked to a commodity. Notes can also be structured so that the performance element is linked to units or shares in funds, such as commodity-index funds.

For fund-linked structures, the issuer must bear in mind the following:
- Any payments due under the note will need to take into account the ability

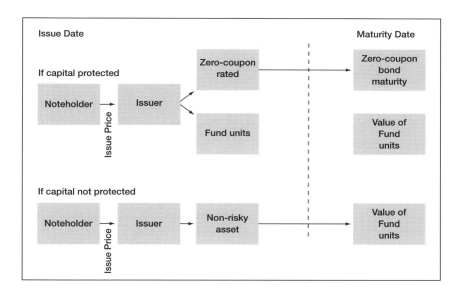

of the issuer to redeem the underlying investment in the fund units. Unlike futures, options, ETFs or ETCs, which are liquid instruments, fund units (depending on the fund) may be redeemable only on certain dates. For example, the issuer may be able to effect a redemption of fund units only on a monthly settlement date or, in certain cases, on quarterly settlement dates. There may also be certain notice requirements and other procedures to comply with prior to redemption. Some funds have restrictions on the aggregate amount of redemptions per settlement date. The note documentation needs to track or otherwise build in contingencies to allow for these events.

- Valuation of fund units will be based on the most recent net asset value (NAV) calculation of the fund, which may quickly become outdated, depending on the liquidity and volatility of the fund. There may be a higher risk to the issuer of hedge mismatch if, under the notes, the amount of the performance portion of the note promised to investors is based on NAV, rather than the actual hedge unwind price achieved by the issuer. The common solution for the issuer is to link the payout to the latter; however, for the investor this raises transparency concerns.

- For investors in certain jurisdictions or for certain classes of investors (eg, pension funds or insurance companies), fund-linked notes may provide exposure to this type of underlying which would otherwise not be permitted for legal, regulatory or tax issues which may arise had the investor directly participated in the fund units itself.

(iv) *Collateralised commodity obligations*
Collateralised commodity obligations are a fixed-income type of product styled in a similar fashion to credit derivatives. This structure combines the use of a commodity

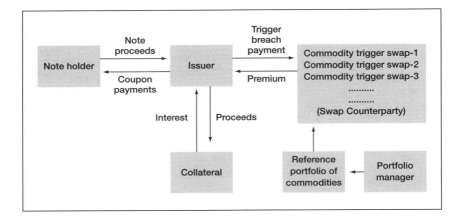

trigger swap, which is sold to an investor/swap counterparty in return for premium payments.

In the diagram above, which gives an example where commodity trigger swaps occur, the issuer issues notes and receives note proceeds from the note holder. At the same time, the issuer sells protection on a basket of commodity trigger swaps and receives a premium amount from the swap counterparty. The issuer typically invests the note proceeds in a collateral asset (ie, a secure asset such as sovereign debt or bonds issued by a highly rated corporate).

The commodity products being referenced are commodity trigger swaps – they are essentially out-of-the-money, European-style put options linked to the price of a commodity/commodity index. The strike price of each option is set at a predefined 'trigger level'. Typically, there will be more than one trigger for each commodity referenced. If the put option becomes exercisable (ie, in the money), the commodity is said to have 'defaulted' or a 'trigger event' has occurred for the purposes of the transaction.

If a trigger event occurs under the commodity trigger swap, the issuer will sell the collateral to make the protection payments due to the swap counterparties. The note holders therefore ultimately bear this risk.

(v)   *Catastrophe bonds*

Catastrophe bonds give investors a high return, which may be reduced if a catastrophic event occurs – for example, a 'wind event' such as a hurricane hitting the coast of Florida.

These fixed-income securities are structured in a similar way to the collateralised commodity obligations described above, except that the interest element and/or principal element can be reduced – usually by a fixed amount – each time a catastrophic event occurs. Catastrophe derivatives usually relate to weather-related events and as such are discussed in further detail in the chapter on weather derivatives.

(e)   Commodity-linked certificates and warrants

A warrant gives an investor the right to buy (in the case of a call warrant) or sell (in the case of a put warrant) a specified quantity of the underlying asset at a particular strike price. Warrants are normally cash settled and tradable. Warrants also typically give investors leverage with respect to the underlying – that is, the investor can gain a return on the underlying asset, just as they could through direct investment in the underlying.

A certificate in most markets is synonymous with the term 'warrant'. Certificates can come in a variety of forms, including 'delta-one' certificates ('tracking' certificates) and 'leveraged' certificates. Some of the common forms of certificates in the market are outlined below.

The terminology used with respect to certificates can be interesting. The underlying asset is typically a futures contract on a particular commodity or a commodity index.

(i)   Airbag certificates

This form of certificate provides protection to an investor up to a specified protection level. The certificate tracks the performance of any underlying commodity. At maturity, if the final price of the certificate is:

- above the initial price, the investor will receive the delta-one (ie, matching) exposure to the underlying asset (see 'Delta-one certificate' below);
- between the protection level and the initial price, the investor will receive its initial investment; or
- below the initial level, the investor will receive a percentage payout based on the amount below the initial price.

So, for example, if the protection level was set at 65% and the commodity price ended up at 70% of the initial price, within the airbag range, the investor would get 100% of the issue price back. If the commodity price ended up at 60% of the initial price, the investor would get 60% of the original issue price back, because the commodity price was outside the airbag range.

(ii)   Auto-callable certificate

If on certain 'call dates' the price of the underlying is above a predefined level, the investor will receive a 'coupon amount' plus the nominal amount on the maturity date and the certificate will terminate. If the trigger level has not been met during the term of the certificate, the investor will typically receive just the nominal amount of the certificate on the maturity date.

(iii)   Booster certificate

This allows investors to receive delta-one exposure to the underlying commodity when the price of the commodity is below a specified strike price and leveraged exposure to the underlying commodity when the price of the commodity is above that specified strike price.

(iv)   *Delta-one certificate*
This can be either of fixed maturity or open ended and it takes the form of a straight 'tracking' certificate which tracks the performance of an underlying commodity. The term 'delta-one' comes from the mathematical term used to describe the correlation of the underlying asset to the derivative – that is, a 1% price change in the underlying asset will result in the same percentage change in the certificate. These certificates are non-principal-protected and do not usually pay an interest amount to the holder.

(v)   *Discount certificate*
This tracks a particular underlying and returns a payout to the holder in line with the value of the underlying. However, the initial investment by the holder is at a discount to what the holder would pay had it invested directly in the underlying. The return on investment is usually capped at an upper limit.

(vi)   *Lock-in certificate*
This allows investors to receive the greater of the performance of the underlying or the 'lock-in level'. The lock-in level will typically be ratcheted – for example, if the underlying commodity reaches 150% of its initial value at least once during the term of the product, the investor will receive a pre-specified amount, and if the underlying commodity reaches 200% of its initial value at least once during the term of the product, the investor will receive a higher pre-specified amount.

(vii)   *Look-back certificate*
This form of certificate typically pays out to investors on maturity an amount linked to a participation in the best performance of the underlying commodity during the term of the certificate.

(viii)   *Mini-future certificate*
This offers investors a leveraged exposure to the underlying commodity – that is, the investor funds only a portion of the certificate, with the issuer financing the remaining portion. These certificates offer delta-one exposure to the underlying asset and will normally have a knock-out feature, whereby the certificate will 'knock out' at a pre-specified level and will pay out an 'unwind amount' to the investor.

(ix)   *Rainbow certificate*
This looks retrospectively to allocate weightings to the constituents of the certificate, based on that constituent's performance. For instance, the underlying asset with the best performance throughout the term of the certificate would be allocated a greater weighting at maturity in order to calculate the payout, and the inverse would be true of the worst-performing underlying asset.

(x)   *Reverse convertible certificates*
This form of certificate pays out a coupon to the investor at maturity plus either:
    •   the initial nominal amount of the certificate, if the final price is higher than

the initial price at maturity; or

- the delta-one exposure to the underlying asset, if the final price is below the initial price at maturity.

(xi)   *Rolling turbo certificate*

This form is similar to a mini-future certificate, except that the proportion of the certificate financed by the issuer and the knock-out level will be adjusted (usually daily) in order to maintain a constant proportion of leverage. As with stop-loss turbo certificates, any unwind amount payable to investors will typically be reinvested in the product instead of being paid out to investors.

(xii)   *Stop-loss turbo certificate*

This is similar to a mini-future certificate, except that any unwind amount payable to investors when a knock-out level has been reached will typically be reinvested in the product instead of being paid out to investors.

(xiii)   *Synthetic convertible certificate*

This provides the investor with income in the form of coupon payments during the term of the product and, at maturity, a return of the initial nominal amount invested, unless the investor opts to convert and receive a predefined amount of the underlying asset.

3.5   **Commodity funds**

A commodity fund is an investment fund that invests in underlying assets comprising commodity-linked assets (eg, physical commodities, commodity futures and commodity-linked securities). For instance, a gold fund is a mutual fund that invests primarily in gold-producing companies (eg, stocks and bonds of gold miners and manufacturers) or gold bullion.

Commodity funds allow investors to participate in commodity price fluctuations without investing directly in futures contracts.

(a)   *Variety of commodity funds*

There is a wide variety of commodity funds, which differ according to:

- legal structure, which dictates whether they have a corporate or a trust structure, whether they are regulated or unregulated, and whether they are open ended or closed ended;
- investment strategy – that is, whether they are passively managed or actively managed; and
- the types of investment in commodities they capture (eg, physical commodities, commodity futures, commodity-linked securities).

(i)   *Legal structures*

The corporate or trust structure will vary depending on the jurisdiction in which the investment fund is set up. For instance, in the United States, mutual funds and closed-ended funds are usually corporate structures, while unit investment trusts are a type of trust structure. In the United Kingdom, investment trusts, investment companies with variable capital (ICVCs) and open-ended investment companies (OEICs) are corporate structures, while unit trusts are trust structures.[6]

A 'regulated' fund is, broadly, a fund that is subject to extensive regulation in respect of its constitution and investment powers, and that can therefore can be marketed more freely to the public. In the United Kingdom, regulated funds can be undertakings for collective investment in transferable securities (UCITS) or non-UCITS. They can take the form of authorised unit trusts or ICVCs.

An 'open-ended' fund means that the number of units in issue regularly expands or contracts as investors come into (subscribe) or leave (redeem) the fund. Thus, for instance, a company with a fixed capital is closed ended. An ICVC or OEIC is open ended.

(ii)   *Investment strategies*

Commodity funds also offer a variety of investment strategies, from active management to passive management:

- active management – the fund manager buys and sells in an effort to outperform a benchmark market or index (active portfolio); and
- passive management – the fund manager seeks to replicate a benchmark market or index and match its performance (passive portfolio).

(iii)   *Types of underlying commodities holding*

Commodity funds themselves capture different types of investment in commodities:

- 'Physical' commodity funds have direct holdings in commodities.
- Commodity funds that hold futures hold commodity-linked derivative contracts (eg, futures).
- Natural resources funds invest in companies that operate in the commodity-related field.
- Combination funds invest in a combination of physical commodities and commodity futures.
- Index-based funds attempt to replicate a certain commodity index. These types of commodity fund are often passively managed and open ended, and take the form of mutual funds (although mutual funds are traditionally actively managed). They are one of the most conventional commodity funds and are further analysed next.

(b)   Open-ended index-based mutual funds

A commodity index-based fund is a type of open-ended investment fund (in the form of either a corporate or trust structure) that holds and manages a basket of commodities or commodity-linked securities in an attempt to replicate the performance of a certain commodity index.

Some key features of open-ended index-based mutual funds are described next.

---

6   In the United Kingdom, some investment funds can also be limited partnerships.

(i)   *Structure, key players and methods of investing*

An investor that wishes to invest in a mutual fund sends cash to the mutual fund. The mutual fund then uses that cash to purchase commodity-linked assets in the market and issues additional fund shares of the mutual fund, which in turn are allocated to the investor. The investor can either buy the fund shares directly or effect the transaction through a brokerage firm.

The mutual fund purchases a basket of commodity-linked assets that mirrors the commodity index portfolio profile. The portfolio is designed to replicate the performance of the targeted commodity index. The mutual fund holds the basket of commodity-linked assets and/or other securities in trust with a custodian for and on behalf of the investors. These assets are legally separate from the assets of the mutual fund.

The key players in a mutual fund's administration are shown in the diagram below.

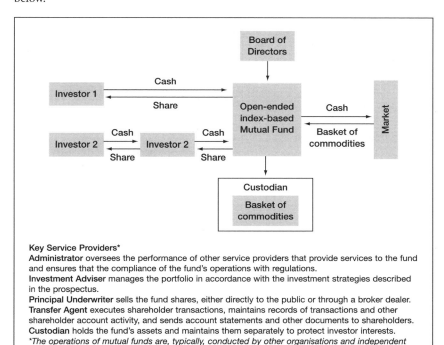

Key Service Providers*
Administrator oversees the performance of other service providers that provide services to the fund and ensures that the compliance of the fund's operations with regulations.
Investment Adviser manages the portfolio in accordance with the investment strategies described in the prospectus.
Principal Underwriter sells the fund shares, either directly to the public or through a broker dealer.
Transfer Agent executes shareholder transactions, maintains records of transactions and other shareholder account activity, and sends account statements and other documents to shareholders.
Custodian holds the fund's assets and maintains them separately to protect investor interests.
The operations of mutual funds are, typically, conducted by other organisations and independent service providers.

(ii)   *Investment return and investors' exit strategies*

At the end of each trading day, the net asset value (NAV) of the mutual fund is calculated. The NAV of a mutual fund is equal to the total value of all assets in the mutual fund's portfolio (based on the closing market prices of those assets), less any liabilities (eg, fees paid to the service providers).

As a result, a mutual fund share's price is calculated by dividing the NAV by the number of outstanding shares. This is the price at which investors will buy fund shares from the mutual fund.

An investor that wishes to disinvest from the mutual fund can redeem its fund share directly at the mutual fund's NAV, as calculated at the end of each trading day. As a result, any investor redeeming or purchasing a fund share on a certain day obtains the same price, regardless of the time of day at which the purchase or redemption is made. A mutual fund does not allow speculative investors to take advantage of the daily fluctuations of its basket of underlying assets.

When investors in open-ended mutual funds redeem their fund shares, the fund shares are returned to the mutual fund in exchange for cash. As a result, the mutual fund may have to liquidate a portion of its underlying positions (ie, sell portfolio securities) to fund the redemption.

(iii)   *Ring fencing*
Mutual funds hold assets in ring-fenced, segregated accounts or ring-fenced fund companies. In the case of a failure of the mutual fund, the investor has recourse directly to the pool of underlying assets. An investor in a mutual fund should therefore bear no credit risk other than to the underlying assets, because it owns a *pro-rata* interest in the basket of underlying assets. In other words, if the mutual fund becomes insolvent, the basket of underlying assets will be returned to the investors, and not to the other creditors of the mutual fund.

(iv)   *Investor protection*
A mutual-fund type of structure offers some protection for investors due to its legal structure, which can be regulated in various jurisdictions (eg, OEICs), and its governance, with regular accounts and reports.

(v)   *Limited tradability*
Open-ended mutual funds are not traded on exchange, and this limits liquidity. Even though they can be bought on margin, open-ended mutual funds cannot usually be shorted. Therefore, unless an investor enters into a bespoke fund derivative referencing a mutual fund, it can take exposure only to the upward price movements. In addition, there are no exchange-traded mutual fund options.

(vi)   *Costs for investors*
The costs (or 'expense ratio') incurred by investors mainly consist of management fees. These cover the costs associated with buying and selling underlying securities to accommodate investors' purchases and redemptions. An index fund typically has lower management fees than a regular mutual fund.[7] The reason for this is that an index fund is not actively managed. Thus, fund managers need only maintain the appropriate weightings of the underlying assets to match the commodity index performance (passive management technique).

---

7   An average non-index fund has an expense ratio of around 1.5%, whereas many index funds have an expense ratio of around 0.2%.

In addition to management fees, investors may be subject to early withdrawal fees depending on the type and prospectus of the mutual fund, and/or delays in receiving back an investment. There are usually no brokerage commissions as fund shares are not traded on an exchange market.

(vii)   *Minimum investments*
Some mutual funds require minimum investment amounts from investors.

(viii)   *Tax treatment*
Tax treatment at investor level usually depends on where the investor is tax resident and where the mutual fund is established. As a general principle, the sale of portfolio securities by open-ended mutual funds (for the purpose of redeeming fund shares to the exiting investor or rebalancing the underlying portfolio to replicate a new version of the commodity index) may potentially generate taxable gains at the fund level that can ultimately result in taxable distributions to remaining investors and exiting investors.

In addition, investors may receive taxable dividend income from the underlying securities due to the tax transparency of the investment vehicle.

3.6   Commodity exchange-traded products
The main characteristic which is shared by all exchange-traded products described below, and which differentiates them from index-based funds, is that they are traded on an exchange market.

(a)   *ETFs*
An ETF[8] is a fund-type investment vehicle that holds a portfolio of physical commodities and/or commodity-linked financial instruments (eg, forwards, futures, options, commodity-linked securities) designed to reflect a market commodity index. It allows its investors to buy and sell shares that represent a fractional ownership of such underlying portfolio on an exchange market.

The first ETF was launched in the United States on the American Stock Exchange in 1993 by State Global Advisors, with the introduction of the SPDR Trust. It was a S&P 500 index fund with an underlying portfolio designed essentially to replicate the performance of the S&P 500 index. This was not a commodity ETF, but the general principles remain the same. The first ETF introduced in the United Kingdom was in 2000.

For terminology purposes for the remainder of this section, the term 'ETF' refers to the fund-type investment vehicle, while the term 'ETF share' means the financial instrument issued by the ETF and held by the investor.

ETFs can be categorised in accordance with different criteria. First, 'commodity' ETFs can be divided into four types of ETF depending on the type of commodity underlying:

---

8   Currently almost $700 billion of assets is held in 950 ETFs globally across 41 different exchanges.

- ETFs that track an individual commodity, such as gold, oil or soybean;
- ETFs that track a basket of different commodities;
- ETFs that invest in a group of companies that produce a commodity; and
- ETFs that invest in other ETFs and give investors exposure to many different sectors.[9]

Secondly, ETFs can be categorised as 'index-based' ETFs – these usually track the price of a particular commodity or group of commodities that comprise an index by using futures contracts.[10] Index-based ETFs are typically passively managed and are those studied further in this section.

Although present in Europe for some time, actively managed ETFs were not introduced in the United States until early 2008, when the Securities and Exchange Commission (SEC) approved their launch. Unlike traditional index-based ETFs, which are designed to track an index, actively managed ETFs permit the fund manager to buy and sell securities and derivatives according to a stated investment strategy, described in the prospectus, without regard to a corresponding commodity index.

The key features of ETFs are set out next.

(i)   *Structures, key players and methods of investing*
The legal form of an ETF varies from jurisdiction to jurisdiction. For example, in the United States, there are three legal structures for ETFs: managed investment companies (open-ended index funds); unit investment trusts; and grantor trusts. The majority of US ETFs are open-ended index funds. In Europe, ETFs are mostly UCITS III compliant (open collective funds).

ETFs are also subject to different regulations depending on jurisdiction and the exchange market on which they are traded. In the United States, traditional ETFs are regulated by the SEC under the Investment Company Act of 1940. However, there is a particularity for commodity-based ETFs which do not invest in securities: this type of ETF is regulated by the Commodity Futures Trading Commission. In Europe, an ETF fund may need to comply with UCITS rules.[11]

For the purpose of describing the methods of investing in an ETF, it is important to distinguish between 'authorised participants' and other investors. An 'authorised participant' is usually an institutional investor or market maker which has signed a participant agreement with the ETF sponsor. Becoming an authorised participant allows the entity to transact directly with the fund on an 'in-kind' basis.

An ETF fund can issue new ETF shares and redeem existing ETF shares on any trading day, in a process referred to as 'creation' and 'redemption', which is open to qualifying entities that have registered as authorised participants with the fund. This mechanism allows an authorised participant to exchange a portfolio of commodity-linked assets and receive ETF shares in return (ie, creation). Similarly, an authorised

---

9   The first ETF wrap portfolio was launched in 2007.
10   However, some ETFs also back themselves with the actual commodity in storage.
11   For example, European regulations do not permit investment in fewer than five underlying constituents or securities in a UCITS III ETF.

participant can redeem ETF shares and receive portfolio assets (ie, redemption).

Creations may take place only in blocks, called 'creation units'. The size varies, but is typically 50,000 shares.

ETF shares are subsequently sold by authorised participants to retail investors through the secondary market. Retail investors can also buy from, or sell such ETF shares to, other investors on the secondary market.

The diagram below sets out the structure, key players and creation/redemption process of ETF shares in a US ETF.

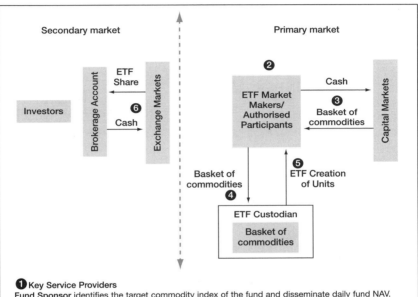

❶ Key Service Providers
Fund Sponsor identifies the target commodity index of the fund and disseminate daily fund NAV.
Investment Manager is responsible for all underlying securities trading decisions.
Custodian is responsible for the safe-keeping of assets, trade processing, settlement and clearance.
Fund Distributor is responsible for approving all creation orders of the EFT shares. The fund sponsor can choose to be distributor or engage third party provider.
Authorised Participant (AP) place orders to creat or redeem ETF shares in large blocks and execute transactions to investors.
Transfer Agent provides maintenance of AP activity records.

❶ A Fund Sponsor (referred as well sometimes as the 'fund manager' and index creator (ie, the firm that create and maintain indices) agree to target a certain commodity index;
❷ The Fund Sponsor then enters into an agreement with the APs the manage the ETF fund and its ETF shares. Such agreement empowers the APs to create and redeem ETF shares. The fund sponser gives APs a portfolio composition file that lists the components and weightings of underlying commodity-linked securities the mirror the target index;
❸ APs then buy or borrow the commodity-linked securities from the capital markets such that it mirrors the index;
❹ The basket of securities/commodities is delivered to the custodian which verifies that it is an approximate mirror of the index;
❺ In exchange, the AP receives a 'creation unit'. The creation unit is broken up into ETF shares, which represent a fraction of the creation unit. The fund sponsor issues ETF shares to the APs. The tota value of these ETF shares equals that of the creation unit.
❻ The APs sell these ETF shares on the open market like any publicly-traded stock (or has the option of holding ETF shares in their name.

There are mainly two options to track the performance of an index with its underlying assets: physical ETFs and swap-based ETFs.

In physical ETFs (also called 'cash-based ETFs'), the ETF fund holds a basket of underlying commodity-linked securities that replicate the targeted commodity index in terms of components and weightings, and tracks the performance of the index by buying and selling the underlying securities.

Physical ETF

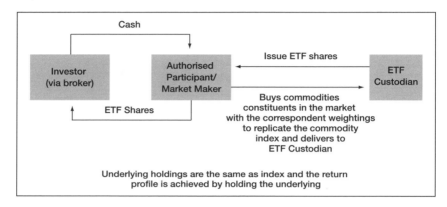

In a swap-based ETF, the ETF replicates the index performance through the use of swaps. Swap-based ETFs buy non-indexed securities and 'outsource' the index tracking to a third party by entering into a swap agreement. They gain their economic exposure to a commodity index via swaps.

Swap-based ETF

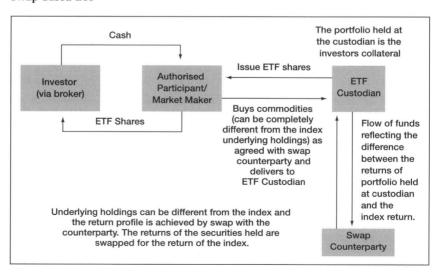

Mechanism of the swap agreement

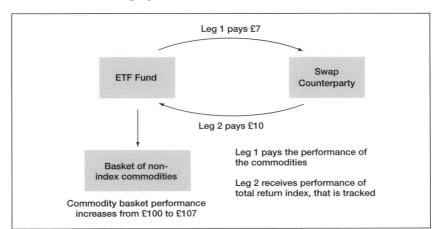

Leg 1 pays £7

ETF Fund

Swap Counterparty

Leg 2 pays £10

Basket of non-index commodities

Leg 1 pays the performance of the commodities

Leg 2 receives performance of total return index, that is tracked

Commodity basket performance increases from £100 to £107

Swap-based ETFs introduce a third-party credit risk that can be minimised through credit default swaps and collateralisation.[12]

(ii)   *Trading, pricing and exit strategies*
ETF shares are listed on a national securities exchange and are bought and sold by retail investors like common stock throughout the trading day in the secondary market. ETF shares from US ETF funds are primarily traded on the American Stock Exchange, but some are also traded on the NYSE Arca, NYSE AltNext and NASDAQ. ETF shares from UK ETF funds are primarily listed on the London Stock Exchange. Investors (if they are not authorised participants) are required to purchase or sell ETF shares through a stock brokerage account in a process identical to the purchase or sale of any other listed stock.

As an exit strategy, an investor may either sell its ETF share during the day on the market exchange or, if the investor is an authorised participant, redeem its ETF share at the end of the trading day. Small investors cannot transact directly with the ETF.

The price of an ETF share is determined in a similar way to those of commodity mutual funds, but with some variations as further explained below.

Because of the open-ended feature of an ETF (ie, the process of daily creation and redemption), ETF shares can be purchased at the end of each trading day for their NAV, which is calculated based on the total assets of the ETF fund, subtracting expenses and dividing by the number of ETF shares outstanding.[13] This value is generally determined at the close of each trading day. The value is used to price creation and redemption units and is disseminated to the public before the market opens the following day.

---

12   If the ETF is UCITS compliant, it is required to collateralise 90% of counterparty exposure (swap counterparty) – that is, the counterparty exposure to the swap counterparty is capped at 10% of the fund's net asset value. The remaining counterparty risk can be also removed by buying a credit default swap.
13   This is the same calculation as for commodity mutual funds.

However, ETF shares can also be traded intra-day on the secondary market. ETF shares experience price changes throughout the day as they are bought and sold (an intra-day indicative value usually gets updated every 15 seconds). However, an ETF share generally trades at a price that is close to its NAV. Indeed, the creation/redemption process is intended to mitigate pricing imbalances, since authorised participants may create new ETF shares and offer them for sale in the secondary market. However, there are times when an ETF can trade at a premium to or at a discount to its NAV. This can occur because:

- there is an imbalance in buying and selling interest in an ETF;
- the underlying components of the ETF (ie, the basket of securities that comprise the ETF) are not trading during the same hours as the ETF shares; or
- the trading in a component security is halted.

In addition, the ETF share may be priced to anticipate a future price in the underlying when it opens for trading.

In a redemption process of ETF shares to an authorised participant, the ETF does not have to sell any of its holdings to fund large shareholder redemption. The authorised participants are redeemed 'in-kind'.

(iii)   *Access to underlying securities in case of insolvency*
ETFs benefit from the mutual-fund-type structure – that is, investors have access to underlying assets in case of failure of the ETF fund. As further described below, ETFs bear no credit risks compared to ETNs.

(iv)   *Enhanced tradability and liquidity*
Investors in ETF shares may enter the same types of order that are placed for shares of stock (ie, securities lending, limit orders, options, purchases on margin, ability to sell short). A speculative investor can thus bet on the direction of shorter-term market movements through the trading of an ETF share (speculative trading strategies).

(v)   *Minimum investment level*
An investor can purchase as little as one share, which constitutes a share of a creation unit, which in turn is a share of the underlying portfolio. Investing in commodities is cost prohibitive for most retail investors because they cannot afford to buy in lot sizes. ETFs allow retail investors to buy commodity lots in much smaller pieces, such as a single ETF share. Therefore, ETFs open up commodity investments to new categories of investor.

(vi)   *Tracking error*
An investor in a physical ETF bears a tracking risk – that is, there is a possibility that the ETF's returns will differ from the return on the underlying index it is tracking. The reason for this tracking error is that the index tracks the return of the underlying securities, but it is not traded. The ETF, on the other hand, is traded daily and it is the trading of the ETF that causes the variation in returns with the index. For

example, if all of the commodity-linked securities in the index are up during the day, the index will also be up. However, if investors in the ETF sell because they do not feel good about the prospects of the market looking forward, the ETF will be down. Nonetheless, this is not a major concern as the divergence between the index and its ETF is relatively minor and the two tend to revert back to each other.

(vii)   *Cost-effective access to an asset class*
There are two types of cost at investor level:

- Management fees (also called 'expense ratio' or 'investor fee') – the ETF charges a management fee that is deducted directly from its assets,[14] expressed as an annualised percentage. It is included in the daily published NAV and thus is incorporated in the bid and asked prices in the secondary market. ETFs generally have a lower expense ratio than their mutual fund counterparts. One of the reasons that ETFs are shielded from the costs associated with buying and selling shares is to accommodate authorised participants' purchases and redemptions.
- Brokerage commissions and/or transaction costs – these typically apply to ETF share purchases and sales depending on the fee structure of the individual investor's securities account. When an investor buys and sells ETF shares, it pays the same commission charge to the broker that it would pay on any regular order.

(viii)   *Tax efficiency*
The tax treatment at investor level will depend on where the investor is tax resident and where the ETF is established.

Generally, ETFs are more likely to be tax efficient than open-ended mutual funds. Unlike open-ended mutual funds, which typically fund investor redemptions by selling portfolio securities, ETFs usually redeem investors in kind, which should not result in realised capital gains at the fund level that must later be distributed to investors.

ETFs usually sell portfolio assets only when the underlying securities rebalance. This low turnover rate will typically result in fewer taxable distributions to investors. When an ETF is forced to sell a commodity-linked asset to change its composition (eg, when an index rebalances), the investors have to pay tax on whatever the capital gain was when the commodity was sold.

(b)   **ETNs**
An ETN is a senior, typically unsecured, unrated note issued by an underwriting bank, designed to replicate the price fluctuation of a particular commodity or commodity index. ETNs were first issued by Barclays Bank PLC on June 12 2006 (the iPath ETN).

For terminology purposes in the remainder of this section, the underwriting bank issuing the ETN is referred to as the 'issuer'.

---

14   The prospectus of the ETF will detail the fees and method of calculation.

The key features of ETNs are described next.

(i)   *Legal structure and key players*

ETNs are similar to ETFs in that they are a means of investing in commodity indexes, but they differ in legal structure: an ETF is a fund with an underlying basket of assets, whereas an ETN is a debt security with no underlying basket of assets.

An investor in an ETN is effectively lending money to the issuer in exchange for the commitment by the issuer to provide, upon maturity of the ETN, a return tied to an index (minus investor fees). In other words, investors buy an obligation similar to a forward contract. Most ETN issuers are large financial institutions with investment-grade credit ratings.

The diagram below highlights the ETN structure and key players.

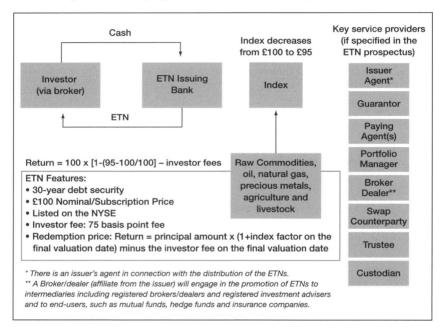

In terms of regulatory framework, US ETNs are registered not under the Investment Company Act 1940, but under the Securities Act 1933. US commodity ETNs are not regulated by the Commodity Futures Trading Commission. However, futures contracts underlying the relevant market index may be regulated by the Commodity Futures Trading Commission.

For the purpose of understanding an ETN, it may be helpful to compare the main characteristics of an ETN with a traditional bond or note.

Characteristic	In a traditional bond or note?	In an ETN?
Distribution of periodic coupon payments	Yes (except zero-coupon notes)	No
Principal repayment	Yes, equal to the nominal (except zero-coupon notes)	Yes, proportional to the performance of a market commodity index minus applicable fees (1)
Principal protection	Yes	No (unless specifically specified in the prospectus) (2)
Maturity date	Yes	Yes

(1) Typically, the return will be calculated as the principal amount of the securities times the index factor on the final valuation date, minus the investor fee on the final valuation date. The index factor can be the percentage difference between the index level on the redemption date or maturity date and the index level on the trade date (starting date); or can be more complex, such as taking the index level at four different dates and averaging them together (the percentage difference between the average of the four dates and the starting date is the return). Some ETNs can also seek to track the leveraged long or leveraged short performance of an index. For example, an ETN can be designed to give double exposure by offering two times the performance of the index over a specific time period; or an inverse leveraged ETN that aims to provide double short exposure may be constructed to provide two times the inverse performance of the index. Thus, for instance, a double short ETN where the index went down 50% would provide the investor with a return of 100%; similarly, if the index went up 50%, the investment loss would be 100%.

(2) However, losses do not exceed the amount of the investment.

(ii) *Trading, pricing and exit strategies*
Similar to shares of an ETF, ETNs, as publicly traded securities, are liquid trading instruments. ETNs are traded on major exchanges, such as the NYSE Arca and SETS (London Stock Exchange's premier trading), during normal trading hours. ETNs are also bought and sold by investors through a broker in a similar manner to ETF shares and ordinary stock.

However, unlike ETF shares, ETNs do not have a NAV. The sale price of an ETN takes into account all relevant factors, including:
- supply and demand in the marketplace (ie, liquidity in the marketplace);
- perceived value and direction of the underlying index or asset class it is tracking;
- the expected total return; and
- the creditworthiness of the issuer.

This latter point is a major difference from an ETF share. An ETN's value is affected by the credit rating of its issuer. For example, the value of an ETN may drop despite no change in the underlying index, due instead to a downgrade in the issuer's credit rating.

An intra-day 'indicative value', published by Bloomberg, is intended to approximate the intrinsic economic value of the ETN. Additionally, the daily indicative value of an ETN is calculated and published at the end of each trading day.

In terms of exit strategies, an investor can withhold the debt security until its maturity date, or trade it on the secondary market exchange or redeem the debt security with the issuer, subject to fulfilment of certain conditions.

When the ETN is held to maturity, the investor will receive a cash payment that is linked to the performance of the index during the period beginning on the trade date and ending at the maturity date, less investor fees. Typically, ETNs do not offer principal protection.

ETNs can also be liquidated before their maturity:

- by sale on the exchange in the secondary market during trading hours;
- by early redemption (if specified in the prospectus), redeeming a large block of securities directly to the issuer, subject to the procedures described in the relevant prospectus;[15] or
- following a specified issuer call event (if specified in the prospectus).

The ETN prospectus often incorporates an early repurchase/redemption feature. This is subject to procedures described in the relevant prospectus, but typically it allows 'qualified' investors to elect on a daily or weekly basis to redeem notes at a predetermined price. Early repurchase is not available to investors for less than a specified minimum amount or minimum number of securities (typically, 50,000 notes). An early redemption charge[16] may apply.

The ETN prospectus may also define a specified issuer call event, whereby individual investors (not qualified for redemption election) can sell their ETNs to the issuer at a specified issuer call event. This comprises call features that allow the issuer to call the ETN at the issuer's discretion following the occurrence of certain market events defined in the prospectus.

(iii) *Credit risk of the issuer*

The ETN is effectively a promise to the investor that the issuer will pay the note according to the terms laid out in the ETN prospectus. As a result, an investor in an ETN bears the credit risk of the issuer of the note (ie, if the issuer goes bankrupt, the investor may not receive the return that was promised). For instance, both Lehman Brothers and Bear Stearns issued ETNs. Lehman Brothers launched three ETNs in early 2008 under the Opta brand name. Following the bankruptcy of Lehman

---

15   The issuer may from time to time, in its sole discretion, reduce, in part or in whole, the minimum redemption amount. Any such reduction will be applied on a consistent basis for all holders of units at the time the reduction becomes effective.

16   The charge is intended to allow the issuer to recoup brokerage and other costs incurred in connection with an early redemption.

Brothers in October 2008, investors had their money tied up in the firm's bankruptcy estate. Furthermore, as ETNs are debt securities, an ETN sponsor does not necessarily hold the underlying assets tied to the ETN's payout.

Usually, ETNs are not secured; however, while not required to, ETNs may use collateral. For instance, the Lyxor ETN issued in Europe has effectively been collateralised with European government bonds and benefits from a guarantee from a financial institution.

(iv) *Enhanced tradability and liquidity*
Like ETF shares, ETNs are highly liquid instruments.

(v) *Access to difficult-to-reach markets*
Like ETFs, ETNs are available on a wide range of commodity indices. In addition, they offer exposure to assets that cannot be achieved through a fund – for example, single commodities (not available in a mutual fund structure). ETNs offer more adequate coverage in terms of markets compared with ETFs.

(vi) *Cost-effective access to an asset class*
An ETN investor faces two types of expense:
- investor fee (also called an 'issuer fee', 'expense ratio', 'tracking fee') – the investor fee is calculated cumulatively through the term of the ETN, based on the yearly fee and the performance of the underlying commodity index, and increases each day based on the level of the index on that day; and
- brokerage fee and commission – because ETNs are traded like stocks, brokerage commissions and transaction costs typically apply to ETN purchases and sales depending on the investor's account type.

(vii) *No principal protection*
Usually, ETNs do not offer principal protection. For example, the investor fee reduces the amount of return at maturity or upon redemption so that, if the value of the underlying decreases or does not increase significantly, the investor may receive less than the principal amount of investment at maturity or upon redemption.

(viii) *Tax treatment*
The tax treatment at investor level will depend on where the investor is tax resident and where the issuer was established. ETNs generally offer a tax-efficient way to invest.

However, the tax treatment in ETNs in the United States is uncertain. ETNs have been mostly treated for tax purposes as pre-paid contracts. A pre-paid contract is a financial instrument, such as a forward contract. The owner of a pre-paid contract pays an initial amount in order to receive a future contingent payment based on the value of an index at a specified time. The difference between the purchase price of the ETN and the price at which it was sold should be treated as a capital gain for income tax purposes.[17] There is usually no interest payment. The timing of realisation of gains or losses on the ETNs is based on when investors buy and sell their investment. Since the entire gain is treated as a capital gain, the investor can defer any gain until the security either is sold or matures. Delaying the tax event is valuable because the amount that would have been paid as tax can continue to accumulate wealth.

In the United Kingdom, ETNs are eligible for capital gains tax treatment. The Lyxor ETN launched in 2009 in the United Kingdom got a tax opinion so as to be eligible for capital gains tax relief in the United Kingdom.

(ix)   Other key features

No tracking error: There is no tracking risk involved in holding an ETN because the return is not based on the underlying securities. The issuer guarantees the investor a return that is an exact replica of the underlying index, minus investor fees.

No rating: The creditworthiness of an ETN is itself not rated, but instead is based on the creditworthiness of the issuer.

No voting rights: ETNs do not usually have voting rights.

Minimum investment levels: Like ETF shares, ETNs have low minimum investment levels.

(c)   ETCs

ETCs are a sub-category of ETNs. They are investment vehicles (mostly asset-backed bonds in Europe) that track the performance of an underlying commodity index, including total return indices, based on a single commodity.

ETCs are listed securities backed by a commodity – either physical commodities[18] or commodity futures. ETCs provide investors with a legal structure that is secured, listed and investable (many institutional investors are prevented from buying physical commodities or even commodity derivatives).

In Europe, ETCs can be regarded as secured, undated, zero-coupon notes that trade through an open-market platform. The first ETC was a gold product named Gold Bullion Securities and launched in 2003 by the company ETF Securities. ETF Securities has since then launched an entire platform of commodity ETCs.

ETCs come in two main forms:
- 'Single-commodity' ETCs follow the spot price of a single commodity. Investors can buy single-commodity ETCs such as gold and oil or more exotic variants such as zinc and lean hogs.
- 'Index-tracking' ETCs follow the movement of a group of associated commodities; investors can invest in index-tracking ETCs giving exposure to a range of underlying assets, from broad indices to specific sub-indices such as energy or livestock, and all in one trade.

In the United States, ETCs can be issued through grantor trusts.

Some key features of ETCs are described next.

---

17   As of October 2008, the Internal Revenue Service (IRS) of the United States had not made a definitive ruling on the tax treatment of ETNs. In addition, the IRS is reviewing the tax treatment of ETNs and may consider taxing them as interest, rather than at lower capital gain rates.

18   For example, a physical gold bullion ETC is collateralised by allocated gold bullion.

(i) *Structure, key players and methods of investing*

ETCs are open-ended, asset-backed securities, created and redeemed on demand by the issuer. They are created through an authorised participant. Other investors buy ETCs from the authorised participant on the secondary market. The monthly roll to track the commodity index, custodianship and management is effectively outsourced to the issuer and 'commodity exposure provider' in return for an annual management fee.

The structure and creation process for ETCs is shown in the diagram below.

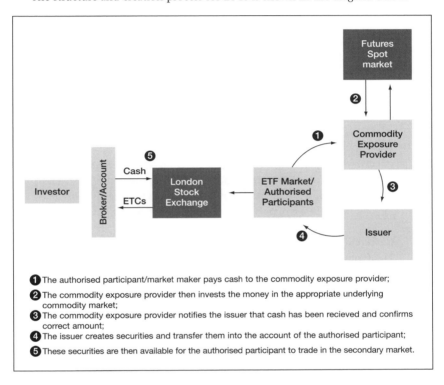

❶ The authorised participant/market maker pays cash to the commodity exposure provider;

❷ The commodity exposure provider then invests the money in the appropriate underlying commodity market;

❸ The commodity exposure provider notifies the issuer that cash has been recieved and confirms correct amount;

❹ The issuer creates securities and transfer them into the account of the authorised participant;

❺ These securities are then available for the authorised participant to trade in the secondary market.

(ii) *Pricing and trading*

Ordinary investors (ie, not authorised participants) buy and sell ETCs through regular brokerage accounts.

ETCs are traded and settled on a regulated exchange, in the same way as any share, ETF share or ETN.

The pricing of ETCs is not subject to supply and demand forces, due to their open-ended feature (ie, created and redeemed on demand). Indeed, the open-ended nature of these securities creates an arbitrage opportunity, should the price drift away from the NAV.

(iii) *Counterparty exposure*

Some precious-metals ETCs are backed by physical holdings. However, ETCs usually benefit from third-party guarantees. As a result, an ETC investor has counterparty exposure to third parties guaranteeing the securities' performance.

(iv)   *Other key features*
Minimum investment size: Like ETNs, the minimum investment size is low.

Tax treatment: Current advice from the London Stock Exchange suggests that there is no stamp duty on trades in those ETCs in the United Kingdom.

3.7   Other structured commodity products

(a)   *Managed futures funds*
A commodity pool operator is a person or a limited partnership that gathers money from investors, combines it in one pool and invests it in commodity futures contracts and options.

These funds are also known as 'commodity pools'. They are managed by a 'commodity trading adviser' in accordance with a trading programme set out in the disclosure documents. The main disadvantage of such product is the difficulty of assessing past performance.

Commodity trading advisers specialise in technical buying and selling of nearby positions based on short-term trends (which can create volatility in short-run prices). They are similar to hedge funds in this regard, but tend to concentrate on the nearby, looking for arbitrage opportunities and other short-term potential.

(b)   *Commodity hedge funds*
The term 'hedge funds' covers many different types of structure and investment, with few similarities between them. Hedge funds are unregulated funds in the United Kingdom – at least for the time being (although changes are likely to take place in 2010 and 2011). They will typically allow participants to redeem on a frequent basis (monthly or quarterly), and will therefore be open ended. Strategies involve high levels of leverage and short selling (to bet on falls in the market and profit from them). Hedge funds tend to be more flexible in their investment approach, enabling them to change direction quickly. There are also some specialist commodity hedge funds trading in just a single commodity, which in some instances are willing to play the physical commodities for future resale on exchange or over the counter.

Investors in hedge funds are typically institutional investors and high-net-worth individuals.

Exchange-traded commodity derivatives

Dharini Collins
Nanak Keswani

1. Introduction

The financial markets of the 16th to 18th centuries pioneered organised trading of derivatives contracts; and the first underlying assets to benefit from derivatives trading were commodities. Historically, commodity derivatives were used by producers of commodities to protect themselves against falling prices or lack of demand for their product while they incurred the costs of production, with commercial users of commodities looking to protect themselves against rising commodity prices erasing their profit margins.

The earliest instances of pure commodities trading date back to at least 2000 BC, when metals and other commodities were the trading currencies of various nation states. For example, evidence of negotiable instruments promising the delivery of pre-specified quantities of lead has been found in the Middle East (originating in Assyria).

Markets evolved so as to formalise a particular time and place for trading goods. These marketplaces developed their own sets of rules and regulations – whether official rules or unspoken conventions – in order to maintain some semblance of order. In London, trading in options and forwards had its origins in Exchange Alley.

In the late 17th century John Castaing began publishing a list of foreign exchange, stock and commodity prices known as "The course of the exchange and other things", which was initially published from Jonathan's Coffee House. This later evolved into the "Daily Official List", published from Garraway's Coffee House, and eventually into the London Stock Exchange. London became the primary European centre for the trading of goods and securities after the French Revolution shut the Paris Bourse and subsequent conflicts in continental Europe prompted traders to migrate from the Amsterdam Bourse to London.[1]

The commodities market is often referred to as the largest non-financial market in the world. The range of commodity-linked instruments available for sale and purchase on regulated exchanges has grown tremendously since the inception of commodities trading, although the commodities market experienced a deceleration in the rate of trading in 2008 following the Lehman collapse, due to concerns about systemic risk. The recent growth of the market is set out in the graph overleaf.

Commodities are normally available for sale (in their simplest form) via futures and options contracts linked to a particular commodity. While hedgers may be interested in taking physical delivery of the underlying commodity at the expiration

---

1   Elizabeth Hennessy, *Coffee House to Cyber Market*.

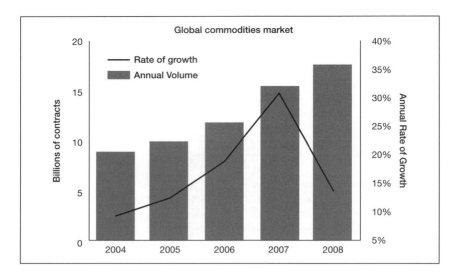

of the futures/option contract, most investors in commodities choose to invest in order to gain exposure to a particular commodity or segment of the market (in which case they will do so via a commodity index). Investors may believe that the market in that commodity/market segment may go up or down, or simply want to diversify their portfolios through an investment in commodities as well as other asset classes. These investors will either invest in cash-settled instruments or sell their physically settled instruments prior to the expiration date.

The tables below set out the size of the exchange-traded commodity derivatives market as at the end of 2008 (and compare it with 2007).

Global Listed Derivatives Volume By Category
Number of Futures and Options Contracts Traded and/or Cleared on Exchanges

Category	2008	2007	% Change
Equity Index	6,488,620,434	5,499,833,555	18.0%
Individual Equity	5,511,194,380	4,400,437,854	25.2%
Interest Rates	3,204,838,617	3,745,176,350	-14.4%
Agricultural	888,828,194	640,683,907	38.7%
Energy	580,404,189	496,710,566	16.8%
Currency	577,156,982	459,752,816	25.5%
Precious Metals	180,370,074	150,976,113	19.5%
Non-Precious Metals	175,788,341	106,859,969	64.5%
Other	45,501,810	26,140,974	74.1%
Total	17,652,703,621	15,526,632,104	13.7%

Note: Based on the number of futures and options traded and/or cleared by 69 exchanges worldwide.

Global listed derivatives volume by region[2]

	Jan-Dec 2008	Jan-Dec 2007	% change
Asia-Pacific	4,974,727,462	4,289,600,329	16.0%
Europe	4,167,116,664	3,592,095,161	16.0%
North America	6,995,493,016	6,137,204,923	14.0%
Latin America	854,405,219	1,048,627,318	-18.5%
Other *	660,961,260	459,104,373	44.0%
Global total	17,652,703,621	15,526,632,104	13.7%

Consists of exchanges in South Africa, Turkey, Israel and Dubai.
Note: Location of exchanges is determined by country of registration.

Breakdown by region (Jan-Dec 2008)

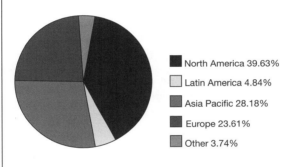

North America 39.63%

Latin America 4.84%

Asia Pacific 28.18%

Europe 23.61%

Other 3.74%

Source: Newedge

Top 20 agricultural futures and options worldwide
Ranked by number of contracts traded and/or cleared in 2008[3]

Rank	Contract	Jan-Dec 2008	Jan-Dec 2007	% change
1	White sugar futures, ZCE	165,485,978	45,468,481	264.0%
2	No 1 soybean futures, DCE	113,681,550	47,432,721	139.7%
3	Soy meal futures, DCE	81,265,439	64,719,466	25.6%
4	Corn futures, CME	59,957,118	54,520,152	10.0%
5	Corn futures, DCE	54,976,724	59,436,742	-7.5%
6	Rubber futures, SHFE	46,461,103	42,191,727	10.1%
7	Soy oil futures, DCE	43,695,993	13,283,866	228.9%
8	Soybean futures, CME	36,373,096	31,726,316	14.6%

continued overleaf

2   *Futures Industry* magazine, March/April 2009.
3   *Futures Industry* magazine, March/April 2009.

Top 20 agricultural futures and options worldwide
Ranked by number of contracts traded and/or cleared in 2008[3]

Rank	Contract	Jan-Dec 2008	Jan-Dec 2007	% change
9	Strong gluten wheat futures, ZCE	27,509,312	38,982,788	-29.4%
10	Sugar #11 futures, ICE Futures US	27,019,704	21,263,799	27.1%
11	Corn options on futures, CME	20,992,582	14,691,277	42.9%
12	Wheat futures, CME	19,011,928	19,582,706	-2.9%
13	Soybean oil futures, CME	16,928,361	13,170,914	28.5%
14	Soybean meal futures, CME	13,354,174	12,213,315	9.3%
15	Soybean options on futures, CME	9,806,935	8,215,582	19.4%
16	Live cattle futures, CME	9,801,360	8,587,973	14.1%
17	Sugar #11 options on futures, ICE Futures US	9,179,779	5,548,668	65.4%
18	Lean hog futures, CME	8,505,138	7,264,832	17.1%
19	Rapeseed oil futures, ZCE	6,429,404	659,612	874.7%
20	Palm oil futures, DCE	6,302,478	339,175	1758.2%

Top 20 energy futures and options worldwide[4]
Ranked by number of contracts traded and/or cleared in 2008

Rank	Contract	Jan-Dec 2008	Jan-Dec 2007	% change
1	Light sweet crude oil futures, CME	134,674,264	121,525,967	10.8%
2	Brent crude oil futures, ICE Futures Europe	68,368,145	59,728,941	14.5%
3	WTI crude oil futures, ICE Futures Europe	51,091,712	51,388,362	-0.6%
4	Natural gas futures, CME	38,730,519	29,786,318	30.0%
5	Light sweet crude oil options on futures, CME	35,255,326	28,398,793	24.1%
6	Henry Hub natural gas swap futures, CME *	31,401,575	16,207,044	93.8%
7	European style natural gas options, CME *	31,158,326	29,921,068	4.1%
8	Fuel oil futures, SHFE	30,810,540	12,005,094	156.6%
9	Gas oil futures, ICE Futures Europe	28,805,192	24,509,884	17.5%
10	NY Harbor RBOB gasoline futures, CME	20,522,571	19,791,439	3.7%

continued overleaf

4   *Futures Industry* magazine, March/April 2009.

Top 20 energy futures and options worldwide[4]
Ranked by number of contracts traded and/or cleared in 2008

Rank	Contract	Jan-Dec 2008	Jan-Dec 2007	% change
11	Crude oil futures, MCX	20,507,001	13,938,813	47.1%
12	No 2 heating Oil Futures, CME	19,583,052	18,078,976	8.3%
13	Henry Hub penultimate swap futures, CME *	12,352,928	10,117,889	22.1%
14	miNY crude oil futures, CME	5,641,145	5,185,214	8.8%
15	Gasoline futures, Tocom	4,054,761	7,529,706	-46.1%
16	European style crude oil options, CME *	3,580,861	1,879,999	90.5%
17	Natural gas options on futures, CME	2,336,287	5,051,879	-53.8%
18	Crude oil average price options, CME *	2,227,738	1,445,930	54.1%
19	Panhandle basis natural gas swap futures, CME *	2,017,371	1,497,748	34.7%
20	ECX CFI futures, European Climate Exchange	1,991,276	980,780	103.0%

* cleared via Clearport

2. Main types of exchange-traded derivatives

2.1 Exchange-traded commodity derivatives v OTC commodity derivatives

An over-the-counter (OTC) financial instrument is a bilateral derivative contract, individually negotiated by the parties and tailored to their specific requirements. The parties take on each other's credit risk when entering into the contract (ie, if there is a default under the contract, each party is subject to the risk that the other party may not perform or deliver its obligations under the contract).

The principal advantage of an OTC contract is the degree of flexibility that the parties enjoy in specifying the terms of the OTC derivative. OTC derivatives are commonly documented using the International Swaps and Derivatives Association (ISDA) suite of documentation[5] and the Futures and Options Association documentation, as well as the documentation platforms of certain other trade bodies – all discussed in detail in the other chapters of this book.

Exchange-traded instruments are standardised instruments traded directly on an exchange. An exchange-traded derivative has a contract specification (ie, a standard set of terms that apply to a specific contract), which details the obligations of each party.

---

5   Note that various jurisdictions have similar forms of documentation produced by the jurisdiction-specific derivatives association (eg, France has a suite of OTC documentation produced by Association Français des Banques; Spain has a suite of documentation produced by Asociacion de Mercados Financieros).

The principal advantage of an exchange-traded derivative is that the trade is effected through a regulated exchange and carries with it the guarantee of the associated clearing house, thereby reducing a party's exposure to the credit risk of its counterparty. Additionally, the parties know what they are getting when they trade: if a party is familiar with the standard specification, there will be no nasty surprises if it enters into the contract at any time.

The liquidity of exchange-traded instruments is far better than that of OTC instruments, because of the standardised nature of the contracts and the fact that they are sold through an exchange. Pricing is more transparent because the exchange will publish prices and because the contracts will be centrally cleared by a clearing-house. A clearing-house is usually an entity related to the exchange, or a commercial entity that acts as a clearing-house in relation to several exchanges. The clearing-house will act as a buyer to every seller and a seller to every buyer. After the parties have contracted 'on exchange', they effectively 'give up' the contract to the clearing-house, which acts as a central counterparty. The parties therefore have exposure only to the central counterparty and not to each other. The clearing-house will be well capitalised and will take margin from the counterparties. Central clearing for the majority of derivatives is the direction in which global regulation is moving.

2.2   Types of commodity derivatives

There are three main types of plain-vanilla commodity derivatives: forwards and futures, options and swaps.

Commodity derivatives are financial instruments that reference a single commodity, a basket of commodities or a single commodity index or basket of commodity indices. An example of a commodity index is the Standard & Poor's (S&P) GSCI (formerly the Goldman Sachs Commodity Index). The range of underlying assets can include traditional commodities such as energy, industrial metals, precious metals, agriculture and livestock, and newer traded markets such as electricity, weather derivatives and freight.

	OTC	Exchange-traded
Forwards	Yes	No
Futures	No	Yes
Options	Yes	Yes
Swaps	Yes	No

Exchange-traded commodity derivatives are either futures or exchange-traded options. The distinction between a derivatives contract from a cash or spot transaction is illustrated in the following examples.

(a) Spot transactions v derivative transactions

In a spot transaction the buyer agrees to purchase, and the seller agrees to sell, a product at the current market price. Delivery in a spot transaction is said to be 'immediate'. However, in practice, there is often a one- or two-day delay between the trade date (the day on which the buy and seller agree to the transaction) and the delivery date (the date on which the buyer pays the purchase price and the seller delivers the product to the buyer). Spot transactions are commonplace in foreign exchange and equity-linked contracts, but not as common in the financial commodities market (as opposed to direct transactions between producers and sellers).

In a forward or futures contract the buyer agrees to purchase, and the seller agrees to sell, a product at some future point in time for an agreed price. The transaction thus does not take place when the agreement is reached between the buyer and seller; rather, it occurs at some future point in time (the actual date being decided at the outset). However, both parties must proceed with the transaction at the specified future date (ie, the delivery date). The party that agrees to buy the underlying asset is said to have a long position in the transaction; conversely, the party that agrees to sell the underlying asset is said to have a short position in the transaction. This is because the party with the long position benefits from the underlying asset price rising by the delivery date; and the party with the short position benefits from the underlying asset falling. A futures contract is a forward contract which is traded on an exchange.

In an options contract the buyer again agrees to purchase, and the seller agrees to sell, an underlying asset at a future point in time for an agreed price. As in a futures transaction, the transaction does not settle when agreement is reached between the buyer and seller, but will instead occur at some future point in time.

In an options contract the buyer has the right (but not the obligation) to proceed with the transaction if it is in the interests of the buyer to exercise that right. If the buyer exercises its rights under the transaction, the seller is required to perform its obligations under the contract. The seller will grant this right for payment of a premium.

As is the case with forwards and futures, the buyer has the long position in an option whereas the seller has the short position. Buyers are also referred to as option holders and sellers as option writers.

Both types of transaction can be physically settled or cash settled. In the former case, a defined quantity of the underlying asset (eg, 1,000 tonnes of cocoa) is physically delivered for payment of the agreed price. In the latter case, the parties settle the transaction by payment of the cash differential between the agreed price and the underlying asset's trading price on the settlement date.

(i)   Futures transaction

The agreement is entered into on the trade date. The following occurs on the delivery date:

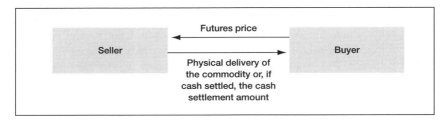

(ii)   Options transaction

The agreement is entered into on the trade date and the buyer pays a premium for the option to the seller, as set out below:

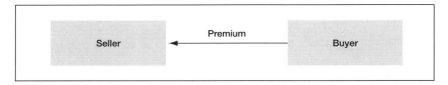

On the delivery date, the date the option expires, the following will occur if the buyer chooses to exercise the option:

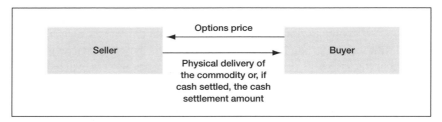

3.   Uses – hedging, speculation, arbitrage

Derivatives are used to manage risk (hedging), to speculate on price movements of an underlying asset (speculation), or to conduct risk-free profit-making arbitrage transactions (arbitrage). Thus, in the case of exchange-traded commodity derivatives:

- hedgers may use futures/options to protect or hedge against adverse price movements in commodity/index movements (eg, a fund manager may look to futures/options to hedge against rising oil prices, as a means of countering the knock-on effect that such a price rise would have on airline shares it holds);
- speculators buy and sell futures/options in order to profit from changes in commodity prices. They are prepared to accept risks that hedgers may not wish to assume; and

- arbitrageurs look to exploit price anomalies. For example, if a future is trading above its fair market value, an arbitrageur can sell (go short on) these futures and buy (go long on) the underlying commodity – so that it can profit from the inflated price of the future – and still be hedged against adverse price movements in the underlying commodity by its long position.

Users of exchange-traded derivatives may include governments, supranationals, banks, companies, asset managers, hedge funds, high-net-worth individuals, private clients and retail investors.

Speculative trading on derivatives gained notoriety with the collapse of Barings Bank in 1995 due to the speculative trading losses incurred by rogue trader Nick Leeson investing in Japanese stock (ie, Nikkei futures).

Such controversies are not exclusive to trading in equities. In February 2008 David Redmond, a commodities trader at Morgan Stanley who shorted oil futures without permission, was banned by the United Kingdom's Financial Services Authority from trading for two years. He exposed Morgan Stanley to a £6 million loss, in breach of its rules, and hid his losses overnight. Although he returned the next day and managed to close his position, even returning a small profit, he was suspended and eventually dismissed for gross misconduct.

In July 2009 PVM Oil Futures, the world's largest independent oil broker, lost almost $10 million following the activities of a rogue trader in the oil futures market. Steve Perkins breached internal rules by acquiring crude-oil futures equal to around 9 million barrels. It is believed that these unauthorised trades led the global crude-oil price to rise to an eight-month high and pushed trading volumes to almost double the current daily output of Saudi Arabia, the world's largest oil exporter.

In spite of these periodic and well-publicised scandals, speculative trading helps to drive liquidity in the market, which helps end-users and hedgers to operate in an effective market.

3.1 Futures

The main difference between forwards and futures is that a forward is a customised transaction entered into between two parties over the counter (off-exchange), whereas a future is the exchange-traded version of a forward. A future is a standardised transaction completed on-exchange via a clearing-house.

A futures contract is a package of terms from which parties can choose a selection of terms that are offered by an exchange. Each futures contract will be for a set quantity of the underlying commodity or index. For example, a party can choose to buy a futures contract linked to cocoa with the delivery month being June 2010. On the delivery date, the buyer of the future will be entitled to the cocoa or a cash equivalent of the value of the a set quantity (as specified in the contract).

Example: Cocoa Futures (No. 401)

Unit of trading	Ten tonnes
Origins tenderable	Cameroon, Côte d'Ivoire, Democratic Republic of Congo (formerly known as Zaire), Equatorial Guinea, Ghana, Grenada Fine Estates, Jamaica, Nigeria, Republic of Sierra Leone, Togo, Trinidad and Tobago Plantation, Western Samoa at contract price. All other growths tenderable at set discounts.
Quality	Please refer to the full contract specification attached below.
Delivery months	March, May, July, September, December, such that ten delivery months are available for trading.
Delivery units	Standard Delivery Unit – bagged cocoa with a nominal net weight of ten tonnes. Large Delivery Unit – bagged cocoa with a nominal net weight of 100 tonnes. Bulk Delivery Unit – loose cocoa with a nominal net weight of 1,000 tonnes [1,2]
Price basis	Pounds sterling per tonne in an Exchange Nominated Warehouse in a Delivery Area which is, in the Board's opinion, in or sufficiently close to Amsterdam, Antwerp, Bremen, Felixstowe, Hamburg, Humberside, Le Havre, Liverpool, London, Rotterdam, or Teesside [2,3]
Minimum price movement (tick size and value)	£1 per tonne (£10)
Last trading day	Eleven business days immediately prior to the last business day of the delivery month at 12:00
Notice day/Tender day	The business day immediately following the last trading day
Trading hours	09:30–16:50
Related documentation	Cocoa Futures Contract (No. 401) Grading and Warehousekeeping Procedures in respect of Cocoa and Robusta Coffee Futures (30/01/09)
Last update	07/07/08

Notes:
1 Where necessary upon tender, a seller may be instructed by the Clearing House to convert a Bulk Delivery Unit into Large and/or Standard Delivery Units, or a Large Delivery Unit into Standard Delivery Units.
2 Bulk Delivery Units are tenderable at a discount of £20 per tonne to the contract price.
3 Contact the Exchange to determine which Delivery Areas have Dual Capacity Warehousekeepers (i.e. those nominated for the storage of Bulk Delivery Units as well as Standard and Large Delivery Units).

Liffe market: London

Trading Platform:
- LIFFE CONNECT® Trading Host for Futures and Options
- Algorithm: Central order book applies a pro-rata algorithm, but with priority given to the first order at the best price subject to a minimum order volume and limited to a maximum volume cap.
- Wholesale Services: Against Actuals.

Contract Standard: Delivery may be made of Cocoa meeting the contract requirements. Please refer to the attached full contract specification.

Clearing: NYSE Liffe Clearing.

Unless otherwise indicated, all times are London times.

The example above is for an NYSE Euronext futures contract (against actual) on cocoa. The contract is for 10 tonnes. If the buyer wants exposure to more than 10 tonnes, it must buy two or more contracts. The buyer can gain exposure to that additional amount of cocoa, on the same terms, only in multiples of 1,000 tonnes. The inflexible nature of the terms of futures contracts is perhaps one of its principal disadvantages. If a buyer wanted exposure to 12 tonnes of cocoa, it may decide instead to enter into a forward contract, under which it can write bespoke terms for the transaction.

The price of a futures contract is calculated by reference to many factors, including:

- the then-current cash or spot price of the underlying product;
- expected future market movements in respect of the underlying product;
- current and expected supply and demand for the underlying asset; and
- associated costs of carry.[6]

Simplistically, if the futures contract price is equal to the spot price plus its costs of carry, then that futures contract is said to be trading at fair market value.

If the futures price is higher than the spot price of the underlying commodity, this is known in the market as 'contango' or a normal market (assuming a liquid underlying commodity) – that is, one would expect the costs of carry of an underlying commodity to increase with time and therefore increase the futures price. If a future is trading above the spot price of the underlying commodity (or if the market is optimistic about the future upward price of the underlying commodity), the future is said to be trading 'at a premium'. The market is also in contango where the longer-dated futures contract prices for a particular commodity are higher than

---

6   Costs of carry in relation to commodity derivatives include the financing costs of the seller in purchasing now the underlying product for delivery at a future date (costs of storage) minus any cash flows generated by the underlying product – for instance, from leasing out the commodity in the example of gold.

those for 'nearby' futures contracts.

However, if the futures price is lower than the spot price of the underlying, this is known in the market as 'backwardation'. This may occur where the current market view is that the price of an underlying commodity is highly inflated (for whatever reason) but is expected to stabilise over time. If a future is trading at a price below the spot price of the underlying commodity (or if the market negatively views the future price of the underlying commodity), the future is said to be trading 'at a discount'. The market is also said to be in backwardation where the longer-dated futures contract prices for a particular commodity are lower than the price of nearby futures contracts. As a futures contract approaches its delivery date, the price of that futures contract must converge with the spot price of the underlying commodity on the delivery date.

A future's price, like the quantity of the underlying, can move only in multiples of its 'tick value'. The 'tick value' is the minimum permitted price movement in a derivative.

Most physically settled futures contracts that are bought and sold on exchange do not reach the delivery date; they are most often traded throughout the life of the contract and the positions are then closed out prior to delivery.

3.2   Options
The main distinction between an option and a future is that in an option contract the buyer has the right (but not the obligation) to proceed with the transaction if it is in the interest of the buyer to exercise that right. However, the seller is required to perform its obligations under the contract if the buyer has exercised its rights under the contract and money is paid up front by the buyer in the form of a 'premium' in order to enter into the option.

(a)   Types of option
There are two types of option contracts: puts and calls. A call option gives the buyer of that option the right to buy (from the seller) the underlying commodity at a fixed strike or exercise price. A put option gives the buyer of that option the right to sell (to the seller) the underlying commodity at a fixed strike or exercise price.

A traded or exchange-traded option contract, as with a futures contract, is a package of terms from which parties can choose a selection that are offered by an exchange.

The following is a list of terms that are frequently uses in relation to options:
- 'Exercise price' or 'strike price' – the agreed price at which the buyer/option holder has the right to buy (call option) or sell (put option) the underlying.
- 'Expiry date' – the last day on which the option may be exercised.
- 'Value date' or 'valuation date' – the date on which the option is valued for settlement.
- 'American option' – an option that can be exercised on any business day up to and including the expiry date.
- 'European option' – an option that can only be exercised on the expiry date of that option.

- 'Bermudan option' – an option that can be exercised on a number of set days before the expiry date.
- 'Asian option' – an option where the pay-off is determined not by the underlying price on the value date, but by the average underlying price over a set period.
- 'Premium' – the amount paid by the buyer of an option for the privilege of buying the right to exercise that option if it is in the buyer's interest to do so.
- 'At the money' – occurs when the strike price of an option is equal to (or nearly equal to) the market price of the underlying.
- 'In the money' – occurs when the strike price of an option is below the current market price of the underlying (for a call option) or above the market price of the underlying (for a put option) (ie, an option that would be worth exercising).
- 'Out of the money' – occurs when the strike price of an option is:
  - above the current market price of the underlying (for a call option); and
  - below the current market price of the underlying (for a put option) (ie, an option that is worthless at that time).

It should be noted that most participants deal in options that are around the at-the-money level. As the underlying price fluctuates, the exchange will create additional strikes so that there are sufficient contracts available to appeal to buyers and sellers.

Example: Cocoa Options (No. 501)
Options on Cocoa Futures

Unit of trading	One Cocoa Futures contract
Expiry months	March, May, July, September, December, such that ten expiry months are available for trading, subject to the option expiring before the underlying future.
Price basis	Pounds sterling per tonne
Minimum price movement (tick size and value)	£1 per tonne (£10)
Exercise day	Exercise by 17:00 on any business day prior to the expiry day
Expiry day	12:00 on the last trading day of the calendar month preceding the expiry month.
Trading hours	09:32–16:50
Related documentation	Options on Commodity Contracts (No. 501)
Last update	06/02/07

Market: London

Trading Platform:
- LIFFE CONNECT® Trading Host for Futures and Options

- Algorithm: Central order book applies a pro-rata algorithm, but with priority given to the first order at the best price subject to a minimum order volume and limited to a maximum volume cap.
- Wholesale Services: None Apply.

Exercise Price Increments: £25 per tonne

Option Premium: The contract price is not paid at the time of purchase. Option positions, as with futures positions, are marked-to-market daily giving rise to positive or negative variation margin flows. If an option is exercised by the Buyer, the Buyer is required to pay the original contract price to the Clearing House and the Clearing House will pay the original option price to the Seller on the following business day. Such payments will be netted against the variation margin balances of Buyer and Seller by the Clearing House.

Clearing: LCH.Clearnet Ltd.

Unless otherwise indicated, all times are London times.

A buyer of a call option would do so expecting the market in the underlying to go up. The buyer of a put option would do so expecting the market in the underlying to go down.

	Buyer	Seller
Call	• Right to buy. • Maximum loss is premium paid. • Maximum gain is unlimited.	• Obligation to sell if exercised. • Maximum gain is premium paid. • Maximum loss is unlimited.
Put	• Right to sell. • Maximum loss is premium paid. • Maximum gain is the exercise price of the option.	• Obligation to buy if exercised. • Maximum gain is premium paid. • Maximum loss is exercise price of the option minus the premium.

While hedging with futures contracts protects the buyer from upside risk, it does not allow the buyer to benefit from any possible downside performance of the underlying commodity and is in fact unprofitable in such circumstances. Hedging with options, however, does afford investors protection against adverse market movements while still permitting the buyer to benefit from any favourable movements in the underlying (ie, by not exercising the option and buying in the spot market instead). The price paid for this flexibility is the premium.

Unlike a basic exchange-traded option written on other asset classes (eg, equity or foreign exchange), an exchange-traded commodity option is actually an option on a futures contract for a commodity (also known as a futures option). Such an option gives the buyer the right to purchase a futures contract at a designated strike price on a future date. The main difference between a futures option and an option on an underlying asset is delivery convenience – a futures contract for 10 tonnes of wheat is significantly easier to deliver than the wheat itself. Typically, investors will not exercise a futures option but will close the option sometime before it expires. A futures option is therefore typically a cash-settled instrument. Cash settlement of a futures option is particularly attractive to investors with insufficient capital to purchase the underlying. This leads us to one of the primary reasons why trading in options is so appealing: leverage.

(b)   *Leverage*

If a speculator believes that the price of a commodity is on the up, why might he buy options on futures for that commodity instead of investing in that commodity directly? The following example provides a compelling argument.

Hypothetical example of leveraged options

On day one, the current price of gold is £500 per troy ounce and the option premium for options on gold traded on the Folgate Exchange is £5.

Mahesh, the investor, has £10,000 to invest and wants to speculate on a potential upward price movement. He could:

- buy 20 troy ounces of gold at £500 per troy ounce; or
- buy call options on 2,000 gold options contracts on the Folgate Exchange, through his broker, for a premium of £5 per contract, with a strike price of £500 per troy ounce; the gold futures contract settles in 20 days' time.

On day 20, the price of gold has increased (as Mahesh expected) to £600 per troy ounce:

- If Mahesh had bought the gold, the 20 troy ounces initially worth £10,000 would now be worth £12,000 – a profit of £2000.
- If Mahesh had bought options, the options on 2,000 gold futures contracts could be exercised with a return of £190,000 as illustrated overleaf.

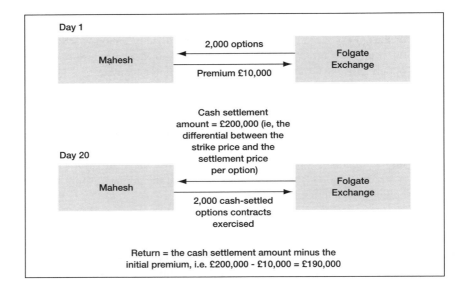

The leverage that the investment in the option has given Mahesh is one of the key benefits of trading in options.

In Mahesh's case, his profit chart could be set out as follows:

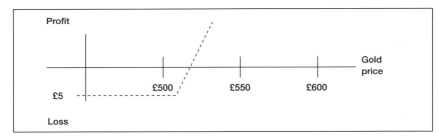

Mahesh, as the buyer of the call option, has his loss limited to the premium paid (£5 per option). He does not begin to make a profit until the price of gold moves beyond £505 per troy ounce (the break-even point). If the price of gold moves to the break-even point, Mahesh's option is considered to be 'at the money'. Where the strike price is below the market value of the underlying, Mahesh's option is considered to be 'in the money' because he can exercise the option and profit from taking delivery of (or receiving the cash equivalent of) the gold for a price lower than the prevailing market price of the underlying.

In the above example, the seller (on the other side of the central counterparty) of the call option to Mahesh would document its profit chart as follows:

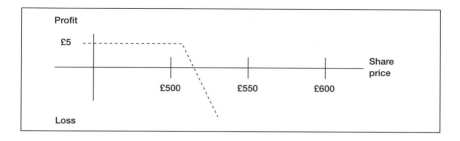

The end seller has its profit limited to the amount of premium paid by Mahesh (£5 per option). The option is considered 'out of the money' (and therefore not worth Mahesh exercising it) until the gold price moves beyond the break-even point of £505 per troy ounce). The potential loss that can be suffered by the end seller is unlimited.

Why would the end seller sell the option?

- If it were speculating on the market going down, it would be confident of making money by pocketing Mahesh's premium.
- By investing the premium received to hedge its positions under the sold options, it may manage the risk of the market going up.

If a writer is selling options 'naked', it means it is doing so unhedged (ie, it is exposed to the full losses it may incur). If the option writer has an existing holding in the underlying commodity as its hedge (or hedges in any other way), its position under that option is considered to be 'covered'.

4. Exchanges

4.1 Trading on-exchange

Exchange-traded derivatives markets have always been order-driven dealing systems (ie, where orders are brought together so that matches can be found between buyers and sellers).

Some exchanges place limits on trading if the price of the future/option moves a certain amount from its opening level (in order to reduce volatility). Most exchanges do not currently impose formal limits on the quantity of contracts that an individual can buy or sell (although as mentioned above, this topic is currently being debated); but they may intervene where they believe there is a risk of market manipulation.

Futures and options are either traded by 'open outcry' or through electronic screen-based trading systems.

In a pit-based 'open-outcry' market, brokers transact (buy and sell) orders on behalf of clients (ie, traders meet at a specified location on the floor of the exchange and attempt to match business through shouting their orders – the essential principle of open outcry is transparency). The Chicago exchanges operate both open-outcry and electronic trading. LIFFE, however, is a wholly electronic trading exchange. Once a trade is struck, the details are entered and published on various websites, including Reuters and Bloomberg.

Either system will provide access only to members of the relevant exchange, so clients will need to submit their orders to a broker for onward execution.

The main functions of an exchange are to:

- facilitate trading (ie, enable buyers and sellers to come together and find a price at which they are willing to trade);
- ensure that trading rules are adhered to; and
- publish the prices of trades.

4.2 Standardisation

A fundamental principle of trading on exchanges is that the goods that the seller delivers should match the buyer's expectations of the goods it will receive. For cash and equity assets, this is easily achieved as homogeneous products are readily discernable.

This is not the case for commodities. Because a specific strain of commodity will not be homogeneous or fungible as in other financial asset classes, there needs to be a predefined specification of underlying commodity built into the contract. It would prove cumbersome to trading if a buyer wanted to conduct an inspection of a seller's products before transacting. Each exchange publishes a set of exchange rules which members must abide by in order to transact on that exchange. All of the exchanges also produce contract terms which apply to the products purchased on exchange. These systems of checks and controls with respect to, among other things, the quality and the source of a product allow a buyer to identify the particular commodity and the particular grade of commodity it is purchasing.

For instance, many different types of crude oil are traded – West Texas Intermediate and Brent Blend to name two. To be classified as Brent Blend on an exchange, crude oil must, among other things, have been sourced from a particular region of the world and have particular traits relating to its colour and sulphur content. Similar specification relate to any other commodity that is traded on exchange.

Contract terms for the products purchased on the exchange will also include rules on how such products should be stored. In this way, the buyer can transact in the confidence that a product should be delivered in a satisfactory state.

4.3 Derivatives exchanges

Traditionally, the Chicago exchanges (the Chicago Board Options Exchange, the Chicago Board of Trade (CBOT) and the Chicago Mercantile Exchange (CME)) were the dominant futures and options exchanges as a result of the historic significance of Chicago in the commodity derivatives marketplace.

Set out below are the top 52 derivatives exchanges (ranked by number of futures and options traded and/or cleared at parent company level).[7]

---

7   *Futures Industry* magazine, March/April 2009.

Rank	Exchange	Jan-Dec 2008	Jan-Dec 2007	% change
1	CME Group (includes CBOT and Nymex)	3,277,645,351	3,158,383,678	3.8%
2	Eurex (includes ISE)	3,172,704,773	2,704,209,603	17.3%
3	Korea Exchange	2,865,482,319	2,777,416,098	3.2%
4	NYSE Euronext (includes all EU and US markets)	1,675,791,242	1,525,247,465	9.9%
5	Chicago Board Options Exchange (includes CFE)	1,194,516,467	945,608,754	26.3%
6	BM&F Bovespa	741,889,113	794,053,775	-6.6%
7	Nasdaq OMX Group (includes all EU and US markets)	722,107,905	551,409,855	31.0%
8	National Stock Exchange of India	590,151,288	379,874,850	55.4%
9	JSE South Africa	513,584,004	329,642,403	55.8%
10	Dalian Commodity Exchange	313,217,957	185,614,913	68.7%
11	Russian Trading Systems Stock Exchange	238,220,708	143,978,211	65.5%
12	IntercontinentalExchange (includes US, UK and Canada markets)	234,414,538	194,667,719	20.4%
13	Zhengzhou Commodity Exchange	222,557,134	93,052,714	139.2%
14	Boston Options Exchange	178,650,541	129,797,339	37.6%
15	Osaka Securities Exchange	163,689,348	108,916,811	50.3%
16	Shanghai Futures Exchange	140,263,185	85,563,833	63.9%
17	Taiwan Futures Exchange	136,719,777	115,150,624	18.7%
18	Moscow Interbank Currency Exchange	131,905,458	85,386,473	54.5%
19	London Metal Exchange	113,215,299	92,914,728	21.8%
20	Hong Kong Exchanges & Clearing	105,006,736	87,985,686	19.3%
21	Australian Securities Exchange (includes SFE)	94,775,920	116,090,973	-18.4%
22	Multi Commodity Exchange of India	94,310,610	68,945,925	36.8%
23	Tel-Aviv Stock Exchange	92,574,042	104,371,763	-11.3%
24	Mercado Español de Opciones y Futuros Financieros	83,416,762	51,859,591	60.9%
25	Mexican Derivatives Exchange	70,143,690	228,972,029	-69.4%
26	Tokyo Financial Exchange	66,927,067	76,195,817	-12.2%
27	Singapore Exchange	61,841,268	44,206,826	39.9%
28	Turkish Derivatives Exchange	54,472,835	24,867,033	119.1%

continued overleaf

Rank	Exchange	Jan-Dec 2008	Jan-Dec 2007	% change
29	Mercado a Termino de Rosario	42,216,661	25,423,950	66.1%
30	Tokyo Commodity Exchange	41,026,955	47,070,169	-12.8%
31	Italian Derivatives Exchange	38,928,785	37,124,922	4.9%
32	Bourse de Montreal	38,064,902	42,742,210	-10.9%
33	Tokyo Stock Exchange	32,500,438	33,093,785	-1.8%
34	National Commodity & Derivatives Exchange	24,639,710	34,947,872	-29.5%
35	Oslo Stock Exchange	16,048,430	13,967,847	14.9%
36	Budapest Stock Exchange	13,369,425	18,827,328	-29.0%
37	Warsaw Stock Exchange	12,560,518	9,341,958	34.5%
38	Tokyo Grain Exchange	8,433,346	19,674,883	-57.1%
39	Athens Derivatives Exchange	7,172,120	6,581,544	9.0%
40	Malaysia Derivatives Exchange	6,120,032	6,202,686	-1.3%
41	OneChicago	4,012,281	8,105,963	-50.5%
42	Kansas City Board of Trade	3,965,924	4,670,955	-15.1%
43	Climate Exchange (includes ECX and CCFE)	3,295,908	1,322,079	149.3%
44	Central Japan Commodity Exchange	3,272,665	6,549,417	-50.0%
45	Thailand Futures Exchange	2,148,620	1,230,666	74.6%
46	New Zealand Futures Exchange	1,459,088	1,651,038	-11.6%
47	Minneapolis Grain Exchange	1,409,002	1,826,807	-22.9%
48	Wiener Boerse	1,129,619	1,316,895	-14.2%
49	Dubai Mercantile Exchange	330,379	223,174	48.0%
50	Kansai Commodities Exchange	183,999	164,743	11.7%
51	Mercado a Termino de Buenos Aires	155,755	177,564	-12.3%
52	US Futures Exchange	22,955	8,110	183.0%

Note: Ranking does not include exchanges that do not report their volume to the Futures Industry Association.

The wave of mergers and acquisitions in recent years has transformed the exchange landscape over the last decade, resulting in a handful of companies that own as many as eight subsidiary derivatives exchanges. In addition, several exchanges have formed subsidiaries to enter new market segments.

Exchange groups[8]	2008 trade volumes	2007 trade volumes	% change
Sydney Futures Exchange	74,605,556	91,121,162	-18.1%
Australian Stock Exchange	20,170,364	24,969,811	-19.2%
Australian Securities Exchange	94,775,920	116,090,973	-18.4%
Bolsa de Mercadorias & Futuros	391,614,615	426,363,492	-8.2%
Bolsa de Valores de São Paulo	350,274,498	367,690,283	-4.7%
BM&F Bovespa	741,889,113	794,053,775	-6.6%
Chicago Board Options Exchange	1,193,355,070	944,472,459	26.4%
CBOE Futures Exchange	1,161,397	1,136,295	2.2%
CBOE Holdings	1,194,516,467	945,608,754	26.3%
European Climate Exchange	2,811,586	1,038,321	170.8%
Chicago Climate Futures Exchange	484,322	283,758	70.7%
Climate Exchange	3,295,908	1,322,079	149.3%
Chicago Mercantile Exchange	1,893,402,536	1,775,429,438	6.6%
Chicago Board of Trade	960,777,756	1,029,568,803	-6.7%
New York Mercantile Exchange	423,465,059	353,385,437	19.8%
CME Group	3,277,645,351	3,158,383,678	3.8%
Eurex 2,165,043,183	1,899,861,926	14.0%	
International Securities Exchange	1,007,661,590	804,347,677	25.3%
Eurex 3,172,704,773	2,704,209,603	17.3%	
ICE Futures Europe	150,138,547	137,432,635	9.2%
ICE Futures US	80,954,781	53,782,919	50.5%
ICE Futures Canada	3,321,210	3,452,165	-3.8%
IntercontinentalExchange*	234,414,538	194,667,719	20.4%
* does not include OTC transactions or ECX products			
Philadelphia Stock Exchange	547,456,114	407,972,525	34.2%
Nasdaq OMX Group (Nordic markets)	143,426,572	143,437,330	0.0%
Nasdaq Options Market (US)	31,225,219	0	NA
Nasdaq OMX Group	722,107,905	551,409,855	31.0%
Liffe UK	809,450,611	695,974,929	16.3%

continued overleaf

Exchange groups[8]	2008 trade volumes	2007 trade volumes	% change
NYSE Arca Options	416,938,764	335,838,547	24.1%
American Stock Exchange	207,285,283	240,383,466	-13.8%
Liffe Amsterdam	142,136,885	159,827,511	-11.1%
Liffe Paris	96,440,021	90,868,890	6.1%
NYSE Liffe	1,837,543	0	NA
Liffe Brussels	1,212,244	1,348,884	-10.1%
Liffe Lisbon	489,891	1,005,238	-51.3%
NYSE Euronext	1,675,791,242	1,525,247,465	9.9%

Note: Volume based on the number of futures and options contracts traded and/or cleared.

4.4 Main UK-based exchanges for commodity derivatives

(a) *ICE Futures Europe*

ICE Futures Europe, formerly called the International Petroleum Exchange of London, is ICE's London-based regulated futures exchange for global energy markets. It is now a fully electronic energy futures exchange and no longer has an open-outcry trading platform. ICE Futures Europe lists the leading global crude-oil benchmarks and sees half of the trade in the world's crude oil and refined product futures in its markets.[9]

(b) *London Metal Exchange*

The London Metal Market and Exchange Company was founded in 1877, but the market traces its origins back to 1571 and the opening of the Royal Exchange. The London Metal Exchange (LME) now offers futures and options contracts for base and non-precious metals such as aluminium, copper, nickel, tin, zinc and lead, plus two regional aluminium alloy contracts – although initially only copper and tin were officially traded.[10] In 2005 the LME launched the world's first futures contracts for plastics, with the introduction of regional plastics contracts in 2007.

The LME provides a transparent forum for all trading activity and as a result helps to 'discover' what the price of material will be months and years ahead. This helps the physical industry to plan forward in a world subject to often severe and rapid price movements.

Open-outcry trading is central to the process of 'discovery'. Prices are derived from the short open-outcry 'ring' trading sessions and are most representative of industry supply and demand. The official settlement price, on which contracts are settled, is determined by the last offer price before the bell is sounded to mark the end of the official ring. Only ring dealing members are entitled to trade in the ring, all of whom are members of the London Clearing House.

---

9   ICE Futures Europe.
10   The London Metal Exchange.

In addition to the open-outcry ring trading sessions, trading occurs across two other trading platforms: through an inter-office telephone market and through LME Select, the LME's electronic trading platform.

Producers of copper or tin, or other commodities listed on the LME, can sell such commodities to one of the global warehouses associated with the LME and receive a warrant in exchange. These communal warehouses are an effective means of sharing the cost of storage between the many industry participants and make it more efficient to compete against other products. The warrant acts as evidence of ownership of the metal. Therefore, if a buyer has acquired the right to take delivery of the metal, then the seller will transfer the warrant to the buyer.

Each day the LME issues detailed figures on how much (by weight) of each metal is in its warehouses, which helps producers and consumers to make correct business decisions.

The LME is a highly liquid market and in 2007 achieved volumes of 93 million lots, equivalent to $9,500 billion annually and between $35 billion and $45 billion on an average business day. Despite its London location, the LME is a global market with an international membership and with more than 95% of its business coming from overseas.[11]

(c)   LIFFE

The London International Financial Futures and Options Exchange (LIFFE) is a futures and options exchange.

The exchange was modelled on the CBOT and the CME. In 1993 LIFFE became the London International Financial Futures and Options Exchange after its merger with the London Traded Options Market. Following a further merger in 1996 with the London Commodity Exchange, a range of soft and agricultural commodity contracts was added to the exchange's offered products.

It is now called NYSE LIFFE and has become part of NYSE Euronext following its takeover by Euronext in January 2002 and Euronext's merger with New York Stock Exchange in April 2007.

LIFFE also developed its own successful trading platform called LIFFE CONNECT, which it has sold to other exchanges including the CBOT.

4.5   Other main derivatives exchanges

(a)   Eurex

Eurex is a global derivatives exchange using a full electronic trading and clearing platform. It is jointly operated by Deutsche Börse AG and SIX Swiss Exchange. The foundation of the exchange was laid in late 1996 when Deutsche Börse AG and the Swiss Exchange signed a memorandum of understanding to create a joint trading and clearing system. Eurex was formally created in 1998 when the Deutsche Terminbörse and the Swiss Options and Financial Futures Exchange merged. On December 20 2007 Eurex completed the acquisition of International Securities Exchange, Inc.

11   London Metal Exchange.

Eurex offers participants the opportunity to trade in carbon dioxide derivatives, gold and silver derivatives and agriculture derivatives. Annual trading at Eurex now exceeds €1.5 billion in the value of contracts each year.[12]

(b)   *CME Group Inc*
The CME Group Inc was formed in July 2007 from the merger of the CME and the CBOT. The CME Group Inc also acquired NYMEX Holdings Inc, the parent company of the NYMEX in 2008.

(i)   *CME*
The CME (colloquially know as the 'Merc') is a financial and commodity derivatives exchange based in Chicago. Founded in 1898 as the Chicago Butter and Egg Board, it was originally a non-profit organisation. The exchange demutualised in November 2000 and went public in December 2002.

Trading is conducted in a variety of products, including commodities, using two platforms: the open-outcry format and (more commonly) the electronic trading platform.

(ii)   *CBOT*
The CBOT, established in 1848, is the world's oldest futures and options exchange. In 1864 the first futures contract was traded on the CBOT. Participants trade through a combination of the open-outcry and electronic trading platforms.

(iii)   *NYMEX*
The NYMEX is a futures and options exchange composed of two divisions: the NYMEX division and the Commodity Exchange Inc (COMEX) division.

The NYMEX division grew out of the Butter and Cheese Exchange of New York, which was founded in 1872. COMEX was founded in 1933 following the merger of the National Metal Exchange, the Rubber Exchange of New York, the National Raw Silk Exchange and the New York Hide Exchange. The two divisions merged in 1994.

It is possible to trade on NYMEX through a combination of open-outcry and electronic platforms. Participants may invest in, among other things, coal, crude oil, electricity and uranium through the NYMEX division. Investors can invest in futures and options that include gold, silver, aluminium and copper through the COMEX division.

NYMEX headquarters at the Wold Trade Center were destroyed by the terrorist attacks on September 11 2001. While it has since moved location to the World Financial Centre, NYMEX has also created a back-up emergency trading facility on Long Island, should its current offices be destroyed for whatever reason.

---

12   www.eurexexchange.com

5.   Principles of clearing and settlement

5.1   Clearing-houses

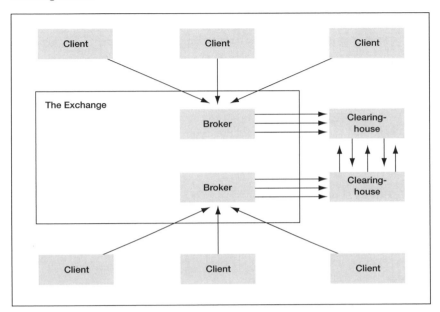

A clearing-house is an organisation, separate from the exchange, which clears transactions.

One of the principal differences between an OTC derivative and an exchange-traded derivative is the management of credit risk. The clearing-house acts as central counterparty and guarantees performance of all contracts.

On exchange, two members will strike a trade, one as buyer and one as seller. Once the details have been confirmed by a matching procedure, the clearing-house is substituted by novation as the seller to every buyer and as the buyer to every seller on a principal-to-principal basis. The clearinghouse is then responsible for the performance of the contract (thereby eliminating credit risk for the buyer and seller).

Clearing-houses are concerned only with contracts with their members (brokers) and not with clients of the brokers (so technically the end client still retains some credit risk on the brokers).

An exchange's clearing-house may be a department of the exchange or a separate legal entity. In most cases a clearing-house will provide clearing services to more than one exchange.

The liquidity of the exchange-traded markets depends on the timely settlement of transactions by a clearing-house.

Defaults by counterparties to an exchange-traded derivative could lead to loss of confidence in the exchange or widespread systemic failure. Interposing a clearing-house between the counterparties lessens this risk, assuring protection for both parties to the trade by requiring them to post collateral (ie, margin). The amount of collateral is adjusted daily (ie, marked to market), thereby disincentivising a party from defaulting.

5.2   Margining

'Margin' is the collateral that must be supplied by both parties to a futures contract, and writers of options contracts, to ensure they have adequate funds to meet their commitments.

In order to trade on-exchange, a trader must set up a margin account with a broker and the initial margin must be deposited into this account. The amount of initial margin that a broker needs to collect is stipulated by the clearing-house (the amount varies according to the type of contract and likely intra-day price movements). This amount is usually a fraction of the cost of buying the actual underlying subject to the futures contract.

Futures contract

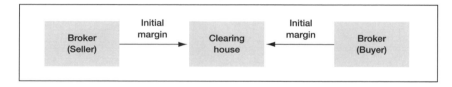

Options contract

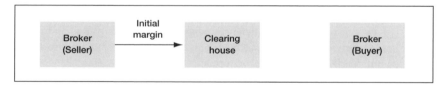

The margining system is designed to provide a measure of protection against default.

At the close of each day, positions will be marked to market so that profits and losses are added to or deducted from the margin account.

If a trader needs to keep topping up the margin account because of adjustments in line with the closing price of the future, this is referred to as 'variation margin'.

Where it is an exchange's practice to trigger a margin call only when a contract has moved by a certain amount, this is referred to as 'margin maintenance'.

The broker manages all margin calls with the trader, and handles payments to and from the clearing house. If a trader does not meet a margin call, the brokers will simply close out the trader's open positions and return the initial margin minus any trading losses and costs.

On some exchanges, the buyer of an option may not be required to pay the whole premium at the outset – but only an amount equal to the initial margin.

Margin need not always be deposited in the form of cash. Certain types of securities are also accepted by brokers as margin; however, a 'haircut' will usually be applied to a securities margin. For instance, if an initial margin of £80 is called for as a cash margin but it is agreed that it can be delivered in a non-cash form, a 20% haircut will mean that securities with a market value of £100 will be required (£100 less 20% = £80).

6. Commodity indices

Investors commonly want exposure to more than just a single commodity. An investor may want exposure to a particular commodities market sector or indeed the entire range of the commodities universe. The main sectors are fuels, agricultural commodities, precious metals, industrial metals and livestock.

The primary way of achieving this is via exposure to a commodity index. Investors do not invest directly in commodity indices; they do so through another financial instrument tracking the relevant commodity index, or they can replicate the index itself by investing in the index constituents in the same weightings as the relevant reference index.

In the context of commodity indices, the constituents are not typically the physical commodity itself but, rather, a commodity-linked futures contract. This peculiarity impacts on the pricing of commodity indices.

The underlying assets of equity indices are shares which are 'non-expiring' assets. On the other hand, the futures contracts which underlie commodity indices must be 'rolled' – that is, sold prior to maturity and a new contract purchased in their place. Rolling incurs costs, which are typically deducted from the value of the index. These costs can create anomalies in the pricing of commodity indices at or around the 'roll period'.

Certain popular indices are referenced in commodity-linked instruments, including structured commodity derivatives. The demand for the underlying constituents of those popular indices (eg, for hedging purposes or to otherwise replicate those indices) could lead to exceptionally high demand for the underlying futures. This could mean that the price of nearby futures contracts on a particular commodity are higher than the longer-dated contracts, creating backwardation in that particular commodity's market where it would otherwise not exist.

Returns on commodity investments can be generated from:

- the increase in a spot price of an underlying commodity (or decrease, if the commodity is being shorted); or
- the yield generated by selling an expiring contract and acquiring another contract with a later maturity date – this is referred to as 'roll yield'. If the market for a commodity is in backwardation, this roll yield will generate positive returns, as the contract being sold is more expensive than the contract being acquired. The inverse is true if the market is in contango.

The main commodity indices include the S&P GSCI and the Commodities Research Board Index, which are long-only investments in commodity futures that are broadly diversified across the spectrum of commodities.

Constituents of commodity indices are typically weighted according to a particular methodology. These may be fairly prescriptive and may include, for example, weighting particular constituents of a commodities index according to worldwide production volumes.

Aside from the main commodity indices, institutions may create bespoke indices tailored to a particular client's needs. In the market, these are referred to as 'bespoke sector indices' and can be innovative in terms of their constituents and methodology. The recent trend in sustainable investments has seen a corresponding rise in investor appetite for 'green' commodity indices.

ISDA suite of commodity derivative documentation

Edmund Parker
Marcin Perzanowski

1. Introduction

The International Swaps and Derivatives Association (ISDA) has produced specific standard documentation for derivatives instruments referencing a wide array of commodities such as gas, electricity, freight, oil, coal, bullion, the weather and emissions allowances, as well as, more generically, agricultural products, paper and metals. A broad church! In other chapters of this book we have highlighted that Frederick Engels and Karl Marx, the communist thinkers, gave 'commodity' a narrower definition than ISDA has done. ISDA's view of what can be included as a 'commodity' could perhaps instead be summarised as: if a derivative has an underlying asset, which is not a debt obligation (credit), an equity obligation or equity index (equity), a fund, an interest rate or a foreign currency, then it is a 'commodity' and will be included in the commodity derivatives documentation platform.

This chapter focuses on the ISDA suite of documentation for derivatives transactions which reference commodities. It also provides an overview of the whole of ISDA's commodity derivatives platform, as well as the products and asset classes covered by it. The subsequent chapter covers the 2005 ISDA Commodity Definitions and related annexes in greater depth.

2. ISDA's suite of commodity derivatives documentation

ISDA is the main trade association for derivatives. It has more than 860 institutions from 57 countries as members. One of its principal roles is to create a documentation platform for over-the-counter (OTC) derivatives transactions. It has obtained legal opinions and updates from leading legal firms and counsel in key jurisdictions on the enforceability of netting, collateral arrangements and commodity derivatives in those jurisdictions.

In addition to the 1992 and 2002 ISDA Master Agreements, ISDA has produced further documentation for reducing counterparty exposure, together with template documentation and definitions for a wide range of derivatives products including commodities, interest rates, currency, inflation, property, credit and funds.

ISDA's suite of documentation for commodity derivatives consists of three interlinking platforms. The primary platform is the same for all of ISDA's suites of derivatives documentation (eg, credit derivatives, commodity derivatives, interest rate derivatives and inflation derivatives). However, the other two platforms are distinct and specific to commodity derivatives trades.

ISDA'S commodity derivatives documentation platform (primary/secondary/tertiary)

1992 or 2002 ISDA Master Agreement

This agreement serves as the principal document binding all ancillary documents together as one agreement. It contains 14 clauses, which cover the basic mechanics of entering into an OTC derivatives transaction – its events of default, termination events and early termination provisions – together with the transaction's administrative side.

Credit support annex

This optional annex allows parties to control credit exposure to each other through a collateral transfer mechanism.

Schedule

Parties may amend the pre-printed ISDA Master Agreement and tailor its rights and obligations to meet their needs.

Asset-specific annexes and confirmations

For cash-settled commodity derivatives transactions, template confirmations have been included within the 2005 definitions and can be found in the exhibits to these definitions.

ISDA has also published a number of asset-specific annexes for physically settled transactions, most of them with template confirmations. Some are included as annexes to the 2005 definitions:

- Bullion A (Sub-Annex B to the 2005 definitions)
- Weather index transactions (Sub-Annex C to the 2005 definitions)
- European gas transactions (Sub-Annex D to the 2005 definitions)
- North American gas transactions (Sub-Annex E to the 2005 definitions)
- North American power transactions (Sub-Annex F to the 2005 definitions)
- Grid Trade Master Agreement transactions (Sub-Annex G to the 2005 definitions)
- EU emissions allowances transactions (Sub-Annex H to the 2005 definitions)
- Freight transactions (Sub-Annex I to the 2005 definitions)

Apart from updates and amendments of the above-listed documents, ISDA has also published the following documents:

- Revised 2009 ISDA Global Physical Coal Annex
- US Emissions Allowance Transaction Annex
- US Crude Oil and Refined Petroleum Products Annex
- ISDA US Wind Event Confirmation

2005 ISDA Commodity Definitions

These 2005 definitions were published on June 30 2005 and constitute 526 pages of definitions used as the market standard for commodity derivatives transactions. This set of definitions updated the 1993 ISDA Commodity Derivatives Definitions.

2006 ISDA definitions

This set of definitions has superseded the 2000 ISDA definitions. They are generally used to document interest rate and currency exchange transactions. Nonetheless, some if its terms have been incorporated into commodity derivatives transactions for any trades with any relevant funding feature.

Best-practice statements

ISDA publishes best-practice statements following various events affecting the price sources. Although not formally binding, they are generally followed by the market:

- Best-practice statements following discontinuation of prices
- Best-practice statements following market disruptions
- Best-practice statements following a change in methodology

3. The primary platform

ISDA's suite of documentation for commodity derivatives draws on the primary platform of the ISDA Master Agreement (as amended by a schedule) and also an optional credit support annex (or, in certain circumstances, a credit support deed) for transfer of collateral.

Parties use either the 1992 ISDA Master Agreement or the 2002 ISDA Master Agreement. After a slow start the latter is becoming more popular among market participants.

Both versions have 14 clauses covering the mechanics of entering into a commodity derivatives transaction (or indeed any derivatives transaction). The 1992 and 2002 versions are similar, and even where parties use the 1992 agreement they often make amendments to incorporate many of the 2002 edition's new provisions. The master agreement sets out events of default, termination events and procedures for early termination, as well as the administrative processes. It is not modified and remains a standard pre-printed form, with amendments to the provisions made by the parties in a pre-printed schedule. Here, they make certain elections and tailor the master agreement to their requirements.

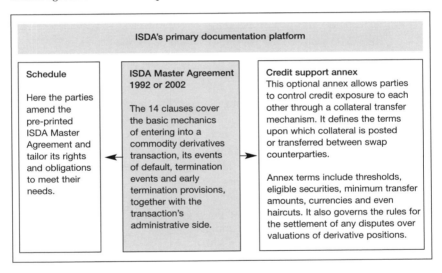

As an option, parties may also enter into a credit support annex (or sometimes a credit support deed). This forms part of the Master Agreement and facilitates the transfer of collateral (either unilaterally or bilaterally) as a means of controlling the parties' risk exposure to each other. The primary platform will continue to be used by the two parties for all of their derivatives transactions (eg, interest rate swaps, currency swaps, equity derivatives, credit derivatives and commodity derivatives).

4. The secondary platform – an overview

The primary platform is complemented by a secondary platform which consists of the 2005 definitions, together with the relevant annexes and template confirmations. Each commodity derivatives confirmation incorporates by reference the 2005 definitions, as well as the parties' ISDA Master Agreement (as amended by the schedule) and, if applicable, a credit support annex.

The 2005 definitions are a booklet of definitions divided into 17 articles. These cover:

- general commodity definitions;
- terms for options and their exercise;
- articles relating to the calculation of fixed and floating payments under swap trades; and
- market disruption events and their consequences.

The principal body of definitions is short – only 22 pages. However, the document also includes nearly 500 pages of annexes. The main body can be used on its own to document most cash-settled commodity derivatives transactions. If the parties want their transactions to be physically settled or want to enter into trades referencing different asset classes, they can incorporate one of the relevant sub-annexes to the 2005 definitions (as set out in the table below), or make bespoke changes to the confirmations themselves.

2005 ISDA Commodity Definitions documents and structure
2005 ISDA Commodity Definitions

Introduction to the 2005 ISDA Commodity Definitions	
Article I	Certain general definitions
Article II	Parties
Article III	Terms and dates
Article IV	Certain definitions relating to payments
Article V	Fixed amounts
Article VI	Floating amounts
Article VII	Calculation of prices for commodity reference prices
Article VIII	Commodity options
Article IX	Rounding
Article X	Bullion transactions
Article XI	Weather index derivatives transactions
Article XII	Physically settled European gas transactions
Article XIII	Physically settled North American gas transactions
Article XIV	Physically settled North American power transactions
Article XV	Physically settled Grid Trade Master Agreement transactions
Article XVI	EU emissions allowance transactions
Article XVII	Freight transactions
Index of terms	

continued overleaf

2005 Commodity Exhibits	
Exhibit I	Introduction, standard paragraphs and closing for a letter agreement or a facsimile confirming a transaction
Exhibit II-A	Additional provisions for a confirmation of a commodity swap/basis swap
Exhibit II-B	Additional provisions for a confirmation of a commodity option
Exhibit II-C	Additional provisions for a confirmation of a commodity cap, collar or floor
Exhibit II-D	Additional provisions for a confirmation of a commodity swaption

Annex to the 2005 ISDA Commodity Definitions	
Sub-Annex A	Commodity reference prices
Sub-Annex B	Bullion transactions
Sub-Annex C	Weather index derivatives transactions
Sub-Annex D	Physically settled European gas transactions
Sub-Annex E	Physically settled North American gas transactions
Sub-Annex F	Physically settled North American power transactions
Sub-Annex G	Physically settled Grid Trade Master Agreement transactions
Sub-Annex H	Physically settled EU emissions allowance transactions
Sub-Annex I	Freight transactions

2005 Commodity User's Guide	

Sub-Annexes B to I cover specific classes of commodity and amend the main body of the 2005 definitions to facilitate transactions relating to those types of asset. After 2005, ISDA also published additional annexes and template confirmations for commodities not covered under the original definitional booklet. They include the following:

- the revised 2009 ISDA Global Physical Coal Annex;
- the US Emissions Allowance Transaction Annex;
- the US Crude Oil and Refined Petroleum Products Annex; and
- the ISDA US Wind Event Confirmation.

Standard commodity derivatives confirmations are aided by incorporating by reference not only the 2005 definitions (together with relevant annexes), but also the more general 2000 or 2006 ISDA definitions. The 2006 definitions are used in documentation for interest rate and currency exchange transactions, but some of their terms are useful for commodity trades that have a relevant funding feature. In the case of the ISDA US Wind Event Confirmation, only the 2006 definitions are referenced, to the exclusion of the 2005 definitions.

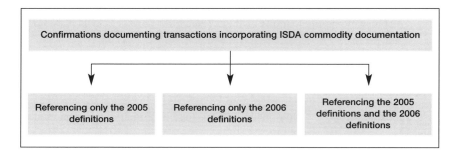

ISDA commodity documentation can be divided in two ways. First, the annexes and template confirmations provide for cash settlement of the relevant transactions, for physical settlement or for both. For example, the main body of the 2005 definitions allows only for cash settlement, whereas under the Bullion Annex the parties can enter into both cash and physically settled trades.

'Cash settlement', also referred to as financial settlement, means that on the settlement of the transaction, one party will make an appropriate payment to the other (ie, there will be no actual transfer of commodities). The final payment will depend on the price of the underlying commodity at the time of settlement. Annexes that only allow for cash settlement include the Freight Annex and the Weather Index Derivatives Annex.

By comparison, 'physical settlement' (or 'settlement by delivery') means that on the settlement of the transaction, one party must deliver the referenced commodity to the other. The EU Emissions Allowances Annex and Gas Annex, by contrast, provide only for physical settlement. More broadly, physical settlement can also mean that the parties must execute or deliver the underlying transaction in a swaption.

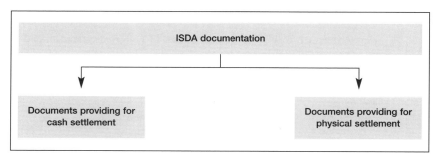

ISDA documentation can sometimes, although not always, be divided along geographical lines. Some of the documents apply only in relation to Europe and some only in relation to North America (which includes the United States and Canada). When the parties enter into a transaction referencing, say, cocoa, no special documentation is required for either region. However, there are different binding regulations and non-binding market practices relating to more regulated underlying commodities such as electricity, power, coal or emissions allowances. Special region-specific annexes cater for those differences.

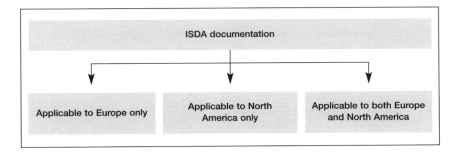

As is explained later, the principal body of the 2005 definitions applies to all cash-settled commodity transactions (with the exception of US wind event swaps) in both Europe and North America. Different documents exist only for physically settled transactions referencing the products set out in the table below.

Product	Europe (ISDA documentation for physically settled transactions)	North America (ISDA documentation for physically settled transactions)
Natural gas	ISDA European Gas Annex (Sub-Annex D to the 2005 definitions)	ISDA North American Gas Annex (Sub-Annex E to the 2005 definitions) Canadian Addendum 2009 Amendment Addendum
Electricity	ISDA GTMA Annex (Sub-Annex G to the 2005 definitions)	ISDA North America Power Annex (Sub-Annex F to the 2005 definitions)
Emissions allowances	EU Emissions Allowance Transaction Document: Version 2.5 and Version 4	US Emissions Allowance Transaction Annex
Crude oil and refined products	No documentation	US Crude Oil and Refined Products Annex
Coal	Appendix 1 to the Revised 2009 ISDA Global Physical Coal Annex	Appendix 2 to the Revised 2009 ISDA Global Physical Coal Annex

The origins of the commodity derivatives markets go back to ancient Egypt and

Mesopotamia. Although standardised documentation is very recent, various market participants used standard documents for effecting these types of transaction before ISDA was even created, or at least turned its attentions to commodities. For this reason, ISDA did not try to reinvent the wheel and draft the paperwork from scratch. To honour various market practices and local rules, ISDA works together with other industry organisations or simply incorporates other standard agreements by reference into its own documents.

For example, the Bullion Annex (Sub-Annex B to the 2005 definitions) is a joint effort by ISDA, the London Bullion Market Association and the Financial Markets Lawyers Group. Other asset-specific annexes incorporate by reference different industry standard rules or agreements – for example, the Grid Trade Master Agreement (published by the Futures and Options Association), or the rules of the London Bullion Market Association and of the London Platinum and Palladium Market.

The ISDA commodity documentation covers not only derivatives transactions, but also simple sale-and-purchase agreements for commodities (also referred to as spot transactions). To reflect this, the original flagship definitional booklet in this area, labelled the ISDA 1993 Commodity Derivatives Definitions, has been revised and renamed as the ISDA 2005 Commodity Definitions. In this connection, the ISDA US Crude Oil and Refined Petroleum Products Annex, published in 2007, can be used only to document spot trades.

ISDA'S secondary platform

2005 ISDA Commodity Definitions
The 2005 definitions were published on June 30 2005 and comprise 526 pages of definitions used as the market standard for commodity derivatives transactions.

2006 ISDA Definitions
These definitions have superseded the 2000 ISDA Definitions (which are incorporated by reference into the 2005 definitions). They are generally used to document interest rate and currency exchange transactions. Nonetheless, they are also often incorporated into commodity derivatives transactions.

Annexes and template confirmations
For cash-settled commodity derivatives transactions, template confirmations have been included within the 2005 definitions and can be found in the exhibits to the 2005 Commodity Definitions
ISDA has also published a number of asset-specific annexes for physically settled transactions, each with template confirmations. Some of these are included as annexes to the 2005 definitions:
• Bullion A (Sub-Annex B to the 2005 definitions)
• Weather index transactions (Sub-Annex C to the 2005 definitions)
• European gas transactions (Sub-Annex D to the 2005 definitions)
• North American gas transactions (Sub-Annex E to the 2005 Definitions)
• North American power transactions (Sub-Annex F to the 2005 definitions)
• Grid Trade Master Agreement transactions (Sub-Annex G to the 2005 definitions)
• EU emission allowances transactions (Sub-Annex H to the 2005 definitions)
• Freight transactions (Sub-Annex I to the 2005 definitions)

Apart from updates and amendments of the above-listed documents, ISDA has also published the following documents:
• Revised 2009 ISDA Global Physical Coal Annex
• US Emissions Allowance Transaction Annex
• US Crude Oil and Refined Petroleum Products Annex
• ISDA US Wind Event Confirmation

5.   The secondary platform – the 2005 definitions together with annexes and exhibits

This section explains the mechanics behind the main definitional booklet for commodity transactions, together with its annexes and exhibits. Each part is analysed in detail in the subsequent chapters, so this section gives a high-level overview. In the next section, we present standard ISDA documents relating to other commodity assets published after the 2005 definitions.

5.1   2005 definitions and the exhibits

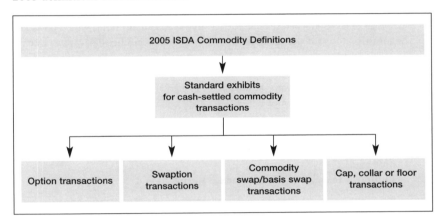

The 2005 definitions were developed to cover a range of commodity derivatives products and underlying commodity assets, as well as to reflect developing market practices in the global derivatives industry. The 2005 definitions succeeded the relatively short ISDA 1993 Commodity Derivatives Definitions and also combine the revised versions of the ISDA 2000 Supplement to the 1993 definitions and the earlier 1997 ISDA Bullion Definitions. This explains their whopping 526 pages!

The purpose of the 2005 definitions, like that of the 1993 definitions, is to provide framework terms, fallbacks and standardised definitions which parties can use in template or bespoke confirmations to document commodity derivatives transactions as efficiently as possible, while also reducing documentation error risk. Even the most complex commodity derivatives products will incorporate the 2005 definitions as a starting point.

The 2005 definitions attach a Sub-Annex A, which is more than 200 pages long and sets out market-standard definitions of various commodity reference prices. Parties can rely on these reference prices when entering into trades, making the documentation process more efficient. ISDA regularly publishes best-practice notes whenever there is a change in, or disruption of, the price sources covered by this sub-annex.

The 2005 definitions are designed to be used primarily with OTC spot, option, forward and swap transactions and are not intended to be used with structured products. However, it is common to adapt the 2005 definitions for use in more complex instruments. As with other ISDA definitions and products, the 2005 definitions are incorporated by reference into transaction confirmations; this definitions document is discussed in depth in the next chapter.

The principal body of the 2005 definitions (ie, without the annexes) is designed to be used only to document cash-settled commodity transactions, as it includes no provisions for physical settlement. As the 2005 definitions apply to assets as diverse as frozen concentrated orange juice, electricity and weather, clearly it would be difficult to include uniform provisions for physical settlement for all those types of commodity. To enter into a physically settled trade, the parties must either amend the confirmation themselves or make use of one of the annexes to the 2005 definitions or other standard ISDA documents.

ISDA has published several exhibits to the 2005 definitions, which provide template confirmations for the most common types of commodity derivatives transaction:

- options;
- swaptions;
- commodity swaps and basis swaps; and
- commodity swaps which are a cap, collar or floor.

The templates incorporate the 2005 definitions by reference and are documented as cash-settled transactions only.

5.2   Bullion transactions – Sub-Annex B to the 2005 definitions

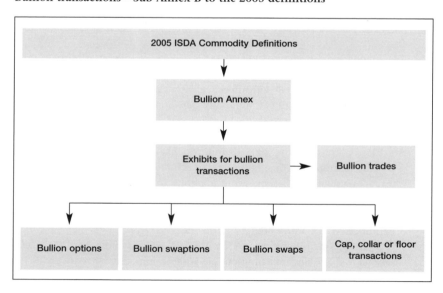

Sub-Annex B to the 2005 definitions (the Bullion Annex) covers both cash and physically settled transactions referencing bullion (ie, gold, silver, platinum or palladium). The annex is a joint effort by ISDA, the London Bullion Market Association and the Financial Markets Lawyers Group. Essentially, it is a revised and updated version of the 1997 ISDA Bullion Definitions.

The annex amends the 2005 definitions to the extent that the market practices for trading bullion differ from those applicable to other commodities. The annex also includes sections covering physical settlement, settlement and novation netting, as well as additional disruption events and their consequences.

If the parties want to enter into a cash-settled transaction referencing bullion, they are not obliged to use the Bullion Annex and may instead rely on the 2005 definitions. However, it is common in the market to incorporate the annex to take advantage of the subtle technicalities included in that document.

The annex is a part of the 2005 definitions and it has been incorporated into the main body of the 2005 definitions as Article X. It is not independent from the 2005 definitions and both documents must be carefully reviewed when drafting confirmations for bullion transactions.

The Bullion Annex also includes exhibits which consist of template confirmations for bullion transactions. It covers the following types of transaction:

- bullion trades (ie, spot and forward transactions);
- bullion swaps;
- bullion swaps which are caps, collars or floors;
- bullion options; and
- bullion swaptions.

Out of these, only bullion trades and bullion options can be physically settled.

5.3   Weather index transactions – Sub-Annex C to the 2005 definitions

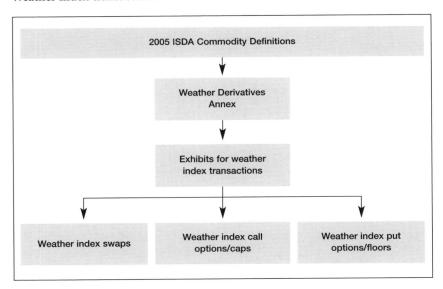

Sub-Annex C to the 2005 definitions (the Weather Derivatives Annex) covers cash-settled transactions referencing weather indices. Unlike other annexes to the 2005 definitions, it does not include provisions governing physical settlement of the trades, as clearly the parties cannot be expected to physically deliver a specified weather. Instead, the transactions are settled by one party making a payment to the other which is linked to the changes in the levels of temperature or precipitation in a given time period.

As weather or weather indices are not commodities in the same way as wool, wheat or gold, this annex amends the 2005 definitions to include all the relevant additional definitions. It also covers additional disruption events and their consequences, as well as extra provisions relating to data correlation and rounding conventions.

The annex is a part of the 2005 definitions and has been incorporated into the main body of the 2005 definitions as Article XI. Unlike the Bullion Annex, the Weather Derivatives Annex will not be incorporated into a confirmation by a mere reference to the 2005 definitions: if the parties wish to take advantage of its provisions, they must specifically agree this in the confirmation (or in the Schedule to their ISDA Master Agreement).

The Weather Derivatives Annex also includes exhibits which consist of template confirmations for weather index transactions. The following types of trades have been covered:

- weather index swaps;
- weather index call options/caps; and
- weather index put options/floors.

5.4   Gas transactions – Sub-Annexes D and E to the 2005 definitions

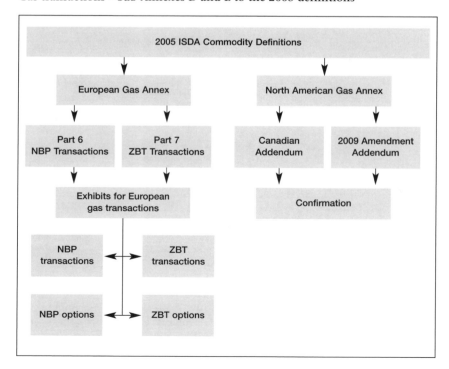

Sub-Annexes D and E cover physically settled gas transactions in Europe and North America respectively. Unlike the Bullion Annex or Weather Derivatives Annex, Sub-Annexes D and E include additional wording which should be included in the Schedule of the ISDA Master Agreement entered into between the parties.

The European Sub-Annex includes two versions of addition paragraphs, depending on the form of gas contract that the parties intend to enter into. There is a form of Part 6 to the schedule which is designed for transactions and options referencing the National Balancing Point (NBP) contracts. These are derivatives contracts where the underlying asset involves the delivery of natural gas within the UK virtual gas trading system. The sub-annex also includes a form of Part 7 which covers Zeebrugge Hub Natural Gas Trading Terms and Conditions (ZBT) contracts. These are derivatives contracts where the underlying asset involves the delivery of natural gas within a complex of terminals in Zeebrugge in Holland, and its related trading hub. In relation to each of Part 6 and Part 7, there are also template confirmations provided for spot (or forward) transactions and for options.

The North American Sub-Annex is simpler, as it contains only one form of Part 6 for all North American gas transactions. If the parties intend to enter into trades with a Canadian element, they should also remember to incorporate the Canadian Addendum. Late in 2009, ISDA also published the 2009 Amendment Addendum, which further clarifies and facilitates trading in physically settled gas, which was followed by the publication of a template confirmation in early 2010.

5.5 Power transactions – Sub-Annexes F and G to the 2005 definitions

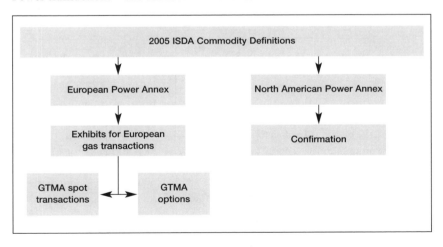

Sub-Annexes F and G cover physically settled power transactions in North America and Europe respectively. Just as with Sub-Annexes D and E above, Sub-Annexes F and G include additional wording which should be included in the Schedule of the ISDA Master Agreement entered into between the parties.

The North American Annex includes a form of Part 6 of the Schedule, which covers all the relevant provisions for physical settlement of North American power transactions. In turn, the European Annex incorporates various clauses from the Grid Trade Master Agreement, as published by the Futures and Options Association. As a result, the main body of the European Annex is shorter, but it also includes two template confirmations: for spot transactions and for option transactions. By contrast, there is no template confirmation for North American trades.

5.6   EU Emissions Allowance Transactions – Sub-Annex H to the 2005 definitions

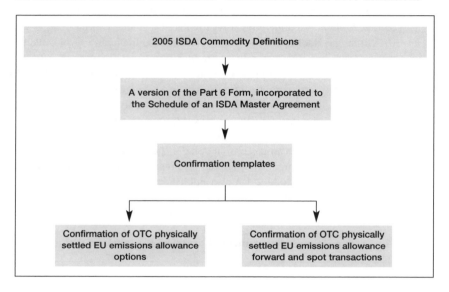

Sub-Annex H to the 2005 definitions is in the same form as the preceding sub-annexes for gas and power transactions. Unlike the Bullion Annex or the Weather Derivatives Annex, it includes a form for Part 6 to the Schedule to an ISDA Master Agreement for EU Emissions Allowance Transactions and a template confirmation.

The Part 6 Form, included in the 2005 definitions, has been revised several times and ISDA has also developed several versions of the template. The latest set of documentation was published on February 11 2008 and market participants should use this to the exclusion of any previously published forms. The frequent changes to the documentation are a result of the complex nature of the underlying assets and reflect the changes to the regulatory framework as established under the laws of the EU Emissions Trading Scheme.

The scheme's main objective is to reduce emissions of carbon dioxide and other gases which are believed to cause global warming. Under the scheme, EU-based companies are granted allowances to emit a specified amount of gases, and these allowances they can later sell on the market (eg, to firms which do not have sufficient allowances to cover their emissions). The programme also provides ways to earn more emissions credits, which can then be traded. Sub-Annex H and the later updates have been created specifically to provide standardised documentation for trading emissions allowances under the scheme.

The programme has been divided into three stages:
- Phase I – from 2005 to 2007;
- Phase II – from 2008 to 2012; and
- Phase III – from 2013 to 2017.

Different rules apply to each phase, which explains why ISDA has published five different versions of the Part 6 Form. However, each of these provides only for physical settlement, which means that one party will need actually to deliver the allowances to the other. If the parties want to have their transactions cash settled, they must do so on a bespoke basis.

ISDA has also published two versions of standard confirmations, which should be used for documenting these types of transaction: one for forward and spot transactions, and one for options. Both documents follow the standard ISDA format for a confirmation. Due to the comprehensive nature of the Part 6 Form, they are relatively short documents setting out specific transaction terms and elections only.

5.7 Freight transactions – Sub-Annex I to the 2005 definitions

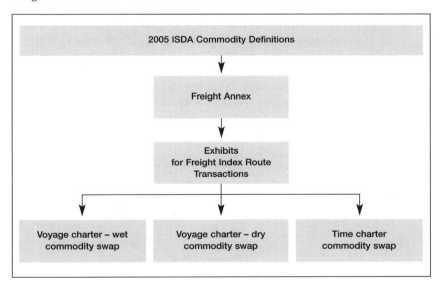

Sub-Annex I to the 2005 definitions covers cash-settled freight index route swaps. To take advantage of this annex's provisions, the parties must remember to refer specifically to it in the confirmation for their trade. The incorporation of the 2005 definitions, without a specific reference to Sub-Annex I, may not be sufficient.

Essentially, the freight derivatives covered in this annex are used for hedging or speculating on the prices charged for carrying goods on a ship. The commodity referenced in each transaction governed by this annex is a 'freight index route', ie a route by which a specified quantity of goods are being shipped.

This is another example of the fact that the 2005 definitions constitute a fallback category for all types of asset. Even though freight rates can hardly be described as a 'commodity', they have been covered in the same ISDA definitional booklet as, for example, coal or gas. On the other hand, the freight rates are often quoted by reference to the commodity being transported, which to some extent explains the link between freight and other commodity derivatives.

The world of freight derivatives is at least 300 years old and highly specialised. Although the main body of Sub-Annex I is just one page long, the annex also includes three forms of confirmation, each containing a number of freight-specific provisions. The document also refers to other industry bodies such as the Baltic Exchange, Forward Freight Agreement Brokers Association and the Worldscale Association.

The exhibit covers confirmations for the following transactions:

- voyage charter – wet commodity swap;
- voyage charter – dry commodity swap; and
- time charter commodity swap.

6. The secondary platform – annexes for commodity assets not covered by the 2005 definitions

The commodity markets are changing constantly and new documentation supplements or replaces older ones. ISDA keeps either updating the annexes to its 2005 definitions or creating new annexes for those commodities which were not covered by the original booklet. This section provides an overview of the documentation for the new asset classes and covers:

- the Revised 2009 ISDA Global Physical Coal Annex;
- the US Emissions Allowance Transaction Annex;
- the ISDA US Wind Event Confirmation; and
- the US Crude Oil and Refined Petroleum Products Annex.

6.1 Revised 2009 ISDA Global Physical Coal Annex

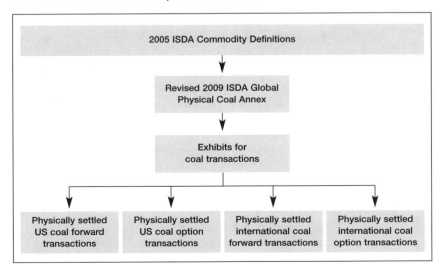

The Revised 2009 ISDA Global Physical Coal Annex is a long and highly technical document which aims to facilitate the purchase and sale of physical coal on a spot or forward basis, as well as trading in options referencing physical coal. As the name suggests, it replaces the old ISDA Global Coal Annex which was published early in 2007.

The Coal Annex is used only for physically settled transactions and the 2005 definitions will still apply to any cash-settled trades. The main body of the annex is quite short, only eight pages long, and includes mainly general and boilerplate provisions, such as:

- credit support documents;
- general rights and obligations;
- *force majeure*;
- payment netting and transaction netting;
- limitation of liability; and
- certain amendments to the ISDA Master Agreements.

The main substantial provisions are included in the appendices to the Coal Annex. Appendix 1 sets out the terms applicable only for US coal (ie, coal sourced at origin solely within the United States). It is based on the Coal Annex of the Master Purchase and Sale Agreement, as published by the Coal Trading Association, and on the Coal Annex to the Master Power Purchase and Sale Agreement, as published by the Edison Electric Institute. It covers:

- the delivery of coal by barge or rail;
- taxes;
- failure to deliver or receive coal;
- delivery and risk of loss;
- substitute coal;
- unit train or truck weighting;
- sampling and analysis;
- quality adjustment;
- rejection and suspension rights; and
- payment.

Appendix 2 governs transactions referencing international coal (ie, everything else other than US coal). It is a much shorter document than Appendix 1 and incorporates large parts of the Standard Coal Trading Agreement, as published by globalCOAL.

The Coal Annex also includes nine exhibits. Exhibits A to D contain various technical details of coal transactions:

- Exhibit A – coal products and product specifications;
- Exhibit B – quality adjustment formulae;
- Exhibit C – quantity variation formulae; and
- Exhibit D – source standards.

ISDA has also published separately template confirmations for coal trades as Exhibits E to I:

- Exhibit E – introduction, standard paragraphs and closing for a letter agreement confirming a physical coal transaction;
- Exhibit F – additional provisions for a confirmation of a physically settled US coal forward transaction;
- Exhibit G – additional provisions for a confirmation of a physically settled US coal option transaction;
- Exhibit H – additional provisions for a confirmation of a physically settled international coal forward transaction; and
- Exhibit I – additional provisions for a confirmation of a physically settled international coal option transaction.

The Coal Annex supplements the 2005 definitions and it is necessary to incorporate the annex in the confirmations for any coal transactions. However, before concluding any trades, the parties must first execute the annex and specify the elective details in Parts (i) to (k) of the document. In Part (i), the parties can make the following elections:

- make the annex applicable with respect to any outstanding coal transactions;
- make the annex applicable with respect to any outstanding credit support for outstanding coal transactions;
- agree the consequence of a *force majeure* event;
- specify whether payment netting shall apply and define its scope;
- decide whether to apply the accelerated payment of damages clause and the financial bookout payment date clause (for transactions referencing US coal only); and
- apply the Standard Coal Trading Agreement dispute resolution clause in respect of their agreement (for transactions referencing international coal only).

In Part (j), the parties should provide the details for notices, and in Part (k) they can agree any modifications to the Coal Annex or any additional provisions.

6.2 US Emissions Allowance Transaction Annex

The US Emissions Allowance Transaction Annex, with a related template confirmation, was published on December 21 2006 and covers the purchase, sale or exchange of an emissions product on a spot or forward basis, or as an option to purchase, sell or exchange an emissions instrument. Similar to the Coal Annex, it supplements the Schedule to the ISDA Master Agreement, but any confirmations should also incorporate the 2005 definitions.

The US Annex relates to:

- instruments traded on the Chicago Climate Exchange;
- nitrogen oxide emissions allowances traded under the NOx SIP Call;
- sulphur dioxide emissions allowances traded under the Clean Air Interstate Rule Programme; and
- any emissions allowances or credits under current or future US state cap-and-trade programmes.

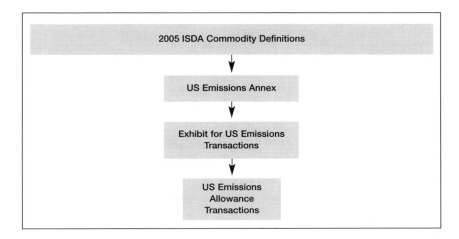

6.3   ISDA US Wind Event Confirmation

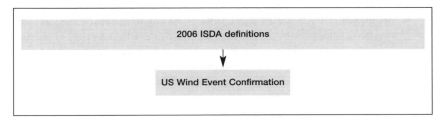

The ISDA US Wind Event Confirmation is another document designed for the US market only. Unlike other documents in this section, it is a standalone confirmation and there is no separate annex. As a result, the template includes four pages of new definitions and is 11 pages long altogether.

Another peculiar feature is that it does not incorporate the 2005 definitions, but instead uses only the 2006 definitions. Therefore, it could be easily argued that this catastrophe derivatives transaction should not be a part of the commodity suite of derivatives. This is also another example that in the ISDA world the term 'commodity' is the ultimate fallback category and includes items which could easily be placed elsewhere.

The US Wind Confirmation can be used to hedge against losses from wind-based natural disasters (or gain exposure to this market). The parties must specify one of three types of wind event and the relevant territory in the United States. If the selected wind event occurs in that region and the amount of damage exceeds the prescribed threshold, a payment will be due from the protection seller to the protection buyer. Therefore, this confirmation is more akin to an insurance contract, although the final payment is not linked to the protection buyer's losses.

6.4   US Crude Oil and Refined Petroleum Products Annex

The US Crude Oil and Refined Petroleum Products Annex was published on June 18

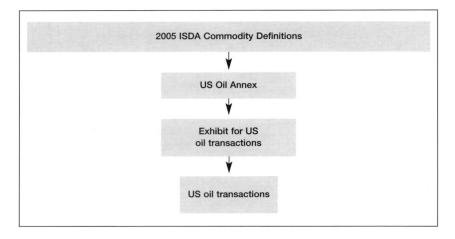

2008. It covers the purchase and sale of physical oil products, which include US pipeline crude oil, refined petroleum products, liquefied petroleum gas and natural gas liquids. The US Annex also facilitates trading in in-tank as well as tank-to-tank transfers, as long as the oil products are not delivered via a vessel or barge.

ISDA has also published one template confirmation to document transactions under the US Oil Annex. The confirmation is very short, as one would expect from a simple sale-and-purchase transaction, and it incorporates by reference the annex as well as the 2005 definitions.

7. The tertiary platform

The tertiary platform for commodity transactions does not really provide any new functionalities for the existing documentation; nor does it cover any additional commodity assets. The commodity markets can be quite volatile and their proper functioning depends on a number of variables. The role of this platform is reactionary, as it provides guidance and support for market participants in case there is any relevant disruption.

Bearing in mind that Sub-Annex A to the 2005 definitions includes more than 200 pages of definitions of commodity prices, it is not surprising that the tertiary documentation platform mostly covers the changes or disruptions relating to the reference prices in this sub-annex. ISDA deals with this in three ways:

- issuing best-practice statements and guidance notes;
- amending Sub-Annex A to the 2005 definitions; and
- producing amendment documentation for affected transactions.

Generally, the first method is preferred by market participants and it has become the usual way for ISDA to deal with any disruptions.

7.1 Best-practice statements and guidance notes

As of early January 2010, ISDA had published 11 best-practice statements and guidance notes. The first was issued on September 14 2001, when the attack on the

World Trade Center resulted in a failure by NYMEX and Platt's to announce or publish the relevant commodity reference prices. At that point, ISDA published a rather technical statement explaining how the affected transactions should be amended to cater for this disruption.

The 2005 definitions include a special section dealing with market disruptions, so any additional statements by ISDA are not really necessary. However, when unique market conditions occur, ISDA feels that such guidance would add to an orderly valuation and settlement of commodity trades. Naturally, the parties are not obliged to follow ISDA's directions, as their relationship is governed only by their bilateral agreement. ISDA's point of view is as follows: "Although parties are not obliged to follow the best practice guidelines … may choose to negotiate an alternative means of addressing the events on a bilateral basis, in light of the current extraordinary circumstances, ISDA strongly encourages market participants to follow these best practice guidelines."

In fact, the vast majority of market participants do follow ISDA's directions.

The 11 best-practice statements published by ISDA can be divided into three main categories, each setting out the consequences of:

- the discontinuance of commodity reference prices;
- changes in methodology; and
- market disruptions.

Discontinuance of prices	Changes in methodology	Market disruptions
Best Practices Statement for Certain OTC Derivatives Transactions Affected by Platt's Discontinuation of Specific Gasoil and Fuel Oil Quotes (Published December 18 2009)	Platt's Best Practices Statement Methodology (Published June 10 2009)	US Exchange Closings on January 2 2007 – Commodity Derivatives (Published January 4 2007)
Best Practices Statement for Certain OTC Derivatives Transactions Affected by Argus' Discontinuation of Specific Gasoline Barge Assessments (Published December 7 2009)	The ISDA Statement of Current Practice Addresses the Treatment of Additional Trading Days on ICE Futures Including Monday, May 28 2007 and Future Trading Days That Have Not Been Announced (Published May 2 2007)	ISDA Best Practices Statement for Certain Energy Products (Announced September 14 2001)

Discontinuance of prices	Changes in methodology	Market disruptions
Best Practices Statement for Certain OTC Derivatives Transactions Affected by Platt's Discontinuation of Specific Diesel Quotes (Published January 28 2009)	Statement of Current Practice Articulated by Certain Members Engaged in OTC Derivatives Transactions Involving Commodity Reference Prices That Reference Brent Blend Crude Oil and Gas Oil Futures Contracts on ICE Futures (Announced December 1 2005)	
Best Practices Statement for Certain OTC Derivatives Transactions Affected by Platt's Discontinuation of Certain Quotes (Published December 23 2008)	ISDA Best Practices Statement for Certain Energy Products (Issued March 25 2003)	
Best Practices Statement for Certain Energy Transactions for OTC Derivatives Transactions Affected by the NYMEX's Discontinuation of its New York Harbor Unleaded Gasoline Futures Contract (Published May 12 2006)		

The statements are generally quite short and technical in nature. In case of any discontinuation of prices, ISDA will normally recommend how the old price should be calculated in the absence of the relevant quote or will advise whether it should be replaced by another quotation.

Whenever a change in methodology occurs, the parties could use standard disruption provisions under the 2005 definitions. However, this may not always be the most efficient approach and, in such circumstances, ISDA advises what changes must be made in the relevant trades. Alternatively, it issues a statement saying that the change is minor and should not affect the transactions. As mentioned above, the parties need not follow the guidance.

Major market disruptions do not happen very often and there are only two guidance notes in this section. One deals with the consequences or failure to publish prices following the September 11 attacks, whereas the other provides for the treatment of the early closure of the exchanges on January 2 2007, which followed the death of former US President Gerald Ford.

7.2 Amendments to Sub-Annex A to the 2005 definitions

Sub-Annex A has been amended only once since the 2005 definitions were published. In October 2005 the New York Mercantile Exchange (NYMEX) announced that it would cease to publish the prices for its New York Harbour unleaded gasoline futures contract. On May 12 2006 ISDA published two items: a best-practice statement, as referred to above, and a supplement to Sub-Annex A.

In the best-practice statement, ISDA argued that the discontinued price should be replaced by the reformulated gasoline blendstock for oxygen blending futures contract. If the parties to a derivatives contract used the discontinued quote in their confirmations, then they could decide whether to follow the guidance note.

The amendment to Sub-Annex A, published on the same date, replaced the prices as recommended in the note. Therefore, for any transactions entered into after May 12 2006, the parties have not had an option to use the discontinued price and can use the new quotation instead. However, to avoid confusion and unnecessary paperwork, ISDA does not normally delete redundant prices.

7.3 Amendment documentation

Instead of producing best-practice statements with recommendations, on one occasion ISDA produced a form of agreement which market participants could use to amend their transactions. "Bi-Lateral Form of Supplement Agreement for Certain Natural Gas Transactions" was published by ISDA on November 25 2008 to address a change to the calendar days used by the NYMEX. It is a short document which amends the definition of 'pricing date' in relation to certain transactions.

8. Miscellaneous documentation

ISDA has also published two further documents, which cannot be properly categorised under any of the primary, secondary or tertiary documentation platforms. These two documents are:
* amendment agreements to incorporate the 2005 definitions; and
* the 2002 ISDA Energy Agreement Bridge.

Both of these were drafted with a view to assisting market participants in documenting and settling their transactions.

8.1   **Amendment agreements to incorporate the 2005 definitions**

The 2005 definitions have replaced the earlier 1993 ISDA Commodity Derivatives Definitions as well as the 1997 ISDA Bullion Definitions. When the new, improved definitional booklet was first published, the entire market was still using the 1993 version. In order to facilitate transition, ISDA has since published two documents: the Amendment Agreement and the Letter Agreement.

The Amendment Agreement is in a form of contract which can be used by the parties to amend the Schedule to their ISDA Master Agreement. If the parties have specified in their Schedule that the 1993 definitions and the Bullion Definitions apply, then the Amendment Agreement would automatically change all those references to the 2005 definitions.

The Letter Agreement performs the same role in relation to any outstanding transactions. If the parties want their commodity derivatives trades to be governed by the 2005 definitions, they can enter into a Letter Agreement and list all relevant confirmations in the annex. Naturally, both documents are entirely optional for parties to use as they see appropriate.

8.2   **2002 ISDA Energy Agreement Bridge**

The 2002 ISDA Energy Agreement Bridge is intended to provide parties to the 1992 ISDA Master Agreement with a means to achieve a form of cross-product netting. The parties do not execute it as a separate document, but instead should add its provisions into Part 5 of the Schedule of their Master Agreement. They should also specify other industry-standard master agreements to which they would want the Energy Bridge to apply.

Following the occurrence of certain events, the parties will be able to terminate their transactions made under all of the selected agreements. The close-out amounts determined under the other agreements will then be incorporated into the close-out amount of their ISDA Master Agreement.

The Energy Bridge has no specific provisions which would make it especially relevant for commodity derivatives, as opposed to, say, credit or equity derivatives. However, there is a plethora of master agreements in the world of commodities, such as the Grid Trade Master Agreement or the Standard Coal Trading Agreement, and all of them could be swept under the Energy Bridge. Probably for this reason it has been included under the commodities section of ISDA's website.

9.   **Current and future developments**

ISDA's work is never done! Swarms of working groups are trying to improve this documentation platform at any one time. This is equally true for commodity derivatives as for credit or equity derivatives. Currently, there are two major projects in the area of commodities.

The first is the update of Sub-Annex A to the 2005 definitions. The old, unused reference prices will be replaced with the current ones and new categories of commodity assets will also be added (eg, polished diamonds and liquid asphalt). The other project is a revision of the current emissions trading documentation. The relevant working group is developing a new form for international emissions allowances and is revising the US emissions allowances template.

ISDA is also busy on other fronts. In today's turbulent times, it often comments on proposed or recent changes in the law which have direct application for commodity derivatives. The most recent example includes a supervisory letter to the Federal Reserve Bank of New York, which it countersigned together with major commodity dealers on December 7 2009.

Introduction to the 2005 ISDA Commodity Definitions

Edmund Parker
Marcin Perzanowski

1. Introduction

If you are involved in over-the-counter (OTC) commodity derivatives, you need to understand the 2005 ISDA Commodity Definitions well enough to be able to review, advise on, or maybe even structure or price commodity derivatives transactions.

The 2005 definitions are the flagship document in ISDA's market-standard documentation platform for commodity derivatives. They provide the operative framework for OTC transactions. They also provide market-standard definitions and detailed fallbacks for when the unforeseen occurs – for example, when a market or trading is disrupted.

Doing the same job as the 2003 ISDA Credit Derivatives Definitions for credit derivatives and the 2002 ISDA Equity Derivatives Definitions for equity derivatives, the 2005 definitions are brought to life through incorporation by reference in an OTC confirmation. The 2005 definitions also contain many templates for those confirmations. A confirmation will also incorporate the parties' ISDA Master Agreement, as amended by its schedule, and possibly a credit support annex as well. In addition to setting out the pricing information for the transaction, the confirmation will select various elections to craft the transaction's terms, definitions and fallbacks, with the efficiency of the 2005 definitions providing market certainty and allowing complex OTC commodity derivatives products to be documented in just a few pages. As with all ISDA transactions, documentation efficiency trumps ease of understanding. To address this, ISDA has published an 18-page user's guide to accompany the 2005 definitions. This chapter goes into a greater level of depth than the user's guide and makes extensive use of diagrams and worked examples to explain this asset class's complexities.

As noted earlier, the terms which are defined in the 2005 ISDA Commodity Definitions are denoted by the use of quotation marks when used for the first time in the book. Thereafter, those terms are spelled without using any capital letters or punctuation marks.

2. History and structure of the 2005 definitions

International Swaps and Derivatives Association Inc (ISDA) was founded in 1985. Organised commodity derivatives markets have existed for hundreds of years. The result of this is that ISDA is the new kid on the block and the darling of the financial institutions and hedge funds – though not of traditional brokers, who were using commodity derivatives long before ISDA showed up. So whereas ISDA definitional booklets such as those for equity and credit derivatives definitions have been driven from a financial institution and hedge fund perspective, the 2005 definitions take greater account of harmonising with existing market practice and organisations, while introducing the robust fallback regime of other derivative asset classes. For example, the provisions relating to trading in the English physical electricity market interact with the Grid Trade Master Agreement published by the Futures and Options Association.

The 2005 definitions were developed to cover a range of commodity derivatives products and underlying commodity assets, as well as to reflect the developing market practices in the global derivatives industry. The 2005 definitions are ISDA's second version of a set of commodity definitions, succeeding ISDA 1993 Commodity Derivatives Definitions. The 2005 definitions also combine the revised versions of the ISDA 2000 Supplement to the 1993 Commodity Derivatives Definitions and the earlier 1997 ISDA Bullion Definitions.[1]

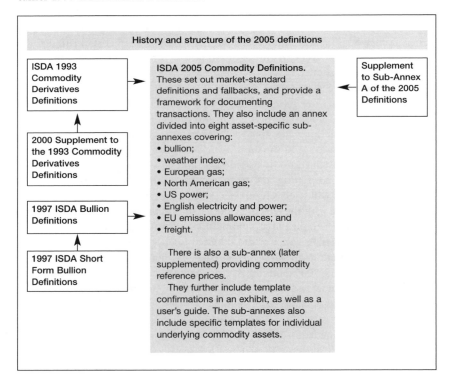

The structure of the 2005 definitions has changed considerably since the 1993 version. Whereas the 1993 definitions had only 42 pages, the new set of definitions (together with the exhibits, annexes and the user's guide) has been expanded into a

---

1   The Bullion Definitions were also available in a short version for use with physically settled transactions and were known as the 1997 ISDA Short Form Bullion Definitions.

huge 526 pages. The 2005 definitions are substantially greater in length, complexity and the range of products covered.

One of the principal reasons for the drafting of the new 2005 definitions was to cover a wider variety of different types of underlying commodity asset.

In *Das Kapital*, Karl Marx viewed commodities as things that are bought and sold, with their value representing a quantity of human labour. The 2005 definitions adapt a broader approach to commodities than Marx; the traditional commodities (eg, gold, copper, gas, cocoa and oil) are covered, but more exotic commodities (eg, electricity, freight, the weather and EU emission allowances) are also included.

The main operative section of the 2005 definitions is quite short – it takes up only 26 of the 526 pages and contains 18 articles. It is quite similar in scope to the 1993 definitions. In addition to the operative section, there is an exhibit which sets out generic template confirmations that can be adapted for use with a wide range of underlying commodity assets. The new definitions also include eight lengthy annexes setting out special provisions for different types of underlying commodity asset.

Some of these sub-annexes provide suggested paragraphs which can be incorporated into an ISDA Master Agreement. For example, the sub-annex for Grid Trade Master Agreement transactions (physically settled electricity) includes provisions to be incorporated into an ISDA Master Agreement adding an electricity-specific additional termination event and event of default. The sub-annex for emissions allowances transactions includes elections relating to which party bears the burden of any penalties imposed when emissions allowances are not delivered on time. The sub-annexes also contain specific template forms of confirmation for the relevant type of underlying commodity asset.

The annexes cover in detail the following types of commodity derivatives transaction:

- bullion transactions (Sub-Annex B);
- weather index transactions (Sub-Annex C);
- European gas transactions (Sub-Annex D);
- North American gas transactions (Sub-Annex E);
- North American power transactions (Sub-Annex F);
- Grid Trade Master Agreement (electricity) transactions (Sub-Annex G);
- EU emissions allowances transactions (Sub-Annex H); and
- freight transactions (Sub-Annex I).

Articles X to XIII of the operative provisions of the 2005 definitions refer to each of the sub-annexes in turn. When parties incorporate the 2005 definitions into a confirmation, only the sub-annex relating to bullion transactions is deemed to be automatically incorporated. If the parties choose to, they can incorporate any of the other sub-annexes either into the schedule to the ISDA Master Agreement or specifically into the confirmation.

The 2005 definitions also include Sub-Annex A. This sets out market-standard definitions of various commodity reference prices. Parties can rely on these when entering into trades, making the documentation process more efficient. Other relatively major differences with the 1993 definitions (as amended by the 2000 supplement) are as follows:

- The definition of the 'calculation period' now covers a wider range of transactions.
- The 'market disruption event' provisions are expanded. There is a new disruption event, namely 'trading disruption', which replaces the previous definitions of 'trading suspension' and 'trading limitation'. The definition of '*de minimis* trading' has been deleted in its entirety for lack of use and the default selection of market disruption event has been revised to conform to the then-current market practice.
- Two of the disruption fallbacks ('postponement – fallback reference price' and 'average daily price disruption') from the 1993 definitions have been dropped and a new disruption fallback is included ('delayed publication or announcement'). Other disruption fallbacks have been modified and the default waterfall of disruption fallbacks has been updated and expanded.
- The 2005 definitions allow the parties to enter into barrier transactions by introducing knock-in and knock-out options. Those have been modelled on ISDA 2002 Equity Definitions.
- The definitions relating to currencies and business days have been amended to conform to the ISDA 2000 definitions.
- The concept of 'common pricing' has been introduced. As explained later in the chapter, it applies only when the transaction refers to more than one commodity reference price.

The 2005 definitions revise and consolidate the Bullion Definitions. Some clauses of the old Bullion Definitions are included in the generic provisions relating to all types of commodity transaction, and some are included in Sub-Annex B. The main differences between the Bullion Definitions and the new 2005 definitions are as follows:

- The responsibilities of the calculation agent in the 2005 definitions are much more detailed.
- The market disruption events and disruption fallbacks have been amended significantly and standardised across different types of commodity asset.
- The 2005 definitions have no specific language relating to additional taxes.
- The 2005 definitions introduce the concept of Bermuda-style options transactions.

The definitions are 526 pages long and are divided into a table of contents, an introduction and preamble, 17 articles, four exhibits, nine sub-annexes and a user's guide. The outline structure is set out next.

2.1   2005 ISDA Definitions documents and structure

3. **Introduction and preamble to the 2005 definitions**

The 17 articles are preceded by both an introduction and a preamble. The introduction informs us that the definitions are intended for use in "privately negotiated commodity transactions", which are governed by either the 1992 ISDA Master Agreement or the 2002 ISDA Master Agreement. That said, they can provide a useful foundation when drafting a structured product.

The introduction continues that the 2005 definitions provide the basic framework for a range of commodity derivatives financial instruments (swaps, basis swaps, options, caps, collars, floors and swaptions), as well as certain physically settled transactions. Furthermore, the introduction tells us that the 2005 definitions have fallback provisions which apply unless the parties provide otherwise in a transaction; and that market participants may adapt or supplement them as they wish.

There is also the usual lengthy liability disclaimer, absolving ISDA from any guilt should market participants misuse the definitions, as well as a reminder that the 2005 definitions do not automatically apply to transactions which incorporated the 1993 definitions or the Bullion Definitions.

The introduction stresses that Sub-Annex B to the 2005 definitions (effectively an update of the old Bullion Definitions) has been endorsed by the London Bullion Market Association and the Financial Markets Lawyers Group – a further example that, contrary to several other ISDA definitions booklets, this one seeks to harmonise with other pre-existing regimes.

The 2005 definitions precede the ISDA 2006 definitions (given in ISDA's general derivatives definitions booklet). In fact, they incorporate by reference various clauses from the predecessor to the 2006 definitions, the 2000 definitions. Considering that only the 2006 version is current, we recommend always specifically incorporating the 2006 definitions by reference into the documentation of all commodity transactions, and providing that all references to the 2000 definitions are deemed to be references to the 2006 definitions.

The introduction does not form part of the 2005 definitions. However, the preamble does, and it states that the definitions and provisions in the 2005 definitions may be incorporated into a document by inserting wording to the effect that the document is subject to the 2005 definitions. The preamble goes on to provide that all terms, definitions and provisions incorporated into a document will be applicable unless otherwise modified; and that is how the transaction framework, standard market definitions and logistical fallbacks are brought into the confirmation. Together with the ISDA Master Agreement, this provides the derivatives documentation infrastructure to create a commodity derivatives transaction.

4. Article I – Certain general definitions

The Article I definitions cover the four distinct areas set out in the diagram below.

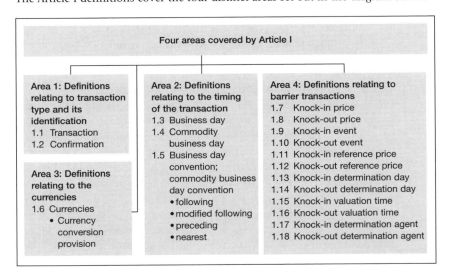

181

4.1 Area 1: Definitions relating to the transaction type and its identification

Article I defines the scope of financial instruments that the 2005 definitions cover in the definition of a 'transaction'.

Definition of 'transaction'		
Group A	**Group B**	**Group C**
• Commodity swap • Commodity basis swap • Commodity cap • Commodity floor • Commodity collar • Commodity index • Commodity forward • Commodity spot	• Bullion transaction • Weather index derivatives transaction • NBP transaction • ZBT transaction • Gas transaction • Power transaction • Grid Trade Master Agreement transaction • EU emissions allowance transaction • Freight transaction	• Any similar transaction to those listed in Group A and Group B • Any option with respect to any transactions in Group A and Group B • Any combination of transactions listed in Group A and Group B • Any other transaction identified as transaction in the relevant confirmation

The chart above shows how broad the definition of a 'transaction' actually is . We can divide the covered trades into three main groups.

Group A includes the main generic types of derivatives transaction (ie, commodity swap, commodity basis swap, commodity cap, commodity floor, commodity collar, commodity index, commodity forward and commodity spot). Group B comprises the commodity-specific transactions; these are further defined in the 2005 definitions and in the relevant sub-annexes.

Group C is a fallback category. It covers any similar transactions to those listed in Groups A and B, as well as any options and any combinations of those transactions. Group C also includes any other transaction identified as a 'transaction' in a confirmation for the purposes of the 2005 definitions.

A 'confirmation' is defined as a document or any other evidence in respect of a transaction confirming its terms.

4.2 Area 2: Definitions relating to the timing of the transaction

This grouping includes the definitions relevant to the timing of the transaction. It covers the types of business day and any applicable business conventions.

Article 1 of the 2005 definitions provides for only two types of day: 'business day' and 'commodity business day'. However, the principal body also includes a number of references to 'bullion business days' (where this term is defined only in Sub-Annex B), as well as to 'seller business days' for option transactions.

Generally, the concept of a business day is relevant only when one party needs to make a payment or make a delivery to the other. A 'business day' is defined as a day on which commercial banks settle payments and are open for business in the place specified in the confirmation (eg, London and New York).

If the parties do not specify a business day in the confirmation, the business day will be determined by reference to Sections 1.5, 1.6 and 1.7 of the 2000 definitions (which are incorporated into the 2005 definitions by reference).

As the 2006 definitions have now replaced the 2000 version as the market standard, we recommend specifically incorporating that references to the 2000 definitions in the 2005 definitions will be deemed to be references to the 2006 definitions and its corresponding provisions. This is especially important if the payments are to be made in Chinese renminbi, Pakistani rupees, Vietnamese dongs, Sri Lankan rupees or Romanian lei, because these currencies are not included in the 2000 definitions but are in the 2006 definitions.

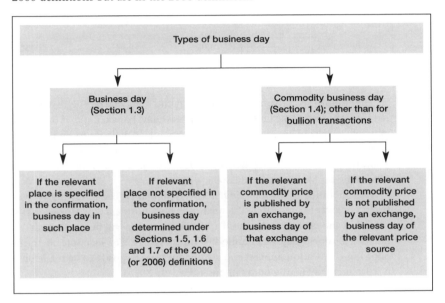

Whereas the term 'business day' is relevant for the transfer of money, the definition of 'commodity business day' is relevant whenever the commodity's reference price must be determined. Accordingly, if an exchange announces or publishes a commodity price, commodity business days will be those days on which that exchange is open for business. If, however, the relevant price is not published or announced by an exchange, commodity business days will be those days on which the relevant price source for that commodity is published.

The above 'commodity business day' definition does not apply to bullion transactions: Sub-Annex B includes a separate definition of a 'bullion business day'.

Furthermore, Section 8.5 of the 2005 definitions also includes a 'seller business day' definition, which applies only to option transactions. It is defined as any day on which banks are open for business in the city where the option seller is located for the purposes of receiving notices.

A calendar day specified in a confirmation may not always fall on a business day – for example, a payment date of June 7 each year. If June 7 falls on a Sunday, as it did in 2009, an alternative date must be taken. Which date this is will be determined by the 'business day convention'. The business day convention is a convention for adjusting any relevant date if that date would otherwise fall on a day that is not a business day or a commodity business day. In respect of both business days and commodity business days, there are four main conventions that the parties can elect to apply in a confirmation.

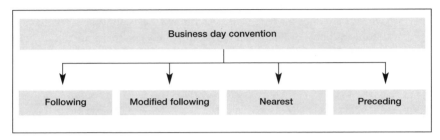

The 'following convention' means that the date will be the first following day that is a commodity business day or a business day. For example, if the confirmation for a five-year confirmation required a payment or delivery to be made on June 7 each year and the parties have elected the following convention and London business days to apply, the payment or delivery for Sunday June 7 2009 would have to be made on Monday June 8 2009.

The 'modified following convention' is similar to the following convention in that the relevant date will be the next following business day. However, if such day will fall in the next calendar month, the relevant day will be the first preceding day that is a business day or commodity business day. For example, if the modified following convention applied and a payment was supposed to be made on Saturday July 31, such payment would fall on Friday July 30.

The 'nearest convention' is slightly more complex. If the date falls on a day other than a Sunday or a Monday, the relevant date will be the first preceding day that is a business day. If, however, the date falls on a Sunday or a Monday, the relevant date will be the first following day. In essence, this means that if the relevant date falls on a Sunday or a public holiday Monday, the relevant date will be Tuesday. If it falls on a Saturday, it will be Friday. However, if there is a public holiday on a day other than Monday, the relevant day will be the first preceding business day.

Finally, there is the 'preceding convention', which says that the relevant date will be the first preceding day which is a business day or a commodity business day.

The parties to a transaction should specify the relevant business day convention in relation to each relevant day in a confirmation. However, if the convention is not specified for a particular date, but is specified for the relevant transaction, such convention will also apply to that date.

4.3 Area 3: Definitions relating to the currencies

This area covers two definitions. 'Currency' is defined as the lawful currency of any country as determined by the parties. It also incorporates by reference Section 1.7 of the 2000 definitions, which sets out the definitions of various currencies.[2]

The other defined term here is 'currency conversion provision'. This is relevant when the reference price of a given commodity is different from the currency of payment that is agreed between the parties. In that case, the parties should agree the mechanism for the currency conversion provision in the confirmation: the 2005 definitions do not provide any fallback mechanism. The ISDA's 1998 FX and Currency Option Definitions can be helpful in this regard.

4.4   Area 4: Definitions relating to barrier transactions

The definitions in Section 1.7 to 1.18 cover 'knock-in/knock-out' transactions. These are often referred to as 'barrier' transactions. They are modelled on the knock-in/knock-out provisions in ISDA 2002 Equity Definitions and are also consistent with the 2005 Barrier Option Supplement to the 1998 FX and Currency Option Definitions.

In a knock-in transaction, a payment or delivery is contingent on the occurrence of a 'knock-in event' on any 'knock-in determination day' at the 'knock-in valuation time'. In turn, a knock-out transaction is a right or obligation that terminates on the occurrence of the specific 'knock-out event' on any 'knock-out determination day' at the 'knock-in valuation time'. For example, a knock-out occurs when a particular level is hit (eg, the price of oil reaches $120 a barrel) and at that point the transaction terminates. No termination payment is payable and no amounts are owed between the parties.

The parties can specify any event as the knock-in event. However, if they mark the knock-in provisions as applicable without setting out the details of the relevant event, they must provide the 'knock-in price'. In that case the obligations under a transaction are contingent on the relevant price of the transaction (the 'knock-in reference price') reaching the level of the knock-in price. The same applies in relation to the 'knock-out price'.

The job of the 'knock-in determination agent' (or the 'knock-out determination agent') is to determine whether a knock-in event (or a knock-out event) has occurred. The parties are free to name the calculation agent or a separate entity to fulfil this role.

5.   Article II – Parties

This short article has only two definitions. A party to a commodity transaction can be either a 'fixed price payer' or a 'floating price payer'.

A 'fixed price payer' makes payments of amounts calculated by reference to a fixed price, or alternatively is obligated to pay a fixed amount. In turn, a 'floating price payer' makes payments calculated by reference to a commodity reference price, or will be obligated to pay a floating amount.

It is not always necessary to have both a fixed price payer and a floating price payer in every transaction. Depending on the parties' commercial intentions, there could be two fixed price payers or indeed two floating price payers.

The terms 'fixed price payer' and 'floating price payer' relate generally only to

2   As referred to above, this should be amended in a confirmation to incorporate the 2006 definitions.

swaps and similar transactions, and may not be used at all if the payments under a trade are subject to a different payment calculation. Article II states that the terms 'fixed rate payer' and 'floating rate payer' do not apply to the following types of transaction: weather index derivatives transactions, NBP transactions, ZBT transactions, gas transactions, power transactions, Grid Trade Master Agreement transactions, EU emissions allowance transactions and freight transactions. Here the parties will have other names: for instance, both weather index derivatives transactions and EU emissions allowance transactions refer to 'buyer', and 'seller'. These terms are set out in the relevant sub-annex.

6.   Article III – Terms and dates

This article provides the basic definitions for transaction timings. Although it looks straightforward, it contains some traps for the unwary.

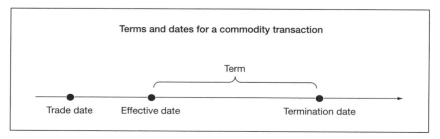

In accordance with the usual ISDA terminology, the 'trade date' is the day when the parties enter into the transaction (ie, the day when they sign the confirmation or otherwise agree terms). On the trade date, the parties will decide the first day on which the transaction's provisions will become operative (the 'effective date'), and the date when the transaction will terminate (the 'termination date'). The period of time from the effective date until the termination date is called the 'term'. Both the effective date and the termination date will be specified by the parties in the confirmation.

Article III also defines three other key dates in a transaction: the 'settlement date', the 'payment date' and the 'expiration date'. For bullion transactions only, the settlement date includes the 'bullion settlement date' and the 'bullion transaction settlement date'.

As the names suggest, the 'settlement date' and the 'payment date' are the dates when the parties settle their transaction obligations. Often, both terms are used interchangeably, but in principle the payment date is the date when an actual payment is made. In contrast, the settlement date is broader and includes, for example, the date the when a party exercises a swaption.

If the parties have not elected a business day convention for a settlement date or payment date, the following business day convention (or the following bullion business day convention, for bullion transactions) will apply by default. In contrast, the termination date will not be adjusted by any business day convention unless the parties have specified otherwise.

The term 'expiration date' applies to option transactions only and it is the last date or, in the case of Asian or European options, the only date when an option can be exercised. This date must be specified in the confirmation.

If the date which has been specified as the expiration date is not a commodity business day, then the first following commodity business day will be the new expiration date.

If a 'market disruption event' (as described in section 10.4 below) occurs on the originally specified expiration date, the first commodity business day on which a market disruption event ceases will be the new expiration date. However, if a market disruption event is still occurring eight commodity business days following the original disrupted commodity business day, that eighth day will be the expiration date, even if the disruption has not ceased by that time.

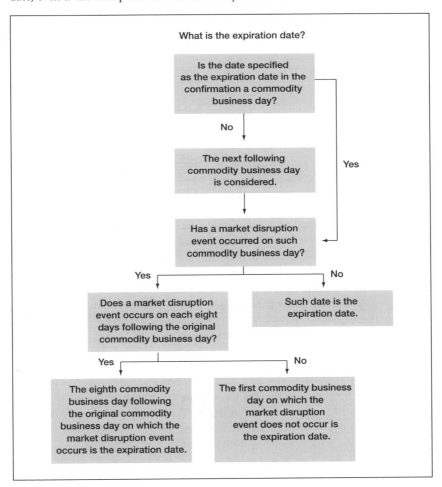

In some option transactions the option buyer can exercise the option only until the 'expiration time' on the 'expiration date'. The 2005 definitions define such time as 9:30am (New York time) on the expiration date, unless the parties specify otherwise. The 2005 definitions lack consistency here; in some sections they refer to New York time and in others to London time. Therefore, it is important always to amend the definition of 'expiration time' in accordance with the parties' needs.

Unfortunately, the 2005 definitions are also unclear as to whether this expiration time fallback applies to all option transactions, or just the few option types specifically referred to in the relevant sub-annexes. Although the term 'expiration time' is defined in the main body of the 2005 definitions, it is not actually used there, and references to it are only present in Sub-Annex B (for bullion transactions) and Sub-Annex D (for NBP options and ZBT options). This term also appears in the 2005 definitions' exhibits. In order to avoid any confusion, we recommend always specifying the expiration time in the confirmation.

7. Article IV – Certain definitions relating to payment

Article IV has various definitions relating to payment. We have divided these into three main areas:

- types of payment;
- types of notional quantity; and
- terms relating to calculations.

7.1 Types of payment

Sections 4.1 and 4.2 provide for two types of payment: 'fixed amounts' and 'floating amounts'. Both definitions are generic and their application is specifically excluded with respect to the following: weather index derivative transactions, NBP transactions, ZBT transactions, gas transactions, power transactions, Grid Trade Master Agreement transactions, EU emissions allowance transactions, freight transactions and any other transactions subject to a different payment calculation.

The 'fixed amount' is defined as an amount payable by the fixed rate payer, which is specified in the confirmation or determined in accordance with Article V of the 2005 definitions. Similarly, the 'floating amount' is defined as an amount payable by the floating rate payer, which is specified in the confirmation or determined in accordance with Article VI of the 2005 definitions. (See sections 8 and 9 below for analysis of the relevant parts of the definitions.)

7.2 Types of notional quantity

Section 4.3 provides three definitions of notional quantity – each is slightly different. The 'notional quantity' is the quantity of the relevant commodity referenced in a transaction. The 'notional quantity per calculation period' is exactly what it says it is, and it is used when there is more than one calculation period for a transaction. Finally, the 'total notional quantity' is the sum of all notional quantities in respect of all calculation periods.

The 2005 definitions further specify that the value of each notional quantity is given in units. 'Units' is defined in Sub-Annex A as the unit of measure of the relevant commodity, as specified in the relevant commodity reference price or in the confirmation. Depending on the commodity, a unit could be, for example, a tonne, an ounce, a megawatt or a gigajoule. The intricacies of the definition of 'commodity reference price' are analysed in detail in section 10 of this chapter.

7.3 Terms relating to calculations

Article IV sets out three definitions relating to calculations: the 'calculation period', 'calculation agent' and 'calculation date'.

The 'calculation period' is a period defined by reference to two dates specified in the confirmation. The first date is the start of the calculation period and the second determines when it ends. Article IV further stresses that such dates need not be determined by reference to the effective date, termination dates or other defined terms in the 2005 definitions.

Not every transaction will have a calculation period. This term is used only when there are periodic payments made under the transaction. Each such periodic payment is made by reference to a calculation period which ends closest in time to the relevant settlement date or payment date.

For each calculation period, there is a 'calculation date' on which the calculation agent will make the relevant calculations and determinations necessary to establish the amounts that need to be paid or delivered under the transaction. There are two definitions for the calculation date: one applicable only to weather index derivatives transactions and one for all other transaction types.

In a weather index derivative transaction, the calculation date is defined by reference to a number of dates following the final date of each calculation period. The number of dates must be specified in the confirmation.

For all other transactions, the calculation date is the earliest date on which the 'calculation agent' can give the notice of the relevant payments that must be made on the settlement date or payment date. This date can occur no later than close of business on the business day (or bullion business day) next preceding the relevant settlement date or payment date.[3] However, if the prices used to make the relevant calculations are published only on the relevant settlement date or payment date, the calculation agent must send the relevant notice at the latest time that will permit the payments due on that date to be made.

Finally, Article IV sets out in detail the obligations of the 'calculation agent'. Section 4.5 sets out nine specific functions of the calculation agent, which can be grouped into four main areas:

- duties relating to calculations;
- duties relating to notifications;
- duties relating to disruption events; and
- any other duties conferred on the agent by the terms of the confirmation.

---

3   The 2005 definitions suggest that the calculation date in this instance can be a 'close of business'. It confuses the date with a specific time during that date. The intention behind this definition was to create an obligation on the calculation agent to send the relevant notice by that time and this is also the market understanding of this provision. The calculation date must then be, at the latest, the first business day preceding the settlement date or the payment date. Where the relevant data is published on the related settlement date or the payment date, that day is the calculation date.

This grouping is set out in the diagram below.

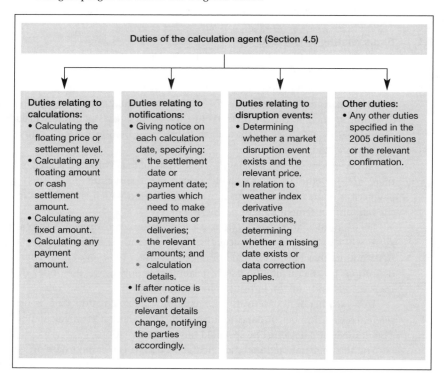

Section 4.5 further specifies that if the calculation agent is required to exercise judgement in any way, it must do so in good faith and in a commercially reasonable manner after consulting the other party (or parties, if the calculation agent is a third party).

8.   Article V – Fixed amounts

This short article sets out the method for calculating fixed amounts. Generally, the parties have two options: they can specify the fixed amount quantum in the confirmation or they can provide a mechanism for determining the amount instead.

Under the default mechanism provided by the 2005 definitions, the parties need only specify a fixed price in the confirmation. This price must always be given by reference to a unit of the underlying commodity. If the parties decide to use this method, the fixed amount payable on a given settlement date or payment date will be calculated in accordance with the following formula:

Fixed amount = notional quantity (per calculation period) × fixed price

9. Article VI – Floating amounts

This article sets out the method for calculating the floating amount. The floating amount is determined using the following formula:

Floating amount = notional quantity (per calculation period) × floating price

This is almost identical to the 'fixed amount' formula, with the only difference being the replacement of 'fixed price' by 'floating price'. However, the definition of 'floating price' is more complex and goes to the heart of the commodity derivatives transaction's economics. The following diagram sets out definition options.

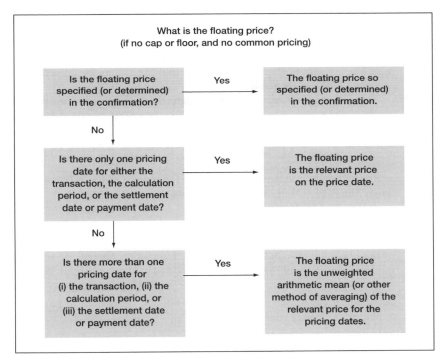

9.1 Standard determination of the floating price – no cap price or floor price and common pricing is not applicable

To determine the floating price for a transaction, we need to follow several steps and answer several questions. First, we must check whether the parties have provided a transaction-specific method for determining the floating price in the confirmation. As anywhere else in ISDA documentation, the parties are free to amend the standard wording of any set of definitions as they see fit. For now, however, we have assumed that the parties decide to follow the standard provisions of the 2005 definitions.

We must therefore check how many pricing dates there are in respect of one payment. A 'pricing date' is a date that is relevant for determining the price of a commodity and the parties can specify one or more of them in the confirmation. If there is just one floating amount payment to be made during the course of the transaction, there must be at least one pricing date specified (or determined) for the entire transaction. However, the floating amount payments often need to be made with respect to each calculation period, or on each settlement date (or payment date), and there must be at least one pricing date in respect of each payment.

For example, the parties to a commodity swap transaction referencing oil could agree that payments under the swap should be made monthly. In the confirmation, they should also specify that, say, the 15th day of each month will be the pricing date. Therefore, on the 15th of each month they will have to check what the relevant price of oil is.

If there is only one pricing date in respect of one payment, the floating price is equal to the relevant price on that pricing date. If more than one pricing date is indicated for a given transaction, calculation period or settlement (or payment) date, the floating price will be equal to an unweighted arithmetic mean of the relevant price for each pricing date. The parties are also free to specify any other method of averaging in the confirmation.

Going back to our example, even though the payments under the swap are made monthly, the parties could designate two dates in a month – say, the 15th and 16th of each month – as the pricing dates. In that case, the floating price for each payment will be equal to the arithmetic average of the prices of oil published on 15th and 16th of each month.

In this section, we have also referred to the concept of the 'relevant price' several times. The 2005 definitions define this term as a price of a given commodity on a given day, as published by the relevant price source and determined as set out in the confirmation. There are various standard price sources for different commodities; the most common are set out in the 200-plus pages of Sub-Annex A. For example, if the parties enter into a commodity derivative transaction referencing sugar, they can specify that the relevant price will be determined in accordance with the commodity reference price (White Sugar Euronext Liffe). This is defined as a price per tonne on deliverable-grade white sugar on Euronext Liffe on the relevant futures contract, as displayed on Reuters screen page 0#LSU. (This is further explained in section 10 of this chapter.)

9.2 Default elections for pricing date and common pricing

The parties are free to specify the pricing date in the confirmation. However, if they do not, the 2005 definitions provide some standard fallbacks.

If the transaction is a European-style option, the pricing date will, by fallback, be the expiration date. This is logical because European options can be exercised only on the last day of their term (as explained in section 11.2 of this chapter). Therefore, the relevant price will have to be determined on that last day (ie, the expiration date).

If the parties have entered into an American-style option, the fallback is for the pricing date to be the exercise date. An American-style option can be exercised at any time during its term, so logically the date when the option is exercised will be the pricing date.

In respect of an Asian-style option, the fallback is for the pricing date to be "each commodity business day during the calculation period". As explained below, an Asian-style option, like a European-style option, is exercisable only on the expiration date, but its value is determined by reference to an average price throughout the term of the transaction. Therefore, each commodity business day in the relevant calculation period under an Asian-style option is a pricing date. Although in relation to other types of option the parties need not specify a calculation period, it is vital that they do so with respect to all Asian-style options. Otherwise, there will be difficulties calculating the relevant values for that transaction.

A Bermuda-style option can be exercised on each specified potential exercise day as well as on the expiration date. The pricing date fallback for this option type is for the pricing dates to be "the potential exercise dates during the exercise period and on the expiration date". This definition is quite surprising, as it suggests that there will always be more than one pricing day in respect of a Bermudan-style option and that the parties need to wait until the expiration date of the instrument in order to be able to determine the floating price. This is not what is normally intended, as the parties should be able to obtain the final price of a transaction on the day that the option buyer decides to exercise the option. So the default pricing date for a Bermudan-style option should have been defined as the exercise date, as it is for the American-style option. Therefore, if the parties elect to undertake a Bermudan-style option, we recommend amending the standard wording of the 2005 definitions in this respect, as required.

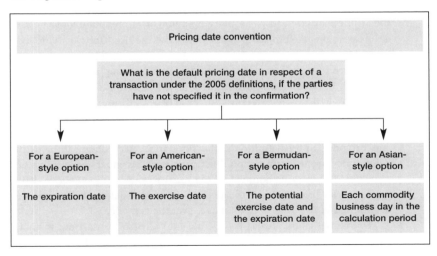

Often, a transaction references more than one commodity. For example, under a basis swap, Party A could pay to Party B a floating amount based on the value of copper and receive a floating amount based on the value of zinc. In that case, the parties may want to determine the prices of both zinc and copper on the same date. If the parties elect 'common pricing' as applicable, then a pricing date in respect of each part of the transaction will not occur until the prices of both commodities are published on the same day.

9.3 Determination of the floating price when a floor price, cap price or collar is applicable

Commodity derivatives are often used to hedge a party's obligations under other transactions. A party might enter into a commodity swap or option transaction to protect itself against the adverse pricing movements in an underlying commodity. For example, an airline might want to be able to buy fuel at no more than a given price at a future date. It could enter into a commodity swap and, in return for a premium, receive a payment if fuel prices rose above the set level at the future date. The payment would reflect the difference between the agreed level and the actual level. If the agreed level was $50 a barrel of oil and actual prices rose to $80 by the future date, the airline would receive $30 a barrel of oil referenced in the transaction.

In the example above, the airline would be a 'fixed price payer', whereas its counterparty would be a 'floating price payer'. Accordingly, the airline would be required to pay a fixed amount equal to $50 for every barrel. In turn, the floating rate payer would have to pay the airline the actual price of oil at the relevant pricing date. If, on such date, the price was $80, then the payment obligations of each party would be offset against each other and only one of them would have to make a payment. In our scenario, the airline would receive $30 for every barrel under the swap. If, however, the actual price of oil was $45 per barrel, then the airline would have to make a payment equal to $5 per barrel ($50 – $45) to its counterparty.

Depending on the actual trading price, the market view of future prices and the agreed level (or fixed price) set at the transaction's outset, to enter into such hedge the airline may need to pay a hefty premium. The premium could be lower if the airline were prepared to accept some portion of the risk. One way of doing so would be to agree a cap price of, for example, $70 a barrel. In that case the counterparty would need to make a payment to the airline only if the price of oil rose above $70 per barrel. In our scenario, this means that at the end of the year the airline would still receive $10 a barrel referenced (instead of $30). However, if the price at the end of the year was $65, the counterparty would not have to pay anything to the airline.

The 2005 definitions allow for this by including the concepts of a 'floor price' and 'cap price' in the definition of the 'floor price'. Accordingly, if the parties specify a floor price in the confirmation, the floating price is equal to the excess of the floor price over the price determined in the usual way, as outlined above. If the parties specify a cap price instead, the floating price is equal to the excess of the price determined in the usual way, as above, over the cap price.

The parties could also agree to enter into a collar transaction. In that case one party would pay a floating amount based on the cap price, whereas the other would pay a floating amount based on the floor price. Therefore, one party would make a payment to the other if the price of the commodity rose above a certain level (the cap price), and the other party would have to make a payment to the first only if the price fell below a defined threshold (the floor price). If, however, the price of the commodity stayed within the 'collar' (ie, it did not rise above the cap price and did not fall below the floor price), no party would need to make any payment to the other.

Hypothetical example: Torre Mining Corporation

Torre Mining Corporation owns several gold mines in West Africa. It has borrowed a large amount of money from a syndicate of banks in order to develop the mines. It hopes that in a few years' time it will be able to make enough profit from the sale of gold to repay the loans. However, it is concerned that the price of gold may fall substantially from the current high level of $900 per ounce.

Vieja Jewellers International is a large corporation which owns almost 100 shops throughout Europe and the United States and sells various pieces of jewellery made of gold, silver and platinum. It has been concerned that the price of gold has recently been on the rise and it would like to hedge its exposure to this commodity. Torre and Vieja (acting through broker intermediaries) enter into a cash-settled five-year collar commodity derivatives transaction, with a floor price of $800 and a cap price of $1,000. The total notional quantity of the transaction is set at 100,000 ounces. If after five years the price of an ounce of gold is more than $1,000, Torre will make a payment to Vieja. If the price is less than $800, Vieja will make a payment to Torre. If, however, the price of an ounce of gold in five years is between $800 and $1,000, neither party makes a payment and the transaction will be terminated.

If, at the end of the term of the transaction, the price is $1,100 per ounce, Torre must pay $100 to Vieja for each ounce referenced. As the notional amount is 100,000 ounces, Torre must pay a floating amount of $10 million to Vieja.

Floating amount = floating price × total notional amount

Floating amount = ($1,100 – $1,000 per ounce) × 100,000 ounces = $10 million

At the same time, Torre can also sell the equivalent amount of gold to third parties at the market price of $1,100. Therefore, it will still make enough profit to start repaying the interest and principal of its loan.

If, at the end of the term of the transaction, the price is $700 per ounce, Vieja must make a floating amount payment to Torre. The payment will also be equal to $10 million.

Floating amount = ($800 – $700 per ounce) × 100,000 ounces = $10 million

However, Vieja will then buy the gold more cheaply on the market at $700 per ounce. Therefore, it should still make a profit out of the drop in commodity price.

If, at the end of the term of the transaction, the price is $900 per ounce, then as the price of $900 is between the floor price of $800 and the cap price of $1,100, no party will need to make any payment to the other. The parties have hedged their exposure to the fluctuations of the price of gold, but it turned out not to be necessary. However, the more important aspect is that they obtained the hedge at zero cost and were both happy with the arrangement.

Considering that Torre actually mines gold and Vieja uses gold in its products, the parties may have decided that it would be cheaper and more cost-effective for them to enter into a physically settled transaction. This would mean that Torre would have to deliver 100,000 ounces of gold at the end of the five-year term.

The payment that Vieja must make to Torre will differ depending on the actual price of gold on the termination of the transaction. If the price stands at $1,100, Vieja will need to pay only $1,000 per ounce (ie, the cap price) for the delivery. If the price is $700, Vieja will need to pay $800 per ounce. If, however, the final price is between $800 and $1,000, Vieja will need to make the market price of gold for the delivery of the agreed 100,000 ounces.

(However, in order to effect physical settlement the parties will need to use the provisions of Sub-Annex B of the Annex to the 2005 definitions, which relates to physically settled bullion transactions. The principal body of the 2005 definitions provides only for cash settlement of all transactions.)

10.   Article VII – Calculation of prices for commodity reference prices

This is the longest and probably most complex article of the 2005 definitions, and it has also undergone the most changes compared with the 1993 definitions and the 2000 supplement. It incorporates the entire Sub-Annex A of the Annex to the 2005 definitions, which forms part of Sections 7.1 and 7.2. Its six sub-sections can be divided into five different, albeit related, areas:

- incorporation of commodity reference prices of Sub-Annex A;
- Sub-Annex A of the Annex to the 2005 definitions;
- correction of the prices by the price source;
- market disruption events; and
- disruption fallbacks.

10.1   Incorporation and corrections of commodity reference prices

If the terms 'commodity reference price' or 'relevant price' appear anywhere in a transaction, the transaction incorporates by reference Sub-Annex A of the Annex to the 2005 definitions. Generally, the sub-annex should be viewed as being part of Sections 7.1 and 7.2 and forming an integral part of the main body of the 2005 definitions. The sub-annex includes hundreds of definitions as to how the price of a specified commodity is determined.

By contrast, the commodity reference prices were included in the principal body of the 1993 definitions. The 2005 version is different for two reasons:

- The inclusion of this very lengthy section in the annex made the main body of the 2005 definitions less bulky and more user-friendly; and
- The intention was that the annex would be amended from time to time to include new or updated definitions of the reference prices, and amending just the annex is easier and more transparent than changing the main body of the document. However, to date Sub-Annex A has been amended only once.

Section 7.2 (the part still included in the main body of the 2005 definitions) specifies that when the parties use the words 'commodity reference price' or 'relevant price', they will be deemed to have incorporated Sub-Annex A as amended through the trade date of the transaction. Therefore, all amendments to the sub-annex will automatically be deemed to be included for any transaction concluded after those amendments were made.

10.2   Sub-Annex A of the Annex to the 2005 definitions

Although this sub-annex is by far the longest part of the commodity documentation, its role is quite straightforward and its application does not cause any major difficulties in practice. It is divided into three sub-sections:

- Section 7.1 contains 196 pages of definitions of commodity reference prices, which cover the following classes of asset: agricultural products, energy, freight, metals, paper, and composite commodity indices. The main difference when compared with the 1993 definitions is the inclusion of some new definitions for agricultural products, coal, wet and dry freight, and composite commodity indices.
- Sections 7.2(a) and 7.2(b) include a few pages of definitions of the price sources (eg, Reuters and Telerate) and of the relevant exchanges (eg, the Baltic Exchange or Euronext Liffe) which are used in Section 7.1.
- Section 7.2(c) includes the 'commodity reference price framework', which facilitates the creation of new reference prices, and it also has various other related definitions.

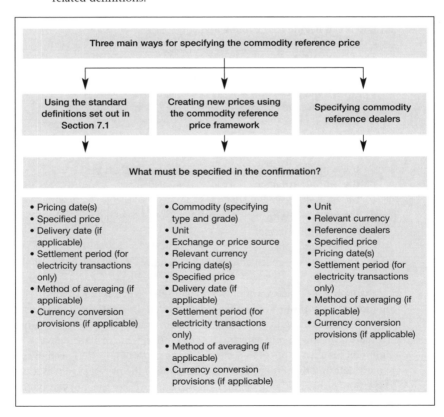

Sub-Annex A provides for three main methods for the parties to specify the commodity reference price for their transaction (see preceding diagram):

- The parties can select a commodity reference price from Section 7.1;
- The parties can create their own commodity reference price using the commodity reference price framework; or
- The parties can elect 'commodity reference dealers', in which case the price will be determined using quotations from four leading dealers.

(a)   *Determining the commodity reference price by using the definitions set out in Section 7.1*

This is the simplest method provided by the 2005 definitions for determining a price for a given pricing date. The parties need to specify one out of hundreds of commodity reference prices set out in Section 7.1, such as White Maize SAFEX for corn or Jet Fuel-Jet 55 Gulf Coast (Waterborne)-Platts US for jet fuel.

However, it is not enough just to specify one of the price codes. The definitions in Section 7.1 make reference to various terms which will be unique for each transaction. Therefore, the parties will always need to provide the details of the 'specified price' and the 'pricing dates' in each confirmation.

The term 'pricing date' has been explained in section 9.2 of this chapter. In turn, the 'specified price' is just a type of price which is published or announced on a given day and it can be one of the following:

- the high price;
- the low price;
- the average of the high price and the low price;
- the closing price;
- the opening price;
- the asked price;
- the bid price;
- the average of the bid price and the asked price;
- the settlement price;
- the official settlement price;
- the official price;
- the morning fixing;
- the afternoon fixing;
- the spot price; or
- any other type specified in the confirmation.

Therefore, the parties will need to consider what types of price of a given commodity are published or announced on a given day, and which one is used for the purposes of calculating the relevant price on the pricing dates for their transaction.

Apart from the pricing date and specified price, which will be relevant for all the commodity reference prices in Section 7.1, the parties may often need to specify the delivery date and the settlement period for some of the prices, as well as the currency conversion provisions and method of averaging. These are not always necessary, though.

As referred to above, the currency conversion provisions are necessary only if a commodity reference price is published in a currency other than the agreed currency of payment. In turn, the method of averaging is relevant only when there is more than one pricing date for a calculation period or a payment date, and the parties would like to amend the default clauses of the 2005 definitions that provide for averaging by way of unweighted arithmetic mean.

The concept of 'delivery date' needs further explanation. The exchanges and the public sources (ie, the places where the prices are published or announced other than exchanges, such as a publication or a magazine) often quote prices of the futures contract on the relevant commodities and those prices depend on the length of the relevant futures contract. The delivery date is the date or month for the delivery of the underlying commodity under that futures contract. Therefore, the delivery date helps to identify the relevant futures contract and, consequently, the price applicable to a given transaction.

The 2005 definitions provide three ways of defining the 'delivery date':
- The parties can specify either a date or a month and year in the relevant confirmation.
- The parties can specify a nearby month for the expiration of the relevant futures contract. For example, if they specify 'first nearby month', the delivery date will be the month of expiration of the first futures contract to expire following the relevant pricing date. Alternatively, the 'eighth nearby month' means that the delivery date will be the month of expiration of the eighth futures contract to expire following the relevant pricing date.
- The parties can agree any other way for determining the delivery date in the confirmation.

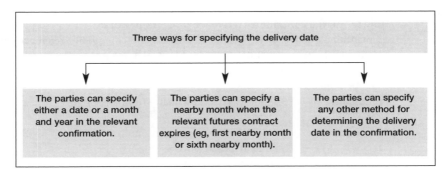

Finally, the parties may need to specify the 'settlement period', but only if they enter into a transaction referencing electricity. As trading in electricity often takes place only on certain days and at certain times during a calculation period, the parties have to specify the applicable dates and times in the confirmation.

(b)   *Determining the commodity reference price by using the commodity reference price framework*

From the legal and documentation perspective, the commodity reference price framework is the most interesting part of this sub-annex, even though it is identical to Section 7.1(c)(ii) of the 1993 definitions and Section 7.1(d)(ii) of the 2000 Supplement. To quote the introduction to the sub-annex, it "allows parties to specify a few key terms in order to tailor a commodity reference price for use in the relevant agreement or confirmation". It can be helpful when a reference price that the parties want to use is not set out in Section 7.1 or when the definitions set out in that section are no longer accurate.

To create a new commodity reference price under the commodity reference price framework, the parties need to specify the following details in the confirmation:

- the relevant commodity (including the type or grade of that commodity);
- the relevant unit (eg, pounds, kilograms, inches, gigajoules, megawatt hours);
- the relevant exchange (if the price of that commodity is announced or published on an exchange), or the relevant price source (if such price is not published or announced on an exchange – for example, a publication or a magazine);
- the relevant currency;
- the specified price (whether the price used in a particular transaction shall be, for example, the high price on the designated date, the opening price, the ask price, the bid price, the morning fixing); and
- if applicable, the delivery date.

Once it is understood how to create commodity reference prices, it is also much easier to understand the reference prices set out in Section 7.1 in Sub-Annex A. Any of the reference prices from Sub-Annex A can also be presented in the format provided for by the commodity reference price framework.

How to use the commodity reference price framework

As mentioned above, it is possible to convert the commodity reference prices defined in Section 7.1 into the format of the commodity reference price framework. For example, the price of corn with the reference White Maize SAFEX could be presented as:

Commodity:	Grade-WM1 yellow maize from any origin
Unit:	Metric tonne
Exchange:	SAFEX (ie, South African Futures Exchange), as displayed on Reuters Screen page 0#MAW
Relevant currency:	South African rand
Specified price:	[this will need to be decided by the parties in the confirmation – for example, the official settlement price]

The parties will also need to give the details of the specified price if they just relied on the commodity reference price as per Section 7.1.

Another example would be the commodity reference price of for jet fuel under the code Jet Fuel-Jet 55 Gulf Coast (Waterborne)-Platts US, which could be translated into:

Commodity:	Jet 55 jet fuel

Unit:	Gallon
Public source:	Platts US, published under the heading "Gulf Coast 7.8 RVP Waterborne: JET 55"
Relevant currency:	US dollars
Specified price:	[this will need to be decided by the parties in the confirmation]

(c)   ***Determining the commodity reference price by using the commodity reference dealer provisions***

Finally, Sub-annex A allows the parties to specify the commodity reference price via commodity reference dealers. If the parties decide to do this, the price for a pricing date will be determined on the basis of four quotations provided by four reference dealers (or bullion reference dealers, in the case of bullion transactions). If the parties elect this method, they will also need to specify the following details in the confirmation:

- the relevant unit (eg, pounds, kilograms, inches, gigajoules, megawatt hours);
- the names of the reference dealers; and
- the relevant currency.

If the parties specify commodity reference dealers as the basis for the commodity reference price but fail to specify the reference dealers, the calculation agent will contact four leading dealers in the relevant commodity market. If the calculation agent obtains four quotations, it will discard the highest and the lowest and use the arithmetic mean of the remaining two figures to determine the relevant price. If the calculation agent obtains only three figures, then it will discard the highest and the lowest one, and the remaining value will be the relevant price for that pricing date. Finally, if there are two or fewer quotations, it will be deemed that the price cannot be determined.

10.3   Corrections of the prices by the price source

Section 7.3 covers the situation when a price used by the calculation agent to determine the relevant price is subsequently corrected by the person or body that originally published that price. If such correction has occurred within 30 days of the original publication (or 90 days in case of weather index derivatives transactions), either party may notify the other of the correction and the amount that is payable as a result. The notification must occur not later than 30 days (or 90 days for weather index derivatives transactions) after the correction has been made.

The relevant party must then make the relevant payment within three business days of the effective date of the notice. Such payment must also include any interest for the period from and including the day on which the payment was originally made, up to but excluding the day of payment following the correction. The interest is calculated by reference to the spot offered rate for deposits in the payments currency in the London interbank market as at 11:00am, London time, on the relevant payment day.

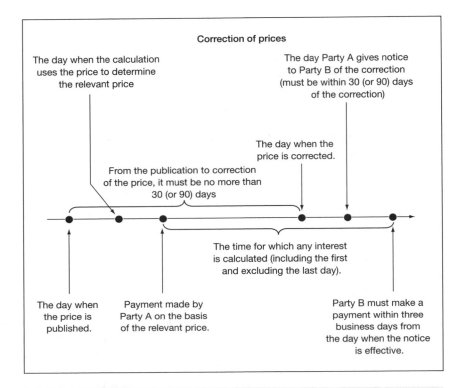

Correction of prices

The day when the calculation uses the price to determine the relevant price

The day Party A gives notice to Party B of the correction (must be within 30 (or 90) days of the correction)

The day when the price is corrected.

From the publication to correction of the price, it must be no more than 30 (or 90) days

The time for which any interest is calculated (including the first and excluding the last day).

The day when the price is published.

Payment made by Party A on the basis of the relevant price.

Party B must make a payment within three business days from the day when the notice is effective.

Hypothetical example: Morland Corporation

Morland Corporation is an international corporation which owns thousands of hectares of fields with orange trees. It is concerned that the price of orange juice may go down and it would like to hedge its position. For this reason, Morland enters into a commodity swap transaction on frozen concentrated orange juice with Flatland International on January 4 2010 on the total notional amount of 1 million pounds-weight of deliverable-grade orange solids. The parties agree that Alacant Brokers will act as the calculation agent, and that the transaction will terminate on January 4 2011.

They choose Frozen Concentrated Orange Juice No1 – NYBOT as the commodity reference price. According to Sub-Annex A, the price of the commodity is made public by the New York Board of Trade and made public on Reuters Screen Page 0#OJ.

On January 4 2010 the price of orange juice is $1.50 per pound. The parties agreed that if the price rises above $1.50, Morland will make a payment to Flatland. However, if the price drops below this level, Flatland will make a payment to Morland.

One year later

On January 4 2011 the price quoted on the relevant Reuters page is equal to $1.40.

On the same date, Alacant calculates that Flatland needs to make a floating amount payment to Morland given by:

Floating amount = ($1.50 per pound – $1.40 per pound) × 1 million pounds
= $100,000

Accordingly, Flatland makes this payment to Morland on January 6 2011.

However, suppose that the price of $1.40 was published by mistake, and it is corrected on January 6 2011 to be $1.55. Flatland spots this only on February 2 2011 and sends a notice to Morland on February 3 2011. In the notice, Flatland specifies that the notice is effective as of February 3. The provisions of Section 7.2 apply considering that:

- there were only two business days between publication of the wrong figure and the correct one (ie, less than 30 calendar days); and
- there were only 29 calendar days between the correction of the figure and the sending of the notice by Flatland (ie, less than 30 days).

This means that Morland must repay the $100,000 that it received from Flatland and, because the price moved against Morland, it must also make the following payment:

Floating amount = ($1.55 per pound – $1.50 per pound) × 1 million pounds
= $50,000

Therefore, Morland must pay to Flatland the money it received originally (ie $100,000), together with the money that it should have paid at that time (ie. $50,000), plus any accrued interest. The interest is to be the spot offered rate for deposits in US dollars in the London interbank market as at approximately 11:00am, London time, calculated from, and including, January 6 2011 (ie, the day that Flatland made the original payment to Morland) to, but excluding, the date that Morland actually makes a payment to Flatland. As Flatland specified February 3 2011 as the effective date of the notice, Morland has until February 7 2011 (ie three business days later) to transfer $150,000 plus interest to Flatland.

10.4 Market disruption events

When the 2005 definitions were being drafted, the working party spent a considerable time redrafting, amending and changing the market disruption events that were set out in the 1993 definitions and the 2000 supplement. The results are contained in Section 7.4 within Article VII. This section:

- sets out the new or revised market disruption events; and
- regulates and sets out what happens if an applicable market disruption event occurs.

We have divided this sub-section of the chapter accordingly.

(a) Description of market disruption events

The 2005 definitions provide for six standard market-disruption events: 'price source disruption', 'trading disruption', 'disappearance of commodity reference price', 'material change in formula', 'material change in content' and 'tax disruption'. Furthermore, the parties can specify and define in the confirmation any 'additional market disruption events'.

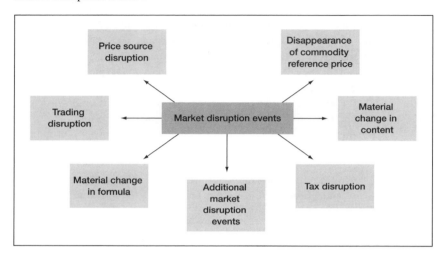

(i) Price source disruption

The first listed market disruption event, 'price source disruption', can apply if the relevant price is determined by an exchange or by any other price source. It occurs when one of four events materialises:

- The price source fails to publish or announce the specified price (or the information necessary for determining the specified price) for the relevant commodity reference price;
- The price source is temporarily or permanently unavailable, or has been discontinued;
- The calculation agent could not obtain at least three quotations from reference dealers (this applies only if the parties have elected commodity reference dealers as the basis for the commodity reference price); or
- The specified price in respect of the relevant commodity reference price differs from the specified price, determined in accordance with commodity reference dealers, by a price materiality percentage. (Naturally, this applies only if the parties have specified the price materiality percentage in the confirmation.)

(ii) Trading disruption

The next market disruption event, 'trading disruption', is new as at 2005. It replaces two disruption events included in the previous definitions: trading suspensions and trading limitation. 'Trading disruption' is defined as "any material suspension of, or any material limitation on, trading in the futures contract or commodity on the exchange or in any additional futures contracts, options contract or commodity on any exchange specified in the confirmation".

Unlike the old definitions of 'trading suspension' and 'trading limitation', the new event clarifies what the key phrases 'material suspension' and 'material limitation' actually mean. Accordingly, a suspension can be considered 'material' in only two circumstances:

- All trading in the relevant futures contracts or the commodity has been suspended for the entire pricing date; or
- All trading on such futures contracts or the commodity is suspended subsequent to opening, provided that:
  - trading does not recommence before the scheduled closing time; and
  - the suspension is announced less than one hour before trading starts.

A limitation of trading will be considered 'material' for the purposes of trading disruption only if:

- the relevant exchange establishes limits on the range within which the price of the futures contract or the commodity can fluctuate; and
- the closing or settlement price of the futures contract or the commodity on such day is at the upper or lower limit of that range.

(iii)   *Disappearance of commodity reference price*
The 'disappearance of commodity reference price' market disruption event has also been changed considerably from the previous version. It is now defined as the occurrence of one of three events:

- the permanent discontinuation of trading in the relevant futures contracts on the relevant exchange;
- the disappearance of the relevant commodity or of the trading in that commodity; or
- the disappearance or permanent discontinuance or unavailability of the specified commodity reference price.

In relation to the third item of the definition, a market disruption event will still occur even if the source of the price is still available or the related futures contracts are still being traded.

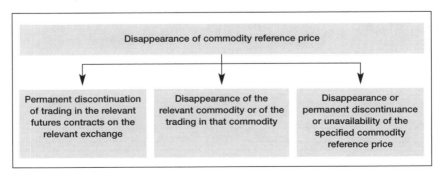

(iv) *Material change in formula or content*
The next two events listed above – 'material change in formula' and 'material change in content' – are self-explanatory and have not been changed when compared with the 1993 definitions.

A material change in formula occurs when there is a material change in the formula or method of calculating the relevant commodity reference price. A material change in content occurs if there is any material change in the content, composition or constitution of the commodity or the related futures contract.

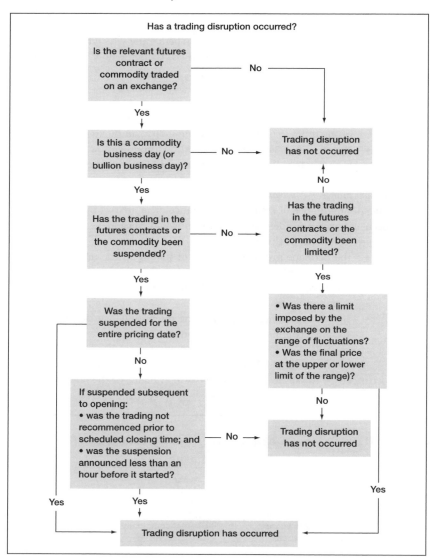

(v) *Tax disruption*

The 'tax disruption' market disruption event has not changed and is defined as any imposition, change or removal of any tax on the relevant commodity which would affect the price of the transaction.

(vi) *Additional market disruption events*

As mentioned above, the parties are also free to define any additional market disruption events. If they decide to disapply the standard market disruption events and use their additional market disruption events instead, they need to be careful when drafting the confirmation. If they specify just 'not applicable' next to the field 'market disruption events' in the confirmation, the 2005 definitions could operate also to disapply any additional market disruption events.[4] Instead, we recommend setting out a full clause stating the intention of the parties.

(vii) *Removal of* de minimis *trading event*

It is also worth noting that the old market disruption event of *de minimis* trading has not been included in the 2005 definitions, as ISDA's working party agreed that it is no longer used in practice and therefore no longer relevant.

(b) **Application and deemed application of the market disruption events provisions**

Under the 2005 definitions, the parties need not specify all market disruption events in order for them to apply. Instead, Section 7.4(d) of Article VII lists events which will be deemed to apply to any transaction other than a bullion transaction or a weather derivative transaction.[5]

Therefore, unless the parties specify otherwise, all market disruption events apart from tax disruption will apply to any transaction other than a bullion transaction or a weather index derivative transaction. However, if the parties specifically list some of the market disruption events to the exclusion of others, then only those events specifically listed in the confirmation will apply.

The definitions also make clear that if the parties elect for the standard market disruption events to apply, they can still designate in the confirmation those commodities for which a material change in formula and a material change in content will not apply.

For a bullion transaction, only the following market disruption events will be deemed to apply: price source disruption, trading disruption and disappearance of commodity reference price. As bullion transactions are standard in the market, the ISDA working party has decided that there is no need for the inclusion of material change in formula and material change in content disruptions to those trades.

---

4 This is due to the last sentence in Section 7.4(c), which is somewhat peculiarly drafted: "The term 'not applicable' when specified in conjunction with the term 'market disruption event' means that the calculation of a relevant price will not be adjusted as a result of any market disruption event (in which case there would also be no cause to specify any additional market disruption events)".

5 Although Section 7.4(d)(i) provides that those events will apply to all transactions other than bullion transactions and does not mention any weather index derivatives transactions, the disruption events for weather index derivatives transactions are separately listed in Section 11 (Sub-annex C) of the 2005 definitions.

The 2005 definitions also clarified what happens if one event is both a market disruption event (or an additional market disruption event) and a termination event under the ISDA Master Agreement. Unless the parties decide otherwise, such event will be deemed only a market disruption event (or an additional market disruption event). However, this is subject to any limiting provisions in the relevant ISDA Master Agreement.

Finally, the last paragraph of Section 7.4 stresses that if the relevant price is unavailable, the parties should first use the fallback provisions which allow for an alternative way of determining the price. Only if this is not available can the parties terminate the transaction.

Deemed application of market disruption events

Market disruption events deemed applicable to all transactions (other than bullion transactions and weather index derivatives transactions, and unless the parties specify otherwise):	Market disruption events deemed applicable to bullion transactions (unless the parties specify otherwise):
• price source disruption; • trading disruption; • disappearance of commodity reference price; • material change in formula; • material change in content; and • tax disruption.	• price source disruption; • trading disruption and • disappearance of commodity reference price.

The parties have an option to disapply the material change in formula and material change in content to specific commodities.

(c) **Disruption fallbacks**

If a market disruption event occurs, the 2005 definitions provide that there will be consequences. These consequences are called 'disruption fallbacks'. The disruption fallbacks provide a basis for an alternative determination of the relevant prices for a transaction or, in certain cases, facilitate its termination once a market disruption event has occurred. Considering their importance in the transaction, the disruption fallbacks received plenty of attention from the ISDA working party which drafted the 2005 definitions.

Section 7.5 of Article VII is divided into three main areas:
- description of various disruption fallbacks available under the 2005 definitions;
- provisions regulating the deemed application of those fallbacks; and
- clauses for the general application of the disruption fallbacks.

(i) *Description of disruption fallbacks*

The 2005 definitions provide for seven standard disruption fallbacks:

- fallback reference dealers;
- fallback reference price;
- negotiated fallback;
- no-fault termination;
- postponement;
- calculation agent determination; and
- delayed publication or announcement.

The 2005 definitions have adopted a 'menu' approach here. The parties will specify the fallbacks that they want to apply in the order that they will apply. If the calculation agent is unable to obtain the relevant price using the first applicable disruption fallback, the next one will apply and so on. The final disruption fallback will provide for termination of the transaction.

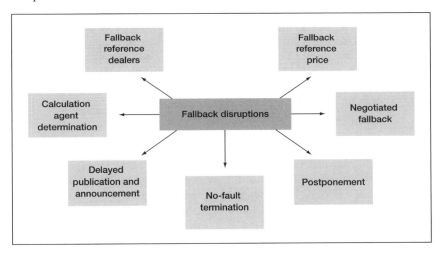

Under the 'fallback reference dealers' disruption fallback, the relevant price will be determined in accordance with the commodity reference price: commodity reference dealers. Obviously, it will not apply if 'commodity reference dealer' is already specified in the confirmation as the basis for the commodity reference price.

The parties can elect 'fallback reference price' as a disruption fallback. In that case, they will also need to specify an alternate commodity reference price. If this fallback applies and if the calculation agent is unable to determine the relevant price using the principal commodity reference price, the alternative commodity reference price will apply.

If the 'negotiated fallback' disruption fallback applies, the parties will negotiate with each other with a view to agreeing on the relevant price. If they have failed to agree the price before the fifth business day (or bullion business day, for bullion transactions) following the pricing date on which the market disruption occurred, the next applicable disruption fallback will apply.

The 'no-fault termination' disruption fallback provides for a termination of the transaction in accordance with the provisions of the relevant ISDA Master Agreement. Accordingly, the relevant market disruption event (or additional disruption event) will constitute a termination event, and the transaction will terminate as if 'illegality' or a *'force majeure'* (as defined in the relevant ISDA Master Agreement) applied. Both parties will be deemed affected parties (as defined in the relevant ISDA Master Agreement).

The 'calculation agent determination' disruption fallback gives the calculation agent a discretionary power to determine the relevant price. However, the calculation agent must take into consideration the latest available quotation for the relevant commodity reference price and any other information that it deems relevant in good faith.

The remaining two fallback disruptions – 'postponement' and 'delayed publication or announcement' – are the most complex in their application, not least because they appear confusingly similar.

'Postponement' was included in previous versions of the definitions, but the 2005 version sets out its application in more detail. If postponement applies, the pricing date will be deemed to be the first succeeding commodity business day (or bullion business day, for bullion transactions) on which the market disruption event (or additional market disruption event) ceases to exist. However, if the market disruption event exists for a number of days equal to the number of 'maximum days of disruption', the next fallback disruption will apply.

Therefore, when electing postponement, the parties should also specify the 'maximum days of disruption' in the confirmation. Considering that the result of postponement is a change in the pricing date, this may also disrupt other payment clauses in the confirmation. For example, it may be impossible to calculate the floating amount as of the original pricing date; therefore, Section 7.5 of Article VII specifies that any determination of the in-the-money amount or floating amount will also be postponed to the same extent. Furthermore, if the other party to the transaction was supposed to make a payment on the same date that the postponed floating amount would have been payable, all such other payments will also be postponed.

The 'delayed publication or announcement' disruption fallback has been introduced in the 2005 definitions and, similar to postponement, it also contemplates that a disrupted price may become available with the period of the maximum days of disruption (as specified in the confirmation). However, unlike postponement, the delayed publication or announcement disruption fallback is retrospective and it preserves the original pricing date (the pricing announcement for which has been delayed). When it applies, the parties hope that the relevant price will eventually be published in respect of that initial pricing date.

Similar to postponement, the delay determining the relevant price may cause disruptions to other payment dates. The determination of the in-the-money amount and the floating amount, as well as the payments of any other amounts payable on the same date, will therefore be delayed to the same extent.

(ii)   *Application and deemed application of disruption fallback provisions*
As with market disruption events, the parties need not specify any disruption fallbacks for certain disruption fallbacks to be deemed applicable. Selected disruption fallbacks are deemed to automatically apply in the order and manner as provided in Section 7.5(d)(i) of Article VII.

The list of deemed fallbacks was drafted by the ISDA working party on the basis of the then-current market practice (or proposed market practice) and applies to all transactions other than weather index derivatives transactions. Although the working group initially considered creating a separate fallback 'waterfall' for bullion transactions, it decided that this could be best dealt with by the inclusion of separate bullion disruption events in Sub-Annex B (bullion transactions), which would apply only to physically settled bullion trades.

If the parties have not provided for any fallbacks in the confirmation, the following fallback disruption will apply to the relevant transaction in this order:

- fallback reference price;
- concurrently:
  - delayed publication or announcement;
  - postponement; and
  - negotiated fallback;
- fallback reference dealers; and
- negotiated fallback.

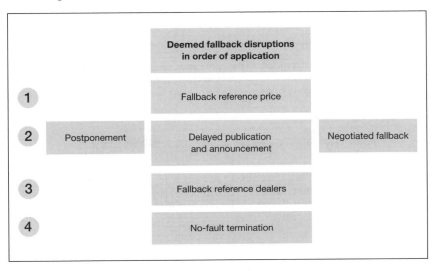

Naturally, the first provision, 'fallback reference price', will apply only if the parties have specified an alternative commodity reference price. Its operation is generally straightforward and its main advantage is that the parties will know almost immediately whether this provision is capable of yielding the relevant price. If it is not, the next fallback will apply.

The second fallback – the concurrent operation of three disruption provisions –

is complex, but it works quite well in practice. When it applies, the parties can start negotiating with a view of agreeing the relevant price under 'negotiated fallback'. If the parties reach a settlement before a price is obtained under 'postponement' or 'delayed publication or announcement', the agreed price will apply as at the relevant pricing date. However, if postponement or delayed publication or announcement yields the relevant price before then, negotiated fallback provisions will cease to operate.

In relation to the deemed application of the fallback provisions under Section 7.5(d)(i) only, the 'maximum days of disruption' for both 'postponement' and 'delayed publication or announcement' is two commodity business day (or bullion business days, for bullion transactions) for both, unless otherwise specified. In the case of conflict between the two fallback provisions, 'delayed publication or announcement' takes precedence over 'postponement'. This means that if the parties have obtained the relevant price through postponement first, they should wait until the end of the period of maximum days of disruption to see whether delayed publication or announcement could also yield the relevant price. If they have obtained a delayed price by that time, it will apply notwithstanding that a postponed price was published earlier. However, if by the end of the period of maximum days of disruption only the postponed price has been published, it will apply as the relevant price for that pricing date.

Whereas the default period for the 'maximum days of disruption' is two commodity business days (or bullion business days) under Section 7.5(d)(i), the standard of operation for negotiated fallback, as described above, is five business days

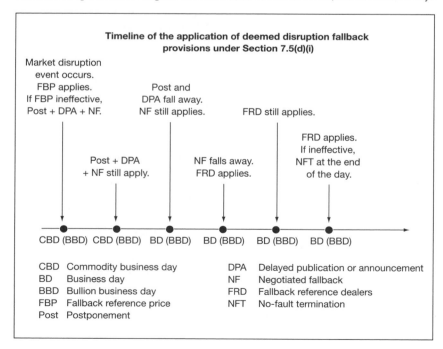

Timeline of the application of deemed disruption fallback provisions under Section 7.5(d)(i)

CBD	Commodity business day	DPA	Delayed publication or announcement
BD	Business day	NF	Negotiated fallback
BBD	Bullion business day	FRD	Fallback reference dealers
FBP	Fallback reference price	NFT	No-fault termination
Post	Postponement		

or bullion business days. Therefore, when all three fallbacks operate simultaneously, there is a potential timing mismatch.

The 2005 definitions solved this by specifying that if negotiated fallback applies simultaneously with both or either postponement and delayed publication or announcement, then negotiated fallback will cease to operate on the first business day (or bullion business day) after the expiry of the 'maximum days of disruption' relating to postponement and delayed publication or announcement. This means that only on the second business day (or bullion business day) after the period of the maximum days of disruption will the parties be able to move on to the next disruption fallback.

Finally, the last two deemed fallback provisions are 'fallback reference dealers' and 'no-fault termination'. Accordingly, the calculation agent will have three business days (or bullion business days) to obtain at least three quotations from the reference dealers. If it does not manage to get those, the transaction will terminate.

Hypothetical example: Cartagena Drinks plc

Cartagena Drinks plc is a dairy producer operating throughout the United States. It hedged itself against the price of milk rising too quickly by entering into a commodity swap agreement on Class III milk on May 26 2009 with Lechia Corporation. Under the terms of the swap, Lechia would make a floating-amount payment to Cartagena half-yearly, starting from June 1 2009, if Class III milk was trading above a set level at the end of the calculation period.

The parties specified the commodity reference price as Milk Class III CME. They included no provisions relating to market disruption events or disruption fallbacks in the confirmation, and specified no value for the maximum days of disruption.

Monday June 1 2009: The selected commodity reference price is defined by reference to the Chicago Mercantile Exchange (CME), or its successor. On June 1 2009 trading on the CME was suspended at 2:30pm due to a serious fault in the operating system and it did not recommence prior to the exchange's scheduled closing time. Thus, the criteria set out in Section 7.4(c)(ii)(A)(2) were met for the disruption to be classed as a trading disruption.

As the parties specified no market disruption events, Section 7.4(d) kicked in and various disruption events were deemed to have been specified for this trade. Trading disruption was included among those default market disruption events. As the parties specified no disruption fallbacks, the default fallback set out in Section 7.5(d)(i) was deemed to apply.

The first fallback is fallback reference price. However, Cartagena and Lechia did not specify an alternative commodity reference price, so this first fallback automatically fell away. This meant that postponement, delayed publication or announcement and negotiated fallback all began to apply on June 1.

Tuesday June 2 2009: The CME did not open for business on Tuesday June 2 so it was not possible to determine the price using postponement or delayed publication or announcement. The parties negotiated to agree the relevant price, but could not settle.

However, if the exchange had opened for business on Tuesday June 2 and it had quoted the price of milk as of 9:00am on June 2 (but not with respect to June 1), this would have meant that the parties had obtained the relevant price under the postponement disruption fallback. At that point the parties could stop negotiating, as the negotiated fallback would cease to apply.

Nevertheless, Cartagena and Lechia woud still need to wait until the end of Tuesday to see whether the exchange would publish the relevant price of milk as of June 1. If the exchange did not do so, the postponed price would apply and the pricing date would be postponed from June 1 until June 2.

Changing the scenario further, if the exchange were to publish the price of milk as of Monday June 1 at 4:00pm on Tuesday, that price would be the relevant price. The pricing date would still remain June 1 2009. However, the relevant settlement date or payment date would be delayed until June 2.

Wednesday June 3 2009: The parties did not obtain a price pursuant to postponed or delayed publication or announcement on June 2. Therefore, both of those disruption fallbacks ceased to operate, but the parties could still reach an agreement pursuant to negotiated fallback.

Thursday June 4 2009: Cartagena and Lechia could not reach an agreement as to the price by the end of June 3. This meant that negotiated fallback fell away and the next applicable disruption fallback (ie, fallback reference dealers) kicked in.

The parties did not specify reference dealers in the confirmation. This meant that the calculation agent had to approach four leading dealers in the market for Class III milk and obtain all least three quotations for the price of milk as of June 1.

Friday June 5 2009: By the end of Friday, the calculation agent had obtained only two quotations for the price of milk as of June 1.

Monday June 8 2009: Saturday June 6 and Sunday June 7 were not business days, so they were disregarded. Monday June 8 was the final date for the calculation agent to obtain three quotations for the price of milk. It failed to do so by the end of Monday. This meant that the transaction terminated at the end of the day in accordance with the no-fault termination fallback.

(iii)   *Other clauses regulating the general application of the fallback provisions*
The deemed provisions, as explained above, will apply only if the parties have not specified any disruption fallbacks in the confirmation themselves. Section 7.5 of Article VII also includes some clauses of general application regulating the operation of fallback disruptions if the deemed provisions are not used.

Even if the deemed provisions do not apply, the parties retain the option to elect for postponement and delayed publication or announcement to apply concurrently. In such a case, delayed announcement or publication will take precedence over postponement, as explained above. Furthermore, if the parties specify both or either of the two disruption fallbacks (to operate either separately or simultaneously), negotiated fallback will automatically apply concurrently with such fallbacks.

However, the automatic inclusion of negotiated fallback will apply only if the parties have not referred at all to this fallback in the confirmation. If they specifically deselected it or if they elected to use it at some other stage, such provisions will apply instead.

Finally, the no-fault termination will apply to all transactions as the ultimate fallback. A transaction will terminate in accordance with its provision even if the parties have not specified it in the confirmation, provided that no other fallback manages to yield the relevant price.

11. Article VIII – Commodity options

An option is a privately negotiated contract between two counterparties. Generally, the buyer of an option acquires a right to buy from (or sell to) the seller of the option a defined amount of assets at a specified price. However, the 2005 definitions are different from other sets of ISDA definitions in this respect, and the option buyer will never actually acquire a right to receive (or sell) any of the underlying commodity assets. Instead, on the expiry of the option, one party will only make a payment to the other.

Although the parties can provide for physical settlement if they incorporate the relevant sub-annexes to the 2005 definitions, Article VIII does not really anticipate this type of settlement in its ordinary sense (ie, the actual transfer of the underlying asset). As noted above, the same applies for swaps or any other instruments governed only by the principal body of the 2005 definitions, so this is a consistent theme throughout the document.

The eight sections of Article VIII cover the following areas:
- the description of an option and the payment of premium;
- the description of different types of option;
- terms relating to the exercise of options; and
- terms relating to the settlement of options.

11.1 Description of an option and the payment of premium

An 'option' is defined in Section 8.1 of Article VIII as a contract between the commodity option seller to the commodity option buyer, which can take one of four forms:
- a grant by the commodity option seller to the commodity option buyer of a right to receive the cash settlement amount (this term is explained later in this section) in respect of the transaction on the settlement date;
- a swaption;
- a right granted to the commodity option buyer of a right to receive any other or contingent rights as specified in the confirmation; or
- an instrument combining any of the three other forms.

A swaption is an option given to the option buyer which allows it either to:
- enter into a swap identified in the confirmation (ie, the underlying transaction); or
- receive a cash settlement amount in respect of that underlying transaction on the settlement date.

The buyer of a swaption has the right to cause the underlying transaction to be effective only if the parties elect 'physical settlement' or 'contract settlement' as applicable. Otherwise, the swaption buyer will only be able to receive the cash settlement amount.

However, the principal body of the 2005 definitions does not allow for physical settlement in the sense that the parties to a transaction would actually exchange commodities. Therefore, the physical settlement of a swaption means only that the buyer will have a right to enter into the underlying swap transaction.

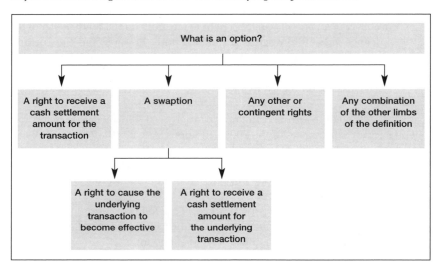

Considering that the 2005 definitions cover a variety of different types of asset class, option transactions relating to certain commodities have their own specific rules and definitions, set out in the annexes to the definitions. Therefore, the following transactions have been excluded from the scope of Article VIII: bullion options, bullion swaptions, weather index call options/caps, weather index put options/floors, NBP options and ZBT options. Each of these is analysed in detail in other chapters of this book.

To enter into a transaction and compensate the commodity option seller for providing the option, a commodity option buyer will normally pay to the seller a specified amount of money ('total premium'). Alternatively, the parties can provide in the confirmation a value for 'premium per unit', which would then be multiplied by the relevant notional quantity to give the 'total premium'. The confirmation should also specify when such payment (or payments) should be made (the 'premium payment date(s)').

11.2   Types of option

There are two main classifications of option transaction. An option could be either a put option or a call option. It could also be either a Bermudan, American, Asian or European option.

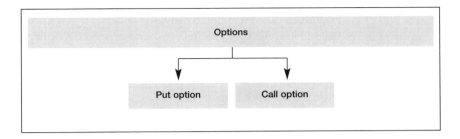

Although the main body of the 2005 definitions does not allow for the actual transfer of commodities, it is easier to understand the difference between a put and a call option if we assume, for now, that options are physically settled. In that case, a physically settled call option would give the buyer a right to purchase a specified commodity from its counterparty at the strike price or a strike price per unit (as specified by the parties in the relevant confirmation). In turn, a put option would give the buyer a right to sell that commodity at a strike price.

In a cash-settled transaction governed by the 2005 definitions, the buyer of a put option will not actually have a right to sell the specified commodity, but it gets the economic equivalent of the same. Instead of selling the commodity, the put option buyer has a right to demand a payment from its counterparty if the floating price (ie, the price of the given commodity on a given day) is lower than the strike price (as provided in the confirmation). Conversely, a call option allows its holder to demand a payment when the actual price (the floating price) is higher than the strike price. (For a fuller description of floating price, please see section 9 of this chapter.)

Another way to categorise different types of option is according to when they can be exercised. The 2005 definitions cover four of the most common types: American, Asian, Bermudan and European.

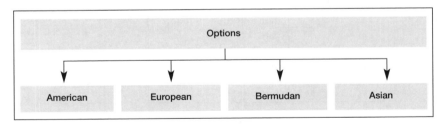

An American option can be exercised on any day during the exercise period (such period as specified in the confirmation). Such day, which can occur at any time before the option's expiry, is called the exercise date if the option is actually exercised on this date (or is deemed to be exercised). However, a European and an Asian option can be exercised only on the day of their expiry (expiration date).

Whereas an American option can be exercised at any time and a European or Asian option only on the expiration date, a Bermudan option is a halfway house. It can be exercised only on specific days during the terms of a transaction as provided in the confirmation (called potential exercise dates), and on the expiration date.

The 2005 definitions are quite imprecise and could suggest that the definition of the exercise date applies only to American options. However, it is a better view that a day on which any option is exercised is called an exercise date in respect of that option. Therefore, the expiration day of an American or Asian option is also an exercise date if the option is actually exercised on this date (or is deemed to be exercised). Article VIII demands that an exercise date be a day which is both:

- a commodity business day; and
- a day when commercial banks are open for business in the city where the option seller is located (seller business day).

Although both European and Asian options can be exercised on the expiration date, the difference between them is quite substantial. In the case of a European (but also a Bermuda or American) option, the calculation agent uses the price of the relevant commodity on the exercise date as the floating price. However, for an Asian option, the calculation agent, when determining the floating price, uses the unweighted arithmetic mean of the relevant prices for each pricing date during the calculation period. Therefore, the value of the Asian option is effectively calculated by reference to the average price of the commodity throughout the term of the transaction.

Types of option	Day when option is exercisable	Days relevant for calculation of the relevant prices
American	Each day during the exercise period	Exercise date (the day when the option is exercised)
European	Expiration date	Expiration date
Bermudan	Each potential exercise date and the expiration date	Exercise date
Asian	Expiration date	Each pricing date in calculation period

11.3 Terms relating to the exercise of options

The main terms relating to the exercise of different types of option have already been explained and analysed in the section above. However, Article VIII also includes some key clauses from a practical perspective.

Section 8.5 provides that automatic exercise will apply to any option unless the parties specify otherwise. This means that the option will be deemed to be exercised at the close of the exercise period for that transaction (ie, the last possible moment when the option could be exercised). However, automatic exercise will not apply to a swaption to cause the underlying transaction to apply.

By comparison, automatic exercise is not deemed to apply for an option governed by the 2002 ISDA Equity Definitions. However, it is generally common practice on the market always to specify automatic exercise as applicable and that is why the working parties included this in the 2005 definitions. After all, the commercial rationale behind an option is to get the benefit of the rising (or falling) prices, without taking any economic risk if the markets are going the other way. Therefore, the default application of automatic exercise makes perfect sense from this perspective.

Unlike the 2002 ISDA Equity Definitions, the 2005 definitions do not give the option buyer a right to disapply automatic exercise during the term of the transaction.

Unless automatic exercise applies to an option, the option buyer can exercise only by giving a notice of exercise to the other party. Such notice can be given orally over the phone and, to be effective, it must be given to the option seller during the hours specified in the confirmation on a seller business day. For an American and a Bermuda option, if the notice is given after the latest time specified, it will be deemed to have been received on the next seller business day in the exercise period. Once served, the notice is irrevocable and it is effective once actually received by the seller.

Thus, the parties should be particularly careful when drafting confirmations for Bermuda options. For example, let us assume that under a Bermuda option the potential exercise dates are March 15 2010 and June 15 2010 and the option buyer must give notice to the option seller by 4:00pm on the relevant day. If the option buyer serves the notice at 4.30pm on March 15, because of the slightly peculiar way the 2005 definitions are drafted, the seller could treat the option as exercised as of June 15. This is particularly dangerous considering that the notice of exercise is irrevocable.

If written confirmation is specified as applicable in the confirmation or if the option seller demands it following the notice of exercise, the buyer must execute a written confirmation setting out the details of the notice. It can be delivered by fax transmission and it must be delivered within one seller business day following the date on which the notice of exercise becomes effective.

11.4 Terms relating to the settlement of options

Under Section 8.7 of Article VIII, on each settlement date for an option transaction, the seller pays to the buyer the cash settlement amount. If the parties are entering into a swaption, they must specify how this amount should be determined in the confirmation. In relation to other options, the following formula will apply, unless specifically amended:

Cash settlement amount = notional quantity × strike price differential

'Strike price differential' is, in turn, defined thus:
- for a call option, an amount which is the excess of the relevant floating price over the strike price; and
- for a put option, an amount which is the excess of the strike price over the relevant floating price.

However, the strike price differential must be a positive number. If it is negative, the option buyer will make no profit from the exercise of the option. Accordingly, the option seller need not make any payments in respect of the cash settlement amount in that case.

> **Hypothetical example: Javier Plantations Corp**
> Javier Plantations Corp owns sugar cane plantations in Latin America and it is concerned that the price of sugar may go down from the current high price of $350 per tonne. It would like to hedge against this risk, but it does not want to enter into a swap, as it would then have to give up the money it makes if the prices continue to rise. It decided to enter into a cash-settled Asian put option with Barbastro Investments Partners, a hedge fund. They choose the commodity reference price to be White Sugar Euronext Liffe, the notional quantity as 100,000 tonnes, and the calculation period will run from March 12 to November 17 2010. November 17 would be the expiration date for the transaction and the strike price is agreed to be $340.
>
> Until late August the price of sugar keeps rising to reach the level of $387 per tonne on July 21. However, it then emerges that there is an oversupply of sugar on the markets and the price starts falling suddenly, until it reaches $284 on November 17 2010.
>
> The calculation agent takes the price of sugar on each commodity business day from March 12 to November 17 and calculates that the unweighted average price during the calculation period was $338.
>
> This means that Barbastro must make the following payment to Javier:
>
> Cash settlement amount = notional amount × strike price difference
>
> Strike price difference is equal to the excess of the strike price over the relevant floating price. Therefore, it is equal to only $2 ($340 – $338). Thus we have:
>
> Cash settlement amount = 100,000 × $2 = $200,000
>
> This means that, as a result of the fall in the price of sugar, Barbastro must pay $200,000 to Javier.

12. Article IX – rounding

The rounding-up provisions have been introduced in the 2005 definitions for the first time. They apply to all transactions other than weather index derivatives transactions, and they provide for the rounding-up of all fixed amounts, floating amounts and cash settlement amounts to the nearest unit of the relevant currency. They also specify that each half of a unit will also be rounded up.

Both Section 9.1 of Article IX and the user's guide make it clear that those provisions are supposed to apply only to those three calculated payment amounts named above and nothing else. In particular, the rounding-up provisions do not apply to percentages or the rounding of commodity-specific prices.

13. **The exhibits and sub-annexes to the 2005 definitions**

This chapter has covered only the principal body of the 2005 definitions and Sub-Annex A of the annex. As referred to at the beginning of the chapter, the document also includes the template confirmations to the 2005 definitions, as well as asset-specific sub-annexes. These are explained and analysed in detail in the following chapters.

Standard commodity derivative confirmations

Marcin Perzanowski

1. Introduction

"When we hear news we should always wait for the sacrament of confirmation." A quote not from the chief executive officer of the International Swaps and Derivatives Association (ISDA), but rather from 18th-century French philosopher Voltaire.

Voltaire's words are not a reference to the way in which derivatives transactions are documented at the beginning of the 21st century; but if they had been, the author of *Dictionnaire Philosophique* could not have been more right.

The 2005 ISDA Commodity Definitions would be useless if the parties could not incorporate their provisions into individual transactions by reference. As is market custom, transactions are entered into on the phone and subsequently confirmed in a 'confirmation'. ISDA has published various forms of template confirmation for documenting commodity transactions with respect to both cash-settled and physically settled trades.

The confirmation takes the form of a countersigned letter setting out the transaction's key dates, elections and specific terms (eg, how the underlying asset is valued and the value that the financial instrument derives from the underlying commodity assets). It also contains administrative information and incorporates by reference the parties' ISDA Master Agreement and the 2005 definitions. These documents provide the framework of a transaction, but the confirmation will take precedence if there are inconsistencies between the confirmation and another document.

2. Template confirmations

The 2005 definitions provide specific provisions for commodity forwards, options and swaps. Articles V and VI cover general terms for swap transactions, whereas Article VIII sets out general terms for options. These articles – along with Article VII, which covers the pricing of each commodity, and Article IV, which sets out calculations and payments – provide the framework and rules for how cash-settled options and swaps are documented using the Exhibits associated with the 2005 ISDA Commodity Definitions. These mechanisms have been fully described earlier in the book, so this chapter focuses on the specific elections included in the template confirmations.

ISDA has produced four general template commodity confirmations, as well as specialised forms of confirmation for specific commodity classes (eg, emissions allowances or bullion). This chapter concentrates on the basic templates as set out in the appendix, whereas the asset-specific forms are covered in detail in the chapters on the sub-annexes to the 2005 definitions.

The appendix consists of two exhibits. Exhibit I provides a sample form for a letter agreement or telex confirming a transaction, which is adapted by the parties to the relevant transaction to become the transaction confirmation.

Exhibit II provides standard terms, set out in separate templates and termed 'additional provisions' for each type of swap or option transaction listed below:

- commodity swap/basis swap;
- commodity option;
- commodity cap, collar or floor; and
- commodity swaption.

These are the most common types of commodity derivatives transaction documented. Depending on which type of transaction the parties have chosen to enter into, the relevant additional provisions will be inserted and adapted as Paragraph 2 of the confirmation to complete the confirmation document as set out as Exhibit I.

This part of the chapter must (in particular) be read in conjunction with the earlier chapter on the 2005 definitions. As the principal body of the 2005 definitions covers only cash-settled transactions, the templates analysed in this chapter should be used only for such trades. Naturally, the parties can amend them appropriately to allow for physical settlement, especially if they use standard language provided in the asset-specific sub-annexes, which are covered in subsequent chapters.

The appendix does not provide standard forms for forward or spot transactions, even though such trades are covered by the 2005 definitions. This omission is not major as forward transactions are less common in the market than exchange-traded commodity futures. In any case, the swap confirmation can easily be adapted for forward or spot trades, if necessary.

3. Exhibit I – Introduction, standard paragraphs and closing for a letter agreement or facsimile confirming a transaction

The first part of each confirmation is an introductory paragraph. This sets out the purpose of the confirmation – that is, to confirm the transaction's terms and detail the framework documentation incorporated by reference (ie, the ISDA Master Agreement, the 2005 definitions and perhaps the 2006 definitions). The confirmation also covers six other areas:

- additional provisions;
- calculation agent;
- account details;
- offices;
- broker/arranger; and
- closing.

Most of these provisions are relevant in any derivatives transaction, but their specific inclusion in the confirmation is not always necessary. The parties need not identify the calculation agent if this has been agreed in the Schedule to the ISDA Master Agreement, unless they want to override its provisions. Similarly, the account details or the offices are also often covered in the Schedule.

Paragraph 1 of Exhibit I is absent, instead providing "Insert relevant additional provisions for the particular transaction from one of Exhibits II-A to II-D". Exhibit II then sets out the relevant additional provisions for swaps, options, collars/floors/caps and swaptions. For example, if the parties wish to enter into a commodity option, they can adapt the sample form confirmation and insert the provisions from Exhibit II-B – Additional Provisions for a Confirmation of a Commodity Option. They will then insert the relevant pricing terms and deal details, as explained later in this chapter.

4.   Exhibit II – Additional provisions

The additional provisions allow the parties to make elections specific to their own transaction, which are then inserted as Paragraph 2 of the confirmation. The additional provisions set out in Exhibit II are broadly similar; each has footnotes to assist parties in making appropriate elections for the particular type of trade.

Each of the additional provisions is relatively short – generally about three to four pages long. The framework used by the additional provisions to make each transaction work is drawn from the 2005 definitions.

4.1   Exhibit II-A – commodity swap or basis swap

The additional provisions for commodity swaps and basis swaps are set out in Exhibit II-A. This is one of the most common over-the-counter commodity derivatives transactions.

In a standard commodity swap, one party, defined as the 'floating price payer', is exposed to the price of the specified commodity and consequently must pay a 'floating amount' to its counterparty. This floating amount represents the actual market fluctuations in the price of the underlying commodity asset. The other party, defined as the 'fixed price payer', is obliged to make payments by reference to a specified fixed price. As a result of the transaction, the fixed price payer trades (or swaps) a fixed amount in exchange for a market-related floating payment with the floating price payer. Naturally, both payments will be offset against each other and only one net amount will be due from one party to the other.

However, some transactions may be structured so that there are two floating price payers in the same transaction. In this case, the parties swap payments which each reference different underlying commodities (or at least different underlying commodity reference prices). For example, one party might make payments calculated on the basis of a gold price, while the other does this for silver. These transactions are called 'basis swap': the parties exchange payments calculated on one basis for those related to another basis.

Each confirmation referencing a commodity swap or a commodity basis swap will be structured as described next.

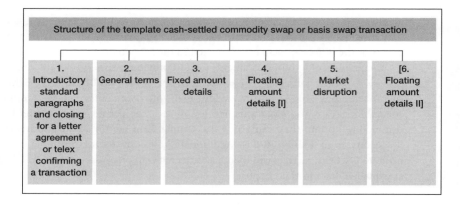

Structure of the template cash-settled commodity swap or basis swap transaction

| 1. Introductory standard paragraphs and closing for a letter agreement or telex confirming a transaction | 2. General terms | 3. Fixed amount details | 4. Floating amount details [I] | 5. Market disruption | [6. Floating amount details II] |

(a) *General terms*

The 'general terms' section of an additional provision is set out first. The parties insert specific details and elections for the transaction for the following terms and definitions from the 2005 definitions:

- the 'trade date' (ie, the date on which the parties agree to enter into the transaction);
- the 'effective date' (ie, the date on which the transaction actually becomes effective);
- the 'termination date' (ie, the date on which the transaction will terminate);
- the 'commodity' (if the transaction is a commodity swap), or 'commodities' (for basis swaps);
- the 'total notional quantity' (ie the amount of commodity, or commodities, relevant for a particular transaction);
- the 'notional quantity per calculation period' (if there is a different notional quantity in each calculation period);
- the 'calculation period(s)' (ie, the period(s) of time by reference to which payments are made);
- the 'settlement period(s)' (this is relevant only for transactions referencing electricity);
- the 'settlement or payment dates' (ie, the dates on which payment or settlement under each transaction will occur);
- 'common pricing' (where more than one commodity reference price is specified for a transaction); and
- the 'business day' (ie, the city by reference to which the business days are determined).

Most of the above terms are self-explanatory and have been covered in detail in the previous chapter. The exception is 'settlement period', which is clarified in the chapter on electricity transactions. If it applies, the parties must also specify the applicable days, the duration and the start time/end time.

The parties will usually specify settlement or payment dates in the 'general terms' section. These are the dates on which the transaction settles and on which the payments must be made. However, if the parties anticipate that their respective payments may not be made on the same date, they should move this paragraph to the 'fixed amount' and/or 'floating amount' sections.

When the confirmation lists more than one commodity reference price, the parties should consider whether to use common pricing. This concept is used to ensure that the prices of both commodity assets referenced in the transaction are published on the same date to assist with the settlement of the trade. If the parties do not specify common pricing as applicable, it is deemed not to apply.

Finally, it is not always necessary to specify the calculation period or notional quantity per calculation period. The calculation period is often included if the parties are obliged to make periodic payments to each other under the terms of the agreement. If a transaction does not provide for a calculation period, the parties delete this part of the template.

(b)   *Fixed amount details*
In the 'fixed amount details' section, the parties will insert specific details and elections for the transaction for the following terms:
- the 'fixed price payer' (ie, the party who makes payments by reference to a fixed price or a fixed amount); and
- the 'fixed amount' or 'fixed price' (ie, the figure by reference to which the fixed price payer makes a payment).

This section is applicable only for commodity swaps, as only they involve a fixed price payer. If the parties enter into a basis swap, there will be two sections for floating amounts (ie 'floating amount details I' and 'floating amount details II').

(c)   *Floating amount details*
In the 'floating amount details' section, the parties will insert specific details and elections for the transaction for the following terms:
- the 'floating price payer' (ie, the party that makes payments by reference to a floating amount);
- the 'applicable spread' (ie, if the parties agree to add an additional spread to the commodity reference price);
- the 'floating price' (ie, the figure by reference to which the floating price payer makes a payment);
- the 'commodity reference price' (ie, the code for the chosen price source as set out in Sub-Annex A to the 2005 definitions);
- the 'unit', 'price source/reference dealers' and 'currency' (this is another way to determine the relevant price);
- the 'specified price' (ie, whether the price will be, among others, the bid price, ask price or morning fixing);
- the 'delivery date' (ie, whether the price will be based on a certain delivery date or a month);
- the 'pricing date(s)' (ie, the day by reference to which the price of the transaction is determined);

- the 'method of averaging' (applicable if there is more than one pricing date in respect of a payment date); and
- the 'currency conversion provisions' (applicable if the commodity reference price is denominated in a currency other than the agreed currency of payment).

This section determines the payments payable by one party to the other by reference to the price of a specified commodity. If the transaction is a basis swap and both parties are floating price payers, then there will be two sections (one labelled 'floating amount details I' and the other 'floating amount details II').

As this is only a template, it includes all the possible standard provisions, although the parties would not include all of them in a single confirmation. For example, the form covers all three main ways to determine the relevant prices relevant to calculating a floating amount:

- election of a commodity reference price from Section 7.1 of the 2005 definitions;
- creation of a commodity reference price using the commodity reference price framework; or
- election of commodity reference dealers, in which case the price will be determined using quotations from four leading dealers.

The easiest method is to pick one of the commodity reference prices from Section 7.1 of Article VII. Naturally, the parties can make any amendments to it if they specify this under the term 'floating price'. They can also add any additional margin to such payment by way of applicable spread.

The terms 'unit', 'price source/reference dealers' and 'currency' will be included only if the parties have not elected a commodity reference price for Sub-Annex A of the 2005 definitions, but instead have decided to use the second or third methods listed above. This has been analysed in depth in the previous chapter.

In some cases the delivery date can be essential to determining a commodity price, but it applies only to a few commodity reference prices. It is relevant when a specific price source publishes several prices by reference to the length of an underlying futures contact. The 'delivery date' is the date or month for delivery of the underlying commodity under that futures contract.

The 2005 definitions provide three ways of defining the delivery date:

- The parties can specify either a date or a month and year in the relevant confirmation;
- The parties can specify a 'nearby month' for the expiration of the relevant futures contract. For example, if they specify 'first nearby month', the delivery date will be the month of expiration of the first futures contract to expire following the relevant pricing date. Alternatively, the 'eighth nearby month' means that the delivery date will be the month of expiration of the eighth futures contract to expire following the relevant pricing date; or
- The parties can agree any other way for determining the delivery date in the confirmation.

The 'specified price' is a type of price which is published or announced on a given day – it can be, for example, a high price, a low price or a morning fixing. Therefore, the parties must consider what types of price of a commodity are published or announced on a given day, and which will be used for the purposes of calculating the relevant price on the pricing dates for their transaction.

A pricing date is a date relevant for determining the price of a commodity; the parties can specify one or more pricing dates in the confirmation. If only one floating amount payment is to be made during the course of the transaction, at least one pricing date must be specified (or determined) for the entire transaction. However, the floating amount payments must often be made with respect to each calculation period or on each settlement date (or payment date), and there must be at least one pricing date in respect of each payment.

In turn, the 'method of averaging' is relevant only when there is more than one pricing date for a calculation period or a payment date and the parties wish to amend the default clauses of the 2005 definitions, which provide for averaging by way of unweighted arithmetic mean (under Section 6.2 of the 2005 definitions).

The 'currency conversion provisions' are necessary only if a commodity reference price is published in a currency other than the agreed currency of payment. In that case the parties should provide how the conversion rate shall be determined.

(d) Market disruption

In the 'market disruption' section, the parties will insert specific details and elections for the transaction for the following terms:

- 'market disruption events' (ie, whether the market disruption events as specified in the 2005 definitions should apply);
- 'additional market disruption events' (ie, any additional event which will constitute market disruption events for the purposes of the 2005 definitions);
- the 'disruption fallbacks' (ie, the consequences of market disruption events);
- the 'fallback reference price' (ie, the price which may apply if the primary reference price is not available); and
- 'maximum days of disruption' (ie, the number of days after which settlement will occur).

As explained in the previous chapter, the 2005 definitions cover in great detail both market disruption events and their consequences – the disruption fallbacks.

The standard market disruption events are 'trading disruption', 'price source disruption', 'disappearance of commodity reference price', 'material change in content', 'tax disruption' and 'material change in formula'. If the parties specify 'applicable' next to market disruption events in the confirmation, then all those market disruption events will apply to the transaction, with the exception of tax disruption.

If the parties specifically list some of the market disruption events to the exclusion of others, then only those listed in the confirmation will apply. Furthermore, if the parties elect for the standard market disruption events to apply, they can still designate in the confirmation those commodities for which 'material change in formula' and 'material change in content' will not apply.

The parties are also free to define any additional market disruption events. If they decide to disapply the standard market disruption events and use their additional market disruption events instead, they need to be careful when drafting the confirmation. If they specify only 'not applicable' next to market disruption events, the 2005 definitions could also operate to disapply the additional market disruption events. For this reason, we recommend setting out a full clause stating the intention of the parties if they decide to include any additional events.

As with market disruption events, the parties need not specify disruption fallbacks in the confirmation, as some of them will be deemed applicable by virtue of the operations of the 2005 definitions. As soon as a market disruption event has occurred, they will apply by default in the following order with a view to ensuring that the parties can obtain the relevant price for the specified commodity:

- 'fallback reference price';
- concurrently,
  - 'delayed publication or announcement';
  - 'postponement'; and
  - 'negotiated fallback';
- 'fallback reference dealers'; and
- 'negotiated fallback'.

The parties should remember to specify an alternative price source for the transaction under 'fallback reference price' if they want to take advantage of the first default disruption fallback. As for 'maximum days of disruption', they should include this section only if they want to depart from the default provisions. Under the 2005 definitions, the maximum days of disruption are three or five commodity business days, depending on the context.

4.2   Exhibits II-B – commodity option

As explained in the previous chapter, an option is a privately negotiated contract between two counterparties. Generally, the buyer of an option acquires a right to buy (or to sell) to the seller of the option a defined amount of assets at a specified price. However, the 2005 definitions are different from other sets of ISDA definitions in this respect and the option buyer will never actually acquire a right to receive (or sell) any of the underlying commodity assets. Instead, the options are cash settled and, on the expiry of the option, one party will only make a payment to the other.

This standard template includes most of the terms applicable for commodity swaps, as included in Exhibit II-A and explained in section 4.1 above. However, it is structured slightly differently and includes various terms applicable only to options. This part of the chapter concentrates on the additional provisions relevant to options in order to avoid duplication with the section above.

The template is structured as described next.

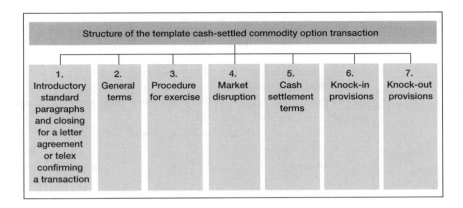

Structure of the template cash-settled commodity option transaction

1. Introductory standard paragraphs and closing for a letter agreement or telex confirming a transaction	2. General terms	3. Procedure for exercise	4. Market disruption	5. Cash settlement terms	6. Knock-in provisions	7. Knock-out provisions

(a) ***General terms***

The 'general terms' section of an additional provision is set out first. The parties will insert specific details and elections for the transaction for the terms and definitions from the 2005 definitions. The following terms are the same as for the commodity swaps/basis swaps set out above:

- the 'trade date' (ie, the date on which the parties agree to enter into the transaction);
- the 'commodity' (if the transaction is a commodity swap), or 'commodities' (for basis swaps);
- the 'total notional quantity' (ie the amount of commodity, or commodities, relevant for a particular transaction);
- the 'notional quantity per calculation period' (if there is a different notional quantity in each calculation period);
- the 'calculation period(s)' (ie, the period(s) of time by reference to which payments are made);
- the 'settlement period(s)' (this is relevant only for transactions referencing electricity);
- the 'settlement or payment dates' (ie, the dates on which payment or settlement under each transaction will occur);
- 'common pricing' (where more than one commodity reference price is specified for a transaction);
- the 'business day' (ie, the city by reference to which the business days are determined);
- the 'effective date' (ie, the date on which the transaction actually becomes effective);
- the 'floating price' (ie, the figure by reference to which the floating price payer makes a payment);
- the 'commodity reference price' (ie, the code for the chosen price source as set out in Sub-Annex A to the 2005 definitions);
- the 'unit, price source/reference dealers and currency' (this is another way to determine the relevant prices);
- the 'specified price' (ie, whether the price will be, for example, the bid price,

ask price or morning fixing);
- the 'delivery date' (ie, whether the price will be based on a certain delivery date or a month);
- the 'pricing date(s)' (ie, the day by reference to which the price of the transaction is determined);
- the 'method of averaging' (applicable if there is more than one pricing date in respect of a payment date); and
- the 'currency conversion provisions' (applicable if the commodity reference price is denominated in a currency other than in the agreed currency of payment).

The above provisions can be found in the 'general terms' and 'floating amount details' sections of Exhibit II-A. Here, they have been combined to form a single part of the document. In addition the 'general terms' section includes the following option-specific clauses:
- the 'seller' (ie, the seller of the commodity option);
- the 'buyer' (ie, the buyer of the commodity option);
- the 'option style' (ie, whether the option is American, European, Bermudan or Asian in style);
- the 'option type' (ie, whether the option is a call or a put);
- the 'strike price per unit' (ie, the price at which the buyer can exercise the option);
- the 'total premium' (ie, the premium paid by the buyer to the seller); and
- the 'premium payment date(s)' (ie, the date(s) when the premium is to be paid).

Those terms are largely self-explanatory and have been covered in detail in the previous chapter. The parties must specify which of them is a buyer and which is a seller under their transaction, and the amount of total premium payable by the buyer to the seller on the selected premium payment date. They must also decide whether the buyer will acquire a right to sell the commodity (a put) or to buy it (a call) at the specified price (the strike price per unit). Finally, the confirmation will provide whether the buyer can exercise the option at any time during its term (American style), at its end (European or Asian style), or only on a handful of selected days (Bermudan style).

If the parties have specified the option type as Asian, they should remember to insert the calculation period provisions. Otherwise, this may not be necessary.

(b) **Procedure for exercise**
This section of the template is specifically for option transactions and the parties will insert here specific details and elections for the following terms:
- the 'exercise period' (ie, the dates and times when an option can be exercised);
- the 'potential exercise date(s)' (ie, the date or dates when a Bermudan-style option can be exercised);
- the 'expiration date' (ie, the last day when an option can be exercised);

- the 'expiration time' (ie, the time of the day when an option can be exercised);
- 'automatic exercise' (ie, whether the option should be exercised automatically when it is 'in the money' for the buyer immediately prior to its expiry);
- 'written confirmation' (ie, whether the buyer needs to confirm its exercise notice in writing);
- the 'seller business day' (ie, the city where the seller of an option is located); and
- the seller's location, telephone or fax number for purposes of giving notice.

All the terms above are analysed in detail in the previous chapter. As with parts of the previous template, many of those terms will be used only if the parties have agreed to depart from the default position under the 2005 definitions. For example, if the parties fail to specify the expiration time, it will be deemed to be 9:30am New York time.

In a similar manner, automatic exercise will apply to any option unless the parties specify otherwise. This means that the option will be deemed to be exercised at the close of the exercise period for that transaction (ie, at the last possible moment when it could be exercised).

If written confirmation is specified as applicable in the confirmation, the buyer must execute a written confirmation setting out the details of the notice. It can be delivered by fax transmission and it must be served within one seller business day following the date on which the notice of exercise becomes effective.

The provisions set out in this part should also be tailored appropriately to different option types. For example, potential exercise dates will be relevant only for Asian-style options. The exercise period will encompass several days for an American-style option, but it will include only several hours for Asian, European or Bermuda-style options.

(c)   ***Market disruption***
The 'market disruption' section is identical to that in Exhibit II-A (see above).

(d)   ***Cash settlement terms***
This section of the template is specific for option transactions and the parties will insert here specific details and elections for the following terms:
- cash settlement (the parties must specify whether it is applicable); and
- the settlement date(s) (ie, the date or dates when an option will be settled).

As mentioned already, the main body of the 2005 definitions and the exhibits analysed in the chapter cover only cash-settled transactions. Therefore, the parties should make any changes in this section carefully if they instead want to allow for physical settlement.

(e)   ***Knock-in provisions and knock-out provisions***
As discussed in the previous chapter, an option to which 'knock-in' provisions apply

becomes effective only on the occurrence of the specified knock-in event. Conversely, if 'knock-out' provisions have been selected, the option can be no longer exercised following the knock-out event. The 2005 definitions provide various options and default fallbacks, which were analysed in the previous chapter.

4.3 Exhibits II-C – commodity cap, collar or floor

As analysed in detail in the previous chapter, 'transactions with caps, collars or floors' are essentially types of commodity swap. Under a 'traditional' swap, the floating price payer is obliged to make a payment which is equal to the relevant price of the commodity (ie, the then-current market price) multiplied by the specified notional amount (and is also netted against the fixed amount payable by the fixed price payer).

However, if the parties introduce a cap, the amount payable will represent only the excess of the selected cap price over the actual market price. Conversely, if the parties have agreed a floor price, the amount payable will be determined by reference to the excess of the market price over the floor price. Depending on the level of the cap or floor price, the parties distribute the amount of risk between themselves.

If there is a collar, one party pays a floating amount by reference to the floor price and the other by reference to the cap price. Therefore, one party makes a payment to another if the price of the commodity rises above the specified level (ie, the cap price), and the other party makes a payment to the first only if the price falls below a defined threshold (ie, the floor price). If, however, the price of the commodity stays within the collar (ie, it does not rise above the cap price and does not fall below the floor price), then no party need make any payment to the other. For a worked example, please see the previous chapter.

In terms of documentation, Exhibit II-C is almost identical to Exhibit II-A and is structured as follows.

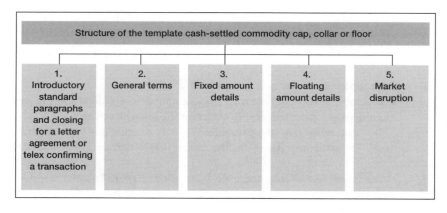

The main difference between Exhibit II-A and Exhibit II-C is that Exhibit II-C includes space for a figure representing the cap price or the floor price in the 'floating amount details' section of the confirmation.

If the parties enter into a collar transaction, they will delete the 'fixed amount details' section, as each party will be obliged to make a payment by reference to the floating amount. Instead, they should include separate 'floating amount details' sections for each party. However, unlike a basis swap, the payments will still be made in respect of only one commodity and they will be determined by reference to a single commodity reference price.

4.4 Exhibits II-D – commodity swaption

A 'commodity swaption' is an option given to the option buyer which allows it either to:

- enter into a swap identified in the confirmation (ie, the 'underlying transaction'); or
- receive a cash settlement amount in respect of that underlying transaction on the settlement date.

Consequently, the template set out as Exhibit II-D is divided into two sections. The first part provides the terms for the exercise of the option, while the second includes the terms relevant for the swap and applies only once the option in the first part has been exercised (or is deemed to have been exercised).

Exhibit II-D is structured as described next.

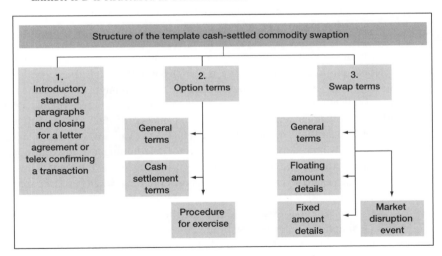

(a) Option terms

As the main economic terms of the transaction are set out in the part of the template relating to the 'swap terms', the 'option terms' section is rather short and includes only the mechanical provisions.

The 'general terms' part is much shorter than in Exhibit II-B and has only the following definitions:

- the 'trade date';
- the 'option style';
- the 'option type';

- the 'seller';
- the 'buyer';
- the 'total premium';
- the 'premium payment date(s)'; and
- 'physical/contract settlement'.

Most of the terms are identical to those in Exhibit II-B and the only new term is 'physical/contract settlement'. The buyer of a swaption will have the right to cause the swap to be effective only if the parties elect 'physical settlement' or 'contract settlement'. Otherwise, the swaption buyer will be able to receive only the cash settlement amount. This has been explained in the previous chapter.

The principal body of the 2005 definitions does not allow for physical settlement in the sense that the parties to a transaction would exchange actual commodities. Therefore, the physical settlement of a swaption means only that the buyer will merely have a right to enter into the swap under the terms presented in the 'swap terms' section.

The 'cash settlement terms' section includes the following items:

- 'cash settlement' (ie, whether it applies);
- the 'settlement date' (ie, when the payment is to be made); and
- the 'cash settlement amount' (ie, the method as to how this figure should be determined).

Although this looks very similar to the corresponding section in Exhibit II-B, its role and purpose in this template is completely different. If the parties elect cash settlement as applicable, this means that the swaption buyer cannot cause the swap to become effective. If the buyer exercises the option, it will receive only a payment (the cash settlement amount), which should reflect the value of the underlying swap. The 2005 definitions do not include a definition of the cash settlement amount, so the parties will need to specify the means for determining it in the confirmation.

Finally, the 'procedure for exercise' section includes the following terms:

- the 'exercise period' (ie, the dates and time when an swaption can be exercised);
- the 'potential exercise date(s)' (ie, the date or dates when a Bermuda-style swaption can be exercised);
- the 'expiration date' (ie, the last day when a swaption can be exercised);
- the 'expiration time' (ie, the time of the day when a swaption can be exercised);
- 'automatic exercise' (ie, whether the swaption should be automatically exercised when it is 'in the money' for the buyer immediately prior to its expiry);
- 'written confirmation' (ie, whether the buyer needs to confirm its exercise notice in writing); and
- the seller's location, telephone or fax number for purposes of giving notice.

All of those terms also appear in Exhibit II-B, but the definition of 'seller business day' has been missed out for swaptions. Considering that the 2005 definitions require an exercise notice to be served on the seller business day, its omission in Exhibit II-D appears to be a drafting mistake. For clarity, we recommend inserting it for all commodity swaption transactions.

The function of 'automatic exercise' has been changed in relation to swaptions. Whereas it is deemed to apply for all options unless specifically disapplied, the parties to a swaption must specifically elect it if they want to make use of its mechanism. Otherwise, it will not apply.

(b)   Swap terms

Perhaps unsurprisingly, this part of the template is almost identical to the additional terms set out in Exhibit II-A, and sets out the following terms.

General terms	Fixed amount details	Floating amount details	Market disruption events
Commodity	Fixed price payer	Floating price payer	Market disruption event(s)
Total notional quantity	Fixed amount/ fixed price	Floating price	Additional market disruption event(s)
Notional quantity per calculation period		Commodity reference price	Disruption fallback(s)
Effective date		Unit; price source/reference dealers; currency	Fallback reference price
Termination date		Specified price	Maximum days of disruption
Calculation period		Delivery date	
Settlement period(s) (including applicable days, duration and start/end time)		Currency conversion provisions	
Settlement/payment date(s)		Method of averaging	

There are minor differences with Exhibit II-A, mostly relating to the fact that the 'swap terms' section of the template covers only commodity swaps and not basis swaps. Thus, the term 'common pricing' has not been included and there is space to reference just one commodity. Furthermore, the term 'applicable spread' has been omitted. For an explanation of those terms, see section 4.1 on commodity swaps above.

However, the underlying transaction of a swaption need not necessarily be a commodity swap. If the parties want to enter into a swaption referencing a basis swap, floor, cap or collar, they can do so using Exhibit II-D. They would then keep the 'option terms' part of the template, but they would need to amend the swap terms as appropriate.

5. Conclusion

The exhibits to the 2005 definitions are forms of confirmation for simple commodity transactions and are a good example of how the 2005 definitions can work in practice. The parties are free to amend them as they wish, which will of course be necessary for more complex structures.

We started this chapter with Voltaire. He is often misquoted as saying, "I disapprove of what you say, but I will defend to the death your right to say it." With a final parallel, the exhibits should be used only for cash-settled transactions, as the principal body of the 2005 definitions does not cover trades where one party must physically deliver the relevant referenced asset to the other. But the 2005 definitions defend your right to say it; for physically settled transactions, the parties can amend the templates and include the relevant provisions.

Alternatively, they can use the forms of confirmations appended to one of the sub-annexes of the 2005 definitions. For example, Sub-Annex B specifically covers physically settled bullion transactions and should be used if the parties expect the delivery of gold, silver, platinum or palladium on termination of the transaction.

Bullion transactions

Marcin Perzanowski

1. Introduction

Vladimir Lenin was wrong when he remarked that "gold would be used to plate the inner surfaces of public urinals". When the capitalist foundations of our society are being tested, huge financial institutions fail or are nationalised and the indices are at their all-time lows, investors can always rely on gold. With the price of this precious metal well above $1,000 per ounce in mid 2010, the gold markets are thriving despite the current crisis environment. The numerous television commercials for various 'cash for gold' companies offering to buy unwanted gold necklaces and earrings bear witness to this.

Selling and delivering your family inheritance by post is one way of effecting physically settled bullion transactions, but it is certainly not the method that the International Swaps and Derivatives Association (ISDA) recommends to its members. Instead ISDA, together with the London Bullion Market Association (LBMA) and the Financial Markets Lawyers Group, has endorsed Sub-Annex B to the Annex to the 2005 ISDA Commodity Definitions, known as the 'Bullion Annex'. This annex is a revised version of the 1997 ISDA Bullion Definitions, which for clarity and convenience have now been combined with and form part of the 2005 definitions.

The Bullion Annex covers both cash and physically settled bullion transactions and amends the 2005 definitions to the extent that the market practices for trading bullion differ from those applicable to other commodities. As the bullion market is both old and specialised, the differences may seem small and rather technical, but they should not be underestimated. Although it is not strictly necessary to use the Bullion Annex to document a cash-settled bullion transaction, precisely to take advantage of those subtle technicalities we recommend that the annex should be incorporated into all bullion agreements.

The annex is not a separate document in its own right and its provisions have been incorporated into the main body of the 2005 definitions as Section 10 (Article X); the numbering of the Bullion Annex reflects this accordingly. The annex should not be read in isolation from the principal section of the 2005 definitions and, when drafting a confirmation of bullion transactions, both documents should be carefully reviewed.

The Bullion Annex is set out as follows.

2005 ISDA Commodity Definitions documents	
Sub-Annex B to the 2005 ISDA Commodity Definitions	
Article X	Bullion transactions
Section 10.1	Bullion transaction
Section 10.2	General definitions with respect to bullion transactions
Section 10.3	Bullion trades
Section 10.4	Bullion options
Section 10.5	Settlement by delivery
Section 10.6	Cash settlement
Section 10.7	Netting
Section 10.8	Bullion swaptions
Section 10.9	Gold Offered Forward Rate (GOFO)
Section 10.10	Bullion swap
Section 10.11	Additional taxes

This chapter analyses in detail each part of the annex, together with the template confirmations included as exhibits, using hypothetical examples.

2.   General definitions

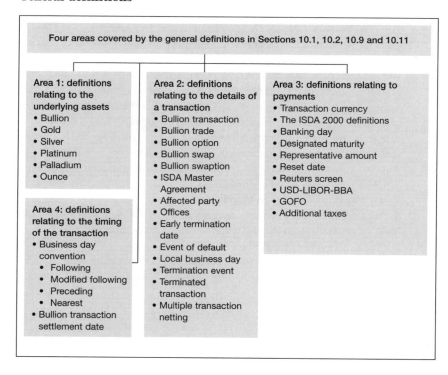

Various general definitions are set out in Sections 10.1, 10.2, 10.9 and 10.11 of the annex. Some of these defined terms may appear to be identical to those set out in the principal body of the 2005 definitions, but they rarely are. A number of technical adjustments and variations warrant the inclusion of this separate annex.

The definitions cover the four distinct areas set out in the diagram above.

2.1   Area 1: definitions relating to the underlying assets

The most important term here is probably 'bullion' itself. It has been defined as either gold, silver, platinum or palladium.

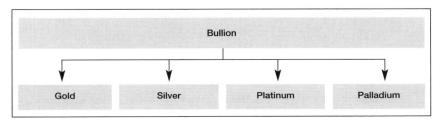

Each of 'gold' and 'silver' has been defined by reference to gold (or silver) bars or unallocated gold (or silver) complying with the rules of the LBMA relating to fineness and good delivery.

'Palladium' and 'platinum', in turn, mean palladium (or platinum) ingots or plate or unallocated palladium (or platinum) complying with the rules of the London Platinum and Palladium Market (LPPM) relating to good delivery and fineness.

The annex also defines the unit of measurement for each type of bullion: an 'ounce'. However, an ounce has one meaning for gold and a separate one for the other precious metals. An ounce used by reference to gold means a fine troy ounce, whereas when describing the amount of silver, platinum or palladium, it is simply a troy ounce.

2.2   Area 2: definitions relating to the details of a transaction

The Bullion Annex defines a 'bullion transaction' as any of the following:

- a 'bullion trade';
- a 'bullion option';
- a 'bullion swap'; or
- a 'bullion swaption'.

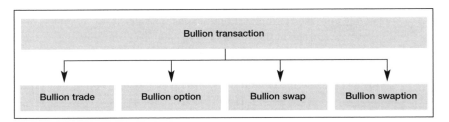

Each type of bullion transaction is later explained in detail in the relevant sections of the annex. However, in principle, a 'bullion trade' is a spot or a forward transaction referencing bullion; a 'bullion option' is an option on any type of bullion; a 'bullion swap' is a swap referencing bullion; and a 'bullion swaption' is simply a swaption with its underlying transaction being a bullion swap.

Furthermore, the Bullion Annex defines the 'ISDA Master Agreement' as the agreement that the relevant bullion transaction supplements and forms part of. Therefore, this term covers both the 1992 ISDA Master Agreement and the later 2002 ISDA Master Agreement. The annex also incorporates by reference the following definitions from the ISDA Master Agreement: 'affected party', 'offices', 'early termination date', 'event of default', 'local business day', 'termination event', 'terminated transaction' and 'multiple transaction netting'. As the term 'multiple transaction netting' appears only in the 2002 ISDA Master Agreement, it will be effectively incorporated only if the parties use this standard form of contract.

The ISDA working parties anticipated that the Bullion Annex may also be incorporated by reference to transactions governed by master agreements other than the ISDA Master Agreement. In that case, the references to a particular provision of the ISDA Master Agreement will be construed as applying to the equivalent provisions in that other standard-form document. However, it is unclear how this would work in practice, so we recommend using the Bullion Annex only for transactions governed by the ISDA Master Agreement.

2.3 Area 3: definitions relating to payments

The Bullion Annex includes various provisions relating to currencies, rates and taxes.

The 'transaction currency' has been defined as the currency in which the 'contract price', for bullion trades, or the 'bullion strike price', for bullion options, is expressed.[1] Naturally, the parties are always free to amend this default provision in the confirmation. This term is relevant when calculating and making payments due from one party to another.

The annex also incorporates by reference the following definitions from the 2000 definitions: 'banking day', 'designated maturity', 'representative amount', 'reset date', 'Reuters screen' and 'USD-LIBOR-BBA'. Naturally, this should now be amended in the confirmation to refer to the current 2006 definitions. In any case, all these definitions (apart from 'USD-LIBOR-BBA', which does not appear in the annex) are used to define the term 'Gold Forward Offered Rate' (GOFO).

GOFO is the gold equivalent to the London Interbank Offered Rate and represents the rate at which dealers will lend gold to swap against US dollars. Section 10.9 of the Bullion Annex provides that the calculation agent will establish it by obtaining quotations from various market makers. However, the word 'GOFO' appears nowhere else in the annex or in the template confirmations; it was included in the 2005 definitions only because various ISDA members suggested that this term be covered somewhere in the standard ISDA documentation. The ISDA working group decided that the Bullion Annex would be the most appropriate place.

---

1   The terms 'contract price' and 'bullion strike price' are defined later in this chapter.

As the term 'GOFO' is a standard rate in US dollars, if the counterparties wish to include it in their transaction, they may prefer to use one of the templates set out in the 2006 definitions with the appropriate amendments.

Finally, Section 10.11 specifies that the party may agree to include in the confirmation any additional provisions relating to any tax, levy, import duty or any other charge imposed by any government or taxing authority. However, the annex provides no standard fallbacks in this area.

2.4 Area 4: definitions relating to the timing of the transaction

As referred to elsewhere in this book, the standard definition of 'commodity business day' does not apply to bullion transactions. Instead, the Bullion Annex introduces the new term 'bullion business day', which is defined as any day on which banks are open for business in all of:

- London;
- New York; and
- the location where the relevant payments are to be made.

In addition, if a transaction is physically settled, that day must also be a scheduled trading day in the market for the relevant bullion in the delivery location.

Section 10.2(c) sets out four options for the 'bullion business day' convention: 'following', 'modified following' (also referred to as 'modified'), 'nearest' and 'preceding'. They are defined in the same way as the business day conventions for commodity business days as set out in Section 1.5(a) of the 2005 definitions.

Section 10.2 also includes the definition of a 'bullion transaction settlement date'. As the name indicates, it is the 'bullion business date' when the parties are obliged to perform their obligations under a transaction by either delivering the required amount of bullion or making the relevant payment.

3. Bullion trades

Section 10.3 provides the definitions applicable to bullion trades. A 'bullion trade' itself is defined as any transaction for the spot or forward sale of bullion.

A spot transaction is a simple sale-and-purchase agreement, so it is not actually a derivative instrument. Under the terms of the contract, one of the parties agrees to sell and the other agrees to buy a specified number of ounces of a bullion at the specified price per ounce (defined as the 'contract price'). In the case of a forward transaction, the parties also agree all these terms but the settlement will occur at a defined point in the future.

There are two ways for settlement of a transaction. If the parties have elected 'settlement by delivery', their transaction is physically settled and one of the parties must effect the delivery of the required number of ounces of bullion, whereas the other must make the related payment. The amount of that payment is arrived at by multiplying the contract price by the number of ounces. If settlement by delivery applies, an obligation to deliver bullion or to make the requisite payment has been defined as a 'bullion obligation'. The details of this method of settlement are further analysed in section 6 of this chapter.

Instead of choosing settlement by delivery, the parties can elect 'bullion cash settlement' in the confirmation. If bullion cash settlement applies to a bullion trade which is a forward, the parties exchange the difference between the actual price of the underlying asset at a future date at the contract price set out in the confirmation. This is further explained in section 7 of this chapter.

4. Bullion options

Section 10.4 sets out the provisions for bullion options. Generally, they are very similar to those relating to standard commodity options as described in the main body of the 2005 definitions. In most cases, instead of the definition of, for example, 'call option', as set out in Section 8 (Article VIII) of the 2005 definitions, the Bullion Annex provides an almost identical term labelled 'bullion call option'.

However, there are a couple of important differences between both documents. This section does not analyse the option provision in great detail because this has already been done elsewhere in the book, but it concentrates on the differences between the main body of the 2005 definitions and the Bullion Annex.

4.1 General terms relating to bullion options

The definition of a 'bullion option' is much simpler than that of an 'option' in Section 8.3 of the 2005 definitions. Accordingly, a 'bullion option' is a right, but not an obligation, of the bullion option buyer to purchase (in the case of a 'bullion call option'), or to sell (in case of a 'bullion put option'), a specified number of ounces at the bullion strike price. In turn, 'bullion strike price' is defined as the price per ounce specified in the confirmation.

In the same way as applies to regular options, bullion options can also be categorised as:

- American-style bullion options, which can be exercised only during the bullion exercise period (ie, from the effective date to the bullion expiration date);
- Bermuda-style bullion options, which can be exercised only on the bullion potential exercise dates and the bullion expiration date (as specified in the confirmation); and
- European-style bullion options, which can be exercised only on the bullion expiration date (as specified in the confirmation).

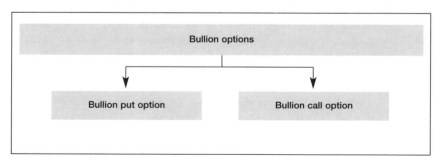

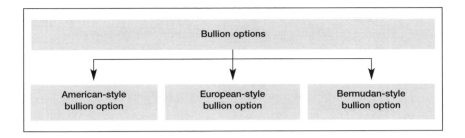

While the definition of the 'expiration date' in the 2005 definitions states that the parties should specify a certain date in the confirmation, the Bullion Annex allows the parties to define the 'bullion expiration date' just by reference to a particular year and month. In that case, the bullion expiration date will fall on the bullion standard date (ie, the day that is two bullion business days before the last bullion business day of that month).

Section 10.4 uses the term 'expiration time' (defined in Section 3.7 of the main body of the 2005 definitions) and 'bullion expiration time' (defined in the Bullion Annex) almost interchangeably. This is probably just a drafting error, but considering that both expiration time and bullion expiration time are defined as 9:30am New York time, this should make no difference in practice. Naturally, the parties are free to amend the definitions of 'expiration time' and 'bullion expiration time' in the confirmation.

Interestingly, the Bullion Annex does not allow for Asian-style options for bullion. Therefore if the parties would like to enter into that option, they would need to rely on the main body of the 2005 definitions with the appropriate amendments. Considering that Asian-style options are not very popular in relation to bullion, their omission from the Bullion Annex should not be an inconvenience.

4.2   Terms relating to the exercise of bullion options

(a)   *Automatic exercise*

Under Section 10.4(c)(ii), automatic exercise also applies to all bullion options unless the parties specifically disapply it in the confirmation. This is the same position as under the main body of the 2005 definitions.

A cash-settled bullion option will be deemed exercised at the expiration time on the expiration date under Section 10.4(c)(ii) only if the buyer would be entitled to any payment on the termination of that option. To determine this, the calculation agent must check whether the 'in the money amount' at that time is a positive number. (The way of determining the in-the-money amount is presented in section 7 of this chapter.)

If, however, the parties have specified settlement by delivery, then the amount to be received by the buyer must be substantial enough for the settlement to make commercial sense. If the difference is negligible, the bullion option buyer may simply buy or sell the relevant quantity of bullion on the market without any adverse consequences in terms of costs.

The Bullion Annex provides a specific formula to determine whether this price difference is negligible enough for the option to remain unexercised. Accordingly, automatic exercise does not apply if the in-the-money amount is smaller than the product of:

- 1% of the bullion strike price; and
- the number of ounces specified in the confirmation.

When calculating the in-the-money amount for the purposes of automatic exercise, the parties need not obtain the relevant price as provided in Article VI of the 2005 definitions. Instead, the bullion option seller determines in good faith what it would quote to market counterparties at the expiration time.

Hypothetical example: Cadiz Corporation and Lechia Mining

Cadiz Corporation and Lechia Mining have entered into a bullion call option for gold, with Lechia as the bullion option buyer, the number of ounces being 100,000 and the strike price being $1,000. Lechia has not exercised the option during the instrument's term, and at the expiration time on the expiration date Cadiz, as the option seller, determines in good faith the price of gold to be $1,001. This means that the in-the-money amount would be equal to:

($1,001 – $1,000 per ounce) × 100,000 ounces = $100,000.

(Details as to how the in-the-money amount is calculated are set out in section 7 of this chapter.)

The product of 1% of the bullion strike price and the number of ounces can be calculated thus:

1% × $1,001 per ounce × 100,000 ounces = $1,001,000.

As $100,000 is less than $1,001,000, automatic exercise has not been triggered and the option is deemed not to have been exercised.

(b) *Exercise by notice to the other party*

If automatic exercise does not apply, or if the option buyer would like to exercise the option sooner than immediately prior to its expiration, then it must send a 'bullion exercise notice' to the other party. Such notice is irrevocable as soon as it is effective, and it may be delivered by telex or other electronic notification providing assurance of receipt (eg, Reuters Dealing 2000-1 or the Bloomberg Trading System). However, the bullion exercise notice cannot be sent by fax unless the parties specifically agree this in the confirmation.

In order for the bullion exercise notice to become effective, the option buyer must deliver it to the option seller before the bullion expiration time (ie, 9:30am New York time). There are also separate rules for the delivery of the notice for American- and Bermuda-style options.

In the case of an American-style bullion option, the notice must be received by the seller before or at 2:00pm in the seller's local time. If the notice is delivered after 2:00pm, it will be deemed to be effective as of the following bullion business day. For a Bermuda-style option, the notice must be delivered before or at the bullion expiration time on a bullion potential exercise date or on the bullion expiration date.

For all types of option, the notice will not be effective if it is received after the bullion expiration time on the bullion expiration date.

The day when an option is exercised, or when it is deemed to be exercised, is the 'bullion exercise date'.

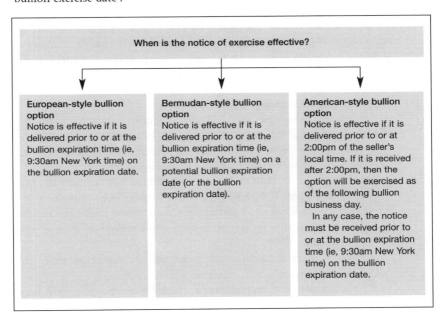

Once an option has been exercised, pursuant to automatic exercise or the receipt of notice, the option is deemed to be a bullion trade with the contract price being equal to the bullion strike price. The option will then be settled, pursuant to either cash or physical settlement provisions, on the 'bullion settlement date' (ie, two bullion business days after the bullion exercise date).

4.3 Terms relating to the payment of premium

The bullion option buyer acquires the bullion option by paying the 'bullion premium' on the 'bullion premium payment date'. Whereas the definition of the 'premium payment date' in the main body of the 2005 definitions states that the parties should specify this date in the confirmation, the Bullion Annex provides a default fallback. Accordingly, the bullion premium payment date is the second bullion business day after the trade date, unless the parties agree otherwise.

If the bullion premium is not received on the bullion premium payment date, the option seller has three options:

- It can accept a late payment of the premium;

- It can send a notice to the buyer and, if the buyer does not make a payment within three local business days of such notice, the seller can treat such option as void; or
- It can send a notice of non-payment and treat it as an event of default under the relevant ISDA Master Agreement if the payment is not made within the applicable grace period (ie, three local business days under the 1992 ISDA Master Agreement or one local business day under the 2002 ISDA Master Agreement).

If the bullion option seller elects for either of the first two methods above, the buyer will be obliged to pay all the seller's out-of-pocket expenses. Such expenses will include any hedging break costs, damages and any other applicable costs, and will be denominated in the same currency as the bullion premium.

4.4 Terms relating to discharge and termination

Section 10(c)(iv) allows for 'opposite' bullion options to be offset against each other and effectively cancelled. This goes back to the fact that if a party sells a put option to its counterparty, and if that counterparty sells an identical put option to the first party, both contracts can effectively cancel each other out.

This section of the Bullion Annex is an additional option and the parties must specify it as applicable if they want to take advantage of its provisions. In order for two option contracts to cancel each other, the following conditions must be met:

- Each option must be in relation to the same bullion (ie, gold, silver, platinum or palladium).
- Each option must have the same bullion expiration time and bullion expiration date.
- Each option must have the same style (ie, they must both be American style, Bermudan style or European style).
- Each option must have the same settlement method (ie, they must both be either cash or physically settled).
- Each option must have the same bullion strike price.
- Each option must be settled in the same location.
- Each contract party must have transacted through the same pair of offices under each option.
- Neither option shall have been executed by delivery of a bullion notice of exercise.

If the above conditions are met, neither party has any obligation under the option contracts on the day on which the last bullion premium has been paid.

However, the above conditions do not require the option contracts to refer to the identical number of ounces. Therefore, if two options satisfy the criteria above but each was made with respect to a different amount of bullion, then the two contracts will be replaced by one with the appropriately adjusted figure for the number of ounces.

5.   Bullion swaps and bullion swaptions

Bullion swaps and bullion swaptions are described in Sections 10.10 and 10.8 of the Bullion Annex, respectively.

The definition of a 'bullion swap' is straightforward. A 'bullion swap' is any transaction where one party pays a fixed amount and the other pays a floating amount based on the application of a 'commodity reference price', as referred to in the main body of the 2005 definitions and set out in its Sub-Annex A. The definition of a 'bullion swap' also includes any caps, collars or floors.

The Bullion Annex provides no further details as to the operation of bullion swaps, as the principal body of the 2005 definitions includes adequate provisions for this type of transaction. As under any commodity swap transaction, physical settlement is not possible because the parties exchange only payments.

In turn, a 'bullion swaption' is defined as a swaption under which the bullion option seller grants a right to the bullion option buyer to cause the underlying bullion swap to become effective. Section 10.8 also provides that the references to bullion options shall be deemed to be references to bullion swaptions. This creates consistency in the operations of both options and swaptions.

6.   Settlement by delivery

The physical settlement of bullion transactions is the main reason why the Bullion Annex was created and its provisions reflect the current market practice which has evolved during the last 200 years. The annex makes references to the two main organisations, the LBMA and the LPPM, and their rules, which provide efficiency and standardisation in the market through their good-delivery lists.

6.1   Types of delivery

There are two ways in which a bullion transaction can be physically settled under the 2005 definitions: the relevant bullion can be delivered on either an allocated or an unallocated basis.

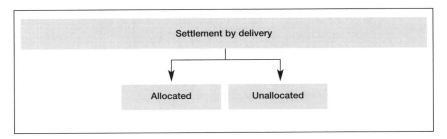

The unallocated basis is the default option under the Bullion Annex, as it is the quickest and most efficient way of settling transactions. To discharge its settlement obligations, a party to a transaction referencing gold or silver must deliver 'loco London' the relevant amount of commodity under the rules of the LBMA by crediting an unallocated account at a member of the LBMA. In the case of platinum or palladium, a party must deliver 'loco Zurich' the relevant amount of commodity under the rules of the LPPM by crediting an unallocated account at a member of the LPPM.

(a) *Conventions in the bullion markets*

The concepts of 'loco London' and 'loco Zurich' (*loco* being Latin for 'in the location') are crucial and their origins date back to the 19th century. At that time, London was the place where gold from the mines of California, South Africa and Australia was refined and sold. Even up to the present day, most global over-the-counter gold and silver trading is cleared through the London clearing system, even though the transaction parties are based throughout the world. Zurich, with weaker traditions, plays an equivalent role for platinum and palladium.

In the case of gold and silver, both domestic and international dealers open bullion accounts with individual London trading houses (ie, 'loco London') and all transfers are effected through the London bullion clearing system. A credit balance on that loco London account with an LMBA member represents a holding of gold or silver in the same way as credit balances on bank accounts represent an amount of money on a deposit account. The same holds true for platinum and palladium accounts in Zurich.

As with an ordinary bank account, an unallocated account with an LMBA or LPPM member does not entitle the creditor to any specific bars or ingots of the relevant bullion. Instead, the creditor has a general entitlement to the precious metal and, in case the relevant bullion dealer goes insolvent, it will be an unsecured creditor.

This is the most efficient way of effecting transactions, but clearly it does not entitle the creditor to the actual bullion. If the account holder wants to receive the actual metal, then specific bars or bullion products will be allocated to the account holder. When a customer has an allocated account, the metals are physically segregated and are identified in a list of bars showing the unique bar number, gross weight, the assay or fineness and its fine weight.

If the parties specify 'delivery on an allocated basis' in the confirmation, then in course of the settlement the transferor will need to identify serial numbers of the relevant bars or ingots of the commodity within a warehouse. Considering that the delivery of bullion may not always be a very straightforward and standardised process, it is surprising that the Bullion Annex provides no fallback mechanisms. Instead, it says that the parties shall specify in the confirmation any additional terms and conditions relating to the delivery method, location, dates and periods, passage of title and risk of loss, insurance, delivery tolerance factors and warehousing costs.

6.2 Additional payments for late delivery

The parties can also specify in the confirmation that 'payment for late delivery' shall apply. If it does and if there is a default in the performance of the delivery obligations, then the innocent party can claim the total costs that it has reasonably incurred, or it would incur, as a result of the late delivery. This amount would normally include insurance, vaulting, transportation and any borrowing costs, and it will be determined by the non-defaulting party acting reasonably and in good faith. However, in order to take advantage of this clause, the innocent party must claim its costs under this section before any termination of the transaction.

6.3 Provisions relating to bullion settlement disruption events

The standard 'market disruption event' from the principal section of the 2005 definitions applies to all cash-settled bullion transactions unless agreed otherwise. However, if settlement by delivery applies, Section 10.5(d) of the Bullion Annex sets out the provisions covering the additional 'bullion settlement disruption events'.

A 'bullion settlement disruption event' is defined broadly and includes any event beyond the control of the parties as a result of which delivery cannot be effected by the method agreed in the confirmation.

The parties should specify in the agreement one of two 'consequences of bullion settlement disruption events' – either 'negotiation' or 'cancellation and payment'. If the parties make no election, the fallback is cancellation and payment.

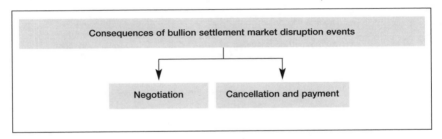

If negotiation has been specified as the applicable consequence, then the bullion transaction settlement date will be the first succeeding day on which delivery can be effected using the method agreed in the confirmation. If, however, delivery cannot be effected by the agreed method on each of the 10 bullion business days immediately following the originally scheduled settlement date, then on the 10th day the parties will have to agree for the delivery by any other method which is commercially reasonable.

For example, if the parties have elected delivery on an allocated basis, but this method is unavailable due to disruption for 10 consecutive bullion business days, then on the 10th day they may need to arrange for delivery on an unallocated basis.

However, if the relevant amount of bullion cannot be delivered in any commercially reasonable method at that time, the parties will negotiate in good faith with a view to agreeing a commercially reasonable method of settling the transaction.

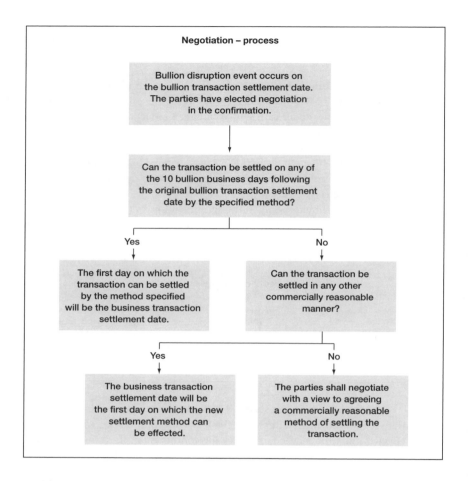

The procedure for cancellation and payment is much simpler. If the bullion settlement disruption prevents the settlement by the specified method on each of the two bullion business days following the original settlement date, then the transaction will terminate. This will be treated as a termination event under the ISDA Master Agreement, with that second day as the early termination date, and the party which was supposed to effect the delivery will be deemed to be the affected party (as defined in the ISDA Master Agreement).

Naturally, if the delivery by the chosen method is possible on the first or the second day following the scheduled settlement date, then that day will be the bullion transaction settlement date.

7. Cash settlement

Cash settlement of commodity transactions is covered in the principal body of the 2005 definitions, so strictly speaking it is not necessary to use the Bullion Annex for cash-settled bullion transactions. However, the annex includes (at Section 10.6) helpful additional provisions and for this reason we recommend always using the

Bullion Annex when documenting transactions referencing bullion.

The provisions for 'bullion cash settlement' can apply, if elected in the confirmation, to 'bullion trades' (ie, spot sales of bullion and forward transactions), as well as to exercised bullion options. As for bullion swaps (or bullion swaps which are a cap, collar or floor), these provisions are not applicable as the parties exchange the defined fixed and floating amounts throughout the term of each transaction.

The obligations of the parties are discharged when one party pays over the in-the-money amount to the other. This amount can be presented using the following formula:

In-the-money amount = (relevant price – contract price) × number of ounces

As discussed earlier in this chapter, the 'relevant price' is the price of a commodity at a given point in time (as determined pursuant to the relevant commodity reference price), whereas the 'contract price' is the price which has been agreed in the confirmation. Also as referred to earlier, the bullion strike price will be deemed to be the contract price for the purposes of calculating the in-the-money amount.

If the relevant price exceeds the contract price and the in-the-money amount has a positive value, then the party which would have been required to deliver the bullion had settlement by delivery applied must make the payment.

If, however, the contract price exceeds the relevant price and the in-the-money amount is negative, then the payment of the absolute value of that amount must be made by the party which would be obliged to make a payment if the transaction were physically settled.

As explained earlier, a bullion option buyer will never be required to make a payment of the in-the-money amount to the seller.

The Bullion Annex also defines the term 'bullion pricing date' as the day that is two bullion business days preceding the bullion transaction settlement date. The bullion pricing date is the date in respect of which the 'relevant price' is determined. This term is not used anywhere in the Bullion Annex, but it is used in the main body of the 2005 definitions. This means that the relevant price should be determined by reference to a day that is two bullion business days before the bullion transaction settlement date.

Hypothetical example: Lilly Jewellery International
Lilly Jewellery International bought a cash-settled European-style call option referencing silver from Fra Mining Corporation on November 20 2009.

The parties agreed the following economic terms for their transaction:
- bullion strike price – $18 per ounce;
- number of ounces – 35,000;
- bullion expiration date – May 13 2010; and
- bullion transaction settlement date – May 20 2010.

Lilly served the notice of exercise to Fra Mining on May 13 2010. Once given, a notice is irrevocable.

The bullion pricing date for this trade is two bullion business days before May 20, which is May 18. On that date, the calculation agent determines the relevant price of silver to be $19 per ounce.

From the time the option is exercised, it is treated as a bullion trade for the purposes of determining the in-the-money amount, whereas the bullion strike price of $18 will be the contract price. This means that the in-the-money amount will be equal to:

$$(\$19 - \$18 \text{ per ounce}) \times 35,000 \text{ ounces} = \$35,000.$$

Therefore, Fra will be obliged to pay $35,000 to Lilly on May 20 2010.

8. Netting

One of the main objectives of ISDA as a documentation platform is to promote efficiency in the derivatives market. One of the most obvious ways that ISDA achieves this goal is through various provisions allowing for netting and set-off of similar transactions. In section 4.4 above of this chapter, we have described the way in which two option transactions can be offset against each other. Section 10.7 of the Bullion Annex provides for two further netting mechanisms.

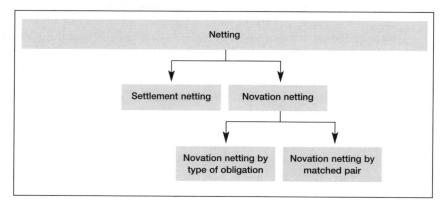

8.1 Bullion settlement netting

Section 2(c) of both the 1992 ISDA Master Agreement and the 2002 ISDA Master Agreement provides for the netting of payments which are made on the same date, in the same currency and in respect of the same transaction. This provision can be amended in both versions of the master agreement so that netting applies across all transactions on the same date and currency between the parties.

Referring to Section 2(c) of the ISDA Master Agreement, Section 10.7(a) of the Bullion Annex allows the parties to net obligations when delivering bullion. If the parties have elected in their ISDA Schedule that payments can be netted only in respect of the same transaction, this will also allow for the netting of the obligations to deliver the same type of bullion, provided that each delivery is due on the same date. However, if Section 2(c) of the related ISDA Master Agreement has been amended to provide for cross-transactional netting, this would also apply with respect to the delivery obligations under any bullion trades between the same parties.

8.2 Bullion novation netting

The parties can also incorporate additional netting provisions in the confirmation by specifying that either 'novation netting by type of obligation' or 'novation netting by matched pair' shall apply. They can take advantage of these provisions only in respect of physically settled transactions (ie, if they have elected settlement by delivery).

The following conditions must be fulfilled in respect of two bullion transactions for novation netting by type of obligation to apply:

- The parties either:
  - enter into one or more bullion trades through the same pair of offices; or
  - have entered, through the same pair of offices, into one or more bullion options which have subsequently been exercised (or are deemed to have been exercised).
- Both transactions have the same bullion transaction settlement date.
- The delivery obligations relate to the same type of bullion or currency.
- The delivery location is identical for both transactions.

If all of those conditions are fulfilled, then as soon as the second transaction has been entered into, both transactions are simultaneously cancelled and replaced by a single bullion obligation for that bullion transaction settlement date.

The details of this single bullion obligation will be determined in a straightforward manner: the delivery obligations in respect of the same bullion will be offset against each other and the resulting bullion obligation will be equal to the difference by which the larger amount of the specified commodity exceeds the smaller amount.

The parties could also elect 'novation netting by matched pair'. This is almost identical to 'novation netting by type of obligation'. The only difference is that the parties must specify the offices between which the netting will apply under the heading 'matched pair offices' of the confirmation.

The Bullion Annex clarifies that a failure to record the new bullion obligations on the books will not affect the validity of the netting arrangements and that the parties are free to agree any cut-off date and time in the confirmation.

Hypothetical example: Lloyd Industries plc and Gez Capital Partners LP

Lloyd Industries plc and Gez Capital Partners have entered into two physically settled bullion transactions, each acting through its London office.

The first transaction is a bullion trade (a forward) referencing 20,000 ounces of platinum with a bullion transaction settlement date of November 26 2009. Under that transaction, Lloyd is the purchaser and Gez is the seller. Lloyd has also bought from Gez a European-style put option referencing 15,000 ounces of platinum, with the bullion expiration date falling on November 26 2009.

Assuming that the option is exercised (or is deemed to have been exercised), the novation netting will apply and both trades will be simultaneously cancelled. As the difference between the bullion trade and the put option is equal to 5,000 ounces, both transactions will be replaced by a single bullion obligation under which Gez will have to deliver 5,000 ounces of platinum to Lloyd on November 26 2009. The new bullion obligation will become binding at the time that the put option is exercised (or is deemed to have been exercised).

9. Exhibits to the Bullion Annex

The forms included in the Bullion Annex (the 'Bullion Templates') are similar to those in the exhibits to the 2005 definitions, which were analysed in the previous chapter and which cover the standard confirmations for commodity transactions. The major differences are as follows:

- The Bullion Templates include additional terms for a bullion trade (ie, for a spot or forward transaction), whereas this type of transaction is not covered in the 2005 exhibits.
- The Bullion Templates cover physical settlement of bullion transactions (ie, settlement by delivery).
- The Bullion Templates adopt the terminology specific to the Bullion Annex – for example, instead of the term 'purchaser', the templates use the expression 'purchaser of bullion'; and instead of 'strike price', they use 'bullion strike price'.

In the same way as in the 2005 exhibits, the Bullion Templates consist of two exhibits. Exhibit I is the "Sample form for a letter agreement or telex confirming a transaction", which is adapted by the parties to the relevant transaction to become the transaction confirmation. Exhibits I in the 2005 exhibits and in the Bullion Templates are identical.

Exhibit II provides standard terms, set out in separate templates and called "Additional provisions", for each type of transaction listed below:

- 'bullion trade';
- 'bullion swap';
- 'bullion option';
- 'bullion swap which is a cap, collar or floor'; and
- 'bullion swaption'.

To avoid duplication, we concentrate below on the main differences between the 2005 exhibits and the Bullion Templates. As an exception, the template for bullion trades is analysed in more detail as there is no equivalent form in the 2005 exhibits.

9.1 Exhibit II-A – bullion trade

This is a very simple template which covers spot or forward transactions referencing bullion. It is structured as described next:

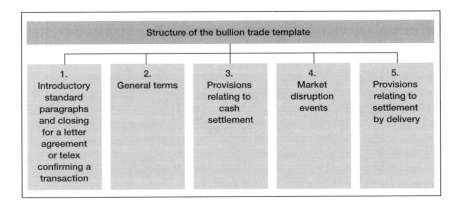

(a) **General terms**

The 'General terms' are set out first. The parties will insert specific details and elections for the transaction for the following terms and definitions from the 2005 definitions:

- the 'reference number' (ie, the internal reference number adopted by the financial institution);
- the 'trade date' (ie, the date on which the parties agree to enter into the transaction);
- the 'purchaser of bullion' (ie, the details of the purchaser);
- the 'seller of bullion' (ie, the details of the seller);
- the 'bullion' (ie, whether the transaction related to gold, silver, platinum or palladium);
- the 'number of ounces' (ie, the amount of bullion relevant for a particular transaction);
- the 'contract price' (ie, the price at which the seller agrees to sell the specified amount of bullion to the buyer);
- the 'bullion transaction settlement dates' (ie, the dates where payment or settlement under each transaction shall occur);
- 'settlement' (ie, whether 'settlement by delivery' or 'cash settlement' shall apply); and
- 'additional provisions for tax' (ie, any additional tax provisions agreed between the parties).

Considering that this is, effectively, a sale-and-purchase agreement, all the terms are largely self-explanatory. The parties enter into the transaction on the trade date and from that date they are bound by its terms. The purchaser agrees to buy a specified number of ounces of the relevant bullion from the seller at the agreed contract price. Under current market practice, bullion is usually measured in ounces and that is why this unit has been included in this template. Naturally, if the parties would like to use any other measurement, they can amend the document accordingly.

The parties will settle the transaction on the bullion transaction settlement date. If this is the same as the trade date, the transaction will be a spot transaction. If the parties decide to choose a future date, it will be a forward.

The parties then decide whether they want cash settlement or settlement by delivery to apply. Depending on their choice, they will include one or the other set of provisions below.

Finally, they can agree any additional tax provisions for their transaction. The Bullion Annex provides no fallbacks here, so the parties must set out their entire agreement relating to taxes.

(b) Provisions relating to cash settlement
This is a shorter, streamlined version of the cash settlement provisions as included in the 2005 exhibits. It covers only three items:

- the 'commodity reference price' (ie, the code for the chosen price source as set out in Sub-annex A to the 2005 definitions);
- the 'price source/reference dealers' (this is another way to determine the relevant prices); and
- the 'delivery date' (ie, whether the price will be based on a certain delivery date or a month).

In most cases the parties to a bullion trade will specify only the commodity reference price and the delivery date in the confirmation. However, if they want to create their own reference price or rely on the reference dealers, they can fill out the relevant section of the template.

When compared with the 2005 exhibits, the following terms have been omitted: 'currency', 'unit' and 'specified price'. However, they may need to be reinserted if necessary to identify the pricing details. They have also been included in the other forms included in the Bullion Templates.

(c) Provision relating to settlement by delivery
Instead of including the cash settlement provisions above, the parties to a bullion trade can elect settlement by delivery to apply. In that case, the template provides the following items:

- the 'delivery location' (ie, London or Zurich);
- the 'consequences of settlement disruption events' (ie, either 'negotiation' or 'cancellation and payment'); and
- other items and conditions.

As explained above, the standard method of physical settlement of bullion trades is on an unallocated basis. This means that the seller's broker will transfer the relevant amount of bullion from the seller's account to the buyer's account. For gold and silver, such account will be located in London, and the parties should select this city as the delivery location. If, however, the buyer acquires platinum or palladium, the account will be located in Zurich.

The parties should also specify what happens if an event occurs beyond the control of the parties as a result of which delivery cannot be effected by the specified method (ie, there is a settlement disruption event); they can elect either negotiation or cancellation and payment to apply. Essentially, 'negotiation' means that the parties will try to negotiate the way to settle the transaction if physical delivery is impossible for 10 successive bullion business days. In turn, 'cancellation and payment' allows for termination of the transaction only two days after a settlement disruption event has occurred.

The parties can also elect that settlement by delivery should apply on an allocated basis. As the Bullion Annex provides no provisions for this mode of settlement, the parties should aim to set out the details in the 'Other items and conditions' section. Naturally, the parties can also insert there any other agreed terms relating to physical settlement.

(d)   Market disruption events

The terms included in this template confirmation are identical to those in the 2005 exhibits and include the following items:

- 'market disruption events' (ie, whether the market disruption events as specified in the 2005 definitions should apply);
- 'additional market disruption events' (ie, any additional event which will constitute a market disruption event for the purposes of the 2005 definitions);
- the 'disruption fallbacks' (ie, the consequences of market disruption events);
- the 'fallback reference price' (ie, the price which may apply if the primary reference price is not available); and
- 'maximum days of disruption' (ie, the number of days after which settlement would occur).

Generally, the market disruption events operate in the same manner for transactions referencing bullion as for those referencing other commodities. However, there is one important difference with respect to the automatic application of market disruption events.

For a bullion transaction, only the following market disruption events will be deemed to apply by default: 'price source disruption', 'trading disruption' and 'disappearance of commodity reference price'. As bullion transactions are very standard in the market, the ISDA working group decided that there is no need for the inclusion of 'material change in formula' and 'material change in content' to those trades, although they would apply for transactions referencing other commodities, unless expressly specified otherwise.

9.2   Other exhibits

The Bullion Templates also include four other exhibits:

- Exhibit II-B for a bullion swap;
- Exhibit II-C for a bullion option;
- Exhibit II-D for a bullion swap which is a cap, collar or floor; and
- Exhibit II-E for a bullion swaption.

Generally, they are very similar to the 2005 exhibits and perform the same function. However, there are certain differences between the Bullion Templates and the corresponding 2005 exhibits, which are highlighted below.

(a) Settlement by delivery

One of the major reasons for the existence of the Bullion Annex is that it allows for physical settlement of bullion transactions. In addition to the bullion trade, the bullion option template also allows parties to elect settlement by delivery. The same wording as in the bullion trade form has also been included in the bullion option template.

The additional provisions for bullion swaps, for bullion swaps which are a cap, collar or floor, and for bullion swaptions do not include the physical settlement provisions – this is not really possible due to the nature of those instruments.

(b) Market disruption events

The market disruption events provisions are identical in the 2005 exhibits and in the Bullion Templates, but different events will be deemed applicable by default. As explained in section 3 of this chapter, only the following market disruption events will be deemed to apply to bullion transactions, unless specifically agreed otherwise: 'price source disruption', 'trading disruption' and 'disappearance of commodity reference price'.

(c) Bullion terminology

The Bullion Templates have been streamlined and adapted for bullion transactions and the terminology has been amended accordingly. Below is the table of the changed terms.

2005 exhibits	Bullion Templates
Commodity	Bullion
Reference dealers	Bullion reference dealers
Notional quantity	Number of ounces
Option style	Bullion option style
Option type	Bullion option type
Seller	Bullion option seller
Buyer	Bullion option buyer
Strike price per unit	Bullion strike price

table continues overleaf

2005 exhibits	Bullion Templates
Premium	Bullion premium
Premium payment date	Bullion premium payment date
Exercise period	Bullion exercise period
Potential exercise date	Bullion potential exercise date
Expiration date	Bullion expiration date

Each term in a pair of terms performs the same function in the respective template. The differences between the respective definitions have been analysed above and can be seen to be relatively minor.

(d)   Basis swaps

Exhibit II-B of the Bullion Templates does not provide for 'basis swaps' in the same way as Exhibit II-A of the 2005 exhibits. However, there is no reason why parties cannot enter into basis swaps referencing more than one bullion commodity reference price if they make the appropriate adjustments to the template. The 'common pricing' option has been included in the bullion swap form, which suggests that the ISDA working group had anticipated such a possibility.

10.   Conclusion

ISDA, with the help of the LMBA, has issued an enormously useful annex to assist market participants to settle their bullion transactions and has provided the market with the efficiency of standardised documentation.

The importance of bullion in general, and gold in particular, has often been underestimated in the last 5,000 years of human history. Lenin was certainly not alone in underestimating its future importance. A number of capitalist economists, including Ludwig von Mises, believed that the price of gold would drop drastically after its demonetisation in 1971. This has not happened and gold remains king, even in the turbulent times of the post-credit-crunch economy. Moreover, the Order of Lenin, the Soviet Union's highest military decoration in the 1940s and 1950s, was made from silver and gold, but those precious metals never made it into use in public urinals.

Weather index derivative transactions

Erica Johansson
David Johnson

1.   Introduction

Accurately predicting the weather is a difficult thing to do. Anyone planning a weekend barbecue based on weather that was forecast to be hot and sunny will have memories of sheltering under nearby trees from unexpected rain. But what if you could buy protection against a change in the weather? Would the rain that ruined your barbecue have been so bad if you had been compensated for it and instead been able to treat your friends at a nice restaurant? Weather derivatives do just that: one party agrees to pay another if a predetermined weather event occurs, in return for a premium.

To take another example, hurricanes such as Andrew (1992) and Katrina (2005), which struck the south-east United States, thankfully do not occur that often, but slight variations in temperature and rainfall occur on a daily basis. What if your business were impacted by these slight variations and you wanted to protect yourself against them? Insurance would not be suitable, since a quantifiable loss would be difficult to prove. However, weather derivatives could be ideal, as evidence of loss is not a prerequisite for payment. Since almost every business in the world is affected by the weather, from utility companies to the tourism industry, the application of weather derivatives is extremely broad.

This chapter explains what weather derivatives are, how they are documented (with particular reference to the 2005 definitions and Sub-Annex C, which covers weather index derivatives transactions). It also discusses the benefits and disadvantages of using weather derivatives, as well as some recent developments in the markets, and provides examples of how weather derivatives have been used to hedge against weather risk.

2.   What are weather derivatives?

Weather risk is usually transferred through variances in weather indices, which transform weather into a fungible product. A typical weather derivative would measure differences in the weather (eg, in relation to temperature, precipitation, snow or wind) against an index. Under a weather derivatives transaction, one or both of the parties must make a payment to the other party on the occurrence of a particular weather event.

Most weather derivatives reference temperature, rain or wind. Less common underlying reference classifications are sunshine, humidity, frost and growing days (for farmers). To give one example, a party may want to enter into a weather derivative in order to hedge against falling temperatures. The party seeking protection from the elements is the buyer and the party selling protection is the seller. The seller is hoping to make more money from the premium paid by the buyer than that which it needs to pay out under the transaction if temperatures should fall. The buyer, on the other hand, is protected from the economic consequences that follow from, for example, a fall in temperature; should the average temperature over a defined period drop below a specified threshold, the seller will pay the buyer a predetermined amount.

One groundbreaking transaction was the weather derivative entered into in 2001 by Corney & Barrow Wine Bars Ltd, a London-based wine bar chain. After reviewing historical sales data, Corney & Barrow realised that, unsurprisingly, it sold more drinks on hot Thursday and Friday afternoons. Under its derivatives transaction, Corney & Barrow paid a one-off premium for the entitlement to receive £15,000 for every Thursday and Friday during the summer that the temperature failed to exceed 24 degrees Celsius, subject to a maximum payout of £100,000 for the contract period (June to September). Buying this protection turned out to be a good decision for Corney & Barrow since the summer of 2001 was unseasonably cold. The transaction helped Corney & Barrow to recoup revenue lost as a result of the cool weather.

In March 2006 the World Food Programme (as protection buyer) entered into a call option transaction with Axa Re (as protection seller) in order to hedge against droughts affecting Ethiopia. The transaction referenced an index linked to rainfall measured at 26 weather stations across Ethiopia, coupled with a countrywide crop-water stress index. The option was triggered when the crop-water stress index rose above a pre-specified level, indicating widespread drought and crop failure. The World Food Programme paid a premium of $930,000. On the occurrence of a drought, Axa Re would pay a maximum of $7.1 million to the World Food Programme. Although no payout was made, since the rainfall that year was above average, this transaction demonstrates the feasibility of using weather derivatives to hedge against disasters.

2.1 Types of weather derivatives

There are two main types of weather derivative. The first type includes derivatives where the aggregate variable (eg, rainfall or temperature); is measured over a predetermined period of time. When the aggregate variable reaches or crosses a certain pre-agreed threshold (ie, it exceeds or falls below that threshold, depending on the agreement of the parties), a payment is due under the transaction. This is the most common kind of weather derivative.

Example 1: degree-day floor fact pattern

Two parties have agreed that, in return for a premium, one party (the protection buyer) will pay the other party (the protection seller) a predetermined amount if the average temperature during the agreed period of time (the month of February) is below 18 degrees Celsius. According to the chart overleaf, a payment will be due since the average temperature in February is 16 degrees Celsius.

Details of how this kind of payment is calculated are set out in section 5.3 below.

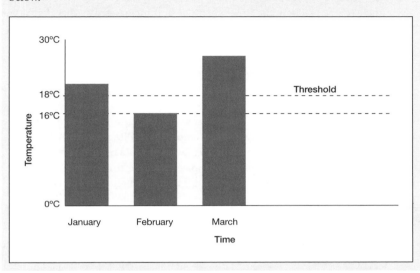

The second type of weather derivative is based on the occurrence of adverse weather events such as storms, tornadoes and hurricanes. If such weather events occur during the contract period at the relevant location, then the protection seller will pay the protection buyer an amount dependent on the severity of the event. Due to the increased popularity of the trading of these kinds of weather derivatives, the International Swaps and Derivatives Association, Inc (ISDA) published the US Wind Event Confirmation in 2009 for use when trading derivatives referencing significant wind events in the United States. See section 6 below for a detailed discussion of this confirmation.

2.2   Who uses weather derivatives and where are they traded?

Any company whose business is affected by weather can benefit from trading weather derivatives. Businesses that are sensitive to the weather include agriculture, utility, food and beverage companies, and the leisure and sport industries. Insurance companies interested in managing their insurance risk also regularly use weather derivatives.

Weather derivatives contract sellers include banks, insurance companies and hedge funds, as well as any other investor seeking exposure to industries affected by weather. From a portfolio risk-management perspective, since weather derivatives are largely immune to systemic risk, they can be a useful hedge against overall market movements.

The biggest participants in the weather derivatives markets are energy and utility corporations. Their involvement is a result of deregulation in these industries and the break-up of state-run monopolies. Whereas historically, energy and utility companies comprise large, state-run companies with generation and distribution arms, deregulation and privatisation have contributed to many companies spinning off their generation capabilities, thereby exposing themselves to supply price increases at precisely the time when demand increases. Weather derivatives can be used to mitigate such risks.

As with any kind of derivative, market participants can combine different derivatives contracts (eg, swaps, caps and floors) to create the desired effect – for instance, through a collar. By way of illustration, the company that is buying protection in the example above could also buy a degree-day cap to secure a payment if the average daily temperature exceeded 24 degrees Celsius. Alternatively, the company could seek to offset the premium payments that it paid to buy the degree-day floor (ie, protection against the temperature falling below 18 degrees Celsius) by selling a corresponding degree-day cap, which would of course expose that company to the risk of a payout obligation. However, if the company is an amusement park company, the risk of the payout under the cap might be acceptable in view of the additional business that it would generate due to the warmer weather.

Most weather derivatives are traded over the counter (OTC). However, weather derivatives are also traded on exchanges, with the CME Group being the leading exchange on which weather derivatives are traded. Unlike bespoke OTC contracts, exchange-traded contracts are standardised contracts traded in an open market with price transparency.

By creating weather indices, the CME Group has made it possible to trade weather like any other indexed investment. Exchange-traded products that are bought and sold on the CME Group exchange include futures and options referencing temperature, hurricanes, snowfall and frost in different cities around the world. Exchange-traded weather products are quantified in terms of how much a particular variable (eg, rain, snowfall, temperature, frost and damage by hurricanes) deviates from the seasonal or monthly average in a prescribed city or region. A dollar amount is attached to each point by which the variable deviates from the average. By way of illustration, the summer weather index on the CME Group exchange is based on a temperature of 18 degrees Celsius at the relevant location.

2.3 The differences between weather derivatives and weather insurance

A product that dates back to before weather derivatives is weather insurance. Parties to an insurance contract agree that the insurer will make a payment to the insured when it suffers a loss. The central difference between weather derivatives and weather insurance is, as one would expect, that under a weather derivatives transaction, the seller of protection has to make a payment regardless of whether the buyer suffers a loss. Insurance contracts also generally rely on there being an insurable interest. Another difference is that weather insurance usually covers high-risk and low-probability events, such as hurricanes or earthquakes. Weather derivatives, on the other hand, often cover low-risk and high-probability events such as an increase or decrease in temperature. While such events are rarely life threatening, they can have a significant financial impact and therefore hedging against them can be advantageous.

A seller of weather derivatives can hedge its exposure under the transaction by entering into complementary agreements. For example, the weather protection seller in the above Corney & Barrow example could have used the premium paid to it by Corney & Barrow to enter into a back-to-back hedge agreement, potentially on better terms, thereby making an arbitrage profit. As mentioned above, many insurance companies use weather derivatives to lay off some of the insurance risk in their portfolios.

3. Status of the weather derivatives market

Trading in weather risk dates back to 1996. The origins of the weather derivatives market was marked by three innovative transactions: one between Koch Industries and PXRe, and two between Koch Industries and Enron. All three transactions were based on tracking variables in the weather through weather indices. The transactions between Enron and Koch Industries were triggered by temperature fluctuations during the winter of 1997. The transactions were structured so that if the temperature rose above a certain level, Koch Industries would pay Enron $10,000 for every degree above it, and if the temperature fell below the same level, Enron would pay Koch Industries $10,000 for every degree below it.

In 1999, leading participants in the weather markets founded the Weather Risk Management Association (WRMA). The WRMA is designed to foster public and corporate awareness of weather risk and promote growth in the weather risk markets. The WRMA also conducts surveys and works with ISDA to standardise documentation for the most common forms of weather derivatives transactions.

Trading in weather derivatives flourished in 2007–2008, with the markets experiencing an increase of 35% in the number of contracts traded compared with the previous year; in terms of notional value, the amounts of traded contracts increased by 76%. However, the weather derivatives markets have not been insulated from the recent downturn. A survey by the WRMA showed that the notional value of all transactions declined by 50% in a year, where the estimated notional value of all weather derivatives was $15 billion in 2008–2009 against an estimated value of $32 billion in 2007–2008. The total number of contracts also declined: 601,000 contracts were traded during 2008–2009 compared with 985,000 contracts in 2007–2008. Most trades take place in North America, although trading also occurs in Asia, Europe and Australia.

4. Advantages and disadvantages of weather derivatives

Many companies could potentially benefit from trading weather derivatives. Below are some of the advantages and disadvantages of using weather derivatives.

4.1 Advantages

Among the advantages of using weather derivatives are the following:
- A company whose business is significantly affected by the weather can hedge against adverse weather conditions.
- Weather derivatives are completely uncorrelated to other asset classes. This also means that they are less sensitive to systemic risk.
- Weather derivatives procure a prompt payout if and when they are triggered (as opposed to weather insurance, where the insured typically needs to prove

that it has suffered an insurable loss before a payment is made).

- A buyer can protect itself against relatively minor fluctuations in weather (whereas insurance generally pays out only on catastrophic events).
- Participants can gain exposure to the weather (and correlated businesses), while avoiding the transaction costs that serve as barriers to entry to such businesses.
- The global nature of weather enables investors to gain exposure to any market in the world (provided that accurate weather data is available – see below).

4.2   Disadvantages

Among the disadvantages of using weather derivatives are the following:

- Many of the potential end users that could benefit from weather derivatives are relatively unsophisticated and do not deal in derivatives on a regular basis. They have therefore been slow in embracing these products.
- It is difficult to identify impartial sources that provide accurate and reliable data.
- Like all forms of derivatives, if used improperly, weather derivatives can lead to excessive risk exposure where companies fail to put sufficient risk controls in place.
- It is hard to estimate the impact that the weather will have on a company's business.
- Since the majority of weather derivatives transactions are traded OTC, the parties are exposed to counterparty risk.
- The novel nature of weather derivatives means that investors will experience barriers to entry in the form of legal costs and training.

5.   Sub-Annex C to the 2005 definitions – weather index derivatives transactions

Sub-Annex C to the 2005 ISDA Commodity Definitions sets out the main provisions and definitions for documenting weather derivatives. Sub-Annex C also contains three template confirmations, which can be used to document:

- weather index swaps;
- weather index call options/caps; and
- weather index put options/floor transactions.

These transactions would normally reference heating degree day (HDD), cooling degree day (CDD) or critical precipitation day (CPD) indices. The 2005 ISDA Commodity Definitions also cover specialised disruption events and disruption fallbacks, which are further discussed below. The selection of a data provider, the source of information and disruption fallbacks are all important, as the calculation of the amounts payable under a weather derivatives transaction depends on the accuracy of the information provided.

5.1 General definitions

Section 11.1 of the 2005 ISDA Commodity Definitions defines a 'weather index derivatives transaction' as:

- any transaction that is an OTC weather index swap transaction, OTC weather index call option/cap transaction, OTC weather index put option/floor transaction or any other similar transaction (including any swaption with respect to any of these transactions);
- any combination of these transactions; and
- any other transaction identified as a weather index derivatives transaction in the related confirmation.

The party hedging itself against adverse weather conditions is usually the 'weather index buyer' and the party selling protection the 'weather index seller'. However, under a weather index swap, both parties can be required to make a payment, depending on which threshold is triggered (see section 5.4(a) below of this chapter). Normally, the weather index buyer would pay a premium (ie, a price) to the weather index seller for entering into the transaction. Under the 2005 ISDA Commodity Definitions, the premium is payable on the 'premium payment date', which is the date specified as such in the confirmation.

The 'calculation period' is the period which the transaction covers. A weather index derivatives transaction can cover a single calculation period or multiple calculation periods

The 'data provider' is the provider of either temperature data or precipitation data, as specified by the parties in the confirmation. The 'weather index station' or 'location' is the relevant intended source of weather index data in the specified location. Usually the data provider is a state meteorological authority, an exchange or another third-party data provider.

5.2 Weather index stations or locations

Section 11.17 of the 2005 ISDA Commodity Definitions sets out 28 different weather index stations or locations, which the parties can choose from. These include meteorological institutions in a variety of countries, including Austria, Australia, Belgium, Canada, Switzerland, the Czech Republic, Germany, Denmark, Italy, Japan, Korea, Mexico, New Zealand, Spain, Finland, Sweden, South Africa, the United Kingdom and the United States.

The parties to a weather index transaction must specify the particular weather index station's data to be used when making the relevant calculations for a transaction. If, for example, 'SE-SMHI' is selected as applying in the confirmation, then data provided by the Swedish Meteorological and Hydrological Institute – Sweden's national meteorological authority responsible for observing, collecting and providing the meteorological data for the reference location in Sweden – will be used. The equivalent institute in the United Kingdom is the United Kingdom's national meteorological authority, the Meteorological Office Agency of the Ministry of Defence (GB-MET).

As for the United States, the 2005 ISDA Commodities Derivatives Definitions cover three US meteorological authorities:

- the National Oceanic and Atmospheric Administration;
- the US National Meteorological Authority, which is responsible for observing, collection and providing meteorological data for the United States and the National Climatic Data Centre; and
- the National Weather Service, which is responsible for providing weather and flood warnings, public forecasts and advisories for the United States, including its territories, adjacent waters and ocean areas.

Both the National Weather Service and the National Climatic Data Centre are divisions of the National Oceanic and Atmospheric Administration.

The parties can also specify a 'fallback weather index station' (FWIS) and a 'second fallback weather index station' (SFWIS) in case the relevant data is unavailable from the nominated weather index station. If the parties fail to specify a fallback and a second fallback, then the fallbacks 'FWIS disruption fallback' and 'SFWIS disruption fallback' will not apply (see section 5.5 below).

5.3 Weather index units

In a weather index derivatives transaction, the notional amount is an amount calculated per 'weather index unit', a number derived from one of the CDD, HDD or CPD methods.

The use of CDDs and HDDs in weather derivatives is based on the US practice of hedging the cost of energy in relation to heating or cooling. Both CDDs and HDDs are measured against a reference temperature (normally 18 degrees Celsius or 65 degrees Fahrenheit). For every degree below the reference temperature, one HDD is added to the number of weather index units that are used as a measurement for calculating the cost of heating. Naturally, most transactions measuring HDDs cover the winter months. CDDs, on the other hand, are a measurement of the costs involved in cooling the temperature – for every degree above the reference temperature, one CDD is added to the total number of weather index units. In contrast to HDDs, transactions referencing CDDs usually cover the summer months.

CDDs are determined in accordance with the following formula: for any day during the relevant calculation period, the CDD is a number equal to the greater of the daily average temperature for that day minus the CDD reference level and zero. The daily average temperature is the arithmetic average of the maximum and minimum temperatures in degrees Celsius or Fahrenheit (as the case may be) at the relevant location for that day as reported by the relevant data provider. The CDD reference level is the (temperature in) degrees Celsius or Fahrenheit specified by the parties to the confirmation.

Note the CDD cannot be less than zero since, theoretically, there would be no need for cooling if the temperature were less than the agreed reference level. So when (daily average temperature – CDD references level) $\leq$ 0, the CDD will be zero.

Example 2: calculating a CDD
If the CDD reference level for a transaction measuring the CDD in Stockholm is 18°C and the daily average temperature for June 20 2009 was 20°C, then the CDD for that day is 2 (20 minus 18).

The HDD is determined for any day during the relevant calculation period by taking the HDD reference level and subtracting the daily average temperature (subject to the HDD never being less than zero).

The HDD reference level is predetermined in the 2005 ISDA Commodity Definitions at 18 degrees Celsius or 65 degrees Fahrenheit unless otherwise specified in the confirmation.

Note the HDD cannot be less than zero since, theoretically, there would be no need for heating if the temperature was more than the agreed reference level. So when (HDD reference level – daily average temperature) ≤ 0, the HDD will be zero.

Example 3: calculating a HDD
If the daily average temperature is 16°C and no HDD reference level has been elected to apply in the confirmation, then the HDD is 2 (18 minus 16).

Similarly, if the daily average temperature is -5°C and no HDD reference level has been elected to apply, then the HDD is 23 (18 minus -5).

The CPD reference level is, as the name indicates, the reference level of precipitation, measured in millimetres (mls) or inches as specified in the confirmation. CPD refers to the measured precipitation over a specified time period. 'Daily precipitation' is the measure of precipitation in mls or inches at the relevant location for the relevant day, as reported by the data provider. CPD is determined in accordance with one of the following two methods:

- Unless 'reference level equals zero' is specified to not apply, the CPD for the relevant calculation period is a number equal to:
  - unity, if the daily precipitation for that day is equal to or greater than the CPD reference level: or
  - zero, if the daily precipitation for that day is less than the CPD reference level.
- If 'reference level equals zero' is specified not to apply in the confirmation, the CPD for the relevant calculation period is for a number equal to:
  - unity, if the daily precipitation for that day is greater than the CPD reference level; or
  - zero, if the daily precipitation for that day is equal to or less than the CPD reference 'level.

'Reference level equals zero' is relevant only in relation to weather index derivatives referencing the CPD. If the parties have elected that 'reference level equals zero' does not apply, the CPD will equal zero if the precipitation for the relevant day is equal to the CPD reference level. On the other hand, if the parties have elected that 'reference level equals zero' shall apply (or if they have omitted to state that reference level equals zero shall not apply), then the CPD will equal one if the precipitation for that day is equal to the CPD reference level (see further example below).

> **Example 4: calculating the CPD**
> If the parties have elected that the CPD reference level is 20 mls and that reference level equals zero shall not apply, on a day where the rainfall is measured at 10 mls, then the CPD equals zero as the daily precipitation for that day is less than or equal to the CPD reference level.
>
> If the parties have elected that the CPD reference level is 20 mls and that the reference level equals zero shall apply, on a day where the rainfall is measured at 25 mls, the CPD is one, as the daily precipitation for that day is greater than or equal to the CPD reference level.
>
> If the parties have elected that the CPD reference level is 20 mls and that the reference level equals zero shall apply, on a day where the rainfall is measured at 20 mls, the CPD equals one as the daily precipitation for that day is greater than or equal to the CPD reference level.

Section 11.22 of the 2005 ISDA Commodity Definitions provides that temperature data and precipitation data shall be rounded to the same degree of accuracy as the data that was (or would have been) provided by the data provider on the relevant calculation date. If 'rounding of weather index units' and the relevant degree of accuracy are specified in the confirmation, then the weather index units shall be rounded in accordance with that methodology. They can, for instance, be rounded up to either the nearest whole weather index unit (with one half-unit being rounded up) or to the nearest half weather index unit (with one quarter-unit being rounded up).

5.4   Calculating payment amounts

Calculating payment amounts under a weather index derivatives transaction is based on measuring the 'settlement level' against the weather index level or the weather index strike level. Depending on the relevant formula that applies (see below), the difference between the two will be multiplied by the 'notional amount'. This amount will, subject to any threshold that applies, be the amount payable by either the weather index buyer or the weather index seller to the other party.

The settlement level is specified by the parties in the confirmation. It can, for instance, be:

- the cumulative number of weather index units for each day in the calculation period;
- the average number of weather index units over a period (ie, the cumulative number of weather index units for each day in the calculation period divided by the number of days in the calculation period); or
- the maximum or minimum number of weather index units for any day in the calculation period.

Example 5: one possible calculation of the settlement level

If the settlement level given in the first bullet point above (ie, the cumulative number of weather index units for each day in the calculation period) is applied to Example 2 above, where the CDD reference level for the transaction was 18, the daily average temperature was 20 degrees Celsius and the CDD was 2, then the settlement level is 2 (assuming that the calculation period only covers one day).

The 'weather index level' and 'weather index strike level' are the number of weather index units specified as such in the confirmation. Subsections (a) to (c) below describe how the payment amount is calculated in respect of weather index swaps, weather index call options/caps and weather index put options/floors.

The 'maximum transaction payment amount' and the 'maximum payment amount' are the amounts specified as such in the confirmation. The maximum transaction payment amount is the maximum amount payable by either the weather index buyer or the weather index seller to the other party under a transaction. The maximum payment amount works as a cap on the amount payable in respect of a calculation period. If there is only one calculation period under the transaction, this puts a limit on the maximum amount payable under the transaction (similar to the maximum transaction payment amount).

(a)   *Calculating a payment amount for a weather index swap*

The template for a confirmation for OTC weather index swap transactions (see Exhibit I-A to Sub-Annex C of the 2005 ISDA Commodity Definitions) incorporates the following provisions for calculating a payment amount for a weather index swap:

- If the settlement level in respect of a calculation period is greater than the weather index level, then the weather index seller shall, except to the extent by which such amount exceeds the maximum transaction payment amount in respect of the weather index seller, pay to the weather index buyer on the relevant payment date an amount equal to the lesser of:
  - an amount equal to the excess of the settlement level over the weather index level multiplied by the notional amount; and
  - if applicable, the maximum payment amount per calculation period in respect of the weather index seller.
- If the settlement level in respect of a calculation period is less than the weather index level, then the weather index buyer shall, except to the extent by which such amount exceeds the maximum transaction payment amount in respect of the weather index buyer, if applicable, pay to the weather index seller on the relevant payment date an amount equal to the lesser of:
  - an amount equal to the excess of the weather index level over the settlement level multiplied by the notional amount; and
  - if applicable, the maximum payment amount per calculation period in respect of the weather index buyer.
- If the settlement level in respect of a calculation period is equal to the weather index level, neither party shall be required to make a payment on the relevant payment date.

Example 6: calculating the payment amount for a weather index swap

The weather index swap confirmation between the parties sets the weather index level at 3. The notional amount is €10,000, the maximum transaction payment amount is €100,000 and the maximum payment amount is €50,000, in respect of both parties.

Using the figures from Examples 2 and 5, above, we have that the CDD reference level for the transaction is 18, the daily average temperature is 20 degrees Celsius, the CDD is 2, and the settlement level equals 2 (assuming that the calculation period covers only one day).

Since the settlement level in respect of the calculation period is less than the weather index level, the second set of provisions, described above, apply. Accordingly, the weather index buyer shall pay the weather index seller an amount equal to €10,000 on the relevant payment date.

Settlement level < weather index level, so

Payment amount = (Weather index level – settlement level) × notional amount
= (3 – 2) × €10,000
= €10,000

(b)   Calculating a payment amount for a weather index call option/cap

The template for a confirmation of OTC weather index call option/cap transactions (see Exhibit I-B to Sub-Annex C to the 2005 ISDA Commodity Definitions) incorporates the following provisions for calculating a payment amount for a weather index call option/cap:

- If the settlement level in respect of a calculation period is greater than the weather index strike level, then the call option seller shall (except to the extent by which such amount exceeds the maximum transaction payment amount) pay to the call option buyer on the relevant payment date an amount equal to the lesser of:
    - an amount equal to (A) the excess of the settlement level over the weather index strike level multiplied by (B) the notional amount; and
    - if applicable, the maximum payment amount per calculation period.
- If the settlement level in respect of a calculation period is equal to or less than the weather index strike level, neither party shall be required to make a payment on the relevant payment date.

A weather index call option/cap transaction is triggered when the weather index strike level is met in respect of the relevant calculation period. As mentioned above, the weather index strike level is the number of weather index units specified in the confirmation.

Example 7: calculating the payment amount for weather index call options/caps

The weather index call option/cap confirmation between the parties sets the weather index strike level at 4. The notional amount is €10,000, the maximum transaction payment amount is €100,000 and the maximum payment amount is €50,000, in respect of both parties.

Using the figures from Examples 2 and 5 above, we again have that the CDD reference level for the transaction is 18, the daily average temperature is 20 degrees Celsius, the CDD is 2, and the settlement level equals 2 (assuming that the calculation period covers only one day).

Since the settlement level in respect of the calculation period is less than the weather index strike level, the second set of provisions described above applies. Accordingly, neither party shall be required to make a payment under the transaction.

(c)   *Calculating a payment amount for a weather index put option/floor*
The template for a confirmation of OTC weather index put option/floor transactions (see Exhibit I-C to Sub-Annex C to the 2005 ISDA Commodity Definitions) incorporates the following provisions for calculating a payment amount for a weather index put option/floor:

- If the settlement level in respect of a calculation period is less than the weather index strike level, then the put option seller shall, except to the extent by which such amount exceeds the maximum transaction payment amount, pay to the put option buyer on the relevant payment date an amount equal to the lesser of:
  - an amount equal to (A) the excess of the weather index strike level over the settlement level multiplied by (B) the notional amount; and
  - if applicable, the maximum payment amount per calculation period; or
- If the weather index strike level in respect of a calculation period is equal to or less than the settlement level, neither party shall be required to make a payment on the relevant payment date.

Similarly to a call option transaction, the put option transaction is triggered when the weather index strike level is met. If the settlement level exceeds the weather index strike level, then an amount becomes payable by the put option seller to the put option buyer, to the extent that such amount does not exceed the maximum transaction payment amount (and is less than the maximum payment amount).

Example 8: calculating the payment amount for weather index put options/floors
The weather index put option/floor confirmation between the parties sets the weather index strike level at 4. The notional amount is €10,000, the maximum transaction payment amount is €100,000 and the maximum payment amount is €50,000, in respect of both parties.

Using the first set of figures from Example 3 above, where the HDD reference level for the transaction is 18, the daily average temperature is 16 degrees Celsius and the HDD is 2, the settlement level equals 2 (assuming that the calculation period covers only one day).

Since the settlement level in respect of the calculation period is less than the weather index strike level, an amount equal to €20,000 will be paid by the put option seller to the put option buyer on the relevant payment date.

Settlement level < weather index strike level, so

Payment amount = (Weather index strike level - settlement level) × notional amount

$$= (4 - 2) \times €10,000$$
$$= €20,000$$

(d)   *Data correction*

The payment amount can also be subject to data correction where the data used to determine the payment amount was incorrect and the wrong amount was paid by one party to the other. In the event that the data provider within the specified correction period publishes or makes any correction or adjustment to the reported daily maximum or minimum temperature or the daily precipitation at the relevant location, and if the payment amount was determined on the basis of the incorrect data or on the basis of a primary disruption fallback (see section 5.5 below), then the calculation agent shall determine a correction amount. The correction amount is equal to the net difference between the payment amount as originally calculated and the payment amount as calculated using the corrected, published or adjusted data.

In order for data correction to apply, the parties must include such provision in the confirmation. The correction amount shall be paid by the relevant party within two business days of written notice by the calculation agent of the correction amount.

5.5   Disruption fallbacks

As mentioned above, it is important that the parties to a weather index derivatives transaction elect for disruption fallbacks to apply in case the relevant temperature or precipitation data is unavailable.

The 2005 ISDA Commodity Definitions distinguish between 'primary disruption events' and 'secondary disruption events'. A primary disruption event applies when the data provider fails to publish data either entirely or in its final edited form (as determined by the calculation agent in good faith) in respect of the relevant maximum or minimum temperature or precipitation data. The maximum or minimum temperature or the daily precipitation for that day will instead be determined by using the first applicable primary disruption fallback elected by the parties in the confirmation that provides the parties with the relevant data.

The secondary disruption event applies if data correction is specified to apply in the confirmation (see section 5.4(d) above). If the calculation agent determines in good faith that the data provider has failed to publish data or failed to publish data in its final edited form, and this affects the calculation of a payment amount, then the calculation agent shall determine a correction amount. As mentioned above, the correction amount shall be equal to the net difference between the payment amount originally calculated and the payment amount as it would have been calculated had the relevant data for that day been determined in accordance with the first applicable secondary disruption fallback.

The parties can elect for one of the following primary disruption fallbacks or secondary disruption fallbacks to apply (when referred to as such) in the confirmation:

- 'fallback data';
- 'synoptic data';
- 'FWIS';
- 'SFWIS';
- 'negotiated fallback'; and
- 'no-fault termination'.

The primary disruption fallbacks and secondary disruption fallbacks will apply in the order that they are specified in the confirmation.

(a) Fallback data

The 'fallback data' disruption fallback provides that the maximum or minimum temperature or daily precipitation for the relevant day will be the data reported by the 'alternative data provider', which is the party specified as such in the confirmation.

(b) Synoptic data

Under the 'synoptic data' disruption fallback, the maximum or minimum temperature or daily precipitation for the relevant day is determined by using meteorological data which has not been subject to the ultimate quality control in its final edited form (but which has been subject to one or more quality controls, integrity processes or verification processes). Where synoptic data has been derived from a mixture of different processes, including automated and manual processes, the relevant synoptic data for the relevant day shall be deemed to be the data derived from the automated process.

(c) FWIS disruption fallback

The 'FWIS' disruption fallback provides that the fallback for the missing data shall be the data reported by the data provider at the fallback weather index station. This means that in order for the FWIS disruption fallback to apply, the parties must specify a fallback weather index station in the confirmation.

(d) SFWIS disruption fallback

Similarly, the 'SFWIS' disruption fallback provides that the relevant data shall be deemed to be the data reported by the data provider at the second fallback weather index station. In order for the SFWIS disruption fallback to apply, the parties must specify a second fallback weather index station in the confirmation.

(e)   ***Negotiated fallback***

As the term indicates, negotiated fallback provides that the parties, on the occurrence of a primary or secondary disruption event, shall in good faith negotiate with each other with a view to coming to an agreement in respect of the relevant data (or a method by which such data can be determined). If the parties have not reached an agreement within three business days of the calculation date of the relevant calculation period in the case of a primary disruption event, or the last day of the correction period in relation to a secondary disruption event, then the next fallback provision shall apply.

(f)   ***No-fault termination***

If none of the applicable primary or secondary disruption fallbacks provides the parties with a maximum or minimum temperature or with the daily precipitation figure, as appropriate, then the weather index derivatives transaction will terminate in accordance with the no-fault termination.

In accordance with the no-fault termination, the transaction will be terminated as if a termination event and an early termination date had occurred on the day the no-fault termination became the applicable primary or secondary disruption fallback. The calculation of the settlement amount shall be based on there being two affected parties and, if the transaction incorporates the 1992 ISDA Master Agreement, as though 'loss' applies under Section 6(e) of the ISDA Master Agreement.

6.   Wind event confirmation

As mentioned above, ISDA published a template Wind Event Confirmation in 2009 for trading exposure to catastrophic wind events in the United States. This template enables parties to hedge against losses from wind-based natural disasters in the United States (or gain exposure to this market). It is anticipated that this template will be primarily utilised by insurance market participants and investors seeking exposure to this kind of risk.

The parties to the Wind Event Confirmation must specify a 'wind event' (see section 6.1 below) for a chosen 'covered territory' (which may be the entirety of the United States or a particular geographic area within the United States). On the occurrence of a 'covered event' (ie, a wind event covered by the confirmation), if the estimated amount of damage exceeds the covered event threshold, a payment will be due from the protection seller to the protection buyer.

6.1 Types of wind event

USA wind event definitions (with key differences highlighted in bold)		
USA Wind Event 1	USA Wind Event 2	USA Wind Event 3
"Any catastrophic event occurring in or affecting the Covered Territory, where the perils identified in the most recent Loss Report with respect to such event include the peril(s) of wind (howsoever described in a Loss Report), including storm, hurricane, tempest, tornado, cyclone, typhoon, hail, or any combination thereof (including all flood following such perils) …"	"Any catastrophic event occurring in or affecting the Covered Territory, where the perils identified in the most recent Loss Report with respect to such event include the peril(s) of wind (howsoever described in a Loss Report), including storm, tempest, tornado, cyclone, hail, or any combination thereof (including all flood following such perils); **provided, however, that the perils of named tropical storms, typhoons and/or hurricanes (and all flood following such perils) will be excluded …"**	"Any catastrophic event occurring in or affecting the Covered Territory, where the perils identified in the most recent Loss Report with respect to such event **are defined as the peril(s) of named tropical storms, typhoons and/or hurricanes (including all flood following such perils) …"**

As indicated in the preceding table, there are three different definitions of wind event for the parties to choose amongst:
- USA Wind Event 1;
- USA Wind Event 2; and
- USA Wind Event 3.

USA Wind Event 1 is the broadest definition. USA Wind Event 2 does not include the "perils of named tropical storms, typhoons and/or hurricanes (and all flood following such perils)". USA Wind Event 3, on the other hand, is exclusively limited to those perils.

6.2 Calculating payment amounts
Payments are calculated based on one of two formulae.
The first formula has a binary outcome and provides that the protection seller will pay the protection buyer a pre-specified percentage of the agreed notional amount of the transaction.

Example 9: calculating the binary payment amount (floating amount)
The parties specified a notional amount of $1 billion and a percentage of 50% in the confirmation, then the payment due would be $500 million on the occurrence of a covered event.

Alternatively, if a linear-loss payment method is chosen, on the occurrence of a covered event the protection seller (ie, the floating rate payer) will need to pay the protection buyer an amount equal to the following:

- if the reference amount relating to the covered event is equal to or greater than the covered event threshold and less than the exposure cap, then the product of (x) and (y), where:
  - (x) = (a), the reference amount minus the covered event threshold, divided by (b), the exposure cap minus the covered event threshold; and
  - (y) = 100% of the notional amount;
- if the reference amount relating to the covered event is equal to or greater than the exposure cap, then 100% of the notional amount, provided that, the floating rate payer's total liability under the transaction shall not exceed the notional amount.

Example 10: calculating a linear payment amount (floating amount)
If the parties specified a covered event threshold of $100 million, an exposure cap of $200 million and a notional amount of $50 million, and a reference amount of $175 million was specified in the loss report, then the payment due by the credit protection seller would be $37.5 million pursuant to the first calculation method outlined above.

$$\text{Floating amount} = \frac{(\text{Reference amount} - \text{covered event threshold})}{(\text{exposure cap} - \text{covered event threshold}))}$$
$$\times (100\% \times \text{notional amount})$$
$$= \frac{(\$175\text{ million} - \$100\text{ million})}{(\$200\text{ million} - \$100\text{ million}))} \times (100\% \times \$50\text{ million})$$
$$= \$37.5\text{ million}$$

If the same figures were selected by the parties in the confirmation but the reference amount specified in the loss report was $300 million, then the floating amount due would be the notional amount of $50 million, pursuant to the second calculation method outlined above.

6.3   Data for determining how to calculate the payment amount
The reference amount used when calculating the payment amount is the figure included in the loss report (a catastrophe bulletin originated and disseminated by the report publisher) as the estimated market loss (the estimated amount of insured property damage or loss resulting in the estimated insurance payment for the covered territory). The reference amount may be subject to adjustment if the figure for estimated market loss in the loss report includes expenses or workers'

compensation losses in the amount of estimated insurance industry losses, then such amounts will be deducted from the reference amount.

The report publisher is the Property Claims Service, a division of the Insurance Services Offices, Inc. The definition of 'report publisher' contains provisions for determining a successor report publisher if the service ceases to provide loss reports or materially changes its methodology and the calculation agent determines that such changes make loss reports published by the service unsuitable for the purposes of the confirmation.

6.4   Risk period
For a wind event to fall within the definition of a 'covered event', it must have a 'date of loss' that occurs during the relevant risk period. The risk period is specified by the parties to the confirmation and is not subject to any business day convention. Date of loss, on the other hand, is specified in the applicable loss report subject to the following adjustment: if the risk period expires while a reference event causing a loss is in progress, then the date of loss for such reference event shall be deemed to be the date specified in the applicable loss report as the date of commencement of such reference event.

7.   Conclusion
The weather affects many businesses. Because it is difficult to predict the weather, companies can benefit from protection against changes in the weather through the use of weather derivatives. Since their advent in 1997, the weather derivatives markets have expanded substantially, with utility and insurance companies being the most active participants. In comparison with insurance products, weather derivatives have the advantage of not requiring the protection buyer to prove a loss before a payment is due.

Weather derivatives are not, however, without their disadvantages. Many potential users of weather derivatives are relatively unsophisticated and therefore do not capitalise on this technology. It is also difficult to identify impartial and accurate providers of weather data that is needed to form the foundation of the weather derivatives markets.

Documentation produced by ISDA in the 2005 Commodity Definitions provides a framework for trading various forms of weather derivatives and includes template confirmations in the form of swaps, caps and floors, as well as supporting definitions. Such confirmations and definitions set out, among other things, the methods for calculating payments, correcting data, and procedures for identifying fallback data sources. ISDA has also recently published a template Wind Event Confirmation, which facilitates the standardisation of transactions referencing wind-based natural disasters.

Most experts believe that global warming contributes to erratic and unpredictable weather. Since weather derivatives can, when used effectively, mitigate the financial impact from variations in weather, it is a reasonable estimate that their popularity will increase throughout the 21st century.

Gas derivative transactions

Edmund Parker

1. Introduction

Natural gas is one of the world's primary energy sources, along with coal and oil. One definition of 'natural gas' is "any hydrocarbon or mixture of hydrocarbons and non-combustible gases which, when extracted from the subsoil of the earth in its natural state separately or together with liquid hydrocarbons, is in the gaseous state".[1] So that is our underlying asset for this category of derivatives.

Used mainly for residential heating, electricity generation and transportation, gas meets almost one-quarter of the world's energy needs. It is extracted from gas fields and oilfields, with the biggest proven reserves being in Eastern Europe and the Middle East.

Gas is more difficult to transport than oil; it must be carried by pipeline or in liquefied form (liquefied natural gas). The high costs of transportation have resulted in regional trading markets in Asia, Europe and the United States, mainly dependent on pipeline networks and the hubs into which they flow. Liquefied natural gas is transported by sea.

The principal gas production areas supplying Europe are Russia, the Netherlands, Norway and Algeria; and for the United States, Canada. The gradual deregulation of energy markets in the United States and Europe has led to a gas trading market.

The gas market is a volatile one. A mild or warm winter can cause huge variations in demand. A new pipeline can increase supply and drive down prices. A political dispute, such as that in 2009 when Russia turned off the gas supply to pipelines crossing Ukraine, can cause a shortage of supply and drive up prices.

The gas market is standardised. In Europe, gas is bought and sold in therms, while in the United States it is traded in units of 100 cubic feet.

As well as volatility and volume, different market participants have an interest in seeing the price of gas move in opposing directions. These include gas producers and suppliers, major corporate users, as well as speculators and market makers.

A gas derivative is a financial instrument which derives its value from the underlying asset of natural gas. This chapter looks at the various types of gas derivatives and their uses. It also examines the documentation infrastructure, in particular that provided by the International Swaps and Derivatives Association, Inc (ISDA) through the 2005 ISDA Commodity Definitions in Sub-Annex D for Europe and Sub-annex E for North America, and their related templates. In addition, we

---

1   Zeebrugge Hub Natural Gas Trading Terms and Conditions (2004).

discuss the basic infrastructure of gas supply and how the spot trading market works, because an understanding of this is essential to understand gas derivatives.

ISDA's gas derivatives documentation is a relatively late arrival to the market, introduced only in the last few years. Sub-Annex D, the European Gas Annex, therefore dovetails with two other sets of market-standard documentation for gas derivatives:

- the Short-term Flat NBP Trading Terms and Conditions, for use with transactions settled on the National Balancing Point; and
- the Zeebrugge Hub Natural Gas Trading Terms and Conditions, for use with transactions settled on the Zeebrugge Hub.

We also discuss the substance of these platforms and their interaction with the ISDA platform.

2. Gas infrastructure

2.1 Pipelines and hubs

Gas is extracted from gasfields and oilfields and then flows through pipelines to storage facilities or terminals, some of which are known as physical hubs. There are several large physical hubs in Europe and the United States where gas arrives, and several major gas pipelines converge and deposit gas in terminals.

A physical hub also provides a trading point for buyers and sellers of natural gas. Sellers include producers, suppliers and traders; and buyers include suppliers and large industrial customers. These trades will have standardised trading terms and will use the transaction infrastructure to allow for the liquid trading of gas. The best way to visualise a trading hub is as a bank; instead of money, customers deposit gas. Just as in a bank, the deposited asset is mixed with all other deposited assets of the same class. Other parties can then make withdrawals, if agreed by the depositors. At a bank, the parties making withdrawals would be entities to which the customer wanted to make a payment (eg, a mortgage provider by direct debit). At a physical trading hub, the party making the withdrawal, or off-take of gas, is a transaction counterparty, one to which the customer has agreed to sell a corresponding quantity of gas.

It is the hub's job to match deliveries of gas with off-takes, following trade nominations by the party delivering the gas and the party off-taking it.

2.2 The Zeebrugge Hub

Zeebrugge in Belgium is the largest trading hub in Europe. Roughly 15% of natural gas consumed in continental Europe passes through the gas infrastructure located in Zeebrugge. It is also the meeting point for several major pipelines converging on three major terminals and is therefore an ideal location in which to site a physical hub.

Zeebrugge's three major terminals are the LNG Terminal, the Zeepipe Terminal and the Interconnector Terminal. Zeebrugge's gas infrastructure is operated by the independent transmission system operator Fluxys and links Siberia to Germany and the United Kingdom, and Norway to Italy and Southern Europe. Fluxys also operates

Belgium's natural gas transportation, its storage infrastructure and it transport grid.

The LNG Terminal is a terminal for liquefied natural gas carried by sea from all over the world. The Zeepipe Terminal receives gas from Norway, in part through an 814-kilometre (km) pipeline which runs from the Norwegian Sleipner area of the North Sea to Zeebrugge. The Interconnector Terminal connects the Fluxys Grid (a 3,700km pipeline grid, which in turn connects to other gas grids), to a 230km pipeline running below the North Sea from Bacton in the United Kingdom to Zeebrugge. In the United Kingdom, the pipeline connects into the UK grid.

The hub provides Europe's largest spot trading market, as well as an online trading exchange, and is a point of reference for trading natural gas around the world. It was established in 1999 as the first short-term trading hub in Europe.

A subsidiary of Fluxys, Huberator, facilitates trading on the Zeebrugge Hub. Huberator has almost 80 members. These include financial institutions such as Barclays, Deutsche Bank, Goldman Sachs, JP Morgan, Morgan Stanley and RBS; and gas producers and suppliers operating through their respective trading arms, such as RWE, Eni and Gas Natural. Huberator also keeps a central record of trades.

The hub provides an infrastructure for physical and financial gas transactions. It facilitates over-the-counter transactions on standard terms and provides screen-based trading on a trading platform. Members sign up to the hub's Zeebrugge Hub Natural Gas Trading Terms and Conditions. Alternatively they can sign up to the European Federation of Energy Traders (EFET)'s ZBT 2004 Appendix or put in place their own agreement.

The Zeebrugge Hub Natural Gas Trading Terms and Conditions provide standard terms for the sale and purchase of gas, on both a spot and a derivatives basis. They set out quality requirements and provisions relating to risk and also establish a procedure for confirming trades, together with a form of confirmation that includes the following:

- representations and warranties between the parties; and
- procedures for terminating and closing-out transactions following a default by one of the parties, together with the calculation of settlement amounts.

EFET released its ZBT 2004 Appendix Version 1.0 in June 2006. This is an appendix to its General Agreement for Gas and is designed to cover spot and option gas transactions for the delivery of gas on the Zeebrugge Hub. The appendix is effectively the Zeebrugge Hub Natural Gas Trading Terms and Conditions, together with the ZBT Option Transactions Annex, which amends the terms and conditions.

Any and all future ZBT transactions are automatically subject to the General Agreement (Gas), as amended by the ZBT Appendix, unless the terms of such ZBT transactions state otherwise.

2.3 The National Balancing Point Hub

A trading exchange for deliveries and off-takes of gas within a single pipeline system is called a virtual balancing point. Here the virtual hub acts as a market maker, provides back-office functions and facilitates the transportation of gas within the pipeline network.

The National Balancing Point (NBP) is a virtual hub for the United Kingdom and is the largest of its kind in Europe. It is also the pricing and delivery point for the Intercontinental Exchange Natural Gas Futures Contract.

Just as with the Zeebrugge Hub, the NBP has its own set of standardised documentation for spot and derivatives trading of gas. The governing documentation terms are known as the Short-Term Flat NBP Trading Terms and Conditions (Ref: NBP 1997). As with the ZBT Terms (ie, quality requirements and provisions relating to risk), these set out procedures for confirming trades, representations and warranties, and procedures for terminating, closing out and settling transactions.

3. Principal sources of market information

Trading in natural gas and the related derivatives is possible only if reliable market prices are available. These come in the form of published indices and trading prices, derived from actual market prices paid. The principal providers of natural gas prices in Europe are:

- the Dow Jones Energy Service;
- the Energy Argus Daily;
- the Heren Report;
- the International Petroluem Exchange (IPE);
- the On-the-Day Commodity Market; and
- Platt's European Natural Gas Report.

For North America, the principal providers of natural gas prices are:

- the Canadian Gas Price Reporter;
- Gas Daily;
- Gas Daily Price Guide;
- 10X Group;
- Inside Ferc;
- Natural Gas Week;
- NGI's Bidweek Survey;
- NGX; and
- NYMEX.

Prices are also available for liquefied natural gas, with these prices provided by Argus, NYMEX and Opis.

A vast range of gas prices are available, far more than for any other commodity. For example, the 2005 ISDA Commodity Definitions has 70 pages of definitions of reference prices for natural gas and four for liquefied natural gas.

4. Overview of ISDA documentation platform for gas derivatives trading

The diagram following sets out the principal ISDA documentation platform for documenting gas derivatives. The ISDA Master Agreement (both the 1992 and 2002 versions), as amended by a schedule and possibly credit support documentation, forms the primary platform.

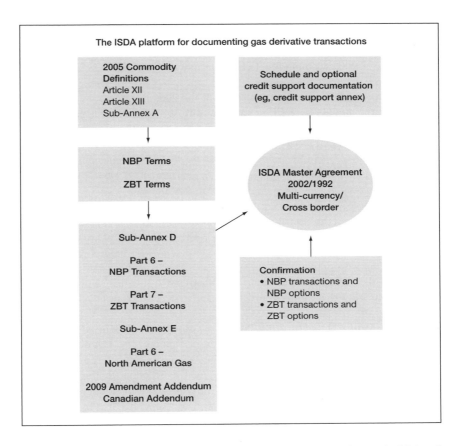

The ISDA platform for documenting gas derivative transactions

This primary platform is supplemented by a secondary platform of additional sections in Sub-Annex D, which may be incorporated into the schedule to facilitate either or both of European ZBT transactions and NBP transactions. The 2005 ISDA Commodity Definitions also form part of the secondary platform. So too does Sub-Annex E: this sets out an additional section of the ISDA Master Agreement for North American Natural Gas Transactions, as well as a Canadian addendum. In 2009 a further addendum was published with amendments to supplement Sub-Annex E.

As a tertiary platform, ISDA has produced template confirmations for derivatives transactions relating to the NBP (NBP transactions and NBP options); and transactions relating to the Zeebrugge Hub (ZBT transactions and ZBT options).

Each confirmation is structured to reference prices set out in Sub-Annex A to the 2005 Commodity Definitions. As mentioned above, this includes 70 pages of definitions for reference prices for natural gas and four for liquid natural gas.

Confirmation templates are set out in Sub-Annex D of the Annex to the 2005 Commodity Definitions, which relates to European transactions. A template confirmation for Sub-Annex E, which relates to North American transactions, was first published in early 2010.

The template confirmations incorporate the primary platform of the ISDA Master

Agreement (which will also include the gas transaction-specific secondary platform), as well as the secondary platform of the 2005 definitions.

The 2005 Commodity Definitions provide the fallbacks and framework for natural gas derivatives.

Article XII of the principal body of the 2005 Commodity Definitions provides that the provisions relating to physically settled European gas transactions are published in Sub-Annex D: the European Gas Annex. Specifically, Article XII states:

> The remaining provisions of this Article XII are published in Sub-Annex D of the Annex to these Commodity Definitions, which may be amended from time to time. The parties may elect that Sub-Annex D apply to an agreement or a Transaction by taking the action described in Sub-Annex D [the European Gas Annex].

Identical wording is set out in Article XIII, except that the reference here is to Sub-Annex E: the North American Gas Annex.

The European Gas Annex and the North American Gas Annex amend the 2005 definitions to the extent that the market practices for natural gas differ from those applicable to other commodities. The annexes are not separate documents in their own right and their provisions are incorporated into the main body of the 2005 Commodity Definitions as Article XII and Article XIII respectively.

5. Sub-Annex D of the 2005 ISDA Commodity Definitions: overview

Sub-Annex D, the European Gas Annex, is 29 pages long. It is designed for use with physical transactions carried out on the Zeebrugge Hub and the NBP only.

It consists of a "form of Part [6] of the Schedule to the 2002 ISDA Master Agreement or the 1992 ISDA Master Agreement (Multicurrency – Cross Border) for NBP Transactions and NBP Options"; and an "Appendix 1 to the 2002 ISDA Master Agreement or the 1992 ISDA Master Agreement (Multicurrency – Cross Border)", which provides forms for NBP transactions and NBP options.

Sub-annex D also sets out a "form of Part [7] of the Schedule to the 2002 ISDA Master Agreement or the 1992 ISDA Master Agreement (Multicurrency – Cross Border) for ZBT Transactions and ZBP Options"; and an "Appendix 2 to the 2002 ISDA Master Agreement or the 1992 ISDA Master Agreement (Multicurrency – Cross Border)", which provides forms for ZBT transactions and ZBP options.

6. Sub-Annex D of the 2005 ISDA Commodity Definitions: NBP transactions

Part 6, when incorporated into the schedule to the ISDA Master Agreement, is titled "Provisions relating to NBP Transactions and NBP Options". It is divided into seven paragraphs, covering:

- incorporation of NBP Terms;
- NBP transactions and NBP options;
- applicable NBP Terms;
- additional provisions for NBP transactions and NBP options;
- close-out of NBP transactions;
- amendments to NBP Terms;
- additional provisions for NBP options; and
- payment instructions.

6.1 Incorporation of NBP terms

Paragraph (a) incorporates by reference the Short-Term Flat NBP Trading Terms and Conditions (ref: NBP 1997). These are defined collectively as the 'NBP Terms', the standard trading terms and conditions for the NBP.

The incorporation paragraph then states that the NBP Terms are deemed amended so that they are relevant only for NBP transactions and NBP options (ie, transactions entered into on the NBP and options to enter into those transactions).

6.2 NBP transactions and NBP options

Paragraph (b) provides that the ISDA Master Agreement will govern any NBP transaction or NBP option that the parties enter into, with the ISDA Master Agreement trumping the NBP Terms if there is any inconsistency.

6.3 Applicable NBP Terms

Paragraph (c) applies certain terms from the NBP Terms, disapplies others and suggests that certain others are optional. The applied, disapplied and optional terms are set out in the table below.

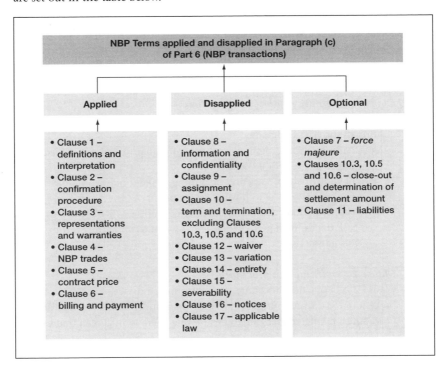

Paragraph (c) deems that the following clauses apply from the NBP Terms:

- Clause 1 – definitions and interpretation;
- Clause 2 – confirmation procedure;
- Clause 3 – representations and warranties;

- Clause 4 – NBP trades;
- Clause 5 – contract price; and
- Clause 6 – billing and payment.

Paragraph (c) also provides for the parties to specify optionally Clauses 7, 10.3, 10.5 and 10.6 and Clause 11 as applicable. Clauses 10.3, 10.5 and 10.6 cover close-out and determination of settlement amount following a termination event. Clause 11 exempts either party from being liable for consequential and/or indirect losses, except in the case of fraud, intentional default or gross negligence.

However, the following clauses are deemed not to apply:
- Clause 8 – information and confidentiality;
- Clause 9 – assignment;
- Clause 10 – term and termination, excluding Clauses 10.3, 10.5 and 10.6;
- Clause 12 – waiver;
- Clause 13 – variation;
- Clause 14 – entirety;
- Clause 15 – severability;
- Clause 16 – notices; and
- Clause 17 – applicable law.

Of the provisions deemed to apply, even optionally, these clauses can be summarised as set out next.

(a) Clause 1 – definitions and interpretation

Clause 1 of the NBP Terms provides several definitions which are used in derivatives confirmations. These include:
- 'daily quantity', defined as "the daily quantity of gas agreed between the parties as such for a transaction";
- 'day', defined as "a period beginning at 0600 hours on a day and ending at 0600 hours on the following day"; and
- 'supply period', defined as "the period during which... the parties shall make NBP trades, such period commencing and terminating on the days agreed for the transaction".

(b) Clause 2 – confirmation procedure

Clause 2 sets out the procedure for confirming transactions. This is a more formal procedure for documenting transactions than under standard ISDA documentation procedures, taking greater care to ensure that there is an agreed trade.

(c) Clause 3 – representations and warranties

Clause 3 sets out two representations which the parties make to each other. First, they represent that during the supply period they will maintain all necessary licences and consents. Second, they represent that they will remain a party to the network code. This has now been updated by the Uniform Network Code and is the regulatory set of rules for gas industry participants using the NBP.

(d)   Clause 4 – NBP trades
Clause 4 covers the matching of trades (ie, matching the gas delivered by the seller with that off-taken by the buyer).

It also provides the fallbacks for what happens when one party breaches its obligations to make an effective trade nomination, or deliver or off-take the gas. More specifically:

- Clause 4.1 covers trade nominations;
- Clause 4.2 covers a breach by the seller;
- Clause 4.3 covers a breach by the buyer; and
- Clause 4.4 covers the payment and amount of compensation following a breach.

(i)   Clause 4.1 – trade nominations
Trade nominations are nominations made by the parties to Transco, the operator of the NBP. Effectively, the seller is notifying the operator that it is delivering a quantity of gas for the account of its counterparty, the buyer. The buyer, for its part, is notifying the operator that it will be off-taking the same quantity of gas.

To facilitate the trade nomination process, Clause 4.1 provides that for each day in the supply period on which the daily quantity is greater than zero, each party will make an accurate trade nomination to the NBP. The NBP's trading infrastructure will then balance the parties' accounts.

One nomination will be by the seller, the party delivering the gas. The other will be by the buyer, the party off-taking the gas.

(ii)   Clause 4.2 – breach by the seller
Clause 4.2 sets out the consequences of breaches by the seller if it fails to make an effective trade nomination under Clause 4.1.

If guilty of a breach, the seller must pay the buyer compensation for each day it is in breach. The amount payable is based on one of two alternative formulae, which the parties may choose as applicable.

The first formula involves calculating the 'system marginal buy price' (SMBP) as a first step. This is defined as the price in pence per kilowatt-hour calculated by Transco on the basis of an average of all trades for that day, plus a premium. The affected transaction's contract price (CP) is then subtracted from the SMBP. The resulting amount is then multiplied by the transaction's daily quantity (DQ). The formula for compensation is therefore: $(SMBP - CP) \times DQ$.

If the amount is positive, the seller will pay this amount to the buyer (no payment will be made if the amount is negative or zero). The calculation is repeated and amounts may fall due for each day of the breach.

The second formula operates in the same way as the first, except that SMBP is replaced by the system average price (SAP), which is a price in pence per kilowatt-hour calculated by Transco on the basis of an average of all trades for that day, but without the premium.

(iii)   *Clause 4.3 – breach by the buyer*
         Clause 4.3 sets out the consequences of breaches by the buyer in making an effective trade nomination under Clause 4.1. If guilty of a breach, the buyer must pay the seller compensation for each day it is in breach. Like Clause 4.2, the amount of compensation payable is based on one of two formulae, which the parties may elect as applicable.

         The first formula involves first calculating the 'system marginal sell price' (SMSP), as described above. The SMSP is then subtracted from the affected transaction's CP. The resulting amount is then multiplied by the DQ. The formula for compensation is therefore: (CP -SMSP) × DQ.

         If the amount is positive, the buyer will pay this amount to the seller (if it is negative or zero, no payment will be made). The calculation is repeated and amounts fall due for each day of the breach.

         The second formula operates in the same way as the first, except SMSP is replaced by SAP (as described above).

(iv)   *Clause 4.4 – payment of compensation*
         Clause 4.4 provides that any compensation amounts described above may be offset by the party owed them against other amounts owed by it for NBP transactions between the parties.

(e)   **Clause 5 – contract price**
         Clause 5 provides that the buyer agrees to pay the seller, for each NBP trade, a sum calculated by multiplying the transaction's contract price per unit of gas by its daily quantity.

(f)   **Clause 6 – billing and payment**
         Clause 6 provides that all transactions between the parties must be settled monthly in arrears on the basis of a monthly statement. This monthly statement must be sent on or before the 10th day of a calendar month and paid within 10 days.

(g)   **Clause 7 – force majeure**
         Under Clause 7, if a *force majeure* event occurs, preventing delivery or off-take of gas, then the parties' obligations will be suspended. The non-claiming party can then give three business days' notice to terminate if it believes that the event may continue for seven consecutive days.

(h)   **Clause 10 – term and termination**
         Clauses 10.3, 10.5 and 10.6 are square bracketed in Part 6. These provisions relate to closing out NBP transactions and the parties may either apply these or rely on the general close-out provisions set out in their ISDA Master Agreement.

         Clause 10.3 provides that any termination of a transaction will not affect rights or obligations which have previously accrued.

         If Clause 10.5 is not elected to apply, then following an event of default or termination event under the parties' ISDA Master Agreement, the parties will calculate the close-out amount for each gas transaction in the same way as they would for an interest rate swap, a credit default swap or an equity derivatives option.

In the case of a 1992 ISDA Master Agreement, this would mean that the close-out amount for each transaction would be calculated according to the first or second payment method, and the market quotation or loss payment measurement. In the case of a 2002 ISDA Master Agreement, close-out amount would be calculated in accordance with the definition of 'close-out amount' in that agreement.

If Clause 10.5 is elected to apply, the close-out amount of gas transactions only will instead be calculated according to the NBP Terms. The parties may elect for this clause to apply, where they are either mainly dealing with NBP transactions under their master agreements or alternatively entering into back-to-back transactions and wish to avoid the possibility of a mismatch in any close-out amounts. Where Clause 10.5 is elected, the following provisions will apply.

(i)   *Terminating party is buyer*

Where the terminating party is a buyer for a particular transaction (following an event of default or termination event under the parties' ISDA Master Agreement), the close-out amount for that transaction will be calculated using the following formula: $(MV - RV) - I$.

Here MV stands for 'market value', which is calculated using its own formula: $D \times DQ \times GRP$. D is the number of days from and including the termination date to the end of the supply period. This number is then multiplied by DQ. The resulting figure is then multiplied by the 'gas reference price' (GRP), which is calculated by taking an average of three price quotes published respectively by Heren, Argus and the IPE (as defined in the NBP Terms).

Once the MV is calculated, the buyer (as the terminating party) then subtracts the 'RV' from the MV. The RV is an amount calculated using the formula: $D \times DQ \times CP$, where CP is the contract price of the terminated transaction.

Once the RV has been deducted from the MV, the final stage for calculating the close-out amount for such a terminated transaction is to subtract I from the resulting figure, where I is the discounted amount that reflects the present-day value as of the termination date of RV - MV, using the London Interbank Offered Rate.

(ii)   *Terminating party is seller*

Where the terminating party is the seller (following an event of default or termination event under the parties' ISDA Master Agreement), the close-out amount for each transaction is calculated by following this formula: $(RV - MV) - I$.

The definitions of 'RV', 'MV' and 'I' are the same as when the terminating party is the buyer. So to calculate a termination amount, the terminating party for a transaction, where it is the seller, will deduct the transaction's MV from its RV and will then subtract the discount amount from the resulting figure.

For any group of terminated transactions, the terminating party may be the seller in some and the buyer in others. A termination amount will need to be calculated for each terminated transaction on this basis and these will need to be netted against each other as part of calculating the wider settlement amount under the parties' ISDA Master Agreement.

(iii)   *Fallbacks*
Clause 10.6 provides a fallback for the terminating party where the price quotations necessary for calculating are unavailable or unreasonable. If this is the case, the terminating party may instead take an average of three reasonable quotations.

(i)   **Clause 11 – liabilities**
Clause 11 provides that neither party is responsible to the other for indirect or consequential losses, save for cases of fraud, intentional default or gross negligence.

6.4   Additional provisions for NBP transactions and NBP options
Paragraph (d) sets out eight additional provisions which are deemed to apply to NBP transactions and NBP options in addition to the provisions of the NBP Terms incorporated by reference in Paragraph (c). Some of these are elections and are square bracketed; others are not. The additional provisions mainly apply or disapply additional events of default or termination events for certain actions relating to NBP Transactions.

The first additional provision establishes that it will be an additional event of default under the ISDA Master Agreement if there is a material adverse change in a party's financial standing that affects its ability to perform its obligations, as compared with the transaction date. This must be accompanied by a request from the other party for it to provide reasonable security for the performance of its obligations within five business days of a request. Due to the subjective nature of such a provision, any party that is requested to have one in its ISDA Master Agreement would do well to resist this clause.

The second additional provision provides that it will be an additional termination event under the ISDA Master Agreement if a party's representation under Clause 3 of the NBP Terms proves to have been materially incorrect or misleading when made. This is also an optional election and will apply if the parties do not want a breach of representation to be an event of default.

The third additional provision establishes that a failure to deliver gas will not constitute an event of default under the ISDA Master Agreement. Instead, the relevant provisions of the incorporated NBP Terms will apply.

The fourth additional provision provides that if a party fails to accept or deliver gas or to make a nomination or notification, this will not constitute an event of default.

The fifth additional provision applies if the parties are using a 2002 ISDA Master Agreement. It provides that Section 5(b)(ii) of the ISDA Master Agreement will not apply. Section 5(b)(ii) is the termination event for *force majeure* (and there is no corresponding provision in the 1992 ISDA Master Agreement). Instead, the parties will rely on the detailed *force majeure* provisions set out in Clause 7 of the NBP Terms, which is incorporated by reference into Part 6 – NBP Transactions and Options.

The sixth additional provision establishes that if a transaction terminates under Clause 7.2 of the NBP Terms (ie, by reason of *force majeure*), then this will not be deemed to be a termination event or an event of default under the parties' ISDA Master Agreement.

The seventh additional provision is also bracketed as an optional election. It provides that each representation under Clause 6 of the NBP Terms is a representation for the purposes of the parties' ISDA Master Agreement. The effect of this is that if there is a breach of this representation, it will be an event of default under the parties' ISDA Master Agreement. The seventh additional provision is offered as an alternative to the second additional provision, which instead makes the breach of representation a termination event under the parties' ISDA Master Agreement.

The eighth additional provision provides that, notwithstanding anything else in the schedule to the ISDA Master Agreement (eg, a New York governing law clause), the NBP Terms will be governed by English law.

6.5 Close-out of NBPN transactions

Paragraph (e) provides mechanisms for NBP gas transactions to be closed out on a different basis from other derivatives transactions documented under the parties' ISDA Master Agreement. Furthermore, it provides certain alternative elections depending on whether the parties are using a 1992 ISDA Master Agreement or a 2002 ISDA Master Agreement.

If the parties are using a 2002 ISDA Master Agreement, they will specify in paragraph (e) that, for NBP transactions, the close-out amount will be determined in accordance with Clause 10.5 of the NBP terms. If they are using a 1992 ISDA Master Agreement, they will specify in paragraph (e) that if, under that agreement, they have specified market quotation as the payment measure, then it will be deemed that a market quotation cannot be determined for each terminated transaction that is a NBP transaction.

Under the 1992 ISDA Master Agreement, if a market quotation for a terminated transaction cannot be determined, the fallback is for the early termination amount to be determined in accordance with the agreement's definition of 'loss'. Paragraph (e) then provides that 'loss' for NBP transactions will be determined in accordance with Clause 10.5, rather than the definition in their ISDA Master Agreement.

6.6 Amendments to NBP Terms

Paragraph (f) sets out six additional provisions amending certain of the definitions in the NBP Terms in order properly to integrate them within the ISDA Master Agreement. For example, the definition of 'transaction' is substituted by 'NBP transaction', to clarify that NBP transactions are treated differently from other derivatives transactions documented under the parties' ISDA Master Agreement.

6.7 Additional provisions for NBP options

Paragraph (g) sets out seven additional provisions which are deemed to apply for NBP options. Each of these are elections and so square bracketed, suggesting that the parties may or may not decide to incorporate them into their ISDA Master Agreement Schedule.

The first section of additional provisions provides an alternative definition of both 'call' and 'put', as well as 'option buyer' and 'option seller', and definitions relating to premiums, prices and exercises, all tailored to apply to NBP options.

In particular, the definition of 'reference price' set out in the 2005 Commodity Definitions is replaced by a new definition which provides that during the supply period this will be the arithmetic average of the Argus price, the Heren price, the Platt's price and the IPE price quoted on the option's expiration date. These four prices are then defined as follows:

- the 'Argus price' is the price reported in *Energy Argus Daily European Natural Gas* and published by Petroleum Argus Ltd;
- the 'Heren price' is the price reported in *The Heren Report European Spot Gas Markets*;
- the 'Platt's price' is the price reported in *Platt's European Natural Gas Report*; and
- the 'IPE Price' is the price published on the International Petroleum Exchange for the IPE Natural Gas Futures Contract for that supply period.

The second section provides that each confirmation for an NBP option will be documented in substantially the same form as the template set out in Part 6.

The third section provides that an NBP option will expire without any payments becoming due if the option buyer does not exercise it by the expiration time on the expiry date. In these circumstances a buyer must physically exercise an option to get any benefit.

The fourth section of additional provisions provides a mechanism for automatic exercise of NBP options. This provision deems automatic exercise is applicable unless otherwise specified. Its provisions work such that the option is deemed to be exercised at its expiration time if the in-the-money amount payable to the buyer is equal to or exceeds the product of 10% of the strike price and the daily quantity for that day or supply period.

The remaining additional provisions include additional terms making the premium payer responsible for value-added tax payments; and where the buyer pays the premium late, several options are provided which the parties may include as remedies for the seller. The parties may include some, all or none of these in Part 6.

6.8 Appendix 1 to the ISDA Master Agreement

Part 6 also contains an appendix setting out a template form of confirmation for NBP transactions, as well as a template form of confirmation for NBP options. The full title of the appendix is "Appendix 1 to the 2002 ISDA Master Agreement or the 1992 ISDA Master Agreement (Multi-Currency-Cross-Border)".

(a) Part I – form of confirmation of NBP transaction

The template NBP transaction confirmation is a short document comprising three paragraphs. The first two of these provide that the confirmation constitutes a confirmation under the parties' ISDA Master Agreement. The third paragraph states that the parties intend to undertake NBP trades in accordance with the NBP Terms.

The main body of the template sets out space for the parties to insert the trade date as well as the identities of the buyer and seller. The price of the gas during the supply period (see first bullet point below) is the contract price, which is also specified here.

It also provides definitions for:

- 'supply period' – the period during which gas will be supplied by the buyer;

- 'daily quantity' – the quantity of gas which the seller will deliver each day within the NBP and which the buyer will off-take; and
- 'total quantity' of the same to be supplied during the supply period.

The template then sets out space for the parties to specify any special conditions which they wish to apply to the transaction.

Hypothetical example of an NBP transaction: Kirk Corporation and Devora Holdings

Kirk Corporation is a major British gas supplier and has huge demands for gas for its customers, which are satisfied by producers from across Europe. Devora Holdings is a gas producer with gas fields across Eastern Europe. Kirk Corporation wants to lock in its prices for its British customers. Devora Holdings is concerned that if another European pipeline from a new gas field comes online earlier than expected, prices could fall, so it too is keen to fix its prices.

Both parties trade through the NBP. They enter into an NBP transaction using the template ISDA confirmation set out in Appendix 1 of Sub-Annex D of the 2005 Definitions.

They complete the template as follows: the seller is Devora Holdings and the buyer is Kirk Corporation. The parties wish to enter into the transaction for the month of October 2010. They specify the supply period as October 1 2010 to October 31 2010 (inclusive).

They then specify the daily quantity and total quantity of gas to be supplied as a number of gigajoules per day and for the entire supply period. Finally, the parties specify the contract price: the amount per gigajoule of gas that Kirk Corporation will pay Devora Holdings for the gas that it delivers on the NBP.

(b) *Part II – form of confirmation for NBP option*
The template NBP option is also a short document. It sets out the same three paragraphs as the NBP transaction template.

The option template takes a similar form to standard ISDA option templates. It provides space for the parties to specify the trade date, and which party is the buyer and which the seller.

The commodity is specified as natural gas and the template provides for the transaction to be physically settled. This means that the settlement provisions set out in Part 6 will apply.

The parties can choose for the option to be a call option or a put option under 'option type'. Under 'option style', they may specify for the transaction to be:

- European (ie, the buyer can exercise only the option on the expiration date);
- American (ie, the buyer can exercise the option on any exercise date); or
- daily expiring (ie, a new option is deemed to be in place during each day of the transaction's term).

The template's default is for automatic exercise not to apply, but this provision may be negotiated on a transaction-by-transaction basis.

The parties will add the supply period. The template provides here two separate bracketed sections, depending on whether the transaction is a daily-expiring option or an American or European option. If the parties are entering into daily-expiring transactions, they will specify here that the supply period is any day "on which this option is exercised from the Start Day to the End Day (inclusive)". In the case of an American or European option, the parties will specify the start day and end day, as well as the expiration date, and an amount specified in therms for the supply period quantity.

The template then provides for the parties to specify daily and total quantities of gas. This is done on a per-gigajoule basis.

Finally, the parties will specify the premium, total premium and premium payment date, as well as the reference price (see the amendments to the NBP Terms discussed in section 6.6 above).

The template also contains a form for NBP transaction which is attached to the NBP option confirmation. This takes the same form as the NBP transaction template and is the transaction that the parties will enter into if the buyer exercises its option under the transaction. The parties will fill this document out in accordance with the terms which they have agreed.

7. **Sub-annex D of the 2005 ISDA Commodity Definitions: ZBT Transactions**
Part 7, when incorporated into the schedule to the ISDA Master Agreement, is titled "Provisions relating to ZBT Transactions and ZBT Options". It is divided into nine parts:
- incorporation of ZBT Terms;
- ZBT transactions and ZBT options;
- applicable ZBT Terms;
- applicable provisions for ZBT transactions and ZBT options;
- close-out of ZBT transactions;
- amendments to ZBT Terms;
- amendments to ZBT Option Transactions Annex;
- additional provisions for ZBT options; and
- payment instructions.

7.1 **Incorporation of ZBT Terms**
Paragraph (a) incorporates by reference the ZBT Terms and the ZBT Options Transactions Annex by reference. These are then defined collectively as the 'ZBT Terms'.

The incorporation paragraph then states that the ZBT Terms are deemed amended so that they are relevant only for ZBT transactions and options (ie, transactions on the Zeebrugge Hub and options referencing those transactions).

7.2 **ZBT transactions and ZBT options**
Paragraph (b) provides that the ISDA Master Agreement will govern any ZBT transaction or ZBT option which the parties enter into, with the master agreement trumping the ZBT Terms in the event of any inconsistency.

7.3 Applicable ZBT Terms

Paragraph (c) applies certain terms from the ZBT Terms, disapplies others and suggests that certain others are optional. The applied, disapplied and optional terms are set out in the table below.

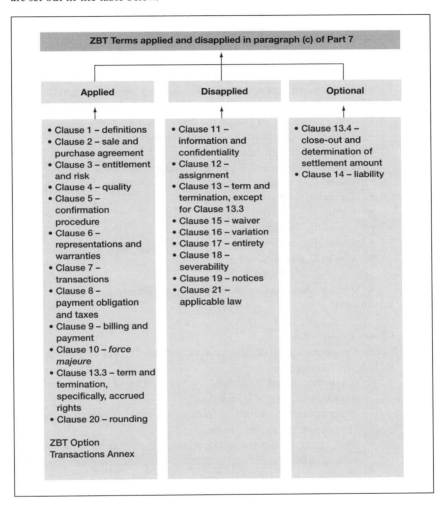

Paragraph (c) deems that the following clauses are incorporated by reference:

- Clause 1 – definitions;
- Clause 2 – sale and purchase agreement;
- Clause 3 – entitlement and risk;
- Clause 4 – quality;
- Clause 5 – confirmation procedure;
- Clause 6 – representations and warranties;
- Clause 7 – transactions;

- Clause 8 – payment obligation and taxes;
- Clause 9 – billing and payment;
- Clause 10 – *force majeure*;
- Clause 13.3 – term and termination, specifically, accrued rights; and
- Clause 20 – rounding.

Paragraph (c) also optionally provides for the parties to specify Clause 13.4 and Clause 14 as applicable. Clause 13.4 covers close-out and the determination of settlement amount following a termination event. Clause 14 carves out either party from being liable for consequential and/or indirect losses, except in the case of fraud, intentional default or gross negligence.

However, the following clauses are deemed not to apply:
- Clause 11 – information and confidentiality;
- Clause 12 – assignment;
- Clause 13 – term and termination, except for Clause 13.3;
- Clause 15 – waiver;
- Clause 16 – variation;
- Clause 17 – entirety;
- Clause 18 – severability;
- Clause 19 – notices; and
- Clause 21 – applicable law.

Of the provisions deemed to apply, even optionally, these can be summarised as set out next.

(a)   *Clause 1 – definitions*
Clause 1 provides several definitions which are used in any ZBT confirmation. These include the following:
- 'quantity', which is defined as "a quantity of Natural Gas expressed in Gigajoule under the Transaction";
- 'daily quantity', which is defined as "the Quantity agreed under the Transaction for a given Day";
- 'day', which is defined as "a period beginning at 0600 hours on a day and ending at 0600 hours on the following day and any date of any Day shall be the date of its beginning ...";
- 'hourly quantity', which is defined as "the Quantity agreed under the Transaction between the parties for a given hour of a given Day"; and
- 'supply period', which is defined as the period agreed by the parties in the transaction.

The definitions section also provides useful definitions relating to the measurement of quantities of gas. It first defines 'joule' as the industry definition – ISO 1,000 SI units – for a quantity of heat. It then defines 'megajoule' as 1 million joules and 'gigajoule' as 1,000 megajoules. Gigajoules are the standard unit of measurement for gas used in gas derivatives transactions.

(b)   **Clause 2 – sale and purchase agreement**
Clause 2 provides that the seller agrees to sell and deliver, and the buyer agrees to buy and take, "a Quantity of Natural Gas at the Zeebrugge Hub".

(c)   **Clause 3 – entitlement and risk**
Under Clause 3, the seller warrants to the buyer that it has the right to transfer the referenced gas and that the associated risks pass to the buyer at the Zeebrugge Hub.

(d)   **Clause 4 – quality**
Clause 4 provides that any natural gas delivered at the Zeebrugge Hub must comply with certain standards. These are the prescribed standards of International Zeebrugge Terminal Fluxys, which is the part of the Fluxys Transmissions System immediately downstream from the Interconnector terminal.

(e)   **Clause 5 – confirmation procedure**
Clause 5 sets out the procedure for confirming transactions. This is a more formal procedure for documenting transactions than under standard ISDA documentation procedures, with greater care taken to ensure that there is an agreed trade.

(f)   **Clause 6 – representations and warranties**
Clause 6 sets out two representations which the parties make to each other. First, they represent that during the supply period they will maintain all necessary licences and consents. Second, they represent that they will remain party to a hub services agreement with the hub operator (unless the hub operator or the party exercises its termination rights). The hub services agreement is an agreement which provides for the dispatching, matching and allocation of services at the Zeebrugge Hub with Huberator SA, the hub operator.

(g)   **Clause 7 – transactions**
Clause 7 covers the matching of trades and their physical settlement, and provides the fallbacks for what happens when one of the parties breaches its obligations to make an effective trade nomination, or to deliver or off-take the gas. More specifically:

- Clause 7.1 covers trade nominations;
- Clause 7.2 cover a breach by the net buyer;
- Clause 7.3 covers a breach by the net seller;
- Clause 7.4 covers deliveries and off-takes of natural gas;
- Clause 7.5 covers failure by the net buyer to off-take natural gas;
- Clause 7.6 covers a failure by the net seller to deliver the natural gas; and
- Cclause 7.7 covers the payment and quantum of compensation following such a breach.

(i)   *Clause 7.1 – trade nominations*
Trade nominations are nominations made by the parties to the hub operator. Effectively, the net seller is notifying the hub operator that it is delivering a quantity

of natural gas for the account of its counterparty. The buyer, for its part, is notifying the hub operator that it will be off-taking this quantity of natural gas from the terminal. The seller will be continually delivering gas into one of the Zeebrugge terminals, the buyer the same, and carrying out multiple transactions with many different counterparties; so it is vital for the functioning of the market that the hub operator matches deliveries with off-takes.

Of course, although there may be only one transaction outstanding between the parties at any one time, it is more likely that there will be many.

Where the parties are acting in a trading capacity, one party might be a buyer under some transactions and a seller under others, and vice versa. However, for the purposes of making a trade nomination, it will net its positions and will be either a net buyer or a net seller.

To facilitate the trade nomination process, Clause 7.1 provides that for each day and each hour within the supply period where the daily quantity is greater than zero, each party will make a trade nomination to the hub operator for both the daily quantity and the hourly quantity of referenced gas.

(ii)   *Clause 7.2 – breach by the (net) buyer*
Clause 7.2 sets out the consequences of breaches by the net buyer in making an effective trade nomination under Clause 7.1.

If a breach occurs, the net buyer must pay the net seller compensation for each hour of breach. The amount of compensation payable is based on a formula.

The formula involves first calculating the GSP, which is defined as 0.5 times the value of the Zeebrugge Day-ahead Base Index for Natural Gas (ZIG Day-ahead) or the Zeebrugge Weekend Base Index for Natural Gas (ZIG Weekend), last published by Dow Jones on the day of the breach. The index level is expressed as a euro amount per gigajoule. The ZIG Day-ahead will be the relevant index if the breach occurs on a weekday (other than a Friday or Monday, which can be a public holiday in England and Wales); the ZIG Weekend will be the relevant index at all other times.

The GSP is then subtracted from the affected transaction's contract price (CPD). If there is more than one transaction, a weighted average is taken.

The resulting amount is then multiplied by the hourly quantity (HQ) or net hourly quantity (NHQ) – depending on whether there is more than one affected transaction. The formula for compensation is therefore: (CPD - GSP) × (HQ or NHQ).

If the amount is positive or zero, then the net seller will pay this amount to the net buyer (if it is negative, no payment will be made). The calculation is repeated for each hour of the breach.

(iii)   *Clause 7.3 – breach by the (net) seller*
Clause 7.3 sets out the consequences of breaches by the net seller in making an effective trade nomination under Clause 7.1.

If a breach occurs, the net seller must pay the net buyer an amount in compensation for each hour of breach. The amount of compensation payable is based on a formula similar to that set out in Clause 7.2.

Again, this formula also involves first calculating the GSP. Here, though, this is defined as 1.5 times the value of either the ZIG Day-ahead or the ZIG Weekend last published on the day of the breach.

The CPD is then subtracted from the GSP; as previously, if there is more than one transaction, a weighted average is taken.

The resulting amount is then multiplied by the HQ or NHQ (depending on whether there is more than one affected transaction). The formula for compensation is therefore: (GSP - CPD) × (HQ or NHQ).

If the amount is positive, the net buyer will pay this amount to the net seller (if it is negative or zero, no payment will be made). The calculation is repeated for each hour of the breach.

(iv)   *Clause 7.4 – deliveries and off-takes*
Under Clause 7.4, the net seller agrees in respect of each hour of a day within the supply period to make available to the net buyer the net hourly quantity of natural gas. The net buyer, for its part, agrees to off-take the same.

(v)   *Clause 7.5 – failure to off-take by the (net) buyer*
Under Clause 7.5, if the net buyer fails to off-take the agreed quantity of gas from the hub, it must pay compensation to the net seller. This amount is calculated on the basis of a formula.

This formula also involves firstly calculating the GSP which, as with Clause 7.2, is defined as 0.5 times the value of either the ZIG Day-ahead or the ZIG Weekend last published on the day of the breach.

The GSP is then subtracted from the CPD; as previously, if there is more than one transaction, a weighted average is taken.

The resulting amount is then multiplied by the sum of the HQ or NHQ (depending on whether there is more than one affected transaction), less the actual quantity (Q) of gas off-taken by the net buyer. The formula for compensation is therefore: (CPD - GSP) × [(N)HQ - Q].

If the amount is positive, the net buyer will pay this amount to the net seller (if it is negative or zero, no payment will be made). The calculation is repeated for each hour of the breach from the period starting at the end of any automatic off-take period until the end of the day immediately following that period. Days under the ZBT Terms run from 06:00 one day until 06:00 the following day.

After that initial period, if the breach is continuing, the net seller can elect for compensation amounts payable to be calculated on the above basis, or alternatively to receive the actual net proceeds of the sale of the gas if it resells this.

(vi)   *Clause 7.6 – failure to make available by the (net) seller*
Under Clause 7.6, if the net seller fails to deliver the agreed quantity of gas to the hub, it must pay compensation to the net buyer. This amount is also calculated on the basis of a formula.

This formula also involves first calculating the GSP which, as with Clause 7.3, is defined as 1.5 times the value of either the ZIG Day-ahead or the ZIG Weekend last published on the day of the breach.

CPD is then subtracted from the GSP; as previously, if there is more than one transaction, a weighted average of the CPD is taken.

The resulting amount is then multiplied by the sum of the HQ or NHQ (depending on whether there is more than one affected transaction), less the actual quantity of gas off-taken by the net buyer. The formula for compensation is therefore: (GSP - CPD) × [(N)HQ - Q].

If the amount is positive, the net seller will pay this amount to the net buyer (if it is negative or zero, no payment will be made). The calculation is repeated for each hour of the breach from the period starting at the end of any automatic off-take period until the end of the day immediately following that period.

After that initial period, if the breach is continuing, the net buyer can elect for compensation amounts payable to be calculated on the above basis or can elect for this to be the actual replacement cost of purchasing the gas from a third party.

(vii)   *Clause 7.7 – payment of compensation*
Clause 7.7 provides that any of the compensation amounts described above are set out and included in a monthly settlement statement, where the parties settle all amounts owed between them under their transactions.

(h)   ***Clauses 8 and 9 – payment obligation and taxes, and billing and payment***
Clause 8 provides that all transactions between the parties are settled monthly in arrears on the basis of a monthly statement. Clause 9 states that this monthly statement must be sent on or before the 10th day of a calendar month and paid within 10 days.

(i)   ***Clause 10 – force majeure***
Under Clause 10, if a *force majeure* event occurs to prevent delivery or off-take of gas, then the parties' obligations will be suspended.

The non-claiming party can then give three business days' notice if it believes that the event may continue for seven consecutive days (where this accounts for at least 25% of the supply period or 60 consecutive days or more). An example of a *force majeure* event would be the Ukraine gas crisis in early 2009, when Russia turned off the gas supply to pipelines crossing Ukraine for a period.

(j)   ***Clause 13.3 – term and termination (accrued rights)***
Clause 13.3 provides that if a transaction terminates, this shall not affect any rights or obligations that have accrued but not yet become due. These instead become due on the date of termination.

(k)   ***Clause 13.4 – term and termination (closing out)***
Clause 13.4 is square bracketed in Part 7 and relates to closing out ZBT transactions. If Clause 13.4 is not elected to apply, then following an event of default or termination event under the parties' ISDA Master Agreement, the parties will calculate the close-out amount for each gas transaction in the same way as they would do for an interest rate swap, a credit default swap or an equity derivatives

option. In the case of a 1992 ISDA Master Agreement, this would mean that the close-out amount for each transaction would be calculated in accordance with the first or second payment method, and the market quotation or loss payment measurement. In the case of a 2002 ISDA Master Agreement, the close-out amount would be calculated in accordance with the definition of 'close-out amount' in that agreement.

If Clause 13.4 is elected to apply, the close-out amount of gas transactions only will instead be calculated in accordance with the ZBT Terms. The parties may elect for this clause to apply, where they are either mainly dealing with ZBT transactions under their master agreements or, alternatively, entering into back-to-back transactions and wish to avoid the possibility of a mismatch in any close-out amounts.

(i)   *Terminating party is the buyer*
Where the terminating party is a buyer (following an event of default or termination event under the parties' ISDA Master Agreement), the close-out amount for each transaction is calculated according to the formula: MV - RV - I.

MV is calculated using the following formula: $(D \times DQ) \times GSPT$. D stands for the number of days from (and including) the termination date to the end of the supply period. This is then multiplied by the transaction's daily quantity (DQ). The resulting figure is then multiplied by the gas settlement price (GSPT), which is calculated by taking an average of at least three representative price quotes published for the termination date for the Zeebrugge Hub that meet certain minimum standards.

RV is calculated using the formula: $(D \times DQ) \times CPT$. As before, D stands for the number of days from (and including) the termination date to the end of the supply period. This is then multiplied by DQ. The resulting figure is then multiplied by the contract price (CPT) of the terminated transaction. The terminating party then subtracts the RV from the MV.

Once the RV has been deducted from the MV, the final stage for calculating the close-out amount for the terminated transaction is to subtract I from the resulting figure. I is defined as a discounted amount which reflects the present-day value as of the termination date of RV less MV, using a Euro Interbank Offered Rate or relevant London Interbank Offered Rate for the transaction currency.

(ii)   *Terminating party is the seller*
Where the terminating party is the seller (following an event of default or termination event under the parties' ISDA Master Agreement), the close-out amount for each transaction is calculated by following the formula: RV - MV - I. 'RV', 'MV' and 'I' are the same as for where the terminating party is the buyer, above.

In relation to any group of terminated transactions, in some the terminating party may be the seller and in others it may be the buyer. A termination amount will need to be calculated for each terminated transaction and these will need to be netted against each other as part of calculating the wider settlement amount under the parties' ISDA Master Agreement.

So to calculate a termination amount, the terminating party for a transaction where it is the seller will deduct the transaction's MV from its RV. It will then subtract the discount amount from the resulting figure.

(iii) *Fallbacks*
Clause 13.4.2 provides fallbacks for the terminating party where the price quotations necessary for calculating the GSPT either are unavailable or would not produce a fair result. If this is the case, the terminating party may instead take the actual unit cost of replacement transactions for those transactions where it is the buyer and the actual unit proceeds of sale for those transactions where it is the seller. Alternatively, if the terminating party has not entered into replacement transactions, it may calculate its loss for each terminated transaction and its out-of-pocket expenses. The definition of 'loss' is broadly similar to the definition found in the 1992 ISDA Master Agreement and reflects the terminating party's total losses, costs and gains in terminating the transaction.

Settlement of the terminated transactions will then take place within the framework of the parties' ISDA Master Agreement.

(l) **Clause 14 – liability**
Clause 14 provides that save for cases of fraud, intentional default or gross negligence, neither party is responsible to the other for indirect or consequential losses.

(m) **Clause 20 – rounding**
Trades on the Zeebrugge Hub are performed in gigajoules per hour at a set temperature, to within two decimal places. Clause 20 sets out some detailed provisions to cater for rounding delivery amounts of gas.

7.4 **Additional provisions for ZBT transactions and ZBT options; close-out of ZBT transactions; and amendments to ZBT Terms**
These provisions, set out in paragraphs (d), (e) and (f) of Part 7, are very similar to the relevant section of the Gas Annex covering NBP Terms. Paragraph (d) sets out additional provisions which mainly apply or disapply additional events of default or termination events for certain actions relating to ZBT transactions. Paragraph (e) provides the mechanics for closing out ZBT transactions. Paragraph (t) makes some minor but consequential changes to some of the definitions included in the ZBT Terms.

7.5 **Amendments to the ZBT Option Transactions Annex**
The ZBT Option Transactions Annex is a separate document that is incorporated by reference to the ZBT Terms and that sets out the relevant provisions for options. Paragraph (g) of Part 7 makes some rather minor changes to that document to ensure it is compatible with the framework provided by the 2005 ISDA Commodity Definitions.

7.6 Additional provisions for ZBT options

Paragraph (h) sets out three additional provisions which are deemed to apply for ZBT options in addition to the provisions of the ZBT Terms incorporated by reference in paragraph (c). Each of these elections is square-bracketed, suggesting that the parties may or may not decide to incorporate these into their ISDA Master Agreement Schedule.

The first section of additional provisions provides an alternative definition of 'reference price', such that during the supply period this will be the arithmetic average of the Argus price, the Heren price and the Platts price quoted on the option's expiration date. These three prices are published prices for the Zeebrugge Hub and are then defined.

The second section of additional provisions provides a mechanism for automatic exercise of ZBT options. This provision deems automatic exercise to be applicable unless otherwise specified. The option is deemed to be exercised at its expiration time if the in-the-money amount payable to the buyer is equal to or exceeds the product of 10% of the strike price and the daily quantity for that day or supply period.

The third section of additional provisions covers late payments of the option premium by the option buyer. Several options are provided which the parties may include as remedies for the seller: the parties may include some, all or none of these in Part 7. First, the seller may choose to accept late payment of the premium. Second, the seller can give the buyer written notice of the non-payment; and if it does not receive the premium within five business days, it may treat the particular transaction as void. Third, with the same notice period the seller may treat the non-payment of a premium as an event of default under the parties' ISDA Master Agreement and terminate all transactions.

If the seller elects to act under the first or second elections, the buyer is obliged to pay its out-of-pocket expenses, plus any damages and interest on the unpaid premium at the buyer's cost of funds, plus 1%, together with certain other break costs.

7.7 Appendix 2 to the ISDA Master Agreement

Like Part 6 of the NBP Terms, Part 7 of the ZBT Terms also contains an appendix setting out a template form of confirmation for ZBT transactions, as well as a form of confirmation for ZBT options. The full title of the appendix is "Appendix 2 to the 2002 ISDA Master Agreement or the 1992 ISDA Master Agreement (Multi-Currency-Cross-Border)".

(a) Part I – form of confirmation of ZBT transaction

The template ZBT transaction confirmation is a short document comprising three paragraphs. The first two provide that the confirmation constitutes a confirmation under the parties' ISDA Master Agreement. The third paragraph states that the parties intend to undertake ZBT trades in accordance with the ZBT Terms.

The main body of the template sets out space for the parties to insert the trade date, as well as the identities of both buyer and seller. It also provides definitions for the 'supply period' (ie, the period during which gas will be supplied by the buyer) and 'hourly quantity' (ie, the quantity of gigajoules which the seller will deliver each hour to the Zeebrugge Hub and the buyer will off-take). Specified too are the 'daily quantity' and 'total quantity' of the same to be supplied during the supply period. The price of the gas during this period is the 'contract price', which is also specified.

Finally, the template sets out space for the parties to specify any special conditions which they wish to apply to the transaction.

> **Hypothetical example of a ZBT transaction: Ana Trading and Tolitou Energy**
> Ana Trading is the energy trading arm of a European gas supplier, which off-takes natural gas from the Zeebrugge Hub. Tolitou Energy is a European gas producer, which delivers natural gas to the Zeebrugge Hub. Ana Trading is facing demands from its customers to lock in its prices. Tolitou Energy, on the other hand, is concerned that if there is a warm winter, gas prices will fall; so it too is keen to fix its prices.
>
> Both parties are members of the Zeebrugge Hub, regularly trade with each other and have an ISDA Master Agreement in place between them. They enter into a ZBT transaction using the template confirmation set out in Appendix 2 of Sub-Annex D of the 2005 ISDA Commodity Definitions.
>
> They complete the template as follows: the seller is Tolitou Energy and the buyer is Ana Trading. The parties wish to enter into the transaction for the month of November 2010. They specify the supply period as November 1 2010 to November 30 2010 (inclusive).
>
> They then specify the hourly quantity, daily quantity and total quantity of gas to be supplied as a number of gigajoules per hour, per day and for the entire supply period. Finally, the parties specify the contract price, namely the amount per gigajoule of gas that Ana Trading will pay Tolitou Energy for the gas that it delivers into the Zeebrugge Hub.
>
> As the parties have a pattern of trading between them, they will make hourly trade nominations to the hub on a net basis.

(b)   Part II – form of confirmation for ZBT option

The template ZBT option is another short document that sets out the same three opening paragraphs as the ZBT transaction template.

The option template takes a similar form to standard ISDA option agreements and the ZBT Terms option template. It provides space for the parties to specify the trade date, and which party is the buyer and which party is the seller.

The commodity is specified as natural gas. The template provides for the transaction to be physically settled, which means that the settlement provisions set out in Part 7 will apply.

The parties can elect under 'option type' for the option to be a call option or a put option. Under 'option style', the parties may specify for the transaction to be European (ie, the buyer can exercise the option only on the expiration date), American (ie, the buyer can exercise the option on any exercise date) or daily expiring (ie, a new option is deemed to be in place during each day of the transaction's term).

The template's default is for 'automatic exercise' not to apply, but this provision may be negotiated on a transaction-by-transaction basis.

The parties will add the supply period. The template provides two separate bracketed sections depending on whether the transaction is a daily-expiring option or an American or European option. If the parties are entering into daily expiring transactions, they will specify here that the supply period is "any day on which this option is exercised from the Start Day to the End Day (inclusive)".

In the case of an American or European option, the parties must specify the start and end day, as well as the expiration date and an amount specified in therms for the supply period quantity. Allied to this, the parties will specify the actual start date and end date. The parties must also specify the expiration date.

The template then provides for the parties to specify hourly, daily and total quantities of gas on a per-gigajoule basis.

Finally, the parties will specify the 'premium', 'total premium' and 'premium payment date', as well as the 'reference price' (the amendments to the ZBT Terms discussed above must be taken into account when ascertaining the reference price).

The template also contains a form for a ZBT transaction which is attached to the ZBT option confirmation. This takes the same form as the ZBT transaction template and is the transaction which the parties will enter into if the buyer exercises its option under the transaction. The parties will fill this out in accordance with the terms they have agreed.

Hypothetical example of a ZBT option: Ana Trading and Tolitou Energy

The ZBT transaction between Ana Trading and Tolitou Energy worked well. At the end of November 2010, both parties feel confident that the gas price will stay stable during December 2010. However, Ana Trading is concerned that prices may rise sharply in January 2011 and it may find it difficult to pass these costs on to its customers.

Ana Trading decides to purchase a call option from Tolitou Energy, giving it the right to enter into a ZBT transaction in January 2011. The parties use the ISDA Commodity form of confirmation of ZBT option set out in Appendix 2 of Sub-Annex D of the 2005 Definitions as a template.

They complete the template as follows: the seller is Tolitou Energy and the buyer is Ana Trading. The commodity is specified as natural gas and the option type as call.

For 'option style', the parties specify daily expiring. This means that a new option is deemed to be in place during each day of the option's one-month term (and the ZBT transaction that the parties will reference will have a one-day supply period). This gives Ana Trading maximum flexibility as prices move. However, it will have to pay a higher premium for this.

The parties specify that 'automatic exercise' should apply. This means that the option is deemed to be exercised at its expiration time on each day in the supply period if the in-the-money amount payable to Ana Trading is equal to or exceeds the product of 10% of the strike price and the daily quantity for that day or supply period.

The parties also specify the supply period. As this is a daily-expiring option, they specify here that the supply period is "any day on which this option is exercised from the Start Day to the End Day (inclusive)", and that the start day is January 1 2011 and the end day is January 31 2011.

For 'expiration date', they specify that this is "for any Day, the London Business Day, immediately preceding that Day". This means that if one of the daily expiring options were to automatically exercise on Thursday January 13 2011, they would enter into a ZBT transaction on Friday January 14 2011.

For 'expiration time' they specify "in respect of each Day, 5.00pm London Time on the Expiration Date". This means that on each day where the conditions for automatic exercise are met, a daily option will exercise at 5:00pm London time and the parties will enter into a ZBT transaction for the following day. For 'exercise period' they specify January 1 2011 to January 31 2011 (inclusive).

The parties then specify the hourly quantity, daily quantity and total quantity of natural gas covered by the option, in gigajoules per hour, per day and for the total period.

The parties will specify the strike price as a euro amount per gigajoule. They will also specify the premium payable by Ana Tranding as the buyer to Tolitou Energy as the seller as a euro amount per gigajoule, and set out the total premium payable. Finally, they specify the date on which the premium is to be paid under premium payment date as January 1 2011 and the reference price as Argus price.

The template confirmation form for the ZBT option also includes a form for a ZBT transaction confirmation to be attached to the ZBT option confirmation and to be issued upon the exercise of the ZBT option. Ana Trading and Tolitou Energy complete this confirmation on the same basis as in the previous example; however, they specify that the supply period is the business day following the exercise of the relevant option.

8. Sub-Annex E of the 2005 ISDA Commodity Definitions: ISDA North American Gas Annex

Sub-Annex E of the 2005 ISDA Commodity Definitions provides additional provisions relating to North America for incorporation into the ISDA Master Agreement as a new Part 6, as well as a further addendum for Canadian transactions.

The North American Part 6 is split into 12 sections. These sections cover:

- credit support documents;
- performance obligations;
- transportation, nomination and imbalances;
- quality and measurement;
- taxes;
- billing, payment and audit;
- title, warranty and indemnity;
- *force majeure*;
- limitation of liability;
- amendments to the main body of the ISDA Master Agreement;
- definitions; and
- elective provisions.

8.1 Credit support documents

Paragraph (a) is broken down into three sub-sections:

- physical gas transactions under this agreement;
- applicability to outstanding gas transactions; and
- credit support documents.

The first sub-section provides that the North American Part 6 applies "solely to transactions between the parties for the purchase or sale of physical gas with delivery points in North America on a Firm or Interruptible basis on a spot or forward basis or as an option to purchase or sell gas (collectively 'Gas Transactions')".

Later on in Sub-Annex E, in the definitions section, a 'firm' basis is defined as where the parties may interrupt their performance only on the basis of *force majeure*. 'Interruptible', on the other hand, is defined as an agreement where the parties can interrupt their performance at any time, although they may have to pay imbalance charges.

The second sub-section provides that the parties can agree to grandfather any previous gas transactions they have outstanding between them so that these are also governed by the ISDA Master Agreement, if this is specified in the elections section of the North American Part 6.

The third sub-section is itself divided into two further sub-sections: outstanding gas credit support and amendments/guaranties. The first additional sub-section provides that if elected in the elections section, collateral will be deemed to be delivered in relation to the ISDA Master Agreement to the extent that collateral has already been provided under grandfathered gas transactions. If the parties already have a credit support annex in place, then this collateral is deemed to be covered by the credit support annex. If they do not, then the existing credit support document is deemed to constitute a credit support document under the ISDA Master Agreement. This would mean that any default under that document would constitute an event of default under the ISDA Master Agreement.

The second additional sub-section provides that the parties will amend any credit support document for grandfathered gas transactions so as to bring any collateral within the ambit of the ISDA Master Agreement. Where the parties have a guarantee in place, this too will be grandfathered; and the parties agree here to make any necessary changes and that the guarantee will be a credit support document and the guarantor a credit support provider under the ISDA Master Agreement. This has the effect that a default under the guarantee will be an event of default under the ISDA Master Agreement. The guarantor, as a credit support provider, will also be brought within the scope of the ISDA Master Agreement's events of default, wherever there is mention of a default by a credit support provider (eg, for bankruptcy).

8.2 Performance obligations

Paragraph (b) is split into three sub-sections. In the first sub-section, the seller agrees to deliver and the buyer agrees to receive the contract quantity of gas on a firm or interruptible basis.

In the second sub-section, two separate options are provided for the parties to specify in the elections section as the consequences of any breach of a transaction entered into on a firm basis.

Under Option A, the 'cover standard' applies to any failure to deliver or off-take gas. It is defined as an obligation for the party not in breach, following an unexpected failure to take or deliver gas, to use commercially reasonable efforts to obtain the gas (in the case of the buyer), or to sell the gas (in the case of the seller) at a reasonable price using alternative sources. Option A provides that the parties use the cover standard, and that their sole remedy following the breach of a firm obligation to deliver or receive gas is as follows:

- For a failure by the seller to deliver gas, the seller must pay the buyer any positive difference between the purchase price paid by the buyer to purchase replacement gas from an alternative source and the contract price (ie, the agreed dollar price that the seller had agreed to deliver gas under the transaction).
- For a failure by the buyer to off-take gas, the buyer must pay the seller the positive difference between the contract price and the resale proceeds of the gas (subject to certain adjustments).
- Where a non-breaching seller cannot resell the gas or a non-breaching buyer cannot purchase the gas from alternative sources, then the non-performing party must pay its counterparty the positive difference between the contract price and the spot price (subject to certain adjustments), multiplied by the difference between the contract quantity and the quantity of gas actually delivered or received.

Calculations under Option A are made on a daily basis. Only amounts owing to the party not in breach are payable.

Under Option B, the spot price standard applies to any failure to deliver or off-take gas. Here, the sole remedy following the breach of a firm obligation to deliver or receive gas is for the party not in breach to pay its counterparty the positive difference between the contract quantity and the actual quantity of gas delivered, multiplied by any positive difference between the contract price and the spot price.

'Spot price' is defined as the price published in *Platts' Gas Daily* as the daily mid-point price in the daily price survey for the geographic location closest to the delivery point for gas under the transaction.

The third sub-section of paragraph (b) provides that the parties can, as an alternative, agree in any confirmation that alternative damages apply following a firm failure or delivery breach. 'Alternative damages' are defined as "damages expressed in dollars per one million British Thermal Units".

8.3 Transportation, nomination and imbalances

Paragraph (c) is divided into three sub-sections. In the first sub-section the parties agree that the seller has sole responsibility for transporting the gas to the delivery point specified in the confirmation and that the buyer has sole responsibility for transporting the gas away from it.

In the second sub-section, the parties agree to coordinate the nominating activities (ie, notifying any transporter or hub of gas being off-taken and delivered to allow it to match a transaction).

In the third sub-section, the parties agree to use reasonable efforts to avoid the imposition of any 'imbalance charges', defined as "fees, penalties, costs or charges" imposed by pipeline companies and local distribution companies for any breach of balance or nomination requirements.

If an imbalance charge is incurred because the buyer off-takes too much or too little gas, then the buyer must cover any imbalance charge. If the seller delivers too much or too little gas, then the seller must pay any imbalance charge incurred. The third sub-section also states that any unpaid imbalance charges will be deemed to be unpaid amounts for the purposes of calculating an early-termination amount if the transaction is closed out under the ISDA Master Agreement following a termination event or an event of default.

8.4   Quality and measurement

Paragraph (d) sets out that the gas delivered by the seller has to meet the pressure, quantity, heating requirements and established procedures of the pipeline company or local distribution company receiving it. It also provides that the unit of quantity of measurement for transactions is "one million British Thermal Units".

8.5   Taxes

Paragraph (e) provides two alternative options for taxes. If selected, Option A (buyer pays at and after the delivery point) obliges the seller to pay any taxes, fees and penalties incurred up to the point that the gas is delivered to the delivery point. The buyer is then responsible for all taxes at the delivery point and after it has off-taken the gas from the delivery point. Option B (seller pays before and at the delivery point) means that the seller pays any taxes, fees and penalties incurred up to the point that the buyer has off-taken the gas from the delivery point (including any taxes at the delivery point).

8.6   Billing, payment and audit

In Paragraph (f) the parties agree to settle their transactions monthly on an invoice basis. Paragraph (f) also provides a mechanism for the parties to check and dispute any invoice.

8.7   Title, warranty and indemnity

In Paragraph (g) the parties agree that title to gas will pass from seller to buyer at the delivery point. The seller further warrants that it has the right to convey and will transfer the goods and merchantable title to the gas, free of encumbrances. The parties also agree here that the seller has responsibility for and assumes liability for the gas up to the delivery point, with this transferring to the buyer at the delivery point.

The seller agrees to indemnify the buyer for claims arising prior to title transfer, and the buyer agrees to the same for claims arising after title transfer.

8.8 *Force majeure*

Paragraph (h) provides detailed provisions covering any *force majeure* event which impacts on a transaction – in particular, in relation to the various events which may or may not constitute a *force majeure* event. Any particular event should be checked carefully to see whether it falls within paragraph (h).

If a *force majeure* event is deemed to occur, neither party will be liable for any failure to perform a firm obligation. The party affected, though, must provide notice to the other. Paragraph (h) specifies that it supersedes the *force majeure* provision in any 2002 ISDA Master Agreement as far as North American gas transactions are concerned.

8.9 Limitation of liability

Paragraph (i) provides that neither party is responsible to the other for consequential losses.

8.10 Amendments to the main body of the ISDA Master Agreement

Paragraph (j) sets out three additional provisions that amend the principal terms of the ISDA Master Agreement. These relate to limiting the provisions relating to delivery so that a failure to deliver gas does not cause an event of default or potential event of default (leading to the potential close-out of the transaction) but is instead dealt with under the provisions described above.

8.11 Definitions

Paragraph (k) sets out various definitions used throughout North American Part 6. There are 22 definitions provided, most of which are described above.

8.12 Elective provisions

Paragraphs (a) to (j) of North American Part 6 contain various elections such as whether gas transactions entered into between the parties before the ISDA Master Agreement should be grandfathered, and performance obligations and taxes. These are described above and the parties' choice is specified in paragraph (l). In addition, the parties may specify here the days on which invoices are to be settled, and whether there is an alternative to the spot index price where this is used as a reference for determining compensation payments.

8.13 Addendums

There are two addendums to North American Part 6. One of these is the 2009 Amendment Addendum. This will not apply where the parties to an ISDA Master Agreement included North American Part 6 before the addendum's publication in 2009, unless specified in a confirmation or updated schedule. Where applicable, the addendum makes changes to the North American Gas Annex, including:

- certain minor amendments to the definition of 'cover standard';
- adding elections for which party bears the burden of any US customs duties where gas is piped in from outside the United States; and
- adding elections for market disruption events, allowing the parties to choose

either that those provided in the 2005 ISDA Commodity Definitions apply or instead a mechanism for selecting a replacement relevant price.

The second addendum is set out in Sub-Annex E and entitled "Canadian Addendum to the ISDA North American Gas Annex". As the title suggests, it is designed to apply where an aspect of a gas transaction involves Canada, either if the delivery point is in Canada or if the gas is exported from Canada. In particular, it replaces some references to US dollars with references to Canadian dollars. The addendum also provides certain alternative tax provisions.

Power derivative transactions[1]

Edmund Parker

1. The electricity market: an ideal underlying commodity derivative asset

We have the likes of Michael Faraday and André-Marie Ampère (discoverers of electro-magnetism) and Thomas Edison (the developer of the durable incandescent light bulb) to thank. Every time we turn on a light, we tap into an enormous infrastructure, founded on the research and inventions of these pioneers.

And what an infrastructure it is. The electric current flowing to the light bulb is generated by electro-magnetic generators located at power stations. These are driven by steam produced from burning coal or gas; kinetic energy drawn from hydro-electric dams or windmills; or the heat produced by a nuclear reactor. The electric energy generated at a power station is then transformed and stepped up to a higher voltage and transmitted in bulk through overhead and/or sea or underground power lines to electricity substations in population centres. Here the electricity is transformed again and stepped down to a lower voltage and distributed to homes, offices and industries. Generation, transmission and distribution: the three stages in the electricity supply chain. Combined with consumption, this means that there are classes of market participant which have diametrically opposed interests in seeing high or low electricity prices. These include power stations and distributors, major corporate users, speculators and market makers.

Electricity has several other features which make it an ideal underlying asset class in a commodity derivative transaction. It is difficult to store. Demand is highly volatile too: for example, there is more demand during the day than at night, and more in winter than in summer. Matching electricity supply and demand is more urgent than in many commodity asset classes. The vast grid networks further make for a large market: substantial amounts of power are transmitted from Canada to the Southern United States, and across the member countries of the European Union, for example. The big privatisations of the 1990s created many regional electricity trading markets too.

The many tradable regional electricity markets are standardised. There is a norm of buying and selling electricity in megawatt hours (units of 1 million watt hours and 3.6 million megajoules).

---

1   This chapter overlaps to some extent with "Overview of documentation produced by the Futures and Options Association", which discusses the UK electricity market and the Grid Trade Master Agreement (GTMA). Certain sections of the description of the operation of electricity trading and the provisions of the GTMA which are incorporated by reference into ISDA documentation are repeated in this chapter.

2. What are power derivatives?

A power derivative is a financial instrument which derives its value from the underlying asset of the price of megawatt hours of electricity. The power derivatives market is principally a physically settled market. This is made up of two categories of derivative. The first is forward transactions; here one party, a buyer, agrees to purchase an agreed amount of electricity over a future period for a price agreed at the transaction's outset. The second is option transactions; here the option buyer purchases the right to enter into a transaction where it can purchase (in the case of a call option), or sell (in the case of a put option), agreed amounts of electricity over a future period for a price agreed at the option's outset.

> **Hypothetical example of a physically settled power forward transaction: Bloomingdale Power and Bruce Generation**
>
> Bloomingdale Power is an electricity supplier. The market is competitive and Bloomingdale Power has limited ability to pass on costs to its consumers. Bruce Generation is a power company which owns 50 power stations. Bruce Generation's costs are fixed, so a fall in electricity prices harms its profitability.
>
> Derivatives to the rescue! The parties enter into a physically settled power forward transaction.
>
> Bloomingdale Power is the buyer and Bruce Generation the seller. They enter into the transaction in the summer, and Bloomingdale Power agrees to purchase an agreed quantity of electricity every day during the winter months, for an agreed price specified in dollars per kilowatt hour. Both parties are happy: by forgoing the upside of a potential reduction in electricity prices, Bloomingdale Power has hedged itself against higher electricity prices; and by forgoing the upside of a potential increase in electricity prices, Bruce Generation has hedged itself against falling electricity prices.

Participation in the physical power market has high barriers to entry: you must be an electricity generator, transmitter, distributor or large consumer. A cash or 'financial' derivatives market also exists, although this is not nearly as large as the physical market. Several electricity futures contracts are traded on exchanges, such as NYMEX. These futures contracts can provide commodity reference prices for over-the-counter (OTC) derivatives transactions, allowing bespoke products to be documented which swap the differential in different electricity commodity reference prices, or which settle on a periodic basis the differential between a fixed price and the current commodity reference price. These contracts are traded by hedge funds and the commodity desks of banks.

In this chapter we look at the various types of power derivative and their uses; as well as the documentation infrastructure provided by the International Swaps and Derivatives Association, Inc (ISDA) through the 2005 ISDA Commodity Definitions in Sub-Annex F for North America Power Transactions and Sub-Annex G for GTMA Transactions (ie, the Grid Trade Master Agreement transactions in the UK market), and related templates.

We also discuss the electricity trading market in general, as this is essential to an understanding of how power derivatives work; and we discuss Sub-Annex A of the 2005 definitions, which provides a plethora of electricity commodity reference prices – particularly useful for cash-settled power transactions.

ISDA's power derivatives documentation is a late arrival in the market. Sub-Annex F therefore interacts with an established market-trading platform for trading electricity. We also discuss the substance of the GTMA platform and its interaction with the ISDA platform.

3.   The electricity trading market

Electricity trading began in the 1990s with the large spate of privatisations that was initiated in the United Kingdom by Margaret Thatcher in 1990, which then spread infectiously across other developed nations.

Nord Pool was one of the first trading markets to gain momentum. Here electricity is traded in a combined pool for the Nordic countries (Finland, Sweden, Denmark and Norway). The market is both a physical (or spot) trading market, involving the actual delivery and supply of electricity, and a financial market where pricing differentials are traded through derivatives on a forward basis.

Trading markets now exist in Australia, Europe (in Benelux, France, Germany, the Nordic countries, Spain, Switzerland and the United Kingdom) and North America. In Australia, electricity passing through regional reference nodes is traded. These include trading markets for the regional reference nodes (ie, delivery points) in Queensland, Victoria, South Australia and Tasmania.

Benelux has a trading market for electricity passing across the Tennet High Voltage Grid; France has one for electricity passing across the RTE High Voltage Grid; and the United Kingdom has one for electricity being carried on the National Grid.

In the United States, there are a number of large separate electricity trading markets, including for the California/Oregon area, Palo Verde, Mid-Columbia and New England.

Those trading electricity fall into three principal categories:

- the generators – the power companies which own the power stations and generate the power;
- the suppliers – the companies that transport the electricity from the generators to the substations and into homes, offices and industries; and
- the non-physical market – the banks and hedge funds trading and making a market in electricity as a separate asset class.

The electricity market is highly regulated, so market participants are usually restricted by a regulatory code and trade on the basis of standardised documentation. This trading may be on a spot (ie, immediate) basis or a derivative (usually forward) basis.

3.1   The UK electricity trading market

Let's take the UK market as an example of the sort of trading infrastructure and regulatory environment that is currently in place. Something similar will exist for all of the jurisdictions mentioned above. To understand the power derivatives market for a particular trading market, you must understand that market's regulatory and trading regime.

The trading infrastructure in the United Kingdom is regulated by the Energy Act 2004. Trading and transmission is documented under the British Electricity Trading and Transmission Arrangements (BETTA), with bilateral trading between generators, suppliers, traders and customers across a series of markets being governed by the Balancing and Settlement Code. Other countries have similar regimes.

The code sets out the rules governing the operation of the balancing mechanism and the imbalance settlement process, and the relationships and responsibilities of all market participants. In particular, the code provides for:

- a mechanism for contracting parties to notify all volumes of electricity to be supplied under contract (notifications are made to Elexon, the market operator);
- the balancing mechanism in which National Grid, as system operator, accepts offers and bids for electricity from generators and suppliers close to real time, to enable it at all times to balance the system, and is responsible for balancing generation and demand and resolving transmission constraints; and
- a settlement process for charging participants whose notified contracted positions do not match corresponding metered volumes of electricity.

All licence holders (ie, transmission, generation, supply and distribution) are required to be registered within the code. Parties that are exempt from holding a licence (eg, non-physical traders) may sign up to the code if they wish and, in practice, investment banks do so and participate in the market. All generators and suppliers have energy accounts with Elexon.

Electricity is generated, transported, delivered and used continuously in real time, and supply must always match demand as electricity cannot be stored.

However, for the purposes of trading and settlement, electricity is considered to be generated, transported, delivered and used in half-hour periods called 'settlement periods'. For each half-hour, those with demand for electricity (eg, suppliers) will assess in advance what the demand will be. They will then contract with generator(s) for that volume of electricity. Contracts can be struck up to an hour before the settlement period which the contract is for (this cut-off is known as 'gate closure' and contracts cannot be struck after this time). In the half-hour itself, generators are expected to generate and deliver their contracted volume of electricity and suppliers are expected to use their contracted volume of electricity.

Generators with additional capacity (ie, those that have not contracted for the full volume that they can generate in any half-hour) can make that additional volume available to the system operator and can set the price they wish to receive for that additional volume.

Similarly, a generator can state that it will reduce the volume being generated and can set a price for reducing their generation. Suppliers that are flexible enough can offer to reduce their demand to make additional volumes of electricity available to the system operator and can set the price they wish to receive for that additional volume. Similarly, flexible suppliers can say to the system operator (the National Grid) that it can increase demand for a set price.

These are called bids and offers.

	Offer	Offer price (per MWh)	Bid	Bid price (per MWh)
Generator	Proposal to increase generation.	Price requested for increase in generation.	Proposal to reduce generation.	Price offered for a decrease in generation.
Supplier	Proposal to reduce demand.	Price requested for decrease in demand.	Proposal to increase demand.	Price offered for an increase in demand.

The National Grid will, in real time and as required, match supply and demand in each half-hour by accepting bids or offers depending on whether they need to increase or reduce electricity generation to meet demand.

Afterwards, metered volumes are collected for the half-hour from generators and suppliers, and compared against their contracted volumes (which are adjusted for any bids or offers accepted). All parties have their contracted volumes compared to determine whether the volumes they bought and sold match. If the contracted volumes don't match the metered volumes, the generators and the suppliers must either buy or sell to the grid additional electricity. These differences are referred to as imbalances and settlement is the process of calculating the volumes of imbalance and the prices to be paid for these imbalances. Settlement also results in other related charges and payments being worked out.

Notifications determine the imbalance exposure of the parties and are made in a single notification process by the parties The notifications are made via a 'notification agent' (either one of the counterparties or an independent notification agent), which must be authorised by the parties with the central system to submit notifications on behalf of the parties. Contract notifications for a settlement period must be received by gate closure (contract volumes may be changed up to the gate closure by overwriting previously notified volumes). After the gate closure, during the hour before the relevant settlement period, Elexon and the National Grid calculate whether each of the Balancing and Settlement Code parties is in balance by comparing the volume of power delivered or off-taken by a party from the system against that party's energy account. If the physical position does not match the notified contractual position, the party is out of balance; to the extent that there is a shortfall (a party is 'short'), Elexon will charge that party the 'system buy price' and to the extent that the party is 'long', it will be paid the system sell price.

	Generator (G)	Supplier (S)
System sell price	Paid to G if over-generating	Paid to S if under-consuming
System buy price	Paid by G if under-generating	Paid by S if over-consuming

The system sell price and the system buy price are established by Elexon for the relevant settlement period in relation to the cost incurred by the National Grid in purchasing additional power or contracting with generators to decrease the generation or with the suppliers to increase their off-take. The difference between the system sell price and the system buy price may be very significant, with the system buy price being extremely high while the system sell price is very low, thereby encouraging parties to ensure they are not short.

4.   Principal sources of market information

Trading in electricity and derivatives needs reliable market prices. This is particularly so for the cash-settled market. These market prices come in the form of published indices and trading prices derived from actual market prices paid. The principal providers of electricity prices in Europe include APX Group for the Netherlands; Powernext for France; the European Energy Exchange for Germany; Nord Pool for the Nordic countries and the London Energy Brokers' Association for the United Kingdom.

For North America, the principal providers of electricity prices include Dow Jones, ICE and NYISO.

A vast range of electricity prices are available. ISDA's 2005 definitions, for example, have 16 pages of definitions of reference prices for Europe and 16 pages of definitions of reference prices for North America.

5.   Overview of ISDA documentation platform for power derivatives trading

The diagram on the next page sets out the principal ISDA documentation platform for documenting power derivatives. The ISDA Master Agreement (1992 or 2002 version), as amended by a schedule and possibly credit support documentation, forms the primary platform.

This primary platform is supplemented by a secondary platform of the 2005 definitions. In particular, additional sections in Sub-Annex F (Physically Settled North American Power Transactions) may be incorporated in the schedule to the ISDA Master Agreement to facilitate physically settled derivatives referencing electricity generated in North America. Likewise, Sub-Annex G (Physically Settled GTMA Transactions) provides an additional section of the ISDA Master Agreement to provide a documentation infrastructure for parties wanting to enter into physically settled derivative transactions referencing electricity on the UK National Grid. For cash-settled OTC derivatives or derivatives referencing electricity in other jurisdictions, the parties will need to document these transactions using their own

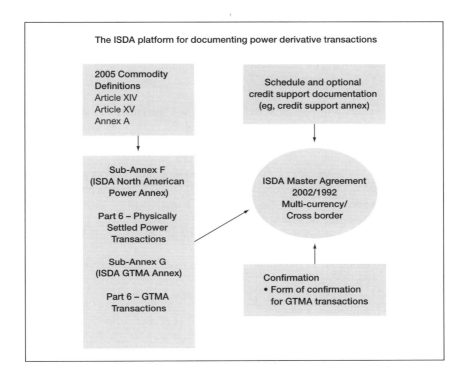

The ISDA platform for documenting power derivative transactions

bespoke documentation, or adapting the other templates provided in the 2005 definitions. As mentioned above, Sub-Annex A of the 2005 definitions provides a broad range of electricity commodity reference prices.

As a tertiary platform, ISDA has produced two template confirmations for derivatives transactions relating to GTMA transactions. These template confirmations incorporate the primary platform of the ISDA Master Agreement and should also incorporate the secondary platform of the 2005 definitions. One confirmation provides a template for a forward transaction, the other for an option transaction. The 2005 definitions provide the fallbacks and framework for power transactions.

Article XIV of the principal body of the 2005 definitions provides that the provisions relating to physically settled North American power transactions are published in Sub-Annex F of the Annex: the ISDA North American Power Annex. The form of words is as follows:

The remaining provisions of this Article XIV are published in Sub-Annex F of the Annex to these Commodity Definitions, which may be amended from time to time. The parties may elect that Sub-Annex F apply to an agreement or a Transaction by taking the action described in Sub-Annex F [the European ISDA North American Power Annex].

Identical wording is set out in Article XV (Physically-Settled GTMA Transactions) except that the reference here is to Sub-Annex G: the ISDA GTMA Annex.

This ISDA North American Power Annex and the ISDA GTMA Annex amend the

2005 definitions to the extent that the market practices for physical power differ from those applicable to other commodities. Each annex is not a separate document in its own right and its provisions are incorporated into the main body of the 2005 definitions as Article XIV and Article XV respectively.

6.   Sub-Annex F of the 2005 definitions (the North American Power Annex)
Sub-Annex F, the North American Power Annex, is 12 pages long. It is designed for use with physical transactions carried out referencing electricity in the United States and Canada only.

The North American Power Annex consists of a Form of Part 6 of the Schedule to the 2002 ISDA Master Agreement or the 1992 ISDA Master Agreement (Multicurrency – Cross Border) for North American Power Transactions.

Part 6 in this context is divided into 10 paragraphs:
- power transactions under the agreement: credit support documents;
- obligations and deliveries;
- remedies for failure to deliver or receive, and limitation on conditions precedent;
- payment;
- limitation of liability;
- taxes;
- title, risk of loss, and indemnity;
- miscellaneous;
- certain modifications to the agreement; and
- elective provisions.

We now look at each of these in turn.

6.1   Power transactions under the agreement: credit support documents
Paragraph (a) (Power Transactions under this Agreement: Credit Support Documents) is broken down into three sub-sections:
- power transactions;
- applicability to outstanding power transactions; and
- credit support documents.

The first sub-section (power transactions) sets out the North American Power Annex's stall: it applies solely to transactions for the purchase, sale or transfer of electricity on a spot or forward basis or as an option to purchase or sell electric energy ('power transactions').

The second sub-section (applicability to outstanding power transactions) provides a grandfathering provision. If the parties specify in the elective provisions section at the end of this Part 6, then they will 'grandfather' any previous power transactions they have outstanding between them, meaning that these will be governed by their ISDA Master Agreement.

The third sub-section (credit support documents) is itself divided into two further subsections: outstanding credit support and amendments/guaranties. The first additional sub-section (outstanding credit support) provides that, if elected in the elective provisions section, then to the extent that collateral has already been provided under grandfathered power transactions, collateral will be deemed to be delivered in relation to the ISDA Master Agreement.

If the parties already have a credit support annex in place, this collateral is deemed to be covered by the credit support annex; if they don't, the existing credit support document is deemed to constitute a 'credit support document' under the ISDA Master Agreement. This would mean that any default under that document would constitute an event of default under the ISDA Master Agreement.

The second additional sub-section (amendments/guaranties) provides that the parties will amend any credit support document for grandfathered power transactions to bring any collateral within the ambit of the ISDA Master Agreement.

If the parties have a guarantee in place, this too will be grandfathered; and the parties agree here to make any necessary changes, and that the guarantee will be a 'credit support document' and the guarantor a 'credit support provider' under the ISDA Master Agreement. This has the effect that a default under the guarantee will be an event of default under the ISDA Master Agreement. The guarantor, as a credit support provider, will also be brought within the scope of the ISDA Master Agreement's events of default wherever there is mention of a default by a credit support provider (eg, for bankruptcy).

6.2 Obligations and deliveries

Paragraph (b) (Obligations and Deliveries) is split into three sub-sections.

In the first sub-section (seller's and buyer's obligations), the seller agrees to deliver, and the buyer agrees to receive the agreed 'quantity' of electricity to an agreed 'delivery point': boilerplate stuff. The first sub-section also provides that the seller is responsible for costs and charges up to the delivery point, and the buyer is responsible for these at and beyond the delivery point.

In the second sub-section (transmission and scheduling), the seller has the responsibility for transporting the electricity to the delivery point specified in the confirmation, while the buyer must transport the electricity away from it.

In the third sub-section (*force majeure*), there are provisions covering any *force majeure* which impacts on a transaction – in particular, in relation to the various events which may or may not constitute a *force majeure* event. Any particular event should be checked carefully to see whether it falls within the paragraph's scope.

If a *force majeure* event is deemed to have occurred, neither party will be liable for any failure to perform its obligation. The party affected by the *force majeure* must provide notice to the other and try to remedy the *force majeure*. The paragraph specifies that that it supersedes the *force majeure* provision in any 2002 ISDA Master Agreement as far as North American power transactions are concerned.

6.3 Remedies for failure to deliver or receive, and limitation on conditions precedent

Paragraph (c) (Remedies for Failure to Deliver or Receive; Limitation on Conditions Precedent) is split into three sub-sections.

The first sub-section (seller failure) provides that following the breach of an obligation by the seller to deliver electricity, the seller must pay the buyer any positive difference between the purchase price paid by the buyer to purchase replacement electricity from an alternative source and the 'contract price' (ie, the agreed dollar price that the seller had agreed to deliver electricity under the transaction). If 'accelerated payment of damages' is specified as an election in paragraph (j) (Elective Provisions), the seller must pay this amount within five local business days; if not, it must pay the amount on the date on which payment would otherwise have been due.

The second sub-section (buyer failure) provides that following the breach of an obligation by the buyer to off-take electricity, the buyer must pay the seller the positive difference between the contract price and the resale proceeds of the electricity (subject to certain adjustments). If 'accelerated payment of damages' is specified as an election in paragraph (j) (Elective Provisions), the buyer must pay this amount within five local business days; if not, then it must pay the amount on the date on which payment would otherwise have been due.

The third sub-section (limitation on conditions precedent) amends Section 2(a)(iii) of the ISDA Master Agreement. This section makes it a condition precedent to payment or delivery for a party that its counterparty have not committed an event of default or potential event of default. The third sub-section amends this provision so that if an event of default or potential event of default has occurred and is continuing for longer than 10 'NERC' business days (these are business days defined by the North American Electric Reliability Council), then if no early termination date has been designated, the condition precedent will fall away.

This is a significant change to the ISDA Master Agreement and prevents a non-defaulting counterparty which is out of the money from failing to perform or close out a power transaction, where its counterparty is in default.

6.4   Payment

Paragraph (d) (Payment) provides for the parties to agree to settle their transactions monthly. However, options premiums are settled two local business days after invoicing. Paragraph (d) also provides for power transactions to be netted against each other.

6.5   Limitation of liability

Paragraph (e) (Limitation of Liability) provides that neither party is responsible to the other for consequential losses.

6.6   Taxes

Under paragraph (f) (Taxes), the seller pays any taxes, fees and penalties incurred up to the point that the electricity is delivered to the delivery point. The buyer is then responsible for all taxes at and after the delivery point.

6.7   Title, risk of loss, and indemnity

In paragraph (g) (Title, Risk of Loss and Indemnity) the parties agree that title to the electricity will pass from seller to buyer at the delivery point. The seller further warrants that it has the right to convey and will transfer good and merchantable title in the electricity, free of encumbrances. The seller agrees to indemnify the buyer for claims arising prior to title transfer, while the buyer agrees to the same for claims arising after title transfer.

The parties also agree to indemnify each other against taxes for which the other is liable.

6.8 Miscellaneous

Paragraph (h) (Miscellaneous) provides three separate sub-sections. The first relates to tariffs, the second to severability and the third to the Federal Energy Regulatory Commission (FERC) standard of review as well as certain covenants and waivers.

The first sub-section (tariffs) is an elective provision, which provides that the seller agrees to provide service to the buyer and the buyer agrees to pay the seller for this service in accordance with the 'seller's tariff'. 'Tariffs' are defined as the "Federal Energy Regulatory Commission tariffs": permitted rates which may be charged for services related to the physical settlement of electricity transactions.

The second sub-section (severability) is an elective provision, which provides that if any provision of the agreement is declared unlawful due to a regulatory event, the parties shall use their best efforts to amend the transaction to allow it to survive.

The third sub-section (FERC standard of review; certain covenants and waivers) is also an elective provision. If selected in paragraph (j) (Elective Provisions), certain covenants and waivers will apply if a transaction's terms are modified following a review by the US FERC.

6.9 Certain modifications to the agreement

Paragraph (i) (Certain Modifications to this Agreement) sets out additional provisions which amend the principal terms of the ISDA Master Agreement.

These relate to limiting the provisions relating to delivery, so that a failure to deliver electricity does not cause an event of default or potential event of default (leading to the potential close-out of the transaction) but is instead dealt with under the provisions described above.

In addition, Paragraph (i) provides that if any power transaction cannot be liquidated or terminated on an early termination date (following an event of default or termination date), in the reasonable opinion of the non-defaulting or non-affected party, then the relevant power transactions will be terminated as soon as reasonably practicable.

Paragraph (i) also sets out various definitions used throughout Part 6 – North American Power Annex. There are 13 definitions provided, most of which are described above.

6.10 Elective provisions

Paragraphs (a) to (i) of Part 6 – North American Power Annex contain various elections, such as whether power transactions entered into between the parties prior to the ISDA Master Agreement should be grandfathered, performance obligations and taxes. These, and others, are described above and the parties' choice is specified in paragraph (j).

7. **Sub-Annex G of the 2005 definitions (the ISDA GTMA Annex)**

Sub-Annex G of the Annex is 29 pages long. It is designed for use with physical transactions carried out on the UK National Grid only. It also interacts with the Grid Trade Master Agreement (Version: June 2004) published by the Futures and Options Association (FOA) (see chapter entitled "Overview of documentation produced by the Futures and Options Association" for an in-depth discussion of this agreement).

The ISDA GTMA Annex consists of a form of Part 6 of the Schedule to the 2002 ISDA Master Agreement or the 1992 ISDA Master Agreement (Multicurrency – Cross Border) for GTMA Transactions, and options to enter into 'grid trades'. There is also an Appendix 1 to Part 6, where the parties will make certain elections within the ISDA Master Agreement; Appendix 2, which sets out a form of confirmation for forward transactions; and Appendix 3, which sets out a form of confirmation for option transactions.

Part 6 (GTMA Transactions) is divided into four paragraphs covering:
- GTMA transactions under the agreement: credit support documents;
- Applicable GTMA terms;
- Additional provisions for GMTA transactions; and
- Amendments to GTMA.

Certain elections are then made in an appendix.

We now look at each of these paragraphs in turn.

7.1 **GTMA transactions under the agreement: credit support documents**

Paragraph (a) (GTMA Transactions under this Agreement: Credit Support Documents) sets out that its provisions relate solely to grid trades or options to enter into grid trades (ie, trades referencing transactions on the UK National Grid). These transactions are then defined as 'GTMA Transactions'.

Paragraph (a) also provides that any GTMA transaction entered into after the effective date specified in the elections in Appendix 1 will be subject to the parties' ISDA Master Agreement, even if they have previously been documenting these types of transaction under another documentation platform: another grandfathering provision. This will also be the case where the parties already have outstanding transactions between them from before the effective date specified in Appendix 1. These trades will be grandfathered into the ISDA Master Agreement (ie, a default under such a transaction would be a default under the ISDA Master Agreement, and the master agreement's payment and close-out netting provisions would apply too).

7.2 **Applicable GTMA terms**

The Grid Trade Master Agreement was introduced to develop a generic framework for OTC electricity trading. It is the market standard set of terms for forward electricity derivatives and is produced by the Futures and Options Association. The GTMA Annex piggybacks the main agreement, but on a selective basis. Paragraph (b) (Applicable GTMA Terms) applies certain of its terms and suggests that certain others are optional only – in addition, the 2005 definitions and ISDA Master Agreement will apply a more robust derivatives regime.

Paragraph (b) deems that the following clauses apply from the GTMA:

- Clause 2.2 (Confirmation Procedure);
- Clause 3.3 (Representation and Warranties);
- Clauses 4–6 (Notifications and Notification Agent);
- Clause 8 (Billing and Payment);
- Clause 9 (*Force Majeure*); and
- Clause 12.6 (Termination).

Paragraph (b) also deems certain other boilerplate clauses to apply and provides an election for the parties to add that the GTMA Options Annex (also produced by the FOA) applies. The GTMA Options Annex provides additional provisions to enable the parties to the GTMA to enter into option transactions under the GTMA. These are option transactions to enter into a grid trade in exchange for a premium.

Of the provisions applied, Clause 2.2 provides a more detailed procedure for agreeing confirmations than that set out in the ISDA Master Agreement. Clause 3.3 provides a representation made between the parties that they will remain parties to the Balancing and Settlement Code, and will comply with its obligations under the code and the relevant credit-related tests specified in the code.

Clauses 4 to 6 relate to notifications and the notification agent. Here each party undertakes to appoint and timely authorise (and maintain the authorisation of) the notification agent in respect of its energy account. Notifications allow the matching of trades between a buyer and a seller, for the delivery and off-take of electricity. Clause 9 provides alternative *force majeure* provisions to the 2002 ISDA Master Agreement for power transactions.

The nomination provisions in the GTMA Terms also cover:

- the parties' obligation to make 'nominations' to the notification agent (stating the information required for the notifications to Elexon);
- the consequences of a failure by a party to appoint or authorise the notification agent; and
- various circumstances where an effective notification has not been made.

Under Clause 8 of the GTMA, the seller prepares and sends to the buyer (on or before the fifth banking day of the following month) a written monthly statement specifying volumes and prices for the transactions carried in the previous month. The party from which a settlement amount is owed should make the payment by the later of the 10th banking day of that following month or the fifth banking day after receipt of the monthly statement (subject to netting if statement amounts are payable by each party to the other).

Clause 12.6 of the GTMA relates to termination. By incorporation of this provision, for any GTMA transaction after the occurrence of an event of default the non-defaulting party can take any action necessary to terminate and relevant notifications.

Of the other important provisions deemed to apply, these exclude consequential and/or indirect losses, except in the case of fraud, intentional default or gross negligence; and allow for certain matters to be referred to an expert.

7.3   Additional provisions for GTMA transactions

Paragraph (c) (Additional Provisions for GTMA Transactions) sets out six additional provisions which are deemed to apply for GTMA in addition to the provisions of the GTMA terms incorporated by reference in paragraph (b).

Certain of these are elections are square-bracketed; others are not. The additional provisions: deem certain definitions to pertain; apply an additional event of default and termination event; modify the trade notification and nomination provisions; and modify the close-out mechanism and the scope of events of default for GTMA transactions.

The first additional provision provides that the definitions section of the GTMA is deemed to be incorporated to the extent relevant for the other GTMA terms incorporated under paragraph (b) (Applicable GTMA Terms) described above.

The second additional provision provides that it will be an additional termination event under the ISDA Master Agreement if a party breaches Clause 3.3 (Representation and Warranties), or Clause 4 or 5 (Notifications and Notification Agent), of the incorporated GTMA terms and the 'compensation threshold' that the parties have specified in Appendix 1 is exceeded. If this occurs, all GTMA transactions will be deemed 'affected transactions', meaning that all GTMA transactions will terminate and be closed out.

The third additional provision provides that it will be an additional event of default under the ISDA Master Agreement if a party fails to perform a material obligation in respect of a GTMA transaction, and the failure is not remedied within five local business days.

The fourth additional provision relates to notifications. It broadens Section 2(a)(i) of the ISDA Master Agreement to make it an obligation to comply with GTMA trade nomination procedures. The fourth additional provision also provides for where a party does not have to comply with its obligations to pay or deliver under Section 2(a)(iii) of the ISDA Master Agreement because the counterparty has incurred an event of default or potential event of default under the ISDA Master Agreement. In these circumstances, if the defaulting/potentially defaulting party is the 'ECV notification agent' (ie, the party which conveys the trade nominations or 'electricity contract volumes'), then the innocent party may require the ECV notification agent to cease complying with its obligations under Clause 5 (ECV Nominations) of the GTMA.

The fifth additional provision broadens the definition of 'specified transaction' under the ISDA Master Agreement to include all electricity transactions entered into by the parties (and their credit support providers and specified entities, set out in the schedule to the ISDA Master Agreement). This expands the ISDA Master Agreement's event of default for 'default under a specified transaction'.

The sixth additional provision is relevant only where a 1992 ISDA Master Agreement is in place. It provides that if 'market quotation' is the payment measure specified in the schedule, then it will be deemed that a market quotation cannot be determined for each terminated transaction which is a GTMA transaction – meaning that 'loss' (as defined in the GTMA) will be the applicable payment measure. This definition of 'loss' takes account of the specific nature of the GTMA marker. The parties may elect whether this additional provision should apply in Appendix 1 (see section 7.5 below).

7.4 Amendments to GTMA

Paragraph (d) (Amendments to GTMA) sets out 11 additional provisions which amend the GTMA.

These provisions amend certain of the definitions in the GTMA so that they properly integrate with the ISDA Master Agreement. For example, the definition of 'transactions' is deemed to be a reference to 'GTMA Transactions' to clarify that GTMA transactions are treated differently from other derivative transactions documented under the parties' ISDA Master Agreement. The definition of 'confirmation' is also amended to make it consistent with the ISDA Master Agreement, while deeming the form of any confirmation to be consistent with the templates provided in the ISDA GTMA Annex. Finally, a bracketed provisions is set out disapplying the *force majeure* provisions of the 2002 ISDA Master Agreement in favour of those in the GTMA.

7.5 Appendix 1 (GTMA Transactions Elections)

Appendix 1 (GTMA Transactions Elections) to Part 6 (GTMA Transactions) provides various elections that will apply to its other sections. These include specifying an 'effective date', defined as the start date for when new GTMA Transactions between the parties will be covered. The parties' can also elect here whether existing GTMA transactions between them will be grandfathered, so that they too will be covered by the ISDA Master Agreement.

The parties will specify in Appendix 1 the quantum of any 'compensation threshold', as an amount per month. This is relevant for the additional termination event described in section 7.3 above. They will also specify whether the market quotation/loss provisions of a 1992 ISDA Master Agreement shall be modified as described above, or whether the automatic exercise of options provisions in the GTMA are to be modified by the parties to fit with the types of transaction they wish to document.

7.6 Appendix 2 (Form of Confirmation)

Appendix 2 (Form of Confirmation) sets out a template form of confirmation for GTMA transactions. The confirmation is for a forward transaction and, as such, locks in a price for the sale and purchase of electricity over an agreed period.

The transaction confirmation is a short document. It sets out two opening paragraphs. These provide that the confirmation is a binding agreement to undertake a GTMA transaction for a grid trade; and that the confirmation is governed by the parties' ISDA Master Agreement. Although not included in the template, the parties should also specify that the 2005 definitions apply.

The main body of the template sets out space for the parties to insert the identities of the buyer and seller and their respective energy accounts.

It also provides for the 'time transaction agreed'. This is equivalent to the trade date. Included too are the 'settlement periods (for which grid trades are to be made)' – that is, which of the 48 half-hourly settlement periods in any day are applicable for the transaction. Specified too is the 'total volume' in megawatts of electricity that will be supplied across all of the settlement periods, as well as the volume of electricity that will be supplied in each settlement period. The price of the electricity during this period is the 'contract price', and this is specified here too in terms of pounds per megawatt-hour.

Finally, the template provides an enhanced confirmation procedure, requiring a signed confirmation to be returned within two local business days.

> **Hypothetical example of a GTMA transaction: Marc-Etienne Energy and Sebire Power**
>
> Marc-Etienne Energy is a major British electricity supplier and has huge demands for electricity, which are satisfied by a variety of electric power producers. Sebire Power is a corporation that owns a range of power stations in the United Kingdom. Sebire Power wants to lock in its prices for its UK customers. Marc-Etienne Energy is concerned that if there is a warm winter, prices could fall, so it is also keen to fix its prices.
>
> The parties have a history of trading under the GTMA with each other. However, their trading relationship has recently broadened, and the parties have also begun to enter into gas derivatives as Sebire Power also has interests in gas fields and Marc-Etienne Energy also provides gas to its customers. The parties enter into an ISDA Master Agreement (so that they can trade both gas and electricity under a single agreement, together with other derivative asset classes) which includes, as an additional section, the Part 6 (GTMA Transactions) provisions.
>
> The parties then enter into a GTMA transaction using the template ISDA confirmation set out in Appendix 2 of Sub-Annex G of the 2005 definitions. They complete the template as follows: the 'seller' is Sebire Power and the 'buyer' is Marc-Etienne Energy. The parties wish to enter into the transaction for the months of January and February 2011. They specify the 'settlement periods (for which grid periods are to be made) as "each Settlement Period in January 2011 and February 2011".
>
> They then specify the 'total volume' of electricity to be supplied as a number of megawatt hours for the entire transaction term, as well as the volumes for each settlement period. Finally, the parties specify the 'contract price': the amount per megawatt hour of electricity that Marc-Etienne Energy will pay Sebire Power for the electricity it delivers.

7.7   Appendix 3 (Form of Option Confirmation)

The template form of option confirmation for GTMA options is also a short document. It sets out the same two opening paragraphs as the GTMA transaction template.

The option template takes a similar form to standard ISDA option agreements. It provides space for the parties to specify the trade date, and which party is the buyer and which the seller.

The confirmation will have the benefit of the GTMA Options Annex. This annex to the GTMA was introduced to provide the necessary additional provisions to enable parties to the GTMA to enter into option transactions under the GTMA. The options transactions provided for are options to enter into a grid trade in exchange for a premium.

The confirmation is divided into two parts: Part A (Option Transaction) and Part B (Grid Trade Transaction). Part A sets out the terms of the option, while Part B sets out the terms of the grid trade transaction which the parties will enter into if the option is exercised.

Under Part A, pursuant to the GTMA Options Annex, the parties may enter into American- or European-style options or 'banking day daily settled' and 'true daily settled' options. Under a European-style option, the buyer can exercise the option only on the expiration date; and under an American-style option the buyer can exercise the option on any exercise date.

For 'banking day daily settled' and 'true daily settled' styles of options, which are option styles specific to GTMA transactions, exercise rights are determined by reference to EFA days.[2] A 'banking day daily settled option' is defined as "a style of Option which may be exercised only on the relevant Expiration Date (which is a Banking Day) and which relates to an EFA Day that corresponds to a day following the Expiration Date up to and including the next Banking Day following that Expiration Date". A 'true daily settled option' is defined as an option "which may be exercised only on the relevant Expiration Date and which relates to the EFA Day that corresponds to the day following that Expiration Date".

The parties will specify under Part A whether the transaction is a call option or a put option. Under a call option, the option buyer has the right to enter into a grid transaction with the seller if the option is exercised. Under a put option, the option buyer has the right to enter into a grid transaction as seller if the option is exercised. They will specify the 'strike price' – this will be the same figure as the 'contract price' under the terms of the grid trade transaction, and it will be the price at which electricity is bought and sold if the option is exercised.

The parties will also specify under Part A the option's 'expiration date' and 'expiration time', as well as term and strike price (expressed in pounds per megawatt-hour); 'total premium' and 'premium payment date' will also be specified.

Part B of the template sets out the form of GTMA transaction, which is provided in Appendix 2. The parties will complete the details and this will be the transaction which the parties will enter into if the buyer exercises its option under the transaction.

Hypothetical example of a GTMA option: Marc-Etienne Energy and Sebire Power

The GTMA transaction between Marc-Etienne Energy and Sebire Power went well. At the end of 2011, both parties feel confident that the price of electricity will stay stable during January 2012. However, Marc-Etienne Energy is concerned that prices may rise sharply in February 2012.

As Marc-Etienne Energy is not confident of this, it decides to hedge itself by

---

2   An EFA day runs from 23:00 hours (inclusive) on a day and ends at 22:59 hours (inclusive) on the next day.

purchasing a call option from Sebire Power, giving it the right to enter into a GTMA transaction in February 2012. The parties use the "Form of Confirmation of GTMA Option" set out in Appendix 3 of Sub-Annex G of the 2005 definitions as a template. Sebire Power believes that electricity prices will go down and so welcomes the premium which it will earn from the transaction.

The parties complete the template as follows: the 'seller' is Sebire Power, and the 'buyer' is Marc Etienne Energy. The 'option type' is specified as 'call'.

For 'option style', the parties specify 'European'. This means that the option can be exercised only on its expiration date, which in turn is specified as February 1 2012 (at this point Marc Etienne Energy will have a good idea of the future direction of energy prices).

'Automatic exercise' is deemed to apply, pursuant to the terms of the GTMA Options Annex. This means that the option is deemed to be exercised at its expiration time on the expiration date if the 'in-the-money amount' payable to Marc-Etienne Energy is equal to or exceeds the product of 10% of the 'total volume' and 'strike price'. 'In-the-money amount', under the GTMA Options Annex, is in turn defined as the amount by which (if any) "(x) the product of the Total Volume times the Reference Price exceeds (y) the product of the Total Volume times the Strike Price".

The 'reference price' was specified in the confirmation as one of the electricity commodity reference prices for the United Kingdom set out in Sub-Annex A to the 2005 definitions.

Under Part B of the transaction, the parties set out the terms of their GTMA transaction, completing the template as follows: the 'seller' is Sebire Power and the 'buyer' is Marc-Etienne Energy. The 'settlement periods for which grid periods are to be made' are stated as "each Settlement Period in January 2012 and February 2012". The total volume of electricity to be supplied, the volumes for each settlement period and the contract price are included too.

Emissions trading

Avanthi Gunatilake
Edmund Parker

1.   Introduction

The columns and clouds of smoke, which are belched forth from the sooty throats of the city's industrial enterprises, made London in a few moments like the picture of Troy sacked by the Greeks. Its inhabitants breathe nothing but an impure and thick mist accompanied by a fulginous and filthy vapour, forcing ladies to clean their complexions with ground almonds and causing the disruption of church services by the constant coughing and spitting of the congregation.[1]

Ever since Evelyn wrote his *Fumifugium: or the inconveniency of the aer and smoke of London* in 1661, the sooty throats of industries around the world have relentlessly devoured fossil fuels and forests, amplifying the greenhouse effect and triggering global warming: 1998 was the warmest year on record around the globe, followed closely by 2007, 2005, 2002, 2003 and 2004.

This ongoing but sudden climate change is putting the world's coastal areas and nearby population centres at risk from rising sea levels caused by melting glaciers and ice caps, and may potentially change existing climatic patterns, resulting in more frequent droughts and occurrences of extreme weather such as hurricanes and monsoons.

Derivatives could save the planet! And International Swaps and Derivatives Association, Inc (ISDA) documentation may be at the forefront. This chapter covers the ISDA documentation platform for emissions trading. The complex nature of the underlying asset and its political ramifications make it essential for the practitioner to understand the rationale for emissions trading, together with the regulatory environment. This chapter covers these areas in detail too.

Nation states have belatedly woken up to the potential dangers of global warming and have begun channelling their energies into the United Nations Framework Convention on Climate Change and the Kyoto Protocol (with the notable exception of the United States, which signed but never ratified the protocol), in a concerted effort to reduce overall greenhouse gas emissions. Among the resulting initiatives are projects to provide economic incentives for nation states and private firms to reduce their greenhouse gas emissions through trading the right to emit them into the atmosphere on an international emissions-trading market. The key emissions trading schemes introduce a 'cap and trade' method whereby a central

---

[1]   J Evelyn, *Fumifugium: or the inconveniency of the aer and smoke of London dissipated*, at p5-16 (London, 1661).

authority issues emissions permits to polluting companies subject to a cap. The polluting companies that are issued with these permits must have a sufficient number of permits to cover their emissions, failing which they must purchase emissions permits from others that pollute less or have otherwise obtained these permits. While maintaining an overall cap, which is lowered over time, this method provides an economic incentive to those that pollute less and imposes an economic burden on those that pollute more: fertile grounds for a derivatives market.

The emissions trading derivatives market consists of financial instruments such as swaps, options and forwards, which derive their value from an underlying asset: the permits giving the right to emit a defined quantity of a greenhouse gas.

Understanding emissions trading requires a greater knowledge of the underlying asset and its regulatory framework than any other derivative. Different rules apply to different countries and greenhouse gases during different periods, all of which are driven by a regulatory infrastructure, including the framework convention, the Kyoto Protocol and the regulatory and legislative actions of its signatories.

Without knowledge of both what global warming involves and the legislative background to emissions trading, a practitioner will not fully understand how emissions trading and its documentation platform function, both now and in the future. With this in mind, this chapter covers issues including:

- the ultimate underlying asset – the greenhouse gas and its relation to climate change;
- a summary of the chain of events from the 1992 Rio Earth Summit, which produced the United Nations Framework Convention on Climate Change, to the resulting 1997 Kyoto Protocol, its coming into effect in 2005 and its development thereafter;
- the Clean Development Mechanism (CDM) and Joint Implementation[2] (JI) 'flexible' project mechanisms for meeting emissions targets, as well as international emissions trading and the interaction between the three mechanisms;
- the mechanics of emissions trading;
- the EU Emissions Trading Scheme (ETS) and a brief look at the developments in the United States for a possible federal emissions trading scheme; and
- the documentation of over-the-counter (OTC) transactions, provided by ISDA for both Europe and the United States.

2. Greenhouse gases and climate change

There is now a consensus among the scientific community that global warming (an increase in the overall temperature of the earth's atmosphere and oceans) is occurring[3] as, over time, the Earth fails to release the sun's energy at the same rate that it absorbs it. This increase in the greenhouse effect has been caused by human activities such as

---

2   Although the term 'joint implementation' was not specifically used in the Kyoto Protocol, it has become the market standard term for this flexible mechanism.
3   Joke Waller-Hunter, executive secretary, United Nations Framework Convention on Climate Change, Bonn, May 2005, foreword to *Caring for Climate: A Guide to the Climate Change Convention and the Kyoto Protocol*.

fossil fuel use and deforestation, pushing up atmospheric levels of greenhouse gases, such as carbon dioxide, nitrogen dioxide and methane. Global warming may increase the Earth's overall temperature by as much as between 2.4 and 6.4 degrees[4] over the next century. The extent of the world's governments' desire to slow or halt this increase will drive the pace of the emissions trading market in future years.

How does the greenhouse effect work?[5,6]

- Solar energy passes through the Earth's atmosphere.
- Some of it is absorbed by greenhouse gases in the atmosphere; some is reflected by the Earth's atmosphere and surface; and the rest is absorbed by, and warms, the earth's surface.
- Through absorption by the Earth's surface, the solar energy is converted into heat, causing the Earth to emit long-wave infrared radiation back towards space.
- Greenhouse gases (eg, carbon dioxide, methane and water vapour), which are the atmosphere's gaseous constituents that absorb and re-emit infrared radiation, send some of this infrared radiation back to the Earth's surface and atmosphere.
- The Earth's surface gains more heat and the infrared radiation is once again emitted.
- Some of the infrared radiation passes through the atmosphere and goes into space.
- The more greenhouse gases that are in the atmosphere, the more the Earth's temperature will increase.

3. The Earth Summit and the United Nations Framework Convention on Climate Change

In 1992 the United Nations Conference on Environment and Development in Rio de Janeiro addressed the increasing evidence of global warming. This conference, which became known as the Earth Summit, agreed a new treaty: the United Nations Framework Convention on Climate Change, which entered into force in 1994. The convention acknowledged that human activities were increasing atmospheric concentrations of greenhouse gases, which in turn were exacerbating the 'greenhouse effect', and that this "will result on average in an additional warming of the earth's surface and atmosphere and may adversely affect natural ecosystems and humankind".

The convention recognised the vulnerability of certain types of geographical areas to climate change, encouraged climate change scientific research and

---

4   Intergovernmental Panel on Climate Change, *Fourth Assessment Report*, 2007.

5   *Caring for Climate: A Guide to the Climate Change Convention and the Kyoto Protocol*, United Nations Framework Convention on Climate Change.

6   *Understanding Climate Change: A Beginner's Guide to the UN Framework Convention and its Kyoto Protocol*; Okangan University in Canada, Department of Geography; US Environmental Protection Agency, Washington; *Climate Change 1995: The Science of Climate Change*, contribution of Working Group 1 to the second assessment report of the Intergovernmental Panel on Climate Change, United Nations Environment Programme and World Meteorological Organisation (Cambridge University Press, 1996); GRID-Arendall.

technology sharing, and agreed an ultimate objective to stabilise greenhouse gas concentrations in the atmosphere at a level which would prevent adverse effects to the climate system, through national policies. Its parties also agreed to record and report their greenhouse gas emissions.

The convention was a framework treaty without enforcement provisions. It committed its parties to meet annually at the Conference of the Parties (COP), which monitors progress and discusses tackling climate change.

The convention was joined almost universally and signatories included all EU member states, the United States, Australia, Canada, China and India. The convention divided its signatory countries into three separate groups: Annex I parties, Annex II parties and the rest, which have become known as non-Annex I parties.

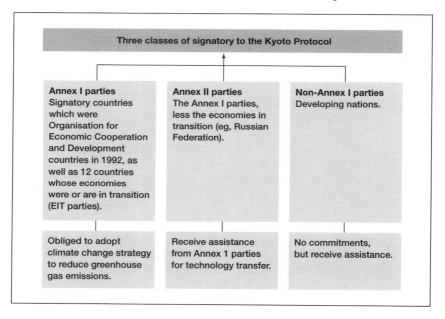

Annex I parties are those signatory countries which were Organisation for Economic Cooperation and Development countries in 1992, as well as 12 countries whose economies were or are in transition (EIT parties). EIT parties include the Russian Federation, Belarus, Bulgaria, Croatia, Hungary and Ukraine. Annex II parties are the Annex I parties, excluding the EIT parties. The non-Annex I parties are for the most part the developing nations.

Each of the convention's three groups was given different obligations. Each Annex I party was obliged to adopt a climate change strategy to reduce its greenhouse gas emissions to 1990 (or in the case of the EIT parties, a later base year) levels by 2000. This target was achieved.

The Annex I parties had to give financial assistance to the non-Annex I parties to assist them in reducing their greenhouse gas emissions and adapting to climate change. They also had to encourage environmentally friendly technology transfer to

EIT and non-Annex I parties. The non-Annex I parties were given no additional specific commitments.

4. Kyoto Protocol

4.1 Ratification and general content

At the third conference, which took place in Kyoto in 1997, the Kyoto Protocol was adopted. This protocol was then refined in the fourth, fifth and sixth conferences and the Marrakesh Accords in 2001.

The protocol focuses on six greenhouse gases:

- carbon dioxide;
- nitrogen oxide (a collective term);
- methane;
- hydrofluorocarbons;
- perfluorocarbons; and
- sulphur hexafluoride.

Carbon dioxide, methane and nitrogen oxide account for almost 75% of greenhouse gas emissions, with carbon dioxide alone accounting for 50%.

The protocol's adherents must achieve legally binding greenhouse gas emissions reductions. They can achieve these targets either by reducing emissions to below a cap or by using three potential flexible mechanisms: the clean development mechanism (CDM), the joint implementation (JI) and/or emissions trading under cap-and-trade systems. The first two are project-based mechanisms that can generate allowances, which can then be traded along with any other allocated allowances under an emissions trading system.

Although all of the protocol's adherents are signatories to the convention, the United States is yet to ratify the protocol. Moreover, India and China are also not bound by the protocol's emissions targets as they are not Annex I parties.

4.2 Commitments to reduce emissions

Each adhering Annex I party must meet a greenhouse gas emissions reduction target. This reduction is benchmarked against 1990 emissions (or in the case of EIT countries, a later benchmark year), and must be met on average through the protocol's compliance period which runs from January 1 2008 to December 31 2012. In addition, Annex I parties must implement climate change policies.

Overall, the Annex I parties must reduce their greenhouse gas emissions by at least 5%. The European Union is treated as a single Annex I party and has an overall emissions reduction target of 8%. It has allocated each EU member state's target internally. This means that some member states may increase their emissions (eg, Portugal by 27% and Spain by 15%), while others must reduce theirs greatly (eg, Germany by 21% and the United Kingdom by 12.5%).

The non-Annex I parties adhering to the protocol have no emissions reductions targets.

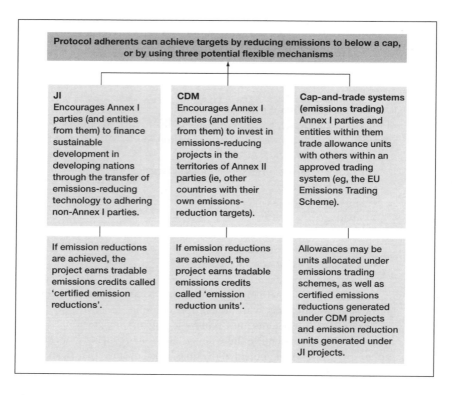

Protocol adherents can achieve targets by reducing emissions to below a cap, or by using three potential flexible mechanisms

JI
Encourages Annex I parties (and entities from them) to finance sustainable development in developing nations through the transfer of emissions-reducing technology to adhering non-Annex I parties.

CDM
Encourages Annex I parties (and entities from them) to invest in emissions-reducing projects in the territories of Annex II parties (ie, other countries with their own emissions-reduction targets).

Cap-and-trade systems (emissions trading)
Annex I parties and entities within them trade allowance units with others within an approved trading system (eg, the EU Emissions Trading Scheme).

If emission reductions are achieved, the project earns tradable emissions credits called 'certified emission reductions'.

If emission reductions are achieved, the project earns tradable emissions credits called 'emission reduction units'.

Allowances may be units allocated under emissions trading schemes, as well as certified emissions reductions generated under CDM projects and emission reduction units generated under JI projects.

4.3   Three flexible methods for emissions reductions

(a)   *Clean development mechanism*

While the adhering Annex I parties could accept greenhouse gas emissions caps, the developing nations could not, and the latter group may increase their emissions in tandem with economic growth. It is inevitable that as these nations industrialise, their emissions will increase. To help tackle this issue without hampering economic development, the protocol introduced the CDM, which encourages Annex I parties (and firms from them) to finance sustainable development in developing nations through the transfer of emissions-reducing technology to adhering non-Annex I parties. If the project implementing the technology results in emissions reductions, the firm or country running the project earns tradable emissions credits (known as 'certified emission reductions'). It is likely that the costs of doing so would be less than if they made the corresponding reduction in emissions in their own country.

Adhering developing nations may, with the prior approval of the CDM Executive Board, carry out their own CDM projects without outside assistance and sell the resulting certified emission reductions into the open market. An example of this could be a Malaysian project to reforest 1 million hectares of its sovereign territory with the certified emission reductions allocated to this 'carbon sink'[7] sold to an EU member state.

---

7   Carbon sinks are projects that remove carbon dioxide from the atmosphere.

The Marrakesh Accords set out the CDM's governing rules in their Modalities and Procedures for a Clean Development Mechanism. These rules have robust procedures which require strong evidence to be shown that a CDM project has caused emissions to be lower than if the project had not happened. The CDM Executive Board supervises all such mechanisms and a designated operational entity, which is a private entity accredited by the board, checks each relevant project and verifies the resulting emissions reductions.[8]

CDM projects include those which can reduce emissions from production, distribution and demand for energy in manufacturing industries, in construction projects, in the chemical industry and through carbon sinks such as afforestation and reforestation projects.

CDM project cycle: a hypothetical example

- Nicol International Industries, a UK corporate and major emitter of carbon dioxide, liaises with the Algerian Energy Ministry to upgrade Algeria's national grid. Algeria and the United Kingdom have both ratified the Kyoto Protocol. The project involves a technology transfer from the United Kingdom, an Annex I party, to Algeria, a non-Annex I party. The Algerian project will make Algerian energy transfer more efficient, resulting in lower carbon dioxide emissions. Nicol believes that the project will qualify as a CDM project.
- Nicol is a participating installation in the EU ETS[9] and so must surrender allowances for all of its carbon dioxide emissions. Nicol has not been allocated enough allowances by the UK government to match its actual emissions. As an alternative to buying allowances on the open market, it plans to register the Algerian project as a CDM and surrender the certified emission reductions it generates to cover the allowances it must submit under the EU ETS.
- Nicol submits the project plan to the CDM Executive Board.
- Leburn Consulting Limited, a designated operational entity appointed by Nicol, and the Algerian Energy Ministry review the project plan and verify that it meets the CDM criteria.
- Nicol registers the approved project with Leburn and the CDM Executive Board.
- Nicol runs and monitors the Algerian project in accordance with the criteria given to it by the CDM Executive Board.
- Two years later the project is complete and Freeland Partners, another designated operational entity, verifies the reduction in carbon dioxide emissions.
- The CDM Executive Board instructs the CDM Registry to credit Nicol's CDM

---

8   The International Emissions Trading Association's *Guidance Note through the CDM Project Approval Process* (Version 1.5, May 2005) states that as of May 1 2005, 28 entities had applied for accreditation as designated operational entities, of which eight had so far been accredited.

9   For an explanation of the EU Emissions Trading Scheme, see section 6 below.

> Registry accounts with the appropriate number of certified emission reductions.[10]
>
> - The CDM Registry deducts 2% of the certified emission reductions from the total issued to Nicol as a CDM levy.[11] These 'deducted' reductions are sold into the market and the proceeds are transferred to an adaptation fund for the developing nations most susceptible to climate change risks.
> - The project is more successful than Nicol anticipated, leaving Nicol with more certified emission reductions than it needs to satisfy its EU ETS quota. Nicol can sell these additional reductions into the market, where they can be bought by countries or private firms.

The CDM Executive Board is made up of representatives from both adhering Annex I and non-Annex I parties. Its responsibilities include:

- formulating policies on CDMs;
- reviewing designated operational entities' decisions;
- deciding whether projects meet the CDM rules;
- deciding the supervisory and regulatory restrictions of CDM projects; and
- having the power to refuse the issue of certified emission reductions when it thinks it appropriate.

The CDM Registry is maintained by the CDM Executive Board. It is a registry which records and accounts for the issue, transfer and holdings of certified emission reductions. Each CDM project has its own account at the registry.

(b)   Joint implementation

The CDM relates to projects in developing nations. By contrast, JI is the protocol's mechanism for Annex I parties, or participating installations in an emissions trading scheme, to earn tradable emissions credits (emission reduction units) for investing in emissions reduction projects in the territories of other Annex I parties (ie, other countries with their own emissions reduction targets). For cost reasons, the host country for a JI project is likely to be an EIT country; this is because bigger emissions reductions can be gained from upgrading antiquated infrastructure than from improving more modern facilities.

The supervisory framework for JI is less robust than that for CDM projects as emission reduction units relate only to the transfer of the location where the emissions reduction is counted. If the host country meets all of the JI eligibility criteria, then it may apply its own procedures to the relevant JI project and issue the units directly. If it does not fulfil all of the requirements, a supervisory committee will oversee the process and decide whether the project meets the JI criteria (and if

---

10   Certified emission reductions can be issued in relation to reductions in any greenhouse gas covered by the protocol (eg, a landfill which captures methane). Importantly, certified emission reductions generated in relation to these other gases can still be surrendered by installations participating in the EU Emissions Trading Scheme to cover their carbon dioxide emissions.

11   This would not have occurred had the project taken place in a Kyoto non-Annex I party deemed to be particularly susceptible to the adverse risks of climate change.

so, how many units the host country can issue). Emissions reductions achieved under JI projects have been eligible to be credited towards the EU ETS since 2008 (ie, during the Kyoto compliance period only).

JI project cycle: a worked example

By 2011 the United Kingdom will be facing high emissions reductions costs and is likely to be struggling to meet its Kyoto target. It decides to invest in upgrading an old Soviet-era Ukrainian power plant with carbon dioxide emissions-reduction technology. Achieving similar emissions reductions in a UK power plant would be far more expensive.

The project is successful and achieves the anticipated carbon dioxide (and sulphur dioxide) reductions. Ukraine issues the United Kingdom with the corresponding emission reduction units, which the United Kingdom counts towards its emissions reduction target.

Ukraine has benefited from the United Kingdom's foreign direct investment, although to prevent double counting the emissions reductions do not count towards Ukraine's target.

(c)   ***Emissions trading***

Emissions trading is the protocol's third flexible mechanism. It allows adhering Annex I parties and the public entities and private firms within them to trade allowance units with other Annex I parties and their public entities and private firms. The allowances may be units allocated under emissions trading schemes as well as certified emission reductions generated under CDM projects and emission reduction units generated under JI projects.

5.   Beyond Kyoto

The latest round of talks, COP 15, took place in Copenhagen in December 2009 and resulted in the Copenhagen Accord of December 18 2009. The accord, a short and a heavily qualified document, was a last-minute gesture and is yet to be signed by the countries.[12] The Kyoto Protocol comes to an end in 2012 so this lack of commitment towards reducing greenhouse gas emissions was disappointing. Nevertheless, the loosely worded Copenhagen Accord will probably come to life during 2010, resulting in a detailed agreement to be reached by COP 16, to be held in Mexico in 2010.

With the disappointing conclusion of COP 15, the price of carbon permits dropped nearly 10% in early trading, finally settling around €12.41 in December 2009. The overall trend nationally and regionally has been towards reducing carbon emissions, and a global accord to this end will probably to be struck in the coming COPs. However, as the IETA notes, governments have missed out on a good opportunity to convince the private sector of the importance of cutting carbon by means such as investing in greener technology on a global scale.

---

12   The final wording of the Copenhagen Accord states that the COP "takes note" of it and it is therefore not a legally binding document.

6.   EU Emissions Trading Scheme

The EU ETS is the European Union's compulsory 'cap and trade' project for trading carbon dioxide emission allowances. It is the most ambitious and comprehensive emissions trading scheme ever created.[13] Roughly 12,000 EU industrial installations, which are responsible for almost half of the European Union's carbon dioxide output, were allocated allowances in the scheme's first stage, with that number expanding in the second stage.[14]

Each allowance represents the right to emit one tonne of carbon dioxide; and each participating installation must surrender allowances equal to its actual carbon dioxide emissions. If its allocated allowances are not sufficient to cover its actual emissions, the affected installation must go into the market and purchase additional allowances to cover the shortfall. Failure to surrender sufficient allowances to cover emissions incurs a penalty per tonne of carbon dioxide emitted; the defaulting firm will also be asked to make good the allowances in the following year. If the affected installation has an excess of allowances, perhaps through generating efficiencies, it can sell these into the market for a profit. The EU ETS aims to reduce carbon dioxide emissions by financially rewarding affected installations that reduce their emissions and penalising those that do not.

Established by the EU Emissions Trading Directive, the EU ETS began life on January 1 2005. It originally applied to each of the European Union's 25 member states (including the 12 2004 accession countries), and became a key mechanism assisting the European Union to meet its Kyoto emissions reduction commitment. Although member states issue allowances to participating installations for carbon dioxide emissions only, these installations can purchase or source certified emission reductions and emission reduction units relating to other protocol greenhouse gas emissions such as methane, and surrender these to help cover their own actual carbon dioxide emissions. This is possible due to the EU Linking Directive, which amended the Emissions Trading Directive.[15] The Linking Directive creates a link between the EU ETS and the protocol's two other flexible mechanisms: CDM and JI. All certified emission reductions and emission reduction units can be linked to the EU ETS and their allowances surrendered to meet emissions quotas, except for those relating to nuclear and sink projects.

---

13   From 2002 to 2006 the United Kingdom operated its own emissions trading scheme. Thirty-four organisations (eg, British Sugar and British Airways) voluntarily accepted emissions reduction targets (including non-carbon dioxide emissions) to reduce their greenhouse gas emissions against 1998 to 2000 levels. Participants that achieve their targets got an 80% reduction in their climate change levy (a business energy tax). Participants could trade allowances in the same way as under the EU ETS. The scheme ended in 2007 with participants migrating to the EU ETS thereafter. In a report appraising the four-year scheme, one lesson noted was that there is a strong case for ensuring that the number of allowances allocated promotes real emissions reductions (*Appraisal of Years 1–4 of the UK Emissions Trading Scheme*, Department for Environment, Food and Rural Affairs, 2006).

14   Installations that produce approximately 46% of UK carbon dioxide emissions are covered in the first stage: *UK Government Review of the UK Climate Change Programme Consultation Paper*, December 2004.

15   2004/101/EC, amending Directive 2003/87/EC.

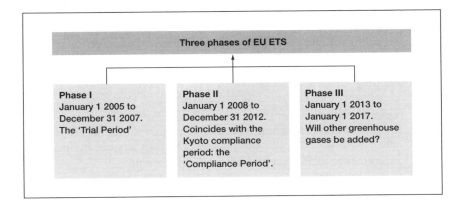

The EU ETS has been divided into three Phases.
- Phase I began on January 1 2005 and ended on December 31 2007.
- Phase II began on January 1 2008 and will end on December 31 2012, coinciding with the Kyoto compliance period.
- Phase III will run from January 1 2013 to January 1 2017.

Participating installations are allocated allowances annually and those not used in one year can be carried over to the next. Surrendered allowances are counted towards each country's Kyoto emissions reduction target.

6.1   EU ETS: Phase I – trial period

Phase I applied to companies which emit carbon dioxide above a set threshold and were involved in:
- energy activities with a thermal capacity of at least 20 megawatts;
- the ferrous metals industry;
- the minerals industry (including cement, ceramics and glass); or
- pulp and paper production.

Phase I was intended as a trial period in establishing the world's largest market for emissions trading. Several lessons were learned during Phase I which highlighted issues such as lack of accurate data to estimate allowances, over-allocation of allowances resulting in high price volatility, and overall lack of progress towards Kyoto targets.

6.2   EU ETS: Phase II – compliance period

EU ETS Phase II commenced on January 1 2008 and will last until December 31 2012. This is the Kyoto compliance period – the timeframe within which the emissions reduction goals set out in Kyoto must be complied with.

As in Phase I, Phase II of the EU ETS covers only one greenhouse gas: carbon dioxide. However, member states may 'opt in' other greenhouse gases. In Phase II the non-compliance penalty increases to €100 per tonne of carbon dioxide, from €40 in Phase I. In addition to the EU member states, three non-members – Iceland, Norway and Liechtenstein – joined Phase II of the EU ETS. Through an amendment to the EU Emissions Trading Directive, the aviation sector will join the EU ETS from 2012.[16]

Learning from Phase I, the European Union has been careful to avoid over-allocation of allowances. The current functioning of the EU ETS is based on the following framework.

(a)   *National Allocation Plans*

The scheme requires each member state to prepare a national allocation plan and submit it to the European Commission. The plan sets out the quantum of the member state's permissible emissions to be assigned to:

- the EU ETS;
- each relevant industrial sector; and
- each affected installation.

In Phase II the EU ETS adopted a tougher stand in reviewing the national allocations plans and the allocations sought were reduced.

(b)   *National registry*

EU Regulation 2216/2004 obliges EU member states to set up a national registry. The online registry records the allowances issued to participating installations, as well as each installation's annual verified emissions and compliance status, and tracks the movements of allowances between accounts (including surrender and cancellation). Participating installations and individuals and organisations that wish to participate in emissions trading are among those that can open registry accounts. The registry also holds the designated national competent authority's accounts into which allowances are surrendered.

(c)   *Community independent transaction log*

All of the registries are supervised by a central administrator which, through the European Union's Community Independent Transaction Log,[17] records and checks each transaction. The log also records any allowance transfers between registries. The ability to transfer allowances between national registries means that EU member states can meet their Kyoto targets while their emissions are above the required threshold. However, the ETS will ensure that corresponding decreases in emissions are made either within the European Union through the trading of allocated allowances and issued certified emission reductions or in non-EU countries through JI or CDM projects.

(d)   *Surrender, cancellation and trading of allowances*

By March 31 each year, each affected installation must report its carbon dioxide emissions during the previous calendar year. The affected installation then has until April 30 to surrender allowances for all of its carbon dioxide emissions to its national

---

16   Aviation Directive (2008/101/EC).
17   Commission Regulation 2216/2004 of December 21 2004.

authority or face a fine. During Phase II this is set at €100 per missing allowance. Once surrendered, the allowances are then cancelled.

Each affected installation is allocated a set number of allowances each year; if it turns out to have more allowances than it needs, it may hold these in its account to be used the following year or it may sell them to another party. Allowances issued under the EU ETS could not be carried over (commonly referred to as 'banking') from Phase I to Phase II, though allowances issued in Phase II can be held over for Phase III. Certified emission reductions and emission reduction units are eligible for surrender against quotas, including those sourced in Phase I.

EU emissions trading: a hypothetical example

Ruthven plc is a large cement manufacturer based in Perth, Scotland. It has been allocated 300,000 emissions allowances per year (each representing an allowance to emit one tonne of carbon dioxide) under the United Kingdom's national allocation plan for Phase II of the EU ETS. At the end of the first year of Phase II, Ruthven prepared its 2008 emissions report, which was checked by an accredited verifier; the amounts are recorded at the UK registry.

The report reveals that Ruthven emitted 480,000 tonnes of carbon dioxide during 2008. Thus, the company had to surrender 480,000 allowances to the UK government account at the registry by March 31 2009. This is 180,000 more allowances than Ruthven was allocated. EU allowances are trading at €20 per tonne on the open market and Ruthven enters into three transactions to buy the missing allowances that it needs:

It enters into a spot transaction on the European Climate Exchange (ECX) with a counterparty to purchase 60,000 ECX carbon financial instruments (these are essentially cash contracts to purchase allowances).

It enters into an International Emissions Trading Association (IETA) emissions allowances single-trade agreement for the EU scheme transaction with Strathallan plc, a local power generating company which had more allowances than it needed, to purchase 60,000 allowances.

It enters into an ISDA-documented transaction to purchase a further 60,000 certified emission reductions from Airlie Projects, a company which has been issued certified emission reductions under a CDM project which it carried out in Tanzania.

The 180,000 allowances cost Ruthven €3.6 million: enough to make a sizeable dent in the company's bottom line. These are credited to Ruthven's registry account. Ruthven then delivers the 480,000 allowances to the UK government on March 31 2009.

In 2009 Ruthven is again allocated 300,000 allowances into its registry account. Ruthven's board decides to upgrade the plant to reduce its carbon dioxide emissions. The upgrade of the plant costs €2 million and is completed in the first quarter.

At the end of the second year of Phase I, Ruthven prepares its 2009 emissions report; once again, the report is checked by an accredited verifier and the amounts are recorded at the UK registry. The report reveals that Ruthven emitted 200,000 tonnes of carbon dioxide during 2009; the plant upgrade paid off and the company has 100,000 more allowances than it was allocated. EU allowances are now trading at €30 per tonne on the open market.

Ruthven enters into a transaction to sell 50,000 allowances to Denny plc, a paper manufacturer which is short of allowances, and 50,000 allowances to Dunning Investments, a speculator which intends to hold the allowances on the expectation that they will rise further in value. The sale of the allowances generates €3 million for Ruthven, more than paying for the cost of the plant upgrade and leaving it with a profit of €1 million.

6.3   EU ETS: Phase III

Phase III is set to run from 2013 to 2020. In January 2009 the EU ETS Reform Directive was published which, if implemented, introduces several bold new developments. It was stated that the goal for the period beyond 2012 was to "expand and improve the functioning of the ETS" in order to reduce greenhouse gas emissions. The proposals include:

- the introduction of a single EU-wide emissions cap, which means allowances for each member at EU level, thereby abolishing national allocation plans;
- expansion of the EU ETS to cover new gases; and
- establishment of a single EU registry, instead of national registries.

In addition, there are several other changes, such as a move towards reducing the free allocation of allowances and an increased commitment to an overall reduction of emissions. The European Union has been faced with strong lobbying from energy-intensive industries, concerned about the impact that the extended ETS could have on business. The directive is intended to be implemented in two stages: Stage 1 by December 31 2009 (which the United Kingdom has done)[18] and Stage 2 by the end of 2012.

7.   Emissions trading in the United States

The United States lags behind the European Union in its efforts to set up an emissions trading scheme. So far, these can be categorised as emissions trading at state level and at federal level.

7.1   State/regional level

At US state and regional level, significant progress has been made in establishing emissions trading schemes.[19] In January 2009 the Regional Greenhouse Gas Initiative (RGGI) commenced. This is the first mandatory, market-based effort in the United States to reduce greenhouse gas emissions. Ten north-eastern and mid-Atlantic states have committed to capping and then reducing carbon dioxide emissions arising from the power sector 10% by 2018.[20]

18   Greenhouse as Emissions Data and National Implementation Measures Regulations 2009.
19   David Hunter, 'Market Developments at the US Federal Level: A Federal Cap-and-Trade Programme within 4 Years', *Greenhouse Gas Market Report* 2008.
20   See www.rggi.org.

7.2 Towards a federal system of emissions trading

In July 2009 the US Congress passed the Clean Energy and Security Act, committing the nation to a 17% reduction in carbon dioxide emissions from 2005 levels by 2020, and introducing a federal emissions trading system. The legislation has four parts:

- a 'clean energy' part that promotes renewable sources of energy and cleaner technology;
- an 'energy efficiency' part that increases energy efficiency across all sectors of the economy, including buildings, appliances, transportation and industry;
- a 'global warming' part that places limits on the emissions of heat-trapping pollutants; and
- a 'transitioning' title that protects US consumers and industry and promotes green jobs during the transition to a clean energy economy.

The bill needs US Senate approval to become law, however, and one year on it has yet to receive approval. The bill nevertheless reflects growing interest in the US carbon market; and if it becomes law, it could create the world's largest carbon market, reaching $1 trillion in size by 2020.[21]

8. Carbon markets

The Kyoto Protocol and the EU ETS provide a framework within which a cap-and-trade scheme can function. However, neither the Kyoto Protocol nor the EU ETS attempted to 'design' the emissions trading market. Firms may take part in trades for a number of reasons:

- to buy allowances to avoid penalties under the scheme;
- to trade and sell excess allowances for gain; or
- for trading purposes or to make a market.

In doing so, entities may utilise derivatives such as forwards, options and swaps to hedge against price volatility, arbitrage against pricing differences of different underlying emissions trading instruments, or secure allowances in advance. These are discussed in detail below.

Point Carbon, a carbon market reporting website, states that the year 2008 saw the overall equivalent of 4.9 billion tonnes of carbon dioxide being traded. This was up 83% from 2007.[22] The latest data shows that in the first quarter of 2009 there was a 37% growth compared with 2008 volume.[23]

8.1 What factors determine the pricing of carbon credits?

A carbon credit is a right to emit carbon dioxide – that is, an allocated allowance or right acquired through JI or the CDM. The volume of carbon credits traded has continued to increase. The factors influencing the price of carbon credits and their

---

21   'Economic Researchers Predict $1 Trillion US Carbon Trading Market by 2010'. New Carbon Finance, www.newcarbonfinance.com.

22   'Carbon market worth almost €100bn in 2008, more than double 2007's figures', Point Carbon, www.pointcarbon.com.

23   Press release, April 27 2009, New Carbon Finance.

supply and demand are complex. They may include economic factors and regulatory developments, such as changes to the EU ETS (eg, including other industries in the scheme).

Any increase in overall carbon dioxide production will mean that more installations will need to purchase allowances. This will inflate allowance prices. This could occur, for example, due to a cold winter driving up energy consumption and forcing power companies to emit more carbon dioxide, or because of an economic boom. Market factors such as liquidity, speculation and anticipated price movements can also affect price.

Factors which can depress carbon credit prices include an economic downturn resulting in a reduction in industrial output; increased carbon credit supply due to more certified emission reductions and emission reduction units arriving on the market; and developments in emissions reduction technology reducing demand for credits.

The general ability for installations to meet their emissions quotas will also drive down prices. A switch away from coal and oil-fired power generation to renewable sources such as wind and hydroelectric power, as well as to gas and nuclear power, could also result in reduced demand for allowances.

Over-allocation or under-allocation of allowances may also impact on prices. In Phase I of the EU ETS, over-allocation of allowances led to high price volatility and eventually rock-bottom prices.

Although allocated allowances, certified emission reductions and emission reduction units[24] are all fungible for the purposes of surrendering allowances, allocated allowances currently trade at a higher price than either certified emission reductions or emission reduction units, due to uncertainty relating to whether these permits will actually arrive and/or fears of fraud in the certification process.

8.2 Use of derivatives in the carbon markets

Trading in carbon credits proved risky in the early days due to price volatility. This risk factor, together with the increasing expansion of the market, led to the development of carbon/emissions derivatives.

Derivatives in the emissions trading arena may be used for three main reasons:

- to give the buyer protection against certain financial risks (eg, a firm in need of buying additional carbon credits may use derivatives as a way of protecting against any future increase in prices);
- as an investment class (eg, a bank may speculate that the price of carbon credits is set to come down in the future and may wish to lock in this gain through a forward contract); and
- for arbitrage or trading purposes (eg, a bank may establish itself as a market maker acting as a central counterparty to buyers and sellers of emissions trading derivatives, and make a profit from the price differential).

The most commonly used types of carbon derivatives in the OTC market include forwards, option and swaps.

---

24   During Phase II only.

(a)   ***Options***

Options are bilateral contracts between an option holder and an option writer. The option writer, in consideration for a premium, grants the option holder the right, but not the obligation, to buy or sell an agreed quantity of carbon credits at a fixed price on a future date.

The most common options are 'put' and 'call' options. Put option holders have the right to sell or deliver carbon credits at an agreed price on a future date. Call option holders have the right to buy or receive carbon credits at an agreed price on a future date.

(b)   ***Forwards***

In forward and futures contracts, the parties agree to buy and sell carbon credits at a future date at an agreed price. Forwards differ from options in that the buyer of a forward contract is obliged to pay the agreed purchase price even if the carbon credits are worth less than the purchase price on the settlement date, while the buyer of an option is not obliged to exercise the option and pay the purchase price.

Use of carbon derivatives: hypothetical example of a forward

Viduli Corporation operates an energy installation in Belgium and does not have sufficient allowances to cover its actual emissions during the next year. In order to avoid a penalty, it decides to purchase carbon credits from the market at the end of the year. However, it is concerned that during the remainder of the year, the price of carbon credits may escalate. Viduli needs to buy 10,000 carbon credits and is happy to pay a price of €20 per tonne of carbon dioxide.

It enters into a forward to buy the 10,000 carbon credits at €20 per tonne of carbon dioxide at the end of the year, replacing the risk of higher carbon prices at a future date with certainty in price (ie, € 200,000).

The end seller of the forward, Italian glass manufacturer Mihika, has invested in green technology and hopes to sell some of the carbon credits allocated to it which are now in excess of its needs. In order to offset some of its investment costs in green technology Mihika looks to sell its excess allowances and lock in the current price. By selling the forwards today, Mihika removes the risk of a drop in carbon credit prices in the future.

Mihika sells the forwards to Strathallan Bank, which is making a market in these forwards, for €180,000. Strathallan Bank then enters into a back-to-back transaction selling the forwards to Viduli for €200,000.

(c)   ***Swaps***

As mentioned above, the trading price of EU allowances can vary from those for certified emission reductions and emission reduction units. The latter two normally trade at a discount due to the uncertainty as to whether these allowances will actually materialise and fears of fraud in the verification process arising in individual projects, resulting in credits being annulled. Where an entity involved in the production or purchase of these units, it may wish to hedge against falls of certified emission reductions or emission reduction units against EU allowances by entering into a swap protecting itself against any downward movement in the trading price.

> **Use of carbon derivatives: hypothetical example of a swap**
> Norton Folgate Industries is a glass manufacturing company. It has noticed that
> the price of certified emission reductions is cheaper than that of EU allowances.
> Norton Folgate will have sufficient allowances to meet its obligations under the
> EU ETS.
>
> To realise a profit, Norton Folgate enters into a physically settled swap with a
> financial institution under which it delivers 30% of its EU allowances in return for
> a corresponding amount of certified emission reductions and a cash amount.
>
> The financial institution has secured the certified emission reductions from a
> Brazilian CDM project and is pleased to have secured a good price for them.
> Norton Folgate can also realise a gain by submitting the certified emission
> reductions in place of its EU allowances.

Cash-settled EU allowance for certified emission reduction swaps are also
possible. In this type of transaction the parties exchange the difference in the trading
price of the two types of credits on a periodic basis. This type of transaction might
be attractive to an entity participating in a CDM project which wanted to ensure that
the price of certified emission reductions did not fall too far below the price of EU
allowances.

(d)   OTC trading

When entering into a carbon trade in the OTC markets, the parties have three
options as regards the documentation platforms they use: ISDA, IETA or the
European Federation of Energy Traders (EFET).[25]

(e)   Trading through climate exchanges

The development of exchange trading is helping the carbon credit market to reduce
credit risk by providing a central counterparty, as well as liquidity, through matching
counterparties, trading standardised and simple contracts, and publishing prices.

There are currently more than 10 European exchanges with exchange-traded
allowance contracts and nearly 40 worldwide. This number is likely to increase as the
market matures and gathers pace. These exchanges include the European Climate
Exchange in the United Kingdom, Powernext in France and Nordpool in Germany.

The European Climate Exchange coordinates the marketing, listing and sales of
ECX carbon financial instruments: futures and cash contracts for EU ETS allowances.
These are listed on ICE Futures (an electronic trading platform). Trades are cleared
through LCH.Clearnet Ltd, which acts as a central counterparty guaranteeing
financial and physical performance.[26]

(f)   Carbon pools

Carbon pools are spot[27] trading platforms. Their members are small emitters that

---

25   See section 9 below.
26   LCH.Clearnet Ltd has a default fund of more than £570 million.
27   Spot transactions are transactions where, once the parties have agreed a contract price, delivery and
      payment occur within a short timeframe.

have been allocated allowances under the EU ETS. The pool matches their buy and sell orders together in an order book. After placing an order, the parties transfer their funds or allowances into their pool account and these are then transferred within the pool.

Advantages of carbon pools include:

- counterparty anonymity;
- the grouping of small buy and sell orders into larger orders together; and
- increased liquidity.

9.   **OTC trading: documenting emissions trading under the EU ETS**

The EU ETS market has a choice of three documentation platforms for OTC transactions, each prepared by a separate trade organisation: ISDA, IETA and EFET. The key differences between the three platforms are outlined below.

Documentation platforms		
Trade organisation	**Organisation description**	**Documentation**
ISDA	ISDA is the dominant derivatives trade association. It has 830 member institutions based in 58 countries, which include almost all the major market players together with law firms and other interested parties.	2005 ISDA Commodity Definitions provide in Sub-annex H a "Form of Part [6] of the Schedule to the ISDA Master Agreement for EU Emissions Allowance Transactions". These emissions trading provisions are inserted into the relevant schedule to the ISDA Master Agreement. This was updated in revised versions, the latest of which was released in February 2008: • Version 2.5 – Schedule to an ISDA Master Agreement for EU Emissions Allowance Transactions. • Version 4 – Schedule to an ISDA Master Agreement for EU Emissions Allowance Transactions (incorporating options).

continued overleaf

Documentation platforms		
Trade organisation	Organisation description	Documentation
IETA	IETA is a non-profit organisation promoting the establishment of market-based trading systems for greenhouse gas emissions and a global greenhouse gas market using CDM, JI and emissions trading. The organisation also acts as an industry lobbying and trade body. Its members include emitters, insurers, brokers, financial institutions, law firms and management consultants.	• Emissions Trading Master Agreement for the EU Scheme (Version 2.1 2005). • Emissions Allowances Single Trade Agreement for the EU Scheme (Version 3.0 2006). • CDM Emissions Reduction Purchase Agreement (Version 3.0 2006).
EFET	EFET is a group of more than 70 European energy trading companies. It is designed to improve conditions for energy trading throughout Europe.	Allowances Appendix to the EFET General Agreement concerning the Delivery and Acceptance of Electricity (Version 3 2008).

ISDA, IETA and EFET's documentation working groups have had a number of meetings together to help harmonise the three documentation platforms, and each organisation's current document reflects this. However, as these three sets of documents had different origins, some differences still remain. This section of the chapter focuses in greater detail on the ISDA documents but highlights the key areas of difference between the platforms.

9.1   The ISDA platform

As illustrated below, the ISDA platform utilises the ISDA Master Agreement and adapts its schedule by incorporating an additional section covering trading EU ETS allowances. The related confirmation is then tailored for emissions trading. As with the other platforms, the parties can trade allocated allowances under the EU ETS,

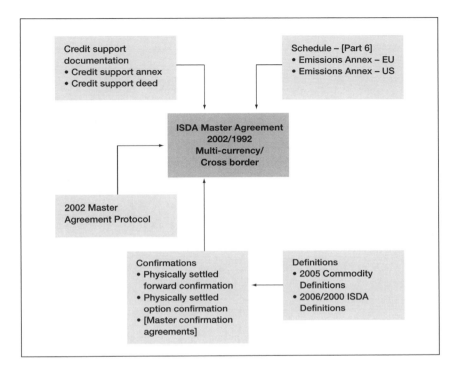

certified emission reductions and emission reduction units. ISDA documentation allows the parties to select either English or New York law as the governing law. However, the parties can adapt the agreement themselves to make any other governing law applicable.

ISDA's platform is most attractive to financial institutions and other entities that are already familiar with ISDA documentation. This is particularly so when both counterparties have already entered into an ISDA master agreement and can then benefit from cross-product netting, as well as reducing basis risk through consistent documentation.

(a)   Sub-Annex H of 2005 ISDA Commodity Definitions

The 2005 ISDA Commodity Definitions provide a form of emissions trading section to insert into the schedule. This is set out in Sub-Annex H as "Form of Part [6] of the Schedule to the ISDA Master Agreement for EU Emissions Allowance Transactions".

This has since been updated by several revised versions, the latest of which was released in February 2008.[28] The EU ETS provisions are 28 pages long and incorporate the 2000 ISDA Definitions by reference. Where there is a funding element to any transaction, users should consider an amendment to incorporate the 2006 ISDA Definitions instead.

---

28   Form of Part [6] to the Schedule to an ISDA Master Agreement for EU Emissions Allowance Transactions (Version 4: February 2008).

The areas covered by the annex are set out in the diagram below.

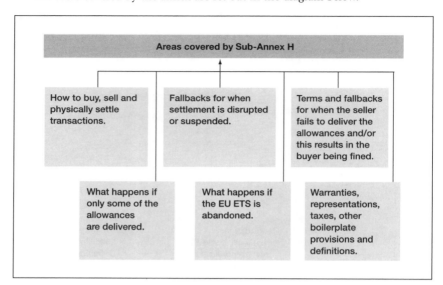

If elected, payments can be netted across products and the parties can net the allowances. The documentation caters for physically settled forward and option transactions. Cash-settled transactions must be drafted on a bespoke basis.

(i)   *Settlement/delivery*

The provisions provide three sets of fallbacks where allowances cannot be delivered. This is a significant issue because of the penalties which can be imposed when an affected installation fails to deliver the required allowances into the EU ETS.

The first fallback is where neither party is at fault (the 'settlement disruption' provisions). The second, introduced in the latest version of 2008, refers to 'suspension events' where one party is unable to perform its obligations due to the occurrence of specific events. The third type of event is where delivery does not take place due to the fault of a party (the 'failure to deliver' provisions).

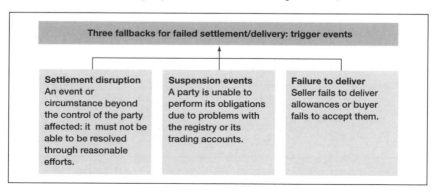

Settlement disruption: A settlement disruption event is an event or circumstance beyond the control of the party affected: it must not be able to be resolved through reasonable efforts, making it impossible for that party to perform its obligations. For the avoidance of doubt, the documentation provides that inability for a party to deliver allowances due to low or non-allocation of allowances to it by an EU member state is not a settlement disruption event.

If a settlement disruption event occurs, either party can elect to suspend the transaction's obligations. The parties will keep trying to settle the transaction, but if they cannot do so within a set timeframe, it will terminate (for more details see the table below). Whether any payments will be made between the parties at this point will depend on what they have negotiated.

Suspension event: A suspension event occurs when a party is unable to perform its obligations under the ISDA agreement for any of the following reasons:

- There is an 'absence of ITL-registry operation' – that is, the lack of establishment or continued functioning of the transaction log established for the scheme or a relevant registry;
- All trading accounts of the party receiving the allowances and/or all trading accounts of the party delivering the allowances are in registries of member states that have not met or do not meet the eligibility criteria listed in Article 17 of the Kyoto Protocol; or
- All trading accounts of the party receiving the allowances and/or all trading accounts of the party delivering the allowances are in registries of member states that have breached their commitment period reserve requirements set out in Decision 11/CMP.1 under Article 17 of the Kyoto Protocol.

If any of these events occurs, the parties are allowed to suspend the settlement of the transaction for the duration of such event. This is subject to certain time limits and a long-stop date (for details see the table below).

Failure to deliver: Through its own fault, a seller can fail to deliver allowances or a buyer can fail to be in a position to accept them. Both instances allow the party not at fault to trigger the 'failure to deliver' fallback provisions by delivering notice to its counterparty. These provisions do not trigger an event of default, but instead postpone settlement while the party at fault attempts to remedy the failure.

Where the seller is to blame, if it manages to deliver the missing allowances on the next delivery business day (or if earlier, the final date for surrendering allowances), it must pay default interest to the buyer. If the seller misses this deadline, the buyer can cancel the seller's obligation to deliver the allowances and demand the replacement cost of buying the missing allowances in the open market. Depending on what the parties have negotiated, this compensation may include reimbursing the buyer for any fine or excess emissions penalty and any related costs arising from the seller's failure. The selection of and interaction between three variables – excess emissions penalty, excess emissions penalty risk period and failure to deliver (alternative method) – in the confirmation will determine the amount that the seller must pay to cover these costs.

If the seller cannot deliver the allowances because the buyer has breached EU ETS requirements, the settlement date will be postponed and the seller may, by notice, request that the buyer meet EU ETS requirements. If the buyer does so, the seller will deliver the allowances and will receive default interest for the period covering the delay.

If the buyer fails to comply prior to the end of the first delivery business day after the notice, or in certain circumstances earlier, the seller may discharge itself from its obligation to deliver the allowances and demand that the buyer pay it the difference between the actual or estimated amount that the seller would receive under an equivalent spot transaction on the final date for surrendering allowances and the original purchase price. The buyer must also pay default interest.

Comparison of types of events that impact on delivery

	Settlement disruption event	Suspension event	Failure to deliver
Delivery	Delivery is suspended until the day on which the settlement disruption event ceases.	Delivery is suspended until the earlier of 10 delivery business days following the cessation of the event or three delivery business days prior to the end of phase reconciliation deadline (April 30 2013) (the delayed delivery date).	In most cases, the receiving party (if not at fault) may serve notice and require the delivering party to remedy the breach. The delivering party must deliver the allowances on or before the first delivery business day after such notice is given, or if earlier, the reconciliation deadline (the final delivery date).

continued overleaf

	Settlement disruption event	Suspension event	Failure to deliver
Long-stop date	Nine delivery business days after the original delivery date (or, where applicable, the reconciliation deadline or three delivery business days preceding the end of phase reconciliation deadline). At this point there will either be an additional termination event or an illegality, (depending on whether the 1992 or 2002 ISDA Master Agreement is used, respectively).	With regard to absence of ITL-registry operation – three delivery business days prior to end of phase reconciliation deadline. For all other suspension events, generally the long-stop date is December 1 of the year immediately preceding the end of phase reconciliation deadline. On the long-stop date, either party may terminate the transaction and it will be considered as the applicable early termination date.	The final delivery date.

continued overleaf

	Settlement disruption event	Suspension event	Failure to deliver
Obligations of the parties	Parties have the ability to select in the confirmation whether they require all obligations to end on settlement disruption. If the election 'no payment on termination for settlement disruption' is selected, all obligations will cease; if not, the suspended obligations will resume on early termination date.	It is deemed that parties had no further delivery or payment obligations after the occurrence of the suspension event. Any payments already made will be reimbursed.	If allowances are delivered on or before the final delivery date, the original delivery date will still apply and the delivering party must pay interest for the delay. If allowances are not delivered on or before the final delivery date, the amount payable by the delivering party will depend on the three elections discussed next.

(ii)   *Calculation of replacement cost where there is failure to deliver*
If the buyer has failed to meet the settlement deadline after receiving the counterparty's notice, there are three standard elections open to the parties to determine how the seller's replacement costs are calculated.

Election one – excess emissions penalty does not apply: An excess emissions penalty is the fine per allowance given to an affected installation for each allowance it fails to submit. An excess emissions penalty risk period is the period of time agreed in the confirmation covering the run-up to that deadline.

The first election is where the excess emissions penalty does not apply to the particular failure to deliver. This will be because either:

- the parties have not selected 'excess emissions penalty' in the confirmation; or
- they have selected it but have also chosen an excess emissions penalty risk period, and the delivery failure occurs before the excess emissions penalty risk period begins.

If this is the case, the buyer can, by notice, cancel the seller's obligation to deliver the allowances, leaving the seller to pay it the difference between the missing allowances' original agreed purchase price and the buyer's estimated or actual cost of purchasing the missing allowances on the delivery date in a spot transaction. In addition, the seller must pay default interest on this amount from the scheduled delivery date.

Election two – excess emissions penalty does apply: The second election is where the excess emissions penalty provisions do apply. This will be either because:

- the parties have selected 'excess emissions penalty' but not defined an excess emissions penalty risk period; or
- they have selected 'excess emissions penalty' and defined an excess emissions penalty risk period, and the delivery failure occurs within the excess emissions penalty risk period.

Following the failure to deliver and notice, the buyer must make reasonable efforts to buy the missing allowances from an alternative source prior to the surrender deadline. If the buyer manages to do so, the seller must then pay the difference between the missing allowances' original agreed purchase price and the actual cost of the allowances bought in. In addition, the seller must pay default interest on this amount from the scheduled delivery date.

If the buyer is unable to buy in all of the undelivered allowances before the surrender deadline, it must attempt to buy in the missing allowances as soon as possible afterwards. The seller must then pay the buyer the difference between the price of the allowances bought after the deadline and the original agreed price, as well as default interest. In addition, the seller must pay the buyer any amount that the buyer has been fined, as well as its related costs.

The buyer must also provide the seller with evidence:

- that the buyer's fine is due, either partially or entirely, to the seller's failure to deliver the allowances;
- of the extent to which the fine results from the failure to deliver; and
- that the buyer could not have used any other allowances it held to avoid the fine.

The buyer must mitigate its losses and, to the extent possible, avoid incurring the fine. The seller must also allocate any losses it makes due to the failure to deliver pro rata among all parties that have failed to make a delivery.

Election three – failure to deliver (alternative method): The final election involves selecting 'failure to deliver (alternative method)' in the confirmation. If this is chosen, following the buyer triggering the failure-to-deliver provisions, the seller must pay the difference between the purchase price of the equivalent number of missing allowances on the final delivery date and the original agreed price, plus default interest.

Where 'excess emissions penalty' is selected in the confirmation together with 'failure to deliver (alternative method)', if the buyer incurs an excess emissions penalty which is directly caused by the seller's failure to deliver within any applicable excess emissions penalty risk period, then in addition to the buyer's replacement cost described above, the seller must reimburse the buyer for any fine that it has incurred but, unlike the second election, not for related costs.

The buyer must also provide the seller with sufficient information for it to make a commercially reasonable assessment of the extent to which the buyer's allowance shortfall was directly caused by the seller's failure to deliver.

The seller's obligation to make the compensatory payment is then conditional upon the buyer demonstrating to the seller's reasonable satisfaction that it has actually incurred and paid the fine, and the extent to which the buyer's liability to pay the fine:

- is directly related to the seller's failure to deliver;
- would have existed even if the seller had delivered the allowances; and
- arose due to any third party failing to deliver it allowances.

If it transpires that the buyer's shortfall in allowances is due to a number of parties (including the buyer and seller), then the seller's compensation payment will be proportionate to its level of fault.

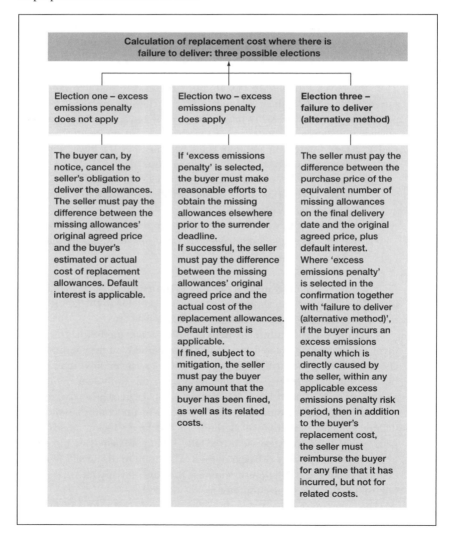

Calculation of replacement cost where there is failure to deliver: three possible elections

Election one – excess emissions penalty does not apply	Election two – excess emissions penalty does apply	Election three – failure to deliver (alternative method)
The buyer can, by notice, cancel the seller's obligation to deliver the allowances. The seller must pay the difference between the missing allowances' original agreed price and the buyer's estimated or actual cost of replacement allowances. Default interest is applicable.	If 'excess emissions penalty' is selected, the buyer must make reasonable efforts to obtain the missing allowances elsewhere prior to the surrender deadline. If successful, the seller must pay the difference between the missing allowances' original agreed price and the actual cost of the replacement allowances. Default interest is applicable. If fined, subject to mitigation, the seller must pay the buyer any amount that the buyer has been fined, as well as its related costs.	The seller must pay the difference between the purchase price of the equivalent number of missing allowances on the final delivery date and the original agreed price, plus default interest. Where 'excess emissions penalty' is selected in the confirmation together with 'failure to deliver (alternative method)', if the buyer incurs an excess emissions penalty which is directly caused by the seller, within any applicable excess emissions penalty risk period, then in addition to the buyer's replacement cost, the seller must reimburse the buyer for any fine that it has incurred, but not for related costs.

(iii) *Other provisions*

Other provisions in the document provide that if the EU ETS is abandoned, neither party will have any obligation to the other, except that the seller shall refund any amounts owed to the buyer with interest. Additionally, the parties agree that:

- on the delivery date, the seller must send the buyer an invoice;
- they will comply with the EU ETS requirements;
- the seller will deliver the allowances free and clear of encumbrances;
- all amounts are exclusive of value added tax (VAT) (although the buyer will pay the seller any VAT or taxes owed);
- they will each take responsibility for any fees and other expenses; and
- they will limit their liability in relation to certain breaches of warranty.

In the schedule's annex, the parties set out their account details, the delivery business day location and the VAT jurisdiction.

(b) **Confirmation of OTC physically settled EU allowance forward**

The confirmation follows the standard ISDA format for a confirmation for a forward transaction. Because of the comprehensive nature of sub-Annex H, it is a relatively short document and sets out specific transaction terms and elections only. In particular, it sets out:

- the trade date;
- the buyer, seller and calculation agent's identities;
- the allowance type, price and number;
- the business, payment and delivery days;
- various failure-to-deliver and excess emissions penalty options; and
- whether any payment will be made if the transaction terminates following a settlement disruption event.

ISDA's published confirmations for options and forwards can also be used and adapted for spot transactions.[29]

In addition, to the extent not already set out in the schedule, the parties may insert their account details, and business day and VAT jurisdiction choices.

(c) **Confirmation of OTC physically settled EU allowance option**

The confirmation follows the standard ISDA format for a confirmation for a forward transaction. The confirmation sets out:

- the trade date;
- the buyer, seller and calculation agent's identities;
- the allowance type, price and number;
- provisions relating to the option itself (number of options, premium payment date, exercise times, etc);

---

29 Under a forward transaction, the parties agree a price for the allowance upfront, but actual delivery and payment take place at a later agreed date. Under an option transaction, either the buyer or seller has the right, but not the obligation, in return for a premium, to deliver or receive the allowances on a future date.

- the business, payment and delivery days;
- various failure to deliver and excess emissions penalty options; and
- whether any payment will be made if the transaction terminates following a settlement disruption event.

(d)   *US emissions allowance transaction annex*

The US Emissions Allowance Transaction Annex was published by ISDA on December 21 2006. It is incorporated by parties into their ISDA master agreement. At the same time ISDA also released a confirmation template.

The annex covers physically settled spot, forward and option emissions trading transactions.

The annex relates to instruments traded on the Chicago Climate Exchange; nitrogen oxide emissions allowances traded under the NOx SIP Call Programme; sulphur dioxide emissions allowances traded under the Clean Air Interstate Rule programme; and any emissions allowances or credits under current or future US state cap-and-trade programmes.

The annex differentiates between 'regulatorily continuing emissions products' and 'regulatorily non-continuing emissions products'. Unless stated otherwise in the relevant transaction confirmation, 'regulatorily non-continuing emissions products' means that the emissions products to be transferred must comply with the rules and relevant regulations of the relevant scheme at both the trade date and the delivery date.

If 'regulatorily continuing emissions products' is specified in the confirmation, then this compliance is applicable only as of the trade date.

Due to its non-specific coverage, the annex is vague, containing none of the tailored provisions relating to excess emissions penalties or detailed fallbacks of the European annex. Such provisions may therefore have to be included in any related confirmation and tailored to the particular cap-and-trade scheme.

ISDA simultaneously released a related two-page confirmation for a physically settled option transaction. Under the confirmation, the parties can select a particular emissions product to be traded. The parties also elect whether an abandonment of the particular scheme should constitute an additional termination event for the transaction, or a transaction unwind with a termination of delivery obligations and a return of any monies, together with accrued interest.

9.2   Comparison of ISDA with IETA and EFET platforms – key differences

The ISDA and IETA standard documents are used by different types of market participant. Whereas financial institutions will be familiar with the ISDA Master Agreement and will use it across a variety of derivatives products, the IETA Emissions Trading Master Agreement for the EU ETS relates only to emissions trading. The specific focus of the IETA Master Agreement means that industrial concerns without large derivatives portfolios or an ISDA master agreement in place are more likely to use the IETA Master Agreement. IETA documentation is governed by English law unless otherwise agreed by the parties.

The EFET platform uses an Allowances Appendix to its General Agreement Concerning the Delivery and Acceptance of Electricity, which is drafted with various

European civil law systems and English law in mind. German law is the default choice of law, although other laws may be selected. The power industry, which has several large market participants, tends to favour the EFET platform due to familiarity with the General Agreement Concerning the Delivery and Acceptance of Electricity.

The three documentation platforms are more similar than they are different. However, there are important differences due to the agreements being updated at different times, and the different aims of the memberships of the three organisations. Market participants need to be aware of the differences in order to be able to use the different platforms and to protect against basis risk where different documentation platforms are used in a chain of transactions.

Although there are several mechanical differences, such as the effect of oral confirmations, the key differences specific to emissions trading relate to:

- excess emissions penalties;[30]
- *force majeure*;
- settlement disruption and failure to deliver;
- differences in payment and delivery dates;
- opting out of physical settlement of delivery obligations; and
- suspension events.

Other differences relate to termination events, close-out payments and netting provisions.

Traders should note that if they buy using one set of documentation, they also need to enter into a sale agreement based on the same documentation. Otherwise, the differences in the terms will result in a risk for the trader.

10. Conclusion

In 1661, when John Evelyn wrote his *Fumifugium*, the pall of smoke above London had become an attraction to tourists, who climbed neighbouring church towers to take a look. Evelyn and other scientists of his day argued that this situation should not continue, because it created an environment that killed people and damaged property. He therefore proposed surrounding the city with a 50-metre "green belt" filled with "such shrubs as yield the most fragrant and odiferous flowers",[31] prohibiting burials within the city and moving the 'sooty throats' that caused pollution far from the capital. The last solution would, he assured readers, yield two principal benefits: not only would London's air regain a "universal serenity" (instead of resembling "Troy sacked by the Greeks"), but relocating noxious industries would open up prime sites within the city for the construction of prestige apartments. In the 17th as in the 21st century, environmental concerns could be turned to a profit.

Parts of this chapter are adapted from a corresponding chapter, "Emissions Trading", *published in* Practical Derivatives: A Transactional Approach *(Globe Law and Business, London, 2006).*

---

30   The excess emissions penalties in particular are more detailed in the ISDA Master Agreement and contain additional options. It is likely that subsequent versions of the corresponding IETA and EFET documentation will also incorporate these changes.
31   Perhaps the earliest reference to a carbon sink.

Freight derivative transactions

Avanthi Gunatilake
Edmund Parker

1. Introduction

Shipping holds the world economy together. More than 90% of internationally traded goods are carried by sea; and globalisation, trade liberalisation and advanced technology will keep driving shipping's growth well into the future.

Freight rates are the prices charged for carrying goods on a ship; they are the underlying asset in freight derivatives. The shipping industry has high freight rate volatility, with dramatic fluctuations in freight rates seen in recent years. For example, from 2003 to mid-2008 freight rates saw an increase of around 300%, followed by a 95% drop in the last quarter of 2008.[1] They even hit zero on some Asia-to-Europe freight routes in early 2009.

Different market participants also have an interest in seeing freight rates move in opposite directions. These include ship owners and makers, importers, exporters and goods manufacturers; added to that are speculators with opposite views on market direction. Freight rates are a commoditised product sourced from reliable data. All of this makes freight rates an ideal asset to underlie a category of commodity derivative. Indeed, in 2008 the freight derivatives market grew to approximately $150 billion[2] – small beer when compared with some derivative classes, but a sizeable market nonetheless and a growing one with most likely a bright future.

A first question to ask, however, is whether a freight rate is a commodity. Arguably, it is no more a commodity than interest rates or foreign exchange (FX) rates. However, banks often trade freight derivatives contracts from their commodities desks; shipping rates for many different routes and ship sizes are commoditised; and the goods transported are often referenced in commodity derivative transactions (eg, coal, iron ore and oil). In addition, the International Swaps and Derivatives Association, Inc (ISDA) has included freight among the underlying asset classes covered under the 2005 ISDA Commodity Definitions, with a special annex for freight derivatives being included in the form of Sub-Annex I to the Annex to the 2005 definitions.

A freight derivative is a financial instrument which derives its value from the underlying asset of a freight rate. A freight rate is, more specifically, a rate to be paid for carrying an agreed quantity of commodities at sea, on a specified voyage on a

---

1   Amir H Alizadeh, Nikos K Nomikos, *Shipping Derivatives and Risk Management*, Palgrave Macmillan (2009).
2   "Freight Derivatives: Beginning of the End or End of the Beginning", Oliver Wyman (2008), Celent.

ship. Instead of a particular voyage, the carriage can be for an agreed time period.

The most common freight derivatives are forwards. These were traditionally individually negotiated by the parties with the help of a broker. Today the freight derivatives market includes freight futures, swaps and options, with centrally cleared and exchange-traded freight derivatives now particularly popular.

Freight derivatives have been around for 300 years at least – long before ISDA was established in 1987 and started standardising and creating interest rate, FX, credit and equity derivatives transactions. As a result, the freight derivatives market mixes old traditions with cutting-edge technology – and not always easily.

This chapter looks at the various types of freight derivative and their uses, as well as the documentation infrastructure – in particular, that provided by ISDA through the 2005 definitions and the related templates. The chapter also looks at the forward freight agreements provided by the Forward Freight Agreement Brokers Association (FFABA), which also utilise the ISDA Master Agreement and the 2005 definitions. We also discuss some of the key terms used in the freight market, as a reasonable knowledge of freight lexicon is vital to an understanding how freight derivatives work.

2. Terminology and the underlying asset

The underlying asset in a freight derivative is a freight rate; and freight rates are filled with nautical terminology. Freight rates are quoted on the basis of cost per metric tonne for transporting cargo on an agreed route, in a vessel of a particular size. These rates will differ according to whether the route is on a 'voyage charter' basis or a 'time charter' basis, the size of the particular vessel transporting the cargo and the route taken, among other factors.

Freight market jargon can be impenetrable to the outsider. Set out in the diagram below and the ensuing narrative is some of the key terminology relevant for freight derivatives transactions. The freight market uses all of this terminology and categories to price freight rates for carrying specified commodities on different types of ship, for different routes on a voyage or time charter basis.

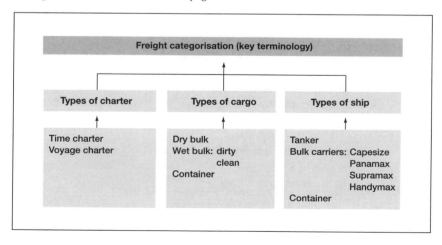

2.1 Charter terminology

Charter terminology covers whether the ship has been chartered on a 'time charter' basis or a 'voyage charter' basis. A 'time charter' means that the ship transporting the cargo has been chartered from a ship owner for a particular period of time – perhaps 15 days. If the ship has been chartered on a 'voyage charter' basis, this means that the ship has been chartered for a particular voyage (eg, from a designated loading port, such as Amsterdam, to a designated discharging port, such as Felixstowe).

2.2 Cargo terminology

Cargoes fall into three principal categories of commodity: 'wet', 'dry' and 'container'. A 'wet' commodity is a liquid such as oil or a chemical. A 'dry' commodity is a raw material such as coal, iron ore or grain. A 'container' cargo is one of finished goods, such as cars or washing machines.

'Wet' cargoes are further subcategorised into 'dirty' and 'clean' for oil. A 'dirty' cargo is an unrefined oil product (eg, crude oil), while a 'clean' cargo is a refined oil product such as jet fuel.

2.3 Ship terminology

The freight market is also categorised by the type of ship which carries a cargo. The principal categories of shipping are bulk carriers, tankers and liners.

(a) Bulk carriers

Bulk carriers are large ships which carry dry commodities in unpackaged form. They are categorised by size, measured in terms of metric tonnes of deadweight (dwt) (ie, the ship's total weight, including fuel, stores, passengers and crew, if it is loaded up to its Plimsoll line).

The four most common categories of bulk carrier are Capesize, Panamax, Supramax and Handymax.

Capesize is the largest category of bulk carrier. These ships are at least 150,000 dwt. Although 172,000 to 175,000 dwt is the standard size, much larger ships do exist. The category is called 'Capesize' because originally ships of this size could not pass through either the Suez Canal or the Panama Canal, and were forced to go around either the Cape of Good Hope or Cape Horn. Although Capesize ships technically encompass tankers (ie, ships which carry oil and chemicals), the market norm is to refer to tankers as a separate category.

The second largest category of bulk carrier is Panamax. These are the largest ships that can pass through the Panama Canal. These ships must be no more than 70,000 dwt.

There are two smaller main categories of bulk carrier: Supramax and Handymax. Supramax vessels are about 52,000 dwt bulk carriers and Handymax 28,000 dwt bulk carriers.

The different types of bulk carrier tend to carry different types of bulk. Capesize and Panamax vessels tend to carry 'major bulk' commodities such as grain, coal and iron ore. Supramax and Handymax vessels tend to carry 'minor bulk' commodities such as sugar and fertiliser.

(b)   *Tankers*

Tankers are ships which carry bulk wet cargoes such as oil or chemicals. They can be of different sizes, such as the smaller general-purpose tankers and medium-range tankers (which fall within the Panamax class). Alternatively, they may be very large, such as the 'very large crude carrier' and the 'ultra large carrier', which are up to 550,000 dwt in size.

(c)   *Other shipping types*

The container market is serviced mainly by container ships. Container ships are smaller than Capesize, to allow them to pass through the Suez Canal. Smaller general cargo vessels also make up a large part of the world's fleet.

3.   Reasons for volatility in the underlying asset

Freight rates are volatile: prediction of future demand rests on sentiment about the future direction of world trade and the global economy, with divergent and unreliable forecasts in this area correlating with volatility in the future direction of freight rates. Ships run on fuel, so movement in the oil price directly impacts on freight rates. Particular freight rates are often directly referenced to the commodities being carried (eg, coal or iron ore). Movements in the pricing of the underlying commodity can also impact on the freight rate.

There are also particular points in the globe where disproportionate amounts of the world's shipping must pass. Sometimes these points coincide with extreme weather conditions, while others, such as the Suez Canal, may be in political hotspots. In both cases the climate (meteorological and political) may impact on freight rates.

4.   Types of freight derivative

There are four principal types of freight derivative financial instrument: forward freight agreements (FFAs), futures, options and swaps.

4.1   Forward freight agreements

An FFA is a bilateral, over-the-counter (OTC) forward contract. One party (the seller) agrees to receive a floating (or variable) freight rate in exchange for other party (the buyer) paying it a fixed freight rate. Both rates are usually for the same agreed route. The contract will settle at an agreed future date.

FFAs are usually documented under an English-law market-standard template confirmation. This is produced by the FFABA. The FFABA's current FFA template is subtitled the "FFABA 2007 Terms", and it updates the previous FFABA 2005 Terms and FFABA 2000 Terms.

The FFABA is an independent organisation of Baltic Exchange broker members founded in 1997. The organisation's objectives include:

- promoting trading of FFAs;
- developing market-standard documentation and underlying assets (eg, indices and route) for OTC freight derivatives and exchange-traded products;
- encouraging high standards of market conduct; and
- acting as a forum for members to resolve problems.

The template confirmation sets out the FFABA 2007 Terms, which provide that the applicable transaction is to be governed by the parties' ISDA Master Agreement. If the parties don't have an ISDA Master Agreement in place, the confirmation deems the 1992 ISDA Master Agreement incorporated by reference.

In this case, it deems certain elections too. These include allowing multi-transaction netting and choosing dollars as a termination currency.

The confirmation also incorporates the 2005 definitions by reference, giving each transaction the benefit of its market-standard definitions, its framework and its fallbacks.

The FFA template confirmation structures its fixed versus floating exchange by setting out an agreed freight rate, called the 'contract rate'. The contract rate is for an agreed route, called the 'contract route'. Both the contract route and the contract rate reference a specified time period, defined as the 'contract period' – this is usually one month.

The contract rate will usually be a rate for a specific contract route published by the Baltic Exchange (see section 5.1). It will be published either in the form of dollars per tonne of cargo or, in the case of tanker routes, by reference to a nominal freight rate published by an organisation called Worldscale (see section 5.3).

In addition to 'contract rate', 'contract route' and 'contract period', the FFA references and defines a 'settlement rate'. This is the unweighted average of the rates for the contract route(s) published by the Baltic Exchange over the settlement period. 'Settlement period' is defined in the FFA as an agreed number of Baltic Exchange Index publication days for the applicable contract period, up to and including the settlement date.

The parties will specify the quantity of freight to which the FFA relates (eg, 10,000 tonnes). This is called the 'contract quantity'.

The above provisions interact so that the transaction will settle on the settlement date. The FFA defines 'settlement date' as "the last Baltic Exchange Index publication day of each Contract Month."; and the parties may specify one or several 'contract month(s)' in their negotiated confirmation. The contract month can be the next calendar month, or it could be a specified month in many months' time (eg, March 2014).

On the settlement date, the FFA template provides that a 'settlement sum' will be paid from one party to the other. This will be from the party that is out of the money to the party that is in the money. This settlement sum is the difference between the contract rate and the settlement rate multiplied by the 'quantity' (ie, tonnage referenced) for the contract period.

'Contract rate' is discussed above, but 'settlement rate' is defined in the confirmation as the unweighted average of the rates for the contract route over the settlement period. The 'settlement period' is in turn defined as the number of Baltic Exchange Index publication days for the relevant contract month up to and including the settlement date.

If the settlement rate is higher than the contract rate, the seller pays the buyer the settlement sum. However, if the settlement rate is lower than the contract rate, the buyer pays the seller the settlement sum.

The settlement sum is then payable the later of either two London business days after the in-the-money party presents its invoice or five London business days after the settlement date (whichever is the sooner).

If the parties specify more than one contract month, then the FFA is technically a swap transaction, as there will be a series of payment exchanges on multiple settlement dates. If this is the case, the contract quantities may vary from month to month.

The parties are also free to specify a number of contract rates – this would create a basket transaction. If this is the case, the contract quantities may vary between contract rates.

The most commonly traded FFAs relate to the four principal types of vessel for bulk routes: Capesize, Panamax, Supramax and Handysize.

Hypothetical example of an FFA: Dominic Grain Exporters and Griffiths Welsh Shipping

Dominic Grain Exporters and Griffiths Welsh Shipping have entered into an FFA. This is documented pursuant to the parties' ISDA Master Agreement, under the market-standard FFA published by the FFABA – the FFABA 2007 Terms.

The FFA references a Handymax freight rate for Rotterdam to Capetown, a 'contract route' reported by the Baltic Exchange. On the trade date, the Baltic Exchange quotes the contract rate as $17 per tonne.

Dominic Grain Exporters agrees to receive a Handymax floating freight rate in exchange for paying a fixed Handymax freight rate (applicable at the trade date). Dominic Grain Exporters is the buyer and Griffiths Welsh Shipping is the seller. The 'contract quantity' they agree is 10,000 tonnes.

Dominic Grain Exporters is concerned that the Handymax freight rate may go up. This would cut its margins on its grain exports, due to the increased costs of transportation. On the other hand, Griffiths Welsh Shipping, a ship owner, is concerned that if the freight rate for its key Handymax route goes down, this will reduce its profitability. Both parties are prepared to forgo a potential upside to hedge against the potential downside.

The 'settlement rate' is defined as the "unweighted average of the rates for the Contract Route(s) published by the Baltic Exchange over the Settlement Period". The settlement period consists of each Baltic Exchange Index publication date in each contract month. Dominic Grain Exporters and Griffiths Welsh Shipping specify each month of the next year as a contract month; and specify the 'quantity by contract month' (ie, tonnage covered) as 50,000 tonnes per contract month.

On the first settlement date, the contract rate of $17 per tonne is higher than the settlement rate of $15 per tonne. Therefore, Dominic Grain Exporters pays a settlement sum of $2 × 50,000 (ie, $100,000) to Griffiths Welsh Shipping. On the second settlement date, the contract rate of $17 per tonne is lower than the settlement rate of $18 per tonne. Therefore, Griffiths Welsh Shipping pays a settlement sum of $1 × 50,000 (ie, $50,000) to Dominic Grain Exporters.

Similar variations occur during the rest of the contract, which result in the
parties successfully hedging their respective positions.

4.2 Futures and centrally cleared OTC derivatives[3]

(a) Exchange trading and clearing markets
In addition to OTC FFAs, freight futures and hybrid FFAs are other forms of freight
derivative. Futures operate in a similar manner to OTC FFAs but are traded on an
organised exchange, subject to clearing, and on more standardised terms.

In a market of few players, the Baltic Exchange provides the largest world market
for freight derivatives trading. The exchange does not itself provide any futures
contracts. However, individual FFAs based on the exchange's indices are traded on
exchange. Some of these are centrally cleared by LCH.Clearnet (LCH).

LCH is a major central counterparty (CCP) and player in all categories of
centrally cleared derivatives in Europe. As with all CCPs, the original counterparties
give up their transaction to the CCP and LCH then acts as a buyer to every seller and
a seller to every buyer, taking margin from the original parties to cover credit
exposure.

LCH provides central clearing for a number of different standardised contracts for
both wet and dry, time charter and voyage charter routes for Supramax, Handymax,
Capesize and Panamax vessels. These standardised contacts are based on the FFABA
FFA.

Other exchanges and players in the futures and central clearing market are now
gaining momentum.

Inmarex Group is a major player in the physically settled commodity derivatives
market. It makes a market in several commodity derivatives – in particular, freight
derivatives. Its principal products involve Supramax, Panamax and Capesize FFAs. It
also provides an electronically traded futures contracts on the Baltic Exchange's
Baltic Dry Index, and certain dry bulk and tanker routes.

Nos Clearing is a member of the Inmarex group and provides clearing and
settlement services for the freight derivatives market.

Electronic trading in general is increasing in the freight derivatives market. This
now makes up about 5% of the overall market. Two companies – ICAP Hyde (ICAP)
and Simpson, Spence & Young – also provide electronic broking for contracts based
on the Baltic Exchange freight indices.

In Asia, the Singapore Stock Exchange provides an exchange facility for freight
derivatives (principally FFAs), with an affiliate providing clearing services.

(b) The growth of clearing in freight derivatives
Until the mid-1980s, the freight derivatives market was mainly an OTC market.
Transactions were specifically tailored by brokers to physical market participants,
such as ship owners and corporations for hedging purposes. Since the late 1990s, the

---

3   Certain statistics in this section are drawn from "Freight Derivatives: Beginning of the End or End of the
Beginning", Oliver Wyman (2008), Celent.

centrally cleared (or hybrid) FFAs described above have become common. Celent, a financial research and consulting firm, estimates that clearing will grow to nearly 100% by 2015.[4] Regulatory developments driven by the European Union in 2010 are likely to accelerate this. Already by 2008, the total number of dry trades cleared or hybrid trades had increased to 58% from 30% in 2007.[5]

4.3   Swaps

In a forward contract there is one exchange of payments at a future date of a fixed amount against a floating amount. If a financial instrument has a series of payment exchanges, it should correctly be termed a swap. But there is correct terminology and there is market usage; and the freight derivatives market long precedes ISDA and its OTC credit, equity, interest and foreign-exchange derivatives markets. An FFA can have a single exchange of payments or, if the parties specify a number of contract months, a series of payment exchanges; the market will still refer to it as a forward, though.

ISDA, a latecomer to the freight derivatives market, has introduced three swap templates through the 2005 ISDA Commodity Definitions. These are financial instruments that its members – mainly those in the financial institution sphere – will feel more comfortable using, as they are structurally similar to other OTC commodity derivative instruments. The swap templates provided by ISDA are discussed further below.

4.4   Options

Another type of freight derivative is an option. Options are the most recent type of freight derivative to be introduced into the market and they allow the holder the right (but not the obligation) to buy or sell an FFA at a future date for a specific price in return for payment of a premium.

Options, unlike FFAs, give the holder the flexibility to walk away from the contract if the market is no longer favourable. ISDA is currently debating adding a freight option template. Inmarex already offers freight derivatives options for trading and clearing. It offers automatic exercise Asian-style options (ie, there are a number of potential exercise dates and the option will settle on the first date (if any) when the option is in the money), referencing Baltic Exchange index-linked FFAs.

Inmarex's traded freight options settle against the arithmetic average of the underlying FFA, over the number of index days in the month, with the settlement amount being the positive difference between the FFA's underlying index's average value and the option's strike price on the last day of each month.

---

4   See note 3.
5   '2008 Freight Derivative Trading Volumes Up', Baltic Exchange, www.balticexchange.com/default.asp?
        action=article&ID=4879.

5. Principal sources of freight market information

Trading in freight derivatives is possible only if reliable market prices are available. These come from published indices, freight rates and trading prices. The principal provider of current freight market information is the Baltic Exchange. For tankers, Platts is important; and for wet route rates published by both the Baltic Exchange and Platts, the prices published by Worldscale are used as a nominal base.

5.1 The Baltic Exchange

The Baltic Exchange publishes prices for both dry and wet routes, and voyage charter and time charter routes. These routes have standardised parameters, including for different sizes and types of vessel, as well as for different cargoes – the main categories outlined in section 2 are all used. The published routes are used both as a negotiating point in fixture lists matching ships with cargoes and an underlying asset to reference in a freight derivatives contract.

The Baltic Exchange also publishes several indices. These indices are composed of different published Baltic freight routes, weighted in accordance with the index's rules. The indices and their components are also referenced in freight derivatives transactions – in particular, for centrally cleared FFAs and ISDA template confirmations. They allow parties to take a 'long' or 'short' position on the future direction of the index. The exchange generates transparency and liquidity for FFA trading. Alternatively, the individual routes comprising the index are referenced.

(a) A brief history of the exchange

The Baltic Exchange started life in 1744 at the Virginia and Maryland coffeehouse in Threadneedle Street, London. As for many of the early London exchanges, the choice of location reflected its users: merchants and sea captains agreeing prices for transporting goods around the world.

The exchange is now located at St Mary's Axe in the City of London and things have moved on since its coffeehouse days. Today it has more than 570 members, including ship owners, traders, brokers and other market professionals, and it is a self-regulating market.

The Baltic Exchange:
- provides independent information;
- acts as a trade organisation for its members;
- provides standardised business practices;
- matches freights with cargoes through its fixture list;
- acts as a trading venue for buying and selling ships; and
- acts as a freight derivatives trading exchange.

It currently has no traded futures contracts of its own, but its published freight routes and indices are referenced in the freight derivatives traded both on and off exchange.

The exchange uses a panel of international shipping brokers to assess and publish daily prices for mor than 50 different freight routes. It does this for dry routes and for wet routes, including for gas. These prices are always based on a notional vessel

– that is, one of a specific deadweight, which has certain other qualities such as flying a particular national flag and being of a certain age.

The routes may be for time charters or voyage charters. As mentioned above, the routes are also organised into weighted indices. These are grouped according to vessel specifications – for example, tankers and their routes (eg, through the Suez or Panama canals or round the Cape of Good Hope).

The Baltic Exchange began publishing these daily freight index prices in 1985. To begin with, its Baltic Freight Index covered 13 voyage routes for various cargoes, among them the transporting of 110,000 metric tonnes of coal from Queensland to Rotterdam and 20,000 tonnes of barley from Antwerp to the Red Sea. The weightings of each route within the index were (and are) variable.

The exchange continually introduces and discontinues new routes, as well as introducing, discontinuing and merging different indices.

In 1989 the index was expanded to cover Panamax routes (ie, routes through the Panama canal). In 1993 four time charter routes were added (ie, routes where the vessel is hired for a particular period of time). These routes included a transatlantic round voyage of 45 to 60 days and a transpacific voyage of 35 to 50 days.

In 1997 the exchange began publishing the Baltic Handy Index (BHI). This index consisted of the following four time charter routes and two voyages. This was based on a 'Baltic handymax' vessel of 43,000mt dead weight, which was less than 15 years old and was a 'self-trimming' bulk carrier. The notional vessel would carry a national flag (rather than a flag of convenience), and have certain other specifications. The BHI was later superseded by the Baltic Handymax Index (BHMI).

In 1998 the exchange introduced five tanker routes. These included the Middle East to Japan in a 250,000 metric tonne vessel and the Caribbean to the US Gulf in a 70,000 metric tonne vessel. This was successful and two years later the exchange introduced the Baltic International Tanker Routes (BITR), which comprised seven routes. This number was later expanded.

Also in 1998 the exchange introduced the Baltic Panamax Index (BPI). This initially consisted of four time-charter and three voyage routes which utilised the Panama Canal. The notional vessel this time had a 70,000mt dwt, not aged over 15 years with "3.0 million cuft. Grain, loa max. 230m, capable of about 14kn (l) on 30mt fuel oil and no diesel at sea" – nautical terms indeed.

Later, the BPI superseded the original BFI, and the definition of the notional vessel was refined.

In 1999 the Baltic Capesize Index (BCI) was launched. It consisted of four time charter routes and seven voyage routes. The index began with an index level of 1000 points. Later the same year, the Baltic Exchange Dry Index (BDI), an equally weighted composite of the BPI, BCI and BHI, was launched. It aimed to provide a general dry-bulk market indicator.

In 2001 the exchange launched the BITR Index. This consisted of nine dirty routes (ie, for crude oil) and three clean routes (ie, for refined products). This was later divided into two separate indices: the Baltic Dirty Tanker Index for dirty routes and the Baltic Clean Tanker Index for clean routes.

In 2005 the Baltic Exchange Supramax Index (BSI) was introduced, consisting of time charter routes and voyage routes. Here the notional vessel had a deadweight of 54,254mt.

In 2006 the exchange launched the Baltic Exchange Handysize Index (BHSI), which covered notional vessels of "28,000 mt dwt self trimming single deck bulkcarriers" on several time charter routes.

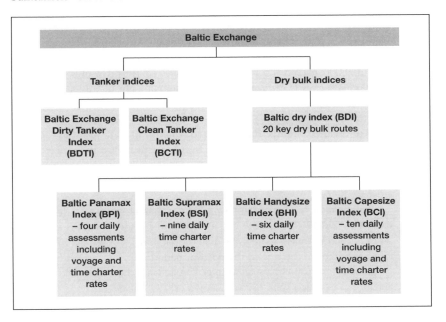

5.2 Platts

Although more than 30% of the world's dry cargo fixtures (ie, matches between cargoes and vessels) and 50% of the tanker fixtures are traded on the Baltic Exchange, it is not the only information provider. Platts is another main source of freight rates, which can be referenced in freight derivative transactions.

Platts is a member of the McGraw-Hill Companies (rating agency Standard & Poor's is also a member). It is an information provider and, like the Baltic Exchange, it provides freight pricing for a large number of routes; in particular, it is referenced for dirty and clean tanker freight routes. Its Dirty Tankerwire service provides freight rates for dirty tanker routes and its Clean Tankerwire service provides freight rates for clean tanker routes. Sub-Annex A of the 2005 ISDA Commodity Definitions references five voyage charter routes for dirty tankers and 13 voyage charter routes for clean tankers which are Platts prices.

5.3 Worldscale

Prices for dry routes are published by reference to a US dollar price. The custom for wet routes is different, with the Baltic Exchange, Platts and other market data providers publishing their pricing for wet routes by reference to 'Worldscale' points, which adjust a dollar nominal freight rate.

Here's an example. The 2005 ISDA definitions provide a definition for "FREIGHT-BALTIC-EXCHANGE-DIRTY TANKER ROUTED1". This is defined as the "that day's Specified Price, stated in Worldscale Points" for transporting wet cargo from the Middle East Gulf to the US Gulf in a 280,000 metric tonne vessel. So what are Worldscale points?

(a) *Worldscale, Worldscale freight rate schedules and Worldscale points*

Worldscale is a joint venture between Worldscale Association (London) Limited and Worldscale Association (NYC) Inc. It operates as an online platform providing more than 320,000 flat rates for previously requested freight routes, on the basis of a standard-sized vessel carrying a standard cargo at a given daily hire rate. These rates are published annually and are supposed to represent the average market rates at the time of publication.

Worldscale's origins date back to the immediate post-war period, when requisitioned shipping in the process of being returned to its owners by the British government was allowed to be used for transporting freight on the basis of fixed rates. These were set out in schedules split by voyage, cargo and vessel, and priced at a per-tonne rate.

Freight rates caught on and a number of market scales were in use throughout the 1950s and 1960s. These scales, as Worldscale is today, were then used as a basis point for parties to negotiate individual transactions – as opposed to providing actual rates, as had been the case in the postwar period.

In 1969 the principal scales merged to become the Worldwide Tanker Nominal Freight Scale, which soon became known as 'Worldscale'.

Worldscale operates on a system of 'points of scale'. It publishes a rate for each of its 320,000-plus freight routes. These are published once a year on the basis of previous data. Parties then negotiate these dollar figures by adjusting them by 'Worldscale points'. Each point represents a percentage point of adjustment to the published rates. One hundred points means the published rate itself (or Worldscale Flat); 40 points means 40% of the published rate; and 180 points means 180% of the published rate. These figures are expressed with the prefix 'WS', so in the preceding example these would be expressed as WS100, WS40 and WS180.

So Worldscale provides both individual prices for freight rates and a method of adjustment of these. Where a tanker route is published by the Baltic Exchange or Platts, this price is published in terms of Worldscale points, which adjust the annual fixed rate published by Worldscale.

6. Common uses and principal users of freight derivatives

Recent market volatility has increased the importance of freight derivatives for hedging risk. Ship owners, ship operators, importers, traders and certain manufacturers are just some of the parties which may be directly affected by fluctuations in freight rates. To manage the risk of freight rate volatility, they may trade long or short in freight derivatives, depending on whether they wish to hedge against freight rates increasing or decreasing.

The 'paper market' for freight derivatives refers to those parties that are hedging freight prices, not to cover their own costs but instead for speculative or arbitrage purposes. These participants include investment banks, hedge funds and dedicated subsidiaries of shipping companies looking to profit from price volatility, making a spread from matching buyers with sellers, and proprietary trading based on their market assumptions. The growth seen in the freight derivatives trading in recent years can be partly attributed to increased trading by these investors.

Freight derivatives are also used in ship financing transactions as part of a lender's security package. The shipbuilding industry has huge financing needs and in the current economic climate lenders are particularly keen to address freight rate volatility risk. As with other types of hedging instrument linked to a financing transaction (eg, interest rate swaps or currency swaps), a freight swap may be used to ensure the certainty of the projected income/freight charges which make up the repayments.

Further, financial institutions may use freight derivatives as means of diversifying their portfolios, especially in situations where there is excess exposure to a sector.

Many major banks act as a market maker for freight derivatives on behalf of borrowers, accessing the market as a principal and then selling on the position through a back-to-back transaction.

When Hurricane Ivan hit the Gulf of Mexico in 2005, it caused massive damage and oil infrastructure prices in the FFA market rose to record highs. Oil price is a major contributor to freight prices, and this resulted in FFA prices going through the roof. The volatility attracted the attention of other derivatives market participants: the clearing-houses, the investment banks and the hedge funds. They have brought both liquidity and technology to the market, and with them greater market sophistication to a traditional market.

7. Documenting freight derivatives: the ISDA platform

There are two main sets of documents used for documenting OTC freight derivatives such as forwards and swaps using the 2005 definitions, together with the ISDA Master Agreement: the ISDA template confirmations set out in the 2005 definitions and the FFABA form of FFA, discussed in section 4 above.

Centrally cleared and exchange-cleared transactions will mostly use the FFABA form of the FFA as their base. Transactions between traditional brokers and participants in the physical markets, such as ship owners and manufacturers, will also tend to use FFAs.

ISDA is most likely to be used in transactions between financial institutions and transactions with other players in the physical market, such as hedge funds and speculators. FFAs are discussed above; below we discuss the ISDA platform and template confirmations.

7.1 Overview of the ISDA documentation platform

The diagram overleaf sets out the principal ISDA documentation platform for documenting freight derivatives. The ISDA Master Agreement (the 1992 or 2002 version), as amended by a schedule and possibly credit support documentation, forms the primary platform. As explained above, these will also provide the primary

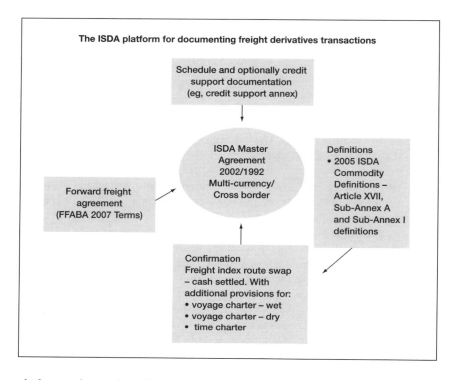

platform and secondary platforms for FFABA FFA transactions. As a tertiary platform, ISDA has produced three template confirmations.

Each confirmation is structured to reference routes published as part of one of the Baltic Exchange's indices. The three templates are all for swap transactions. One is structured as a voyage charter for a wet clean tanker route; another as a voyage charter for a dry Capesize route; and the third as a time charter for a Capesize route, either dry or wet.

These templates are set out in Sub-Annex I of the Annex to the 2005 definitions. They incorporate the primary platform of the ISDA Master Agreement, as well as the secondary platform of the 2005 definitions.

The 2005 definitions provide the fallbacks and framework for freight derivatives. Article XVII of the principal body of the 2005 definitions provides that the provisions relating to freight derivatives are published in Sub-Annex I of the Annex to the 2005 definition: the Freight Annex. Thus:

Article XVII

Freight Transactions

The remaining provisions of this Article XVII are published in Sub-Annex I of the Annex to these Commodity Definitions, which may be amended from time to time. The parties may elect that Sub-Annex I apply to an agreement or a Transaction by taking the action described in Sub-Annex I [the Freight Annex]

This Freight Annex amends the 2005 definitions to the extent that the market practices for freight differ from those applicable to other commodities. This annex is not a separate document in its own right and its provisions are incorporated into the main body of the 2005 definitions as Article XVII. The 2005 definitions also provide a section of market-standard definitions for market-standard price definitions for certain freight routes in its Sub-Annex A.

The 2005 definitions, the Freight Annex and the related template confirmations are analysed below.

7.2   Sub-Annex A of the 2005 ISDA Commodity Definitions

Wedged deep between Article XVII and Sub-Annex I in the 2005 definitions is Sub-Annex A. It includes a section on freight. This has 15 pages of market-standard definitions for freight derivatives underlying prices. The definitions fall into four principal areas: Baltic Exchange Wet Dry Bulk Routes, Baltic Exchange Wet Bulk Routes, Platts Clean Tankerwire and Platts Dirty Tankerwire.

The Baltic Exchange Dry Bulk Routes definitions cover time-charter and voyage-charter routes for each of Capesize, Panamax and Handymax classes of vessel. The definitions specified for Capesize, for example, include "Freight-Baltic Exchange-Capesize Index Route C8_03", which is defined as the price for any pricing date published on the Baltic Exchange's website under "Market Information: Indices: Baltic Exchange Capsize Index: C8_03: 172,000 mt Gibraltar/Hamburg trans Atlantic RV: Average in USD".

Other definitions reference voyage charter prices for carrying specific commodities such as iron ore, coal, grain and soya.

7.3   Sub-Annex I of the 2005 ISDA Commodity Definitions: the Freight Annex

Sub-Annex I of the Annex, the Freight Annex, is a relatively short annex when compared with those on other underlying assets such as emissions and bullion.

It consists of two pages of additional provisions and definitions; it also has one exhibit which has a form of introductory paragraph, letter agreement and closing for a freight derivatives transaction; and three exhibits which take the form of templates for additional provisions for cash-settled freight index constituent swaps. These additional provisions are for a voyage charter wet commodity swap, a voyage charter dry commodity swap and a time charter commodity swap.

The Freight Annex provides that the parties may elect to use the provisions of Sub-Annex I by specifying this in the relevant confirmation. Alternatively, they can use one of the template confirmations.

The annex should not be read in isolation from the principal section of the 2005 definitions. The Freight Annex is set out overleaf:

2005 ISDA COMMODITY DEFINITIONS DOCUMENTS
SUB-ANNEX I TO THE 2005 ISDA COMMODITY DEFINITIONS
Article XVII   *Freight Transactions*
Section 17.1   Freight Transaction
Section 17.2   General Definitions with respect to Freight Transactions
Exhibits to Sub-Annex I (the template confirmations)

The Freight Annex adds several new definitions to Article XVII. It adds a definition of 'freight transaction' as a new Section 17.1. This is defined as "a Transaction in respect of which the Commodity specified in the related Confirmation is a 'Freight Index Route'".

A new Section 17.2 then provides certain "General Definitions with respect to Freight Transactions". These definitions include 'freight index route' – the underlying commodity asset. This is defined as being "the route, expressed as load port to discharge port, in respect of which the Commodity Reference Price specified in the related confirmation is quoted". The commodity reference prices it refers to are set out in Sub-Annex A and are those discussed above.

These general definitions also set out a definition of 'multiplier'. This allows the parties to add leverage to a transaction – most relevant for the paper market. The time charter commodity swap template is the only one which includes the multiplier as standard.

The general definitions also contain two definitions relating to rates: 'contract rate' and 'flat rate'. The 'contract rate' is the fixed portion of payments exchanged under the swaps templates. The contract rate is used for calculating a 'fixed amount' payable by a party on a settlement date in a transaction and is defined as being the price per relevant unit specified in the transaction.

Furthermore, Section 17.2 defines 'flat rate'. This is a variable rate and is relevant to the template for wet transactions only. The flat rate can either be a 'fixed rate' or a 'floating rate'. Confusingly, this is relevant for both the floating leg and the fixed leg of a transaction. If 'fixed rate' is specified, this will be the dollar amount per metric tonne equal to Worldscale's New World Tanker Nominal Freight Scale for the freight index route for the 'trade date' for that freight transaction.

If 'floating rate' is specified, this will be the dollar amount per metric tonne equal to Worldscale's New World Tanker Nominal Freight Scale for the freight index route for the 'pricing date' for that freight transaction.

Dry commodity swaps exchange fixed contract rates for a floating amount, in a similar way to an FFA.

Section 17.2 also provides certain definitions in relation to Worldscale rates. These include defining the Worldscale organisation itself, as well as what Worldscale points and Worldscale rates are. These concepts are described above and are relevant only for wet commodity swaps.

(a)   Exhibit I to Sub-Annex I

Exhibit I is a "Sample Form for a Letter Agreement or Telex Confirming a Transaction", which is adapted by the parties to the relevant transaction to become the transaction confirmation. It follows the standard ISDA format.

The first part of the confirmation is an introductory paragraph. It sets out the purpose of the confirmation – that is, to confirm the transaction's terms and to detail the framework documentation incorporated by reference (ie, the ISDA Master Agreement and the 2005 definitions). The confirmation also covers six other areas:

- the parties' names;
- the provisions of Exhibits II-A through II-C which apply;
- calculation agent;
- account details/offices;
- broker/arranger; and
- closing for agreement or telex.

Most of these areas would be relevant in any derivatives transaction. The standard second paragraph, though, is absent, instead taking the form "Insert relevant additional provisions from one of Exhibit II-A through II-C". Exhibit II then provides the relevant additional provisions for each type of a voyage charter wet commodity swap, a voyage charter dry commodity swap and a time charter commodity swap.

For example, if the parties wish to enter into a voyage charter wet commodity swap, they can adapt the sample form confirmation and insert the provisions from Exhibit II-A. They will then insert the relevant pricing terms, deal details and elections in the confirmation.

(b)   Exhibits II-A to II-C – Additional provisions for commodity swaps

There are three sets of additional provisions set out in Exhibits II-A to 11-C of the Freight Annex. These allow the parties to make elections specific to three types of transaction. These are then inserted as an additional paragraph 2 of the confirmation (ie, the form in "Exhibit I to Sub-Annex A" set out above). The three exhibits are broadly similar. Each has footnotes to assist parties in making appropriate elections for the particular type of trade.

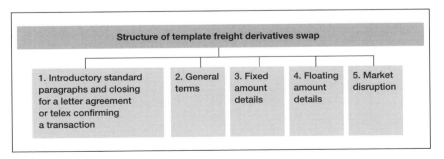

(i)   *Exhibit II-A to Sub-Annex I*

Exhibit II-A to Sub-Annex I sets out a template for a "Voyage Charter – Wet Commodity Swap".

General terms: The exhibit sets out a general terms section first. Here the parties insert specific details and elections for the transaction for the following terms and definitions from the 2005 definitions:

- 'Notional quantity per calculation period' – the 'notional quantity' is the quantity – in this case tonnage – of the freight rate referenced (eg, 10,000 tonnes of iron ore). The parties specify a 'notional quantity per calculation period' because there may be more than one calculation period for a transaction, and they may elect to adjust the notional quantity for different calculation periods.
- 'Total notional quantity' – this is the sum of all notional quantities in respect of all calculation periods.
- 'Commodity' – this is specified as the 'freight index route' – that is, the route expressed as load port to discharge port in respect of the commodity reference price (with the commodity reference price being specified in the floating amount details section).
- 'Trade date' – this is the date on which the parties agree to enter into the transaction.
- 'Effective date'- this is the first day on which the transaction's provisions become operative.
- 'Termination date' – this is the agreed date when the transaction will terminate.
- 'Calculation period(s)' – these are each period defined by a reference to the two dates specified here in the confirmation. For each payment amount calculated by reference to a calculation period, the relevant calculation period will be the one which ends closest in time to the relevant settlement date or payment date.
- 'Settlement date(s)' or 'payment date(s)' – these are the dates on which the parties settle their transaction obligations.
- 'Business day convention' and 'commodity business day convention' – these relate to adjustments for payment dates and for taking exchange-published prices respectively.

Fixed amount details: The fixed amount details section of the template covers the fixed amount payments under the swap. It provides for a 'fixed rate payer' to pay 'fixed amounts' to the counterparty.

The template provides for the fixed rate to take one of two forms, depending on whether the 'flat rate', which is set out in the 'floating amount details' section, is fixed or floating.

If the flat rate is 'fixed' (ie, the dollar amount per metric tonne is equal to Worldscale's New World Tanker Nominal Freight Scale for the freight index route for the trade date), then the template provides for the fixed rate to be defined as "(Worldscale Rate * Flat Rate/100) * Notional Quantity per Calculation Period"

(* representing multiplication and / division).

Because the underlying asset is a wet route, the formula provides for the flat rate to be multiplied by the Worldscale rate. The amount is then divided by 100 because parity in the Worldscale ratings is 100. The resulting figure is then multiplied by the 'notional quantity per calculation period' (ie, the tonnage figure).

If the flat rate is 'floating', the dollar amount per metric tonne will be equal to Worldscale's New World Tanker Nominal Freight Scale for the freight index route for the 'pricing date'; and the pricing dates will be specified in the floating amount details.

If this is the case, then the template provides for the fixed rate to be defined as "the product of (a) the unweighted arithmetic mean of the Worldscale Rate multiplied by the Flat Rate divided by 100 for each Pricing Date in the Calculation Period; and (b) the Notional Quantity per Calculation Period".

Despite the aesthetic differences between these two descriptions, the only difference is that the Worldscale rate is taken for each pricing date (usually each commodity business day) during the calculation period, and the rate will therefore vary between pricing dates if the New World Tanker Nominal Freight Scale for that freight index route is updated (which is usually annually).

Floating amount details: The floating amount details section of the template covers the floating amount payments under the swap. It provides for a 'floating rate payer' to pay 'floating amounts' to the counterparty.

The template provides for the floating rate to take one of two forms, depending on whether the 'flat rate' is fixed or floating.

If the flat rate is 'fixed' (ie, the dollar amount per metric tonne will be equal to Worldscale's New World Tanker Nominal Freight Scale for the freight index route for the 'trade date'), then the template provides for the fixed rate to be defined as "[(Floating Price * Flat Rate/100) * Notional Quantity per Calculation Period".

Section 6.2 of the 2005 definitions sets out the options for a definition of 'floating price'. This is summarised in the table on the next page.

If the flat rate is 'floating', the dollar amount per metric tonne will be equal to Worldscale's New World Tanker Nominal Freight Scale for the freight index route for the 'pricing date', and the pricing dates will be specified in the floating amount details.

If this is the case, then the template provides for the fixed rate to be defined as "the product of (a) the unweighted arithmetic mean of the Relevant Price multiplied by the Flat Rate divided by 100 for each Pricing Date in the Calculation Period; and (b) the Notional Quantity per Calculation Period".

The 'relevant price' is the price of the commodity reference price on a given day. The particular 'commodity reference price' is specified in the floating amount details, with the template suggesting "FREIGHT-BALTIC EXCHANGE – CLEAN TANKER INDEX ROUTE TC 1" as a price taken from Sub-Annex A.

The parties also specify the 'pricing dates'. If there is more than one pricing date, the template provides for the price taken to be averaged. If the parties would like to amend the default clauses of the 2005 definitions, which provides for the 'average' to be taken by way of unweighted arithmetic mean, the floating amount details section includes a 'method of averaging' section for the parties to amend this.

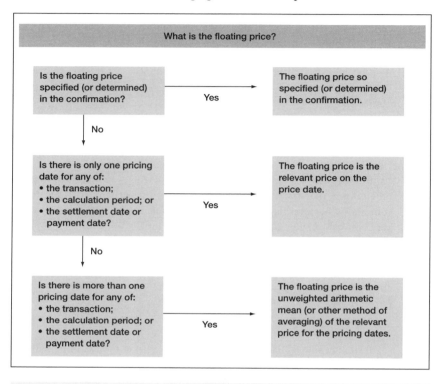

Hypothetical example of a voyage charter wet commodity swap: Yacoub Shipping and Olivia Refining Corp

Yacoub Shipping is a Japanese shipping conglomerate with a fleet of oil tankers. Its most profitable route is the "FREIGHT-BALTIC EXCHANGE – CLEAN TANKER INDEX ROUTE TC 1", for which the Baltic Exchange provides a daily price, and is a route between the Middle East and Japan for tankers carrying highly refined oil products. If the market rate for carrying freight across this route declines, this will impact on Yacoub's profits.

Olivia Refining Corp is a sophisticated Egyptian oil-refining corporation. It relies heavily on transporting its finished refined oil products across the "FREIGHT-BALTIC EXCHANGE – CLEAN TANKER INDEX ROUTE TC 1" route. A rise in freight costs will have a significant negative impact on Olivia's profits.

Both parties are willing to forgo the upside of a change in freight rates to obtain protection against the potential downside. Through their broker, the parties enter into a voyage charter wet commodity swap using the template documentation set out in the first exhibit to Sub-Annex I of the 2005 definitions.

The parties agree the terms of the transaction on September 15 2010, the trade date, with the transaction due to come into effect on September 20 2010, the effective date. They agree that the swap will have a term of exactly three years, meaning that September 15 2013 is specified as the termination date.

The 'commodity' is specified as 'freight index route', which means that they specify "FREIGHT-BALTIC EXCHANGE – CLEAN TANKER INDEX ROUTE TC 1" as the commodity reference price.

The parties want the swap to settle quarterly, so they specify that the payment dates will be March 15, June, 15, September 15 and December 15 in each year, commencing on December 15 2010 and ending on the termination date in 2013.

Yacoub and Olivia also specify that each calculation period will start on one payment date and end on the business day preceding the next one, apart from the first calculation period, which commences on the effective date.

They also specify that the 'notional quantity per calculation period' will be 100,000 metric tonnes – that is, 100,000 metric tonnes of refined oil products.

Olivia is keen that freight rates do not exceed current rates, so it becomes the 'fixed price payer'. Yacoub wants freight rates not to fall below current rates, so it is the 'floating price payer'.

The commodity swap references a wet route. This means that it is priced according to the New World Tanker Nominal Freight Scale for the freight index route for 2010. Freight rates have reduced by 10% since the start of the year, but remain volatile. The parties agree to a Worldscale rate adjusted downwards by 10% and so insert 90 Worldscale points as the Worldscale rate (ie, WS90).

For the purposes of the flat rate, they agree to make this a 'fixed rate'. The price published in Worldscale's New World Tanker Nominal Freight Scale for the freight index route for the trade date, September 15 2010, is $10 per metric tonne.

On each payment date, Olivia will be obliged to pay Yacoub the fixed amount. This is inserted into the confirmation as "(Worldscale Rate * Flat Rate/100) * Notional Quantity per Calculation Period". This translates to 90 * $10/100 * 100,000 per calculation period (ie, $900,000). This is not the amount payable, however. This figure will be netted against the floating price payable by Yacoub on each payment date.

On each payment date, Yacoub is obliged to pay Olivia the floating amount. This is set out in the confirmation as "(Floating Price * Flat Rate/100) * Notional Quantity per Calculation Period".

The pricing dates for the transaction are specified as being "Each Commodity Business Day during the Calculation Period". The floating price is therefore the unweighted arithmetic mean of the relevant price (ie, FREIGHT-BALTIC EXCHANGE – CLEAN TANKER INDEX ROUTE TC 1) for the pricing dates.

For the first calculation period, the unweighted arithmetic mean of the relevant price is $12. This means that "(Floating Price * Flat Rate/100) * Notional Quantity per Calculation Period" is 12* $100/100 * 100,000 per calculation period (ie, $1.2 million).

The floating price payable by Yacoub is netted against the fixed price payable by Olivia (ie, $900,000). On the first payment date, Yacoub pays Olivia $300,000.

Market disruption: The 2005 definitions list several market disruption events in their Section 7.4(c). These events result in a disruption, which means that the ordinary method of determining the price under the trade is no longer possible – perhaps resulting in the trade terminating. These market disruption events are:

- 'price source disruption', which relates to the failure or unavailability of market prices;
- 'trading disruption', which relates to a material suspension or limitation of trading at the relevant exchange;
- 'disappearance of commodity reference price', which relates to the discontinuation of trading of the relevant contract in the exchange, the disappearance of the relevant commodity or the unavailability of the relevant index;
- 'material change in formula', which relates to a material change in the formula for the method of calculation of the relevant index;
- 'material change in content', which relates to a material change in the content, composition or constitution of the relevant contract; and
- 'tax disruption', which relates to a change in a tax which directly affects the price under the contract.

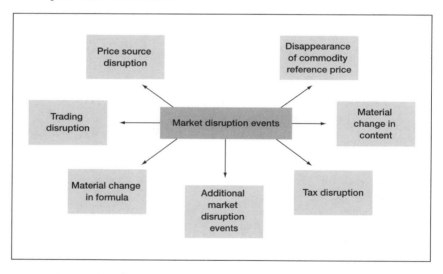

The 'market disruption' section of the template confirmation provides for three specific fallbacks for freight derivatives in relation to 'disappearance of commodity reference price', 'material change in formula' and 'material change in content'.

For each of these, if a successor commodity reference price is published by the price source (eg, the Baltic Exchange or Platts) to reflect amendments which were announced as forthcoming on or before the trade date, then this will not constitute a market disruption event and the successor commodity reference price shall apply instead.

When a market disruption event or an additional market disruption event occurs, instead of terminating the trade, the parties may decide to calculate the payment under the trade in accordance with an alternative method. This is known as a disruption fallback and, subject to a few exceptions, must be specified in the confirmation. The notes to the template suggest including 'negotiated fallback' as a disruption fallback so as to include the FFABA forming a panel to provide missing rates or pricing information on a pricing date.

Each template allows the parties to add any additional market disruption events or delete any or all of the above market disruption events. If the parties do not specify any market disruption event in the confirmation, the default position under Section 7.4(d)(i) is that all of the above market disruption events, other than the tax disruption event, apply to the transaction.

Finally, the templates provide for the parties to elect a 'fallback reference price' and 'maximum days of disruption'. If the parties specify an alternative commodity reference price as the fallback reference price and a calculation agent is unable to determine the relevant price using the principal commodity reference price, then the alternate commodity reference price will apply.

'Maximum days of disruption' is relevant to several of the market disruption events for determining a relevant price or moving to an alternative disruption fallback. If the parties wish to specify the standard number of maximum days of disruption, they should do so here.

(ii)   *Exhibit II-B to Sub-Annex I*
The "Alternative Provisions for a Confirmation of a Voyage Charter – Dry Commodity Swap", set out in Exhibit II-B to Sub-Annex I, operate much the same as the wet commodity swap template discussed in (i) above. There are, however, some differences and these are highlighted next.

The payment formulae for both the 'fixed amount details' section and the 'floating amount details' section are different from those in the wet commodity swap template. This reflects the different way that dry freight routes and wet freight routes are priced.

The fixed rate is defined by reference to a 'contract rate'. 'Contract rate' is defined in Section 17.1 of the sub-annex as being "a price, expressed as a price per relevant unit, equal to the price specified as such" for the fixed-price payer. The contract rate will be specified as a dollar amount per metric tonne.

The template specifies that the fixed rate is calculated by using the following formula: "Contract Rate * Notional Quantity per Calculation Period."

The floating amount is also calculated slightly differently from the wet commodity swap, using the following formula: "Floating Price * Notional Amount per Calculation Period."

The 'commodity reference price' suggested is the "FREIGHT-BALTIC EXCHANGE-CAPESIZE INDEX ROUTE C2".

(iii)   *Exhibit II-C to Sub-Annex I*
The "Alternative Provisions for a Confirmation of a Time Charter Commodity Swap", set out in Exhibit II-C to Sub-Annex I, operate the same as the dry commodity swap

template discussed in (ii) above, with some minor differences.

In the general terms section, the only difference is the addition of a 'multiplier', which allows the parties to add leverage to any transaction. The formulae for both 'fixed amount' and 'floating amount' can be multiplied by any specified 'multiplier'.

Because the template deals with time rather than voyage, the 'contract rate' is specified as an amount of "US dollars per day".

The 'commodity reference price' suggested is the "FREIGHT-BALTIC EXCHANGE-CAPESIZE INDEX ROUTE C8_03".

8.   Conclusion

We need ships to carry goods by sea, and this need will only increase while globalisation and trade liberalisation continue.

The price of carrying those goods will also remain volatile for as long as the global economy's fortunes fluctuate, more or fewer ships of differing sizes become available or cease to be available, and the bargaining power of the various parties involved in shipping changes. A wealth of macro- and micro-economic factors additionally have an influence.

Freight rates have all the ingredients to be a perfect derivatives product: volatility, sophisticated parties and, increasingly, liquidity brought about by the paper traders. Commoditised and reliable pricing, standardised derivatives products and underlying assets are important too.

With freight rates forming an important part of the general price of world goods, and freight derivatives being an asset class which is capable of being separately traded, the future looks bright for this derivatives genre to be a future star.

Overview of documentation produced by the Futures and Options Association

Danuta Rychlicka

1. Introduction

Those whose work revolves around drafting and negotiating documents appreciate that good financial documentation plays a vital role in ensuring smooth operations and liquidity in financial products markets, and is a powerful driver of market growth. Standardised documentation has multiple benefits: as well as creating greater predictability and certainty regarding the financial contracts at issue, it streamlines the negotiation process, reduces the time, costs and resources involved and, once the documentation is in place, facilitates administrative controls, thereby reducing operational risk.

This is why the efforts made by various industry associations to create and maintain standard documentation are so important. This chapter covers the documentation library of the Futures and Options Association (FOA) as it relates to commodity derivatives. A principal part of the documentation library comprises a model set of terms of business for dealings in futures and other exchange-traded derivatives. These terms have been produced and are maintained by the FOA and are available to its members via the FOA website. Additionally, the FOA library contains documentation in which the FOA participated in drafting at various levels, which FOA members may find relevant and useful.

2. Futures and Options Association

The FOA is a London-based European industry association gathering together organisations and institutions involved in or carrying on business in futures, options and other derivatives, or which use such products in their business.

The FOA was formed in 1993 in an attempt to consolidate the then-multiple existing trade associations. Following the initiative of the Bank of England and various futures industry participants, a formation committee chaired by Sir Brian Williamson, former chairman of Liffe, started work in October 1993 with 100 founder members, aiming to combine the membership and aims of organisations such as the Commodities Traders Group, the London Markets Action Group, the UK Managed Futures Association, the Clearing and Settlement Association and the Joint Exchanges Committee. On September 28 2007 the FOA entered into an arrangement

---

1   The FIA is an international trade organisation for the futures industry linking more than 35 of the largest futures commission merchants, which are estimated to be responsible for over 90% of all public customer business executed on US contract markets.

for closer cooperation with the US-based Futures Industry Association (FIA).[1] The new arrangement aimed to facilitate communication between the two associations and to create and promote a unified view on global issues that affect their members, in particular members of both organisations. The cooperation includes the formation of joint committees and reciprocal access to board meetings.

The FOA currently brings together around 175 international organisations and institutions, including banks and financial institutions, brokers, commodity trade houses, energy market participants, fund managers, exchanges, clearing houses, systems providers, lawyers, accountants and consultants. The complete list of current members is available on the FOA website.

The principal role of the FOA is to represent the interests of its members in the public and regulatory domains, as well as to monitor and respond to proposed and actual changes in the regulatory environment and to support the businesses of its members by providing necessary and up-to-date guidance, documentation and information to its members.

3. Documentation platform

The FOA has taken a similar approach to the International Swaps and Derivatives Association (ISDA) and has undertaken the task of producing a multi-product documentation platform for market participants involved in exchange-traded derivatives, including futures and options. In order to accommodate the wide variety of products which the documentation covers and the requirements of exchanges on which the products are traded, the FOA client documentation has been built as a set of standardised basic client terms and a set of supporting modules covering specific topics, which together may be used in a number of combinations to create the most suitable documentation tailored to the needs and requirements of the relationship of a firm and its clients.

The FOA has produced a user's guide to provide basic guidance as to the scope and use of the documentation and the structure of the FOA documentation library. Every document included in the FOA library includes more detailed guidance notes which explain the options available to parties when negotiating the various modules and consequences of choosing one particular option over another, including explanations of consequential changes required in the remainder of the document to ensure that the particular option or concept is carried across the provisions.

Finally, the detailed document-specific notes include thorough explanation of the various rules, compliance with which requires incorporation of the particular provisions in the documents. Thanks to various consultations and input from regulatory experts as well as market practitioners, the users of the FOA documentation have a set of law- and regulation-compliant modules. Helpfully, the notes also include references to the relevant rules so that the person producing or negotiating an FOA-based agreement is always aware which provisions in the agreement are indispensable in order to ensure compliance with those rules that must always be complied with, and which provisions are necessary only in relation to certain types of client, transaction or market.

The documentation library available through the FOA website includes documentation produced by the FOA itself, as well as other futures- and options-related documents in the drafting of which the FOA has participated as co-author or consultant.

The FOA has gathered and makes available to its members the documentation described next.

3.1   FOA documentation

(a)   *General FMSA Library*

The General Financial Services and Markets Act (FSMA) Library is available in its historic version and an updated version of September 2009, and includes the following:

- Basic terms:
  - eligible counterparty terms;
  - professional client terms;
  - professional client agreement (execution-only); and
  - retail client terms.
- Exchange-specific modules:
  - Euronext Liffe;
  - Euronext Brussels;
  - LME; and
  - SGX.
- Specialised modules:
  - agency module;
  - custody module;
  - disclosure of compensation for deposits;
  - equities module;
  - fixed-income securities module;
  - futures and options module;
  - futures and options product information module;
  - metals and soft commodities module;
  - oil and gas module;
  - short-form netting module;
  - short-form two-way netting module;
  - default, netting and termination module (two-way netting);
  - title transfer securities and physical collateral annex; and
  - trustee annex to netting module.
- Special guidance papers:
  - product information risk disclosure checklist.
- Non-UK modules:
  - Hong Kong;
  - Japan;
  - Singapore; and
  - United States.

(b) *FOA Master Netting Agreement*[2]

Having regard to the importance of the netting risk and to ensure that effective netting arrangements are put in place to allow parties to net off profitable and losing transactions and thereby limit their loss when an event of default occurs without the risk that such arrangements may be challenged in insolvency scenarios, the FOA has developed the Master Netting Agreement (MNA). Following the requirement of the Financial Services Authority (FSA) that netting arrangements be supported by legal opinions, the FOA has secured positive legal opinions from key jurisdictions around the world which are available to its members and hence enable compliance with the FSA rule that firms must have a legal opinion addressed to them.

The following forms of MNA have been produced and are available from the FOA:

- 'MNA one-way'; and
- 'MNA two-way'.

(c) *Energy Market Participants and Oil Market Participants*[3] *Library*

The Energy Market Participants and Oil Market Participants (EMP/OMP) Library includes two sets of terms produced for two types of customer (as per the Conduct of Business Sourcebook categorisation): intermediate customers[4] and market counterparties.[5] The EMP/OMP documentation covers only dealing in designated investments, including over-the-counter (OTC) energy derivatives (including forwards) and contracts for difference (including those that are energy related). The EMP/OMP Library consists of the following documents:

- Basic terms (including netting module):
    - intermediate customer terms; and
    - market counterparty terms.
- Specialised modules:
    - agency;
    - e-trading terms; and
    - electronic order routing.
- Account opening and money laundering:
    - opt-up letter (private to intermediate);
    - opt-up letter (intermediate to market counterparty);
    - disapplication and opt-out side letter;
    - money laundering checklist; and
    - money laundering process chart (corporates).

---

2   For analysis of the FOA netting provisions, please see section 9.4(i) herein on Module I.

3   An Energy Market Participant (EMP) is a firm whose permission covers no investment business except energy market activity, and which is not a professional firm or another type of investment firm such as a bank or a mortgage lender, and is not an OMP. An OMP (Oil Market Participant) is subject to similar requirements as an EMP, except that its activity is limited to investment business related to oil markets.

4   'Intermediate customers' are investors that have some experience and have either appropriate expertise in-house or the means to pay for professional advice when this is needed.

5   'Market counterparties' are clients experienced in financial products and markets who are either sufficiently sophisticated to operate within a light-touch conduct-of-business regime without the application of regulatory protections or counterparties (mainly authorised firms) operating within the inter-professional regime.

(d) Power Trading Forum documentation

There are two Power trading Forum documents:

- the ROC Trading Master Agreement (March 2005); and
- the Grid Trade Master Agreement (GTMA) and the GTMA Option Annex (June 2004).

3.2 Other industry documentation (created in cooperation with the FOA)

(a) Give-up agreements

Give-up transactions: 'Give-up' is a procedure which involves three brokers and occurs most often as a professional courtesy in situations when a broker receives an order from its client but is too busy to execute that order. The broker arranges for the executing broker to place the trade, but on its behalf (ie, as if the broker has executed the trade itself). Consequently, the records show a transaction between the broker of the client and the broker with which the executing broker completes the transaction (the 'sell-side broker'), even though the trade is actually executed between the executing broker and the sell-side broker. The broker of the client and the sell-side broker also receive the commission, while the executing broker gets nothing. The term originates from the fact that the broker that executes the transaction must 'give up' the commission to another broker.

International Uniform Execution Services (Give-Up) Agreement: The International Uniform Brokerage Execution Services Give-up Agreements are market-standard agreements used by participants of the futures industry to document give-up transactions. The agreements were initially produced in 1995 by the FIA Law and Compliance Division in consultation with the FOA and the Managed Funds Association, and in cooperation with leading law firms and exchanges. Following the changes in the way that futures contracts are traded, in particular the use of electronic order-routing systems, the agreement was updated in 2006 and a specific version designed for use with give-up transactions on the London Metal Exchange (LME) was created. Due to the establishment of the FIA Electronic Give-Up System (EGUS), the agreement was updated again in 2008 to accommodate the industry changes brought about by the technical developments.

The agreement has been created in two versions:

- Customer Version 2008 – a tripartite agreement between the executing broker, the clearing broker and the customer; and
- Trader Version 2008 – either a tripartite agreement between the executing broker, the clearing broker and the trader (acting on its own behalf and, if authorised, on behalf of the customer) or, if the trader is not authorised to act on behalf of the customer, also the customer, a fourth party.

Similarly to other standardised industry documents, any changes to the agreements must be clearly indicated to avoid inadvertently misrepresenting that the documents are in the standard form without modifications. With the introduction of EGUS, the parties were given the possibility to enter into such agreements electronically. When negotiating and executing the agreement via EGUS, the parties present each paragraph of the agreement in two columns, with the original text in the left-hand column and changes to the language of the agreement in the right-hand column. This allows any changes to the agreement to be drawn to the parties' attention immediately.

In order to comply with specific requirements of the LME's rules, several LME versions of the agreement were created and were then updated and broadened in 2008. Eight versions of the LME Customer Agreement and eight versions of the LME Trader Agreement (covering various combinations of various parties to the agreement being for LME members, Category 4 LME members or non-members) are available for download through the FOA website.

(b)   ***Exchange of Futures for Physicals Transaction Agreements***
The FOA has also made available through its website the International Uniform Exchange of Futures for Physicals (EFP) Transaction Agreement. This agreement was primarily developed by the FIA in consultation with the Managed Funds Association, the FOA and several US and UK exchanges. The agreement is designed to simplify and facilitate the documentation of EFPs[6] by establishing a common approach to the legal and commercial obligations of the parties to an EFP.

The agreement has been created in two versions:

- Customer Version 2006 – a tripartite agreement between the customer, the dealer and the customer's clearing broker; and
- Trader Version 2006 – with the trader as an additional party.

As for the give-up agreements, the parties must clearly highlight any changes to the standard form of the agreements to avoid representing that the documents are in the standard form without modifications.

The specifics of the General FSMA Library are set out in the following sections.

4.   Standardisation

The FOA documentation library comprises the Standardised Client Documentation, which is specified in the FOA User's Guide as including:

- the Standardised Client Documentation (which is available in WORD format for downloading and use by firms to create their own documentation); and
- the Standardised Client Documentation with Guidance Notes (which is available only to participating firms for their internal use and is not intended for circulation or reuse).

The FOA documentation, similarly to ISDA documentation, is standardised – that is, for use by the parties without making significant changes in the documents – and

---

6   An EFP is an off-market transaction in which a position in the underlying is traded for a futures position so that a future position may be closed out. It is often effected by two hedging parties, one long and one short, making a private deal in the cash market when they no longer need their (equal and opposite) futures contracts to hedge. The hedging parties then request that the contracts be nullified by the exchange (without making a trade on the floor) in order to ensure that neither contract results in the requirement to deliver. EFPs are rare and are also known as exchange-for-physicals transactions, against-actuals transactions, cash-futures swaps or ex-pit transactions.

therefore transaction-specific details and changes should be introduced via a schedule of amendments (the Individually Agreed Terms Schedule) which forms part of the agreement and in the relevant confirmations for the particular types of transaction (confirmations are not included in the FOA library). However, unlike ISDA documentation, the FOA documents are designed as 'benchmark' documents only; therefore, the FOA guidance allows for changes in the main body of an agreement, provided that such changes are sufficiently highlighted.

The standardised documents are date stamped to indicate the version which is used. The documents are subject to regular amendments – at the time of writing, the latest available versions of documents are dated September 2009.

5. Regulatory and exchange requirements

Although the FOA documentation is not intended to be comprehensive and cover all aspects of every type of transaction (and therefore parties must separately produce confirmations for transactions), it does includes all those provisions which are required by relevant regulatory and exchange rules (see below) in client agreements of this kind. The documentation also includes market-standard commercial terms of business and those terms which are commonly used in relation to the majority of investment services and products (eg, terms relating to settlement of transactions).

As regards regulatory requirements, the documentation has been drafted in full compliance with the requirements of the United Kingdom's FSMA 2000, the FSA Conduct of Business Sourcebook Instrument 2007, the FSA Handbook of Rules and Guidance, the FSA Client Assets Sourcebook and the FSA Systems and Controls Sourcebook, all as amended to implement the EU Markets in Financial Instruments Directive (MiFID) (2004/39/EC). The documentation also considers as relevant the rules of the London Code of Conduct for Non-investment Products, the voluntary code of good practice for market practitioners.

Following the recent financial crisis, the client terms of business were revised and updated in 2009 to reflect the regulations of the Banking Act 2009, the new disclosure and transparency rules for contacts for difference, the extension of MiFID, the Capital Requirements Directive and Systems and Controls Sourcebook requirements to non-MiFID and Capital Requirements Directive firms, the extension of MiFID client assets regulation to non-MiFID firms and amendments to the Client Assets Sourcebook and various other amendments, including those to the Money Laundering Regulations and those introduced by the Companies Act 2006 and the Rome Convention.

As regards documentation requirements of exchanges, the following exchanges have been contacted by the FOA and have provided information on any additional terms required by them to be included in client documentation:

- the Chicago Board of Trade;
- the Chicago Mercantile Exchange;
- EDX;
- EUREX;
- Frankfurt;
- Euronext.Liffe;
- Euronext Amsterdam;

- Euronext Brussels;
- Euronext Paris;
- the Hong Kong Stock Exchange;
- ICE Futures;
- the Korea Exchange;
- the London Metal Exchange;
- the London Stock Exchange;
- the New York Mercantile Exchange; and
- the Singapore Exchange Limited.

Those requirements of various exchanges which were common or required also by other regulations are covered in the basic terms and properly annotated in the guidance notes to avoid parties deleting them. In certain cases, requirements of an exchange have been included in a separate module, with the parties having an option to add such module as required.[7]

6. Governing law and jurisdiction

The documents in the FOA library are intended to be enforceable under English law and be compatible with the UK regulatory requirements for client documentation after the implementation of MiFID. The governing clause in the standard-terms module has recently been updated to reflect the parties' choice of law governing non-contractual obligations pursuant to Rome II.[8]

However, the FOA has reviewed client documentation requirements of certain non-UK jurisdictions in relation to cross-border business for the Bahamas, Bermuda, the British Virgin Islands, the Cayman Islands, Guernsey, Hong Kong, Japan, Jersey, Singapore, South Korea, Switzerland and the United States, and supplementary terms have been prepared in respect of Hong Kong, Japan, Singapore and the United States.

7. Clients and products

As mentioned above, the FOA standardised documentation is intended to provide terms of business covering a wide range of investments and products and multiple categories of client.

7.1 Clients

The FOA standardised documentation includes three basic sets of terms for client agreements, to be used in relation to clients categorised in accordance with MiFID:[9]

- for eligible counterparties, the Eligible Counterparty Agreement, relevant

---

7   See sections 8 and 9 below.
8   Rome II Convention (864/2007/EC).
9   Through the use of categories of client, MiFID recognises that investors have different levels of knowledge, skill and expertise and that regulatory requirements should reflect this. MiFID generally adopts two main categories of client, retail and professional, with a separate and distinct third category for a limited range of business, eligible counterparty (ECP). Different regulatory protections are attached to each of these categories, resulting in the retail category (the less experienced, knowledgeable and sophisticated) investors being afforded a higher level of protection than that afforded to investors in the professional or ECP category.

only to certain types of MiFID investment business;
- for professional clients:
  - the Professional Client Agreement (full version); and
  - the Professional Client Agreement – execution only (an abridged version for firms acting as execution brokers in connection with a give-up agreement); and
- the Retail Client Agreement for retail clients.[10]

7.2 Products

The FOA documentation covers only dealings in certain business and product areas, and designated investments (including arranging deals involving, and advising on, such investments), but there may be other investment activities which require specific other client-related provisions.

The FOA standard terms cover the following product range:
- equity products;
- fixed-income products;
- financial futures;
- exchange and OTC traded metals and soft commodities; and
- oil and gas.

8. Documentation structure

The FOA documentation comprises a set of 'modules', each containing a set of provisions covering particular subjects. Different modules cover different areas of interest, including specific lines of investment business (eg, securities, commodities, oil and gas) or exchange-specific terms.

The basic sets of terms comprise 12 basic modules (Modules A to K, illustrated overleaf), which include general and boilerplate provisions essential for any legal agreement, as well as certain terms required by laws and regulations in connection with providing investment services. Some additional terms applicable only to specific products, clients or types of transaction have been included in separate modules which the parties may elect to add to the basic terms as required. These additional modules may be appended as annexes or built into the body of the documentation.

Accordingly, the modules can be combined by the parties as required to produce a finished document with some of the modules included in the documentation and other elements (eg, exchange-specific modules) removed. However, the parties must be aware that just as the addition of product-specific modules will not affect the validity or sense of the remainder of the document, removal of any of the modules contained in the basic sets of terms may have undesired commercial consequences or may affect the legal validity of the agreement, and therefore should be carefully considered by the parties.

---

10   In accordance with Conduct of Business Sourcebook 8.1.2, if a firm carries on designated investment business, other than advising on investments, with or for a new retail client, the firm must enter into a written basic agreement, on paper or other durable medium, with the client, setting out the essential rights and obligations of the firm and the client.

Basic terms modules

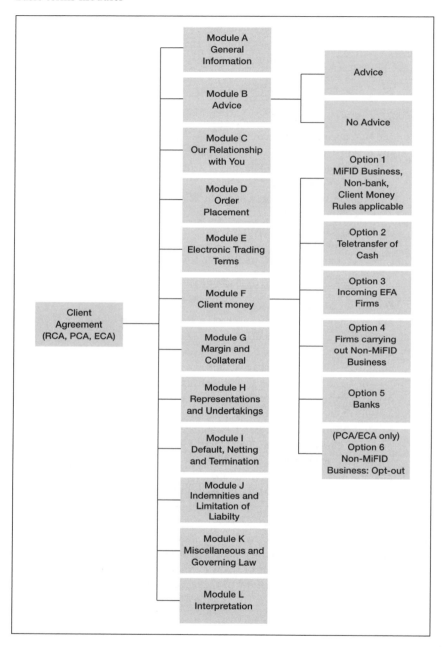

The additional (supplemental) modules may be divided into five categories as illustrated below:

- product-specific modules;
- netting modules;
- agency and custody modules;
- exchange-specific modules;
- non-UK client-specific modules; and
- other modules.

Supporting modules

Product-Specific Modules	Netting Modules	Agency and Custody Modules	Exchange-Specific Modules	Non-UK Client-Specific Module
Metals and Soft Commodities	Two-Way Netting	Agency	LIFFE	Hong Kong
Oil and Gas	Short Form Netting (One Way)	Custody	Euronext Brussels	Japan
Futures and Options	Short Form Netting (Two Way)		London Metal Exchange Guidance Note	Singapore
Futures and Options Product Information	Trustee Annex*		Singapore Exchange (SGX)	USA
Fixed Income	Title Transfer Securities and Physical Collateral Annex*		Other Module: Disclosure of Compensation for Deposits	
Equities				

* FOA guidance notes on this module are available to FOA members.

9. Documentation assembly

The assembly of documentation for a particular client will involve the following stages.

9.1 Categorisation of the client

The firm must determine whether the client is a retail client, a professional client or an eligible counterparty (if the client is a professional client, firms have an option to choose the execution-only version of the Professional Client Agreement), and select the appropriate basic set of terms (the Eligible Counterparty Agreement, the

Professional Client Agreement, the Professional Client Agreement (execution only) or the Retail Client Agreement).

9.2 Selection of modules

The firm must determine:

- which modules included in the basic terms apply and which do not apply to the business of the transaction types to be entered into with the client; and
- which supporting modules apply to the particular business, type of transaction or client.

Any modules which the parties wish to remove may be either deleted or disapplied in the Individually Agreed Terms Schedule.

However, as suggested by the FOA in its User's Guide, unless the documentation is used as a supplement to or in conjunction with other general terms and conditions of business between the firm and the client (eg, a prime brokerage agreement), the following basic-terms modules should never be removed by the parties, in order to avoid the risk of the agreement being legally ineffective:

- Module A – Introduction;
- Module B – Advice;
- Module C – Our Relationship with You;
- Module D – Order placement;
- Module I – Default, Netting, and Termination;
- Module K – Miscellaneous and Governing Law; and
- Module L – Interpretation.

If any modules have been removed, replaced or added, the firm should explain to the client the reasons for such removal, replacement or addition of supplemental modules to the basic Retail Client Agreement, Professional Client Agreement or Eligible Counterparty Agreement.

9.3 Amendments to original text

In accordance with the recommendations of the FOA, any amendments to the text of the basic terms or any supplemental module should be clearly marked 'Client Agreement – Summary of Provisions'.

9.4 Basic modules

All three sets of basic terms follow the same general pattern of modules.

(a) Module A – Introduction

Module A consists of two clauses:

- 'General information'; and
- 'Right to cancel'.

(b) Module B – Advice

The Retail Client Agreement and the Professional Client Agreement provide two options regarding the scope of services that the firm may provide to the client:

- Option 1: advice – this option should be elected if the firm intends to, or may, provide advice or personal recommendation to the client; and
- Option 2: no advice – this option assumes that advice will never be given to the client and execution-only services will be offered to the client.

(c)   ***Module C – Our Relationship with You***

Module C differs among the three client agreements because of different regulations applying to retail and professional clients. Module C describes confidentiality obligations of the firm in relation to information and data about, or provided by, the client.

(d)   ***Module D – Order Placement***

Module D covers one of the most important areas in the agreement, specifying the agreed methods of the placing of order instructions. The parties are free to agree which method(s) of placing instructions they will use to suit their particular business. Given the risks involved and the scope for errors, Module D puts the firm in a strong position, giving it the rights to:

- refuse orders;
- set limits on orders (and limit the number of open positions);
- execute transactions by crossing the client's orders; and
- aggregate orders with its own and its clients' orders.

The module also excludes the firm's liability for non-execution of the client's orders, as well as liability for the actions or omissions of any intermediate broker or agent which the firm may use (at its entire discretion) to carry out any transactions. At the end of each trading day, the firm sends to the client confirmations for the transactions executed on that day on behalf of that client.

(e)   ***Module E – Electronic Trading Terms***

With the development and adoption of electronic methods of trading across the industry, the Electronic Trading Terms module has been added to the client agreements to address the commercial and legal problems which may be raised by the use of electronic order routing and to facilitate electronic communication between the firm and the client. Due to the broad array of electronic services that firms offer to their clients and the variety of licensing requirements, the electronic trading terms in this module are drafted to be general and may require amendments (eg, to the definitions of 'electronic services or systems') and additional specific provisions to cover the range and nature of the electronic services actually provided to the client appropriately.

Module E includes general provisions relating to:

- the client's access to electronic services, restrictions which the firm may impose on the use of such services, and the circumstances in which the firm is authorised to suspend or terminate the client's use of the services;
- the client's obligation to provide and maintain the system (including hardware, software, network connections and anti-virus protections);

- exclusion of the firm's liability in connection with providing the electronic services; and
- indemnity due to the firm from the client in a case of virus introduction to the system.

(f)   Module F – Client Money

The implementation of MiFID, which came into force on November 1 2007, resulted in certain amendments to UK legislation, including the Financial Services and Markets Act 2000 (Regulated Activities) Order 2001 (SI 2001/544) and the FSA Handbook Rules. Regarding client assets (including client money and custody), the MiFID requirements were initially and temporarily added to the existing non-MiFID rules as additional chapters to the Client Assets Sourcebook in order to provide for the custody and client-money requirements applying to firms carrying on MiFID business. Following the FSA's review of its client assets regime, revised rules came into force on January 1 2009. One of the key changes to the Client Assets Sourcebook was a merger of the non-MiFID rules relating to custody and client money and the MiFID rules, thereby adopting and consistently applying the MiFID standards to all firms (with a few necessary exceptions).

However, those investment firms which hold client assets only in the course of their non-MiFID business may opt out by agreeing with professional clients and eligible counterparties that money that would otherwise be client money will not be subject to Client Assets Sourcebook protection. Such opt-out is not available to a firm which conducts MiFID business even in relation to activity which is outside the scope of its MiFID business.

The 2009 review of the FOA documentation took into account the 2009 amendments to the Client Assets Sourcebook and implemented consequential changes in the client money module of its client agreements by removing the fourth option which applied to "(a) firms which were not subject to MiFID and (b) MiFID investment firms in respect of their non-MiFID business". Firms which hold client assets or client money in the course of non-MiFID business have been added to the first option. Accordingly, the client agreements now offer five sets of provisions regulating holding client assets and client money by a firm (certain provisions are available in the Professional Client Agreement and the Eligible Counterparty Agreement, but not in the Retail Client Agreement).

(g)   Module G – Margin and Collateral

The margin module specifies margining arrangements which apply between the firm and the client, including the form of acceptable margin and the treatment of posted margin in default situations. The disclosure of margin requirements applicable to the client and, in the case of retail clients, the provisions of information about consequences of failure by the client to post margin are required under the Conduct of Business Sourcebook, as well as the rules of some markets (eg, the London Metal Exchange).

Margin may be posted in the form of cash or non-cash assets. Because acceptance of non-cash margin gives rise to additional issues and regulations regarding valuation, custody over the client's assets and security matters, as the default the standard-form client agreements allow only cash margin which, if posted as an outright title of transfer, excludes application of the client money rules. If the parties agree that non-cash margin is acceptable, the margin will be subject to security interest in favour of the firm; if the firm holds security interest in the client's assets, it will have to comply with the client money rules if the asset is cash or the custody rules if the asset is not cash (in which case the parties should consider adding the custody module provisions).

Given the importance of margin as collateral covering the firm's credit risk, the provisions of the module vest numerous decisions and determination in the discretion of the firm, subject only to applicable regulations or rules of markets. In accordance with the module, the firm may exercise its discretion when determining:

- the amount of margin call (reasonable discretion as to the amount required to provide the firm with appropriate protection);
- a form of acceptable non-cash collateral and currencies of cash collateral; and
- the value of non-cash collateral (absolute discretion).

Following the occurrence of an event of default or termination of the client agreement, the module gives the firm the following rights:

- right of retention of cash collateral (beyond what is required under any market rules, if there are any other outstanding obligations between the parties);
- right to sell all or any part of the margin; and
- right of set-off of any cash margin owed by the firm against any due and payable obligations owed by the client to the firm.

Two further aspects of margin and collateral need to be highlighted.

(i) *Security interest*

As regards security interest over non-cash margin, the module provides that the client grants the first fixed charge in favour of the firm over all of the present and future non-cash collateral provided in relation to the agreement. The parties should consider what form of security interest is most appropriate for each type of non-cash collateral and ensure that the registration requirements and other actions required in order to perfect the security interest are satisfied.[11] Pursuant to the module, the client undertakes to take any additional steps which may be required to perfect the security and to refrain from granting any other security, or transferring or assigning any of the security interest. To avoid the risk of recharacterisation of the fixed charge as a floating charge, the agreement prohibits the client from substituting or withdrawing any of the secured assets without the consent of the firm.

To the extent that the margin constitutes 'financial collateral', the module gives the firm the right to charge the margin in its own name and the right of

---

11 From October 1 2009, Part 25 of the Companies Act 2006 regulates the registration of charges granted by companies incorporated in England and Wales; charges granted by overseas companies are subject to the Overseas Companies Regulations 2009.

appropriation (foreclosure and retention of secured assets towards discharge of secured obligations).

(ii)   *Title Transfer Securities and Physical Collateral Annex (to the netting module)*
Where the firm intends to take collateral using outright transfer of margin rather than creating a security interest, the Title Transfer Securities and Physical Collateral Annex supplements the client agreement, with appropriate provisions covering the legal consequences of the legal and beneficial ownership passing to the firm. The annex provisions cover the following areas:

- margining requirements, including transfer of acceptable margin, redelivery obligation on termination of the agreement, and substitution of collateral during the life of the agreement;
- manufactured dividend and interest payment by the firm in relation to transferred margin;
- calculation of the 'default margin amount' on an event of default;
- representations and warranties in relation to transfer of margin; and
- dispute resolution provisions.

(h)   **Module H – Representations and Undertakings**
This module covers representations given by the client at the conception of the agreement. The representations which are common to all three client agreements (Retail Client Agreement, Professional Client Agreement and Eligible Counterparty Agreement) include:

- power and authority;
- due authorisation of signatory;
- binding obligations and no contravention with law, regulation or agreement binding on a client;
- no event of default or potential event of default;
- acting as principal and sole beneficial owner;
- no misleading information; and
- margin beneficially owned and free from any security interest (other than routinely imposed in a clearing system where it is held).

As a result of the different features of clients, the Retail Client Agreement and the Professional Client Agreement include additional representation as to:

- age and ability to act; and
- willingness and ability to sustain total loss of funds as a result of a transaction and (optionally) suitability of investment vehicle for the client.

The covenants common to the Retail Client Agreement, the Professional Client Agreement and the Eligible Counterparty Agreement include:

- no speculative orders or orders breaching law; and
- provision of further information promptly upon the firm's request.

In relation to retail and professional clients, the following additional obligations are explicitly imposed:

- maintenance of continuing authorisation and power;
- prompt notification to the firm of any event of default (or potential event of default) in relation to the client or credit support provider; and
- compliance with applicable law and regulation.

(i) *Module I – Default, Netting and Termination (and supporting netting modules)*

The netting provisions in Module I of the client agreements have been widely based on the FOA Master Netting Agreement. Except for the Eligible Counterparty Agreement, in which the module effectively provides for two-way netting, the provisions of Module I in the standard-form Retail Client Agreement and Professional Client Agreement envisage one-way netting, pursuant to which only the firm can net its exposure on the occurrence of a default under the agreement. If the one-way netting approach is not suitable in relation to a client, the standard Module I may be replaced with the Default, Netting and Termination Module (Two-way Netting), available from the FOA documentation library; or if the firm wishes to limit the netting provisions, in particular as regards applicable events of default, a shortened version of Module I (in both a one-way and a two-way netting version) may be used. The list of events of default in the short-form modules is limited to four events and their description is less detailed. The parties may use short-form modules as a starting point and, by reference to the long-form module, may amend or widen their provisions as required.

Each of the FOA netting modules has the same structure, divided into four clauses covering the following areas:

- Clause 10 – Events of default;
- Clause 11 – Netting;
- Clause 12 – Rights on default; and
- Clause 13 – Termination without default.

The netting will apply only to those transactions which the parties have specified as 'netting transactions' in the schedule.

(i) *Events of default*

The list of events of default in the netting module may be shortened or lengthened by the firm, depending on the relationship and creditworthiness of the client, in order best to serve the interests of the relationship between the parties. The list proposed in Module I is long and exhaustive, and not all of the events would be applicable to every client.

The main events of default present in each netting module (including the short-form and eligible counterparty agreement module) are:

- non-performance, including failure to pay, failure to make delivery and failure to comply with other terms of the agreement which may constitute an immediate event of default or, at the option of the parties, may become an event of default if it continues for a specified period of time following notification of default;
- voluntary insolvency, including any proceeding which proposes liquidation

or reorganisation or any other relief under bankruptcy or insolvency law;

- insolvency, including involuntary proceedings seeking the liquidation or reorganisation of a party or any other arrangement or relief under bankruptcy or insolvency law; and
- untrue representation or warranty – that is, a representation or warranty given (or deemed to be given) under a client agreement or credit support documentation that proves to have been false or misleading in any material respect at the time it was given (or deemed to be given).

The long-form netting modules in the Retail Client Agreement and the Professional Client Agreement also include the following events:

- inability to pay debts, including by reason of death of a physical person, bankruptcy or insolvency or when the debts are capable of being accelerated;
- repudiation of obligations under the client agreement or any security of credit support document;
- dissolution of a party or removal from a register;
- potential violation of applicable regulations or good standard of market practice (subject to a subjective test of the firm or non-defaulting party, as applicable);
- material adverse effect on a party's ability to perform obligations under the agreement, where it is desirable for a party's protection or an action is taken which, in a party's opinion, might have a material adverse effect;
- default of the credit support provider, where certain events described above occur in relation to the credit support provider or affect any credit support documentation; and
- cross-default with agreements between the client and the firm or any specific agreements which may be listed in the schedule.

(ii)   *Netting*

On the occurrence of an event of default, the agreement gives the firm a right to net its obligations against those of the client (except where a bankruptcy default occurs and the automatic termination provisions apply). Unless the automatic termination has occurred, (in which case the date of the bankruptcy default automatically and without notice constitutes a liquidation date), the firm may specify, by notice to the client, the date for termination and liquidation of netting transactions (ie, the liquidation notice).

Following the liquidation date, the obligations to make payments are extinguished and are satisfied by settlement of the liquidation amount, which should be determined by the firm as soon as practicable after the liquidation date, and should represent the net aggregate received after netting "the total cost, loss or, as the case may be, gain" in relation to each netting transaction against any gains by the firm. The firm should inform the client of the liquidation amount, whether that amount is positive or negative and which party is liable to pay it.

If the firm wishes to have a discretionary right to terminate and liquidate any other transactions which are outstanding between the firm and the client at that same time, the relevant terms giving this options should be incorporated.

(iii)   *Additional rights on default*
In addition to the rights described above, following an event of default or determination by the firm (in its absolute discretion) that the client will be unable to perform its obligations in the future, the firm has a right, without notice to the client:

- instead of returning equivalent investments, to pay fair market value of such investments;
- to sell the client's investments in the firm's possession to realise funds to cover any amounts due from the client; or
- to close out, replace, reverse or take any other action in relation to any outstanding transaction to cover, reduce or eliminate the firm's loss or liability in respect of dealings with the client.

This firm-friendly provision is commonly challenged by clients, which try to remove it or, if not possible, qualify it so that the firm must always act reasonably.

(iv)   *Termination without default*
Either party may terminate the client agreement by 10 days' written notice of termination to the other party. On termination of the agreements, all amounts payable by the client to the firm become immediately due and payable; however, the termination will not affect any outstanding rights, obligations or transactions until all obligations have been fully performed.

(v)   *Trustee Annex to the Netting Module (September 2009 version)*
Where the firm enters into netting arrangements with a counterparty that is a trust under English law, several additional issues arise which must be carefully considered when documenting such arrangements. To assist firms in dealing with trustees, the FOA has produced (and recently updated) the Trustee Annex and Guidance Notes, which explain the most important trust-related issues for firms to address. The Trustee Annex includes the special provisions which must be incorporated into the client agreement to achieve effective netting when dealing with trustees. These provisions include:

- additional representations;
- warranties and covenants which should be sought from trustees; and
- additional events of default specific to a party organised as an English law trust.

In order to avoid the risk of discontinuity of effective netting arrangements with an appointment of a new trustee after the date of execution of the client agreement, an Adoption Form has been added to the Trustee Annex, pursuant to which the incoming trustee adopts the agreement and all outstanding transactions.

(j)   ***Module J – Indemnities and Limitation of Liability***
This module reflects a market-standard approach in agreements of this kind, excluding and largely limiting the liability of a firm.

Pursuant to the provisions in Module J, liability of the firm is limited to losses which are a reasonable and foreseeable consequence of, or arise directly from, the firm's (or its representatives' or employees') gross negligence, wilful default or fraud (but liability of the firm for any consequential damage, loss of profit and goodwill is excluded). Furthermore, to the extent possible pursuant to FSA regulations, the firm's liability for non-performance is excluded if such failure is caused by *force majeure* or a failure of a third party.

On the other side, the client must fully indemnify the firm for any costs, losses and expenses incurred in relation to the client's accounts and transactions.

(k) Module K – Miscellaneous and Governing Law

The Miscellaneous and Governing Law module covers the usual boilerplate provisions which cover various operational issues. The most significant of them are described below.

(i) Amendments

The agreement gives the firm an express and one-sided right to amend the agreement, specifying further that if an amendment is material, the firm should notify it to the client "in good time" (which may be freely agreed by the parties – the document suggests a period of "at least 10 business days"). Such amendment becomes effective on the date specified in the notice.

Any other amendments, which may include any non-material amendments and amendments requested by the client, must be agreed in writing between the parties.

Although the drafting does not make it clear, it seems that the one-sided right to impose amendments has been included to enable the firm easily and quickly to implement any amendments required by law or regulatory authorities, while the mutual-agreement regime will apply to any other amendments that the parties may wish to make to the agreement. Unless the parties agree otherwise, the amendments have no retroactive effect.

(ii) Electronic communication, recording of calls and recordkeeping

As most communication between the client and the firm are made electronically, the agreement confirms that communications using electronic signatures will have the effect of written communications, and that orders and instructions will be validly evidenced by email or other electronic means. In compliance with the requirements of the United Kingdom's Telecommunications Regulations to inform customers if calls are recorded, the agreement provides that telephone conversations with clients will be recorded as evidence of the terms and information regarding orders and instructions given by the client.

Under MiFID, the records which the firm is required to keep for five years are evidence of dealings between the parties which the client undertakes in the agreement not to contest.

(iii) Investor protection schemes

Pursuant to the Conduct of Business Sourcebook, firms carrying on MiFID business are required to disclose to the client information regarding any compensation scheme of which the firm is a member. The 2007 version of the agreement refers to the UK Financial Services Compensation Scheme, under which claimants may receive up to £48,000 in compensation.

(iv)   *Complaints procedure*

Module K in the Retail Client Agreement incorporates an additional clause which provides basic information about the complaint handling process. It is a regulatory requirement that the firm provide such information to retail clients at or around the time when they enter into the agreement or when the client files a complaint. The approach taken by the authors of the Retail Client Agreement was to provide basic details in the agreement itself, with the client having the option to request further information.

(v)   *Transfer and assignment of the agreement*

In order to preserve the rights of close-out netting and set-off, the client cannot assign, charge or transfer its rights or obligations under the agreement without the firm's consent. Any assignment, charge or transfer made in violation of this restriction will be invalid. There is no similar restriction in relation to the firm.

(vi)   *Set-off*

Pursuant to the agreement, the firm may, at any time and without notice to the client, offset any amounts owed by the client to the firm against any amount owed by the firm to the client. The firm may exercise this right regardless of whether the obligations are current or future, or actual or contingent. In case of contingent obligations, the firm has full discretion as to the valuation of such obligations, subject only to such ascribed value being commercially reasonable.

(vii)   *Governing law and jurisdiction*

All the FOA client agreements are governed by English law, subject to any rules which may apply by reason of the transactions being connected to a specific market. The parties may select other laws to govern their relationship before signing the agreement. The choice of governing law is also subject to the Rome Convention, which gives a natural person the right to request that the contract be governed by the law of the jurisdiction of that person's domicile.

Pursuant to the jurisdiction clause, the parties submit to the jurisdiction of the English courts. These provisions may be superseded by specific provisions applying to arbitration (eg, in the Liffe module).

(l)   **Module L – Interpretation**

Module L (in the same form in each of the Retail Client Agreement, the Professional Client Agreement and the Eligible Counterparty Agreement) includes definitions of 14 terms used in the client agreements as defined. The parties may amend the definitions as required to reflect the specifics of the transactions. Of all the definitions, two require additional commentary: 'market' and 'transaction'.

The definition of 'market' has been drafted in two alternative versions: one to be used where the parties intend to list the markets in the schedule and the other where no schedule will be used. However, in its second alternative the definition does not cover non-European Economic Area markets; therefore, if the parties wish these markets to be covered, they should either use the schedule or amend the second definition as required.

The definition of 'transaction' is important as it determines the scope and application of the agreement. As explained in the FOA notes, this definition must be wide enough to cover all relevant transactions, but not so wide as to avoid bringing into the client agreement transactions governed by other netting agreements. In relation to commodity futures, the underlying commodity may not be an investment and transactions in it may not be covered if not traded on the 'market' (as defined), and may need special mention in the definition of 'transaction'. Special mention may also be needed for collective investment schemes, funds and other investments based on the above, some of which may not be market traded. There is provision for the scope of the definition to be widened or reduced in the schedule. If the definition of 'transaction' is extended to cover additional types of product (eg, funds), the agreement may need to include supporting modules from the FOA documentation library.

(m) Individually Agreed Terms Schedule

This schedule plays the same role as a schedule to any framework master agreement – that is, it allows the counterparties to adapt the agreement to meet their specific trading and business requirements.

The schedule deals with the following matters:

- Transaction – the parties may include here any additional types of transaction that they agree should be governed by the agreement. The parties may also specify which transactions (under which circumstances) will be or become 'netting transactions' (and therefore subject to netting provisions), and which transactions shall be excluded (being covered by other netting arrangements or not suitable for netting).
- Markets – the parties may list applicable markets if the first alternative has been elected (see definition of 'market' in (l) above).
- Automatic termination – parties may elect if and when automatic termination shall apply (but this should be deleted if the Default, Netting and Termination module is not used).
- Base currency – the parties should elect the base currency (unless the netting module is deleted). The default currency is British pounds, which parties may wish to amend. If two-way netting provisions are used, the parties should specify base currency for both counterparties.
- Capacity and condition on payment – it is not necessary to include these clauses.
- Obligations – this part of the schedule relates to the set-off rights of the parties. If the firm wishes to be able to offset against obligations of the client under other instruments, those obligations may be listed in the schedule.

When executing the client agreement, the parties sign the Acknowledgments Schedule, which consists of Part A – Signatures and Part B, which includes a list of acknowledgments that a firm must obtain from a client. The list is not comprehensive and therefore, when drafting the schedule, it should be carefully reviewed and supplemented as required to ensure that all necessary acknowledgments and consents will be obtained from the client.

9.5 Professional Client Agreement – execution-only business

The Professional Client Agreement for execution-only business has been drafted for use by the firms which, in relation to a client, act solely as an execution broker and provide only execution services, excluding any settlement services or providing advice in relation to transactions. Therefore, this version of the Professional Client Agreement is limited to Module A – Introduction, which combines some of the provisions covered in Module A of the full-form client agreements and certain additional provisions specific to the role and activities of the firm acting as an execution broker for the client.

Further, this version of the client terms has been drafted so that it supplements a give-up agreement (the FIA/FOA International Uniform Execution Agreement), which the document assumes that the parties have entered or will enter into in addition to the Professional Client Agreement. Firms which, in their capacity as execution brokers, have entered into a give-up agreement may augment that agreement by entering into the Professional Client Agreement and thereby ensuring their compliance with the FSA conduct-of-business rules.

Due to its limited scope, this version of the Professional Client Agreement does not provide full contractual protection to the firm and therefore firms may consider supplementing it with other clauses from the long-form Professional Client Agreement. Any additional clauses may be added in Schedule I to the agreement.

It is important to reiterate that this version is based on certain assumptions as regards the firm – namely that the firm:

- acts as an executing broker (ie, does not provide clearing services);
- has entered into or will enter into a give-up agreement with the client;
- is not providing client money protection;
- is not taking any margin or other collateral; and
- does not wish to impose close-out netting.

If these assumptions are incorrect, appropriate modifications to the agreement or the addition of supporting modules will be needed.

The execution-only business version of the Professional Client Agreement covers the following areas:

- obtaining and accepting instructions from the client, and the timing for execution of accepted orders;
- the consequences of aggregation of the client's orders with orders of the firm or other clients of the firm;
- rights of the firm on the occurrence of an event of default or other non-performance by the client (including actions available to the firm pursuant

to the give-up agreement);
- the right to terminate the agreement by either party with 10 days' written notice;
- limitation of the firm's liability (save for reasonably foreseeable consequences, losses arising directly from gross negligence, wilful default or fraud, or death or personal injury resulting from negligence);
- indemnities from the client for any losses suffered by the firm in connection with the client's account; and
- boilerplate provisions, governing law and jurisdiction.

The events of default under the execution-only business version of the Professional Client Agreement, on the occurrence of which the firm may exercise its rights under the give-up agreement, include:
- non-performance – failure by the client to perform any of its obligations under, at the option of the parties, only this agreement or any agreement between the client and the firm and, where such failure is capable of remedy, not remedying it within an agreed time after serving a notice by the firm;
- insolvency proceedings – any insolvency proceedings, including the appointment of an insolvency officer, are commenced either voluntarily by the client or by its creditors;
- insolvency – the client is unable to pay its debts when they are due; and
- a composition arrangement with the creditors of the client.

The Acknowledgment Schedule used in this context includes acknowledgments and representations which the firm should seek or is required to obtain from the client pursuant to the Conduct of Business Sourcebook and the Client Assets Sourcebook. The list of the acknowledgments is not complete and may include acknowledgments which are not relevant for particular clients. The acknowledgments should be carefully reviewed and supplemented as necessary.

Although the execution-only version of the Professional Client Agreement provides a good starting point for negotiation of documentation with the client for execution services, firms should ensure that they are negotiated in the context of, and giving consideration to, the provisions of the give-up agreement.

9.6   Selected supporting modules

(a)   Product-specific modules

(i)   Futures and Options Product Information (September 2007 version)
The Futures And Option Product Information Module has been prepared to facilitate compliance with the Conduct of Business Sourcebook requirements regarding the provision of information by firms to their retail and professional clients about the designated investments offered to clients. Such information should explain the nature of, and the risk particular to, the specific type of designated investment in sufficient detail to enable the client to take decisions on an informed basis. It must

also, where relevant to the specific type of designated investment and the level of knowledge of the client, include a description of:

- the risks associated with that type of designated investment, including an explanation of leverage and its effects and the risk of losing the entire investment;
- the volatility of the price of designated investments and any limitations on the available market for such investments;
- the fact that an investor might assume, as a result of transactions in such designated investments, financial commitments and other additional obligations, including contingent liabilities, additional to the cost of acquiring the designated investments; and
- any margin requirements or similar obligations, applicable to designated investments of that type.[12]

This information, as well as any material change to such information, must be provided by the firm in good time before it carries on designated investment business or ancillary services with or for a retail client.[13]

In compliance with these rules, the FOA has produced the Futures And Options Product Information Module, which includes a description of various investment opportunities and products which may be the subject of transactions under the client agreements. The following products are explained in the module:

- futures;
- options;
- contracts for difference;
- contingent liability and limited liability transactions;
- securitised derivatives; and
- warrants.

The module also explains the risks connected with the way in which the markets operate and the consequences of occurrences such as suspension of trading or transaction settlement failure. As with all other modules, the firm will determine which product information is appropriate and should be provided to the client.

(ii)   *Futures and Options Module (September 2009 version)*

The Future and Options Module includes terms which are particular to futures and options, but common to commodities futures and financial futures. As such, the module does not cover any particular aspects that are characteristic to commodities or financial derivatives, and therefore it should be used in conjunction with the Metals and Soft Commodities Module (see (iii) below) and/or the Oil and Gas Module (see (iv) below), where parties enter into commodities transactions, and with the Fixed Income Securities and Equities Modules, where the parties trade financial derivatives. As regards the type of transaction to which the module applies, Clause 1

---

12   See Conduct of Business Sourcebook 14.3.2R (1) and (2).
13   Conduct of Business Sourcebook 14.3.9R.

of the module cross-refers to the definition of a 'transaction' as agreed in the client agreement.

The Future and Options Module is divided into four sections covering the following areas:

- trading arrangements;
- clearing services;
- non-cash settled financial futures; and
- EFP transactions.

Within the above sections, certain provisions apply only in relation to particular exchanges or execution and settlement arrangements between the parties. The EFP transactions section complements the Uniform EFP Transaction Agreement and covers both EFP transactions in which a physical contract is replaced by a futures contract and reverse EFP transactions where one or more futures contracts are closed out and replaced by a physical contract.

(iii)   *Metals And Soft Commodities Module (June 2007 version)*
The Metals and Soft Commodities Module has been prepared for transactions relating to, or contemplating delivery of, any base metals, precious metals or agricultural products, including commodities deliverable by transfer of a warehouse warrant ('warrant-based commodities').[14] If the parties intend to enter into transactions relating to commodity futures or EFPs in relation to any commodity, the Futures and Options Module should also be added to the agreement.

The Metals And Soft Commodities Module consists of the following main sections:

- Market disruption – this includes provisions allowing the firm to take certain actions (including closing out outstanding transactions, requesting immediate delivery of additional commodities or declining to enter into any new transactions) if market disruptions or price volatilities occur which may result in the market value of the relevant commodity moving to an unusual level.

- Title and quality – pursuant to this section, the client represents (at the date of the agreement and each time that the client enters into a transaction relating to a commodity) that the commodities in possession of or delivered to the firm are and will remain free of any encumbrances or security (other than a warehouse's general lien where commodities are held in a warehouse, but subject to the client's liability for any payment obligations due to the warehouse). By virtue of this section, the client covenants that it delivers commodities with full or limited (as the case may be) title guarantee, with the legal title to the commodities passing at the later of delivery of the relevant commodity or payment by the client, if delivery is made by the firm. As

---

14   A 'warehouse warrant' is a document of possession to the specific lot of material against which it was issued, evidencing entitlement to a commodity issued by the warehouse company (usually an exchange-approved facility). Warrants which are regulated by exchange may be used as the means of delivering commodities under exchange contracts.

regards warrant-based commodities, the legal title is transferred at the time when the relevant warehouse warrant is delivered. Any commodity delivered in relation to market-traded futures which is intended to be traded on the relevant market must comply with the requirements of that market.

- Delivery of commodities – this section provides that delivery of warrant-based commodities is effected by the transfer of warrants. However, if the warrants are in the firm's possession, such delivery is effected:
  - by appropriation by the firm of the requisite number and amount of warrants (where delivery is due from the client); or
  - by segregation by the firm of the requisite number and amount of warrants (where delivery is due from the firm).

Transfer of warrants held in SWORD[15] is effected by transfer between the parties' SWORD accounts. In its unamended form, the section provides that any costs incurred in connection with physical delivery of commodities are to be borne by the client. The parties may alter the provisions of the module to suit their factual delivery arrangements or ignore the provisions where other terms relating to the relevant commodities include specific mechanisms for delivery.

- Custodianship – pursuant to this section, the firm may provide custodian services to the client in relation to commodities or documents of title which the client acquired from the firm pursuant to a transaction. This section sets out the terms on which the firm would provide custodian services to the client, including the extent of the firm's responsibility.

As already mentioned, the module also intends to cover warrant-based commodities, including warrants held in SWORD, and therefore it includes certain specific provisions which are square bracketed for ease of identification. Where warrants are held in SWORD, these provisions should be incorporated in order to ensure that the agreement complies with the SWORD regulations and operating procedures. Where a client does not have a SWORD account, the firm may agree to hold its SWORD-eligible warrants in its own SWORD account on behalf of the client, but may also cause the client to lodge the warrants in SWORD. Where the firm holds SWORD warrants in its own account on behalf of a client, it acts as bailee only (rather than custodian) and therefore assumes no fiduciary duties. The SWORD-related provisions in the module also include the necessary consents and representations by the client to enable the firm to deal with the warrants on the terms of the SWORD regulations.

Finally, the module includes a set of provisions for use in transactions which involve delivery of bullion.[16] The provisions assume that the firm does not operate a bullion custodial service, but maintains an account at a custodian (named in the

15 SWORD is a secure electronic transfer system for London Metal Exchange warrants and a central depository and database for London Metal Exchange warrants. It has been in operation since July 1999 and allows for the ownership of London Metal Exchange warrants to be transferred between SWORD members in a matter of seconds.
16 Bullion includes gold, silver, palladium and platinum.

module) and that any deliveries are effected via the custodian account. The module also assumes that the bullion is held on an unallocated basis, and therefore that no covenants or warranties are given by the delivering party as to the title to the bullion. In order to ensure a satisfactory quality of bullion, the module requires that all deliveries of bullion as a minimum meet the "specifications and requirements of London good delivery or equivalent market standard laid down by the London Bullion Market Association or the London Platinum and Palladium Market".

The parties may amend the bullion provisions in accordance with their factual account and custodian arrangements.

(iv)   *Oil and Gas Module (September 2009 version)*
The Oil and Gas Module applies to transactions relating to, or contemplating the delivery of, energy commodities such as gas oil, fuel oil and natural gas. Similar to the Metals and Soft Commodities Module, if a firm intends to enter into any commodity future transactions or EFPs in relation to any energy commodity, the Futures and Options Module should be added to the agreement.

The Oil and Gas Module largely follows the language and structure of the Metals and Soft Commodities Module sections described above, save for those provisions which are specific to the type of commodities which are the subject of the module, such as terms relating to the delivery of commodities. A wide variety of specific arrangements in relation to the delivery of gas and oil are in use across the market and most parties would normally agree such arrangements separately. If the parties have agreed no such delivery arrangements in the 'Delivery' section, the module provides some fallback arrangements which have been based on those applicable to deliveries to LCH.Clearnet Ltd.

(b)   The Agency and Custody Modules

(i)   *Agency Module (September 2009 version)*
The Agency Module includes provisions for use in the transactions in which the client acts as agent for counterparties approved (in writing) by the firm. Unless the parties agree otherwise, only the agent is treated as the client of the firm for the purposes of the Conduct of Business Sourcebook and not the counterparties (although this does not relieve the firm from obligations which the firm may owe to the counterparties under the general law relating to agency).

For the purposes of credit approval and money laundering regulations, prior to placing an order the agent should disclose to the firm the identity and certain information about the counterparty on behalf of which it is acting. The extent to which information about the counterparty must be disclosed will depend on the type of counterparty and the agent. The firm maintains a separate account (or accounts) for each counterparty.

The Agency Module envisages that the agent may act for more than one counterparty. If this is the case, the agent must promptly allocate specific trades to relevant counterparties; otherwise it remains personally liable for the performance of the transaction. When the agent acts as agent for multiple counterparties, it has a number of additional administration duties regarding documentation and notifications and is fully responsible for investment decisions with respect to each counterparty. The firm's responsibility for the counterparties' compliance with any law or regulation is expressly excluded.

The Agency Module disapplies the representations and undertakings in Module H of the agreement and replaces it with a specific set of representations to be given by the agent as the agent for each counterparty and on its own behalf. These include certain additional representations relating to money laundering regulations.

As regards margining arrangements, the Module G of the agreement applies to agency transactions with reference to the client being deemed to refer to the agent. Any delivery of payment obligations by the firm is discharged by delivery or payment to the agent, regardless of the interest of a counterparty.

The netting provisions of the Agency Module have been drafted to ensure that the Netting Module (Module I) applies separately in respect of each counterparty, so that any positions of such counterparty may be effectively terminated and liquidated if an event of default occurs in respect of an individual counterparty or the agent (a default by the agent triggers termination and liquidation in respect of each counterparty's account). A default of a single counterparty will trigger termination and liquidation only in respect of that counterparty's account.

The Agency Module also includes an optional indemnity clause, which the firms may seek to incorporate if there are ambiguities as to the identity of counterparties (a disclosed principal is primarily liable for indemnities as a matter of law).

(ii)   *Custody Module (September 2009 version)*

As regards custody services, the FOA client agreements do not envisage that a firm will provide a full custody service, but may at most take custody of a client's assets as an incidental part of its offering dealing, arranging or advisory services. Despite the incidental nature of such custody agreements, the custody provisions of the FSA Handbook of Rules and Guidance may be triggered. The Custody Module (September 2009 version) is intended to be used in such circumstances to cover the necessary aspects of the regulations, even though it does not provide the full range of protection or have the scope of a typical full-service custody agreement.

Before the merger of the non-MiFID rules relating to custody and client money and the MiFID rules, two separate custody modules were available in the FOA documentation library: the Custody Module for MiFID business and the Custody Module for non-MiFID firms. Following the consolidation of the FSA rules, the non-MiFID Custody Module became redundant and has effectively been replaced by a revised version of the Custody Module which applies to both MiFID and non-MiFID firms subject to exceptions (eg, where a client provides margin by way of full transfers to the firm of the legal and beneficial title to security assets).

The Custody Module regulates the safe custody services which the firm may provide and includes provisions relating to the appointment of a custodian, the use of sub-custodians, the registration of custody assets, acting on instructions of the client in relation to custody assets and the scope of the firm's responsibilities. The final section of the Custody Module includes provisions relating to use of custody assets by the firm for securities lending (or other) purposes. Such use is subject to the express consent of a client required pursuant to the Client Assets Sourcebook.

(c) **Exchange-specific modules**

(i) *Liffe[17] Schedule*

The Liffe Schedule has been produced for use by those firms and clients that enter into transactions which are subject to the Liffe Rules.

The Liffe Rules require that all Liffe members (unless they enter into an agreement with another member of Liffe) include in their client documentation certain prescribed provisions set out in Liffe General Notice 399. The provisions cover areas such as the matching and allocation of contracts, allocation on delivery or exercise, margining, exclusion of liability, arbitration, governing law, jurisdiction and changes to the agreement. In order to ensure that the client documentation fulfils the requirements of the Liffe Rules, most of the prescribed provisions have been incorporated in the main body of the client agreements. The Liffe Schedule supplements the client agreement as regards those Liffe provisions which are more specific and therefore are better placed in a separate schedule which the parties may use at their option.

Pursuant to the Financial Services and Markets Act 2000, Liffe is obliged to ensure that its business is conducted in an orderly manner and that it provides proper protection to investors. This obligation is reinforced in the Liffe Rules, pursuant to which Liffe should at all times endeavour to maintain a fair and orderly market and to have effective arrangements to facilitate the efficient and timely finalisation of the transactions executed under its systems. However, as business on Liffe may from time to time be suspended, restricted or closed, the Liffe Rules also require that Liffe's liability towards clients be excluded. In line with the rules, the Liffe Schedule includes an explicit exclusion of liability of Liffe for "any loss, damage, injury or delay, whether direct or indirect, arising from any circumstances described above or any failure of some or all market facilities or from any act or omission of Liffe ... or from any breach of contract by or any negligence arising of Liffe". The liability of a firm is excluded to the same extent.

The Liffe Schedule further provides that any disputes arising in relation to contracts which are subject to the Liffe Rules must be referred to arbitration under the Liffe Rules before they may be brought before a court.

The Liffe CONNECT[18] section of the Liffe Schedule should be used only in relation to business conducted for clients that are in Liffe CONNECT. This section lists the additional powers which Liffe has in relation to operations on Liffe CONNECT, including cancelling all outstanding orders on default of the member or failure of a trading host.

---

17 Liffe (the London International Financial Futures and Options Exchange) is a futures exchange based in London. It is part of NYSE Euronext following its takeover by Euronext in January 2002 and Euronext's merger with the New York Stock Exchange in April 2007.

18 Liffe CONNECT® is a derivatives trading system which was designed and developed by Liffe to replace its open-outcry trading floor. It is a fully electronic exchange trading equity options, bond and index futures, short-term interest-rate futures, financial options and commodity products. Its special design and architecture allows customers to build or purchase trading applications according to their business needs, and to integrate those applications into other lines of business and business systems.

(ii)   *Euronext Brussels (July 2007 version)*
Unlike Euronext Amsterdam or Euronext Paris, both of which prescribe no specific terms for use in client documentation, Euronext Brussels imposes specific client documentation requirements which have been gathered in the Euronext Brussels Module and included in the FOA documentation library for use by firms as required.

The module has a form of information memorandum which aims to provide an overview of the operations of the Euronext. Liffe markets for derivatives products in Brussels and explain risks which may be involved in using the products admitted to the market. Under Belgian law, such an overview must be provided to a client before any transaction is entered into between the client and the member of Euronext Brussels. The memorandum has been prepared by Euronext Brussels and approved by the Belgian Banking and Finance Commission.

The information memorandum consists of:

- obligations of the members of the Euronext Brussels derivatives market towards their clients;
- Belgian derivatives, including an overview of the derivatives admitted to Euronext Brussels and the risks connected to transactions involving these derivatives;
- operations of the Euronext Brussels derivatives market, including information about the risks inherent to the operation of the market; and
- additional information explaining the risks connected with OTC transactions and currency risk.

(iii)   *London Metal Exchange Guidance Note (July 2007 version)*
Although the London Metal Exchange requires no mandatory terms or conditions to be included in client documentation, it expects its members to have client agreements in place whose provisions are consistent with London Metal Exchange rules. The FOA client documentation has been prepared in compliance with this requirement and applicable provisions have been included in the standard documentation. The London Metal Exchange guidance note lists the recommended specific provisions, identifying the relevant rules and those parts of the FOA standard documentation that include the provisions applying those rules.

(d)   *Other module – Disclosure of Compensation for Deposits*
Following the 2009 update to the documentation, a new module has been added – the Disclosure of Compensation for Deposits Module. This module includes information on the compensation arrangement in which the firm participates and gives three options for use by:

- UK domestic firms covered by the Financial Services Compensation Scheme;
- non-European Economic Area firms which are covered by compensation schemes in their country of origin; and
- European Economic Area firms which may 'top up' the cover provided by the country of origin to the level provided by the UK Financial Services Compensation Scheme in respect of deposits which the firms accept through their UK branches.

The information contained in this module must be disclosed to any protected deposit holder that is or is likely to be an 'eligible claimant' (as defined in the FSA Glossary), and therefore it has been produced and included in the FOA documentation library.

10.   Power trading forum documentation

(a)   Grid Trade Master Agreement

(i)   Basics of electricity trading

The Grid Trade Master Agreement has been prepared for use with transactions trading electricity in England and Wales. To understand the contractual relationship created between parties to the agreement, you must understand the basics of the electricity trading.

UK electricity market participants include:

- suppliers, which buy electricity to sell on to customers;
- generators, which sell electricity to suppliers; and
- non-physical traders – organisations without a physical demand for or ability to generate electricity, but which trade electricity.

Under the United Kingdom's Energy Act 2004, the British Electricity Trading and Transmission Arrangements (BETTA) were introduced on April 1 2005, replacing the previous New Electricity Trading Arrangements in England and Wales, and the separate arrangements that existed in Scotland and the British Grid System Agreement. The arrangements under BETTA are based on bilateral trading between generators, suppliers, traders and customers across a series of markets and are governed by the Balancing and Settlement Code (BSC).

The BSC sets out the rules governing the operation of the 'balancing mechanism' and the 'imbalance settlement' process, and it also sets out the relationships and responsibilities of all market participants. In particular, the BSC provides for:

- a mechanism for contracting parties to notify all volumes of electricity to be supplied under contract (notifications are made to Elexon);
- the balancing mechanism, in which NGC, as system operator, accepts offers and bids for electricity from generators and suppliers close to real time to enable it to balance the system at all times; (it has responsibility for balancing generation and demand and for resolving transmission constraints;) and
- a settlement process for charging participants whose notified contracted positions do not match corresponding metered volumes of electricity.

All licence holders (ie, transmission, generation, supply and distribution entities) must be registered within the BSC. Parties exempt from holding a licence (eg, non-physical traders) may sign up to the BSC if they wish and, in practice, investment banks do so and participate in the market. All generators and suppliers have energy accounts with the market operator, Elexon Limited.

Electricity is generated, transported, delivered and used continuously in real time, and supply must always match demand as electricity cannot be stored. However, for the purposes of trading and settlement, electricity is considered to be generated, transported, delivered and used in half-hour periods called 'settlement periods'. For each half-hour, those with demand for electricity (eg, suppliers) assess in advance what the demand will be. They then contract with generators for that volume of electricity. Contracts can be struck up to an hour before the relevant settlement period (where this cut-off is known as 'gate closure' and contracts cannot be struck after this time). In the half-hour itself, generators are expected to generate and deliver their contracted volume of electricity and suppliers are expected to use their contracted volume of electricity.

Generators with additional capacity (ie, those that have not contracted for the full volume that they can generate in any half-hour) can make that additional volume available to the system operator and can set the price they wish to receive for that additional volume. Similarly, a generator can state that it will reduce the volume being generated and can set a price for reducing its generation. Suppliers that are flexible enough can offer to reduce their demand to make additional volumes of electricity available to the system operator and can set the price they wish to receive for that additional volume. Similarly, flexible suppliers can say to the system operator that it will increase demand for a set price. These are called bids and offers.

	Offer	Offer price (per megawatt hour (MWh))	Bid	Bid price (per MWh)
Generator	Proposal to increase generation	Price requested for increase in generation	Proposal to reduce generation	Price offered for a decrease in generation
Supplier	Proposal to reduce demand	Price requested for decrease in demand	Proposal to increase demand	Price offered for an increase in demand

The system operator (National Grid) will, in real time and as required, match supply and demand in each half-hour by accepting bids or offers depending on whether it needs to increase or reduce electricity generation to meet demand.

Afterwards, metered volumes are collected for the half-hour from generators and suppliers, and compared against their contracted volumes (which are adjusted for any bids or offers accepted). All parties have their contracted volumes compared to determine whether the volumes they bought and sold match. If the contracted volumes do not match the metered volumes, the generators and the suppliers must either buy or sell to the grid additional electricity. These differences are referred to as 'imbalances', and 'settlement' is the process of calculating the volumes of imbalance and the prices to be paid for these imbalances. Settlement also enables other related charges and payments to be worked out.

(ii)   *Notifications*

The notifications determine the imbalance exposure of the parties and are made in a single notification process by the parties The notifications are made via a 'notification agent' (either one of the counterparties or an independent notification agent), which must be authorised by the parties with the central system to submit notifications on behalf of the parties. Contract notifications for a settlement period must be received by gate closure (contract volumes may be changed up to the gate closure by overwriting previously notified volumes). After the gate closure, during the hour before the relevant settlement period, Elexon and NGC calculate whether each of the BSC parties is in balance by comparing the volume of power delivered or taken by a party from the system against that party's energy account. If the physical position does not match the notified contractual position, the party is out of balance and, to the extent that there is a shortfall (the party is 'short'), Elexon will charge that party the 'system buy price'; and to the extent that the party is 'long', it will be paid the 'system sell price'.

	Generator (G)	Supplier (S)
System sell price	Paid to G if over-generating	Paid to S if under-consuming
System buy price	Paid by G if under-generating	Paid by S if over-consuming

The system sell price and the system buy price are established by Elexon for the relevant settlement period in relation to the cost incurred by NGC in purchasing additional power or contracting with generators to decrease the generation or with the suppliers to increase their off-take. The differences between the system sell price and the system buy price may be very significant, with the system buy price being extremely high while the system sell price is very low, thereby encouraging parties to ensure they are not short.

(iii)   *Making and documenting trades*

Electricity is traded using the following methods:
- Grid Trade Master Agreements or other power purchase agreements – long-term power supply contracts, usually bespoke power purchase agreements for the basic amount needed to match demand (baseload) contracted for bilaterally via OTC contracts; and
- power exchange trades (used for spot and futures contracts to 'fine tune' baseload in accordance with the expected volume)

The Grid Trade Master Agreement was introduced to develop a generic framework for OTC electricity trading and has been accepted as the standard set of terms under which the majority of forwards take place. Pursuant to the agreement, the parties may enter into such transactions relating to a trade of electricity which can be notified and taken into account for settlement purposes under the BSC.

Details of individual transactions are documented in standard-form confirmations. Any amendments to the terms of the Grid Trade Master Agreement, as well as certain elections to be made by the counterparties which are to apply to all trades between the counterparties, are specified in a separate schedule (Schedule 2 – Agreement information).

The Grid Trade Master Agreement consists of the main body of the agreement and the following attachments:

- Schedule 1 – Definitions and interpretation;
- Schedule 2 – Agreement information;
- Schedule 3B – Contract party notification agent approach;
- Schedule 4 – Transitional provisions;
- Annex A – Form of confirmation;
- Annex B – Form of notice of ability to submit ECV notification; and
- Annex C – Form of position for ECV notification.

The terms contained in the main body of the Grid Trade Master Agreement cover the following areas:

- confirmation procedure (Clause 2);
- representations and warranties (Clause 3);
- notifications and notification agent (Clauses 4–6 and 9);
- billing and payment (Clause 8);
- termination (Clause 12); and
- other provisions and boilerplate clauses (including taxes, confidentiality obligations, assignment, amendments and waivers, notices, governing law and jurisdiction).

Confirmations: Details of each transaction are documented in a separate confirmation which includes the following information:

- who the seller and the buyer are (including details of their energy accounts with Elexon);
- the time when the transaction has been agreed;
- the settlement periods for which grid trades are to be made;
- the settlement period volume (if not specified, deemed zero);
- the contract price (exclusive of taxes); and
- any special conditions which apply to the transaction.

A form of confirmation is attached to the Grid Trade Master Agreement as Annex A. The master agreement and all confirmations form a single agreement between the parties and, similarly to the ISDA Master Agreement, if the parties have not executed the Grid Trade Master Agreement at the time they enter into a transaction, the parties agree to use all reasonable efforts promptly to negotiate, execute and deliver the Grid Trade Master Agreement. Unless parties otherwise agree, confirmations are send by fax by the seller to the buyer. The buyer has two banking days either to accept or to comment on the terms in the confirmation.

Representations and warranties: The parties to the Grid Trade Master Agreement are required to give the usual contractual representations and warranties, as well as specific ones, including the parties representing that they are, and will remain at all times during each transaction term, parties to the BSC and will comply with its obligations under the BSC, and the relevant credit-related tests specified in the BSC.

Notifications and notification agent: The notifications and notification agent provisions regulate the following matters:

- Appointment and authorisation of the notification agent – pursuant to these provisions, each counterparty undertakes to appoint and authorise in a timely manner (and maintain the authorisation of) the notification agent in respect of its energy account. In case the notification agent ceases or is unable to act, the parties should appoint a new notification agent. If at any time (and for so long as) there is no notification agent acting, the relevant provisions relating to the notification agent are replaced by Schedule 3B (Contract party notification agent approach) and the party which has been specified as 'fallback ECV notification agent' in Schedule 2 (Agreement information) or, if the parties failed to so specify, the buyer, becomes the notification agent.
- Notifications – the notification provisions cover the following areas:
  - the requirements relating to the parties' obligation to make relevant nominations to the notification agent (stating the information required for the notifications to Elexon) which should be submitted in time to enable the notification agent to make appropriate notifications to Elexon before the gate closure; and
  - consequences of a failure by a party to appoint or authorise the notification agent as well as various circumstances where (other than in a case of *force majeure*) due to a failure or a party, an effective notification to Elexon has not been made.

Billing and payment: Pursuant to Clause 8 of the Grid Trade Master Agreement, the seller prepares and sends to the buyer (on or before the fifth banking day of the following month) a written monthly statement specifying volumes and prices for the transactions carried in the previous month. The party which owes a settlement amount should make the payment by the later of the 10th banking day of the following month or the fifth banking day after receipt of the monthly statement (subject to netting if the statement amounts are payable by each party to the other).

Termination: The termination provisions distinguish between two types of termination event:

- events of default which give the non-defaulting party a right to terminate the transactions and designate the 'early termination date'; and
- termination events (illegality and change in taxes), which give both parties a right to designate the early termination date.

Following the occurrence of an event of default by a party, the non-defaulting party may designate the early termination date in respect of all outstanding transactions by giving at least 20 days' notice (the early termination date being not earlier than the day when the notice is effective).

The events of default under the Grid Trade Master Agreement include the occurrence of the following events (in relation to a party or, where applicable, the credit support provider):

- insolvency;
- untrue or misleading representation or warranty;
- failure to pay (subject to a grace period of three banking days);
- persistent notification default;
- breach of a material obligation (other than the two points immediately above and subject to a grace period of five banking days);
- default of a party or a credit support provider under a credit support document;
- cross-default (if elected and subject to cross-default threshold specified by the parties in Schedule 2 – Agreement information);
- default under a derivatives transaction; and
- material adverse change.

On or as soon as possible after the early termination date, the non-defaulting party shall in good faith calculate the termination payment in accordance with the election made by the parties in Schedule 2 – Agreement information. The parties may elect one of two payment methods:

- 'loss', which means an amount that the non-defaulting party determines to represent its total losses and costs (or gain, as the case may be) incurred in connection with the termination of the transactions; or
- 'market amount', which means either:
  - the sum of the 'market quotation' for the transaction and the losses and costs (or gains) in respect of any payment resulting from the suspension; or
  - if the market quotation cannot be determined and would not produce a commercially reasonable result, the non-defaulting party's loss for the transactions.

'Market quotation' is defined as the average of quotations received from three leading traders in England and Wales, being amounts that the traders would charge from the non-defaulting party in consideration of entering into a 'replacement agreement' (ie, an agreement preserving the non-defaulting party's economic equivalent of any payment that it would, but for the occurrence of the early termination date, have received after that date). The party is not required actually to enter into a replacement agreement.

The payment of the termination payment should be made, if due from the defaulting party, within two banking days of notification of the termination payments (the 'termination payment date') or, if due from the non-defaulting party, within 30 banking days of the termination payment date.

The other termination events are illegality and changes in tax.

If after the date on which a transaction is entered into, it becomes unlawful for a party to perform its rights or obligations under the Grid Trade Master Agreement or any credit support document because of a change in any applicable law, either party may elect to terminate, liquidate and accelerate the affected transactions in accordance with the default termination provisions (described above) applied with prescribed changes. So either party may designate the early termination date; and if both parties are affected, each party determines the termination payment and the amount payable is the algebraic average of the two determinations.

If the parties have specified in Schedule 2 – Agreement information that the change in taxes provisions apply to a party and, after the date on which a transaction is entered into, that party (the 'affected tax party') becomes obligated to pay or make deductions for or on account of a tax arising from a change in tax law or an action taken by a taxing authority, the affected tax party (but not the other party) may elect to terminate, liquidate and accelerate those transactions in accordance with the default termination provisions (described above) applied with prescribed changes. So either party may designate the early termination date; and if both parties are affected, each party determines the termination payment and the amount payable is the algebraic average of the two determinations.

Suspension: In addition to the termination rights, following the occurrence of an event of default (or a potential event of default), the non-defaulting party has the right to suspend any payments under the agreement and compliance with the notification provisions.

Other provisions: Of the remaining provisions, which include the standard contractual terms, the four below are worth mentioning:

- A 'banking day' is defined as a day (other than a Saturday or Sunday) on which clearing banks in London are open for general business.
- The Grid Trade Master Agreement contains a *force majeure* provision which the parties may rely on, but only in relation to inability to issue the required notification to Elexon for reasons beyond the control of the notifying party.
- The Grid Trade Master Agreement jurisdiction provisions allow parties to refer any disputes arising under or in connection with the agreement to an independent expert appointed by agreement between the parties (or if the parties fail to reach an agreement, by the president of the Law Society of England and Wales).
- If there are any changes to the BSC which affect the ability of a party to comply with the terms of the Grid Trade Master Agreement, then at the written request of either party the parties should in good faith seek to agree appropriate amendments to the Grid Trade Master Agreement to accommodate the changes to the BSC (or if they fail to reach an agreement, they may refer the matter to the independent expert (see above)).

Grid Trade Master Agreement Options Annex: The Grid Trade Master Agreement Options Annex has been introduced to provide the necessary additional provisions and thereby enable parties to the Grid Trade Master Agreement to enter into 'option transactions' under the Grid Trade Master Agreement – 'option transactions' being agreements to enter into one or more options to enter into a grid trade in exchange for a premium. Pursuant to the Options Annex, the parties may enter into call or put options exercised as American- or European-style options, or as 'banking day daily settled' and 'true daily settled' options (the two latter ones determined by reference to an EFA day).[19]

The Options Annex has been drafted as an annex to, and to form part of, Schedule 2 – Agreement information. If the parties to the Grid Trade Master Agreement decide they wish to enter into options transactions, certain amendments will apply to the Grid Trade Master Agreement, including:

- a new clause regulating the payment of premium by the option buyer to the option seller;
- a new Clause 24 providing for the exercise of options;
- a new Clause 25 on the effect of the exercise and settlement of options; and
- amendments to Schedule 1 – Definitions and interpretation, including a set of additional options-related definitions.

Annex 2A, which forms part of the Options Annex, includes a form of option confirmation in which the parties shall specify details of each option transaction (Part A) and the underlying grid transactions (Part B) to which the option relates.

(b)   *Renewables Obligation Certificate Trading Master Agreement*

(i)   *Renewables obligation*
The 'renewables obligation' is an obligation placed on all licensed electricity suppliers in the United Kingdom to source an increasing proportion of electricity from renewable sources. It is the United Kingdom's principal measure for promoting the generation of renewable electricity, which was introduced in 2002 by secondary legislation under the Electricity Act 1989. The renewables obligation is administered by the Gas and Electricity Markets Authority (Ofgem) and requires electricity suppliers to source an increasing percentage of the electricity they sell from renewable sources each year. Accredited renewable energy generators are awarded one 'renewables obligation certificate' (ROC) for each megawatt-hour (MWh) of renewable electricity that they produce.[20] They can then sell the ROCs on the open market to suppliers that need them to make up their shortfall and meet their renewables obligations in each 12-month period (running from April to March). Where suppliers do not have sufficient ROCs to cover their renewables obligation, they must 'buy out' their shortfall by paying a set amount (the 'buy-out price') per missing ROC into a fund (the 'buy-out fund'). The buy-out price is a fixed price and is adjusted in line with the Retail Prices Index each year. The proceeds of the buy-out fund are paid back to suppliers in proportion to how many ROCs they have presented.

---

19   An EFA day runs from 23:00 hours (inclusive) on a calendar day and ends at 22:59 hours (inclusive) on the next day.

20   A ROC is a green certificate issued by Ofgem under the Electricity Act 1989 and pursuant to the Renewables Obligation Order 2002 or the Renewables Obligation (Scotland) Order 2002, as applicable, for eligible renewable electricity generated within the United Kingdom and supplied to customers in the United Kingdom by a licensed supplier. One ROC is issued for each MWh of eligible renewable output. ROCs are issued into the ROC Register and are electronic certificates.

The renewables obligation has for some time been the subject of criticism as being unnecessarily complicated and burdensome when compared with equivalent measures implemented in other European countries, as well as having a technology-neutral approach as a result of which all renewable sources attracted one ROC for each MWh of electricity produced. That criticism was addressed in the Renewables Obligation Order 2009, which came into force on April 1 2009 and introduced, among other changes, a concept known as 'banding', which eliminates the earlier approach and differentiates the volume requirements per ROC for different renewable energy technologies.

(ii)   *Making and documenting trades*
The ROC Trading Master Agreement has been prepared for use with transactions relating to effecting transfers of ROCs from the seller to the buyer. A transfer of a ROC is effected by its sale by the seller and purchase by the buyer, followed by a transfer of that ROC from the seller's ROC account to the buyer's ROC account.[21] Similarly to other standardised documentation, details of individual transactions are documented in standard-form confirmations, while any amendments to the terms of the ROC Trading Master Agreement, as well as certain elections, are made by the counterparties in a separate schedule to the ROC Trading Master Agreement (Schedule 2 – Elections).

The structure of the ROC Trading Master Agreement largely follows the structure of the Grid Trade Master Agreement. The main body of the agreement is appended with the following attachments:

- Schedule 1 – Definitions and interpretation;
- Schedule 2 – Elections; and
- Annex – Form of confirmation.

The terms contained in the main body of the ROC Trading Master Agreement cover the following areas:

- confirmation procedure (Clause 2);
- representations and warranties (Clause 3);
- ROC transfers (Clauses 4–7);
- billing and payment (Clause 8);
- termination (Clause 12); and
- other provisions and boilerplate clauses (including taxes, confidentiality obligations, assignment, amendments and waivers, notices, governing law and jurisdiction).

Each of these categories is described further below.

Confirmations: Details of each transaction are documented in a separate confirmation, each of which includes the following information:

- trade date and the time when the transaction has been agreed;

---

21   A 'ROC account' is an account on the ROC Register, which is a register established and maintained by Ofgem in respect of ROCs.

- who the seller, the buyer and (if applicable) the broker are;
- obligation period(s);
- obligation period volume in MWh and the number of instalments in which the volume will be transferred;
- corresponding generating station types;
- contract price(s);
- long-stop date(s) and applicable volumes;
- buy-out recycling benefit (if any); and
- any special conditions which apply to the transaction.

The master agreement and all confirmations form a single agreement between the parties. The standard form of confirmation does not anticipate that the parties have not executed the ROC Trading Master Agreement at the time they enter into a transaction and does not include the usual ISDA-like wording allowing parties to enter into the ROC Trading Master Agreement at a later stage.

Unless the parties agree otherwise, confirmations are sent by fax by the seller to the buyer. The buyer has three banking days either to accept or to comment on the terms in the confirmation.

Representations and warranties: The parties to the ROC Trading Master Agreement are required to give the usual contractual representations and warranties. Additionally, the seller must represent that it has a good legal and beneficial title to all the ROCs that are being transferred to the buyer, and that on the day of transfer the ROCs are in full force and effect and no circumstances exist under which Ofgem could revoke the ROCs.

ROC transfers: Pursuant to each transaction, the seller sells and the buyer purchases one or more ROCs; the subject of the ROC transfer and the title in each purchased ROC passes from the seller to the buyer on the ROC transfer date (ie, the date the ROC first appears on the buyer's ROC account).

The procedure which must be followed in relation to effecting a ROC transfer is illustrated overleaf.

If either party fails to fulfil its obligations in relation to the ROC transfer (except by reason of *force majeure*), that party must compensate the counterparty by paying it, for each ROC in respect of which a ROC transfer failure has occurred, an amount calculated in accordance with the ROC Trading Master Agreement.

Having regard to the power of Ofgem to revoke any ROCs which were issued on the basis of inaccurate information, ROC Trading Master Agreement Clause 7 (Revocation) includes provisions regulating the procedure which the parties should follow if any ROC which is subject to a transaction is revoked by Ofgem after the ROC transfer request date.

Billing and payment: The billing and payment provisions in the ROC Trading Master Agreement are very similar to the corresponding terms of the Grid Trading Master Agreement, in that the seller prepares and sends to the buyer (on or before the fifth banking day of the following month) a written monthly statement specifying volumes for the obligation period which have been subject to ROC transfers, as well as the prices for the transactions carried out in the previous month.

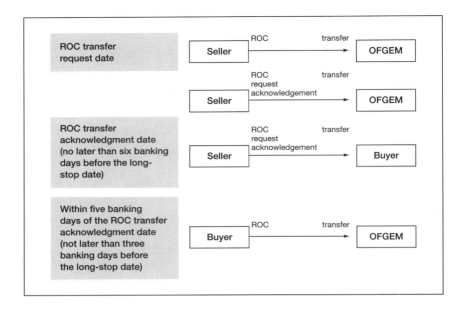

The party from which an amount is owed should make the payment by the later of the 10th banking day of that following month or the fifth banking day after receipt of the monthly statement (subject to netting if statement amounts are payable by each party to the other). In connection with the payments to the buy-out fund, the ROC Trading Master Agreement provides for the method and time of payments of amounts due in respect of the fund.

Termination: The termination provisions largely follow the Grid Trading Master Agreement, including the methods of calculation of termination payment ('market amount' and 'loss' – see above).

The few differences include additional events of default in the ROC Trading Master Agreement (ie: revocation for fraudulent behaviour; providing false information; merger without assumption; and credit event on merger – with the latter two based on the similar events of default in the ISDA Master Agreement).

Similarly to the Grid Trading Master Agreement, after the occurrence of an event of default (or a potential event of default), in addition to the termination rights the non-defaulting party has the right to suspend any payments under the agreement and compliance with its obligations in relation to ROC transfers.

Other provisions: As the ROC Trading Master Agreement follows the structure and language of the Grid Trading Master Agreement, the majority of the boilerplate provisions in the ROC Trading Master Agreement, subject to minor or necessary changes, mirror the language in the Grid Trading Master Agreement. If any changes are made to the regulation relating to ROCs as a result of which ROCs cease to have value, are revoked without replacement or are discontinued, then any transaction in relation to which ROC transfer date has not occurred may be terminated by either party and no termination payment will be payable.

The European Federation of Energy Traders

Ellen Doubtfire
Aimee Lewis

1. Introduction

"EFET promotes and facilitates European energy trading in open, transparent and liquid wholesale markets, unhindered by national borders or other undue obstacles."[1] This chapter discusses how the European Federation of Energy Traders (EFET) fulfils this purpose with energy derivatives, a sub-set in the commodity derivatives universe.

In 2001 American television host Jay Leno quipped, "Enron is now officially out of the energy business. They are now in a new business: confetti." He may well have been referring to energy derivatives contracts now being in shreds. Prior to its infamous 2001 bankruptcy, Enron was one of the world's leading energy companies and a key participant in Europe's energy markets – in particular, energy derivatives markets. European energy markets were in the early stages of growth and the Enron bankruptcy stifled a promising new market. The crisis of confidence led to a significant reduction in the size and number of participants in Europe's energy markets, and a robust single wholesale energy market throughout Europe has since failed to materialise.

Despite these obstacles, the European energy sector has been subject to fundamental change over the last 10 years and progress is being made. Much of this transformation is a result of the establishment of, and subsequent work by, EFET. Alongside EFET, market participants and regulatory authorities have made important commitments to improving market transparency and liquidity, with the ultimate goal of creating a single European market in electricity and gas. As a result of these efforts, wholesale trading – particularly in electricity – has been successfully established in a number of European regions.

Competitive wholesale energy markets are desirable and derivatives play a key part in these. The connection of the pool of supply with the pool of demand means that competitive wholesale markets result in increased trading efficiency, which in turn benefits the end consumer in terms of both cost savings and enhanced choice. Developing competitive and efficient wholesale markets in electricity and gas is a complex task. Unlike commodities such as agricultural products, both electricity and gas are restricted to their respective networks, and access to the power grids and gas pipelines is essential.

---

[1] EFET's Statement of Purpose; EFET booklet – *The Past and Future of European Energy Trading*: www.efet.org/.

Another challenge specific to the electricity and gas markets is the unbundling of the monopoly infrastructure that continues to exist in many countries, particularly in the gas sector. Despite privatisation in the 1990s in certain countries such as the United Kingdom and Norway, existing power grids and gas pipelines are generally completely or partially state-owned enterprises. The status quo of these state monopolies or large vertically integrated companies is maintained due to the many and varied barriers to entry into the European energy market.

2.   What is EFET?

Energy trading in Europe was virtually non-existent until the late 1990s, except in the United Kingdom and certain Scandinavian countries. Despite this slow start, things began to change rapidly as borders throughout Europe began to open and the established monopoly suppliers started to feel the first effects of competition. Many of Europe's biggest utility companies also began setting up trading functions. It was in the wake of these changes that EFET was founded in 1999. EFET was established as an industry association of market-orientated companies, represented by open-minded managers, with a view to bringing structure to and promoting an open energy market in Europe.

EFET is a non-profit organisation whose membership, although quite limited during its infancy, is now made up of more than 90 energy trading companies from 23 European countries. A current list of EFET's members is set out in the table below.

Company	Country	Company	Country
Regular members			
Actogas	Germany	ALPIQ	Switzerland
Barclays Capital	United Kingdom	BG International	United Kingdom
BKW FMB	Switzerland	BP	United Kingdom
British Energy	United Kingdom	Bulgargaz	Bulgaria
Cargill International	Switzerland	Centrica	United Kingdom
CEZ	Czech Republic	Citi	United Kingdom
Compagnie Nationale du Rhone	France	Deutsche Bank	Germany
Dong	Denmark	E & T Energie	Austria

Company	Country	Company	Country
Regular members (continued)			
E.On Energie	Germany	E.On Ruhrgas	Germany
EDF Trading	France	Edison	Italy
EDP Energya	Portugal	EFT	United Kingdom
EGL	Switzerland	Electrabel	Belgium
EnBW	Germany	Endesa	Spain
Eneco	Netherlands	Enel Trade	Italy
Energy Holding	Romania	ENI	Italy
EOS	Switzerland	Essent Trading International	Netherlands
Fortum	Finland	Gas Natural	Spain
Gaselys	France	GasTerra	Netherlands
Gazprom	United Kingdom	Goldman Sachs	United Kingdom
HSE	Slovenia	Hydro	Norway
Iberdrola	Spain	JP Morgan Chase	United Kingdom
Lumius	Czech Republic	Macquarie Bank	United Kingdom
Mercuria Energy Trading	Switzerland	Merrill Lynch	United Kingdom
Morgan Stanley	United Kingdom	MVM	Hungary
MVV Energie	Germany	Nidera Handelsmaatschap	Netherlands
Nuon	Netherlands	PGE Electra	Poland

Company	Country	Company	Country
Regular members (continued)			
Plurigas	Italy	Public Power Corporation	Greece
Raetia Energie	Switzerland	RAO Nordic	Finland
RBS Sempra Energy Europe	United Kingdom	RheinEnergie	Germany
Rudnap group	Serbia	RWE Supply & Trading	Germany
Shell Energy Trading	United Kingdom	Slovenske Elektrarne	Slovak Republic
SPE	Belgium	Stadtwerke Munchen	Germany
Statkraft Energi	Norway	Statoil	United Kingdom
Syneco	Germany	Tiwag	Austria
Total	United Kingdom	Trianel	Germany
Union Fenosa	Spain	Vattenfall	Sweden
VERBUND- Austriam Power Trading	Austria	Wingas	Germany

Company	Country	Company	Country
Associate members			
Acquirente Unico	Italy	AET	Germany
AXPO AG	Switzerland	BNP Paribas	United Kingdom
Calyon	United Kingdom	Conoco Phillips	United Kingdom
Delta	Netherlands	Dresdner Bank	United Kingdom

Company	Country	Company	Country
Associate members (continued)			
Electromagnetica	Romania	ENOI	Italy
EPS	Serbia	GEN-I	Slovenia
ENTEC	Germany	Gunvor International	Switzerland
HEP Trade	Croatia	IEG Netherlands	Netherlands
KELAG	Austria	KOM-STROM	Germany
Mark-E	Germany	MOL	Hungary
Nexen	United Kingdom	Scottish Power	United Kingdom
SJB Energy Trading	Netherlands	Stadtwerke Hanover	Germany
Stadtwerke Leipzig	Germany	TEI Energy	Italy
Vitol	Switzerland	Vivid Power	Bulgaria
ZMB	Germany		

Since 2005, all new EFET members must sign up to a set of guiding principles before their membership is accepted. These are EFET's 10 Pillars of Good Conduct:

Companies engaged in trading in energy markets will:
1. Respect and promote free and fair competition as the basis for trading sustainable traded energy markets.
2. Not engage in any activities which would amount to market abuse, market manipulation or fraud, or relay information known or strongly suspected to be false or misleading.
3. Deal with each other in accordance with established market practices and the standards expected of professional market counterparties.
4. Deal with customers fairly and with integrity, and manage any conflicts of interest that may arise appropriately.
5. Organise their energy trading business effectively, respecting appropriate segregation of staff duties, and exercise diligent control over trading functions.

6. Establish effective risk management policies and control procedures governing the key risks managed by their energy trading functions.
7. Establish compliance policies setting out the company's procedures for fulfilling all legal and regulatory obligations and any related corporate governance rules relating to energy trading functions.
8. Ensure that their traders are suitably qualified and properly supervised to carry out their duties, including where appropriate to have taken relevant industry examinations.
9. Prohibit their employees from giving or receiving bribes and from indulging in other corrupt behaviour in all circumstances; and establish policies governing gifts and hospitality, highlighting acceptable and unacceptable practices.
10. Maintain accounts related to trading transactions and risk books in accordance with relevant accounting standards, and respecting normal audit practices.

EFET's main activities are managed by its four committees (gas policy, electricity policy, legal, and business process optimisation). The committees are further divided into various sub-groups that focus on particular energy trading issues or market areas. EFET's sub-groups are made up of national organisations, taskforces, working groups and project groups. Both EFET committees and its sub-groups operate under the supervision of the EFET Board.

Since its establishment, the role and ambit of EFET's work has grown significantly. Presently, EFET carries out its activities in four main areas:

- power, gas and emissions market design;
- energy policy and regulation;
- standardisation of energy contracts; and
- standardisation of electronic transaction data.

2.1 Standardisation

At the heart of EFET's goal of creating a single, liquid European energy market lies one of its key challenges: the harmonisation and standardisation of Europe's many and varied energy trading markets, practices and rules. Part of EFET's work in achieving this goal involves the standardisation of contracts, business processes and electronic data exchange.

(a) Standardised contracts

One of EFET's key accomplishments has been the development and production of standardised contracts, particularly derivatives contracts, which are generally accepted by market participants to be the industry standard.

EFET produced its first standard electricity contract at the end of 1999 and the standard trading contract for gas was completed in 2002. Like the ISDA documentation discussed in other chapters of this book, these standard contracts are largely market standard-form documents that can be customised through their corresponding annexes and appendices.

Section 3 below discusses EFET's standardised documentation in further detail.

(b)   Business processes and data exchange standardisation

EFET began developing standards for electronic data exchange in 2001. This aspect of standardisation has been highlighted as one of the main areas of focus for the future, mitigating operational risk and providing significant cost savings. EFET's work in this area is to be coordinated predominantly by EFETnet.[2]

EFETnet is a software platform developed by and for EFET to facilitate energy trading and is used by energy companies, banks and brokers throughout Europe. EFETnet provides an infrastructure for traders to exchange electronic data. It operates on a cost-sharing basis and is intended to realise and deliver the benefits of electronic data exchange standardisation developed by EFET.

Electronic deal confirmation matching (eCM) has been earmarked by EFET as a key business process for developing standards for electronic data exchange. Implementing EFET's standards for eCM and ensuring compliance with EFETnet software was EFETnet's initial task; now, following a pilot phase, energy traders can use EFETnet for fully automated deal confirmation matching.

Business processes and data exchange standardisation are discussed in further detail in section 3.8 below.

2.2   Policy and regulation

One of EFET's core activities is "advocating policies and regulatory measures which allow electricity and gas trading to develop freely in parallel, and which minimise obstacles to trading in related instruments and products, including futures and forwards, other derivatives, emission allowances and 'green' certificates".[3]

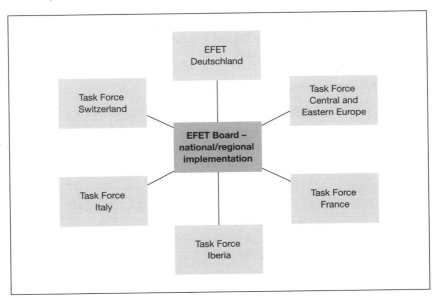

---

2   See www.efetnet.org.
3   EFET Statement of Activities, www.efet.org/default.aspx?page=6663.

The scope of EFET's work goes beyond European-wide regulatory and policy issues. Over the past 10 years, EFET has focused on issues at a regional or national level, as well as particular geographical markets. Indeed, at a very early stage, EFET's members recognised that certain geographical areas would be critical to the development of a proper European energy market. The result of this vision was the establishment of national taskforces in 2000 in both France and Germany, for electricity and gas respectively. Since then, further taskforces have been set up, including a dedicated taskforce for Central and Eastern Europe.

In promoting policies and regulatory measures, EFET has published a number of position papers setting out its views on current issues in the European energy market. These are available on the EFET website (www.efet.org).

The position papers, together with other publications issued by EFET (presentations, discussions, analyses and letters), are categorised into EFET's principal areas of focus:

- the electricity market;
- the gas market;
- energy liberalisation;
- renewable energy and emissions; and
- financial regulation.

Key areas of European energy policy and regulation in which EFET will continue to support and push for progress are market integration and regulatory harmonisation. Further developments in the transparency of information and liquidity of the energy markets, together with the resolution of difficulties in cross-border access, also feature high on the agenda. A significant recent development has been the establishment of the EU Emissions Trading Scheme, an initiative which EFET will continue to advocate.

3. Documentation platform

3.1 Gas

What binds us together is our shared goal of establishing robust and liquid gas trading throughout Europe. We never forget that competition can only occur if there are competitors. A substantive gas market needs gas traders as much as companies need the market to monetise their gas assets, balance their portfolios or manage price risk.

Colin Lyle, chair of EFET's Gas Committee[4]

Growth of the European gas market has trailed behind that of electricity. Monopolisation, cross-border issues and a lack of competition and information have prevented the development of an efficient and liquid wholesale gas trading market. One of EFET's primary goals is to eradicate these problems, which continue to plague the European gas market.

---

4   EFET website, EFET booklet – *The Past and Future of European Energy Trading:* www.efet.org/.

(a) **Standard documentation**

EFET's derivatives documentation platform operates in a similar manner to ISDA documentation. EFET utilises a primary platform of general agreements which operate in a similar manner to ISDA master agreements. These general agreements are then amended, modified or supplemented through separate election sheets and/or appendices, just as one would amend an ISDA master agreement through an ISDA schedule. This primary platform is used by the relevant parties for all power and/or gas transactions.

EFET's secondary platform consists of a confirmation under which each individual transaction is documented. Each confirmation supplements and forms part of the relevant general agreement; in addition, specific definitions are incorporated by reference into each general agreement. In this way, EFET's documentation encompasses the 'single agreement' concept utilised by ISDA. Parties may further amend the terms of the general agreement by making various elections on a separate election sheet, which allows individual transactions to be customised.

(b) **EFET General Agreement (Gas)**

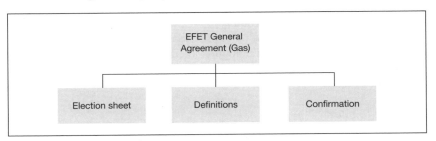

EFET's members introduced the EFET General Agreement Concerning the Delivery and Acceptance of Natural Gas in 2002 as the first standard trading contract for gas. The expanse of EFET's gas documentation has since grown significantly and now includes a number of country- and hub-specific appendices.

The latest version of the General Agreement (Gas) (Version 2.0(a)) was released on May 11 2007 and was drafted with a range of European civil law systems and English law envisaged. It has two governing law options – English and German – although the default choice of law is English. Other laws may be selected in the accompanying election sheet.

Together with its annexes and election sheet, the General Agreement (Gas) operates to govern all individual transactions entered into by the parties for the purchase, sale, delivery and acceptance of natural gas (each such transaction being an 'individual contract').

The General Agreement (Gas) is split into 23 sections and sets out standard provisions which are incorporated by reference into each individual contract, forming integral terms:

- subject of the agreement (Section 1);
- definitions and construction (Section 2);

- concluding and conforming individual contracts (Section 3);
- primary obligations for the delivery and acceptance of and payment for natural gas (Section 4);
- primary obligations for options (Section 5);
- delivery, measurement, transportation and risk (Section 6);
- non-performance due to *force majeure* (Section 7);
- remedies for failure to deliver or accept the contract quantity (Section 8);
- suspension of delivery or acceptance (Section 9);
- term and termination rights (Section 10);
- calculation of termination amount (Section 11);
- limitation of liability (Section 12);
- invoicing and payment (Section 13);
- value added tax (VAT) and other taxes (Section 14);
- floating prices and fall-back procedure for market disruption (Section 15);
- guarantees and credit support (Section 16);
- performance assurance (Section 17);
- provisions of financial statements and tangible net worth (Section 18);
- assignment (Section 19);
- confidentiality (Section 20);
- representations and warranties (Section 21);
- governing law and arbitration (Section 22); and
- miscellaneous (eg, notices and communications, amendments, third-party rights) (Section 23).

(i)   *Election sheet*
The parties can customise the standard provisions of the General Agreement (Gas) by making certain elections on the annexed election sheet. Elections made apply to each individual contract and override any contradictory provisions in the body of the General Agreement (Gas). The election sheet also allows for additional provisions not addressed in the General Agreement (Gas) to be specified.

(ii)   *Annexes*
Annexed to the General Agreement (Gas) are different forms of confirmation which record and confirm the specific terms of individual contracts. There are four different types of confirmation:
- fixed price (Annex 2A);
- floating price (Annex 2B);
- call option (Annex 2C); and
- put option (Annex 2D).

Each confirmation enables the parties to specify terms in relation to pricing, quantities and mechanics of delivery. The option confirmations also include details of the option itself – namely, particulars in relation to exercise and premium. The type of confirmation utilised by the parties will be determined by the characteristics of the transaction.

Each confirmation supplements and forms part of the General Agreement (Gas). In the event of any inconsistency between the terms of an individual contract and the General Agreement (Gas), the terms of the individual contract will prevail.

(iii)   *Definitions*
Definitions used in the General Agreement (Gas) are set out in Annex 1. These definitions are standard and are incorporated into both the General Agreement (Gas) and each individual contract.

(iv)   *Appendices*
EFET has produced a number of country-specific appendices which allow parties to customise the General Agreement (Gas) for the purposes of trading in one of the applicable countries or at one of the applicable gas hubs. A summary of each appendix is set out below.

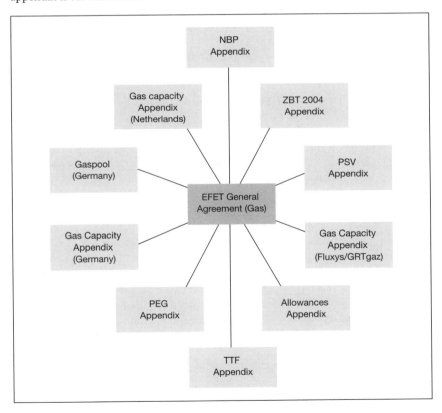

Allowances Appendix: The Allowances Appendix was produced by EFET to cater for emissions trading, allowing participants of European emission trading schemes to buy, sell or transfer emission allowances. The Allowances Appendix modifies, supplements and amends certain provisions of the General Agreement (Gas) in order to facilitate the trading of 'allowances'. The latest version of the Allowances Appendix (Version 2.0) was released on July 17 2008.

Despite replacing many provisions of the General Agreement (Gas) in their entirety, the Allowances Appendix operates in a similar manner to the General Agreement (Gas), acting as an 'umbrella' agreement, while individual 'allowance transactions' are evidenced by separate confirmations.

The Allowances Appendix is split into two parts. Part I sets out the general terms, which mirror the 23 sections set out in the General Agreement (Gas), and Part II incorporates the election sheet and additional provisions.

Definitions are annexed to the Allowances Appendix at Annex 1. Annex 2A contains the form of confirmation of allowance transactions (comprising, among other terms, the delivery schedule and any special terms and conditions).

Gaspool Appendix: Prior to the establishment of the Gaspool virtual trading point, virtual trading points for high-calorific-value gas ('H gas') were separately operated by:

- Gasunie Deutschland Transport Services GmbH (GDTS) (in its joint market area with DONG Energy Pipelines GmbH and StatoilHydro Deutschland GmbH); and
- ONTRAS-VNG Gastransport GmbH and WINGAS Transport GmbH & Co KG in their respective market areas.

The GDTS virtual trading points were operated by BEB Transport GmbH & Co KG. As such, Version 1.0 of the Gaspool Appendix was called the BEB Appendix.

EFET issued the BEB Appendix on September 28 2007. When GDTS took over operations of the high and low calorific value natural gas transportation networks of BEB Transport, EFET published a new Version 2.0 of the BEB Appendix on December 31 2008, which was renamed the Gasunie Deutschland Appendix (GUD Appendix).

EFET has since published a draft letter for parties that are using the GUD Appendix. This letter provides that, as of October 1 2009, the H gas transportation system of GDTS forms part of the joint market area 'GASPOOL'. GASPOOL has been set up by various market area network operators as a joint market area and single virtual trading point, and is run by GASPOOL Balancing Services GmbH ('Gaspool').

Together with the draft letter, EFET has published Version 1.0 of the Gaspool Appendix. This replaces the GUD Appendix for all individual contracts for delivery at the Gaspool virtual trading point. Parties using the GUD Appendix can transfer all existing GUD transactions for natural gas, or existing individual contracts at the ONTRAS and WINGAS virtual trading points, onto Gaspool Appendix terms by signing up to the letter.

The Gaspool Appendix incorporates by reference Gaspool's network access conditions. It modifies, amends and supplements certain provisions of the General Agreement (Gas) and governs all individual contracts concerning the delivery and acceptance of natural gas at the Gaspool virtual trading point. Parties can specify additional provisions and any amendments to the Gaspool Appendix. Forms of confirmation are set out in Annex 2. These mirror the four forms of confirmation set out in the General Agreement (Gas), covering fixed-price transactions, floating-price transactions, call options and put options.

Gas Capacity Appendix (Germany): The Gas Capacity Appendix (Germany) was published for use solely in connection with the Gas Regional Initiative (GRI) Day Ahead Pilot – the day-ahead capacity trading pilot for secondary capacity on the interconnection points between Oude Statenzijl, Bunde and Ellund. Version 1.0 of this appendix was released on May 20 2008 and developed specifically in accordance with the rules of a number of transmission system operators (TSOs): WINGAS Transport GmbH & Co KG, E.ON Gastransport AG & Co KG, DONG Energy Pipelines GmbH and BEB Transport GmbH.

This appendix is intended to modify certain provisions of the General Agreement (Gas) to facilitate the purchase, sale and transfer of gas capacity by the parties in connection with the GRI Day Ahead Pilot. The general terms of the Gas Capacity Appendix (Germany) are set out in Part I, with the election sheet and additional provisions/amendments sheet at Part II. Defined terms are included at Annex 1 and the form of confirmation for individual transactions concluded under this appendix is attached as Annex 2(A).

Gas Capacity Appendix (Fluxys/GRTgaz) (France/Belgium): EFET released the Gas Capacity Appendix (Fluxys/GRTgaz) (Version 1.0) on December 31 2008. This appendix covers the secondary gas market on the Belgian and French transmission systems and was developed in conjunction with the rules of Fluxys NV/SA (the TSO of Belgium) and the rules of GRTgaz (one of the French TSOs). The appendix was also developed in accordance with the rules of Capsquare. Capsquare is the capacity platform operator and is a joint initiative between Fluxys and GRTgaz to foster liquidity in the secondary market for capacity in their networks. The appendix incorporates the risk and credit management provisions for capacity products, as available on the Capsquare platform, and provides for documentary cover of capacity trades in general.[5]

This appendix is set out in a similar manner to the Allowances Appendix, with the general terms set out in Part I and the election sheet and additional provisions/amendments in Part II. Definitions are then set out at Annex 1 and the form of confirmation for gas capacity transactions at Annex 2(A). This confirmation provides particulars of each gas capacity transaction, including the relevant TSO, gas capacity details and the nature of the gas capacity transaction.

Gas Capacity appendix (Netherlands): The Gas Capacity Appendix (Netherlands) (Version 1.0) was introduced by EFET on December 7 2007. It was developed in line with the rules of Gas Transport Services BV (the TSO of the Netherlands), and is used in relation to individual contracts concerning the transfer and acceptance of gas capacity in the Netherlands. The appendix is laid out in the same format as the Gas Capacity Appendix (Germany).

PEG Appendix (France): Version 2.0 of the PEG Appendix (France) was released by EFET on March 31 2008. This appendix covers the delivery and acceptance of natural gas on the French gas network. 'PEG' means a *'point d'échange de gaz'*, 'title transfer point' or 'gas exchange point', as defined in the relevant transportation contract. The 'transportation contract' is the contract concluded between a shipper and the relevant network operator, being either GRTgaz or TIGF, for access to the related delivery point.

---

5   Capsquare website: www.capsquare.eu/.

The PEG Appendix is used to govern individual contracts entered into in relation to the delivery and acceptance of natural gas at a 'PEG delivery point'. The 'PEG delivery point' is each of the title transfer points in the main network of either GRTgaz or TIGF.

Any and all future PEG transactions are automatically subject to the General Agreement (Gas), as amended by the PEG Appendix, unless the terms of the particular PEG transaction state otherwise.

Certain defined terms used in the PEG Appendix are set out in Annex 1. The PEG Appendix also incorporates by reference definitions (or their French translations) used in the relevant transportation contract published by either GRTgaz or TIGF. Four forms of confirmation are laid out at Annex 2, which mirror the types of confirmation annexed to the General Agreement (Gas).

PSV Appendix (Italy): EFET prepared the PSV Appendix (Italy) together with *Associazone Italiana di Grossisti di Energia e Trader* (AIGET), the Italian association of energy traders. This appendix is dual language (Italian and English) and provides for the English version to prevail in cases of dispute. At the time of preparation, EFET and AIGET hoped that the "dual language translations will foster the increased take-up of these standard contracts by the Italian market players in energy trading".[6]

Version 1.0 of the PSV Appendix was introduced in January 2007 and was drafted in cooperation with Italian and foreign traders. It covers all individual contracts which deal with the delivery and acceptance of gas at Punto di Scambio Virtuale (PSV), being the virtual trading point established by the relevant network operator, Snam Rete Gas SpA (SRG), and located between the entry and exit points of the national transportation network. It also incorporates aspects of the PSV manual and the Italian gas market in general into the mechanics of the General Agreement (Gas).

Any and all future PSV transactions are automatically subject to the General Agreement (Gas), as amended by the PSV Appendix, unless the terms of the particular PSV transaction state otherwise. Annex 2 of the PSV Appendix sets out forms of confirmation for PSV transactions, produced in both Italian and English.

NBP Appendix: The NBP Appendix (Version 1.0) was introduced by EFET in December 2006. This appendix applies to all individual contracts entered into for the delivery and acceptance of natural gas at the National Balancing Point (NBP) in the United Kingdom. The NBP is a virtual trading location for the sale and purchase of UK natural gas. It is the most liquid gas trading point in Europe and is also the pricing and delivery point for the InterContinental Exchange natural-gas futures contract.

Certain terms and provisions of the Short Term Flat NBP Trading Terms & Conditions 1997 ('NBP Terms') are incorporated by reference into the NBP Appendix. Part I of the NBP Appendix sets out the general terms, which amend and supplement the General Agreement (Gas). Elections to customise the NBP Appendix are set out in Part II. The forms of confirmation for NBP contracts are annexed at Annex 1 and follow the same format as the PSV and PEG Appendices.

Any and all future NBP contracts are automatically subject to the General Agreement (Gas), as amended by the NBP Appendix, unless the terms of the

---

6   EFET Press Release 23/07, "A new EFET documentation for the Italian energy market".

particular NBP contract state otherwise.

TTF Appendix (Netherlands): Not unlike the NBP, the Title Transfer Facility (TTF) is a virtual trading point for natural gas in the Netherlands. It was established by NV Nederlandse Gasunie in 2003 and permits gas trading within the Dutch gas network. The TTF is operated by Gas Transport Services BV (GTS) and offers parties the ability to transfer gas already in the GTS system to another market player.

The TTF "serves to promote gas trading ... and can serve as a virtual entry point in the portfolio of a shipper or trader who buys gas on TTF, or as a virtual exit point in the portfolio of a shipper or trader who sells gas on TTF".[7]

The TTF Appendix (Version 2.0) was introduced in July 2006. It governs all individual contracts which relate to the delivery and acceptance of gas at the TTF and is laid out in the same way as the NBP Appendix. In addition to the defined terms at Annex 1, the Transmission Service Conditions (which are published by GTS) are integrated into the TTF Appendix and provide an extra layer of definitions where terms are not defined in the appendix itself or in the General Agreement (Gas).

Any and all future TTF transactions are automatically subject to the General Agreement (Gas), as amended by the TTF Appendix, unless the terms of the particular TTF transaction state otherwise.

ZBT 2004 Appendix (Netherlands): Version 1.0 of the ZBT 2004 Appendix was released in June 2006. This appendix governs all individual contracts entered into for the delivery and acceptance of gas (and options on such delivery and acceptance) at the Zeebrugge Hub. The Zeebrugge Hub is operated by Huberator SA, a subsidiary of Fluxys SA, and is the leading international short-term gas market in continental Europe.[8]

As with the NBP Appendix, certain additional terms and provisions are incorporated by reference into the ZBT Appendix – being the 2004 release of the Zeebrugge Hub Natural Gas Trading Terms and Conditions ('ZBT Terms'), together with the ZBT Option Transactions Annex, which amends, supplements and forms part of the ZBT Terms. Definitions contained in the relevant Hub Services Agreement are also incorporated into the ZBT Appendix by reference. The ZBT Terms and the Option Transactions Annex are standard trading agreements which aim to facilitate trading and liquidity at the Zeebrugge Hub.

Any and all future ZBT transactions are automatically subject to the General Agreement (Gas), as amended by the ZBT Appendix, unless the terms of such ZBT transactions state otherwise.

Discrepancies between the General Agreement (Gas), relevant appendices and individual contracts: If there is a discrepancy between the General Agreement (Gas) and the relevant appendix used to supplement and amend its terms, the relevant appendix will prevail in relation to all individual contracts governed by that appendix. In the event that the terms of the individual contract conflict with the relevant appendix and/or the General Agreement (Gas), the terms of the individual contract will prevail.

---

7   Gas Transport Services BV website: www.gastransportservices.com/shippers/gts/ttf_gas_exchange/.
8   Huberator website: www.huberator.com/.

(v)   Gas Committee

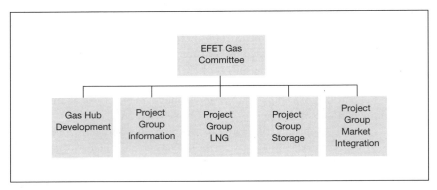

EFET's Gas Committee "foresees the development of transparent and liquid traded gas markets throughout Europe. To this end, the Committee focuses on the improvement of the interconnection and liquidity across Europe's widely varying national gas markets".[9] Members of the Gas Committee liaise with interested parties such as regulators and TSOs on an ongoing basis in relation to developments within the European gas market.

The Gas Committee is assisted by five sub-groups, each of which is responsible for managing one of the main barriers to liquid gas-trading markets:

- Gas Hub Development;
- Project Group LNG;
- Project Group Market Integration;
- Project Group Information; and
- Project Group Storage.

Since its establishment, the Gas Committee has prepared and released a wide range of position papers which set out EFET members' stance on policy and regulatory issues within the European energy markets. Such opinions have subsequently been incorporated into various European directives. Copies of all position papers issued by the Gas Committee are available on EFET's website.

3.2   Electricity

EFET is closest to its goals of openness and transparency in relation to electricity trading. Since its establishment in 1999, EFET has been instrumental in developing a framework in which wholesale electricity is transacted inside the European Union.

Yet despite dramatic progress made over the last decade, the creation of a single European energy electricity market is still a distant goal. Many challenges lie ahead in terms of opening up European borders and breaking down barriers to entry, which EFET remains committed to achieving.

---

9   EFET website, EFET Organisation, Gas Committee: www.efet.org/Default.aspx?page=6871.

(a) *EFET General Agreement (Power)*

The EFET General Agreement Concerning the Delivery and Acceptance of Electricity was introduced by EFET's members to govern and facilitate the trading of electricity across Europe. The current version (Version 2.1(a)) was introduced on September 21 2007 to bring the General Agreement (Power) into line with the General Agreement (Gas), by including a new Section 14 ("VAT and Taxes").

The General Agreement (Power) is structured in the same way as the General Agreement (Gas), with the standard provisions of the master agreement being amended and supplemented by the relevant annexes and election sheet in order to govern all individual contracts entered into for the purchase, sale, delivery and acceptance of electricity.

The General Agreement (Power) is split into 23 sections and the provisions covered mirror those set out in the General Agreement (Gas). Relevant definitions can be found at Annex 1. As per the General Agreement (Gas), certain elections can be made on the annexed election sheet to customise standard provisions and specific terms of individual contracts are documented through entry into a form of confirmation. Parties may also enter into an allowances appendix to facilitate the purchase, sale and transfer of allowances.

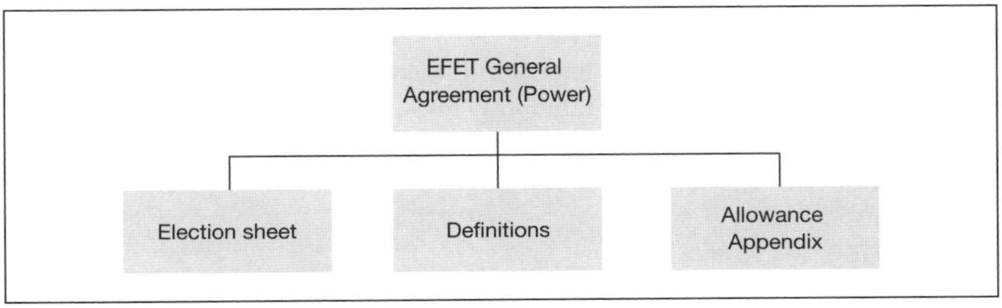

(b) *Electricity Committee*

EFET established the Electricity Committee shortly after its formation in 1999 to operate as a central voice for the electricity trading community. The Electricity Committee's mission is to identify obstacles to electricity trading throughout Europe and to propose solutions. The Electricity Committee has come to hold an important role in ensuring a minimum set of transparency rules and representing the interests of EFET's members. Driven by the practical views and opinions of traders, it exerts influence over EU law makers and regulators, operating as a successful lobby and policy crew. Several of its key position papers have helped to shape the reform agenda of the European Commission and the individual EU member states.

3.3 Coal

(a) *globalCOAL*

"globalCOAL is the world's leading online coal trading platform, providing a fast, effective and transparent route to the international physical and financial coal markets."[10] It was founded by leading members of the world coal industry as an online trading platform in order to promote the development of international coal markets and to enhance the efficient trading of coal products. Its mission has been to provide fast, anonymous and open access to physical and financial coal markets and to facilitate the trading of standardised coal contracts between market participants.

globalCOAL has achieved its mission through a number of innovations, including the creation of a range of standardised quality specifications, which have been embedded in its Standard Coal Trading Agreement (SCoTA®). SCoTA has been adopted by EFET's members and is widely established as the contract of choice for the sale and purchase of coal across global markets.

(b) **SCoTA**

SCoTA was introduced by globalCOAL in May 2001 as a means of altering the way that business is conducted in the coal market by enabling the creation of tradable standard products.

Acting as a master agreement, SCoTA provides a consolidated set of accepted terms and conditions and a range of coal quality specifications and delivery points for international coal sales and purchases. Although it can be used offline in bilateral and brokered deals, SCoTA also governs each and every transaction executed on the globalCOAL online trading platform.

In order to ensure that it remains relevant and effective, and captures new market opportunities, SCoTA is continuously revised and enhanced by globalCOAL working in collaboration with its market members in order to ensure that it responds to market developments. The latest version, SCoTA v7, was released in June 2009.

(c) ***Coal Credit Annex***

EFET's members introduced the Coal Credit Annex (CCA) to SCoTA as a means of amending and supplementing the terms of SCoTA and all transactions entered into pursuant to SCoTA to provide for and enhance credit support. The CCA is intended to have retrospective effect such that all SCoTA transactions entered into by the relevant parties both prior to and as from the specified 'Coal Credit Annex effective date' become subject to the terms and conditions of SCoTA, as modified by the CCA.

The CCA is divided into four parts. Part I sets out general provisions and specifies prevailing terms in the event of any inconsistency. As such, if there is any inconsistency between SCoTA and the CCA, the CCA will prevail. In the event of any inconsistency between the CCA and the terms of an individual transaction, the terms of the individual transaction will prevail for the purposes of that transaction only.

Part II sets out general amendments to the following clauses of SCoTA:
- definitions (Clause 1) (including amendments to the definitions of 'event of default', 'specified transaction', 'commodity', 'insolvency event', 'material adverse change' and various other definitions);
- obligations (Clause 3);

---

10   Mission statement on globalCOAL's official website: www.globalcoal.com/home.

- performance assurance and credit (Clause 14);
- failure to deliver or take delivery (Clause 15);
- remedies in respect of an event of default (Clause 16);
- assignment/novation (Clause 19); and
- governing law (Clause 27).

Part III allows for the customisation of the general amendments set out in Part II, enabling parties to make certain elections to alter further the terms and scope of application of SCoTA. Part IV allows for any additional amendments to be specified.

(d)   ***globalCOAL Product Licensing Agreement***
Access to the use of globalCOAL's documentation in bilateral coal sale-and-purchase transactions requires companies to become 'licensed users' by signing the globalCOAL Product Licensing Agreement (PLA).

The PLA grants licensed users the right to use certain products, indices and standards developed by globalCOAL for the purposes of entering into or arranging transactions for the trading of coal. Licensed users must comply with the restrictions set out in the PLA in relation to the use of globalCOAL's products and trademarks and are prohibited from granting sub-licences. Licensed users must enter into transactions for the sale or purchase of coal only with third parties licensed on the same terms.

globalCOAL currently has more than 350 licensed users. globalCOAL is entitled to terminate a licence granted pursuant to the PLA at any time upon one week's prior written notice or immediately upon any breach of the terms of the PLA. In the event of termination, the licensed user must immediately cease the use of globalCOAL products and trademarks.

3.4   Cross-Product Master Agreement
In 2003 EFET partnered with the International Energy Credit Association (IECA) to establish standardised bilateral netting arrangements between counterparties in the European energy markets. The selected approach was to adopt the existing Cross-Product Master Agreement (CPMA) prepared by the Bond Market Association (published in February 2000) and to adapt its standard terms by way of an accompanying schedule.

In developing the Schedule, EFET and the IECA were concerned to limit the alteration of the terms of the underlying agreements subject to the CPMA and to uphold a general framework while accommodating a range of requirements of various market participants.

(a)   ***Structure***
The Schedule is split into two modules – an elective module (Division 1) and an amending module (Division 2). Division 1 is split into the following parts, allowing for amendments to be made to the corresponding sections under the CPMA:
- principal agreements, excluded agreements and uncovered transactions (Part I, which deals with the scope of the CPMA and allows parties to select which

contractual relations should be covered (termed 'principal agreements') and which are to be excluded);

- events excluded from the definition of 'close-out event' (Part II, which requires parties to define the triggers for operation of the CPMA);
- additional representations (Part III);
- governing law (Part IV);
- assignment (Part VII);
- optional provisions (Part VIII); and
- credit support (Part IX).

Division 2 allows for further amendments to be made to simplify and improve the CPMA from a European commodities perspective.

Annex A to the CPMA contains a simple form of NBP master agreement which amends the NBP Terms to include provisions in relation to close-out netting. This avoids the need for parties to include NBP contracts under the scope of the CPMA.

Annex B contains a form of cross-product Credit Support Annex (CSA), a description of which is set out next.

3.5   Credit Support Annex

EFET's CSA documents the terms on which parties to the General Agreement (Gas) and/or General Agreement (Power), and individual contracts entered into pursuant thereto, agree to provide one another with credit support as collateral for outstanding obligations. The CSA is structured similarly to the ISDA Credit Support Annex.

The CSA is spilt into 14 sections, as follows:

- definitions and interpretations (Section 1);
- valuation agent and determination of valuations (Section 2);
- credit support obligations (Section 3);
- return of eligible credit support (Section 4);
- minimum transfer, thresholds and independent amounts (Section 5);
- exchange of eligible credit support (Section 6);
- transfer of title, representations and no security interest (Section 7);
- dispute resolution (Section 8);
- interest income on cash (Section 9);
- material reason (Section 10);
- termination of the agreement (Section 11);
- expenses (Section 12);
- bank accounts (Section 13); and
- specifications (Section 14).

Appendix 1 to the CSA sets out defined terms. Section 14 (Specifications) allows for the parties to make certain elections/amendments in relation to various of the defined terms set out in Appendix 1, including (but not limited to): 'threshold amount', 'minimum transfer amount', 'valuation time', 'eligible currency' and 'independent amount'.

3.6   EFET VAT Agreement

EFET's members introduced the VAT Agreement – Change in Place of Supply of Electricity/Natural Gas – Value Added Tax in November 2005, as a means of modifying EFET's gas and electricity master agreements and the individual contracts entered into to include additional representations in relation to VAT. Such additional representations were introduced for the purposes of Articles 8(1)(d) and (e) of the EU Turnover Tax Directive (77/388/ECC) – the intention being to establish a uniform basis of VAT assessment across the European Union.

(a)   Scope of application

The front page of the VAT Agreement allows for the parties to elect the scope of its application. The parties choose a 'VAT Agreement effective date', from which the additional representations contained in the VAT Agreement are to take effect. Such representations are deemed to be repeated each time the parties enter into, schedule, deliver, receive and/or settle any individual contract, agreement, transaction or trade pursuant to the specified master agreements at any time thereafter.

In addition, parties may elect for the provisions of the VAT Agreement to apply to any/all agreements, individual contracts, trades or transactions entered into between the parties that incorporate by reference the ZBT Terms or the NBP Terms.

(b)   Structure

The VAT Agreement is arranged into six sections, as follows:

- effect of the VAT Agreement (Section 1);
- additional VAT representations (Section 2);
- covenant and undertaking with respect to VAT representations (Section 3);
- misrepresentations (Section 4);
- indemnification for VAT misrepresentations (Section 5); and
- counterparts (Section 6).

The VAT representations set out in Section 2 are divided into 'Party A representations' and 'Party B representations', and relate to:

- the place of supply of the natural gas/electricity delivered under the specified master agreement(s); and
- the establishment(s) to which the supply of such natural gas/electricity is made, including VAT number(s) of such establishment(s).

Each party covenants, pursuant to Section 3, to notify the other party of any change in the accuracy of the representations set out in Section 2 within 20 business days of such change. The parties elect for one of two provisions under Section 4 to apply in the event that any representation proves to have been incorrect or misleading in any material respect when made or repeated.

(c)   VAT Annex

The VAT Annex contains the same provisions as the VAT Agreement. However, it will only form part of the master agreement(s) to which it is physically annexed at the time of execution. The VAT Annex can therefore be used as a more selective way of limiting the scope of the additional VAT representations.

3.7 Legal opinions

To ensure that EFET's standard documentation is legally enforceable in European legal systems, EFET has commissioned and made available to its members legal opinions in a number of European countries. These opinions cover insolvency, close-out netting and other key issues relating to enforcement of the EFET master agreements.

EFET's members can order the required legal opinion(s) via an order form on the EFET website.[11] The order form sets out a list of European countries, alongside the relevant EFET master agreement and the cost of an update for each country and each agreement. Members can choose a combined legal opinion on more than one EFET master agreement. The order form also specifies the law firm responsible for producing the legal opinion(s).

As part of its future focus, EFET's Legal Committee intends to increase the number of jurisdictions for which it has obtained legal opinions and perhaps to extend the scope of the opinions to address enhancements to the corresponding master agreements.

3.8 EFET Standards

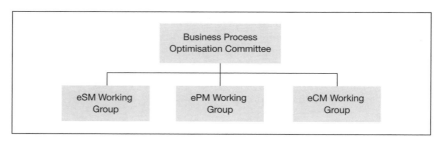

EFET's Back Office Group was formed in 2003 and "focuses on the standardisation of data exchanges and industry processes"[12] to improve efficiency in the European energy trading market. Its activities are performed by specialist project workgroups which are overseen by the Business Process Optimisation Committee. The project workgroups are:

- the Payment Netting Working Group;
- the Electronic Position Matching (ePM) Working Group;
- the eCM Working Group; and
- the Benchmarking Working Group.

---

11   Legal opinion order form 2009, available at www.efet.org/Standardisation/Legal_Opinions_4844.aspx ?urlID2r=24.

12   EFET website, EFET Organisation, Back Office Group: www.efet.org/Default.aspx?page=6869.

These project workgroups have been at the forefront of a number of EFET projects that aim to enhance process efficiency and reduce cost and operational risk in the energy trading environment. The industry itself does not have 'standard' electronic communication standards and hence industry participants have difficulty integrating their business processes. EFET identified the solution to this problem as the establishment of a set of common electronic communication standards which would be adopted by individual organisations: the so-called 'EFET Standards'. It identified those aspects of the energy trading industry in need of standardisation as trade confirmations, scheduling and logistics, clearing and settlement, and quotes.

Defining the EFET Standards is the responsibility of the EFET project workgroups. Once defined, these standards are of general application and apply to all electronic messages exchanged between parties in the energy trading industry. EFET has taken a prioritised approach to the development of the EFET Standards. The first stage of the standardisation process was entrusted to the eCM Working Group. Subsequent phases followed suit and extended the coverage of the EFET Standards to other business processes. EFET's strategy is to develop a set of global standards covering the complete business requirements of traders. The eCM project is an important initial step towards this overall goal.

(a)   eCM

As mentioned above, the eCM Working Group was tasked with dealing with the first phase of standardisation. Its aim was to define a 'standard electronic confirmation process' – that is, to develop a set of electronic communication standards for the exchange and validation of electronic trade confirmations for power and gas. This project was driven by the urgent need for the Back Office Group to automate manual confirmation processes.

The process of automated trade confirmation enables parties to carry out confirmation matching electronically instead of by manual transfer and is seen as a major improvement on the fax-based process. It also helps to eradicate a number of issues with the fax confirmation process, particularly the reduction in cost and operational risk linked to manual processing and complexity in the confirmation matching process.

The eCM standards are incorporated into a single document with a number of chapters and sections. EFET has released a number of versions of the eCM standards, each a revision of the previous version. The latest, Version 3.3, was published in December 2007 to include financial instruments.

(b)   ePM

The ePM initiative builds on the work of the eCM project and extends coverage of EFET's standards into an additional process area. This project covers the business process concerning the exchange and comparison of electronic documents that describe counterparty data. The ePM project was driven by the need for the Back Office Group to improve the quality of position data within counterparty organisations for the overall benefit of each company and the broader industry.

An accurate record of an individual organisation's position in relation to each of its counterparties is an important aspect of any commodity trading business. However, prior to the ePM project there was no existing process for position matching between counterparties which could be used as a foundation for developing a uniform process capable of electronic automation. Position matching was done manually, leading to operational risk and innumerable difficulties as a result of a lack of general agreement between individual organisations as to standard comparative data. As such, the ePM project is not really streamlining an existing process, but actually creating a new process which will add value to the energy trading industry. It will do this by improving each organisation's awareness and accuracy of its overall position.

As with the eCM project, the documentation for electronic position matching is a single document released under the control of the joint EFET Back Office Group on behalf of the EFET Board. Each chapter within the document is controlled by the ePM Working Group and is subject to revision. The latest version of the ePM Standards is Version 1.1, which was issued in December 2007.

(c)   **eSM**

The electronic settlement management (eSM) project deals with the business process concerning the exchange and comparison of electronic documents that describe counterparty settlement data. Similarly to the ePM initiative, this project was driven by the need for the Back Office Group to improve the quality of settlement data within counterparty organisations. The objective of the project was to define a 'standard electronic settlement matching process' to eradicate some of the problems with the paper-based settlement process then used within the energy/commodity trading environment.

Settlement terms are already highly standardised because of the existence of only a few master agreements under which most trades are settled, but the settlement process itself is difficult to automate. This is a result of a lack of standardisation between industry participants as to how they implement their back office procedures. Further, two separate settlement processes exist for financial and physical deals, which only adds to the complexity. As such, developing a single defined global process for managing both types of settlement, together with a set of standardised documents, would increase efficiency and reduce operational risk.

The eSM project workgroup is sponsored by the EFET Board and controlled by the Back Office Group. It joined forces with the LEAP Settlement Group,[13] which also has an interest in standardising the settlement process. The final draft of these standards was released in July 2009.

4.   Conclusion

We foresee energy markets throughout Europe, in which traders efficiently intermediate in the value chain on the basis of clear wholesale price signals, thereby optimising supply and demand and enhancing security of supply, to the overall long term benefit of economy and of society.[14]

---

13   www.energyleap.org/.

Well-functioning wholesale markets in electricity and gas are essential. As well as providing benefits to the consumer of increased competition and choice, these markets help to optimise supply and demand and uphold EU competitiveness in a global context. Yet despite some significant progress in Europe's electricity markets, numerous obstacles have hindered development of the gas market. One of EFET's major achievements has been the introduction of its standardised documentation platform. These contracts, now widely accepted by market participants as the industry standard, facilitate energy trading throughout Europe. This aids the development of the open and liquid wholesale European energy market that EFET so desires.

In order for these markets to continue to develop and integrate effectively, EFET must build on the important work it has done thus far, most notably in energy policy and regulation, energy market design, and contractual and electronic data standardisation.

As Europe's energy markets have developed over the years, so has EFET as an organisation. Its role and scope have grown considerably since its creation in 1999, much of which has helped to make the European energy sector what it is today. Even though there is still a long way to go, EFET is committed to achieving its vision and fulfilling its purpose, in cooperation with other players in the energy industry.

As EFET has aptly stated: "Over the past ten years, EFET has become the voice of energy traders across Europe. In the next decade, with the same dedication and optimism, we will continue our cooperation with all other interested parties and authorities on the way to establishing a truly modern, open, transparent, sustainable and liquid wholesale energy market in Europe."[15]

---

14 EFET's Vision; EFET booklet – *The Past and Future of European Energy Trading*: www.efet.org/.
15 EFET booklet, *A Single European Energy Market? Traders' Fears and Hopes at Ten Years*.

Overview of other documentation platforms for OTC commodity derivatives

Amandeep Kharaud

1. Introduction

In a case of art eating itself, commodity derivatives contracts themselves are commoditised. This is the case with all derivatives: users want standardised and efficient documentation, allowing them to trade quickly while protecting their rights. The situation is more complex with commodity derivatives because of the range of underlying assets and the diverse nature of those interested in them.

In the equity derivatives arena, the underlying assets are shares and share indices. One of the parties to an over-the-counter (OTC) equity derivatives transaction is usually a financial institution, and so the documentation platform provided by the International Swaps and Derivatives Association (ISDA) is dominant.

In the commodity derivatives world the underlying assets could be, for example, coal, bullion, carbon dioxide emissions credits, or freight. End-users trading in coal forwards may be producers with no interest in bullion; glass manufacturers trading in emissions credits may be interested in trading in emissions credits alone. This has led to several industry bodies establishing individual documentation platforms for specific types of commodity derivatives transaction.

Documentation platforms

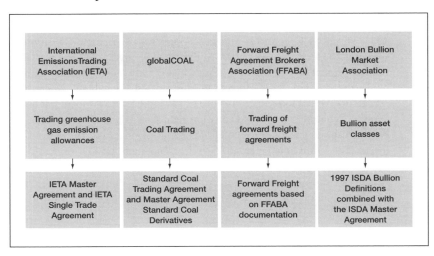

The documentation platforms established by ISDA, the European Federation of Energy Traders (EFET) and the Futures and Options Association are covered in other dedicated chapters in this book. This chapter looks at four other industry bodies – the International Emissions Trading Association (IETA), globalCOAL, the Forward Freight Agreement Brokers Association (FFABA) and the London Bullion Market Association (LBMA) – and the derivatives documentation that they have produced, respectively covering greenhouse gas emission allowances, coal, freight agreements and bullion asset classes.

2. Overview of various other organisations

2.1 International Emissions Trading Association

The IETA was founded in June 1999. The organisation has established a documentation framework for trading greenhouse gas emission allowances. The IETA's members include more than 160 international companies from both Organisation of Economic Cooperation and Development (OECD) and non-OECD countries. Members of the IETA include multinational companies, emitters of greenhouse gas emissions, solution providers, brokers, insurers, financial institutions and law firms. The IETA has partnerships with the World Bank, Eurelectric, the World Business Council for Sustainable Development and the California Climate Action Registry. The association states that it is dedicated to assisting with the objectives that have been compiled under the UN Framework Convention on Climate Change.[1] One of the convention's goals is to work towards greater climate protection through the reduction of greenhouse gas emissions.

The UN Framework Convention on Climate Change acknowledged that human activities are increasing the greenhouse effect and contributing to global warming. The convention agreed an ultimate objective to stabilise greenhouse gas concentrations and was joined almost universally. The convention divided signatory countries into three separate groups: Annex I parties; Annex II parties; and the rest, which have become known as non-Annex I parties.

Annex I parties are those signatory countries which were OECD countries in 1992, as well as 12 countries whose economies were or are in transition (generally speaking, the former Eastern Bloc). Annex II parties are the Annex I parties excluding the transitional parties. The non-Annex I parties are mostly developing nations.

Further substance was added to the convention at later conferences. At the third conference, which took place in Kyoto in 1997, the Kyoto Protocol was adopted. This allowed signatories to achieve emission reduction targets by reducing emissions to below a cap or by using three potential flexible mechanisms: the clean development mechanism, joint implementation and/or emissions trading under cap-and-trade systems. The first two are project-based mechanisms that can generate allowances, which can then be traded along with any other allocated allowances under an emissions trading system. The United States is yet to ratify the protocol.

---

1   For further details see www.ieta.org/ieta/www/pages/index.php?IdSiteTree=1248.

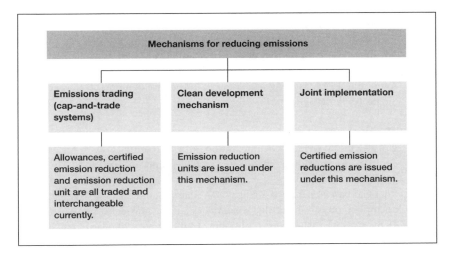

The EU Emissions Trading Scheme is the European Union's compulsory cap-and-trade project for trading carbon dioxide emission allowances. Approximately 12,000 EU industrial installations, which are responsible for almost half of the European Union's carbon dioxide output, were allocated allowances in the scheme's first stage, with that number expanded in the second stage.

Each allowance represents the right to emit one tonne of carbon dioxide and each participating installation must surrender allowances equal to its actual carbon dioxide emissions. If its allocated allowances are insufficient to cover its actual emissions, the affected installation must purchase additional allowances to cover the shortfall from the market. Failure to surrender sufficient allowances to cover emissions incurs a penalty per tonne of carbon dioxide emitted, and the defaulting firm will also be asked to make good the allowances in the following year. If the affected installation has an excess of allowances, perhaps through generating efficiencies, it can sell these into the market for a profit. The scheme aims to reduce carbon dioxide emissions by financially rewarding affected installations that reduce their emissions and penalising those that do not.

These installations can also purchase or source certified emission reductions (emission allowances generated under joint implementation projects), and emission reduction units (emission allowances generated under clean development mechanism projects), and surrender these to help to cover their own actual carbon dioxide emissions. The IETA produces a number of documents that its registered members can access in order to document trades in relation to greenhouse gas allowances and reductions. The IETA documentation is based on the EU scheme which controls the amount of greenhouse gas emissions that are emitted into the atmosphere.

The IETA standard documents relate to only one type of commodity – emission allowances – whereas the ISDA documentation can be used in relation to a variety of commodity products and derivatives, such as equity or credit-based derivatives. Financial institutions which are more accustomed to the ISDA documentation may prefer to use the ISDA documentation rather than the more tailored IETA documents.

Where a party has entered into a number of different transactions with a person, it may wish to take advantage of cross-product netting through the use of the ISDA documentation. Those that do not have an ISDA Master Agreement already in place or do not enter into a large number of derivative transactions would be more likely to use the IETA Master Agreement and, in the case of a one-off transaction, the IETA Single Trade Agreement.

2.2   globalCOAL

globalCOAL provides documentation and a trading system for coal trades, in addition to providing coal-related services and information. The organisation provides documentation for both physical settlement of coal trading and pure financial-based coal trades. globalCOAL has a Standard Coal Trading Agreement to document physically settled coal trades and a Master Agreement Standard Coal Derivatives for cash-settled coal trades. Trading on its Standard Coal System allows a participant to trade with the counterparty that provides the best trade price, as trading is conducted on an anonymous basis; anonymity is retained until the trade has been executed.

globalCOAL has more than 90 registered members, including a number of financial institutions and companies that are located worldwide. In addition, coal news and calculation tools are provided in its service to members. In order to become a member or globalCOAL, a usage agreement must be signed and the annual fee can range from $1,000 to $6,000, depending on the type of membership. In addition, a commission of between 2.5% and 10% is payable (a market-maker membership is negotiated in relation to the fee and commission that is payable).

2.3   Forward Freight Agreement Brokers Association

The FFABA is an independent organisation of Baltic Exchange broker members and was founded in 1997. The organisation's objectives include:

- promoting the trade of forward freight agreements;
- developing market-standard documentation and underlying assets (eg, indices and routes) for OTC freight derivatives and exchange-traded products;
- encouraging high standards of market conduct; and
- acting as a forum for members to resolve problems.

The association produces the market-standard English law template Forward Freight Agreement. This is a bilateral OTC forward contract. The association's current Forward Freight Agreement template is subtitled "FFABA 2007 Terms" and provides that the applicable transaction is to be governed by the parties' ISDA Master Agreement.

Forward freight agreements derive their value from freight rates. Freight rates are quoted on the basis of the cost per metric tonne to transport cargo on an agreed route in a vessel of a particular size. They vary according to, among other factors:

- whether the route is on a voyage basis or a time charter basis;
- the size of the particular vessel transporting the cargo; and
- the route taken.

2.4   London Bullion Market Association

The LBMA was formed in 1987 to represent the wholesale gold and silver bullion market in London. Central banks, producers, refineries, fabricators and traders throughout the world enter into OTC transactions in relation to gold and silver. The LBMA provides a specification with regard to the standard of the quality of the gold and silver bars that must be maintained in order to be listed with the organisation. Trading documentation has been produced by the LBMA, and the organisation also reviews and updates standards and helps to foster good trading practices. The LBMA has developed standardised documentation for use when parties enter into forward, option and gold interest rate derivatives transactions.

The LBMA has also worked with ISDA to produce the 1997 ISDA Bullion Definitions. If these definitions are incorporated into the bullion-related confirmations pursuant to the ISDA Master Agreement, this incorporates the bullion transactions in relation to the netting provisions under an ISDA Master Agreement so that there will be cross-product netting. The LBMA has also developed with ISDA standalone agreements and confirmations which would bring the derivatives transaction under the provisions and scope of the 1992 Master Agreement. The bullion definitions are also set out in Sub-Annex B of the 2005 ISDA Commodity Definitions.

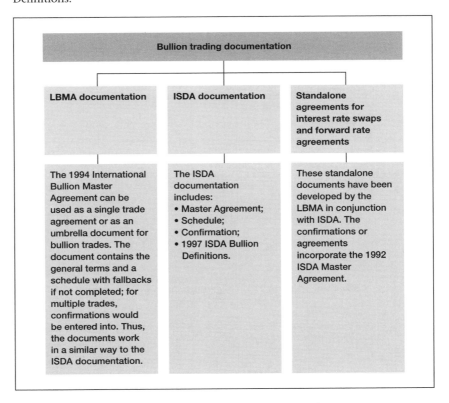

3.   Standard documents

3.1   IETA documents

The diagram on the next page shows the plethora of IETA-produced documents and details when each should be used. They are described in more detail next.

(a)   Emissions Allowances Single Trade Agreement for the EU Scheme (Version 4)

The Emissions Allowances Single Trade Agreement is a long-form confirmation which can be used by parties that trade with another party occasionally. It is an alternative to using the Emissions Trading Master Agreement, which contains the general terms with a number of elections that need to be made among the parties; each trade is confirmed in a short-form confirmation which usually runs to two pages. The latest version of the single trade agreement was produced in August 2008, with changes to correspond with the latest version of the Emissions Trading Master Agreement and to allow for the contracting parties to transact more than one delivery of emission allowances under a single agreement. The single trade agreement contains 11 sections, as follows:

- interpretation and construction;
- general obligations, representations and warranties;
- allowance transfers;
- price, taxes and payment;
- *force majeure* and suspension event;
- transfer failure;
- default and consequences;
- limitation of liability
- confidentiality;
- miscellaneous; and
- definitions.

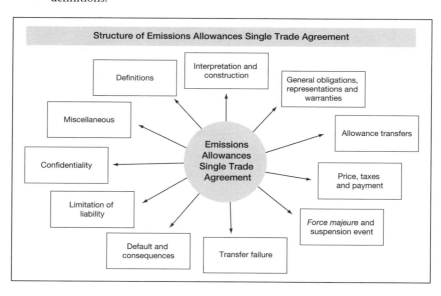

IETA documentation

Emissions Allowances Single Trade Agreement for the EU scheme	Emissions Trading Master Agreement for the EU scheme	Clean Development Mechanism Emission Reduction Purchase Agreement	Transition Agreement	Template Amendment Agreement	Option Annex
Used for one-off transaction for the sale and purchase of emissions allowances.	Provides an umbrella document for more than one transaction entered into between two parties which are buying and selling emission allowances and entering to options.	Used to buy and sell emissions reductions to be received in the future in relation to an approved emission reduction project.	Allows counterparties to move from Version 2 to Version 2.1 of the IETA Master Agreement so that all existing and future transactions entered into or that will be entered into between the parties will be governed by the Version 2.1 provisions.	Allows counterparties to move from Version 2.1 to Version 3 of the IETA Master Agreement so that all existing and future transactions entered into or that will be entered into between the parties will be governed by the Version 3 provisions.	This annex is incorporated into the Emissions Allowances Master Agreement for the EU scheme to allow option transactions to be entered into between the parties.

Where the parties are transacting with a party on a one-off basis, this is the most sensible document to use.

The single trade agreement can be used for the transfer of allowances, certified emission reductions and emission reduction units under the EU scheme rules. It contains a schedule which can allow the parties to provide details of the delivery dates and quantities under the single trade agreement. The allowance transfers are electronic and allowances will be transferred to the receiving party's account with the registry of the relevant member state. If the delivering party fails to deliver, it must pay the replacement cost of the quantities of allowances that were to be delivered under the single trade agreement. The agreement also provides events of default with reference to the receiving party and the delivering party – provisions for both parties include termination rights with determinations in relation to event of default loss. The event of default provisions include failure to deliver or accept, failure to pay, breaches of warranties, and insolvency.

(b) **_Emissions Trading Master Agreement for the EU scheme (version 3)_**
The Emissions Trading Master Agreement facilitates emissions trading whereby the parties enter into a number of trades with each other; the master agreement makes it easier to document the individual trades as and when they are entered into and reduces transaction costs. The master agreement contains the general terms applicable to the parties in relation to any emission trades that they enter into with each other. So when an individual trade is entered into between the two parties, only the individual terms of that trade need be documented under a confirmation, such as the allowance type, allowance amount, delivery date and price.

As a result of moving into Phase II of the EU Emissions Trading System, IETA last produced a revised version of the Emissions Trading Master Agreement in February 2008. The revised version also harmonises provisions with the ISDA and EFET master agreements. Therefore, it is no surprise that the boilerplate provisions are substantially similar to those of the ISDA Master Agreement. The IETA Master Agreement has the following sections:
- interpretation and construction;
- confirmation procedure;
- general obligations, representations and warranties;
- allowance transfers;
- effecting transfers;
- transfer failure;
- value-added taxes;
- billing and payment;
- _force majeure_ and suspension event;
- confidentiality;
- assignment;
- termination;
- liabilities; and
- miscellaneous.

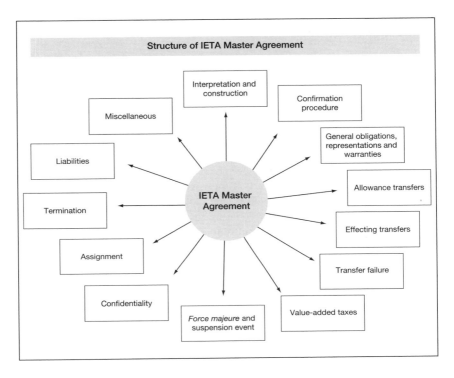

The IETA Master Agreement is similar to the single trade agreement in that the provision for a failure to transfer evaluates the receiving party's actual loss. The IETA Master Agreement introduces the concept of 'excess emission penalty'. This applies to the receiving party if the failure to deliver allowances renders the receiving party in default for not surrendering allowances equal to its actual emissions – as a result of which the receiving party must pay the excess emission penalty. There are also event-of-default provisions which would allow for early termination by the non-defaulting party – events of default provisions include non-payment, breach of representations and warranties, failure to perform a material obligation, insolvency, failure of compliance under the credit support, cross-default, material adverse change (including credit rating and financial covenant-related provisions) and illegality.

The IETA Master Agreement differs from the ISDA documents as it schedules in full the definitions, agreement information and form of confirmation, whereas ISDA splits these into different documents and they are not contained in the master agreement. The ISDA definitions are documented separately and are incorporated into each confirmation, and the master agreement is amended through the schedule to the master agreement, which is a separate document. The IETA Master Agreement is much simpler and is specific to emissions trading, whereas both the ISDA schedule and the ISDA definitions must be adapted by incorporating additional provisions which cover trading EU Emissions Trading Scheme allowances.

(c) ***Clean Development Mechanism Emission Reduction Purchase Agreement (Versions 2 and 3)***

(i) *Version 2 of the agreement*

The Clean Development Mechanism Emission Reduction Purchase Agreement version 2, which was published in August 2004, is a forward contract in relation to the purchase of certified emission reductions, which will be issued under the clean development mechanism. The certified emissions reductions can be issued under the Kyoto Protocol or under other relevant international UN Framework Convention on Climate Change rules. This allows the sale of certified emission reductions before the actual issuance on the basis that these will be generated in the future by a project that has already been approved. This allows the buyer to ensure that it has bought adequate allowances to surrender against its actual emissions, and the seller can receive cash for reducing the emission discharge as a result of entering into a project.

Hypothetical example: Shergill Industries

Shergill Industries plc, a UK corporate and an emitter of greenhouse gases, contacts the Indian Ministry of Environment and Forest to invest in upgrading Punjab's power plants in the Jalandar region. India, a non-Annex I party, ratified the Kyoto Protocol in 2002. The project involves a technological transfer from the United Kingdom, an Annex I party, to India. The Indian project will make the plants work more efficiently, resulting in lower greenhouse gas emissions. Shergill thinks that this project will qualify as a clean development mechanism project. Shergill is a participating company in the EU Emissions Trading Scheme and must surrender equivalent allowances for all its greenhouse gas emissions. Shergill has a greater amount of greenhouse gas emission per year than the allowances allocated to it by the UK government. Currently, emissions allowances are trading at a high price and therefore, as an alternative to buying at these high prices on the open market, Shergill plans to register the Indian project as a clean development mechanism project and surrender the certified emission reductions that it generates from the project to cover the total allowances that it must submit under the EU Emissions Trading Scheme.

Shergill makes a submission of the project plan to the Clean Development Mechanism Executive Board. Simon-Hart Energy Consultancy Limited, a designated operational entity appointed by both Shergill and the Indian Ministry of Environment and Forest, reviews the project plan and verifies that the project meets the clean development mechanism criteria. Shergill thus registers the approved project with Simon-Hart and the Clean Development Mechanism Executive Board.

Shergill runs and monitors the Indian project in accordance with the Clean Development Mechanism Executive Board's criteria. After three years of work, the project is complete and another designated operational entity, Nicol Scots LLP, verifies the reduction in greenhouse gas emissions.

Once the verification is made and the Clean Development Mechanism Executive Board is provided with this, it instructs the Clean Development Mechanism Registry to credit Shergill's Clean Development Mechanism Registry accounts with the number of certified emission reductions due to Shergill as a result of the reduction through the project.

The Clean Development Mechanism Registry deducts 2% of the certified emission reductions from the amount issued to Shergill as a clean development mechanism levy. This deduction is sold into the open market and the proceeds are transferred to an adaptation fund for those developing nations most susceptible to climate change risks.

It is then discovered that the project has been more successful than was originally anticipated, so this has resulted in excess certified emission reductions in Shergill's Clean Development Mechanism Registry accounts than required for surrender under the EU Emissions Trading Scheme. Shergill sells these additional reductions into the open market and these are bought by other nations and private firms.

The Clean Development Mechanism Emission Reduction Purchase Agreement (Version 2) is divided into 15 articles:
- definitions and interpretation;
- conditions precedent;
- purchase and sale of certified emissions reductions;
- options to acquire additional or sell excess emission reductions;
- price and payment;

- verification, validation, registration and baseline;
- monitoring plan;
- verification and certification;
- project operation and management;
- certified emission reductions;
- representations and warranties;
- failure to generate or transfer a minimum amount;
- events of default;
- termination; and
- miscellaneous provisions.

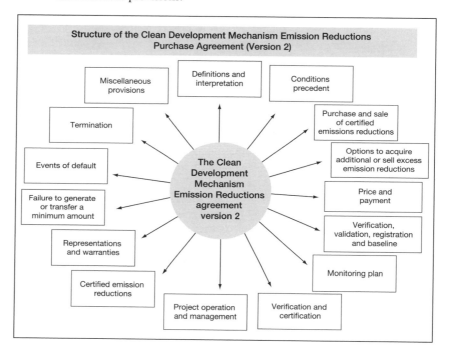

The agreement also lists six schedules, which cover:
- a description of the project;
- a table setting out the minimum amount of greenhouse gas reductions that must be generated by the project and forwarded to the buyer as certified emission reductions each year;
- a description of the clean development mechanism project-monitoring plan to be set out;
- a form of option notice for purchasing additional or excess certified emission reductions;
- a form of letter from the designated national authority of the clean development mechanism project approving the project and the future issue of certified emission reductions generated through the project; and

- if a letter of credit is provided under the agreement, a copy of this.

(ii)   *Version 3 of the agreement*
The agreement was revised and a new Version 3 was published in September 2006. This new version must be read in conjunction with the Clean Development Mechanism Code of Terms. The code sets out a number of terms which can be incorporated into the Clean Development Mechanism Emission Reduction Purchase Agreement. Version 3 of the agreement has nine sections:

- details of the parties and the recitals;
- definitions and interpretation and term;
- conditions precedent;
- obligations of the seller;
- obligations of the buyer;
- representations, warranties and undertakings;
- termination;
- governing law and dispute resolution; and
- miscellaneous.

The agreement also contains two schedules and an annex, which relate to:

- incorporated provisions from the code;
- the commercial terms in relation to the project, delivery, payment and notice details; and
- an annex of the project documentation referred to in the commercial terms.

The code contains a standardised set of contract terms which will be regularly updated to reflect new decisions of the Conference of the Parties to the UN Framework Convention on Climate Change serving as the Meeting of the Parties to the Kyoto Protocol and the Clean Development Mechanism Executive Board. The code runs to 33 pages with eight articles, similar to those in the actual agreement:

- definitions and interpretation;
- conditions precedent;
- obligations of the seller;
- obligations of the buyer;
- representations, warranties and undertakings;
- termination;
- dispute resolution; and
- miscellaneous.

The revised version seems to be a mechanism to reduce transaction costs through incorporation of provisions from the code, rather than a longer and more negotiated agreement.

(d)   ***Transition Agreement***
The Transition Agreement came about as a result of the release of a revised IETA Master Agreement in June 2005 (Version 2.1), which updated the previous version

(Version 2, dated July 2 2004). The Transition Agreement was released in October 2005 to allow parties which had originally entered into Version 2 to apply Version 2.1 to apply to all existing and future transactions. Certain elections must be made in this agreement and these are documented in Annexure 1. These elections must be made as a result of the additional provisions contained in Version 2.1, which relate to:

- the seller's holding account details;
- whether the excess emissions penalty applies;
- the payment due date;
- whether physical netting of deliveries applies;
- the *force majeure* termination payment provisions;
- applicable law provisions; and
- certain other miscellaneous provisions.

The Transition Agreement also contains a Part 2 in Annexure 1, which would allow the parties to include any other amendments to the IETA Master Agreement on which they agree.

(e)   *Template Amendment Agreement*
Similar to the Transition Agreement, the Template Amendment Agreement was created to allow parties to update their IETA Master Agreement from Version 2.1 to Version 3, which was published to address delivery issues in Phase 2 of the EU scheme. The Template Amendment Agreement allows the parties to replace their IETA Master Agreement with Version 3 in relation to both existing and future transactions. There are some minor elections in relation to account and notice details for the parties, so there are substantially less elections to be made in the Template Amendment Agreement as compared with the Transition Agreement. As with the Transition Agreement, parties can include any other amendments to the IETA Master Agreement that they agree in the Template Amendment Agreement.

(f)   *Options Annex*
In addition to immediate settlement and forward contracts being traded, options can be entered into in relation to emissions reductions (whether call or put options). The Options Annex would form part of Schedule 2 of the IETA Master Agreement – the agreement information section. The Options Annex is to be inserted as a new Part 3 of Schedule 2 and contains provisions on option transactions, the exercise of options, the effect of exercise and additional definitions that are needed. The Options Annex also contains a form of confirmation for option transactions which is inserted into the IETA Master Agreement as Schedule 3A.

3.2   globalCOAL

(a)   *Standard Coal Trading Agreement*
The Standard Coal Trading Agreement allows the sale and purchase of coal which is to be physically settled (by spot or forward transactions or options to purchase or sell physical coal). The Standard Coal Trading Agreement was first published in May

2001 and there have been a number of updating versions since then. The agreement has been constantly revised and amended to ensure that market developments are taken into account, particularly as the market in relation to coal is a fast-paced environment.[2] There are changes to port regulations, international law and trading practices which result in new versions of the Standard Coal Trading Agreement. The latest version was published in July 2009 and is Version 7. The Standard Coal Trading Agreement is a standard-form document used for trading physically settled coal. It has two parts: the first is a transaction summary and the second contains the terms and conditions.

The transaction summary covers:

- the relevant standard specification;
- the amount of coal to be bought or sold per delivery period;
- the price;
- the origin of the coal;
- the delivery point; and
- details of the buyer and seller.

The terms and conditions contain 27 clauses dealing with:

- definitions;
- interpretation;
- obligations;
- representations, warranties and undertakings;
- financial settlement;
- nominations;
- laytime and demurrage (this relates to the time allowed for loading of the vessel at the delivery point and the financial compensation if this is exceeded);
- delivery;
- title and risk;
- weighing/sampling/analysis;
- quality and contamination;
- rejection of the shipment;
- price, payment, netting and close-out;
- performance assurance and credit;
- failure to deliver or take delivery;
- remedies in respect of an event of default;
- *force majeure*;
- disputes;
- assignment or novation;
- agents;
- confidentiality;
- exclusion of certain warranties and condition (including limitation of liability;
- limitation of liability;
- notices and communication;

---

2   globalCOAL website, under the Standard Coal Trading Agreement section.

- waiver;
- amendment;
- exclusion of third-party rights; and
- governing law.

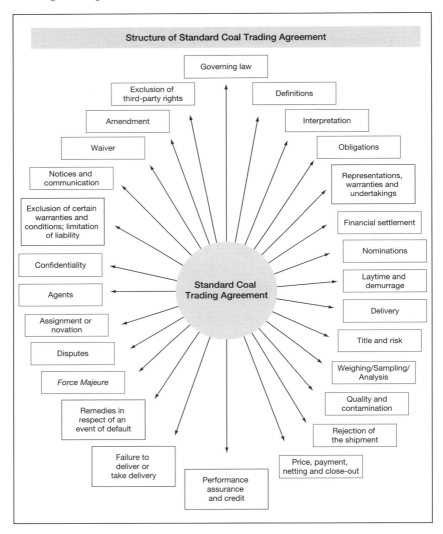

Structure of Standard Coal Trading Agreement

Governing law

Exclusion of third-party rights

Definitions

Amendment

Interpretation

Waiver

Obligations

Notices and communication

Representations, warranties and undertakings

Exclusion of certain warranties and conditions; limitation of liability

Financial settlement

Confidentiality

Nominations

Agents

Laytime and demurrage

Assignment or novation

Delivery

Disputes

Title and risk

Force Majeure

Weighing/Sampling/Analysis

Remedies in respect of an event of default

Quality and contamination

Failure to deliver or take delivery

Rejection of the shipment

Performance assurance and credit

Price, payment, netting and close-out

Standard Coal Trading Agreement

Part 2 of the Standard Coal Trading Agreement contains the general terms and conditions. The terms and conditions contain a number of coal-specific clauses with regard to the quality of the coal and shipping-related matters. There are also 10 schedules which detail different specifications and the applicable specification would be indicated in Part 1, the transaction summary. The schedules have varying specifications in relation to the coal and sub-section topics, and each schedule has varying information and provisions. The schedules provide terms applicable for coal trading hubs around the world; these outline the main terms and conditions of coal delivery to the hub. The headings covered include:

- nominations;
- laytime and demurrage;
- delivery;
- weighing/sampling/analysis;
- price, payment, netting and close-out;
- failure to deliver or take delivery;
- representations, warranties and undertakings; and
- governing law.

Schedules A and B relate to coal originating from one or more of South Africa, Australia, Colombia, Poland, Russia and the United States. Schedule C relates to coal originating in Colombia; Schedule D to F relates to coal originating in Indonesia; Schedules G and H relate to coal from Australia; and Schedules I and J refer to coal originating from South Africa.

The Standard Coal Trading Agreement contains three appendices:

- a standard close-out agreement for coal in a form for a single settlement month;
- a standard financial settlement agreement for coal where physical delivery is forgone; and
- a standard agreement on index settlement of shipment tolerances – this agreement takes into account the actual amount of coal shipped comparative to the quantity as prescribed in the contract.

Hypothetical example: Hain Coal Trader Ltd and Fireplace plc

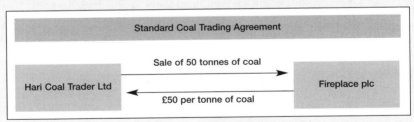

Fireplace plc is a supplier of coal to residential properties in the United Kingdom and wishes to lock in the current price as it has entered into contracts of supply at a set rate for delivery in six months' time. Coal is currently trading at £50 per tonne and Fireplace has factored this into its supply contracts with a delivery date in six months.

Hari Coal Trader Ltd is a producer of coal in Colombia. Hari Coal would like to lock in the current price for future sales in six months' time to ensure that it receives £50 per tonne.

Hari Coal and Fireplace enter into a Standard Coal Trading Agreement with

> Schedule C attached, as the coal is originating from Colombia and the delivery point is Colombia.
>
> Hari Coal delivers coal to Fireplace in six months' time in the United Kingdom and Fireplace pays £50 per tonne even though the cost per tonne may have changed.

In addition to the Standard Coal Trading Agreement, parties must, before the first transaction, agree in writing the performance assurance required. Further local rules must be adhered to and these take precedence over the agreement. There is also a provision allowing cash settlement rather than physical settlement. If an event of default occurs, the Standard Coal Trading Agreement can be terminated by the non-defaulting party and the loss is calculated under each transaction. Default events include:

- failure to pay;
- failure to provide performance assurance;
- material breach of representations or warranties;
- a material breach;
- any agreed cross-default threshold being exceeded;
- failure to pay under any other agreement with the counterparty; and
- insolvency-related provisions.

ISDA has produced a physical coal annex which allows for documentation of the purchase or sale of physically settled coal on a spot or forward basis, as well as trading in options to purchase or sell coal. This annex has a similar structure to other commodity-specific annexes produced by ISDA. Incorporation of the annex allows cross-product netting under the ISDA Master Agreement. The Standard Coal Trading Agreement is incorporated into Appendix 2 of the coal annex produced by ISDA and relates to coal sourced outside the United States (ie, international coal); this increases the harmonisation of provisions documenting physically settled coal trades and is the accepted document used by market participants prior to the ISDA coal annex being created.

(b) *Master Agreement for Standard Coal Derivatives (MaSCoD)*
globalCOAL has provided a Master Agreement for Standard Coal Derivatives since May 2003 and the latest, Version 3(g), was published in January 2008. The agreement makes provisions in relation to the documentation of derivatives transactions (ie, coal-based financial agreements which would be cash settled and traded on globalCOAL's system). This would include futures and options entered into which would be cash settled only. Parties can also enter into index-based swaps and these are listed in the schedule to the agreement. They can be entered into for hedging or speculative purposes. The coal derivatives transactions will be documented under ISDA documentation and the Master Agreement for Standard Coal Derivatives make reference to this. Essentially, the agreement is to document the allowing of trading by the party entering into it on its platform, and that the party agrees to document the derivatives agreements under ISDA documentation.

The Master Agreement for Standard Coal Derivatives has the following sections:

- introduction – this describes the system provided and the purpose of the agreement;
- definitions;
- terms of ISDA instruments;
- documentation;
- representations and warranties;
- whole agreement; and
- governing law.

The agreement essentially documents the terms for trading on globalCOAL's trading platform and ensures that standardised ISDA documentation is used to document the coal derivative transactions entered into on its platform.

3.3 Forward Freight Agreements

(a) General

The Forward Freight Agreement template confirmation structures its fixed versus floating exchange by setting out an agreed freight rate called the 'contract rate'. The contract rate is for an agreed route, namely the 'contract route'. Both the contract route and the contract rate reference a specified period – the Forward Freight Agreement defines this as the 'contract period', which is usually one month.

The contract rate will usually be a rate for a specific contract route published by the Baltic Exchange. It will be published either in the form of dollars per tonne of cargo or, in the case of tanker routes, by reference to a nominal freight rate published by Worldscale.

In addition to the contract rate, contract route and contract period, the Forward Freight Agreement also references and defines a 'settlement rate'. This is the unweighted average of the rates for the contract route(s) published by the Baltic Exchange over the settlement period. 'Settlement period' is defined in the Forward Freight Agreement as an agreed number of Baltic Exchange Index publication days for the applicable contract period, up to and including the settlement date.

The parties will specify the quantity of freight to which the Forward Freight Agreement relates (eg, 10,000 tonnes). This is called the 'contract quantity'.

The above provisions interact so that the transaction will settle on the settlement date. The Forward Freight Agreement defines 'settlement date' as "the last Baltic Exchange Index publication day of each Contract Month"; the parties may specify one or several contract month(s) in their negotiated confirmation. The contract month can be the next calendar month or could be a specified month in many months' time (eg, March 2014).

On the settlement date, the Forward Freight Agreement template provides that a 'settlement sum' will be paid from one party to the other. This will be from the party which is out of the money to the party which is in the money. This settlement sum is the difference between the contract rate and the settlement rate, multiplied by the quantity (ie, tonnage referenced) for the contract period.

'Settlement rate' is defined in the confirmation as the unweighted average of the rates for the contract route over the settlement period. In turn, the settlement period is defined as the number of Baltic Exchange Index publication days for the relevant contract month up to and including the settlement date.

If the settlement rate is higher than the contract rate, the seller pays the buyer the settlement sum. However, if the settlement rate is lower than the contract rate, the buyer pays the seller the settlement sum.

The settlement sum is then payable either two London business days after the in-the-money party presents its invoice or five London business days after the settlement date (whichever is sooner).

There are two further points to note. First, if the parties specify more than one contract month, the Forward Freight Agreement is technically a swap transaction, as there will be a series of payment exchanges on multiple settlement dates. If this is the case, the contract quantities may vary from month to month. Second, the parties are also free to specify a number of contract rates – this will create a basket transaction and, if this is the case, the contract quantities may vary between contract rates.

Hypothetical example: Dominic Grain Exporters and Griffiths Welsh Shipping
Dominic Grain Exporters and Griffiths Welsh Shipping have entered into a Forward Freight Agreement. This is documented pursuant to the parties' ISDA Master Agreement, under the market-standard Forward Freight Agreement published by the FFABA.

The Forward Freight Agreement references a Handymax freight rate for Rotterdam to Capetown: this is a contract route reported by the Baltic Exchange. On the trade date, the Baltic Exchange quotes the contract rate as $17 per tonne.

Dominic Grain Exporters is concerned that the Handymax freight rate may go up; this would cut its margins on its grain exports due to the increased costs of transportation. On the other hand, shipowner Griffiths Welsh Shipping is concerned that if the freight rate for its key Handymax route goes down, this will reduce its profitability. Both parties are prepared to forgo a potential upside to hedge against the potential downside.

Dominic Grain Exporters agrees to receive a Handymax floating freight rate in exchange for paying a fixed Handymax freight rate (applicable at the trade date). Dominic Grain Exporters is the buyer and Griffiths Welsh Shipping is the seller. The contract quantity agreed is 10,000 tonnes.

The settlement rate is defined in the unweighted average of the rates for the contract route(s) published by the Baltic Exchange over the settlement period. The settlement period consists of each Baltic Exchange Index publication date in each contract month. Dominic Manufacturing and Griffiths Welsh Shipping specify each month of the next year as a contract month and specify the quantity by contract month (ie, tonnage covered) as 50,000 tonnes per contract month.

On the first settlement date, the contract rate of $17 per tonne is higher than the settlement rate of $15 per tonne. Therefore, Dominic Transportation pays a settlement sum of $2 × 50,000 (ie, $100,000) to Griffiths Welsh Shipping. On the second settlement date the contract rate of $17 per tonne is lower than the settlement rate of $18 per tonne. Therefore, Griffiths Welsh Shipping pays a settlement sum of $1 × 50,000 (ie, $50,000) to Dominic Manufacturing.

Similar variations occur during the rest of the contract, which result in the parties successfully hedging their respective positions.

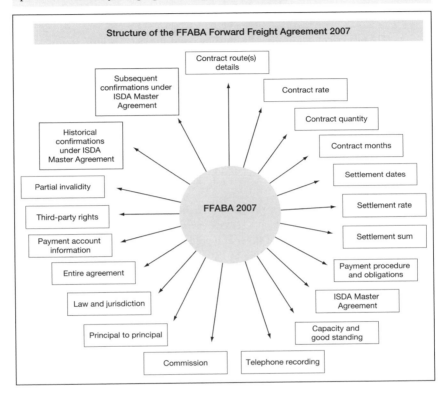

Structure of the FFABA Forward Freight Agreement 2007

3.4   1994 International Bullion Master Agreement Terms

The 1994 International Bullion Master Agreement works similarly to the ISDA Master Agreement, as it provides a set of general terms which govern all bullion-related transactions entered into by the counterparties; the individual confirmations provide the individual transaction details. The Bullion Master Agreement can be used as an umbrella document for the spot, forward and options entered into between the parties, and provides for close-out and netting of outstanding bullion transactions. Alternatively, it can be used as a single trade agreement. In effect, it is a single-product netting agreement when used as a master agreement. The Bullion Master Agreement will apply if executed by the parties, but will also be presumed to apply if one party is acting through an office in London and no other bilateral agreement has been signed.[3]

Two versions of the Bullion Master Agreement have been published: one is governed by English law and the other by New York law. One difference between the

---

3   See www.lbma.org.uk/london/stddocun on this point.

agreements is that the New York law version does not provide for automatic close-out and liquidation, so it applies only if that is specified in the schedule; whereas in the English law version this applies automatically to all outstanding bullion transactions in relation to certain specified events of default relating to the insolvency of the defaulting party.

Hypothetical example: ARK Bullions and Rings R'Us Ltd

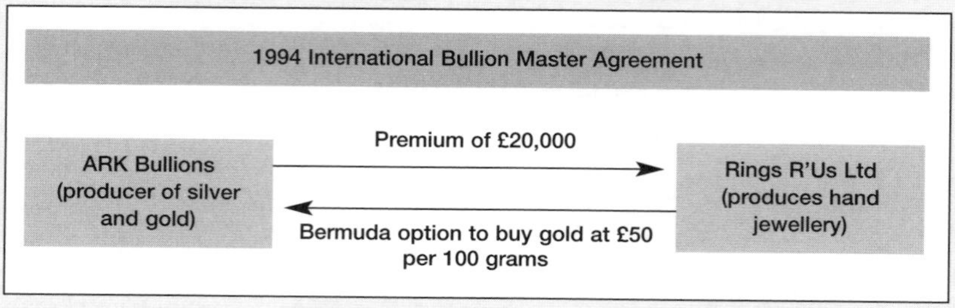

Rings R'Us Ltd is a producer of hand jewellery and wishes to purchase an option to purchase gold at a set rate every six months for the next two years. ARK Bullions is a producer of silver and gold in South Africa.

Gold is currently trading at £50 per 100 grams and Rings believes that gold prices will rise, so it wishes to be able to purchase at the current rate in the future and is willing to pay a premium for the right to purchase at this rate.

ARK and Rings enter into a Bullion Master Agreement on the basis that this will be an umbrella document as they may wish to purchase further options or forward contracts in relation to bullion from ARK in the future.

The Bullion Master Agreement Terms has 12 sections (as well as a supplementary schedule):

- definitions;
- bullion transactions;
- bullion options – premium;
- bullion options – discharge and termination;
- bullion options – exercise and settlement;
- bullion transaction – settlement and netting;
- representations, warranties and covenants;
- close-out and liquidation;
- illegality, impossibility and *force majeure*;
- parties to rely on their own expertise;
- miscellaneous (including currency indemnity, assignments, telephonic recording, termination, time of essence, taxes); and
- law and jurisdiction.

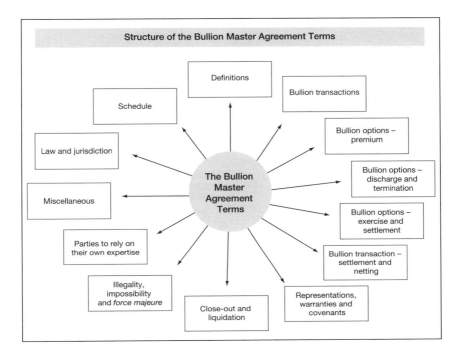

The schedule to the Bullion Master Agreement Terms is divided into 15 parts and covers the following:

- base currency;
- designated offices;
- matched-pair novation netting offices;
- novation netting offices;
- settlement netting offices;
- threshold amount;
- scope of agreement;
- confirmation procedures;
- discharge and termination of bullion options;
- netting of premiums;
- notices;
- payment and settlement instructions;
- process agent;
- withholding tax; and
- adequate assurances.

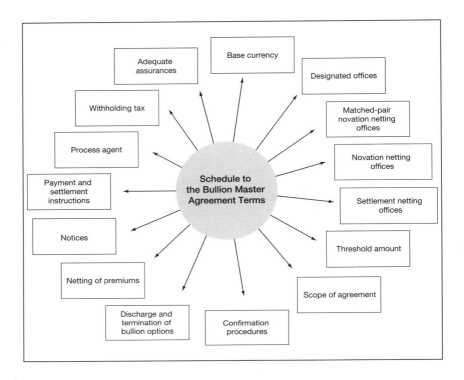

The New York law version covers the same scope as the English law version, but the schedule to the New York law version has three additional parts covering automatic termination, Federal Deposit Insurance Corporation Improvement Act representations, and other metals. The New York law version can be extended to apply not only to silver and gold, but also to other metals. The ISDA documentation for bullion transactions, contained in the ISDA Commodity Definitions, covers a greater variety of derivatives transactions, such as bullion swaption and a bullion swap which is a cap, collar or floor.

4. Conclusion

The documentation platforms discussed above have each been formed specifically for one type of commodity and can therefore focus on the issues that are unique to that commodity. These focused documentation platforms will ensure that the documentation for trading that commodity is reviewed and updated as required, whereas ISDA may require assistance from these organisations to ensure that its documentation is also reflective of current market needs. As well as providing competition in the market for the most effective trading documentation, this leads to a collaborative approach which is evident from the documentation platforms and ISDA. This will ensure the harmonisation of documentation provisions, as well as greater liquidity within these commodity markets.

IETA has collaborated with both the ISDA and EFET with regard to the IETA Master Agreement so that there is greater harmonisation of IETA-produced documents with these other platform documents. ISDA has incorporated into its coal annex the Standard Coal Trading Agreement produced by globalCoal, and globalCoal has mandatory rules ensuring that coal derivatives must be documented under the ISDA documentation platform. This indicates recognition by the documentation platforms that they must work together with each other to ensure that there is harmonisation and greater liquidity of commodities as a result of the standardised documentation of trades. The FFABA also incorporates the ISDA Master Agreement as a result of understanding the weaknesses and flaws of its previous documentation. There is a drive by organisations to ensure that the documentation is comprehensive and that the market is working at its optimum, with certainty and efficiency being paramount. The LBMA has worked closely with ISDA to produce documentation so that the trading of silver and gold bullions is comprehensively provided for.

The scope of the documentation covered by ISDA and the documentation platforms discussed in this chapter are rather similar, as these organisations have worked together to provide documentation that is best placed to deal with the current trading markets with reference to the specific commodity. Where competing documentations is offered by different documentation platforms, what the parties choose depends on the sophistication of the parties and what they are accustomed to and familiar with.

Tax aspects of commodity derivative transactions

Sandy Bhogal
Catriona Nicol

1. Introduction

Buried among the many reasons set out earlier in this publication for using commodity derivatives is tax efficiency. Commodity derivatives are used in tax planning and tax structuring. As a result, they attract the attention of tax collectors and are regularly subject to tax avoidance provisions.

Getting it wrong can be very expensive. This chapter is a general outline of the taxation of commodity derivative contracts. It primarily considers the tax consequences for UK corporation taxpayers using commodity derivatives and reflects the law as at November 1 2009. Tax consequences will be different in every country and can be particularly complex where the counterparties are in two different countries, with the relevant underlying asset being in a third.

Similar issues to those outlined in this chapter for the United Kingdom may also arise in other countries. They may, however, be very different and consideration of the specific tax issues for a jurisdiction should always be central to structuring any commodity derivative contract.

2. History

To understand why the UK tax code for derivative contracts has developed in the way it has, one must consider certain historical factors.

The opening chapter of this book defines a 'derivative' as a financial instrument referencing an underlying commodity asset or other variable, from which the financial instrument's price or value is derived, entered into by the parties for a purpose. Therefore, where the tax code looks immediately to classify an amount as falling within a particular category, derivatives can be problematic. The 'character' of an amount (eg, whether it is capital, income or exempt) is of primary importance when assessing the tax treatment. The other main issues are timing (eg, accrual,

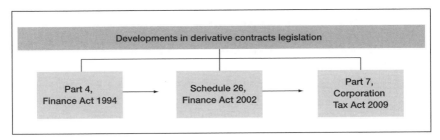

yield-to-maturity, receipt) and source (which matters for any withholding tax and foreign tax credit analysis).

The United Kingdom tried to solve this problem by enacting legislation in the Finance Act 1994. This created a payments-based code for certain types of derivative contract. This legislation was comprehensively revised and enacted as Schedule 26 to the Finance Act 2002.

The new law moved the tax treatment of derivative instruments closer to the accounting treatment. In addition, the provisions in the Finance Act 1994 had applied to six very narrowly defined groups of contract. The revised provisions in Schedule 26 were drafted much more widely and were based heavily on accounting and financial services concepts and definitions. Indeed, the definitions of 'options', 'futures' and 'contracts for differences' set out in the current legislation relating to the taxation of derivative contracts are based on those in the Financial Services and Markets Act 2000, allowing the courts to be guided by case law related to regulated activities should they need to consider these definitions in a tax context.

Following the introduction of Schedule 26, extensive amendments were made to the legislation by the Finance Act 2004 and a number of regulations were laid before Parliament in 2004 and 2005 to reflect the UK adoption of International Accounting Standards.

The main legislation governing the taxation of derivative contracts was rewritten to Part 7 of the Corporation Tax Act 2009 as part of the Tax Law Rewrite Project. However, the provisions are substantively the same as those previously contained in Schedule 26.

The tax treatment of derivative contracts under Part 7 is heavily linked to the accounting treatment. One consequence of this is that a sound understanding of the accounting principles as they relate to derivative contracts is valuable in order to understand fully the tax treatment. This also means that the frequent changes in accounting practice require regular consequential amendments to the legislation.

3.   Accounting standards relating to derivatives

A detailed discussion of the accounting treatment of financial instruments is outside the scope of this chapter. Relevant standards are, nevertheless, thus:

- IAS – International Accounting Standards;
- IFRS – International Financial Reporting Standards;
- UK GAAP – UK Generally Accepted Accounting Practice;
- IAS 32 – establishes principles for presenting financial instruments as liabilities or equity and for offsetting financial assets and financial liabilities;
- IAS 39 – establishes principles for recognising and measuring financial assets, financial liabilities and some contracts to buy or sell non-financial items;
- IFRS 7 – requires entities to provide disclosures in their financial statements that enable users to evaluate the significance of financial instruments for the entity's financial position and performance; and the nature and extent of risks arising from financial instruments to which the entity is exposed; and
- IFRS 9 – an intended entire replacement for IAS 39.

IAS 32, IAS 39 (eventually IFRS 9) and IFRS 7 are the international accounting standards which are relevant for derivatives. IAS 32 and IAS 39 have been incorporated into UK GAAP by Financial Reporting Standard (FRS) 25 and FRS 26, but the content of the former two standards are anyway being reviewed and revised as a result of the recent financial crisis.

'Financial instruments' are defined in IAS 32 as any contract that gives rise to both a financial asset of one entity and a financial liability or equity instrument of another entity. A 'financial asset' comprises: cash; a contractual right to receive cash or another financial asset; a contractual right to exchange financial assets or liabilities with another entity on terms which are favourable; or an equity instrument of another entity. A 'financial liability' is defined as a contractual obligation to deliver cash or another financial asset to another entity, or to exchange financial instruments with another entity under conditions that are potentially unfavourable.

Contracts to buy or sell non-financial items are within the scope of IAS 39 if they can be settled net in cash or another financial asset.

IAS 39 defines a 'derivative' as a financial instrument or other contract with all three of the following characteristics:

- Its value changes in response to the change in a specific interest rate, financial instrument price, commodity price, foreign exchange rate, index of prices or rates, credit rating or credit index, or other variable, provided in the case of a non-financial variable that the variable is not specific to a party to the contract;
- It requires no initial net investment or an initial net investment that is smaller than would be required for other types of contract that would be expected to have a similar response to market factors; and
- It is settled at a future date.

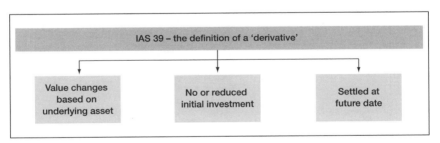

4. Taxation of derivative contracts in the United Kingdom

Part 7 of the Corporation Tax Act 2009 applies only to UK corporation tax payers – in particular, UK tax-resident companies and UK permanent establishments of non-UK tax-resident companies. Special rules relating to the taxation of derivative contracts apply in relation to groups, collective investment schemes and insurance and mutual trading companies.

The effect of Part 7 is that profits arising to a company from its derivative contracts are chargeable to corporation tax as income, except in certain circumstances where the gains and losses will be taxed as capital.

Profits and losses arising from commodity derivative contracts which fall within the Part 7 regime will be taxable only as income under Part 7, as chargeable gains treatment is available only where the underlying subject matter of the contract is or relates to qualifying ordinary shares, land or certain tangible movable property (from which commodities are specifically excluded).

Part 7 sets out a number of rules relating to the taxation of derivative contracts and, in particular, identifies:

- the derivative contracts to which the rules apply;
- the profits and losses, and credits and debits, which are to be brought into account; and
- various anti-avoidance measures.

Under Section 699 of Part 7, the provisions of Part 7 take priority over all other areas of the Corporation Taxes Acts. However, Section 700 of Part 7 provides that the loan relationships rules in Part 5 of the Corporation Tax Act 2009 take priority over the derivative contract rules in Part 7. Where a company is party to a loan relationship as a result of terms contained within a derivative contract, and a profit or loss accrues to the company on that derivative contract, that amount will be brought into account under loan relationship rules rather than the derivative contract regime (except in the case of a loan relationship with an embedded derivative, as discussed below).

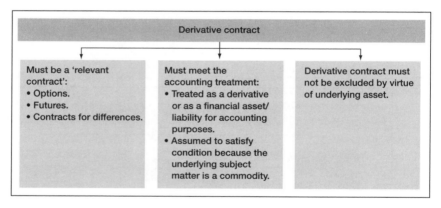

4.1 Entering the derivative contract regime

In order to fall within the provisions of Part 7, a derivative contract must meet the following conditions:

- It must be a 'relevant contract';
- It must satisfy the accounting conditions; and
- It must not be excluded from being a derivative contract by virtue of its underlying subject matter or any provision of the Corporation Tax Acts.

(a) 'Relevant contract'

As a preliminary interpretative point, where one or more derivatives transactions between two parties are executed under the same ISDA master agreement, they will be regarded as part of the same transaction. However, for tax purposes, each individual transaction or trade – whether or not it is covered by the same ISDA master agreement – will be treated as a separate transaction. Each 'relevant contract' will therefore be considered individually under the provisions of Part 7.

Section 577 of Part 7 defines a 'relevant contract' as "an option; a future; or a contract for differences". This limits the legislation's scope to contracts deriving their value from underlying assets subject to changes in market prices or other factors. The definitions of 'options', 'futures' and 'contracts for differences' are set out in Sections 580 to 582 of Part 7 and are based on those in the Financial Services and Markets Act 2000.

For much of Part 7, it does not matter whether a derivative contract is an option, future or a contract for differences, provided that it constitutes a 'relevant contract' under one of these definitions. Relevant contracts which are contracts for differences are also subject to certain special rules.

(i)   *Options*

'Option' is not defined in Part 7 (although Section 580(1) of the 2009 Act explicitly states that an option includes a warrant) and therefore takes its ordinary meaning. Her Majesty's Revenue & Customs (HMRC) guidance distinguishes an option from other types of derivative contract. It does so on the basis that the option holder has a choice: it has a right, but not an obligation, to buy or sell a specified underlying asset on or before a future date.

Subject to certain exceptions, cash-settled options are excluded from the definition of an 'option'. This is on the basis that they fall within the definition of 'contracts for differences' and are therefore subject to some provisions which apply only to contracts for differences.

> **Hypothetical example of an option; Green Ltd and Yates Ltd**
>
> Green Limited enters into a cash-settled European option with Yates Limited to purchase 100,000 therms of gas at 74 pence per therm in three months' time. Should the price of gas rise, Green Limited will exercise that option and Yates Limited will then have to make a payment to Green Limited reflecting the difference in price between the current market price (the strike price) and 74 pence. This derivative contract is an option, as Green Limited has the choice as to whether it exercises its rights. However, as the option is cash rather than physically settled, the derivative contract will constitute a contract for differences for the purposes of Part 7 of the 2009 Act, rather than an option.

(ii)   *Futures*

A 'future' is defined in Section 581 of Part 7 as "a contract for the sale of property under which delivery is to be made (i) at a future date agreed when the contract is made, and (ii) at a price so agreed". A price is treated as agreed even when it is left to be determined by reference to a market or exchange price. The same is true where the contract provides for a variation in the price to take account of any variation in quantity or quality upon delivery.

As with options, cash-settled futures are excluded from this definition. This is on the basis that they fall within the definition of 'contracts for differences' (and are therefore subject to those provisions which apply only to contracts for differences).

(iii)   *Contracts for differences*

Contracts for differences is the broadest category of 'relevant contract'. It is subject to several exclusions. Under Section 582 of Part 7, a 'contract for differences' is defined as "a contract, the purpose or pretended purpose of which is to make a profit or avoid a loss by reference to fluctuations in the value or price of property described in the contract, or an index or other factor designated in the contract". 'Pretended' in this context does not imply any presence of fraud or deceit on the part of the holder, but instead that the holder aimed or aspired to make a profit.

A contract cannot be a contract for differences if it constitutes an option, future, contract of insurance, capital redemption policy, contract of indemnity, guarantee, warranty or loan relationship.

However, a cash-settled future or option would fall within the definition of a 'contract for differences', as discussed above, along with a swap transaction.

(b)   **Accounting conditions**

The definitions of 'options', 'futures' and 'contracts for differences' are very wide. In a regulatory context, limitations are placed on the scope of these terms by the Financial Services and Markets Act 2000 (Regulated Activities Order) 2001. In a tax context, the scope is limited by excluding contracts which would not be treated as derivative contracts in a company's accounts.

Under Section 579 of Part 7, a relevant contract must satisfy one of the following three accounting conditions in order to fall within Part 7:

- The relevant contract is treated for accounting purposes as a derivative;
- The relevant contract is treated as a financial asset or liability for accounting purposes; or
- The contract's underlying asset is a commodity; or where the relevant contract is a contract for differences, the underlying asset is land, tangible moveable property (other than commodities which are tangible assets), intangible fixed assets, weather conditions or creditworthiness.

Many derivative contracts, regardless of the underlying asset, will meet one of the first two accounting conditions. Where neither of these is met, a derivative contract referencing and underlying commodity can satisfy the accounting condition because of its underlying subject matter. This is regardless of whether it is an option, future or contract for differences. The third leg of the 'accounting conditions' test unusually distinguishes between contracts for differences, and options and futures.

The tax legislation does not provide guidance on the meaning of 'commodity' for these purposes. The term should be given its normal meaning. HMRC guidance states that it should generally be clear whether the underlying subject matter of a contract is a commodity. Futures over agricultural products, metals, and fuel and oil products are all traded on recognised futures exchanges, and all constitute 'commodities'. However, commodities are not limited to tangible and storable assets – for example, electricity constitutes a commodity.

(c) *Contracts excluded because of underlying subject matter*
Under Section 589(1) of Part 7, a relevant contract will not be a derivative contract under Part 7 if its underlying subject matter consists of, or is treated as consisting wholly of, excluded property. The 'excluded property' definition includes intangible fixed assets in the case of options and futures.

However, this qualification will not affect the inclusion of a derivative contract which has commodities as its underlying subject matter.

4.2 Taxation of derivative contracts
Where a derivative contract falls into the Part 7 regime, the general rule is contained in Section 595 of Part 7. This provides that amounts to be brought into account are those amounts recognised in determining the company's profit or loss in accordance with generally accepted accounting principles. These amounts include all profits and losses of the company which arise to it from its derivative contracts. They also include all expenses incurred by the company under, or for the purposes of, those contracts.

Where a company prepares its accounts in accordance with IAS (or failing that, UK GAAP), those standards constitute generally accepted accounting practice for the purposes of Schedule 26.

To determine a company's profit and loss, the following must be considered:
- the amount recognised in the company's profit and loss account;
- the income statement or statement of comprehensive income for that period;
- the statement of total recognised gains and losses;
- the statement of recognised income and expense;
- the statement of changes in equity or statement of income and retained earnings for that period; and/or
- any other statement of items recognised in calculating the company's profits and losses for that period.

(a) *Expenses*
Section 595(4) of Part 7 limits the expenses which can be brought into account in relation to a derivative contract. In particular, expenses are treated as being incurred for the purpose of a derivative contract only if they are incurred directly:
- in bringing the derivative contract into existence;
- in entering into or giving effect to any of the related transactions;
- in making payments under any of those contracts or as a result of any of those transactions; or
- in taking steps to ensure the receipt of payments under any of those contracts or in accordance with any of those transactions.

(b)   The Disregard Regulations

The Loan Relationships and Derivative Contracts (Disregard and Bringing into Account of Profits and Losses) Regulations 2004 (the 'Disregard Regulations') have effect for accounting periods beginning on or after January 1 2005.

As discussed above, for the purposes of the derivative contracts legislation, either IAS or UK GAAP may constitute generally accepted accounting practice when determining the profits and losses associated with derivative contracts. However, there are differences in the application of these two standards. This is particularly so for the treatment of derivative contracts used for hedging. Various changes were made to the rules contained in Schedule 26 (which were the legislative provisions in effect at that time) by the Finance Act 2004, which also provided for additional regulations to be made.

Accordingly, the Disregard Regulations specifically apply to derivative contracts which are commodity contracts (among other derivative contracts). They provide for changes in the fair value of certain derivative contracts to be left out of account for tax purposes when they are recognised in accounts – in some cases, to be brought back into account for those purposes when the contract matures or is otherwise disposed of.

(c)   Miscellaneous provisions

(i)   'Embedded derivatives'

Under Sections 584 to 586 of Part 7, in certain circumstances, rights and liabilities under a contract may themselves be treated as a 'relevant contract'. In particular, this applies where a company which is party to a hybrid derivative (which is a relevant contract which satisfies Section 579(1)(b) or 579(1)(c) of Part 7), a loan relationship or a contract which is neither a hybrid derivative nor a loan relationship treats certain rights and liabilities under that agreement as being divided, in accordance with generally accepted accounting principles, between:

- rights and liabilities under the embedded derivative; and
- the remaining rights and liabilities under the contract.

Part 7 will treat the rights associated with the derivative contract as a 'relevant contract' in its own right.

Hypothetical example of an embedded derivative; Green Ltd and Yates Ltd

Green Limited enters into a contract with Yates Limited to purchase 10,000 tonnes of cocoa for £2,000 per tonne for immediate delivery and payment. The sale and purchase contract also provides that Green Limited has the option to purchase a further 5,000 tonnes of cocoa for £2,000 per tonne in three months' time. Three months later, the price of cocoa in the market has risen to £2,100 per tonne. Green Limited decides to exercise the option and purchases the additional quantity of cocoa from Yates Limited.

Under Section 586 of Part 7, the agreement would be treated as consisting of two contracts – firstly, a sale-and-purchase agreement relating to the cocoa; and

---

secondly, a commodity option (the embedded derivative). Provided that the commodity option meets the other requirements to qualify for Part 7 treatment, then any profits and losses arising from that contract will be taxed under Part 7.

The rights and obligations associated with the rights and obligations under the sale-and-purchase contract will be taxed in accordance with the relevant provisions of the Corporation Tax Act 2009.

Where a loan relationship contains an embedded derivative, the profits and losses arising under each contract will be taxable under the respective parts of the Corporation Tax Act 2009 and the priority rules will have no effect in this area – profits and losses arising from the loan relationship will be taxable under Part 5 of the Corporation Tax Act 2009, and profits and losses arising from the embedded derivative will be taxed in accordance with Part 7.

(ii) *Exchange gains and losses*
Section 606 of Part 7 provides that the profits and losses arising to a company from its derivative contracts under Section 595(3) of Part 7 include any exchange profits or losses arising from that derivative contract.

There are exceptions. In particular, this section does not apply where either the exchange gain or loss arises in relation to a derivative contract whose underlying asset consists wholly or partly of currency. The section is also not applicable where the exchange gain or loss results from the translation from one currency to another of the profit or loss of part of the company's business.

(iii) *Company ceasing to be a party to a derivative contract*
Section 608 of Part 7 of the 2009 Act provides for a situation where a company ceases to be a party to a derivative contract in an accounting period, but does not bring all profits and losses into account at the time of cessation. For example, the accounting policies of the company may treat part of the profit or loss as deferred income or loss, bringing these into account in later accounting periods.

In these circumstances, the company must bring into account credits and debits in respect of so much of those profits or losses as have not been reflected in the accounts following the close-out. This is designed to ensure that all deferred income is brought into account.

(iv) *Transfers within groups*
Chapter 5 of Part 7 makes provision for where, as a result of a transaction or a series of transactions, a company replaces a member of the same group of companies as a party to a derivative contract. Both companies must be within the charge to corporation tax. One of the most common methods of transferring the rights and liabilities is by way of assignment.

Where one company replaces another, Sections 625 to 628 of Part 7 determine the credits and debits which can be brought into account. In essence, the transferor is treated as disposing of the transfer for an amount equal to the notional carrying value of the derivative contract. This is an amount which would have been its value in the accounts of the transferor had the accounting period ended immediately before the transfer. The transferee is treated as acquiring the contract for an amount equal to the notional carrying value.

Where some level of discount has been applied, this will increase the amount that the transferor is treated as having received. It will not affect the consideration that the transferee is treated as having paid.

These provisions can be disapplied by anti-avoidance legislation. This provides that the above treatment will not apply where the transferor is a party to the transaction or series of transactions for tax avoidance purposes under which the derivative contract will be transferred on by the transferee. This is also the case if another provision countering tax avoidance applies to a disposal which would otherwise be within these provisions.

Sections 630 to 632 of Part 7 provide that where the transferee leaves the group within six years of a transaction or series of transactions falling within the above provisions, there will be a deemed assignment of its rights and liabilities under the derivative contract (similar in concept to the degrouping provisions found in Section 179 of the Taxation of Chargeable Gains Act 1992). The transferee will be treated as having assigned its rights and liabilities under the relevant derivative contract for an amount equal to their fair value immediately before the transferee ceased to be a member of the group, and having immediately reacquired them for consideration of the same amount.

(d) Withholding tax

Under Section 980 of the Income Tax Act 2007, where the profits and losses of a derivative contract are calculated in accordance with Part 7, there is no obligation to make a deduction in respect of income tax from a payment made under a derivative contract.

4.3 Anti-avoidance and unallowable purpose

The anti-avoidance provisions which specifically relate to derivative contracts are contained in Chapter 11 of Part 7 of the Corporation Tax Act 2009. The provisions are extensive, reflecting the fact that derivatives have long been an attractive tax-structuring tool due to the fact that significant fluctuations in income can be generated without any requirement to own the underlying asset (and therefore without the corresponding risk of ownership).

(a) 'Unallowable purpose'

Section 690 of Part 7 provides that where a derivative contract has an "unallowable purpose", the company may not bring into account so much of any exchange credit or any debit in respect of that contract as is referable to the unallowable purpose.

The distinction should be noted that while only exchange credits are excluded from being brought into account, all debits are excluded. An 'exchange credit' is defined as a credit which is attributable to any exchange gains arising to the company from a derivative contract.

Relief is available where the company has "excess accumulated net losses" under

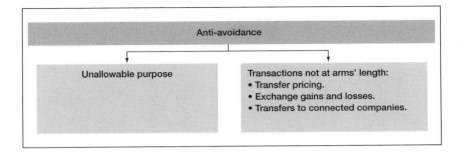

Section 692 of Part 7. In these circumstances, debits which have been excluded for an accounting period may be relieved in that or a later accounting period if there are non-excluded losses against which they may be offset.

However, the priority rule still applies – so where an amount cannot be brought into account due to this section, it is treated as having been brought into account for the purposes of the priority rule and therefore cannot be brought into account under any other provision of the Corporation Tax Acts.

For these purposes, Section 691 of Part 7 provides that a contract is said to have an 'unallowable purpose' if the purposes for which the company is a party to the derivative contract include a purpose which is not among the business or other commercial purposes of the company. This is also the case if the company enters into transactions which are related transactions by reference to that derivative contract.

Sections 691(3) and (4) of Part 7 apply where tax avoidance is one of the purposes for which the company either is a party to the derivative contract or enters into transactions which are related transactions by reference to that derivative contract. The sections provide that the tax avoidance will not constitute a business or commercial purpose where it is the main purpose, or one of the main purposes, of being party to the contract or entering into the related transactions.

Following consultation on the taxation of foreign profits in 2008 and 2009, there were moves by HMRC and HM Treasury to extend the application of the unallowable-purpose rules as they apply to derivative contracts. These proposals have now been dropped.

(b)   Transactions not at arm's length

(i)   Transfer pricing
The transfer pricing provisions contained in Schedule 28AA to the Income and Corporation Taxes Act 1988 also apply in relation to Part 7.

In particular, where an amount is treated as profits or losses (the 'imputed amount'), or as expenses incurred by a company under or for the purposes of its derivative contracts or related transactions, the related credits and debits are to be brought into account as if they were actual profits, losses or expenses.

(ii)   Exchange gains and losses
Section 694 of Part 7 applies where a company is party to a derivative contract and

an exchange gain or loss arises in relation to that contract. If, as a result of the application of Schedule 28AA, the company's profits and losses are calculated for tax purposes as if it were deemed not to be a party to the contract, then any exchange gains or losses which arise will be left out in determining the profits and losses to be brought into account under Part 7.

A similar determination is made if the application of Schedule 28AA would result in the profits and losses being calculated for tax purposes as if the terms of the contract had been agreed by two parties at arm's length. Here, the credits and debits to be brought into account will be those determined on the basis of the terms which would have been agreed had the parties been acting at arm's length.

(iii)   Transfers to connected companies

Section 695 of Part 7 deals specifically with tax avoidance relating to the use of options. It applies where one company pays an amount to another company for the grant of an option; and as a result of a failure to exercise in full the rights under the option, there is a transfer of value between the companies.

The section applies only where the companies are connected (for these purposes, if one company controls the other or both companies are controlled by a third party), and one company is not subject to corporation tax.

Where these conditions are met, the first company must bring into account a credit of the appropriate amount for the period in which the option expired or would have expired if none of the rights were exercised under it. The 'appropriate amount' for these purposes means the amount that the first company initially paid to the second company where the option expired; or that amount less an amount referable, on a just and reasonable basis, to the rights which were exercised.

4.4   International aspects

(a)   Derivatives held by non-UK resident companies

The provisions of Part 7 apply only to companies which are resident in the United Kingdom or trade through a permanent establishment in the United Kingdom. Where a derivative contract is held by a non-UK resident company which does not have a permanent establishment in the United Kingdom, profits and losses arising from the derivative contract are outside the scope of UK tax.

(b)   Redomiciliation and change of tax residence

It is becoming increasingly common for companies to migrate their tax residence. Section 609 of Part 7 is directed at situations where a derivative contract moves outside the UK tax net as a result of the company which holds the derivative contract ceasing to be chargeable for UK corporation tax.

In such circumstances, the company is treated as having made a deemed disposal and acquisition – it has assigned its rights and liabilities under the contract for consideration of an amount equal to their fair value immediately before the cessation of its UK tax residence, and immediately reacquired those rights and liabilities for consideration of the same amount.

'Fair value' is defined under Section 710 of Part 7 as the amount which a company would obtain or would have to pay to an independent person dealing at arm's length for the transfer of the company's rights under the contract and the release of all the company's liabilities under it.

4.5   Additional legislation

While the majority of the legislation relating to the taxation of derivative contracts is contained within Part 7, additional provisions are contained in other parts of the UK tax code – in particular, the Income Tax (Trading and Other Income) Act 2005 and the Taxation of Chargeable Gains Act 1992. These pieces of legislation will apply where a derivative contract falls outside the ambit of Part 7 – in such a case the derivative contract will generally be taxed under capital gains legislation.

Section 779 of the Income Tax (Trading and Other Income) Act provides that where a gain arises to a person in the course of dealing in commodity or financial futures or traded options, no liability to income tax will arise.

Section 143 of the Taxation of Chargeable Gains Act 1992 relates to commodity and financial futures and qualifying options. If, other than under Section 779 of the Income Tax (Trading and Other Income) Act, gains arising to any person in the course of dealing in commodity or financial futures or in qualifying options would constitute profits or gains chargeable to tax under Chapter 8 of Part 10 of the Corporation Tax Act 2009 or Chapter 8 of Part 5 of the Income Tax (Trading and Other Income) Act, then the outstanding obligations under any futures contract entered into in the course of that dealing and any qualifying option granted or acquired in the course of that dealing shall be regarded as assets to the disposal of which the Taxation of Chargeable Gains Act 1992 applies. Accordingly, any profits or gains will be subject to corporation tax on chargeable gains.

Section 143 of the Taxation of Chargeable Gains Act 1992 applies to commodity futures which are being dealt in on a recognised futures exchange, while a 'traded option' is defined as being an option which at the time of disposal is listed on a recognised stock exchange or a recognised futures exchange.

5.   UK-resident individuals

The majority of derivative contracts will be held by parties that are corporation tax payers. However, in certain circumstances, UK-resident individuals may also be a party to a derivative contract. Part 7 does not apply to such individuals; instead, the general UK tax rules apply.

The following discussion is based on the assumption that the individual is not acquiring and disposing of derivative contracts so frequently that he is treated as carrying on a trade.

Where an individual makes a profit, gain or loss on a derivative contract, this can be treated in one of three ways:

- The individual is outside the scope of UK tax – either income tax or capital gains tax – as the profit or gain is treated as being derived from a betting transaction and therefore not taxable;
- The individual is taxed on any profit in accordance with the income tax

rules; or

- The individual is taxed on any profit in accordance with the capital gains tax rules.

5.1 Outside the scope of UK tax

Any profit or gain derived from a derivative contract will be outside the scope of UK tax if it is treated as arising from a 'betting' transaction. However, if the gain is treated as arising from 'speculation', any profit or gain will be subject to either income tax or capital gains tax.

Cooper v Stubbs 10 TC 29 suggests that in order to determine whether a profit or gain from a derivative transaction will be treated as deriving from 'betting' or 'speculation', it is necessary to look at the identity and the intentions of the counterparty to the derivative contract.

5.2 Capital gains or income tax?

If the profit or gain from the transaction is treated as arising from speculation, rather than from betting, then it is necessary to work out whether the profit or gain will be taxed in accordance with the income tax or capital gains tax rules.

The relevant capital gains tax rules are contained in Section 143 of the Taxation of Chargeable Gains Act 1992, as discussed in section 4.5 above. Capital gains tax would be charged upon disposal of the asset at a (current) rate of 18%.

Should the derivative contract not fall within the provisions of Section 143, the profit or gain is likely to be taxed in accordance with the income tax rules. Currently, the top rate of UK income tax is 50%, imposed on income over £150,000.

6. VAT treatment of commodity derivatives

A detailed discussion of the value added tax (VAT) consequences associated with the holding of a commodity derivative contract is outside the scope of this chapter. However, a few brief points should be noted, as set out below.

The VAT treatment of a commodity derivative will vary depending on whether the derivative contract is to be cash settled or physically settled.

6.1 Cash-settled derivative contracts

A cash-settled derivative contract will qualify as an exempt financial instrument (Value Added Tax Act 1994, Schedule 9, Group 5, Item 1 and recast Sixth Directive 2006/112/EC, Article 135 1(d)). For the purposes of this contract, the place of supply will be determined by the location of the counterparty. Thus, in a situation where the counterparty is based outside the United Kingdom, the derivative contract will be outside the scope of UK VAT.

6.2 Physically settled derivative contracts

Where a derivative contract can or will be physically settled, there may be VAT consequences associated with this contract – even where there is no intention actually to physically settle the contract.

The VAT consequences will depend on a number of factors, including the location of the parties to the contract and the underlying subject matter. Typically, the VAT treatment will follow the VAT treatment of the underlying subject matter – and the derivative contract is therefore likely to attract VAT at the current rate (although certain commodities, such as food products, may be subject to a reduced rate).

The main exception to this is where a physically settled commodity derivative is traded on a 'qualifying terminal market', which includes the London Metal Exchange and the London Bullion Market, in which case the transaction may be treated as zero-rated for the purposes of VAT. Each exchange has specific rules to determine whether a transaction may be zero-rated.

> **Hypothetical example of VAT treatment of an option**
> Green Limited, which is located in the United Kingdom, enters into a physically settled European option with Yates Limited, which is also located in the United Kingdom, to purchase 1,000 ounces of gold at $900 per ounce in three months' time. Green Limited also pays a premium to Yates Limited of $10,000 for entering into this contract. Six months later, the gold price has risen to $1,000 per ounce and Green Limited exercises its right under the option to purchase gold from Yates Limited.
>
> For the purposes of the VAT analysis, the option between Green Limited and Yates Limited will be made up of two separate supplies. Firstly, the premium paid by Green Limited under the option – which relates to the right to buy the gold – will be treated as a standard-rated supply of services. The supply of gold by Yates Limited to Green Limited following exercise of the option will be treated as a supply of goods and subject to VAT.

7.   Conclusion

The chargeability of any profits or losses arising from a derivative contract to UK tax will have a significant impact on the profitability of a commodity derivative transaction. The law relating to the taxation of derivative contracts is extensive, particularly those provisions applicable to those parties liable to corporation tax. Any parties contemplating entering into a derivative contract that do not give due consideration to the direct and indirect tax consequences of a transaction may find that the taxman rains on their parade!

UK and EU regulatory aspects of commodity derivatives

Miles Bake

1. Introduction

Greed and fear: for as long as there have been markets, their oscillations have been driven by these twin devils. It is the job of regulation to tame these demons. This translates into three key policy objectives:

- to make markets operate fairly;
- to protect customers and investors; and
- to prevent so-called 'negative externalities' causing havoc (ie, problems created by the firm, but borne by the financial markets and wider society).

Regulators over the ages (and we are talking ages – King Hammurabi of Mesopotamia was regulating the use of derivatives some 4,000 years ago[1]) have sought to do this by deploying various tactical levers. Some attach to the instruments themselves (e.g., onion futures were banned by US Congress in the 1950s). Some are targeted at the firms using them, by way of outright business restrictions and by encouraging trading on safer platforms. Such approaches are being contemplated by regulators today. Throughout, it is notable that commodity derivatives, by the nature of their underlying reference points (ie, their link to the vital real economy of foodstuffs, metals and fuels), are qualitatively different from other sorts of derivatives, and so attract different market participants and regulatory challenges.

This chapter covers how regulators in the European Union (and specifically the United Kingdom) have approached these challenges, and it identifies some of the directions in which this area might develop.

2. EU framework

2.1 Background and policy considerations

The rationale behind the regulation of commodity derivatives is the same as for the regulation of any other financial instrument, especially complex financial instruments – to correct a perceived market failure, in order to:

- provide an appropriate degree of investor protection by setting minimum standards;
- promote market integrity (ie, through price discovery, transparency and the prevention of abuse); and

---

1   *The Economist*, November 14 2009, p 14.

- prevent systemic problems through prudential oversight.

To do this, regulation can attach to three things:
- to firms themselves (eg, in how they conduct their business or management systems);
- to instruments, by focusing on the qualities, characteristics and terms of the contracts; and
- to the markets on which these are traded (eg, by establishing minimum standards of disclosure).

In practice, regulatory objectives would be met through a combination of (ideally, harmonised) policies across these three areas. Broadly speaking, regulation has developed in this way through EU legislation, albeit at an uneven pace, via the European Commission's financial services action plan; the regulation of commodity derivatives and the firms using them has arisen more recently through the Markets in Financial Instruments Directive (MiFID) and the Market Abuse Directive.

2.2   Regulation on firms and instruments – MiFID

For much of their historic existence, commodity derivatives stood outside the formal EU regulatory framework relating to firms and instruments. For example, the EU Investment Services Directive (93/22/EEC), passed in 1993, did not capture these instruments within its scope.

The effects of various destabilising market events (eg, Enron and Amaranth) called this approach into question, as did the growth in the number of firms offering investment services based on commodity derivatives.[2]

Consequently, when the Investment Services Directive was being overhauled and modernised in the early part of this century, EU legislators took the step of bringing commodity derivatives as an instrument – and accordingly, firms trading in commodity and so-called 'exotic' derivatives[3] – within the regulatory sphere. This was achieved through MiFID[4] (which was implemented in the United Kingdom on November 1 2007).

MiFID tersely describes the rationale for extending into these areas in its opening recitals: "It is appropriate to include in the list of financial instruments certain commodity derivatives and others which are constituted and traded in such a manner as to give rise to regulatory issues comparable to traditional financial instruments."[5] Investor protection and market integrity are paramount among these regulatory issues.

There is no scope for EU member states to impose super-equivalent measures or 'gold-plating' to the MiFID rules. Thus, in theory, there should be a harmonised and

---

2   See www.fsa.gov.uk/Pages/About/What/International/basel/csg/comsg/index.shtml.
3   An 'exotic' derivative is one based on esoteric references such as weather, freight rates or emissions. See paragraph 2.2(a).
4   MiFID comprises two directives – an overarching 'level one' directive setting out the framework for the MiFID regulatory regime and a detailed implementation directive (Directive 2004/39/EC and Directive 2006/73/EC respectively) – and implementing regulations, Regulations 1287/2006.
5   Directive 2004/39/EC, Recital (4).

consistent level of protection throughout the European Union (consistent with the directive's single-market goals).

To try to encapsulate as sprawling a directive as MiFID in a sentence is challenging. The main point is that investment firms which provide certain services in relation to designated financial instruments must observe MiFID standards of business. MiFID also provides a passport for firms to provide those services throughout the European Economic Area (EEA). Thus the following three-stage test should be used to determine whether MiFID applies:

- Is it a MiFID investment?
- Is it a MiFID investment firm?
- Is it a MiFID service or ancillary service?

(a)   *MiFID instruments*

For the purposes of this chapter, commodities and exotic derivatives would typically fall within the MiFID definition of 'financial instruments'. The most obviously relevant definitions include the following for commodity derivatives:

Options, futures, swaps, forward rate agreements and any other derivative contracts relating to commodities that...

- *...must be settled in cash or may be settled in cash at the option of one of the parties (other than by reason of a default or other termination event)... [or]*
- *...can be physically settled provided they are traded on a regulated market and/or MTF (multilateral trading facility)... [or]*
- *...can be physically settled, not otherwise mentioned [i.e. not traded on a regulated market and/or MTF] and not being for commercial purposes, which have the characteristics of other derivative financial instruments, having regard to whether,* inter alia, *they are cleared and settled through recognised clearing houses or are subject to regular margin calls.*

A 'commodity' is defined as "any goods of a fungible nature that are capable of being delivered, including metals and their ores and alloys, agricultural products, and energy such as electricity".[6]

'Exotic derivatives' are defined as "options, futures, swaps, forward rate agreements and any other derivative contracts relating to climatic variables, freight rates [or] emission allowances...that must be settled in cash or may be settled in cash at the option of one of the parties (other than by reason of a default or other termination event)".

There is a further catch-all definition, bringing within MiFID "any other derivatives...which have the characteristics of other derivative financial instruments".[7]

One of the important points about these definitions is that the MiFID relates, as its name suggests, to financial instruments. It is for this reason that the first limb of the definition covers commodity derivatives that are:

- cash settled (ie, closely akin to a financial transaction);

---

6   Commission Regulation (EC) No 1287/2006.
7   Directive 2004/39/EC, Annex I, Section C, paragraphs (5)–(7) and (10).

- physically settled, but traded on certain financial markets; or
- like financial instruments and not for commercial purposes.

This is intended to provide a carve-out from MiFID for derivatives primarily designed for the hedging of, or transactions in, commodities as a matter of commerce (ie, getting commodities to market, rather than as financial tools or speculative instruments).

This distinction between commodity derivatives for finance and commodity derivatives for commercial purposes reflects the fact that the majority of trades in commodity derivatives are carried out by firms that are active in the market for the underlying commodity (eg, electricity generators and gas refiners) hedging their supply chain. Evidence from industry to the European Commission indicates that, for example:

- in Norway, two-thirds of commodity derivatives trades are carried out by firms that also trade the commodities in the cash markets; and
- in the United Kingdom, some 60% of authorised firms involved in commodity derivatives investment activities also operate commercially in the underlying commodity market.[8]

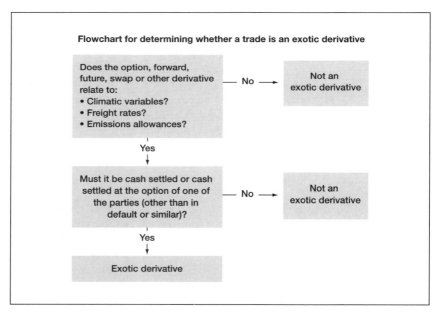

8   CESR/08-752, CEBS 2008 152 rev October 15 2008 (hereafter in this chapter the CEBS/CESR paper), p.15 paragraph 22.

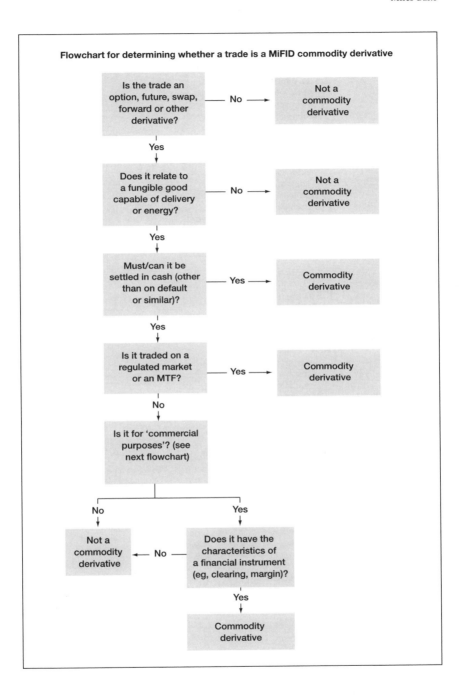

Flowchart for determining whether a trade is a MiFID commodity derivative

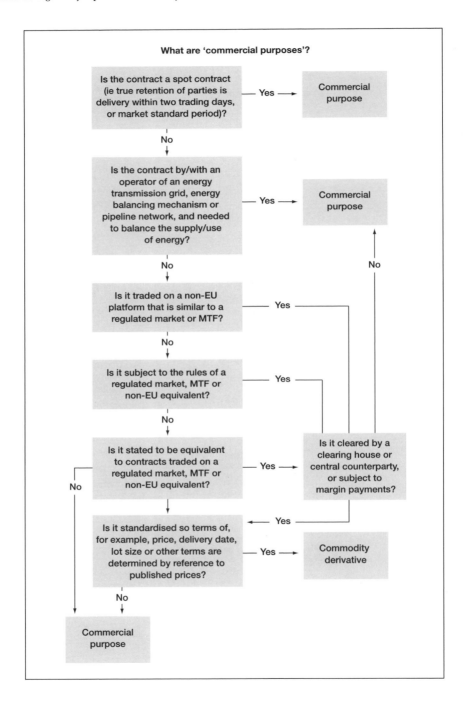

One of the problems with using a test of commercial purpose in the definition of 'commodity derivatives' is that it potentially brings in an unstable element of subjectivity (ie, what I may think of as a commercial purpose, you may think of as rank financial speculation). Moreover, where a trade may well have overlapping characteristics and purposes, the definition on its own is clearly insufficient for market participants or in the interests of legal certainty. Taking this into account, the MiFID implementing regulation provides guidance on the question of whether a trade would be characterised as having a commercial purpose.

The MiFID implementing regulation is regrettably not drafted in model plain English. For guidance on the concept of the 'commercial purpose' for 'other' commodity derivatives, it provides what is set out next.

Guidance box 1

1. For the purposes of Section C(7) of Annex I to Directive 2004/39/EC [i.e., 'other' commodity derivatives], a contract which is not a spot contract within the meaning of paragraph 2...and which is not covered by paragraph 4 shall be considered as having the characteristics of other derivative financial instruments and not being for commercial purposes if it satisfies the following conditions:

(a) it meets one of the following sets of criteria:

(i) it is traded on a third country trading facility that performs a similar function to a regulated market or an MTF;

(ii) it is expressly stated to be traded on, or is subject to the rules of, a regulated market, an MTF or such a third country trading facility;

(iii) it is expressly stated to be equivalent to a contract traded on a regulated market, MTF or such a third country trading facility;

(b) it is cleared by a clearing house or other entity carrying out the same functions as a central counterparty, or there are arrangements for the payment or provision of margin in relation to the contract;

(c) it is standardised so that, in particular, the price, the lot, the delivery date or other terms are determined principally by reference to regularly published prices, standard lots or standard delivery dates.

2. A spot contract for the purposes of paragraph 1 means a contract for the sale of a commodity, asset or right, under the terms of which delivery is scheduled to be made within the longer of the following periods:

(a) two trading days;

(b) the period generally accepted in the market for that commodity, asset or right as the standard delivery period.

However, a contract is not a spot contract if, irrespective of its explicit terms, there is an understanding between the parties to the contract that delivery of the underlying is to be postponed and not to be performed within the period mentioned in the first subparagraph.

...

4. A contract shall be considered to be for commercial purposes for the purposes of Section C(7) of Annex I to Directive 2004/39/EC, and as not having the

characteristics of other derivative financial instruments for the purposes of Sections C(7) and (10) of that Annex, if it is entered into with or by an operator or administrator of an energy transmission grid, energy balancing mechanism or pipeline network, and it is necessary to keep in balance the supplies and uses of energy at a given time.

A similar, and no less linguistically stodgy, approach is followed for 'other' exotic derivatives.

Guidance box 2

2. In addition to derivative contracts of a kind referred to in Section C(10) of Annex I to Directive 2004/39/EC, a derivative contract relating to any of the following shall fall within that Section if it meets the criteria set out in that Section and in Article 38(3):

(a) telecommunications bandwidth;

(b) commodity storage capacity;

(c) transmission or transportation capacity relating to commodities, whether cable, pipeline or other means;

(d) an allowance, credit, permit, right or similar asset which is directly linked to the supply, distribution or consumption of energy derived from renewable resources;

(e) a geological, environmental or other physical variable;

(f) any other asset or right of a fungible nature, other than a right to receive a service, that is capable of being transferred;

(g) an index or measure related to the price or value of, or volume of transactions in any asset, right, service or obligation.

For the purposes of Section C(10) of Annex I to Directive 2004/39/EC, a derivative contract relating to an underlying referred to in that Section or in Article 39 shall be considered to have the characteristics of other derivative financial instruments if one of the following conditions is satisfied:

(a) that contract is settled in cash or may be settled in cash at the option of one or more of the parties, otherwise than by reason of a default or other termination event;

(b) that contract is traded on a regulated market or an MTF;

(c) the conditions laid down in paragraph 1 [in Guidance Box 1, above] relating to commodities derivatives [see box above] are satisfied in relation to that contract.

However, the division of the commodity derivatives market by regulators into financial and commercial is not necessarily static, as markets and investment opportunities evolve. This has been the subject of an ongoing EU consultation.

(b)   *MiFID standards*

We have established that commodity and exotic derivatives with the characteristics of a financial investment fall within the scope of MiFID. What are the implications of this? And for whom?

MiFID applies to investment firms and to credit institutions (in so far as the latter provide MiFID investment services or perform MiFID investment activities).[9] An 'investment firm' is technically defined as "any legal person whose regular occupation or business is the provision of one or more investment services to third parties and/or the performance of one or more investment activities on a professional basis".[10] In other words, any business proferring investment services to third parties or engaging in investment activities on its own behalf must comply with MiFID (subject to any exemptions).

'Investment services' and 'investment activities' are also defined by MiFID. To recite the full extensive lists here would not be valuable – keen readers can look at Annex 1, Sections A and B of EU Directive 2004/39/EC. Suffice it to say that in the context of commodity or exotic derivatives, MiFID investment services and activities include:

- transmitting orders;
- executing client orders;
- providing investment advice;
- dealing on one's own account; and
- in relation to the underlying commodity or variable, doing any of the above in connection with the commodity derivative.

So, if the firm is performing such activities in relation to MiFID-qualifying commodity or exotic derivatives, it falls within MiFID's scope. What, then, are the key implications of being caught by MiFID?

The first key point is what MiFID does not do. It does not say that an investment firm can perform activities/services only in relation to MiFID investments (here, commodity or exotic derivatives). Quite the reverse. It says that if you do MiFID business in those investments, then these are the standards you must meet. Going back to the regulatory theory at the start of this chapter, the point is that if you are a MiFID firm doing MiFID business in these commodity derivatives, for reasons of market integrity and consumer protection these are the standards and operational requirements by which you must abide.

(c) Key MiFID requirements
The following are key MiFID requirements:
- Organisation – this covers a multitude of virtues and basically sets out the systems and functions that a firm must put in place.
- Outsourcing – rules on outsourcing functions (eg, the terms of business with third-party providers) are imposed on MiFID firms.
- Safeguarding of client assets – this covers the required procedures for record keeping, segregation of funds, accounting for holding client assets and

9   Directive 2004/39/EC, Article 1.1.
10   Directive 2004/39/EC, Article 4.1. The definition extends to capture natural persons and non-legal entities in certain relatively remote circumstances.

509

utilising them during the period of custody.

- Managing conflicts of interest – this requires the firm to act honestly and fairly.
- Client classification – each client of a MiFID firm must be categorised as either a retail client, a professional client or an eligible counterparty. Different levels of client protection apply, depending on the category of the client.
- Best execution – this has been subject to considerable detailed elaboration by the Committee of European Banking Supervisors (CEBS), but in essence requires a firm, when dealing with a retail or professional client, to obtain "the best possible result... to the extent that it executes an order or a specific part of an order following specific instructions from the client".[11]
- Transparency obligations – these include obligations to provide data on trades, including prices. The extent of this obligation varies depending on whether the trade is on a regulated market or on a multilateral trading facility.

(d)   *Specific exemptions from the MiFID*

There are two major exemptions from the scope of the MiFID, which are relevant for our purposes. The first, set out in Article 2.1(i), covers:

persons dealing on own account in financial instruments, or providing investment services in commodity derivatives or [exotic] derivatives...to the clients of their main business, provided this is an ancillary activity, when considered on a group basis, and that the main business is not the provision of investment services within the meaning of [MiFID] or banking services under Directive 2002/12/ED.

The second, set out in Article 2, is an exemption for "persons whose main business consists of dealing on own account in commodities and/or commodity derivatives". This exemption covers commodity derivatives only; it does not cover exotic derivatives.

The overall effect of these two exemptions is relevant to traders in commodity and exotic derivatives that act as part of a commercial commodities business rather than a financial business (eg, hedging by a steel producer). It is also relevant for hedging and incidental investment activities.[12]

Again, this relates to the objectives of regulation: it is the view of European regulators that such standalone commodity-derivatives trading firms do not pose risks to the financial market and its participants, and therefore should not be subject to strict financial regulation.

The effect of this is that no firm within the exemption is required to apply MiFID rules (eg, client categorisation, transparency, internal systems and controls).

The rationale for these carve-outs is that these activities would not provide a source of counterparty risk to other market participants and accordingly should not fall within

---

11   Directive 2006/73/EC, Article 44.
12   Response from the European Securities Markets Expert Group (ESME) Sub-group on Commodities, page 52.

the scope of prudential regulation.[13] In its implementing regulation, the European Commission anticipated that the effect of these two exemptions was to "exclude significant numbers of commercial producers and consumers of energy and other commodities, including energy suppliers, commodity merchants and their subsidiaries".

The validity of this exemption is the subject of ongoing review by the commission (see below).

2.3   Capital Requirements Directive

(a)   Introduction and purpose

At the start of this chapter (see section 2.1), we noted that the aims of regulation include investor protection, market integrity and the prevention of systematic or externality risk. MiFID, broadly speaking, deals with the first two. For systemic risk – and the so-called 'prudential' oversights and standards that govern this area – we turn to the field of capital requirements.

The Capital Requirements Directive (CRD) consists of two linked directives: the Banking Consolidation Directive (2006/48/EC) and the Capital Adequacy Directive (2006/49/EC). The Banking Consolidation Directive effectively governs the operations of banks and other credit institutions, and includes requirements as to how much capital they are required to hold in respect of their non-trading (ie, banking) book. The Capital Adequacy Directive extends the scope of the Banking Consolidation Directive to certain classes of investment firm and addresses the prudential question of how much capital must be held by investment firms, banks and other credit institutions in respect of each of their trading books. The CRD also imposes certain operational restrictions (eg, on large exposures to linked counterparties) and provides a pan-EEA passport for banking activities.[14]

The CRD relates to commodity derivatives in two ways.

First, at a firm-wide level, the parameters of the directive – its scope, in terms of who and what is subject to it – are set out according to which sorts of firm pose systemic risk, based on the kinds of business they do. It is for this reason that banks – which, as we have seen, can pose significant systemic risk – are captured, whereas firms that have been perceived not to pose a systemic risk (eg, hedge funds) are not subject to the directive's strictures. As we shall see, commodity derivatives businesses may or may not fall within the scope of the CRD, depending on whether they are part of larger institutions that do fall under the directive's scope.

Second, once a firm falls within the directive's scope, its assets are subject to risk weighting which is calibrated, broadly speaking, on how risky the asset is (in terms of ability to recover liquid value). The risk weighting determines how much capital (equity and subordinated debt) the firm must have (or hold) in respect of those assets. The higher an asset's risk weighting, the more capital must be held against it and, accordingly, the more expensive (in terms of capital costs) it is for the firm to

---

13   *Ibid*, Recital 25.
14   The trading book is defined in Article 11 of the Capital Adequacy Directive as "all positions in financial instruments and commodities held either with trading intent or in order to hedge".

hold the asset. Where a firm has a position in a commodity derivative, it will potentially be an asset against which capital must be held. By this mechanism, as we shall see below, regulators calibrate assets according to their riskiness – although at a theoretical level, the precise risk weightings are not a subject of academic or political consensus, and the risk weighting in itself can be a factor in shaping a market (eg, if something is cheaply or expensively risk weighted, it will attract or repel investors).

(b)   Capital requirements at instrument level

The CRD distinguishes between assets held on the firm's trading book and those held on its non-trading book (colloquially known as its banking book). Banking book and trading book assets attract different capital requirements (the basis for this being that a trading asset has a qualitatively different risk profile from a 'hold-to-maturity' banking asset).

(i)   Banking book

The banking or non-trading book comprises those assets which a firm subject to the CRD holds which are not part of its trading book (ie, not held with trading intent). CRD firms are required to calculate their capital requirements in respect of credit risk and dilution risk for all items on their banking books.[15]

A firm can do this using either the standardised approach or the internal ratings-based approach. The principle is the same: the 'exposure value' for each asset is calculated and then multiplied by a risk weighting, which translates into a capital requirement. For derivatives, these are known as the 'counterparty credit-risk capital requirements' – that is, the capital required to cover the risk of the derivatives counterparty defaulting before settlement.

For commodity and exotic derivatives (using the MiFID definitions), the standardised approach involves calculating the exposure value of the position in accordance with Annex III of the Banking Consolidation Directive,[16] which takes into account any exposure value and netting.

Annex III sets out the methods by which the requirements may be determined. A CRD firm using the standardised approach may, for commodity and exotic derivatives, use:

- the mark-to-market method; or
- for over-the-counter (OTC) and long-settlement transactions[17] only, the standardised method.

The mark-to-market method[18] involves three stages:

- First, calculate the current market values so as to obtain the current replacement cost of all contracts with positive values.

---

15   Article 75(a) of the Banking Consolidation Directive.
16   Article 78.2 of the Banking Consolidation Directive.
17   In this context, long-settlement transactions are those where a counterparty undertakes to deliver a commodity against cash or other commodity, or vice versa, at a contractual settlement or delivery date that is more than the lower of the market standard for this type of transaction or five business days from the trade date. Annex III, Point 3 of the Banking Consolidation Directive.
18   Annex III, Part 3 of the Banking Consolidation Directive.

- Second, calculate a figure for the potential future credit exposure by multiplying the notional principal amount or underlying value by the applicable multiples in one of two tables (see below). Table 1 is the default table; CRD firms can use Table 2 for non-gold derivatives if their national regulator has given them permission to do so – the permission will depend on whether the firm has a 'significant' commodities business and diversified commodities portfolio, but cannot yet use the internal ratings-based approach.
- Finally, add together the current market value and the potential future credit exposure to obtain the exposure value.

The exposure value is then multiplied by the applicable counterparty risk weighting to obtain the counterparty risk-weighted exposure amount.

Table 1

Residual maturity	Contracts concerning gold	Contracts concerning non-gold precious metals	Contracts concerning commodities other than precious metals	MiFID exotic and other derivatives
One year or less	1%	7%	10%	10%
> One year, ≤ five years	5%	7%	12%	12%
> Five years	7.5%	8%	15%	15%

Table 2

Residual maturity	Non-gold precious metals	Base metals	Agricultural products	Other, industrial energy
One year or less	2%	2.5%	3%	4%
> One year, ≤ five years	5%	4%	5%	6%
> Five years	7.5%	8%	9%	10%

The standardised method for OTC derivatives and long-settlement transactions[19] is a formula for calculating the exposure for each 'netting set' (ie, set of transactions with a single counterparty subject to a legally enforceable common netting agreement,[20] such as an ISDA Master Agreement).

The formula takes into account:

- the current market value of the portfolio of transactions within the netting set;
- any collateral assigned to that netting set;
- a risk factor to be applied to the transactions and the collateral; and
- a credit counterparty risk multiplier for each hedging set.

Hedging sets are determined by the similarity of the instruments. In terms of commodities, the Banking Consolidation Directive gives the following guidance as to what constitutes a 'similar investment':[21]

- for precious metals, those in the same metal;
- for electrical power, deliveries to the same peak or off-peak load within any 24-hour interval; and
- for any other commodity, the same commodity.

In each case, indices are treated separately (ie, not similar).

The credit counterparty risk multiplier applicable to commodity derivatives also varies depending on the type of underlying commodity, as illustrated by Table 3.

Table 3

Hedging set	Credit counterparty risk multiplier
Electric power	4%
Gold	5%
Non-gold precious metals	8.5%
Other commodities	10%
Other derivatives	10%

Under the internal ratings-based approach, CRD firms may deploy a third method for deteriorating the exposure value, using internal models. This essentially involves applying a fixed multiplier (1.4× is the default, but firms may be permitted

19   Annex III, Part 5 of the Banking Consolidation Directive.
20   Annex III, Part 5 of the Banking Consolidation Directive. The criteria for the netting agreement that we set out appear in Annex III, Part 7.
21   Annex III, Part 5, Point 17 of the Banking Consolidation Directive.

514

lower multipliers, subject to a floor of 1.2×) to 'effective' exposures (which involves taking the average of the destitution of exposures on netting set), together with a host of 'conduct of business' requirements on the firm, including the management of market, liquidity, legal and operational risks and stress-testing.

'Central counterparties' are legal entities interposed between counterparties to contracts, being the seller to every buyer and the buyer to every seller.[22]

In a trade involving central counterparties, all counterparty risk is located solely with that central counterparty; therefore, an exposure value of zero is given (ie, no risk capital need be held against it). This makes for a powerful capital incentive to use central counterparties for derivatives trades of all types, including commodity and exotic derivatives. As discussed below, it is now EU policy to encourage use of central counterparties.

(ii)   *Trading book*

The trading book comprises positions held "for trading purposes and which are subject mainly to market risks" – specifically, "with trading intent [ie, to benefit from short-term resale or short-term price differentials] or in order to hedge other elements of the trading book".[23] Because of this, the capital to be held against settlement and counterparty credit risk in the trading book needs to be calculated.

For settlement risk, where settlement is late, capital needs to be held based on the difference between the agreed settlement price and the current market value, multiplied by a scaling factor depending on the lateness; or, where delivery is 'free' (ie, a party has delivered and not received payment, or paid and not received delivery), capital needs to be held based on the banking-book approach to the probability of that counterparty defaulting (see (i) above).[24]

A counterparty credit risk requirement for OTC derivatives and commodities lending or borrowing transactions based on commodities in the trading book should also be calculated, using the same rules for calculating counterparty credit risk as in the banking-book treatment.[25]

(iii)   *All business*

In respect of all business activities, for all positions involving commodities risk an amount of capital needs to be held.[26] 'Positions' includes both proprietary positions and positions arising from client servicing or market making.[27]

The capital requirement for such positions is divided into a number of components, each representing a discrete risk associated with a position. In broad terms, the situation for commodity derivatives (other than gold) is as follows.[28]

The first task is to establish the net position in a particular commodity derivative.

22	Annex III, Point 2 of the Banking Consolidation Directive.
23	Article 11.1 of the Capital Adequacy Directive.
24	Annex II of the Capital Adequacy Directive paragraphs 1–4.
25	Annex II of the Capital Adequacy Directive, paragraphs 5 and 6.
26	Article 75(c) of the Banking Consolidation Directive.
27	Article 11.2 of the Capital Adequacy Directive.
28	This is a complex area and the given summary is just a guide to the analysis that will be required for a commodity derivative held in the trading book.

In this regard, highly correlated commodities may be considered the same for netting purposes. For the purposes of netting involving commodity options, the delta-adjusted commodity option may be netted against any positions in the underlying commodity.[29]

For exchange-traded futures and centrally cleared OTC derivatives, the position risk will be the margin required by the exchange or clearing-house.

Otherwise, the position risk is calculated in one of three ways:

- Under the maturity ladder approach, the position risk requirement is the aggregate of a spread (based on the position's maturity), a carry (based on the position and the spot price) and an outright amount for unmarked positions (based on the outright rate, the spot price and the position). This approach has been criticised (eg, by the Committee of European Securities Regulators (CESR) and the CEBS),[30] as being far too blunt a methodology for commodity derivatives, which "could lead to overestimating or underestimating capital requirements", particularly as the netting rules assume correlations which are not necessarily accurate (eg, delivery of electricity in one hour of a day (peak) can be uncorrelated to delivery of electricity at a different time (off-peak), which the maturity ladders do not reflect).
- A simplified approach, which is the sum of:
  - 15% of the net position, multiplied by the applicable spot price; and
  - 3% of the gross position, multiplied by the applicable spot price.
- An extended maturity ladder approach, which may be used by firms with a significant commodities business and a diversified commodities portfolio. This is essentially the same as the maturity ladder approach, but has a more nuanced approach to the spread, carry and outright rates, which are varied according to the nature of the underlying commodity (ie, precious metals (excluding gold), base metals, agricultural products and the rest).

For more sophisticated firms – analogous to firms using the internal ratings-based approach for the banking book – an internal model-based approach may be used. This involves calculating the capital requirement using a value-at-risk methodology. As far as this relates to commodities, any risk arising from less-than-perfect correlation should be captured in the model.

Counterparty credit risk should be calculated as it would be under the banking book rules (see (i) above).

To deal with large exposures for positions that would also constitute large exposures under the banking book rules, a ratcheted multiplier (based on the excess exposure over the exposure limit) is applied to the capital charge.

Gold is treated for trading book capital purposes not as a commodity, but as a foreign currency. Therefore, to the extent the firm's net gold position exceeds 2% of

---

29   Capital Adequacy Directive, Annex IV, paragraph 10: "The delta used shall be that of the exchange concerned, that calculated by the competent authorities or, where none of those is available, or for OTC options, that calculated by the institution itself, subject to the competent authorities being satisfied that the model used … is reasonable."
30   CEBS/CESR consultation, p 65, paragraph 264.

its total own funds, the capital requirement for foreign exchange risk is the net gold position multiplied by 8%.

(c) European Commission reform proposals for derivatives markets

Since the financial crisis broke, and particularly given ructions in the fabric of credit counterparty risk arising from Lehman Brothers' insolvency and AIG's collapse, regulators the world over have been looking to reduce the chains of interconnectedness in derivatives markets, particularly credit default swaps.

Part of the toolkit of regulators in the area is to encourage use of central counterparties for clearing OTC and other derivatives. One of the findings from the Lehman Brothers crisis was that participants in the OTC market had little clear idea of who the counterparties of their counterparties were: since the creditworthiness of all counterparties was being questioned, such uncertainty fuelled fear.

It is in this environment that a centralised counterparty acts like a fire break – a clearance in a forest across which an incendiary front cannot pass, insulating parties from other market participants.[31] Of course, in such a situation the credit quality of the central counterparty must be unassailable.

It is because of these considerations that the European Commission has recently brought forward preliminary proposals for a regulatory – in particular, prudential – framework which promotes the use of centralised counterparties. The commission's thinking in relation to derivatives is set out in a communication entitled 'Ensuring Efficient, Safe and Sound Derivatives Markets; Future Policy Actions', published on October 26 2009. The communication sets out policy parameters and objectives which the commission hopes to push forward in 2010.

The communication asserts the commission's wish to allow efficient allocation of resources through a true and clear pricing of risk which, the commission asserts, has been a market shortcoming. Critically, it does not want to prevent certain contracts: "the Commission does not want to limit the economic terms of derivative contracts, neither to prohibit the use of customised contracts nor to make them excessively costly for non-financial institutions."[32] Instead it hopes to incentivise more prudent behaviour (or rather, perhaps disincentivise risky behaviour)[33] through regulation. It considers the role of central counterparties (CCPs) pivotal to this aim: "The crisis has shown, *inter alia*, that market participants did not price counterparty credit risk correctly. Clearing is the way by which this risk is mitigated... The Commission has identified CCP–clearing as the main tool to manage counterparty risks and the G20 shares this view."

The policy implications of this position are multiple.

First, central counterparties themselves should be governed prudently. Accordingly, the commission will prepare legislation for central counterparties to "ensure [their] safety, soundness and proper governance".[34] This will cover central

---

31   The metaphor is taken from a speech by Andrew Haldane, executive director, financial stability at the Bank of England, entitled "Rethinking the Financial Network", in April 2009 (available at www.bankofengland.co.uk/publications/speeches/2009/speech386.pdf).
32   Communication, p 3.
33   Obviously these are two sides of the same coin.
34   Communication, p 4.

counterparties clearing, and commodity and exotic derivatives.

Second, bilateral clearing will be disincentivised through the imposition of margin posting requirements on banks, investment firms and other financial investment firms. This will effectively widen the cost of capital between central counterparty clearing and bilateral clearing – at least as far as financial firms are concerned. For non-financial firms – which would include existing 'specialist commodity firms' – it is not yet clear how far the initial and variation margin requirements would extend.[35]

Third, again to widen the capital cost spread between central counterparty clearing and bilateral clearing, the commission intends to increase the capital requirements on bilaterally cleared derivatives contracts.[36]

Fourth, from an operational point of view, the commission intends to mandate central clearing for standardised derivatives and increase the 'Pillar 2' capital requirement on firms using non-standardised contracts. Given how broadly standardised many commodity derivatives are, since so many are exchange traded, this would seem to be of limited import to commodity derivatives.

Fifth, outright limitations on speculative positions may be contemplated (possibly *in extremis*).

Sixth, pre- and post-trade transparency requirements for the disclosure of prices will be increased, if not for disclosure to the market then at least so that regulators who stand on the heights surveying the financial system can see signs of systemic hurricanes swelling.

At present, the impact that these changes would have on commodity derivatives is only hypothetical. However, it is reasonable to point out that the further provisions of central counterparty clearing may have only a small impact. This is because the majority of commodity derivatives by value are already cleared in this way: as CESR and CEBS point out in their consultation paper, in the United Kingdom alone some $5 trillion of oil derivatives are cleared through a clearing house; and in 2007 some 95.5 million metals contracts were traded via the London Metals Exchange.[37]

A final argument should be reserved specifically for commodity derivatives. Here, the problem with treating commodities homogeneously comes up against the fact that different commodities attract different political and social considerations: platinum and pork bellies may exist side by side in the International Swaps and Derivatives Association (ISDA) definitions, but they do not in EU policy terms. For this reason, a diversified and tailored approach is required (and, in fairness, is being proposed).

For example, the communication cites the G20 Pittsburgh Summit's call "to improve the regulation, functioning and transparency of financial and commodity markets to address excessive commodity price volatility". While some economic purists may quibble with the concept of 'excessive' volatility *per se*, the policy response is a disaggregated one:

- With regard to agricultural products, the commission plans to issue a

---

35   *Id*, pp 4 and 5.
36   *Id*, p 5.
37   Consultation paper on CESR/CEBS's technical advice to the European Commission, May 15 2008 (hereafter, "CEBS/CESR correlations"), p 10, paragraph 27.

statement on the food supply chain in due course in 2010.

- For gas and electricity markets, the commission will be bringing forward proposals in 2010 for wholesale spot market transparency.
- The commission will be examining questions of market integrity for emissions by the end of 2010.
- For the MiFID generally, the commission will be reconsidering the existing commodity firm exceptions (a project already well under way).

(d) *Other CRD requirements*

As mentioned, the CRD is largely about putting in place prudential standards. The preceding sections have discussed how this relates to specific positions in commodity derivatives, but the CRD imposes many more general requirements on firms, including absolute capital (own funds') minima, and operations restrictions such as limitations on the site of exposures to connected counterparties.

(e) *Specialist commodity firms exemption*

While a precise delineation of what sorts of firm are subject to these requirements (in whole or in part – and there are a number of exemptions) is beyond the scope of this chapter, one carve-out is relevant: investment firms where the business consists exclusively of providing investment services in relation to commodity and exotic derivatives are exempt from the CRD's capital requirements.[38]

The rationale for this is that such standalone firms do not post a systemic risk to the financial sector and accordingly it would be disproportionate to subject them to the CRD.

This applies only for standalone specialist commodity derivatives firms. It does not apply to subsidiaries of larger investment firms or credit institutions, which are required to maintain capital in the normal way.

One effect of this is that such specialist commodities firms can gain an EU passport to carry out business across the European Union without being required to meet other CRD standards, which is a quick way in but is not particularly pivotal from a prudential point of view. More significant is the question of whether such an exemption gives these specialist commodities firms a competitive advantage over other firms which must comply with the CRD. This is a question upon which the commission has consulted experts and industry extensively (see section 4 below).

3. The Market Abuse Directive

The Market Abuse Directive (2003/6/EC) requires specialist commodity firms to comply only with the large exposure rules, which are often seen as disproportionate.[39]

There is the possibility that commodity derivatives, to the extent that they are traded on regulated markets, could be susceptible to market abuse. Market abuse is thus governed by the directive, as transposed into EU member states' laws. The

---

38 Article 48.1 of the Capital Adequacy Directive.
39 CESR/CEBS paper, p 58 para 235.

general position is that certain types of behaviour in relation to qualifying investments that are admitted to trading on prescribed markets, or where a request for admission to trading on such a market has been made (or in relation to investments which are related to qualifying investments – that is, where the price of the related investment depends on the price of the qualifying investment) may amount to abuse. Seven kinds of behaviour can constitute market abuse:

- insider dealing;
- improper disclosure of inside information;
- misuse of information;
- manipulating transactions;
- manipulating devices;
- dissemination of information to create a false or misleading impression; and
- market distortion or misleading behaviour.

The definition of 'inside information', which is at the heart of the first three types of market abuse, is different for commodity derivatives compared with for other types of qualifying or related investment. It reads:

In relation to investments which are commodity derivatives, inside information is information of a precise nature which -

    (a) is not generally available,

    (b) relates, directly or indirectly, to one or more such derivatives, and

    (c) users of markets on which the derivatives are traded would expect to receive in accordance with any accepted market practices on those markets.

And by way of guidance as to what is covered by 'misuse of information':

For the purposes of subsection (c), users of markets on which investments in commodity derivatives are traded are to be treated as expecting to receive information ... which is –

    (i) routinely made available to the users of those markets, or

    (ii) required to be disclosed in accordance with any statutory provision, market rules, or contracts or customs on the relevant underlying commodity market or commodity derivatives market.[40]

The reason for this specific definition is that commodity derivatives are so often used for commercial purposes (ie, hedging supply-chain costs and receivables), and as such, traders would have knowledge of the underlying supply and demand market in that commodity.

Take, as an example, a major electricity producer. It may want to hedge the price of electricity and could do this through a derivatives instrument. However, as a major electricity producer, it would also have knowledge of its anticipated levels of electricity production, which may be affected by idiosyncratic factors (eg, whether a new power plant is due to be opened, whether it is on schedule, or whether repairs are needed to a generation facility which will crimp production). The value of the derivative would be partly dependent on the underlying production level, which can

---

40   Sections 118(C)3 and 118(C)7 of the Financial Services Market Act 2000.

be influenced by the electricity producer. This information asymmetry could potentially be abused in the derivatives pricing.

Hence, the definition of 'inside information' for commodity derivatives distinguishes between information customarily made available to the market (and hence counterparties) and information which is not – the definition is intended to be flexible enough to cover the different qualities of underlying commodities. As the CEBS/CESR response put it succinctly: "Derivatives trading [by producers] based on knowledge of their production and supply activities should not generally be regarded as an inappropriate use of information unless that information is expected to be publicly available."[41]

CEBS/CESR note that informational asymmetries can lead to abusive market conduct and in their consultation paper described the admission by BP America to the US Department of Justice that it manipulated the price of February 2004 TET physical propane.[42]

However, CEBS/CESR sidestepped giving a definitive and absolute response, by saying that "issues relating to market abuse should be addressed in the Commission's wider reviews of the Market Abuse Directive".[43]

4.   Review of MiFID, CRD and market abuse positions

The CRD exemption and possible exemptions to MiFID were the subject of negotiation when MiFID was being prepared. Agreement between member states and the European Union was arrived at on the basis that there would follow a more extensive, EU-wide review of the regimes relating to commodity derivatives. For this reason, the Capital Adequacy Directive exemption has an explicit sunset date of no later than December 31 2010, with provision for the European Commission to report on what would be an appropriately prudential supervisory regime for specialist commodity derivatives firms. The MiFID hardwired this review into its provisions.[44]

The commission's review process cannot be accused of being excessively simplistic or rushed. It began shortly after MiFID came into effect, with the commission issuing three calls for advice in December 2007 to:

- the CESR and the CEBS;[45]
- the European Securities Markets Expert Group (ESME) Sub-group on Commodities; and
- the CEDR and the European Regulators' Group for Electricity and Gas (ERGEG).

Each of these calls for advice covered a slightly different area.

4.1   The CESR/CEBS response

The joint call to the CESR and the CEBS was more technical in nature, and

---

41   CEBS/CESR paper, p 17 paragraph 31.
42   CEBS/CESR consultation, p 24 paragraph 80.
43   CEBS/CESR paper, p 30 paragraph 97.
44   Directive 2004/39/EC, Article 65.
45   Each call is available at www.ec.europa.eu/internal_market/securities/isd/mifid_reports_en.htm.

questioned whether the existing regulatory regime and Capital Adequacy Directive/MiFID carve-out could give rise to market failure or regulatory failure (arising from the different treatments of different categories of firm providing investment services relating to commodity derivatives). It also questioned the likely impact of various policy options.

The CEBS and CESR responded by creating a joint taskforce on commodities, issuing a call for advice of their own to the industry and running a consultation in Spring 2008 to inform the commission of their ultimate response in October 2008.

The CESR/CEBS response[46] is an extremely comprehensive paper discussing both the rationale for regulating specialist commodities business and its potential technical content.

On a macro level, its main findings are as follows:

- Most participants in commodity derivatives markets are sophisticated and there is limited potential for significant information asymmetries (and hence abusive market conduct – see below).
- Although there are low levels of transparency on OTC commodity derivatives markets, regulated trading firms in the OTC space do not consider this a deterrent to trading.
- Although activities of specialist commodity derivatives firms may give rise to systemic risk, this is generally lower than for credit institutions and investment firms.[47]

Indeed, CEBS/CESR note that financial interconnectedness between specialist commodity derivatives firms and other financial institutions has not led to significant financial instability, and they cite the collapse of the Amaranth hedge fund in 2006 as supporting evidence, along with the problems at Sumitomo, Enron and Metallgesellschaft.[48]

With regard to the policy implications of the CRD, applying MiFID and the CRD to specialist commodity derivatives firms "would be disproportionate and would lead to regulatory failure".[49] The CESR/CEBS analysis on this was twofold: on the one hand, would it be disproportionate and excessive to make specialist commodity firms subject to the full scope of capital requirements? (Answer – yes.) On the other, did this exemption slow the market and give such firms an unfair competitive advantage? (Answer – no; but does this not mean that member states cannot regulate such firms if they want to, in this respect?) CESR/CEBS took note of the United Kingdom's Financial Service Authority rules which except oil market participants, provided that they are not trading members of a recognised or designated exchange and energy market participants on application.

The policy implications as regards MiFID include the following:[50]

- Further pre- and post-trade transparency in commodity derivatives would not

---

46   Via the CESR/CEBS paper (see fn 8).
47   CESR/CEBS paper p 3 paragraph 12.
48   CEBS/CESR consultations, p 28 paragraph 97.
49   CESR/CEBS paper p 3 paragraph 13.
50   CESR/CEBS paper p 4 paragraphs 15 & 16.

522

bring meaningful benefits – current disclosure practices are sufficient.
- No change to the organisational requirements for business conduct rules is required.
- More relaxed criteria for clients to request to be treated as professional clients, on request, should be permitted.
- The definition of 'commodity derivative' need not be revised.
- It would be desirable to clarify the exceptions to Articles 2.1(i) and (k).

Additionally, CESR/CEBS do not consider that the regulatory regime should be differentiated based on the nature of the underlying commodity. In particular, they concluded that there is no evidence that only investment firms generate different risks from other sorts of investment firm active in commodity derivatives.[51]

In the communication, the commission confirmed that it will take into account ESME's and CESR/CEBS's consultations and advice when formulating its legislative reform proposals.[52]

4.2 The ESME response[53]

The call to ESME requested technical advice on:
- the scope and effect of the Capital Adequacy Directive and MiFID carve-outs;
- record keeping and transparency in relation to non-MiFID gas and electricity derivatives; and
- any proposals for clarifying the Market Abuse Directive.

ESME's response was based on exclusive market analysis (its fact-finding section covers some 35 pages). It considers that, on the MiFID exceptions, "this current position is clearly unsatisfactory".[54] It suggests that the reason for this is that some of the exceptions are interpreted differently by different member states' regulatory bodies, leading to "excessive complexity for firms". Partly, this is due to the overlapping nature of some of these exemptions.

However, ESME's policy recommendations are quite modest. In unequivocal terms, it considers that "the fundamental premises for imposing authorisation requirements – to protect clients or to mitigate systemic risks – do not present themselves in commodity markets to the same degree (if at all) as in financial markets". Accordingly, ESME suggests replacing Articles 2.1(i) and (k) with a single exemption for all firms whose main business consists of dealing on their own account in relation to commodities and/or commodity derivatives or other non-financial (including exotic) derivatives. ESME would finesse this by requiring that the exemption apply only when dealing in wholesale markets with counterparties that are either MiFID eligible counterparties or (an expanded definition of) intrinsically professional clients.[55]

---

51 CESR/CEBS paper, p 5 paragraph 17.
52 Communication p 9.
53 "Review under Articles 65(3)(a), (b) and (d), of the MiFID and 48(2) of the CAD and proposed guidelines to be adopted under the Third Energy Package" (the ESME response).
54 ESME response, p.57.
55 *Id* pp 59–60.

4.3   The CESR/ERGEG response

The terms of reference for CESR/ERGEG were narrower than those for the other reviewing committees. CESR/ERGEG focused only on:

- record keeping;
- transparency (eg, publishing transaction prices); and
- the market abuse regime.

The first two topics were addressed in CESR/ERGEG's report of October 15 2008, in which the joint committees recommended extending the MiFID-standard record of derivatives to other energy supply undertakings. They also recommended publishing post-trade data on standardised electricity and gas supply contracts.[56]

In their assessment of market abuse, CESR/ERGEG noted that the Market Abuse Directory does not apply to physical commodities markets and markets for electricity and gas. Moreover, derivatives are covered only if they are admitted to trading on a regulated market. CESR/ERGEG go on to say that "the commodity derivative specific definition of insider information in MAD is difficult for securities regulators to apply, in the absence of a clear definition of the information that users of commodity markets can expect to receive in accordance with accepted market practices on those markets".[57]

Clearly, CESR/ERGEG consider that the regime for controlling market abuse for commodity derivatives is not adequate. However, their preferred policy is not an amendment of the Market Abuse Directive. Instead "the Commission should consider developing and evaluating proposals for a basic, tailor-made market abuse framework in the energy sector legislation for all electricity and gas products not covered by MAD".[58]

This proposal for a bespoke commodities market-abuse framework – which CESR/ERGEG consider could draw on the model of the Nordic Power Exchange – neatly highlights the fact that while commodity derivatives may look like financial instruments, their behaviour and the related regulatory issues are related to the unique challenges of physical markets in a way that pure financial derivatives (ie, derivatives on financial instruments, such as credit default swaps referencing a listed bond) are not.

4.4   Next steps?

The European Commission initially anticipated that the consultation would result in legislative proposals by autumn 2009. However, more urgent changes to the regulatory landscape driven by the financial market dislocations have since dominated bureaucratic and ministerial attentions. As a result, it would appear that draft legislation on these points is now more likely to appear during 2010, but it would not be surprising to see this pushed back again.

---

56   CESR/ERGEG advice to the commission, October 15 2008 pp 4–13.
57   CESR/ERGEG advice to the commission, October 15 2008 p 4. This may be a harsh criticism – an argument could be made that accepted market practice evolves and therefore any advice which purports to freeze it would potentially become outdated.
58   Id, p 5.

5.   The role of the Financial Services Authority (FSA)

5.1   The Financial Services and Markets Act 2000

With some 433 clauses and 21 schedules, the Financial Services and Markets Act 2000 sets out the main parameters of substantive financial regulation in the United Kingdom. It also establishes the FSA and delineates its scope and powers. This high-level legislation is supplemented by a compendium of delegated legislation in the form of specific regulations.

Under the powers granted to it pursuant to the act, the FSA also has a delegated authority to create rules and give guidance within certain of the areas under its purview. These rules and guidance promulgated by the FSA are contained within the FSA Handbook, which is divided into specific and general areas covering the full range of financial services and products that the FSA regulates.

One of the challenges in explaining the regulatory position in the United Kingdom is that there are effectively two layers of regulation: one originating in the United Kingdom and one imported from the European Union. The overlapping of these two regimes under the regulatory auspices of the FSA means that there is a patchwork of exceptions and overrides, which require careful navigation.

5.2   Implementing MiFID

MiFID is largely implemented in the United Kingdom through the Conduct of Business Sourcebook, part of the FSA Handbook. From a regulatory parameter point of view, the activities covered by MiFID were already covered by the FSA's pre-existing list of regulated activities so it did not change the scope of activities.[59]

5.3   Regulated activities

The Financial Services and Markets Act 2000 contains a general prohibition on non-authorised persons carrying out regulated activities by way of business, unless an exemption applies.[60] Many of these have their origins in earlier legislation from the 1980s. The list of regulated activities is set out in the Financial Services and Markets Act 2000 (Regulated Activities) Order 2001. There are 21 regulated activities in total, the vast majority of which are not relevant here. However, there are some activities centring on investments which could potentially apply to commodity derivatives. This is because, following the introduction of MiFID, the definition of 'investment' in the order tracks that of MiFID.[61]

In addition, as this is an area where the pre-existing Regulated Activities Order has been overlaid with the legally superior MiFID, pre-existing exemptions from the order have had to be made subject to a 'MiFID override': that is, if an order exemption would have the effect of taking an activity outside of the scope of MiFID, a MiFID override brings it back within the regulatory perimeter.

Carrying on a regulated activity by way of a business in the United Kingdom

---

59   Some small tweaks were made for the sake of clarity (eg, specifically including the MiFID activity of operating a multilateral trading facility).
60   Sections 19 and 22 of the Financial Services and Markets Act 2000.
61   As implemented by the Financial Services and Markets Act 2000 (Amendment No 3) Order 2006.

requires FSA authorisation, unless an exclusion is available or the person is otherwise exempt. Failure to do so is a minimal offence.[62] The simple flowchart overleaf indicates what would fall within the regulatory perimeter.

Where a MiFID commodity or exotic derivative is involved, the following are the most likely regulated activities that could apply, depending on the nature of the firm involved:

- accepting deposits;
- dealing in investments as principal;
- arranging deals in investments;
- managing investments; and
- advising on investments.

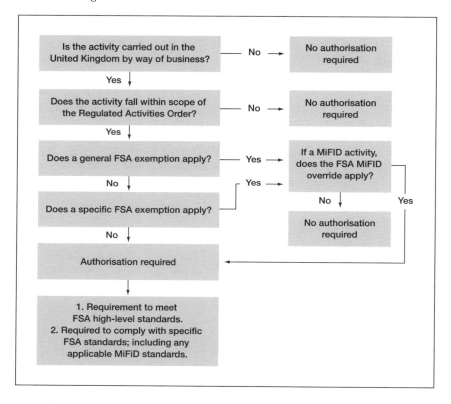

These are all contained in detail in the Regulated Activities Order and further guidance as to the precise scope of each activity is contained in the FSA's Perimeter Guidance Manual (which also forms part of the FSA Handbook). In each case, a patchwork of general and specific exemptions may apply, meaning that each activity should be checked on a case-by-case basis.

If a firm needs authorisation, it should apply to the FSA and ensure that it

---

62   Section 19 of the Financial Services and Markets Act 2000.

subsequently complies with the FSA's principles and applicable conduct of business, reporting, management, capitalisation and other standards.

5.4 Partial exemptions for oil and energy market participants

Prior to MiFID, the FSA recognised that professional participation in oil and energy markets alone does not give rise to the full range of regulatory concerns that authorisation and compliance with the FSA's regime are designed to combat. Accordingly, for such focused firms, partial exemption from the FSA Handbook requirements is available.

Thus, the 'oil market participant exemption' disapplies parts of the FSA Handbook for oil market participants and the same for energy market participants, the necessary changes having been made.

As to what constitutes 'oil market activity', the FSA defines it as:

(a) any regulated activity in relation to an oil investment or to oil, or in relation to a biofuel investment, biofuel, a biomass investment or biomass that is ancillary to activities related to oil investments or oil, which:

(i) is the executing of own account transactions on any recognised investment exchange or designated investment exchange; or

(ii) if it is not the executing of transactions on such exchanges, is performed in connection with or for persons who are not individuals; and

(b) establishing, operating or winding up a collective investment scheme which is an oil collective investment scheme in which individuals do not participate.

A similar definition covers 'energy market activity' on which the definition of an 'energy market participant' rests:

(a) any regulated activity in relation to an energy investment or to energy, or in relation to a biomass investment or biomass that is ancillary to activities related to energy investments or energy, which:

(i) is the executing of own account transactions on any recognised investment exchange or designated investment exchange; or

(ii) if it is not the executing of transactions on such exchanges, is performed in connection with or for persons who are not retail clients;

(b) establishing, operating or winding up a collective investment scheme which is an energy collective investment scheme in which retail clients do not participate.[63]

6. Market/trading offences

In addition to the offence of market abuse, which entered into UK law by way of the Financial Services and Markets Act 2000 and was subsequently amended to accommodate the transposition of the Market Abuse Directive, there are certain UK criminal offences which can attach to financial instruments and financial market conduct. These are not specific to commodity derivatives, applying as they do to market conduct generally, so they are not explored in detail here other than by way of a short overview.

---

63   See FSA Handbook glossary for these and connected definitions.

6.1   Misleading statements

A legacy of the Financial Services Act 1986, Section 397(1) of the Financial Services and Markets Act 2000 effectively reproduced the law prohibiting the making of materially false, misleading or deceptive statements, whether knowingly or recklessly, for the purpose of inducing, or being reckless as to whether it may induce, a person to:

- enter into (or refrain from entering into) certain controlled activities; or
- exercise (or refrain from exercising) rights in relation to a controlled investment.

'Controlled activities' for these purposes are those set out in Part I of Schedule I of the Financial Services and Markets Act (Financial Promotion) Order 2005. 'Controlled investments' are those within Part II of Schedule I of the order. This includes options over certain precious metals (ie, palladium, platinum, gold and silver) and futures, including commodity futures for investment purposes only (ie, not for commercial purposes).[64] The indicators set out in Article 84 of the Regulated Activities Order apply when determining whether something is for investment or commercial purposes.

6.2   Market manipulation

Related to making misleading statements is the offence of market manipulation, and this is set out in Section 367(3) of the Financial Status and Markets Act 2000. This captures "any course of conduct which creates a false or misleading impression as to the market, the price or the value of any investments" and was done for the purpose of creating that impression (ie, it was deliberate). It is a defence for a person to have honestly believed that the act or conduct in question would not create that misleading impression. Again, instruments take the same definition as for the misleading statements offence above.

---

64   Paragraphs 21 and 22, Part II, Schedule I of the Financial Services and Markets Act 2000 (Financial Promotion) Order 2005.

US regulation of commodity derivatives

Jeremiah Wagner

1. Choose your own (derivatives) adventure

In the *Choose Your Own Adventure*™ children's book series,[1] the reader assumes the role of the protagonist and, by making choices throughout the book, guides the plot to one of many possible endings. If you have ever read one of these books, you should recognise the style of the following introduction...

You are interested in reading about how commodity derivatives are regulated in the United States. The current time is unknown, but it is sometime after 2007, when the US sub-prime mortgage crisis triggered a chain reaction of economic events that led to a global recession (often referred to as the 'Great Recession'). There had not been a recession of comparable magnitude since the Great Depression of the 1930s. Governments and regulators around the globe reacted to the Great Recession with great fervour to combat its perceived causes.

Blame for the Great Recession was widespread. Financial wizard Warren Buffett had already singled out derivatives as "financial weapons of mass destruction".[2] Many government officials, experts and industry participants shared this belief; but many did not. The US government introduced numerous measures to regulate derivatives further, but at the time of this story, none has been enacted.

You must now determine whether significant regulatory reform for commodity derivatives has been enacted in the United States or whether it is safe to proceed under the regulatory framework that existed at the time of this writing.

If major US regulation has not been enacted, or you would like to learn about the current structure before anything new comes into force, go to section 2. If you are reading this after major US regulation has been enacted (or are unsure), go to the end of the chapter.

2. Introduction

"It's hard enough to get anyone to listen when you mention derivatives, but if you team them up with commodities, people tend to want to run a mile."[3] Once regulation is factored into the discussion, people want to run a marathon. Make it US regulation and people would soon prefer to compete in an 'iron man' challenge.

This may be a slight over-exaggeration, but the US regulatory framework for

---

1   http://en.wikipedia.org/wiki/Choose_Your_Own_Adventure.
2   Warren Buffett, *Berkshire Hathaway Inc: Letter to the Shareholders of Berkshire Hathaway Inc*, at p15 (2002).
3   Anonymous derivatives trader, *Risk* (January 1995), available at
    www.bus.lsu.edu/academics/finance/faculty/dchance/MiscProf/DerivaQuote/Qt19.htm.

commodity derivatives is multi-faceted, prodigious, often ambiguous and discouragingly complex. Any single commodity derivatives instrument can be affected, or at least implicated, by federal and state laws relating to commodities, banking, securities, bankruptcy, gambling and insurance, each with their own concerns and approach.

This chapter looks at the primary US laws and regulations affecting commodity derivatives, their markets and their market participants – namely, the rules of the Commodities Exchange Act and its regulations as promulgated by the Commodity Futures Trading Commission (CFTC). In addition, this chapter briefly looks at other regulatory schemes (eg, federal and state securities laws) that affect or are important to consider in connection with commodity derivatives transacted in the United States.

3.   Commodity Exchange Act

The Commodity Exchange Act was passed in 1936 in "response to the perceived problems of manipulation of grain markets" through the use of futures contracts.[4] Although it has undergone numerous amendments since then, the act's core underlying principle continues to be the maintenance of an efficient balance between the benefits and risks associated with commodity derivatives and their markets.

The pre-eminent benefits of commodity derivatives (and their markets), as advanced by the act, are risk transfer and price discovery.[5] The act, on the other hand, embodies in its provisions the risk that, if left unchecked, commodity derivatives (and their markets) may facilitate excessive speculation, fraud and various forms of market manipulation, to the detriment of market participants (especially individuals) and in ways that might negatively impact on pricing stability for the underlying commodities.[6]

For the vast majority of its history, the Commodity Exchange Act aimed to balance these benefits and risks through a 'one size fits all' approach, whereby all commodity derivatives were illegal and unenforceable unless traded on a regulated exchange, of which there was only one permitted type – a designated contract market. This approach changed drastically in 2000 when the Commodity Futures Modernization Act of 2000 ushered in a multi-tiered statutory framework whereby "the level of regulation is tailored to the type of market and the risks associated with that market".[7]

---

4   Alan Greenspan, Testimony of Chairman Alan Greenspan, "The regulation of OTC derivatives", before the Committee on Banking and Financial Services, US House of Representatives (July 24 1998) (hereinafter 'Greenspan testimony').

5   7 USC §5 (recognising that commodity derivatives serve to provide a "means for managing and assuming price risks, discovering prices, or disseminating pricing information through trading in liquid, fair and financially secure trading facilities"). 'Price discovery' is premised on the theory that the dissemination of information through a "liquid, fair and financially secure" market will allow pricing to reflect veritable supply and demand in the related commodity more accurately.

6   See id (providing that the Commodity Exchange Act is designed to maintain the benefits of the derivatives markets by deterring and preventing "price manipulation or any other disruptions to market integrity; to ensure the financial integrity of all transactions subject to this chapter and the avoidance of systemic risk; to protect all market participants from fraudulent or other abusive sales practices and misuses of customer assets; and to promote responsible innovation and fair competition among boards of trade, other markets and market participants").

7   CFTC, *Report on the Oversight of Trading on Regulated Futures Exchanges and Exempt Commercial Markets*, at p6 (October 2007).

To understand the multi-tiered approach, it is vital to recognise that under the Commodity Exchange Act any transaction involving a commodity for future delivery or an option must be traded on the most robustly regulated market,[8] unless the transaction otherwise qualifies for an exemption. If the transaction qualifies for an exemption, it may be traded through a lesser regulated market – some of which have little to no regulation. The exact market tier of regulation depends on the specific exemption(s) for which a transaction qualifies.

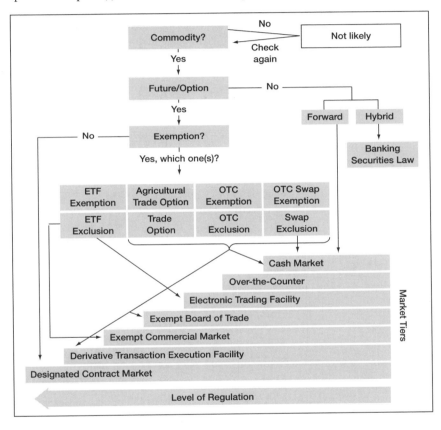

The basic analytical structure (which is schematically set out in the chart above) for determining where in the multi-tiered continuum of market regulation a particular commodity derivative belongs can be broken down into three initial questions:

- Does the transaction involve a commodity?
- Is the transaction for future delivery or an option?
- What exemption(s), if any, does the transaction qualify for?

---

8   7 USC §6(a).

Sections 3.1 to 3.3 of this chapter address these three questions. Sections 3.4 and 3.5 then summarise how commodity derivatives markets and their market participants are regulated under the Commodity Exchange Act. Finally, section 3.6 describes the regulatory provisions designed to ensure the overall well-being of the commodity derivatives markets in the United States.

3.1 What is a 'commodity' under the Commodity Exchange Act?

As used in the Commodity Exchange Act, the definition of a 'commodity' goes far beyond what is generally considered to be a commodity for the purposes of this book (ie, little qualitative differentiation, deliverable cash market).

The term 'commodity' was first defined under the Commodity Exchange Act in 1936. At that time, the definition was limited to a specific list of physical, agricultural products, including grain (eg, corn, wheat, oats), cotton, rice, mill feeds, butter, eggs and Irish potatoes. Over the years the definition was expanded from time to time to include additional agricultural goods, such as various oils, peanuts, soybeans, livestock and livestock products.[9]

In 1974 the US Congress significantly expanded the definition in response to public outcry that speculative trading was causing unwarranted price volatility in goods not then included in the definition. The definition of a 'commodity' was no longer limited to specific physical, agricultural products, but was widened to include "all other goods and articles [other than onions]... and all services, rights and interest in which contracts for future delivery are presently or in the future dealt in".[10]

The conservative, and safest, interpretation of the definition of a 'commodity' under the Commodity Exchange Act is that it encompasses "potentially anything".

3.2 Is the transaction for future delivery or an option?

If a good is a commodity (which we have established is almost certainly the case), the next question is whether the particular transaction by which it is being traded is for future delivery or an option.

(a) Future delivery

The Commodity Exchange Act does not define when a transaction in a commodity is for future delivery (ie, a futures contract); instead, the act defines when it is not. 'Future delivery' is simply defined to "not include any sale of any cash commodity for deferred shipment or delivery",[11] or what is known as a forward contract.

What constitutes a futures contract has been broadly interpreted.[12]

---

9   CFTC website, "Futures Regulation Before the Creation of the CFTC", available at www.cftc.gov/aboutthecftc/historyofthecftc/history_precftc.html.

10   7 USC §1a(4).

11   7 USC §1a(19).

Essentially, any agreement that involves the delivery of a commodity at some point in the future, as long as it is not a forward contract, may qualify as a futures contract subject to regulation under the Commodity Exchange Act.[13]

Forward contracts were excluded on the basis that they were viewed as necessary for bona fide market participants (ie, merchandisers, not speculators) to hedge price risk, ensure adequate supply levels and "facilitate the movement of commodities through the merchandizing chain".[14]

However, the Commodity Exchange Act does not define a 'forward contract' (or deferred delivery), so it has been left to the interpretation of the courts and the CFTC. Without further statutory guidance, the courts and the CFTC have had difficulty establishing a definitive definition.[15]

In defining a 'forward contract', the CFTC and the courts have focused primarily on whether the transaction at issue required delivery of the underlying commodity. Initially, the courts and the CFTC took the consistent view that a transaction would qualify as a forward contract if the subjective intent of the parties was to deliver the underlying commodity.[16]

In 1990 the CFTC diverged from the accordant position when it objected to a New York district court finding that, based on the subjective intent of the parties, Brent oil contracts were future contracts.[17] The CFTC responded by issuing its own interpretation that Brent oil contracts were in fact forward contracts on the basis that the contractual terms required delivery regardless of the parties' intent.[18] As it sits currently, the form of a transaction seems to be the key determinative feature of a forward contract.[19]

However, it is not without risk to rely exclusively on the form of a transaction in determining whether it will be a forward contract, as the courts and the CFTC have "consistently held that, in evaluating whether a transaction involves a futures contract, 'they will assess the transaction as a whole with a critical eye toward its underlying purpose'".[20] It is a much more certain route to execute a transaction under one of the exemptions from the Commodity Exchange Act (as described in section 3.3 below).

(b) Options

An 'option' is defined under the Commodity Exchange Act to be any "agreement,

---

12 See, for example, *Dunn v Commodity Futures Trading Commission*, 519 US 465, 478 (1997), interpreting both options and futures as being for future delivery.

13 Edward F Greene *et al, US Regulation of the International Securities and Derivatives Markets* (9th edn 2008) (hereinafter *Derivatives Regulation*), §14.08[2] ("The CFTC has indicated that it considers any agreement involving the future delivery of a commodity, other than a forward contract or commodity option, to be a futures contract"); see also, Greenspan testimony, *supra* note 4.

14 General Accounting Office (GAO), *Report to Congressional Committees: The Commodity Exchange Act – Legal and Regulatory Issues Remain* (April 1997) (hereinafter GAO 1997), at p19.

15 GAO, *Report to Congressional Committees: The Commodity Exchange Act – Issues Related to the Commodity Futures Trading Commission's Reauthorization* (May 1999) (hereinafter GAO 1999), at p38.

16 *Derivatives Regulation, supra* note 13, §14.08[3][a].

17 GAO 1997, *supra* note 14, at p13, citing *Transnor (Bermuda) Limited v BP North America Petroleum*, 738 F.Supp 1472 (SDNY 1990).

18 See *id*, at p14.

19 See, for example, *CFTC v Michael Zelener*, 373 F 3d 861 (7th Cir 2004) (holding that contracts that were rolled-over every two days were "spot sales for delivery within 48 hours...the magnification of gain or loss over a longer period does not turn sales into futures contracts").

20 *Derivatives Regulation, supra* note 13, §14.08.

contract or transaction that is of the character of, or is commonly known to the trade as, an option, privilege, indemnity, bid, offer, put, call, advance guaranty or decline guaranty".[21]

3.3 Exemptions from the Commodity Exchange Act

If it is determined that a transaction is a futures contract or an option involving a commodity, it must be traded on a regulated market unless it qualifies for an exemption under the act. The exemption(s), if any, for which a transaction qualifies depends on the particular mix of the following key variables:

- the type of instrument (forward, future, swap, option);
- the commodity involved (agricultural commodity, financial commodity, energy commodity);
- the participants (sophisticated parties, retail parties, bona fide hedger); and
- the market on which the transaction is executed (over-the-counter (OTC), trading facility, board of trade).

This section looks only at the key statutory and regulatory exemptions that affect the commodity derivatives that are the subject of this book. There are additional exemptions, but because these relate primarily to non-commodity derivatives (eg, equity, credit default) they are not addressed. Those exemptions that are relevant are tabulated on the next page and described further below.

(a) Statutory exemptions

When the definition of 'commodity' was expanded in 1974, derivatives instruments and their markets had entered a period of rapid and immense expansion (in terms of sophistication, innovation and quantity).

Many of the new derivatives instruments (particularly swap agreements) were traded OTC in reliance on the sole exemption at the time (ie, the exemption for forward contracts). However, the new derivatives were similar in many respects to futures contracts. Market participants consequently feared that these derivatives would be rendered illegal and unenforceable on account of not being traded on a regulated market.[22]

A myriad of actions were taken to provide legal certitude to the new instruments and their OTC markets. For example, almost simultaneously with the amendments in 1974, a separate amendment, often referred to as the Treasury amendment, was passed to exclude certain transactions in government securities and foreign currencies.[23] The CFTC also used its regulatory authority to exempt certain OTC derivatives involving interest rates and other non-agricultural commodities.[24] These

21 7 USC §1a(26).
22 Market participants' concerns were twofold. First, they were concerned that the CFTC might bring enforcement action against counterparties for illegally trading futures contracts off exchange. Second, it was possible that a court could declare a swap agreement to be unenforceable on the basis that it was an illegal contract (thereby giving out-of-the-money counterparties a way to avoid their obligations). See, for example, GAO 1997, *supra* note 14, at p11.
23 7 USC 2(c).
24 See later discussion of the CFTC's exemption for swap agreements.

534

Key exclusions and exemptions for commodity derivatives

Exemption/ Exclusion	Type	Permitted Commodities	Permitted Participants	Requirements	Retained Rules
Swap Exclusion: CEA § 2(g)	Statutory	All, except Agricultural	Eligible Contract Participants	1. Individual negotiation 2. Not on a Trading Facility	None
OTC Exclusion: CEA § 2(d)(1)	Statutory	Excluded Commodities	Eligible Contract Participants	Not on a Trading Facility	None
OTC Exemption: CEA § 2(h)(1)	Statutory	Exempt Commodities	Eligible Contract Participants	Not on a Trading Facility	Anti-Fraud & Anti-Manipulation
Electronic Trading Facility Exclusion: CEA § 2(d)(2)	Statutory	Excluded Commodities	Eligible Contract Participants	1. Principal-to-Principal 2. Electronic Trading Facility	None
Electronic Trading Facility Exemption: CEA § 2(h)(3)	Statutory	Exempt Commodities	Eligible Commercial Entities	1. Principal-to-Principal 2. Electronic Trading Facility	1. Anti-Fraud & Anti-Manipulation 2. Information Rules 3. Significant Price Discovery Rules
Exclusion – Hybrid Securities: CEA § 2(f)	Statutory	All	No restriction	"Predominantly" a security	Subject to US Securities Laws
Exclusion – Bank Products: CEA § 27	Statutory	All	No restriction	1. "Predominantly" banking 2. Identified banking 3. Bankswap agreement	Subject to US Banking Laws
CFTC Swap Exemption: CFTC § 35	Regulatory	All	Eligible swap participants	1. Over-the-counter 2. Qualifying "Swap" 3. Negotiable Terms 4. Counterparty creditworthy	Anti-Fraud & Anti-Manipulation
Trade Option Exemption: CFTC § 32.4(a)	Regulatory	All, except Enumerated Agricultural	Commercial Entities	1. Over-the-counter 2. Business Purposes	Anti-fraud
Agricultural Trade Option Exemption: CFTC § 32 .13	Regulatory	Enumerated Agricultural	Commercial Entities	1. Over-the-counter 2. Business Purposes 3. Transacted through ATOM	Anti-fraud

actions failed to fully assuage market participants' fears.

In the hope of finally providing the legal clarity and certainty that had long been absent from the OTC markets, the Commodity Futures Modernization Act implemented (or otherwise amended) essentially all the statutory exemptions currently in existence under the Commodity Exchange Act. To effect the statutory exemptions, several similar themes, concepts and definitions were integrated throughout the Commodity Exchange Act. To delineate these clearly, the analysis of the statutory exemptions is broken into three sections:

- categories of commodity;
- key definitions; and
- key statutory exemptions for commodity derivatives.

(i)   *Categories of commodity*

The Commodity Futures Modernization Act split the definition of 'commodity' into three broad categories:

- agricultural commodities;
- excluded commodities; and
- exempt commodities;

The category in which the underlying commodity fits affects which exemptions might apply.

The term 'agricultural commodity' is used throughout the Commodity Exchange Act, but is not specifically defined. Instead, it is an amalgam of the agricultural products explicitly listed in the definition of 'commodity' (ie, the 'enumerated agricultural commodities') and any "other goods and articles" that fit the bill.[25] The first grouping is tabulated below.

Enumerated Agricultural Commodities		
• Wheat	• Grain sorghum	• Cottonseed meal
• Cotton	• Mill feeds	• Cottonseed
• Rice	• Butter	• Peanuts
• Com	• Eggs	• Soybeans
• Oats	• Irish potatoes	• Soybean meal
• Barley	• Wool	• Livestock
• Rye	• Wool tops	• Livestock products
• Flaxseed	• Fats and oils	• Frozen concentrated orange juice

Often it is obvious which "other goods and articles" fit the bill. This is the case for non-enumerated goods, such as coffee, sugar, cocoa, dairy products, lumber and similar products. One product type that is not so obvious is the by-product of an agricultural commodity. For example, is ethanol, a by-product of corn, an agricultural commodity or an energy product?

Because of the characteristics of cash markets for agricultural commodities (ie, seasonal, volatile and finite supplies), and their susceptibility to price manipulation,

---

25   7 USC §1a(4).

their related derivative instruments have always been the pre-eminent focus of the Commodity Exchange Act. When the Commodity Futures Modernization Act was enacted, its purpose was to add clarity to OTC derivatives in non-agricultural commodities under the Commodity Exchange Act, not to reverse its historical focus. Thus, most derivatives involving agricultural commodities are not eligible for the statutory exemptions under the Commodity Exchange Act.

Unlike agricultural commodities, financial assets (eg, interest rates and economic indices) do not have a quantifiable and finite supply.[26] Because its architects believed that it is not possible to manipulate a market "where the underlying asset or its equivalent is in essentially unlimited supply",[27] the Commodity Futures Modernization Act created a category for financial commodities that captured "a broad range of interest rate, currency, credit, equity, weather and other derivatives".[28] The financial commodities included in this category are referred to as 'excluded commodities', and are eligible for the most liberal statutory exemptions under the Commodity Exchange Act.[29]

Definition of Excluded Commodity
(1) an interest rate, exchange rate, currency, security, security index, credit risk or measure, debt or equity instrument, index or measure of inflation, or other macroeconomic index or measure;
(2) any other rate, differential, index, or measure of economic or commercial risk, return, or value so long as it is not based in substantial part on the value of a narrow group of non-financial commodities; or is based solely on one or more commodities that have no cash market;
(3) any economic or commercial index based on prices, rates, values, or levels that are not within the control of any party to the relevant contract, agreement, or transaction; or
(4) an occurrence, extent of an occurrence, or contingency (other than a change in the price, rate, value, or level of a non-financial commodity) that is: (a) beyond the control of the parties to the relevant contract, agreement, or transaction; and (b) associated with a financial, commercial, or economic consequence.

'Exempt commodities' are defined under the Commodity Exchange Act to include any "commodity that is not an excluded commodity or an agricultural commodity".[30] Examples of exempt commodities include metals, energy products, bandwidth, chemicals, carbon emissions and other pollution allowances.[31] Exempt commodities are eligible for several of the exemptions under the Commodity Exchange Act, but they tend to be less liberal than those available for excluded commodities. This narrower relief is generally attributable to the fact that exempt commodities are believed to be more susceptible to market manipulation than excluded commodities.[32]

---

26   See generally the report of the President's Working Group on Financial Markets, *Over-the-Counter Derivatives and the Commodity Exchange Act* (November 1999) (hereinafter PWG 1999), at p16, available at www.treas.gov/press/releases/reports/otcact.pdf.

27   Greenspan testimony, *supra* note 4.

28   Daniel P Cunningham and Katherine J Page, *Memorandum for ISDA Members: Commodity Futures Modernization Act of 2000,* (January 5 2001) (hereinafter ISDA memo), at p6.

29   7 USC §1a(13).

30   7 USC §1a(14).

31   ISDA memo, *supra* note 28, at p6.

32   See *id*, at 19.

(ii)   *Key definitions*

In addition to structuring the statutory exemptions to take account of the underlying commodity, the Commodity Futures Modernization Act aimed to limit the application of the statutory exemptions to contractual counterparties that "simply [did] not require the customer protections that may be needed by the general public".[33] The authors of the Commodity Futures Modernization Act also believed that the legal uncertainty which it aimed to address "hampered private sector efforts to utilize electronic trading systems to enhance market efficiency and transparency".[34] To integrate these objectives throughout the statutory exemptions, the act added the following key definitions:

- eligible contract participant;
- eligible commercial entity;
- trading facility; and
- electronic trading facility.

Eligible contract participant: The definition of 'eligible contract participant' includes a number of companies, firms and persons that are considered sophisticated enough to take on and understand the economic risk of a derivative. The definition is divided into three broad categories:

- sophisticated parties trading for their own account;
- select sophisticated parties acting as a broker (or agent) for any eligible contract participant; or
- "any other person that the [CFTC] determines to be eligible in light of the financial or other qualifications of the person".[35]

Some of the sophisticated parties included in the definition are financial institutions (eg, regulated domestic and foreign banks, trust companies, credit unions), regulated insurance companies, regulated investment companies, commodity pools, certain employment benefit plans, government entities (and certain government departments), regulated brokers and various market participants that are regulated under the Commodity Exchange Act.[36]

Also included in the definition is any corporate entity that has:

- total assets exceeding $10 million;
- its obligations guaranteed by an entity with total assets exceeding $10 million; or
- a net worth in excess of $1 million and has entered into the derivative "in connection with the conduct of [its] business or to manage the risk associated with an asset or liability owned or incurred or reasonably likely to be owned or incurred by [it] in the conduct of [its] business".[37]

---

33   Greenspan testimony, *supra* note 4.
34   PWG 1999, *supra* note 26, at p10.
35   7 USC §1a(12).
36   7 USC §1a(12)(A).
37   7 USC §1a(12)(A)(v).

Like corporate entities, individuals with total assets exceeding $10 million are included in the definition, and their economic threshold is similarly reduced, albeit only to $5 million, provided that they enter into the pertinent derivative for bona fide hedging purposes.[38]

Eligible commercial entity: An eligible commercial entity is a subset of the eligible contract participants. Notably, individuals are excluded from the definition altogether.[39]

The definition specifically includes those eligible contract participants that are financial institutions, regulated insurance companies, qualifying corporate entities, certain government entities, regulated brokers and various derivatives market participants that are regulated under the Commodity Exchange Act, provided that in connection with their business they:

- have the ability to take delivery of the underlying commodity;
- incur risk (in addition to price risk) related to the underlying commodity; or
- have requisite experience in certain markets.[40]

An eligible commercial entity is also defined to include any eligible contract participant (other than individuals and state and local government entities) that regularly enters into agreements involving the underlying commodity and has total assets of at least $100 million.[41]

As it did for eligible contract participants, the CFTC may include any other person in the definition that it "shall determine appropriate".[42]

Trading facility: Under the Commodity Exchange Act, a 'trading facility' is:

[A] person or group of persons that constitutes, maintains, or provides a physical or electronic facility or system in which multiple participants have the ability to execute or trade agreements, contracts, or transactions (i) by accepting bids or offers made by other participants that are open to multiple participants in the facility or system; or (ii) through the interaction of multiple bids or multiple offers within a system with a predetermined non-discretionary automated trade matching and execution algorithm.[43]

The definition does not include:

- trading structures that enable only bilateral negotiations without an opportunity for multi-party bidding;
- facilities used by government securities dealers and brokers; and
- facilities that permit non-binding bidding.[44]

Furthermore, a trading structure will not be deemed to be a trading facility solely from the submission of trades to a derivatives clearing organisation.[45]

---

38 7 USC §1a(12)(A)(xi).
39 7 USC §1a(11).
40 7 USC §1a(11)(A).
41 7 USC §1a(11)(B).
42 7 USC §1a(11)(C).
43 7 USC §1a(34)(A).
44 7 USC §1a(34)(B).
45 7 USC §1a(34)(C).

Electronic trading facility: An 'electronic trading facility' is defined as a trading facility "that (A) operates by means of an electronic or telecommunications network; and (B) maintains an automated audit trail of bids, offers, and the matching of orders or the execution of transactions on the facility".

(iii)   Key exemptions

To recap, we have so far determined that:

- a 'commodity' is defined to include "potentially anything";
- futures contracts are broadly interpreted to apply to any contract for future delivery of "potentially anything" (other than a forward contract);
- commodities are categorised as being agricultural, excluded or exempt; and
- certain definitions are central to understanding the statutory exemptions.

Next, we look at the statutory exemptions most likely to affect commodity derivatives.

Swap exclusion: Section 2(g) to the Commodity Exchange Act is often seen as the codification of the CFTC swap exemption (as defined below), and for this reason is referred to as the 'swap exclusion'. Despite its name, the swap exclusion is not limited to swap agreements and is potentially applicable to a vast array of derivatives instruments.

The swap exclusion exempts any OTC derivative (ie, one not traded on a trading facility) involving a commodity, other than an agricultural commodity, that is "subject to individual negotiation" between eligible contract participants.

The Commodity Exchange Act does not explicitly state what is required in order for a transaction to be "subject to individual negotiation". It does not appear to mean that each term of the transaction must be negotiated and thus contain no standardisation. Rather, it appears to require that the terms must be capable of negotiation. However, the requisite level of negotiation (and permissible level of standardisation) is unclear.

Exemptions for excluded commodities: Two exemptions from the Commodity Exchange Act apply solely to derivatives involving excluded commodities. Under either, the qualifying derivative will be fully excluded from regulation under the act. The exemptions are:

- OTC transactions in excluded commodities – Section 2(d)(1) of the act exempts any transaction in an excluded commodity that is between eligible contract participants and is not executed on a trading facility.
- Excluded commodities on an electronic trading facility – derivatives involving excluded commodities that are traded on an electronic trading facility are also exempt, provided that the transaction is between eligible contract participants on a principal-to-principal basis.[46] Electronic trading facilities solely trading these exempted transactions are themselves exempt from regulation pursuant to Section 2(e) of the Commodity Exchange Act (as discussed below in section 3.4(c)).

---

46   7 USC §2(d)(2).

The principal-to-principal requirement generally includes any transaction where the parties are acting for their own account, even where they have entered into an offsetting transaction with another party. In addition, the principal-to-principal requirement does not extend to certain investment managers or fiduciaries acting as an agent for an eligible contract participant. Essentially, the requirement functions to restrict transactions from being effected by certain agents (eg, a broker), including situations where the principal is also an eligible contract participant.[47]

Exemptions for exempt commodities: Like derivatives involving excluded commodities, two exemptions apply solely to derivatives involving exempt commodities. However, these exemptions are not relieved from the Commodity Exchange Act's anti-fraud and anti-manipulation provisions. The exemptions for transactions involving exempt commodities are as follows:

- OTC transactions in exempt commodities – the Commodity Exchange Act exempts any transaction in an exempt commodity that is between eligible contract participants and is not executed on a trading facility. Nevertheless, as noted above, the anti-fraud and anti-manipulation provisions continue to apply (although the anti-fraud provisions do not apply if the parties to the transaction are eligible commercial entities); and[48]
- exempt commodities on an electronic trading facility – derivatives in exempt commodities that are traded on an electronic trading facility are also exempt, provided that the transaction is between eligible commercial entities (as opposed to eligible contract participants) on a principal-to-principal basis.[49] Notably, these electronic trading facilities are regulated as exempt commercial markets (which are defined below in section 3.3(a)).

Exemptions for hybrid securities and bank products: If a hybrid security, which is a "security having one or more payments indexed to the value, level, or rate of, or providing for the delivery of, one or more commodities", is predominantly a security, it will not be subject to the provisions of the Commodity Exchange Act.

A hybrid security is considered predominantly to be a security if:

- the full purchase price is paid "substantially contemporaneously" with delivery of the hybrid security;
- the holder of the hybrid security is not required to make payments in addition to the purchase price (including margin or settlement payments);
- the issuer of the hybrid security is not required to make mark-to-market margin payments; and
- the hybrid security is not marketed as a commodity future (or option) subject to the provisions of the Commodity Exchange Act.

The mark-to-market margin requirement (referred to above) does not "include the

47 See *Derivatives Regulation, supra* note 13, at §14.09.
48 7 USC §§2(h)(1) and (2) (for this, 'eligible commercial entity' does not include an instrumentality, department or agency of a state or local government entity).
49 7 USC §§2(h)(3) and (4).
50 7 USC §§2(f).

obligation of an issuer of a secured debt instrument to increase the amount of collateral held in pledge for the benefit of the purchaser of the secured debt instrument to secure the repayment obligations of the issuer under the secured debt instrument".[50]

Another purpose of the Commodity Futures Modernization Act was to delineate clearly which federal regulatory authority was best suited to regulate certain commodity derivatives.[51] For this reason, the act excluded three categories of commodity derivative offered, entered into or provided by banks that were subject to US banking law.

First, the Commodity Futures Modernization Act excluded certain "identified banking products"[52] that were commonly offered in the United States on or before December 5 2000.[53] Identified banking products that were not commonly offered in the United States before December 5 2000 may also be exempt so long as they are not indexed to the value, level or rate and do not provide for the delivery of any commodity.[54]

Second, covered swap agreements that are "offered, entered into, or provided by a bank" are excluded from the Commodity Exchange Act.[55] Covered swap agreements include:

- any swap agreement that involves any commodity, other than an agricultural commodity, and that is traded OTC by eligible contract participants; and
- any swap agreement that involves an excluded commodity and that is entered into on an electronic trading facility between eligible contract participants (other than those acting as a broker for other eligible contract participants) trading on a principal-to-principal basis.[56]

Finally, any hybrid banking product that is predominantly a banking product is excluded from the Commodity Exchange Act. The predominance test for hybrid banking products mirrors the predominance test for hybrid securities. Even where the CFTC determines that a hybrid banking product is not predominantly a banking product, it is not permitted to regulate the instrument unless it determines that it is in the public interest to do so and has consulted with the Board of Governors of the Federal Reserve System.[57]

(b)   Regulatory exemptions

In addition to the statutory exemptions, the Commodity Exchange Act gives the CFTC the authority to exempt commodity derivatives from the provisions of the act.

The CFTC has the authority to exempt any futures contract or option[58] from any and

---

51   See generally, PWG 1999, *supra* note 26, at p30 (recommending action to provide jurisdictional clarity to hybrid instruments).
52   As defined in 7 USC §27.
53   7 USC §27a.
54   7 USC §27b.
55   7 USC §27e.
56   7 USC §27(d).
57   7 USC §27d; see also 7 USC §27d(c) (providing that the board of governors of the Federal Reserve System may request a ruling by the CFTC to be set aside in the US Court of Appeals for the District of Columbia).
58   7 USC §6c(b) (giving the CFTC the authority to prescribe the terms and conditions by which commodity options may be transacted without violating the Commodity Exchange Act).

all provisions of the act following "notice and opportunity for hearing". Exemptions of futures contracts also require the CFTC to determine that the exemption:

- is "consistent with the public interest";
- will be transacted only by "appropriate persons";[59] and
- will have no "material adverse effect" on its or any regulated exchange's ability to carry-out its regulatory duties.[60]

(i) CFTC swap exemption

The CFTC regulations exempt qualifying "swap agreement[s]...from all provisions of the [CEA]", other than those that "prohibit manipulation of the market price of any commodity".[61] To qualify, a swap agreement[62] must be:

- entered into solely between eligible swap participants (similar to, but a more limited subset of, the eligible contract participants);
- negotiable with respect to its material economic terms;
- affected by the creditworthiness of its counterparties, including in its pricing, cost or credit enhancement; and
- traded over the counter.[63]

Commodity derivatives in non-agricultural commodities have little use for the CFTC swap exemption as its requirements are more cumbersome than those of the swap exclusion and, if applicable, the exemptions relating to excluded and exempt commodities. Commodity derivatives in agricultural commodities, on the other hand, can benefit from the exemption since it is not limited by what type of commodity is involved.

(ii) Exemptions for trade options

Trade options were designed to allow commercial end users (eg, farmers and producers) to manage their exposure to commodity price volatility through OTC option contracts. Although the regulatory framework for commodity options under the Commodity Exchange Act is now very similar to that for commodity futures,[64] its historical course was considerably distinct.

For many years the Commodity Exchange Act maintained a general ban on all options involving enumerated agricultural commodities, whether traded on a regulated exchange or not. Options on all other commodities were permitted to trade on regulated markets but were generally banned from being traded OTC.[65]

---

59 7 USC §6(c)(3) (defining 'appropriate person' to consist of businesses of a qualifying financial stature, but ultimately includes any "other persons that the [CFTC] determines to be appropriate in light of their financial or other qualifications").

60 See *id.*

61 17 CFR §35.2.

62 17 CFR §35.1(b)(1) (defining 'swap agreement' to include, among other things, an "agreement ... which is a rate swap agreement, basis swap, forward rate agreement, commodity swap, interest rate option, forward foreign exchange agreement, rate cap agreement, rate floor agreement, rate collar agreement, currency swap agreement, cross-currency rate swap agreement, currency option, or any other similar agreement").

63 17 CFR §35.2.

64 See generally 17 CFR §34.

65 GAO 1999, *supra* note 15, at p41.

Exemptions for OTC options were thus considered at different times for options that involve the enumerated agricultural commodities and those that did not.

As a result, two classes of trade option were promulgated by the CFTC:

- standard, plain-vanilla trade options; and
- agricultural trade options.

Trade options are OTC options "offered by a person who reasonably believes that the option is being purchased by a commercial entity for purposes related to its business".[66] Trade options are exempt from all the requirements applicable to commodity options except the CFTC regulations prohibiting fraud.[67] However, they do not apply to options on enumerated agricultural commodities.[68]

Agricultural trade options are essentially trade options on enumerated agricultural commodities. Like trade options, agricultural trade options are traded OTC and must be offered only to persons reasonably believed to be a "producer, processor, or commercial user of, or a merchant handling" the underlying commodity (including a related product or by-product), and must be entered into for business purposes. However, unlike trade options, agricultural trade options must either be offered by or purchased through an agricultural trade option merchant, or be transacted between parties that each have a net worth of at least $10 million.[69]

Agricultural trade option merchants are primarily regulated under Parts 3 and 32 of the CFTC regulations. This regulatory framework generally consists of:

- registration requirements;
- financial requirements (eg, agricultural trade option merchants must maintain a net worth of $50,000 at all times);
- restrictions on the contracts and their offer and sale; and
- disclosure and reporting requirements.

3.4 Regulating the markets

The regulatory framework in place prior to the Commodity Futures Modernization Act was seen to inhibit healthy financial innovation and competition.[70] The architects of the act set out to change this by designing "a regulatory environment that would promote continued growth and innovation in both the exchange and OTC derivatives markets and foster competition in a rapidly changing global marketplace".[71] To achieve this, the Commodity Futures Modernization Act overhauled the Commodity Exchange Act in two fundamental ways.

First, the regulatory framework shifted away from a merit-based system to a "system of effective self-regulation of trading facilities, clearing systems, market participants and market professionals" under the ultimate oversight of the CFTC.[72] Before the Commodity Futures Modernization Act, regulated markets were not

---

66 17 CFR §32.4(a).
67 17 CFR §32.4(b); 17 CFR §32.9.
68 17 CFR §32.4(a).
69 17 CFR §32.13.
70 *Derivatives Regulation, supra* note 13, at §14.08.
71 CFTC 2007 Report, *supra* note 7, at p6.
72 7 USC §5.

permitted to trade a new commodity derivative until its merits were found to be in line with public interest. The revised, self-regulatory approach allows the regulated markets to adopt new contracts (through self-certification) and to prescribe their own rules and regulations, provided that overall compliance with certain core principles is maintained.[73]

Second, the one-size-fits-all approach was abandoned. In its place is a multi-tiered approach with a range of markets with varying levels of regulatory oversight. The basic premise of this is that the greater the regulation, the less restriction on market participants, types of commodity and types of transaction permitted.

To effect this multi-tiered system of self-regulation, the Commodity Exchange Act, through its statutory and regulatory exemptions, attempts to enable market participants to match each commodity derivative with the regulated (or unregulated) market that best fits its perceived risk profile (which is based mostly on the related commodity and the contractual counterparties).

Three broad market categories exist for the purposes of regulation under the Commodity Exchange Act:

- regulated markets;
- exempt markets; and
- excluded markets.

This section also looks at foreign markets, but they do not fit squarely within one of the broader categories above.

(a) Regulated markets

Regulated markets are subject to the greatest level of regulation under the Commodity Exchange Act, but permit trading in the widest range of commodity derivative products and among the fullest range of market participants.

(i) Designated contract markets

Designated contract markets were the sole market existing before the enactment of the Commodity Futures Modernization Act and are the most extensively regulated markets under the Commodity Exchange Act. As a trade-off, designated contract

Designated Contract Markets	
1. CBOE Futures Exchange	8. New York Mercantile Exchange
2. Kansas City Board of Trade	9. Commodity Exchange, Inc.
3. Chicago Board of Trade	10. North American Derivatives Exchange, Inc.
4. Minneapolis Grain Exchange	11. ELX Futmes, L.P.
5. Chicago Climate Futures Exchange, LLC	12. NYSE Liffe US LLC
6. Nasdaq OMX Futures Exchange	13. ICE Futures U.S., Inc.
7. Chicago Mercantile Exchange	14. OneChicago LLC Futures Exchange

---

73   *Derivatives Regulation, supra* note 13, at §14.08.
74   7 USC §7 (setting out the criteria, core principles, procedures and other requirements for designation as a designated contract market); *see also* 17 CFR §38, Appendices A and B (providing specific information on the requirements and guidance to applicants seeking to become designated contract markets).

markets are the least restricted by the types of commodity and parties that it may permit on its facilities.

To register as a designated contract market, a trading facility must apply to the CFTC.[74] As indicated above, the Commodity Exchange Act does not explicitly set the designated contract market's rules; instead, it establishes the parameters within which a designated contract market must operate.

Before a trading facility is designated as a designated contract market, it must establish its competencies with respect to the following criteria:

- Prevention of market manipulation – the trading facility must demonstrate its ability to prevent market manipulation through sufficient "market surveillance, compliance, and enforcement practices and procedures".
- Fair and equitable trading – the trading facility must enact and enforce trading rules to ensure fair and equitable trading (including the ability to "detect, investigate and discipline" violations of the rules).
- Trade execution facility – the trading facility must establish procedures by which it will operate and how such procedures will be enforced.
- Financial integrity of transactions – the trading facility must "establish and enforce rules and procedures for ensuring the financial integrity of [its facilities], including the clearance and settlement of the transactions with a derivatives clearing organization".
- Disciplinary procedure – the trading facility must establish and enforce procedures to discipline, suspend or expel members or market participants.
- Public access – the trading facility must make its rules, regulations and contract specifications accessible to the public.
- Ability to obtain information – the trading facility must establish and enforce rules to obtain any information that is necessary for its functions and to carry out information requests from the CFTC.

Following submission of an application, the CFTC will, within 180 days (or 90 days if an expedited process is utilised), accept or deny the trading facility's application to be a designated contract market (in some instances, the CFTC may make its acceptance conditional on further action by the trading facility).

Once a trading facility obtains designated contract market status, it is required to maintain compliance with the initial seven designation criteria, as well as 17 additional core principles. The designated contract market is required to comply with each of the core principles, but "shall have reasonable discretion in establishing the manner in which it complies".[75]

Under the Commodity Exchange Act's self-regulatory scheme, designated contract markets are permitted to implement new rules or to list new products by certifying to the CFTC that the new rule or listing complies with the core principles and other rules and regulations under the act. However, CFTC approval is required

75   7 USC §§7(d)(1).
76   17 CFR §40.4(b) (specifying which changes are deemed to be "not material", including, for example, changes to trading hours, certain changes in lists of approved delivery facilities and changes to minimum price tick).

Core principles for designated contract markets (DCMs)

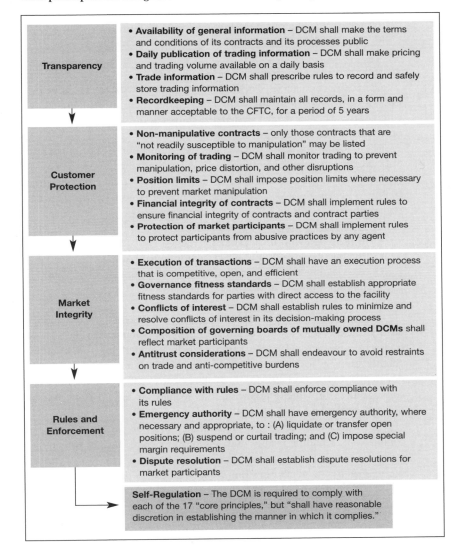

for any material changes[76] to the terms and conditions of commodity derivatives involving an enumerated agricultural commodity.[77]

(ii)   *Designated transaction execution facilities*

Designated transaction execution facilities can operate with less regulatory oversight than designated contract markets because they are limited in the types of underlying

---

77   17 CFR §40.4(a); see also 17 CFR §40.5.

commodity and transaction participant that may use their facilities. The Commodity Exchange Act contemplates two types of designated transaction execution facility:

- regular designated transaction execution facilities; and
- commercial designated transaction execution facilities.

However, as yet no facility has registered as either.

Generally, commercial designated transaction execution facilities may permit trading of derivatives in any commodity, other than an enumerated agricultural commodity, whereas regular designated transaction execution facilities may allow only trading of derivatives in excluded commodities.[78]

The trade-off for commercial designated transaction execution facilities is that only eligible commercial entities trading for their own account may access the facility.[79] On the other hand, to trade on a regular designated transaction execution facility, a person must be only either an eligible contract participant or a person trading through a futures commission merchant[80] that:

- is an eligible contract participant;
- is registered with the CFTC;
- is a member of a futures self-regulatory organisation;[81]
- is a clearing member of a derivatives clearing organisation;[82] and
- has net capital of at least $20 million.

It is possible for either a regular or commercial designated transaction execution facility to expand its list of permitted underlying commodities. Regular designated transaction execution facilities can also include underlying commodities that are "highly unlikely to be susceptible to the threat of manipulation".[83] Commercial designated transaction execution facilities can include enumerated agricultural commodities for which, following the request of any person, the CFTC has prescribed rules and regulations.[84]

Initially, to be a designated transaction execution facility (whether regular or commercial), a trading facility must establish its competencies with respect to the following criteria:[85]

- Deterrence of abuses – the designated transaction execution facility must establish rules to deter abuses and demonstrate its capability to detect, investigate and enforce those rules.
- Trading procedures – the designated transaction execution facility must establish rules defining trading procedures.

---

78   7 USC §§7a(b)(2)(A) to (C) (listing certain types of permissible underlying commodity that have been interpreted by the CFTC to mean excluded commodities).
79   7 USC §7a(b)(2)(F).
80   As defined in Part 029.
81   This prong is also satisfied if the futures commission merchant is registered on a national securities association registered under Section 15A(a) of the Securities Exchange Act of 1934, provided that it is trading only security futures on the designated transaction execution facility. 7 USC §7a(b)(3)(B)(ii).
82   As defined in 7 USC §1a(9).
83   7 USC §7a(b)(2)(E) (giving the CFTC the authority to make such a determination).
84   7 USC §7(e)(2).
85   17 CFR §38, Appendix A.

- Financial integrity of transactions – the designated transaction execution facility must establish rules to ensure the protection of customer funds and the financial integrity of transactions entered into on its facilities.

Once a trading facility is registered as a designated transaction execution facility, it is required to self-regulate its market functions in compliance with the designation criteria above, as well as an additional nine core principles. The designated transaction execution facility core principles are not only less restrictive in pure number than those for a designated contract market but, in several instances, they are also less restrictive in substance. For example, designated contract markets must publish the daily trading information on all actively traded contracts, whereas designated transaction execution facilities need do this only for contracts that perform a significant price discovery function for the underlying commodity.

Derivative trading execution facility core principles		
1. Compliance with rules 2. Monitoring of trading 3. Position limitations or accountability	4. Disclosure of general information 5. Daily publication of trading information	6. Fitness standards 7. Conflicts of interest 8. Recordkeeping 9. Anti-trust considerations

(b) Exempt markets

The next tier of market regulation under the Commodity Exchange Act is exempt markets. Exempt markets are spared from most of the act's provisions, but are further limited by the types of commodity derivative and market participant that may use their facilities. There are two categories of exempt market:

- exempt commercial markets; and
- exempt boards of trade.

(i) Exempt commercial markets

Exempt commercial markets are electronic trading facilities that permit trading only in exempt commodities between eligible commercial entities on a principal-to-principal basis (as previously described in section 3.3(a) above) to be transacted on their facilities.[86]

Exempt Commercial markets	
1. Agora-X, LLC 2. International Maritime Exchange 3. Chicago Climate Exchange, Inc. 4. Natural Gas Exchange, Inc. 5. EOX Holclings LLC 6. NetThmPut 7. GFI Group Inc. – EnergyMatch 8. Nodal Exchange, LLC 9. HoustonStreet Exchange, Inc. 10. OILX	11. ICAP Commodity and Commodity Delivatives Trading System 12. Pmity Energy, Inc. 13. ICAP Shipping Trading System 14. TFSWeather. com 15. ICAPtme 16. TraditionCoal.com 17. IntercontinentalExchange, Inc. 18. WorldPulp.com

86   7 USC §2(e).

An electronic trading facility that intends to operate as an exempt commercial market must notify the CFTC.[87] In addition to the facility's contact details, the notice must include:

- the categories of commodity that it intends to list;
- the derivatives clearing organisation that it intends to utilise; and
- several required certifications.[88]

An exempt commercial market must certify annually that it continues to operate as such.[89]

Exempt commercial markets are subject to ongoing reporting and record-keeping requirements for every transaction on their facilities that averaged five or more trades a day during the last calendar quarter.[90] For these transactions, exempt commercial markets are required to submit weekly reports to the CFTC showing:

- the underlying commodity, the delivery or price-basing location, the maturity date, whether physical delivery is required, the time of execution, the price and the quantity;
- total daily volume and, if cleared, open interest;
- if applicable, the type of option (ie, call or put) and strike prices; and
- any other information required by the CFTC.[91]

Instead of providing weekly reports, an exempt commercial market may grant the CFTC electronic access to its facilities in order to compile and record the same information.[92] The CFTC also has the authority to make a special call to the exempt commercial market for whatever information it deems necessary to enforce the rules and regulations of the Commodity Exchange Act.[93]

Exempt commercial markets are popularly known as the 'Enron loophole' because when Enron Corp collapsed in 2001, it was revealed that the company had what many believed to be an unhealthy affinity for unregulated energy derivatives (ie, exempt OTC derivatives and exempt electronic trading facilities). Since Enron's fall, the Enron loophole has been hotly debated, but it came under increased public ire in 2008 when oil reached record high prices.[94] Unregulated speculation in oil derivatives

---

87   7 USC §2(h)(5)(A).
88   7 USC §2(g)(5)(A)(iii), requiring that the facility certify that:
        • no executive officer or member of the governing board of, or any holder of a 10% or greater equity interest in, the facility is a person described in any of subparagraphs (A) to (H) of Section 8a(2) of the Commodity Exchange Act;
        • the facility will comply with the conditions for the exemption under Section 2(h)(5) of the Commodity Exchange Act; and
        • the facility will notify the commission of any material change in the information previously provided by the facility to the commission pursuant to Section 2(h)(5) of the act.
89   17 CFR §36.3(b)(1)(v). In addition to the information required in the notice, a facility operating as an exempt commercial market must "initially" provide the CFTC with the information required by 17 CFR §36.3(b).
90   7 USC §2(h)(5)(B); see also 17 CFR §36.3(b)(1).
91   17 CFR §36.3(b)(2)(i)(A).
92   17 CFR §36.3(b)(2)(i)(B).
93   7 USC §2(h)(5)(B)(iii).
94   Patrice Hill, "'Enron Loophole' enables oil speculation", *Washington Times* (June 24 2008), available at www.washingtontimes.com/news/2008/jun/24/enron-loophole-keeps-oil-speculation-unleashed/.

on exempt commercial markets was believed to be a significant contributing factor.

The US Congress amended the Commodity Exchange Act in 2008 to close the Enron loophole.[95] Following the amendment, if the CFTC determines that a transaction listed on an exempt commercial market performs a significant price discovery function in relation to the underlying commodity,[96] the exempt commercial market will be subject to regulatory requirements similar to those for regulated markets.

In making any determination that a transaction performs a significant price discovery function, the CFTC must consider the following factors (as well as any other material factors it may later specify by rule):

- price linkage – the extent to which the value of the transaction is linked to (or relies on) the daily or final settlement price, or other major price parameter, of a transaction listed for trading on a regulated market;[97]
- arbitrage – the extent to which the transaction is linked to the price of transactions traded through regulated markets and a market participant's ability to arbitrage the linked transactions effectively;
- material price reference – the extent to which the transaction's price influences a commodity's cash market price; and
- material liquidity – the extent to which the volume of transactions in the commodity being traded on the exempt commercial market is sufficient to have a material effect on a corresponding transaction listed for trading on a regulated market.[98]

The CFTC must conduct at least annual evaluations of the transactions traded on the exempt commercial markets to determine whether they perform a significant price discovery function.[99] To do so, the CFTC has broad authority to request information from exempt commercial markets[100] and exempt commercial markets are required to provide this information in the form and manner required by the CFTC.[101] Additionally, every exempt commercial market is required to notify the CFTC promptly of any transactions with certain characteristics associated with a significant price discovery contract.[102]

However, before making any final determination that a transaction performs a significant price discovery function, the CFTC is required to make notice of its

---

95 However, the Farm Bill of 2008 addressed only exempt electronic trading facilities, not exempt OTC derivatives, which were the exemptions on which Enron primarily relied.
96 7 USC §2(h)(7).
97 'Regulated market' for purposes of this section includes any exempt commercial market on which a significant price discovery contract is traded.
98 7 USC §2(h)(7)(B).
99 17 CFR §36.3(d).
100 7 USC §2(h)(5)(B)(iii).
101 17 CFR §36.3(b)(1)(iv).
102 17 CFR §36.3(c)(2) (mandating that each exempt commercial market is required to notify the CFTC promptly of any transaction averaging at least five trades per day during the most recent calendar quarter and for which the exempt commercial market "sells its price information regarding the [transaction] to market participants or industry publications" or "[w]hose daily closing or settlement prices on 95 percent or more of the days in the most recent quarter were within 2.5 percent of the contemporaneously determined closing, settlement or other daily price of another agreement, contract or transaction").

intention and, for a period of 30 calendar days, allow market participants to provide data, views and arguments with respect to such determination. Within a reasonable time after this comment period has ended, the CFTC must issue an order explaining its final determination.[103]

If the CFTC issues an order determining that a transaction performs a significant price discovery function, each exempt commercial market trading that transaction will be subject to additional regulation similar to that required of the regulated markets. Like the regulated markets, the exempt commercial market will be required effectively to self-regulate its activities, as they relate to a significant price discovery contract, within a set of core principles.

Exempt commercial market core principles	
1. Contracts not readily 2. Monitoring of trading susceptible to manipulation 3. Ability to obtain information 4. Position limitations or accountability 5. Emergency authority	6. Daily publication of trading information 7. Compliance with rules 8. Conflicts of interest 9. Anti-trust considerations

The exact point at which an affected exempt commercial market will be required to demonstrate its compliance with the core principles will depend on whether it is the first time that an order has been issued with respect to a transaction traded through its facilities.[104]

However, an important distinction is that the exempt commercial market, as a whole, is not regulated in this manner; instead, it is the significant price discovery contract that is subjected to the additional regulation.[105] Nevertheless, it is not entirely clear how such a distinction would play out in practice.

(ii)   *Exempt boards of trade*

The other exempt market is the exempt board of trade. Exempt boards of trade are subject to substantially less regulation than designated contract markets, designated transaction execution facilities and exempt commercial markets, but they are also much more limited in the types of commodity and participant permitted on their facilities. Exempt boards of trade are exempt from nearly all of the provisions of the Commodity Exchange Act other than certain of its anti-fraud and anti-manipulation provisions.[106]

Only eligible contract participants are permitted to trade on an exempt board of trade,[107] and the only commodities that may be the subject of transactions on its facilities are those believed to have little risk of being prone to market manipulation. Specifically, the Commodity Exchange Act provides that the underlying commodity must have:

---

103   17 CFR §36.3(c)(3).
104   17 CFR §36.3(c)(4).
105   17 CFR §36.3(c)(5).
106   7 USC §7a-3(c).
107   7 USC §7a-3(b)(2).

- an inexhaustible deliverable supply;
- a sufficiently large deliverable supply and a liquid cash market "to render any contract traded on the Commodity highly unlikely to be susceptible to the threat of manipulation"; and
- no cash market.[108]

The CFTC regulations provide that the commodities satisfying these criteria are excluded commodities and any "other...Commodities as [it] may determine by rule, regulation or order".[109]

Exempt boards of trade	
1. CME Alternative Marketplace, Inc.	4. Longitude LLC
2. IRESE, Inc.	5. GFI Group Inc. – ForexMatch
3. Delivatives Blidge, LLC	6. Swapstream Operating Selvices Ltd.

The process for obtaining status as an exempt board of trade imposes little burden. All that is initially required, in addition to compliance with the limits described above, is for an entity looking to become an exempt board of trade to notify its intent to the CFTC.[110] An exempt board of trade is required to certify to the CFTC by the end of each calendar year that it continues to operate as an exempt board of trade and to ensure that the information initially provided remains up to date.[111] Beyond this there is not much else required of exempt boards of trade, except with respect to transactions that serve a significant price discovery function.

If the CFTC determines that any transaction conducted on an exempt board of trade serves as a significant source of price discovery for the underlying commodity,[112] the exempt board of trade is required to provide the public with certain pricing information on a daily basis.[113]

If an exempt board of trade has reason to believe that any of the transactions on its facility is serving a price discovery function, it is required to notify the CFTC.[114] Following receipt of such notice, the CFTC may, following public notice and a hearing, issue an order of its determination.[115] Following such determination, the

---

108 7 USC §7a-3(b).
109 17 CFR §36.2(a)(iii)(2). For example, the CFTC determined that weather indices are eligible to be traded on exempt boards of trade by an order dated May 30 2002 (available at www.cftc.gov/ucm/groups/public/@iodtefs/documents/file/deawiebots05-02.pdf).
110 7 USC §7a-3(a); see also 17 CFR §36.2(b).
111 17 CFR §36.2(c)(3).
112 17 CFR §36.2(c)(2)(i) (providing that an exempt board of trade "performs a significant price discovery function for transactions in the cash market for a commodity underlying any agreement, contract, or transaction executed or traded on the facility when: (A) Cash market bids, offers or transactions are directly based on, or quoted at a differential to, the prices generated on the market on a more than occasional basis; or (B) The market's prices are routinely disseminated in a widely distributed industry publication and are routinely consulted by industry participants in pricing cash market transactions").
113 7 USC §7a-3(d).
114 17 CFR §36.2(c)(2)(ii).
115 17 CFR §36.2(c)(2)(iii); but see 17 CFR §36.2(c)(2)(v) (providing that an exempt board of trade "may petition the [CFTC] any time to modify or vacate that determination").
116 17 CFR §36.2(c)(2)(iv)(B) (providing that the exempt board of trade "shall make such information readily available to the news media and the general public without charge no later than the business day following the day to which the information pertains").

affected exempt board of trade will be required publicly[116] to disseminate additional pricing data.[117]

(c)   Excluded markets

In some sense, the excluded market category can be thought of as a catch-all for the exempted transactions (and their related markets) that are subject to little to no regulation under the Commodity Exchange Act. These markets face no reporting obligations or any pervasive level of market monitoring. The excluded markets consist of the following:

- OTC markets – the OTC markets are those unregulated markets that develop to trade exempt OTC derivatives, excluded OTC derivatives and trade options, as well as transactions qualifying for the swap exclusion and the CFTC swap exemption. However, some of these remain subject to the Commodity Exchange Act's anti-fraud and anti-manipulation provisions.
- Excluded electronic trading facility markets – these markets consist of electronic trading facilities that are exempt from regulation on the basis that the only transactions permitted on their facilities are those involving excluded commodities between eligible contract participants on a principal-to-principal basis, or they otherwise qualify for the swap exclusion.[118]
- Non-Commodity Exchange Act regulated markets – these markets are not directly regulated by the act but would instead arise in relation to the exemptions for hybrid securities, bank products and the Treasury amendment, as well as several others not addressed in this chapter. These are mostly derivatives that are traded in markets completely outside the reach of the act but are monitored by other US federal regulatory authorities.
- Cash markets – somewhat obvious, but to round out the full spectrum of the multi-tiered market structure, cash (or spot) markets are not regulated under the Commodity Exchange Act (and this includes forward contracts).

(d)   Foreign markets

Derivatives markets located outside the United States (or 'foreign markets', as they are referred to under the Commodity Exchange Act), may permit US customers to trade commodity derivatives through their facilities without registering with the CFTC.[119] The CFTC will grant such relief only to genuine foreign markets.[120]

To receive the CFTC's stamp of approval, a foreign market must request a no-action letter[121] from the CTFC, which, if issued, will state that enforcement action will not be recommended provided that it complies with certain conditions set out in the

---

117   7 USC §7a-3(d); 17 CFR §36.2(c)(2)(v)(a) (providing the information that must be disseminated).
118   7 USC §2(e).
119   7 USC §§6 (a) &(b).
120   Commodity Futures Trading Commission, *Policy Statement: Boards of Trade Located Outside of the United States and No-Action Relief From the Requirement To Become a Designated Contract Market or Derivatives Transaction Execution Facility*, 71 Fed Reg 64,443 (November 2 2006) (hereinafter Foreign Market Policy), Part I.B (interpreting the exclusion of foreign markets under Section 6(a) of the Commodity Exchange Act "to apply only with respect to 'bona fide' boards of trade").
121   17 CFR §140.99.

letter. The conditions that are certain to be required of a foreign market are that it:

- accepts the CFTC's authority to take appropriate action if it later finds that trading on the foreign market has certain adverse consequences;
- agrees to participate in certain information-sharing relationships; and
- provides periodic certification that it is in good standing.[122]

Foreign markets often have less restrictive rules than the US markets subject to the CFTC's regulatory oversight. In some instances, contracts available in the foreign markets are linked to those traded through regulated markets in the United States. It has been argued that excessive speculation through the foreign markets has adversely affected the pricing of underlying commodities in the United States.[123] As a result, the CFTC's no-action letter policy permitting US persons to trade on these foreign markets has been notoriously referred to as the 'London loophole' or the 'Dubai loophole'.[124]

In an effort to address the concerns associated with the London/Dubai loophole, the CFTC has recently amended several no-action letters to impose additional conditions. For example, in 2008, the CFTC amended Dubai Mercantile Exchange Limited's no-action letter to require position limits, daily trading and large-position reports, as well as quarterly reports of positions exceeding the imposed position limits with respect to any Dubai Mercantile contract linked to the price of a contract traded on a designated transaction execution facility or a designated contract market, or the price of a significant price discovery contract traded on an exempt commercial market.[125]

3.5   Regulation of market participants

Before 1974 it was standard practice for exchanges to establish the primary rules and regulations within which their members were required to transact. When the Commodity Exchange Act was amended in 1974, comprehensive provision was made for the implementation of industry-wide, self-regulatory associations designed to maintain the integrity of those participating in the commodity derivatives market.[126] In 1983 the CFTC first authorised the National Futures Association to perform registration functions for certain market participants; it now performs the foremost registration and licensing functions for the CFTC.[127] Over the years the National Futures Association has taken on other essential functions, such as the provision of dispute resolution processes and certain participant disciplinary actions.

Today, registration with the National Futures Association is mandatory for all market participants (other than clearing organisations); thus, industry participants

---

122   Foreign Market Policy, *supra* note 120, at Part IV.
123   Michael Greenberger, "Testimony of Michael Greenberger: Potential Excessive Speculation in Commodity Markets: The Impact of Proposed Legislation", before the House Committee on Agricultural (July 10–11 2008).
124   Cyrus Sanati, "Sewing the Energy Loopholes Shut", *New York Times* (May 30 2008).
125   No-action letter, Amendment to No-Action Letter Issued to the Dubai Mercantile Exchange, 08-10 (July 3 2008).
126   7 USC §21.
127   7 USC §21(o).

Primary market participants regulated under the Commodity Exchange Act

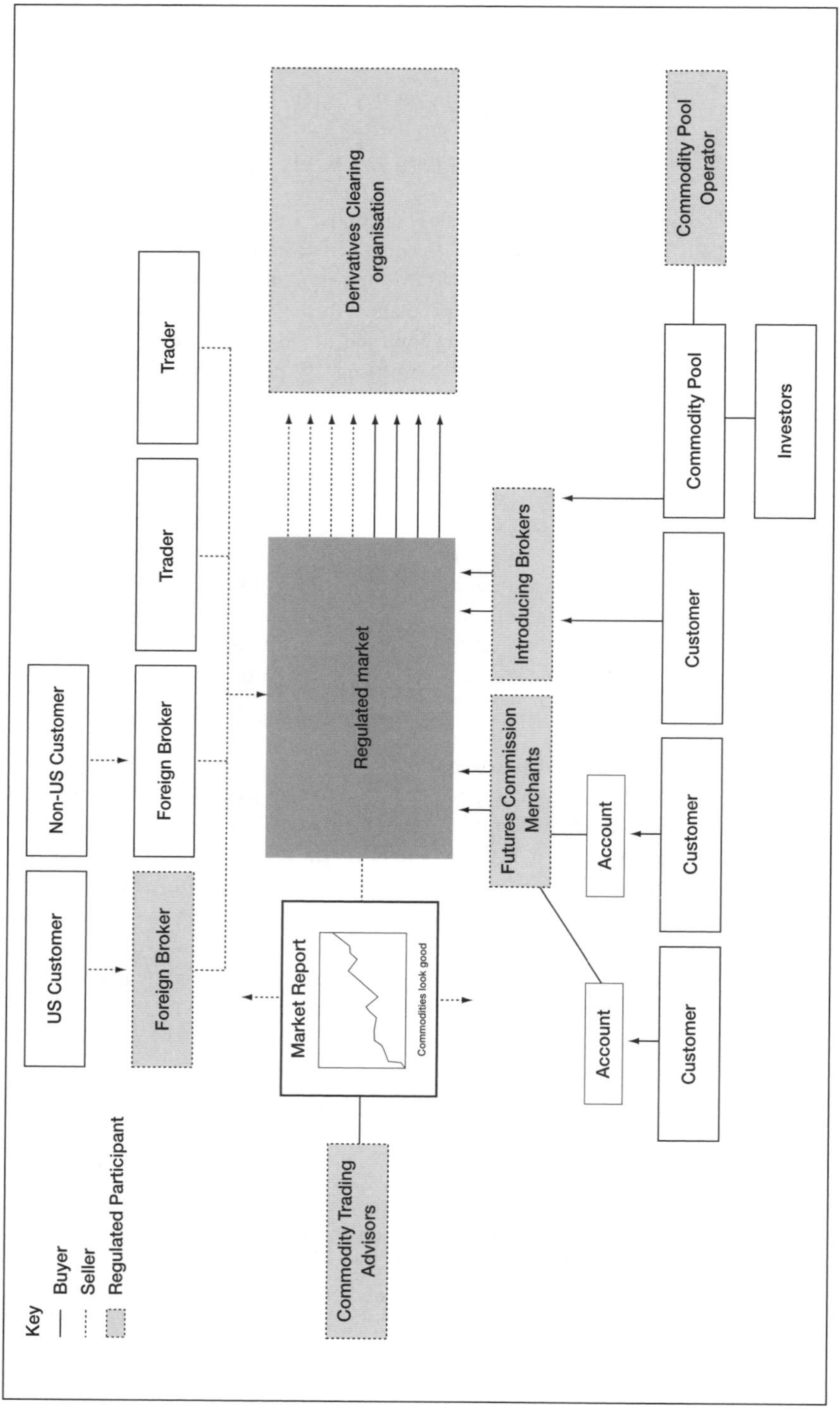

Key

— Buyer

····· Seller

▨ Regulated Participant

Derivatives Clearing organisation

Commodity Pool Operator

Commodity Pool

Investors

Trader

Trader

Foreign Broker

Introducing Brokers

Regulated market

Customer

Non-US Customer

Futures Commission Merchants

US Customer

Foreign Broker

Customer

Account

Market Report

Commodities look good

Account

Customer

Commodity Trading Advisors

must operate within the rules and regulations constructed through the collaborative efforts of the regulated markets, the National Futures Association and the CFTC. Each has its principal areas of authority, but it is the Commodity Exchange Act and the CFTC that provide the structural foundation for the regulation of market participants. For this reason, as well as space limitations, this section provides only a high-level review of the key provisions of the Commodity Exchange Act and the CFTC regulations applicable to industry participants.

The most heavily regulated market participants, and those that are discussed in this section, are:

- futures commission merchants;
- introducing brokers;
- commodity pool operators;
- commodity trading advisers; and
- clearing organisations.

Non-US market participants are also briefly discussed here.

(a) Futures commission merchants

Any individual or entity that solicits or accepts orders for commodity derivatives traded on a designated contract market or a designated transaction execution facility and "accepts any money, securities, or property (or extends credit in lieu thereof) to margin, guarantee, or secure" trades that may result from such solicitation and acceptance must register with the CFTC as a futures commission merchant.[128] Engaging in these activities solely for one's own account does not require registration as a futures commission merchant.[129]

Futures commission merchants must comply with a myriad of regulations, including the following:

- Minimum net capital requirements – futures commission merchants must maintain adjusted net capital[130] in a minimum amount of $500,000.[131]
- Customer funds – futures commission merchants must segregate their customers' funds from their own.[132]
- Customer disclosure – before opening an account for a customer,[133] a futures commission merchant must provide the customer with a prescribed risk disclosure statement.[134]
- Trading standards – futures commission merchants (and their affiliates) are

---

128 7 USC §1a(20) (defining 'futures commission merchant') and 7 USC §6d(a) (requiring futures commission merchants to register with the CFTC); see also 17 CFR §32.3 (imposing requirements on person engaged in futures commission merchant-type activities in relation to options).
129 17 CFR §3.10(c).
130 17 CFR §1.17(c)(1) (defining 'net capital' as the amount by which current assets exceeds liabilities).
131 17 CFR §1.17.
132 7 USC §6d(a)(2).
133 There exist exclusions for customers that are eligible contract participants. See 17 CFR §1.55(f) (providing that risk disclosure statements are not required for institutional customers) and 17 CFR §1.3(g) (defining 'institutional customer' as an eligible contract participant).
134 17 CFR1.55.

required to comply with certain trading standards,[135] including, for example:

- prohibitions against 'front running' (ie, the practice of executing a trade for its own account based on advance knowledge of its customers' pending orders);[136]
- restrictions against trading opposite a customer without consent;[137] and
- prohibitions against disclosing its customers' orders.[138]
- Reporting and record-keeping – futures commission merchants are subject to significant reporting and record-keeping requirements, both with respect to its customers' accounts[139] as well as its own financial stability[140] and trading positions.[141]

Futures commission merchants remain subject to, among other provisions, the Commodity Exchange Act's general anti-fraud and anti-manipulation provisions.

A 'foreign broker', which is a non-US entity that maintains accounts for non-US customers only, is not regulated as a futures commission merchant solely for trading on a US exchange. Nevertheless, foreign brokers will be required to comply with the information and reporting requirements of the exchanges on which they participate.

(b)   Introducing brokers

An introducing broker, like a futures commission merchant, is a person that solicits or accepts orders for transactions on a designated contract market or a designated transaction execution facility. However, unlike a futures commission merchant, an introducing broker does not "accept any money, securities, or property (or extend credit in lieu thereof) to margin, guarantee, or secure any trades" for its customers. A person that has elected to be registered as an associated person of a futures commission merchant is not required to register as an introducing broker.[142]

The regulations to which an introducing broker is subject are similar to those applicable to a futures commission merchant; however, they are generally less rigid, since introducing brokers do not hold customer funds. For example, the minimum adjusted net capital required of an introducing broker has a floor of only $45,000. Also, if the introducing broker has a guarantee from a futures commission merchant that is in compliance with its own minimum adjusted net capital requirements, it is not required to maintain a minimum net capital amount.[143]

---

135   17 CFR §155.
136   17 CFR §155.3.
137   7 USC §6b(a)(iv); see also 17 CFR §155.3(b)(2).
138   17 CFR §155.3(b)(1).
139   17 CFR §1.33.
140   17 CFR §1.10.
141   See eg, 17 CFR §38 and 17 CFR §150.
142   7 USC §1a(23) (defining an 'introducing broker' as "any person...engaged in soliciting or in accepting orders for the purchase or sale of any commodity for future delivery on or subject to the rules of any contract market or derivatives transaction execution facility who does not accept any money, securities, or property (or extend credit in lieu thereof) to margin, guarantee, or secure any trades or contracts that result or may result therefrom").
143   17 CFR §1.17(a)(1)(iii).

(c)   Commodity pool operators

A commodity pool is similar to a mutual fund (or other similar investment fund), except that it is "operated for the purpose of trading" commodity derivatives on a regulated market.[144] The trading of commodity derivatives need not even be the predominant purpose, just a purpose.[145] To finance its investment activities, commodity pools generally sell securities (or similar financial units) to investors.

The Commodity Exchange Act does not regulate the commodity pool itself; rather, it regulates the individual or legal entity that operates the commodity pool or what is referred to as a 'commodity pool operator'.[146] A 'commodity pool operator' is defined under the act to be any individual or entity that operates a commodity pool and, in connection therewith, "solicits, accepts, or receives" funds or other property, "either directly or through capital contributions, the sale of stock or other forms of securities, or otherwise".[147]

Despite the definitional reference to "solicits, accepts, or receives" the CFTC has focused more on the managerial aspects of operation.[148] In other words, in most cases the act does not take the view that the underwriters and investment advisers for the commodity pool fall with the definition of a 'commodity pool operator'.[149]

The CFTC may, by rule, regulation or order, exclude from the definition of 'commodity pool operator' those persons that are "not within the intent of the definition".[150] To date, the CFTC has used this authority sparingly, but has excluded:

- certain foreign operators of offshore funds that have no US investors even though they trade on regulated markets;[151]
- commodity pool operators that are operating a qualifying entity; and[152]
- commodity pool operators operating certain benefit plans that are excluded from the definition of 'pool';[153]

A commodity pool operator and its "associated persons"[154] are required to register with the CFTC and comply with its corresponding regulations, which include the following:

---

144   17 CFR §4.10(d)(1) (defining a 'pool' as "any investment trust, syndicate or similar form of enterprise operated for the purpose of trading commodity interests [(which are generally defined pursuant to 17 C.F.R. §1.3(yy) as commodity futures and options)]"). 'Regulated market' includes in this instance a designated contract market or a designated transaction execution facility with respect to commodity futures, but only a designated contract market with respect to commodity options. 17 CFR §1.3(cc).

145   *Derivative Regulation, supra* note 13, at §12.13.

146   7 USC §6m.

147   7 USC §1a(5).

148   *Derivative Regulation, supra* note 13, at §12.13.

149   See *id.*

150   See *id.*

151   17 CFR §4.13(a)(4).

152   17 CFR §4.5(b), providing that qualifying entity includes:
• investment company registered under the Investment Company Act of 1940;
• a state regulated insurance companies;
• a federal or state regulated bank, trust company or similar depository institution; and
• a trustee of, a named (or delegated) fiduciary of or an employer maintaining a pension plan that is subject to title I of the Employee Retirement Income Security Act of 1974 (ERISA).

153   17 CFR §4.5(a)(iv).

154   7 USC §6k(2) (defining 'associated person' to include any person associated with a commodity pool operator as "a partner, officer, employee, consultant, or agent (or any person occupying a similar status or performing similar functions)").

- Prohibited activities – commodity pool operators are generally required to:
  - operate, in most cases, as a separate legal entity from that of the commodity pool;[155]
  - take all funds from prospective participants in the name of the commodity pool;[156] and
  - segregate the funds of any commodity pool that they manage.[157]
- Disclosure document – commodity pool operators are required to deliver a disclosure document to each prospective participant, which is conceptually similar to a prospectus used in a securities offering under the Securities Act of 1933.[158] The disclosure document is split into two fundamental parts: the general disclosure and the performance disclosure. The general disclosure part lists specific information, such as cautionary legends, business background, risk factors and any other material information that must be included.[159] The performance disclosure part sets out certain required financial information.[160] Before accepting any funds from a prospective participant, the commodity pool operator must obtain that prospective participant's acknowledgement that it has received the disclosure documents.[161]
- Reporting and record-keeping requirements – commodity pool operators are required to provide monthly and quarterly reports to each participant detailing their overall financial position (eg, the net asset value).[162] Additionally, commodity pool operators are required to keep specified "books and records in an accurate, current and orderly manner at its main business office".[163]

Even though a fund operator is not excluded from the definition of a commodity pool operator, it still may qualify for an exemption from the attendant registration requirements. If exempt, many of the disclosure, reporting and record-keeping requirements described above would no longer be applicable for such commodity pool operator. However, unlike fund operators that are excluded from the definition, certain of the provisions would continue to be applicable. Each of the following may qualify for such an exemption:

- a single pool operator – a commodity pool operator that operates only a single commodity pool, receives no compensation other then reimbursement for administrative expenses, and does not advertise in connection with the commodity pool;[164]

---

155   17 CFR §4.20(a).
156   17 CFR §4.20(b).
157   17 CFR §4.20(c).
158   17 CFR §4.21(a) (providing that a disclosure document is to be delivered to each prospective participant "no later than the time it delivers…a subscription agreement" to the prospective participant). Also, under National Futures Association rules this is required, with some exceptions, to be delivered 21 days prior to the subscription agreement.
159   17 CFR §4.24.
160   17 CFR §4.25.
161   17 CFR §4.21(b).
162   17 CFR §4.22.
163   17 CFR §4.23; see also 7 USC §§6n(3) & (4).
164   17 CFR §4.13(a)(1).

- a small pool operator – a commodity pool operator that operates only funds with no more than 15 participants and the combined investment for all of its funds does not exceed $400,000;[165]
- minimal commodity trading – a commodity pool operator which, provided that certain other requirements are satisfied,[166] maintains limited positions in commodity derivatives; and[167]
- limited to qualifying investors – a commodity pool operator which reasonably believes that, on investment, each participant is a qualified eligible person and the investments in the commodity pool are exempt from registration under the Securities Act.[168]

Commodity pool operators that qualify for the above registration exemptions may also be relieved of some of the disclosure, reporting and record-keeping obligations normally required of commodity pool operators.[169]

(d)   Commodity trading advisers

Any person or company that provides advice or analysis regarding commodity derivatives should be mindful of the Commodity Exchange Act's regulatory authority over commodity trading advisers. A commodity trading adviser is any person or company that, "for compensation or profit", advises others on (either directly or indirectly through publications or similar writings), or as part of its "regular business" analyses, the value or the advisability of trading in commodity derivatives on a regulated market and certain OTC commodity options.[170]

An entity providing advice or analysis regarding transactions that are exempt from the substantive regulation of the Commodity Exchange Act alone does not require registration as a commodity trading adviser.

The act also excludes each of the following entities from the definition of a 'commodity trading adviser', where the provision of trading advice or analysis is solely incidental to its business:

- any bank or trust company or any person acting as an employee thereof;
- any news reporter, news columnist or news editor of the print or electronic media, or any lawyer, accountant or teacher;
- any futures commission broker or floor broker;[171]
- the publisher or producer of any print or electronic data of general and regular dissemination, including its employees;

---

165   17 CFR §4.13(a)(2).
166   17 CFR §4.13(a)(3)(i) through (iv).
167   17 CFR §4.13, (providing that a limited position is one in which either: the entire initial margin and premium required to establish such positions is not greater than 5%; or the aggregate net notional value of such positions does not exceed 100%, in each case, of the net liquidation value of the commodity pool.)
168   17 CFR §4.13(4).
169   See, for example, 17 CFR §4.7(b), providing relief from many of the disclosure document requirements where investment interests in a commodity pool operator's managed commodity pools are offered only to certain qualifying participants in an offering that is exempt from the registration requirements of the Securities Act under either Section 4(2) or Regulation S.
170   7 USC §1a(6)(A).
171   As defined in 7 USC §1a(16).

- the fiduciary of any defined-benefit plan that is subject to ERISA; and
- any designated contract market or a designated transaction execution facility.[172]

The CFTC has the direct authority to extend, by rule, regulation or order, this list for "such other persons not within the intent" of the definition.[173] This authority has been used to exclude state-regulated insurance companies and persons excluded from the definition of 'commodity pool operator',[174] in each case where the entity's advice or analysis regarding covered commodity derivatives is "solely incidental" to its business.[175]

Registered commodity trading advisers must comply with the following:

- Prohibited activities – commodity trading advisers are generally prohibited from:
  - soliciting or accepting funds or other property in their name to "purchase, margin, guarantee or secure" any covered commodity derivative of a client unless they are also a registered futures commission merchant;[176]
  - engaging in fraudulent or deceptive advertising;[177] and
  - representing or implying that they have been "sponsored, recommended or approved" by the CFTC or any other US agency.[178]
- Disclosure document – commodity trading advisers are required to deliver a disclosure document to each prospective client for which they seek to direct a trading programme of certain commodity derivatives.[179] The disclosure document is essentially the same as that required of commodity pool operators.[180] Before entering "into an agreement with a prospective client to direct the client's commodity [derivative] account or to guide the client's commodity [derivative] trading", the commodity trading adviser must obtain that prospective client's acknowledgement that it has received a disclosure document.[181]
- Record-keeping requirements – commodity trading advisers, like commodity pool operators, are required to keep specified "books and records in an accurate, current and orderly manner at its main business office"; but, unlike commodity pool operators, they have no significant ongoing reporting obligations to their clients.[182]

---

172   7 USC §1a(6)(B).
173   7 USC §1a(6)(B)(vii).
174   Those excluded by 17 CFR §4.5.
175   17 CFR §4.6(a).
176   17 CFR §4.30.
177   17 CFR §4.41.
178   7 USC §6o(2).
179   17 CFR §4.31(a).
180   Compare 17 CFR §4.34 and 4.35 (establishing the disclosure document requirements for commodity trading advisers) to 17 CFR §4.24 and 4.25 (establishing the disclosure document requirements for commodity pool operators).
181   17 CFR §4.31(b).
182   17 CFR §4.33.

In some cases, commodity trading advisers may obtain relief from some of the registration, reporting and disclosure requirements.[183] For example, many of the disclosure document and record-keeping requirements are eliminated where a commodity trading adviser's trading programme is established solely for certain qualifying eligible persons.[184]

(e) **Non-US market participants**

A person or entity, whether domiciled within or outside[185] the United States, that performs activities similar to those of a futures commission merchant, an introducing broker, a commodity pool operator or a commodity trading adviser solely with respect to commodity derivatives subject to the rules of a non-US regulated market may be subject to regulation under the Commodity Exchange Act. This risk of regulation arises where the non-US market participant directs any of its activities towards US persons. Non-US market participants are prohibited from directing their activities towards US persons unless they are registered with the CFTC or are otherwise exempt from such requirement.[186] Even if exempted, a non-US market participant that directs its activities to US persons remains subject to the anti-fraud provisions under the CFTC regulations and must submit to the jurisdiction of the US courts and the CFTC.[187]

Non-US market participants, other than those performing functions similar to a futures commission merchant, may seek exemption from the registration requirements.[188] However, even though exempt, a non-US market participant acting as a commodity trading adviser or a commodity pool operator is required to disseminate a disclosure document to US persons.[189]

All non-US market participants may seek relief from the registration requirements on the basis that they are subject to comparable regulation in their home jurisdiction.[190] The exemption may not be immediate or uniform, as the CFTC often makes it conditional on additional action and subject to bespoke terms and conditions.[191] Any such exemption does not relieve a non-US market participant

---

183 17 CFR §4.14 (providing several exemptions from the commodity trading adviser registration requirements); and 17 CFR §4.7(c) (providing relief from certain of the disclosure and record-keeping requirements required of commodity trading advisers).

184 17 CFR §4.7(a)(2).

185 If a non-US market participant is not domiciled in the United States, it may request an exemption pursuant to 17 CFR §30.5, provided that it conducts its activities through a futures commission merchant or a non-US market participant that has been exempted from registration pursuant to 17 CFR §30.10.

186 17 CFR §30.4.

187 17 CFR §30.9 (providing that "[i]t shall be unlawful for *any person...*, in or in connection with any... transaction involving *any* foreign futures contract or foreign options transaction" to engage in certain prohibited fraudulent action) (emphasis added); see also 17 CFR §30.5 and 30.10 (each providing that any non-US market participant that is exempted by its provisions is required to submit to the jurisdiction of the US courts and the CFTC).

188 17 CFR §30.5 (non-US market participants that obtain this exemption are required to "engage in all transactions" through a registered futures commission merchant or an exempt non-US market participant futures commission merchant).

189 17 CFR §30.6.

190 17 CFR §30.10; see also 17 CFR §30, Appendix A, providing, among other things, the key elements that will be considered by the CFTC when reviewing whether regulatory scheme is comparable.

191 17 CFR §30.10(a) (providing that exemptive relief "may be granted subject to the terms and conditions as the [CFTC] may find appropriate").

acting as a futures commission merchant from the rules requiring it to segregate the funds of its US customers.[192]

(f) Clearing organisations

Clearing organisations have long been utilised in the United States to reduce counterparty risk for exchange-traded commodity derivatives, but before the Commodity Futures Modernization Act there was little regulatory guidance.

In connection with the Commodity Futures Modernization Act, regulators took the position that clearing organisations had the "potential to reduce counterparty risks", but also tended to "concentrate risk and certain responsibilities for risk management" with a single entity.[193] The regulators' eventual recommendation was that clearing systems still had a net benefit and should be encouraged (especially in the growing OTC market), but within proper regulatory oversight.[194]

On this recommendation, the US Congress, through passage of the Commodity Futures Modernization Act, strived to achieve a balance between the perceived benefits and risks by requiring all cleared trades to be through a regulated clearing organisation, but this by itself would not cause otherwise unregulated OTC transactions to be subjected to regulation. To achieve this, the act introduced two types of clearing organisation: derivatives clearing organisations and multilateral clearing organisations.

(i) Derivatives clearing organisations

The Commodity Exchange Act defines a 'derivatives clearing organisation' as:

A clearinghouse, clearing association, clearing corporation, or similar entity, facility, system, or organization that, with respect to an agreement, contract, or transaction:

- *enables each party to the agreement, contract, or transaction to substitute, through novation or otherwise, the credit of the derivatives clearing organization for the credit of the parties;*
- *arranges or provides, on a multilateral basis, for the settlement or netting of obligations resulting from such agreements, contracts, or transactions executed by participants in the derivatives clearing organization; or*
- *otherwise provides clearing services or arrangements that mutualize or transfer among participants in the derivatives clearing organization the credit risk arising from such agreements, contracts, or transactions executed by the participants.*[195]

Every derivatives clearing organisation must register with the CFTC unless it clears only commodity derivatives exempt from regulation. An otherwise exempt derivatives clearing organisation may voluntarily register as a derivatives clearing organisation.[196] Upon registration (whether required or voluntary), a derivatives

---

192   17 CFR §30.7; see also 17 CFR §30, Appendix B.
193   PWG 1999, *supra* note 26, at p19, stating that clearing organisations may provide stability to the markets "through risk management techniques that may include mutualizing risks, facilitating offset, and netting".
194   See *id.*
195   7 USC §1a(9).
196   7 USC §7a-1(b).

clearing organisation, much like entities in the regulated markets, is required to self-regulate its activities within a specific set of core principles.[197]

(ii)   *Multilateral clearing organisations*
Multilateral clearing organisations were also created under the Commodity Futures Modernization Act, but by an amendment to the Federal Deposit Insurance Corporation (FDIC) Improvement Act of 1991 instead of to the Commodity Exchange Act. The FDIC Improvement Act defines a 'multilateral clearing organisation' as any "system utilized by more than two participants in which the bilateral credit exposures of participants arising from the transactions cleared are effectively eliminated and replaced by a system of guarantees, insurance, or mutualized risk of loss".[198]

Under the FDIC Improvement Act, all OTC derivatives must be traded on a multilateral clearing organisation that is:

- a bank (or similar financial institution) subject to state or federal bank regulation;
- registered as a derivatives clearing organisation under the Commodity Exchange Act;
- registered as a clearing agency under the Exchange Act; or
- supervised by a foreign financial regulator that has been deemed to satisfy appropriate standards by the CFTC or another specified US financial regulator.[199]

Essentially, these multilateral clearing organisations are required to clear those derivatives not required to be cleared by a derivatives clearing organisation.

3.6   Maintaining the integrity of the commodity derivatives markets
At the beginning of this chapter, it was noted that the Commodity Exchange Act recognises commodity derivatives and their markets as providing two essential benefits: price discovery and risk mitigation. However, if not regulated, excessive speculation, market manipulation and fraud could significantly inhibit the culmination of these benefits. The subsequent sections provided a roadmap for determining which instruments, markets and market participants are subject to the provisions of the Commodity Exchange Act, and the parameters under which they are regulated or must self-regulate. This section reviews the key provisions of the Commodity Exchange Act designed to curb excessive speculation, market manipulation and fraud.

(a)   *Preventing excessive speculation*
To protect against excessive speculation that may cause "sudden or unreasonable fluctuations or unwarranted changes in the price of [a] commodity", the CFTC may impose limits on the amounts of speculative trading and speculative positions in the

---

197   7 USC §7a-1(c)(2).
198   FDIC Improvement Act §408(1).
199   FDIC Improvement Act §409.

regulated markets.[200] Violations of position limits are subject to disciplinary action.[201]

The CFTC has established position limits for several agricultural commodities (corn, oats, wheat, various soybean products and cotton).[202] For other commodities, the CFTC requires regulated markets, in accordance with their respective core principles,[203] to impose position limits or accountability position limits[204] in accordance with "acceptable practices" established by the CFTC.[205]

It is standard practice that stricter position limits are implemented for contracts during the month in which they mature.[206] Additionally, where the threat of market manipulation is considered remote – such as when the underlying commodity does not have a cash market (eg, weather derivatives), or has a large or unlimited supply (eg, interest rates, certain energy commodities) – position limits are forgone or accountability position limits are imposed in lieu thereof.

Speculative position limits for any person are determined on a consolidated basis. The positions held by any person are aggregated with those of any person it directly or indirectly controls.[207] Also under this principle, a position limit may be applied to a group of persons (eg, a commodity pool) or persons acting in accordance with an agreement.

Bona fide (or good faith) hedging positions are exempted from position limits. A bona fide hedging position is designed for the purpose of offsetting "price risks incidental to commercial cash or spot operations". The CFTC has enumerated specific, qualifying bona fide hedging positions as well as a process for market participants to request recognition of a non-enumerated hedging position as bona fide.[208]

(b) Preventing market manipulation and fraud

To protect commodity derivatives markets from manipulation and fraud, the Commodity Exchange Act has:

- banned specific transactions that historically have been associated with manipulative and fraudulent action; and
- given the CFTC broad authority to enforce its general anti-fraud and anti-manipulation provisions.

---

200 For this section, 'regulated markets' includes designated contract markets, designated transaction execution facilities and exempt commercial markets where the CFTC has determined that a significant price discovery contract resides.
201 7 USC §6a(b).
202 17 CFR 150.2.
203 See, for example, 7 USC §7(d)(5).
204 Accountability position limits, if exceeded, trigger additional reporting requirements. Generally, market participants holding positions in excess of an accountability position limit will be required to submit additional information to the CFTC or regulated market (as applicable), such as disclosure of all their held positions and additional information regarding the strategy. With this information the CFTC or regulated market (as applicable) can monitor whether the large position is being used to manipulate the market.
205 17 CFR §38, Appendix B.
206 17 CFR §150.2; see also, 7 USC §7(d)(5), mandating that designated contract markets should impose position limits as necessary to prevent market manipulation, "especially during trading in the delivery month".
207 Very generally, control has been interpreted as holding 10% or greater interest in the controlled person.
208 17 CFR §1.3z(2) (establishing the enumerated good-faith hedging transactions) and 17 CFR §1.3z(3) (establishing the process by which market participants may request the CFTC to determine non-enumerated transactions as good-faith hedging).

(i) *Prohibited transactions*

For price discovery to function properly, commodity pricing should be determined in an open and competitive bidding environment. In order to promote such an environment, the Commodity Exchange Act prohibits specific transactions that have historically hindered the market process, including the following:

- Wash sales – these occur where a market participant simultaneously enters into offsetting trades without taking any market risk. By giving the appearance of market activity without any real market risk, wash sales – especially in large volumes – can manipulate the price of a commodity by sending misleading information of supply and demand to the market.
- Fictitious sales – these are transactions that are reported on an exchange, but in fact no transaction has occurred. Similar to wash sales, these can send misleading information to the markets.
- Market corner – cornering (or 'squeezing') the market occurs where a party is able or attempts to increase artificially the price of a commodity in which it holds a long position, while at the same time controlling its physical inventory.
- Bucket orders – a bucket order occurs where a market participant books a trade on behalf of a customer, but does not actually register it with an exchange, instead taking the other side of the transaction. In addition to being fraudulent, bucket orders are detrimental to the price discovery function as they intentionally restrict information from being disseminated and reflected through the market price.

(ii) *Anti-fraud and anti-manipulation provisions*

The anti-fraud and anti-manipulation provisions of the Commodity Exchange Act are two of the main enforcement tools available to the CFTC. However, as previously noted, they do not apply to many of the transactions that are specifically exempted from regulation under the Commodity Exchange Act. In short, these provisions provide as follows:

- Anti-fraud provisions – the act's anti-fraud provisions forbid any person, in connection with a commodity derivative, from:
  - cheating or defrauding any other person;
  - making false reports or statements to another person; and
  - wilfully deceiving any other person by any means whatsoever.[209]
- Anti-manipulation provisions – the general anti-manipulation provision under the act provides that it is a criminal offence for any person "to manipulate or attempt to manipulate the price of any commodity in interstate commerce... or knowingly to deliver or cause to be delivered... false or knowingly inaccurate reports concerning crop or market information or conditions that affect or tend to affect the price of any commodity in interstate commerce". [210]

---

209   7 USC §6b(a).
210   7 USC §13(a)(2).

(iii)   *Restoring orderly trading*

To supplement the anti-fraud and anti-manipulation provision, the CFTC has been given emergency authority to take whatever action is necessary to "maintain or restore orderly trading" whenever it has reason to believe that an emergency exists. An 'emergency' is "in addition to threatened or actual market manipulations and corners, any act of the United States or a foreign government affecting a commodity or any other major market disturbance" disrupting the "forces of supply and demand for such commodity".[211]

Some examples of such emergency action are given in tabulated form on the next page.

4.   Other US regulation

There is little question that the principal US regulatory regime for commodity derivatives is the Commodity Exchange Act. However, this is not the end of the road. There are a number of other speed bumps, forks and potholes that must be navigated with caution when driving a commodity derivative down the US regulatory highway. This section briefly navigates a few of the more consequential perils of the road.

4.1   Securities laws

"Sunlight is said to be the best disinfectant; electric light the most efficient policeman."[212] This famous quote of Justice Louis Brandeis eloquently summarises the key underlying regulatory objective of the Securities Act of 1933 and the Securities Exchange Act of 1934, which is, broadly stated, to prohibit deceit, misrepresentations and fraud in the offering and sale of securities by ensuring that potential investors or purchasers receive sufficient data to make an informed decision.

The US securities laws and the Commodity Exchange Act are similar in that they both aim to prevent fraud and manipulation through the products subject to their respective regulatory jurisdiction. However, there are fundamental differences between their structure and regulatory objectives, which can have significant ramifications as to how a commodity derivative is transacted depending on whether it is subject to the requirements of the Commodity Exchange Act, the securities laws or both.

Derivatives instruments involving securities (eg, equity swaps and fixed-income swaps) are much more likely to be subject to the regulatory provisions of the securities laws than those involving commodity derivatives. However, there are several instances where the securities laws may apply to commodity derivatives and the potential impact of the securities laws in such instances should be given consideration.

(a)   *General*

Although there is some overlap, the Securities Act generally regulates the primary securities market, whereas the Securities Exchange Act contains the crux of the regulations affecting the secondary securities market. The Securities Act requires that any offer or sale of securities in the United States be registered, unless such offer or

---

211   7 USC §12a(9).
212   Louis Brandeis, Other People's Money, at p92 (1914).

CFTC uses of emergency authority

November 1976	December 1977	March 1979	January 1980
Maine Potatoes Traded on NYMEX: This involved a threat of manipulation in an expiring contract. In November 1976, the CFTC declared an emergency and ordered the exchange to impose 100% margins on all accounts and to limit trading in this contract to liquidation only.	Coffee Traded on New York Coffee and Sugar Exchange: This again involved a threat of manipulation in an expiring contract. In November 1977, the Commission, in conjunction with the exchange, declared an emergency and ordered a phased liquidation of all positions subject to a prescribed schedule.	Wheat Traded on CBOT: This again involved a threat of manipulation in an expiring contract. In early 1979, the Commission declared a market emergency and ordered a 1-day suspension of trading so the exchange could take further regulatory action. Subsequently, based on its belief that an emergency continued to exist, the Commission ordered the exchange to suspend all further trading in the contract and to settle any contracts remaining after the delivery period expired at the last prevailing settlement price for that contract.	Soviet Grain Embargo: In January 1980, when President Carter imposed the Soviet grain embargo after the USSR invaded Afghanistan, the Commission declared an emergency and suspended trading for 2 days in futures for wheat, corn, oats, soybeans, soybean meal and soybean oil that were traded on 4 different exchanges. The Commission acted because, in its view, the sudden shock to the market and uncertainties concerning unannounced USDA plans to compensate those affected by the embargo would render the markets temporarily incapable of accurately reflecting the forces of supply and demand. The 2-day suspension gave the markets time to consider the USDA support programs in light of the embargo action.

Source: Commodity Futures Trading Commission, CFTC Emergency Authority Background Letter (June 26 2008), available at www.cftc.gov/ucm/groups/public/@newsroom/documents/file/cftcemergencyauthoritybackgrou.pdf.

sale is exempt from registration.[213] Registration is intended not to act as a stamp of approval, but rather to ensure that sufficient disclosure is available to prospective investors. Once registered, the Securities Exchange Act governs the ongoing reporting obligations of an issuer, oversees the securities trading facilities and regulates the secondary market participants.[214]

If applicable, the US securities laws impose significant disclosure and ongoing reporting obligations that expose affected participants to potentially significant liability. It would not be practical to enter into many commodity derivatives if they were subject to the US securities laws. Therefore, it is important to consider the potential impact of the securities laws and when they may be applicable.

(b)   Is a commodity derivative a security?

Commodity derivatives traded or executed on a designated contract market or designated transaction execution facility are subject to the exclusive jurisdiction of the CFTC, which, as a result, removes such instruments from the provisions of the securities laws.[215] However, a commodity derivative that is exempt from the provisions of the Commodity Exchange Act is potentially subject to the securities laws, provided that it is a security.

A 'security' is defined in both the Securities Act and the Securities Exchange Act by reference to a long laundry list of financial instruments.[216] The definition of 'security' has been interpreted broadly by the US courts to "encompass virtually any instrument that might be sold as an investment".[217]

Before the Commodity Futures Modernization Act, there was a great deal of uncertainty as to whether OTC commodity derivatives were subject to the jurisdiction of the Commodity Exchange Act or the US securities laws. The Commodity Futures Modernization Act clarified this by amending the US securities laws to remove certain qualifying swap agreements from the definition of 'security'.[218]

An excluded swap agreement includes an extensive list of almost any type of derivative transaction, with the exception of a number of traditional security derivatives[219] between certain eligible contract participants,[220] "the material terms of which (other than price and quantity) are subject to individual negotiation".[221]

211	7 USC §12a(9).
212	Louis Brandeis, Other People's Money, at p92 (1914).
213	Securities Act §5.
214	Securities Exchange Act §2.
215	Section 2(a)(1)(A) of the Commodity Exchange Act.
216	Securities Act §2(a)(1); Securities Exchange Act §3(a)(10).
217	*Reves v Ernst & Young*, 494 US 56, 61 (1990) (stating that the US Congress "did not attempt precisely to cabin the scope of the Securities Acts", but rather "enacted a definition of 'security' sufficiently broad to encompass virtually any instrument that might be sold as an investment").
218	Securities Act §2A; Securities Exchange Act §3A (each removing non-security based swap agreements and security-based swap agreements from its respective definition of 'security').
219	15 USC 78c(b) (Gramm-Leach-Bliley Act of 1999).
220	This is limited to the 'eligible contract participants' as defined under the Commodity Exchange Act as of the date of the enactment of the Gramm-Leach-Bliley Act and does not include any additional persons added pursuant to Section 1(a)(12)(C) of the Commodity Exchange Act.
221	15 USC 78c(a) (Gramm-Leach-Bliley Act §206A).

(c)   *If it is a security, then what?*

In most instances a commodity derivative that qualifies for one of the OTC exemptions will be excluded from the definition of a 'security'. Where this is not the case, additional analysis will be necessary to determine whether the commodity derivative is a security. The US securities laws are also clearly applicable to certain commodity derivatives discussed in this book. Most notably, these include structured commodity products (which are predominantly a security) and investment units issued by commodity pools.

If a commodity derivative is a security, it must be registered under the Securities Act unless it qualifies for an exemption. There are several exemptions from the Securities Act, but the most common are:

- private placements to sophisticated purchasers (ie, those "able to fend for themselves"[222]) (Section 4(2); Regulation D; Rule 144A);
- non-US person placements (Regulation S); and
- intrastate placements (Section 3(a)(11); Rule 147).

Some of the anti-fraud provisions of the US securities laws may still apply, but the cumbersome disclosure and ongoing reporting requirements, as well as various other potential areas of liability, are no longer of concern.[223]

4.2   Crossover regulation (energy markets)

Historically, the Securities and Exchange Commission and the CFTC have wrangled over which agency has jurisdiction to regulate certain derivatives products, most commonly those relating to equity instruments. The Commodity Futures Modernization Act did much to clarify the roles of these agencies, but new battles have emerged between the CFTC and other federal regulatory agencies.

(a)   *Federal Energy Regulatory Commission*

The Federal Energy Regulatory Commission (FERC) is an independent agency formed in 1977 to regulate the interstate transmission of electricity, natural gas and oil. Its jurisdiction relates to the spot markets for these commodities as opposed to futures (or other derivatives).

The Energy Policy Act of 2005 significantly expanded FERC's powers by giving it the authority to prohibit "any entity", whether directly or indirectly, from using or employing "any manipulative or deceptive device or contrivance (as those terms are used in Section 10(b) of the Exchange Act)" in connection with the purchase or sale of natural gas, electricity, natural gas transportation services or electricity transmission services under FERC's jurisdiction.[224] This prohibition was not self-enacting; instead, its scope was to be defined through rules and regulations promulgated by FERC.[225]

The final rule adopted by FERC intentionally mirrors Rule 10b-5 of the Securities

---

222   *SEC v Ralston Purina*, 346 US 119 (1953).
223   Exchange Act §10(b); see also 17 CFR §240.10b-5.
224   15 USCA 717c-1; 16 USCA 824v.
225   15 USCA 717c-1; 16 USCA 824v.

Exchange Act and FERC intends to implement its historical precedent as appropriate. Under the rule, it is:

> *unlawful for any entity, directly or indirectly, in connection with the purchase or sale of natural gas, electricity, natural gas transportation services or electricity transmission services subject to the jurisdiction of the FERC:*
> - *To sue or employ any device, scheme, or artifice to defraud;*
> - *To make any untrue statement of a material fact or to omit to state a material fact necessary in order to make the statements made, in the light of the circumstances under which they were made, not misleading; or*
> - *To engage in any act, practice, or course of business that operates or would operate as a fraud or deceit upon any entity.*[226]

While the rule makes no actual mention of manipulation, it is intended to "permit the [FERC] to police all forms of fraud and manipulation that affect natural gas and electric energy transactions and activities the [FERC] is charged with protecting".[227]

The crossover regulatory implications of the rule came to light in 2007 when both the CFTC and FERC brought successive actions against Amaranth Advisors, LLC and certain of its traders, alleging that they used gas futures contracts on the New York Mercantile Exchange to manipulate the price of natural gas. The CFTC challenged FERC's assertion of authority, arguing that it had exclusive authority over the matter because of its exclusive jurisdiction to regulate exchange-traded futures contracts. In August 2009 Amaranth settled with both the CFTC and FERC before any final decision was rendered on the agencies' jurisdictional turf.

(b) Federal Trade Commission

The enactment of the Energy Independence and Security Act in 2007 further muddied the water by ceding to the Federal Trade Commission (FTC)[228] the authority to prescribe rules to prohibit the fraud and manipulation of wholesale oil markets.[229]

The Energy Independence and Security Act did for the FTC what the Energy Policy Act did for FERC, except that the FTC was charged with promulgating rules and regulations aimed at preventing manipulation in the wholesale petroleum markets.[230] The FTC's final rule, like the FERC final rule, was modelled on Rule 10b-5 of the Securities Exchange Act and intended to follow much of its legal precedent, but was not taken verbatim.

The FTC rule provides that:

> *it is unlawful for any person, directly or indirectly, in connection with the purchase or sale of crude oil, gasoline, or petroleum distillates at wholesale, to:*
> - *knowingly engage in any act, practice, or course of business – including the making*

---

226   18 CFR §§1c.1(a) & 1c.2(a).
227   Prohibition of Energy Market Manipulation, 114 FERC ¶ 61,047 (2006).
228   The FTC is an independent US government agency that was established in 1914. The principal functions of the FTC are consumer protection and the prevention of anti-competitive business practices (eg, price discrimination, monopolistic mergers).
229   Energy Independence and Security Act §811.
230   See *id.*

of any untrue statement of material fact – that operates or would operate as a fraud or deceit upon any person; or

- *intentionally fail to state a material fact that under the circumstances renders a statement made by such person misleading, provided that such omission distorts or is likely to distort market conditions for any such product.*[231]

In issuing the rule, the FTC acknowledged that market participants could face overlapping jurisdiction from the CFTC. The FTC noted that it intended to coordinate its efforts with the CFTC when investigating derivatives contracts, but stopped short of adopting an absolute safe harbour for commodity derivatives.[232] The FTC rule was passed only in August 2009, so the extent of its application in cases involving wholesale petroleum derivatives contracts remains to be seen.[233]

4.3   Bank regulation and capital requirements for commodity derivatives

US banks are regulated pursuant to a complex system that functions under both state and federal law. US banks can choose whether they are charted as a state or national bank.

If a bank decides to register as a national bank, it will be primarily regulated by the Office of the Comptroller of the Currency, but it must also become a member of the Federal Reserve System. Federal law generally pre-empts the application of state law to nationally charted banks.

If, on the other hand, a bank chooses to obtain a state charter, it will be governed by both state and federal law. State-chartered banks are given the option to become a member of the Federal Reserve System, in which case they will be subject to its regulations. Where they elect not to join the Federal Reserve System, state-chartered banks will nonetheless be subject to the federal regulatory oversight of the Federal Deposit Insurance Corporation.

One area of US bank regulation which has a direct impact on commodity derivatives is the capital adequacy rules.

(a)   *Capital adequacy rules*

The capital adequacy rules in the United States are derived from the standards published in 2006 by the Basel Committee on Banking Supervision ('Basel II').[234] Basel II sets out the global framework for ensuring that internationally active financial institutions maintain adequate levels of capital (ie, equity). Basel II was split into three broad categories or pillars:

- minimum capital requirements;
- supervisory review; and
- market discipline (ie, disclosure requirements).

---

231   Energy Independence and Security Act §317.3.
232   16 CFR Part 317.1
233   16 CFR Part 317.
234   Basel Committee on Banking Supervision, Bank for International Settlements, International Convergence of Capital Measurement and Capital Standards (2006), available at www.bis.org/publ/bcbs128.pdf.

Of the three pillars, Pillar One – minimum capital requirements – contains the rules in which we are interested.

Pillar One establishes the minimum level of qualifying capital that a bank must hold based on the credit, market and operational risk profile of its assets. As a minimum, a bank is required to have outstanding capital equal to at least 8% of its risk-weighted assets. The risk weighting of an asset adjusts its value in accordance with its perceived exposure to credit, market and operational risk – the higher the perceived risk, the higher the risk-weighting.[235] A different set of risk-weighting rules exists for each type of risk, of which the rules for credit risk and market risk are expressly applicable to commodity derivatives.

(b) Credit risk rules

Basel II developed two approaches by which banks could operate under the credit risk rules. The first approach – the internal-ratings based approach – allows banks to use internal estimates of credit risk. The second approach – the standardised approach – predefines the credit risk weights based on the credit quality of the obligor and, in some instances, the type and the external rating, if applicable, of a particular asset.

In December 2007 US federal bank regulators published final rules implementing their version of the internal ratings-based approach,[236] but have published only proposed rules for the adoption of the standardised approach.[237]

Under both sets of rules, commodity derivatives that use a qualifying central clearing organisation[238] will be assigned a risk-weight asset value of zero and thus will have no corresponding capital requirement under the credit risk rules. While this covers exchange-traded commodity derivatives,[239] those traded OTC, while similar in application, are substantially different under the credit risk rules adopted by the United States.

(i) US standardised rules for commodity derivatives

The US standardised rules for determining the risk-weighted asset value of an OTC commodity derivative are relatively straightforward. Under the US standardised rules, the risk-weighted asset value of an OTC commodity derivative is calculated by

---

235 For example, if a bank held an asset of $100 with a risk weight of 75%, then it would be required to have only $6 (8% × 75% × 100) of outstanding capital, instead of $8 had there not been a risk-weight adjustment.

236 Risk-Based Capital Standards: Advanced Capital Adequacy Framework – Basel II; Final Rule, 72 Fed Reg 69,288 (Dec 7 2007) (to be codified at 12 CFR §pts 3, 208, 225, 325, 559, 560, 563, 567), available at http://edocket.access.gpo.gov/2007/pdf/07-5729.pdf.

237 Risk-Based Capital Guidelines; Capital Adequacy Guidelines: Standardized Framework; Proposed Rule, 73 Fed Reg 43,982 (July 29 2008) (to be codified at 12 CFR §pts 3, 208, 225, 325, 567), available at http://edocket.access.gpo.gov/2008/pdf/E8-16262.pdf.

238 See *id* at 44,007 note 46, (indicating that a "qualifying central counterparty would be defined as a counterparty that: (i) facilitates trades between counterparties in one or more financial markets by either guaranteeing trades or novating contracts; (ii) requires all participants in its arrangements to be fully collateralized on a daily basis; and (iii) the banking organization demonstrates to the satisfaction of the agency is in sound financial condition and is subject to effective oversight by a national supervisory authority".

239 US internal ratings-based rules, *supra* note 237, at 69,410, Section 31(d)(6)(ii); US standardised rules, *supra* note 237, at 44,007, note 46, indicating that the bank regulatory agencies consider a qualifying central counterparty to be the functional equivalent of an exchange and have long exempted exchange-traded contracts from risk-based capital requirements.

first determining an exposure amount and then multiplying that by the risk-weight factor corresponding to the credit quality of the counterparty to the contract.[240]

The exposure amount for a single OTC commodity derivative is calculated under the US standardised rules by adding the following:

- current credit exposure, which is equal to the greater of the mark-to-market value of the OTC commodity derivative and zero; and
- potential future credit exposure, which is equal to the notional principal amount of the OTC commodity derivative, multiplied by a conversion factor corresponding to the underlying commodity (see table)[241] and remaining maturity of the contract.[242]

Remaining maturity	Gold	Precious Metals (other than gold)	Others
≤ 1 year	1%	7%	10%
> 1 ≤ 5 years	5%	7%	12%
> 5 years	7.5%	8%	15%

The exposure amount for multiple OTC commodity derivatives that are subject to a qualifying master netting agreement, such as the International Swaps and Derivatives Association Master Agreement, is calculated using the same inputs as those used for a single OTC commodity derivative. However, several adjustments are made to take into account the overall net exposure amount for all trades under the master netting agreement.[243]

The exposure amount for an OTC commodity derivative (whether single or multiple) may also be revised to take into account the benefit of any financial collateral posted to mitigate the counterparty's credit risk.[244]

(ii)   *US internal ratings-based rules for OTC commodity derivatives*

OTC commodity derivatives fall in the wholesale exposure category under the US internal ratings-based rules. The risk-weighted asset value for each wholesale exposure[245] is derived from the risk-based capital formula, which is calculated on the basis of the following risk parameters:

- probability of default – the bank's estimate of the likelihood that the obligor

240 US standardised rules, *supra* note 237, at 44,037, Section 31(b), providing that a bank "must multiply each exposure amount identified under [Section 31(a)] by the risk weight appropriate to the exposure based on the obligor or exposure type, eligible guarantor, or financial collateral to determine the risk-weighted asset amount for each exposure".
241 See *id* at 44,041, Table 8 – Conversion Factor Matrix for OTC Derivative Contracts.
242 See *id* at 44,041, Section 35(c).
243 See *id* at 44,041, Section 35(d).
244 See *id* at 44,041, Section 35(e); but see also *id* at 44,043, Section 37(a)(3), providing that if the financial collateral is factored into the "exposure amount" that it cannot also be used in credit-risk mitigation rules of Section 37.
245 This is modified where the obligor has defaulted. See US internal ratings-based rules, *supra* note 236, at 69,41, Section 31(e)(2).

(or a guarantor) will default over a one-year horizon;

- loss given default – the bank's estimate of the percentage economic loss that would occur if the obligor defaulted in an economic downturn;
- exposure at default – the bank's estimate of the amount that the obligor would owe the bank at the time of default; and
- maturity – the effective remaining maturity of the exposure.[246]

For the purposes of understanding the risk-weighted asset value of an OTC commodity derivative under the US internal ratings-based rules, the exposure at default can be thought of as the functional equivalent of the exposure amount under the US standardised rules.

The exposure at default for OTC commodity derivatives contracts can be determined by one of two methods under the US internal ratings-based rules. The first method, for all intents and purposes, follows the same approach used to determine the exposure amount under the US standardised rules. The second method – the internal models methodology – allows a bank to use internal models to estimate the exposure at default for an OTC commodity derivative. However, before using the internal models methodology, a bank is required to obtain the approval of its federal bank regulator.

(c) Market risk rules

The US market risk rules[247] require all banks that engage in substantial trading activity[248] to carry sufficient capital to insulate their exposure to market value losses on all of their covered positions.[249] The covered positions subject to the market risk rules include all of a trading bank's positions in its trading account and, of greater relevance, all of its commodity positions (whether or not in its trading account). A commodity position includes any "position for which price risk arises from changes in the value of a commodity".[250]

The market risk rules work in tandem with the US credit risk rules to determine the minimum capital required for a trading bank as a whole. The process for making this calculation occurs in five stages:

- Stage 1 – a trading bank calculates its adjusted risk-weighted assets, which equals the risk-weighted asset value for all of its assets (as calculated under the US credit risk rules) minus the risk-weighted asset values for all of its covered positions (as calculated under the US credit risk rules). Importantly, the adjusted risk-weighted assets are not reduced by positions held in OTC commodity derivatives.

---

246 Robert F Hugi, *et al*, "U.S. Adoption of Basel II and the Basel II Securitization Framework", *North Carolina Banking Institute* (Vol 12, 2008) at 54.

247 12 CFR Part 208, Appendix E. The market risk rules became effective in 1998. Revisions were proposed in 2006, but have not yet been published as final rules.

248 12 CFR Part 208, Appendix E, Section 1(b) (providing that its provisions apply to those whose "trading activity equals 10 percent or more of total assets, or $1 billion or more").

249 12 CFR Part 208, Appendix E, Section 1(a).

250 Risk-Based Capital Rules: Mark Risk (Proposed Rules), 73 Fed Reg 55,958 (Sept 25 2006) (to be codified at 12 CFR §pts 3, 208, 225, 325, 566), available at http://edocket.access.gpo.gov/2006/pdf/06-7673.pdf.

- Stage 2 – the trading bank measures the market risk for its covered positions. A covered position's market risk is the sum of its value at risk and any specific risk. Value at risk is an estimate of the "maximum amount that the value of covered positions could decline due to market price or rate movements during a fixed holding period" within a specific statistical confidence level. The specific risk of a covered position includes non-market-related risks, such as default risk.
- Stage 3 – the trading bank calculates the market risk equivalent asset for each covered position by multiplying its market risk measure (as determined in Stage 2) by 12.5.[251]
- Stage 4 – the trading bank determines the risk-weighted asset value for all of its assets by adding the market risk equivalent asset value for each of its covered positions (as determined in Stage 3) to its adjusted risk-weighted assets (as determined in Stage 1).
- Stage 5 – following completion of Stage 4, the trading bank can determine whether its qualifying capital is at least equal to 8% of its risk-weighted asset value.[252]

As briefly noted at Stage 1, the risk-weighted asset value of OTC commodity derivatives is not excluded from the adjusted risk-weighted assets. This ensures that such a position has sufficient capital held against both the counterparty's credit risk as well as the market risk of the underlying commodity price.

4.4 State regulation

State law has never hidden its contempt for commodity price speculation. The efforts by states to rid commodity prices from the influence of speculators pre-date those of the federal government. The earliest such law dates back to the common law doctrine against difference contracts (also known as the rule against settling differences), which had its heyday sometime in the mid-to-late 19th century.[253] Difference contracts were essentially cash-settled futures contracts for agricultural goods, and the doctrine rendered these contracts unenforceable unless they served a bona fide hedging purpose.[254]

Many states later codified the rule against settling differences by enacting anti-'bucket shop' and anti-gambling laws. Like the rule against settling differences, these laws banned the sale of goods without delivery.[255] While still on the books of many states, anti-bucket shop and anti-gambling laws, as well as many other state laws,

---

251   This is the inverse of 8% (ie, the minimum required capital percentage under the US capital adequacy rules), which effectively converts the market risk measure (as determined in Stage 2) into a risk-weighted asset value. For example, if an asset has a current value of $100 and the market risk measure is $5, the risk-weighted asset value would be $62.50 (and then the minimum required capital, calculated at 8%, would be $5 or the equivalent of 5% of the original $100).
252   12 CFR208, Appendix E, Section 3.
253   Lynn A Stout, "Why the Law Hates Speculators: Regulation and Private Ordering in the Market for OTC Derivatives", *Duke Law Journal* (Vol48:701 1999), at 713.
254   See *id* at 714.
255   See *id* at 721.

have taken a back seat to federal regulation under the Commodity Exchange Act.

The Commodity Exchange Act will generally pre-empt state law that purports to regulate commodity derivatives directly. Furthermore, Section 2(a) of the Commodity Exchange Act confers on the CFTC exclusive jurisdiction over commodity derivatives, which pre-empts any other agency, whether at the federal or state level, from regulating commodity derivatives.

The Commodity Exchange Act, on the other hand, does not pre-empt any state law or regulation affecting a commodity derivative that is traded outside a registered entity[256] or an exempt board of trade.[257] However, the Commodity Exchange Act does expressly pre-empt state anti-bucket-shop and anti-gambling laws from applying to the various OTC transactions and other derivative transactions exempted from regulation under the act.[258] However, this does not apply to "antifraud provisions of general applicability".[259] Moreover, exchanges, organisations and market participants that fail to register as required under the act remain exposed to the full onslaught of existing state law.[260]

In addition, in cases where the US securities laws are applicable, it is necessary to consider whether states' securities laws (more commonly known as 'blue-sky' laws) are implicated (eg, states' blue-sky laws apply to the issuance of securities by commodity pools).

4.5 Other US regulation to consider

There are a slew of other US regulations that, albeit with much less likelihood, could be implicated in connection with a commodity derivative. As an example, commodity pools, commodity pool operators and commodity trading advisers should consider the laws and regulations of the Investment Company Act of 1940 and the Investment Advisors Act of 1940. In addition, market participants are required to comply with various privacy, antitrust and anti-money-laundering laws, and similar regulatory provisions.

5. Where is US regulation of commodity derivatives heading?

"Never let a serious crisis go to waste."[261] While not the regulatory philosophy of all, this has been the mantra of many US legislators and other government officials since the onset of the Great Recession. A number of major bills have been introduced in the US Congress to regulate derivatives further. Existing rules and regulations have been in a state of constant flux. State regulators are chomping at the bit for their share of the action. However, no grand new law has been passed and at times it seems

---

256 7 USC §1a(29) (defining 'registered entity' to include a designated contract market, a designated transaction execution facility, a derivatives clearing organisation or an exempt commercial market required to be registered with the CFTC).

257 7 USC §16(e)(1)(B)(i).

258 7 USC §16(e)(2).

259 7 USC §16(e)(2).

260 7 USC §16(e)(1)(C) (providing that the Commodity Exchange Act does not pre-empt "the applicable of any...State statute...to any person required to be registered or designated under [the act] who shall fail or refuse to obtain such registration or designation").

261 Rahm Emanuel, White House Chief of Staff to President Barack Obama, available at http://online.wsj.com/article/SB123310466514522309.html.

possible that none (or one having little consequence) will be.

While not wholly consistent, the regulatory proposals, thus far, have centred on two key objectives: greater transparency and systemic risk mitigation (ie, greater reliance on central clearing organisations) for the largely unregulated OTC derivatives markets.

If I were to venture a guess, legislation will be passed in the United States to deal with these two main objectives, but with much less impact than is contemplated in the current legislative proposals.

To learn more about the existing proposals, whether new regulation has been enacted and, if so, what the new regulations entail and whether my predictions have panned out, please go to www.globelawandbusiness.com/CMD/.

About the authors

Miles Bake
Regulatory expert
london@mayerbrown.com

Miles Bake joined Mayer Brown in 2005 and specialises in financial regulation and regulation-driven transactions, such as structured finance and regulatory capital trades. He has also advised on the solvent and insolvent restructuring of banks, securitisations and structured investment vehicles. Mr Bake has experience of working with US and European banks and industry bodies, and has spent time in-house at a US bank in London. He frequently writes and comments on developments in EU and UK banking and financial regulations.

Mr Bake has now left Mayer Brown to pursue other opportunities.

Sabine Bertin
Associate
sbertin@mayerbrown.com

Sabine Bertin is an associate at the London office of Mayer Brown International LLP. Dual-qualified in France and England and Wales, she represents commercial and investment banks in a wide range of cross-border structured and project financings. Ms Bertin particularly focuses on the mining finance sector and has experience in a variety of jurisdictions, including Zambia, Mauritania, the Democratic Republic of Congo, Russia and the Republic of Kazakhstan.

Sandy Bhogal
Partner
sbhogal@mayerbrown.com

Sandy Bhogal is a partner in the corporate tax practice at Mayer Brown International LLP. His extensive experience ranges from general corporate tax advice to transactional advice on matters involving corporate finance, banking, capital markets, asset finance and property. Mr Bhogal also has significant experience with corporate tax planning, as well as with advising on the development of domestic and cross-border tax-efficient structures.

He is a member of the International Fiscal Association and the International Chamber of Commerce, and he sits on the Law Society's sub-committee for international taxes. He has written widely on domestic and international tax matters.

Dharini Collins
Senior associate
dcollins@mayerbrown.com

Dharini Collins is a senior associate in the derivatives and structured finance team at Mayer Brown. She has extensive derivatives experience, having previously worked in-house at ABN AMRO Bank NV, working on exchange-traded retail equity derivatives, structured note programmes, fund and commodity-linked products and exotic over-the-counter (OTC) equity derivatives. She has also recently completed a secondment with Citigroup, working in the prime brokerage/equity derivatives legal team, on the portfolio equity swap platform.

Ms Collins advises financial institutions, insurance companies and pension funds on a range of derivatives transactions, including credit, equity and 'securitisation-friendly' derivatives and structured insurance derivative solutions.

Ellen Doubtfire
Associate
EDoubtfire@mayerbrown.com

Ellen Doubtfire is an associate in the finance practice of the London office of Mayer Brown. She specialises in derivatives and structured products.

Avanthi Gunatilake
Associate
agunatilake@mayerbrown.com

Avanthi Gunatilake is an associate in the finance practice of the London office of Mayer Brown. She has worked in a variety of areas, including asset-based lending, structured products and derivatives.

Erica Johansson
Senior associate
ejohansson@mayerbrown.com

Erica Johansson is a senior lawyer in the finance practice at Mayer Brown International LLP's London office, specialising in derivatives and structured finance. She has extensive experience in advising leading financial institutions on derivatives and structured finance transactions, including advising on credit, equity, foreign exchange, index-linked and OTC derivatives, hedging aspects of securitisation, and project finance transactions and derivatives transactions with pension funds. Dr Johansson also advises clients on cash collateralised debt obligations, securitisations, structured notes, repos, repackagings, securities lending and margining arrangements, and banking and finance matters generally.

Dr Johansson has published extensively in the area of intermediated securities and is the sole author of *Property Rights in Investment Securities and the Doctrine of Specificity* (Springer, 2009). She has a law degree from Stockholm University and a PhD from London University, and she has acted as a consultant to the World Bank.

David Johnson
Vice president, Citigroup
David.R.Johnson@Citi.com

David Johnson is currently legal counsel to Citigroup, London, where he specialises in OTC and exchange-traded credit products. His experience includes advising financial institutions on various structured finance and derivatives transactions.

Prior to his move to Citigroup, Mr Johnson was an associate in Mayer Brown International LLP's London office, having graduated with a BA from the University of British Columbia, a MA from Lancaster University and a GDL and a LPC from Nottingham Law School. Mr Johnson is also fluent in French.

Nanak Keswani
Associate
NKeswani@mayerbrown.com

Nanak Keswani is an associate in the finance practice of the London office, having joined Mayer Brown in April 2007. He has extensive experience of OTC and structured derivatives, including credit, equity and commodity derivatives, as well as complex hedging arrangements.

Mr Keswani also has experience acting for arrangers and lenders on a wide spectrum of financing arrangements, ranging from straightforward secured lending and capital market transactions to multi-jurisdictional structured finance transactions, including receivables purchase securitisations, asset-backed commercial paper programmes, collateralised fund obligations and asset-based lending.

Amandeep Kharaud

Associate

akharaud@mayerbrown.com

Amandeep Kharaud is an associate in the finance practice at Mayer Brown International LLP. Miss Kharaud joined Mayer Brown in 2006 as a trainee and qualified into the finance group in 2008. She has been seconded both to Mayer Brown's Chicago office (2007–2008) and to Deutsche Bank's emerging markets group (2009-2010).

Before joining Mayer Brown, Miss Kharaud worked at Goldman Sachs, Bank of America and Clifford Chance. Since joining the firm she has worked on a number of transactions, including the restructuring of Vseukrainsky Aksionerny Bank's $125 million loan participation notes, the asset-based lending refinancing transaction to Liz Claiborne by JPMorgan, the project financing from WestLB for Chilean copper mining by Centenario, the refinancing of Persimmon's bank facilities, and private placements and the issue of a eurobond listed on the London Stock Exchange for a Turkish entity.

Aimee Lewis

Associate

alewis@mayerbrown.com

Aimee Lewis is an associate in the finance practice of the London office of Mayer Brown. She specialises in derivatives and structured products.

Aaron McGarry

Associate

amcgarry@mayerbrown.com

Aaron McGarry is an associate in the finance practice at Mayer Brown International LLP. He focuses on structured finance (in particular over-the-counter credit and equity derivatives for banks, corporates and fund managers), pension-linked derivatives, all aspects of credit default swaps, repackaging and asset-based lending financing.

Catriona Nicol

Associate

cnicol@mayerbrown.com

Catriona Nicol is an associate in the corporate tax practice at Mayer Brown International LLP. She has experience in providing general corporate tax advice as well as transactional advice in corporate and finance transactions. She has co-authored a number of articles on domestic and international tax issues.

Edmund Parker

Partner

eparker@mayerbrown.com

Edmund Parker is a partner at Mayer Brown International LLP; he heads the London office's derivatives practice and co-heads the global derivatives and structured products practice. Mr Parker advises on complex OTC credit and equity derivatives, commodity derivatives, Islamic derivatives, and insurance and pensions-linked derivative structures. He also advises on repackagings, as well as distress situations affecting derivatives.

According to *UK Legal 500 (2008)*, "the [derivatives] practice has been transformed by the arrival of [Parker]", and he "brings a reputation for structured credit and equity derivatives". It has also been said that he "would easily fit into any top-tier derivatives practice" and "he has great expertise" (*Chambers UK (2009)*).

Mr Parker has written extensively on derivatives and related matters, and is sole author of *Credit Derivatives: Documenting and Understanding Credit Derivative Products* and sole editor of *Equity Derivatives: Documenting and Understanding Equity Derivative Products*.

Marcin Perzanowski

Associate

MPerzanowski@mayerbrown.com

Marcin Perzanowski is an associate in the finance practice of the Mayer Brown's London office, having joined the firm in 2006. He has extensive experience in advising on OTC commodity, credit and equity derivatives for banks, corporates, funds and insurance companies. He has worked on portfolio swap agreements, corporate and strategic equity derivatives, fund-linked notes, pension-linked and insurance-linked products, as well as various exotic OTC derivatives.

He has completed two secondments to The Royal Bank of Scotland plc, where he advised on various aspects of derivatives transactions. He has also been seconded to the London office of Wachovia Bank.

Mr Perzanowski's publications include an article on structured credit derivatives and three chapters in Edmund Parker's textbook *Equity Derivatives: Documenting and Understanding Equity Derivative Products*. He is a native Polish speaker and is fluent in English and German.

Danuta Rychlicka

Associate

DRychlicka@mayerbrown.com

Danuta Rychlicka is an associate in the finance practice of Mayer Brown in London and specialises in derivatives work.

Jeremiah Wagner

Lawyer

jwagner@mayerbrown.com

Jeremiah Wagner is currently an associate in the finance practice of Mayer Brown's London office. Prior to joining the London office, he worked in the firms Chicago office.

Mr Wagner has extensive experience across a range of structured finance and derivatives transactions, capital markets and financial regulation. While in the Chicago office of Mayer Brown, he primarily represented issuers and underwriters in publicly and privately offered securitisations under the US securities laws. Mr Wagner's securitisation and structured-finance experience encompasses a vast range of asset classes over multiple jurisdictions, including residential and commercial mortgages, auto loans and leases, dealer floorplan loans, credit-card receivables, trade receivables and synthetic exposures.

All authors are (or recently have been) lawyers working at Mayer Brown

Also by the author

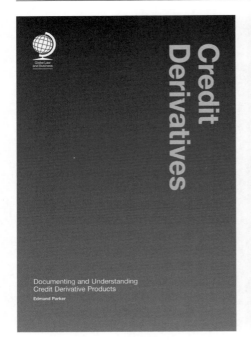

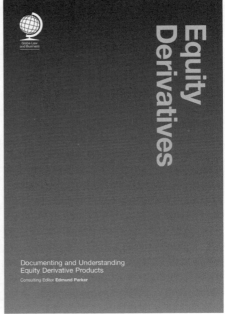

Go to **www.globelawandbusiness.com** for further
details, including a sample chapter and reviews.